Managerial Accounting

CREATING VALUE IN A DYNAMIC BUSINESS ENVIRONMENT

NINTH EDITION

Ronald W. Hilton
Cornell University

With Additional Material from

Managerial Accounting

FOURTEENTH EDITION

Ray H. Garrison, D.B.A., CPA
Professor Emeritus
Brigham Young University

Eric W. Noreen, Ph.D., CMA
Professor Emeritus
University of Washington

Peter C. Brewer, Ph.D., CPA
Miami University—Oxford, Ohio

Accounting for Decision Making and Control

SEVENTH EDITION

Jerold L. Zimmerman
Univeristy of Rochester

Custom Edition for University of Illinois at Urbana-Champaign ACCY 302

Learning Solutions

Boston Burr Ridge, IL Dubuque, IA New York San Francisco St. Louis
Bangkok Bogotá Caracas Lisbon London Madrid
Mexico City Milan New Delhi Seoul Singapore Sydney Taipei Toronto

The McGraw·Hill Companies

MANAGERIAL ACCOUNTING

Creating Value in a Dynamic Business Environment, Ninth Edition
Custom Edition for University of Illinois at Urbana-Champaign
ACCY 302

This book is a McGraw-Hill Learning Solutions textbook and contains select material from the following sources:
Managerial Accounting: Creating Value in a Dynamic Business Environment, Ninth Edition by Ronald W. Hilton. Copyright © 2011, 2009, 2008, 2005, 2002, 1999, 1997, 1994, 1991 by The McGraw-Hill Companies, Inc.
Managerial Accounting, Fourteenth Edition by Ray H. Garrison, Eric W. Noreen and Peter C. Brewer. Copyright © 2012, 2010, 2008, 2006, 2003, 2000, 1997, 1994, 1991, 1988, 1985, 1982, 1979, 1976 by The McGraw-Hill Companies, Inc.
Accounting for Decision Making and Control, Seventh Edition by Jerold L. Zimmerman. Copyright © 2011, 2009, 2006, 2003 by The McGraw-Hill Companies, Inc.
All are reprinted with permission of the publisher. Many custom published texts are modified versions or adaptations of our best-selling textbooks. Some adaptations are printed in black and white to keep prices at a minimum, while others are in color.

2 3 4 5 6 7 8 9 0 SCI SCI 15 14 13

ISBN-13: 978-0-07-784723-4
ISBN-10: 0-07-784723-7
part of
ISBN-13: 978-0-07-784724-1
ISBN-10: 0-07-784724-5

Learning Solutions Consultant: Bridget Hannenberg
Learning Solutions Representative: Ann Hayes
Project Manager: Jennifer Bartell
Printer/Binder: Strategic Content Imaging

Brief Contents

Zimmerman: *Accounting for Decision Making and Control, 7/e*,
ISBN: 0-07-813672-5

Contents

Chapter One

Introduction

Chapter Outline

A. Managerial Accounting: Decision Making and Control

B. Design and Use of Cost Systems

C. Marmots and Grizzly Bears

D. Management Accountant's Role in the Organization

E. Evolution of Management Accounting: A Framework for Change

F. Vortec Medical Probe Example

G. Outline of the Text

H. Summary

A. Managerial Accounting: Decision Making and Control

Managers at BMW must decide which car models to produce, the quantity of each model to produce given the selling prices for the models, and how to manufacture the automobiles. They must decide which car parts, such as headlight assemblies, BMW should manufacture internally and which parts should be outsourced. They must decide not only on advertising, distribution, and product positioning to sell the cars, but also the quantity and quality of the various inputs to use. For example, they must determine which models will have leather seats and the quality of the leather to be used.

How are future revenues and costs of proposed car models estimated? Similarly, in deciding which investment projects to accept, capital budgeting analysts require data on future cash flows. How are these numbers derived? How does one coordinate the activities of hundreds or thousands of employees in the firm so that these employees accept senior management's leadership? At BMW and organizations small and large, managers must have good information to make all these decisions and the leadership abilities to get others to implement the decisions.

Information about firms' future costs and revenues is not readily available but must be estimated by managers. Organizations must obtain and disseminate the knowledge to make these decisions. Decision making is much easier with the requisite knowledge.

Organizations' internal information systems provide some of the knowledge for these pricing, production, capital budgeting, and marketing decisions. These systems range from the informal and the rudimentary to very sophisticated, computerized management information systems. The term **information system** should not be interpreted to mean a single, integrated system. Most information systems consist not only of formal, organized, tangible records such as payroll and purchasing documents but also informal, intangible bits of data such as memos, special studies, and managers' impressions and opinions. The firm's information system also contains nonfinancial information such as customer and employee satisfaction surveys. As firms grow from single proprietorships to large global corporations with tens of thousands of employees, managers lose the knowledge of enterprise affairs gained from personal, face-to-face contact in daily operations. Higher-level managers of larger firms come to rely more and more on formal operating reports.

The **internal accounting system**, an important component of a firm's information system, includes budgets, data on the costs of each product and current inventory, and periodic financial reports. In many cases, especially in small companies, these accounting reports are the only formalized part of the information system providing the knowledge for decision making. Many larger companies have other formalized, nonaccounting–based information systems, such as production planning systems. This book focuses on how internal accounting systems provide knowledge for decision making.

After making decisions, managers must implement them in organizations in which the interests of the employees and the owners do not necessarily coincide. Just because senior managers announce a decision does not necessarily ensure that the decision will be implemented.

Organizations do not have objectives; people do. A discussion of an organization's objectives requires addressing the owners' objectives. One common objective of owners is to maximize profits, or the difference between revenues and expenses. Maximizing firm value is equivalent to maximizing the stream of profits over the organization's life. Employees, suppliers, and customers also have their own objectives—usually maximizing their self-interest.

Not all owners care only about monetary flows. An owner of a professional sports team might care more about winning (subject to covering costs) than maximizing profits.

Nonprofits do not have owners with the legal rights to the organization's profits. Moreover, nonprofits seek to maximize their value by serving some social goal such as education, health care, or welfare.

No matter what the firm's objective, the organization will survive only if its inflow of resources (such as revenue) is at least as large as the outflow. Accounting information is useful to help manage the inflow and outflow of resources and to help align the owners' and employees' interests, no matter what objectives the owners wish to pursue.

Throughout this book, we assume that individuals maximize their self-interest. The owners of the firm usually want to maximize profits, but managers and employees will do so only if it is in their interest. Hence, a conflict of interest exists between owners—who, in general, want higher profits—and employees—who want easier jobs, higher wages, and more fringe benefits. To control this conflict, senior managers and owners design systems to monitor employees' behavior and incentive schemes that reward employees for generating more profits. Not-for-profit organizations face similar conflicts. Those people responsible for the nonprofit organization (boards of trustees and government officials) must design incentive schemes to motivate their employees to operate the organization efficiently.

All successful firms must devise mechanisms that help align employee interests with maximizing the organization's value. All of these mechanisms constitute the firm's **control system**; they include performance measures and incentive compensation systems, promotions, demotions, and terminations, security guards and video surveillance, internal auditors, and the firm's internal accounting system.[1]

As part of the firm's control system, the internal accounting system helps align the interests of managers and shareholders to cause employees to maximize firm value. It sounds like a relatively easy task to design systems to ensure that employees maximize firm value. But a significant portion of this book demonstrates the exceedingly complex nature of aligning employee interests with those of the owners.

Internal accounting systems serve two purposes: (1) to provide some of the knowledge necessary for planning and making decisions (*decision making*) and (2) to help motivate and monitor people in organizations (*control*). The most basic control use of accounting is to prevent fraud and embezzlement. Maintaining inventory records helps reduce employee theft. Accounting budgets, discussed more fully in Chapter 6, provide an example of both decision making and control. Asking each salesperson in the firm to forecast their next year's sales is useful for planning next year's production (decision making). However, if the salesperson's sales forecast is used to benchmark their performance for compensation purposes (control), they have strong incentives to underestimate their budget forecasts.

Using internal accounting systems for both decision making and control gives rise to the fundamental trade-off in these systems: A system cannot be designed to perform two tasks as well as a system that must perform only one task. Some ability to deliver knowledge for decision making is usually sacrificed to provide better motivation (control). The trade-off between providing knowledge for decision making and motivation/control arises continually throughout this text.

This book is applications oriented: It describes how the accounting system assembles knowledge necessary for implementing decisions using the theories from microeconomics,

[1] *Control* refers to the process that helps "ensure the proper behaviors of the people in the organization. These behaviors should be consistent with the organization's strategy," as noted in K Merchant, *Control in Business Organizations* (Boston: Pitman Publishing Inc., 1985), p. 4. Merchant provides an extensive discussion of control systems and a bibliography. In *Theory of Accounting and Control* (Cincinnati, OH: South-Western Publishing Company, 1997), S Sunder describes control as mitigating and resolving conflicts between employees, owners, suppliers, and customers that threaten to pull organizations apart.

finance, operations management, and marketing. It also shows how the accounting system helps motivate employees to implement these decisions. Moreover, it stresses the continual trade-offs that must be made between the decision making and control functions of accounting.

A survey of 2,000 senior-level executives (chief financial officers, vice presidents of finance, controllers, etc.) asked managers to rank the importance of various goals of their firm's accounting system. The typical respondent was in a company with $300 million of sales and 1,700 employees. Eighty percent of the respondents reported that cost management (controlling costs) was a significant goal of their accounting system and was important to achieving their company's overall strategic objective. Another top priority of their firm's accounting system, even higher than cost management or strategic planning, is internal reporting and performance evaluation. These results indicate that firms use their internal accounting system both for decision making (strategic planning, cost reduction, financial management) and for controlling behavior (internal reporting and performance evaluation).[2]

The firm's accounting system is very much a part of the fabric that helps hold the organization together. It provides knowledge for decision making, and it provides information for evaluating and motivating the behavior of individuals within the firm. Being such an integral part of the organization, the accounting system cannot be studied in isolation from the other mechanisms used for decision making or for reducing organizational problems. A firm's internal accounting system should be examined from a broad perspective, as part of the larger organization design question facing managers.

This book uses an economic perspective to study how accounting can motivate and control behavior in organizations. Besides economics, a variety of other paradigms also are used to investigate organizations: scientific management (Taylor), the bureaucratic school (Weber), the human relations approach (Mayo), human resource theory (Maslow, Rickert, Argyris), the decision-making school (Simon), and the political science school (Selznick). Behavior is a complex topic. No single theory or approach is likely to capture all the elements. However, understanding managerial accounting requires addressing the behavioral and organizational issues. Economics offers one useful framework.

B. Design and Use of Cost Systems

Managers make decisions and monitor subordinates who make decisions. Both managers and accountants must acquire sufficient familiarity with cost systems to perform their jobs. Accountants (often called *controllers*) are charged with designing, improving, and operating the firm's accounting system—an integral part of both the decision-making and performance evaluation systems. Both managers and accountants must understand the strengths and weaknesses of current accounting systems. Internal accounting systems, like all systems within the firm, are constantly being refined and modified. Accountants' responsibilities include making these changes.

An internal accounting system should have the following characteristics:

1. Provides the information necessary to assess the profitability of products or services and to optimally price and market these products or services.

[2] Ernst & Young and IMA, "State of Management Accounting," www.imanet.org/pdf/SurveyofMgtAcctingEY.pdf, 2003.

FIGURE 1–1
The multiple role of accounting systems

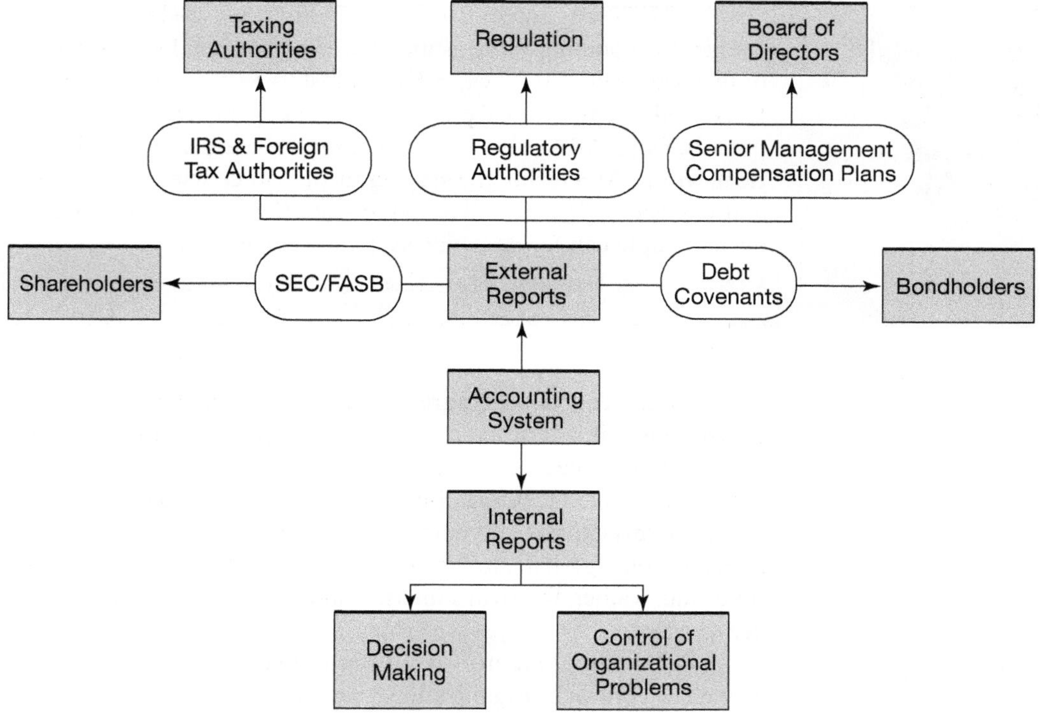

2. Provides information to detect production inefficiencies to ensure that the proposed products and volumes are produced at minimum cost.
3. When combined with the performance evaluation and reward systems, creates incentives for managers to maximize firm value.
4. Supports the financial accounting and tax accounting reporting functions. (In some instances, these latter considerations dominate the first three.)
5. Contributes more to firm value than it costs.

Figure 1–1 portrays the functions of the accounting system. In it, the accounting system supports both external and internal reporting systems. Examine the top half of Figure 1–1. The accounting procedures chosen for external reports to shareholders and taxing authorities are dictated in part by regulators. The **Securities and Exchange Commission (SEC)** and the **Financial Accounting Standards Board (FASB)** regulate the financial statements issued to shareholders. The **Internal Revenue Service (IRS)** administers the accounting procedures used in calculating corporate income taxes. If the firm is involved in international trade, foreign tax authorities prescribe the accounting rules applied in calculating foreign taxes. Regulatory agencies constrain public utilities' and financial institutions' accounting procedures.[3]

Management compensation plans and debt contracts often rely on external reports. Senior managers' bonuses are often based on accounting net income. Likewise, if the firm

[3] Tax laws can affect financial reporting and internal reporting. For example, a 1973 U.S. tax code change allowed firms to exclude manufacturing depreciation from inventories and write it off directly against taxable income of the period if the same method was used for external financial reporting. Such a provision reduces taxes for most firms, although few firms adopted the procedure. See E Noreen and R Bowen, "Tax Incentives and the Decision to Capitalize or Expense Manufacturing Overhead," *Accounting Horizons,* 1989.

Managerial Application: Spaceship Lost Because Two Measures Used

Multiple accounting systems are confusing and can lead to errors. An extreme example of this occurred in 1999 when NASA lost its $125 million Mars spacecraft. Engineers at Lockheed Martin built the spacecraft and specified the spacecraft's thrust in English pounds. But NASA scientists, navigating the craft, assumed the information was in metric newtons. As a result, the spacecraft was off course by 60 miles as it approached Mars and crashed. Whenever two systems are being used to measure the same underlying event, people can forget which system is being used.

SOURCE: A Pollack, "Two Teams, Two Measures Equaled One Lost Spacecraft," *The New York Times,* October 1, 1999, p. 1.

issues long-term bonds, it agrees in the debt covenants not to violate specified accounting-based constraints. For example, the bond contract might specify that the debt-to-equity ratio will not exceed some limit. Like taxes and regulation, compensation plans and debt covenants create incentives for managers to choose particular accounting procedures.[4]

As firms expand into international markets, external users of the firm's financial statements become global. No longer are the firm's shareholders, tax authorities, and regulators domestic. Rather, the firm's internal and external reports are used internationally in a variety of ways.

The bottom of Figure 1–1 illustrates that internal reports are used for decision making as well as control of organizational problems. As discussed earlier, managers use a variety of sources of data for making decisions. The internal accounting system provides one important source. These internal reports are also used to evaluate and motivate (control) the behavior of managers in the firm. The internal accounting system reports on managers' performance and therefore provides incentives for them. Any changes to the internal accounting system can affect all the various uses of the resulting accounting numbers.

The internal and external reports are closely linked. The internal accounting system affords a more disaggregated view of the company. These internal reports are generated more frequently, usually monthly or even weekly or daily, whereas the external reports are provided quarterly for publicly traded U.S. companies. The internal reports offer costs and profits by specific products, customers, lines of business, and divisions of the company. For example, the internal accounting system computes the unit cost of individual products as they are produced. These unit costs are then used to value the work-in-process and finished goods inventory, and to compute cost of goods sold. Chapter 9 describes the details of product costing.

Because internal systems serve multiple users and have several purposes, the firm employs either multiple systems (one for each function) or one basic system that serves all three functions (decision making, performance evaluation, and external reporting). Firms can either maintain a single set of books and use the same accounting methods for both internal and external reports, or they can keep multiple sets of books. The decision depends on the costs of writing and maintaining contracts based on accounting numbers, the costs from the dysfunctional internal decisions made using a single system, the additional bookkeeping costs arising from the extra system, and the confusion of having to reconcile the different numbers arising from multiple accounting systems.

Inexpensive accounting software packages and falling costs of computers have reduced some of the costs of maintaining multiple accounting systems. However, confusion arises

---

[4] For further discussion of the incentives of managers to choose accounting methods, see R Watts and J Zimmerman, *Positive Accounting Theory* (Englewood Cliffs, NJ: Prentice Hall, 1986).

Historical Application: Different Costs for Different Purposes

". . . cost accounting has a number of functions, calling for different, if not inconsistent, information. As a result, if cost accounting sets out, determined to discover what the cost of everything is and convinced in advance that there is one figure which can be found and which will furnish exactly the information which is desired for every possible purpose, it will necessarily fail, because there is no such figure. If it finds a figure which is right for some purposes it must necessarily be wrong for others."

SOURCE: J Clark, *Studies in the Economics of Overhead Costs* (Chicago: University of Chicago Press, 1923), p. 234.

when the systems report different numbers for the same concept. For example, when one system reports the manufacturing cost of a product as $12.56 and another system reports it at $17.19, managers wonder which system is producing the "right" number. Some managers may be using the $12.56 figure while others are using the $17.19 figure, causing inconsistency and uncertainty. Whenever two numbers for the same concept are produced, the natural tendency is to explain (i.e., reconcile) the differences. Managers involved in this reconciliation could have used this time in more productive ways. Also, using the same accounting system for multiple purposes increases the credibility of the financial reports for each purpose.[5] With only one accounting system, the external auditor monitors the internal reporting system at little or no additional cost.

Interestingly, a survey of large U.S. firms found that managers typically use the same accounting procedures for both external and internal reporting. For example, the same accounting rules for leases are used for both internal and external reporting by 93 percent of the firms. Likewise, 79 percent of the firms use the same procedures for inventory accounting and 92 percent use the same procedures for depreciation accounting.[6] Nothing prevents firms from using separate accounting systems for internal decision making and internal performance evaluation except the confusion generated and the extra data processing costs.

Probably the most important reason firms use a single accounting system is it allows reclassification of the data. An accounting system does not present a single, bottom-line number, such as the "cost of publishing this textbook." Rather, the system reports the components of the total cost of this textbook: the costs of proofreading, typesetting, paper, binding, cover, and so on. Managers in the firm then reclassify the information on the basis of different attributes and derive different cost numbers for different decisions. For example, if the publisher is considering translating this book into Russian, not all the components used in calculating the U.S. costs are relevant. The Russian edition might be printed on different paper stock with a different cover. The point is, a single accounting system usually offers enough flexibility for managers to reclassify, recombine, and reorganize the data for multiple purposes.

A single internal accounting system requires the firm to make trade-offs. A system that is best for performance measurement and control is unlikely to be the best for decision making. It's like configuring a motorcycle for both off-road and on-road racing: Riders on bikes designed for both racing conditions probably won't beat riders on specialized bikes designed for just one type of racing surface. Wherever a single accounting system exists, additional analyses arise. Managers making decisions find the accounting system less useful and devise other systems to augment the accounting numbers for decision-making purposes.

---

[5] A Christie, "An Analysis of the Properties of Fair (Market) Value Accounting," in *Modernizing U.S. Securities Regulation: Economic and Legal Perspectives,* K Lehn and R Kamphuis, eds. (Pittsburgh, PA: University of Pittsburgh, Joseph M. Katz Graduate School of Business, 1992).

[6] R Vancil, *Decentralization: Managerial Ambiguity by Design* (Burr Ridge, IL: Dow Jones-Irwin, 1979), p. 360.

Concept Questions

Q1–1	What causes the conflict between using internal accounting systems for decision making and control?
Q1–2	Describe the different kinds of information provided by the internal accounting system.
Q1–3	Give three examples of the uses of an accounting system.
Q1–4	List the characteristics of an internal accounting system.
Q1–5	Do firms have multiple accounting systems? Why or why not?

C. Marmots and Grizzly Bears

Economists and operating managers often criticize accounting data for decision making. Accounting data are often not in the form managers want for decision making. For example, the book value of a factory (historical cost less accumulated accounting depreciation) does not necessarily indicate the market or selling value of the factory, which is what a manager wants to know when contemplating shutting down the factory. Why do managers persist in using (presumably inferior) accounting information?

Before addressing this question, consider the parable of the marmots and the grizzly bears.[7] Marmots are small groundhogs that are a principal food source for certain bears. Zoologists studying the ecology of marmots and bears observed bears digging and moving rocks in the autumn in search of marmots. They estimated that the calories expended

Managerial Application: Managers' Views on Their Accounting Systems

Plant managers were asked to identify the major problems with their current cost system. The following percentages show how many plant managers selected each item as a key problem. (Percentages add to more than 100 percent because plant managers could select more than one problem.)

Provides inadequate information for product costing/pricing	53%
Lack of information for management decision making	52
Unsatisfactory operating performance measures	33
Lack of information for valid worker performance evaluation	30
Performance measures are not meaningful for competitive analysis	27
Performance measures are inconsistent with firm strategy	18
Other	17

Notice that these managers are more likely to fault the accounting system for decision making than for motivation and control. These findings, and those of other researchers, indicate that internal accounting systems are less useful as a source of knowledge for decision making than for external reporting and control.

SOURCE: A Sullivan and K Smith, "What Is Really Happening to Cost Management Systems in U.S. Manufacturing," *Review of Business Studies* 2 (1993), pp. 51–68.

[7] This example is suggested by J McGee, "Predatory Pricing Revisited," *Journal of Law & Economics* XXIII (October 1980), pp. 289–330.

Terminology: Benchmarking and Economic Darwinism

Benchmarking is defined as a "process of continuously comparing and measuring an organization's business processing against business leaders anywhere in the world to gain information which will help the organization take action to improve its performance."

Economic Darwinism predicts that successful firm practices will be imitated. Benchmarking is the practice of imitating successful business practices. The practice of benchmarking dates back to 607, when Japan sent teams to China to learn the best practices in business, government, and education. Today, most large firms routinely conduct benchmarking studies to discover the best business practices and then implement them in their own firms.

SOURCE: Society of Management Accountants of Canada, *Benchmarking: A Survey of Canadian Practice* (Hamilton, Ontario, Canada, 1994).

Historical Application: Sixteenth-Century Cost Records

The well-known Italian Medici family had extensive banking interests and owned textile plants in the fifteenth and sixteenth centuries. They also used sophisticated cost records to maintain control of their cloth production. These cost reports contained detailed data on the costs of purchasing, washing, beating, spinning, and weaving the wool, of supplies, and of overhead (tools, rent, and administrative expenses). Modern costing methodologies closely resemble these 15th-century cost systems, suggesting they yield benefits in excess of their costs.

SOURCE: P Garner, *Evolution of Cost Accounting to 1925* (Montgomery, AL: University of Alabama Press, 1954), pp. 12–13. Original source R de Roover, "A Florentine Firm of Cloth Manufacturers," *Speculum* XVI (January 1941), pp. 3–33.

searching for marmots exceeded the calories obtained from their consumption. A zoologist relying on Darwin's theory of natural selection might conclude that searching for marmots is an inefficient use of the bear's limited resources and thus these bears should become extinct. But fossils of marmot bones near bear remains suggest that bears have been searching for marmots for tens of thousands of years.

Since the bears survive, the benefits of consuming marmots must exceed the costs. Bears' claws might be sharpened as a by-product of the digging involved in hunting for marmots. Sharp claws are useful in searching for food under the ice after winter's hibernation. Therefore, the benefit of sharpened claws and the calories derived from the marmots offset the calories consumed gathering the marmots.

What does the marmot-and-bear parable say about why managers persist in using apparently inferior accounting data in their decision making? As it turns out, the marmot-and-bear parable is an extremely important proposition in the social sciences known as *economic Darwinism.* In a competitive world, if surviving organizations use some operating procedure (such as historical cost accounting) over long periods of time, then this procedure likely yields benefits in excess of its costs. Firms survive in competition by selling goods or services at lower prices than their competitors while still covering costs. Firms cannot survive by making more mistakes than their competitors.[8]

Economic Darwinism suggests that in successful (surviving) firms, things should not be fixed unless they are clearly broken. Currently, considerable attention is being directed

[8] See A Alchian, "Uncertainty, Evolution and Economic Theory," *Journal of Political Economy* 58 (June 1950), pp. 211–21.

at revising and updating firms' internal accounting systems because many managers believe their current accounting systems are "broken" and require major overhaul. Alternative internal accounting systems are being proposed, among them **activity-based costing (ABC), balanced score cards, economic value added (EVA),** and **Lean accounting systems.** These systems are discussed and analyzed later in terms of their ability to help managers make better decisions as well as to help provide better measures of performance for managers in organizations, thereby aligning managers' and owners' interests.

Although internal accounting systems may appear to have certain inconsistencies with some particular theory, these systems (like the bears searching for marmots) have survived the test of time and therefore are likely to be yielding unobserved benefits (like claw sharpening). This book discusses these additional benefits. Two caveats must be raised concerning too strict an application of economic Darwinism:

1. Some surviving operating procedures can be neutral mutations. Just because a system survives does not mean that its benefits exceed its costs. Benefits less costs might be close to zero.
2. Just because a given system survives does not mean it is optimal. A better system might exist but has not yet been discovered.

The fact that most managers use their accounting system as the primary formal information system suggests that these accounting systems are yielding total benefits that exceed their total costs. These benefits include financial and tax reporting, providing information for decision making, and creating internal incentives. The proposition that surviving firms have efficient accounting systems does not imply that better systems do not exist, only that they have not yet been discovered. It is not necessarily the case that what is, is optimal. Economic Darwinism helps identify the costs and benefits of alternative internal accounting systems and is applied repeatedly throughout the book.

D. Management Accountant's Role in the Organization

To better understand internal accounting systems, it is useful to describe how firms organize their accounting functions. No single organizational structure applies to all firms. Figure 1–2 presents one common organization chart. The design and operation of the internal and external accounting systems are the responsibility of the firm's chief financial officer (CFO). The firm's line-of-business or functional areas, such as marketing, manufacturing, and research and development, are combined and shown under a single organization, "operating divisions." The remaining staff and administrative functions include human resources, chief financial officer, legal, and other. In Figure 1–2, the chief financial officer oversees all the financial and accounting functions in the firm and reports directly to the president. The chief financial officer's three major functions include: controllership, treasury, and internal audit. Controllership involves tax administration, the internal and external accounting reports (including statutory filings with the Securities and Exchange Commission if the firm is publicly traded), and the planning and control systems (including budgeting). Treasury involves short- and long-term financing, banking, credit and collections, investments, insurance, and capital budgeting. Depending on their size and structure, firms organize these functions differently. Figure 1–2 shows the internal audit group reporting directly to the chief financial officer. In other firms, internal audit reports to the controller, the chief executive officer, or the board of directors.

The controller is the firm's chief management accountant and is responsible for data collection and reporting. The controller compiles the data for balance sheets and income statements and for preparing the firm's tax returns. In addition, this person prepares the internal reports for the various divisions and departments within the firm and helps the other

FIGURE 1–2
Organization chart for a typical corporation

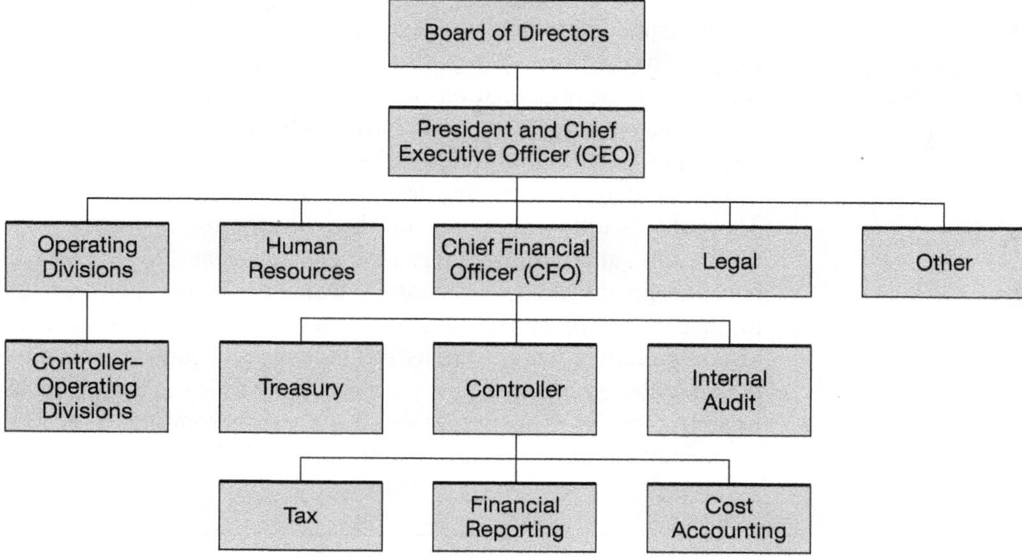

managers by providing them with the data necessary to make decisions—as well as the data necessary to evaluate these managers' performance.

Usually, each operating division or department has its own controller. For example, if a firm has several manufacturing plants, each plant has its own plant controller, who reports to both the plant manager and the corporate controller. In Figure 1–2, the operating divisions have their own controllers. The plant controller provides the corporate controller with periodic reports on the plant's operations. The plant controller oversees the plant's budgets, payroll, inventory, and product costing system (which reports the cost of units manufactured at the plant). While most firms have plant-level controllers, some firms centralize these functions to reduce staff, so that all the plant-level controller functions are performed centrally out of corporate headquarters.

The controllership function at the corporate, division, and plant levels involves assisting decision making and control. The controller must balance providing information to

Managerial Application: Super CFOs (Chief Financial Officers)

CFOs have greater responsibilities than ever before. As an integral part of the senior management team, CFOs oversee organizations that provide decision-making information, identify risks and opportunities, and often make unpopular decisions, such as shutting down unprofitable segments.

Global competition, greater attention on corporate governance, and technological change requires the CFO to have diverse skills, including:

- Deep understanding of the business.
- Knowledge of market dynamics and operational drivers of success.
- Strong analytic focus.
- Flexibility.
- Communication and team-building skills.
- Customer orientation.
- Appreciation for change management.

SOURCE: K Kuehn, "7 Habits of Strategic CFOs," *Strategic Finance* (September 2008), pp. 27–30.

Managerial Application: CFO's Role During a Global Economic Crisis

CFOs' usual duties include managing the firm's financial resources and maintaining the integrity of the financial reporting systems, but these responsibilities became even more critical to their organizations during the global financial crisis of 2008–2009. During normal economic times, firms have ready access to short-term bank loans to finance operations such as inventories and accounts receivable. Seasonal businesses usually borrow while they build inventories and provide their customers credit to make purchases. These short-term loans are repaid when the inventories and receivables are liquidated. But during the subprime mortgage financial crisis starting in 2008, financially weakened banks stopped making these normal loans. CFOs and their treasury staffs started monitoring daily the financial health of the banks who were lending them money. Corporations also rely on their banks to transfer funds across countries and various operations to pay their employees and suppliers. If a firm's bank fails and these critical cash transactions are impaired, the firm's operations are severely compromised. As PNC Bank senior vice president Scott Horan states, firms want "an ironclad guarantee for their cash accounts."

SOURCE: V Ryan, "All Eyes on Treasury," *CFO* (January 2009), pp. 36–41.

other managers for decision making against providing monitoring information to top executives for use in controlling the behavior of lower-level managers.

Besides overseeing the controllership and treasury functions in the firm, the chief financial officer usually has responsibility for the internal audit function. The internal audit group's primary roles are to seek out and eliminate internal fraud and to provide internal consulting and risk management. The Sarbanes-Oxley Act of 2002 mandated numerous corporate governance reforms, such as requiring boards of directors of publicly traded companies in the United States to have audit committees composed of independent (outside) directors and requiring these companies to continuously test the effectiveness of the internal controls over their financial statements. This federal legislation indirectly expanded the internal audit group's role. The internal audit group now works closely with the audit committee of the board of directors to help ensure the integrity of the firm's financial statements by testing whether the firm's accounting procedures are free of internal control deficiencies.

The Sarbanes-Oxley Act also requires companies to have corporate codes of conduct (ethics codes). While many firms had ethics codes prior to this act, these codes define honest and ethical conduct, including conflicts of interest between personal and professional relationships, compliance with applicable governmental laws, rules and regulations, and prompt internal reporting of code violations to the appropriate person in the company. The audit committee of the board of directors is responsible for overseeing compliance with the company's code of conduct.

The importance of the internal control system cannot be stressed enough. Throughout this book, we use the term *control* to mean aligning the interests of employees with maximizing the value of the firm. The most basic conflict of interest between employees and owners is employee theft. To reduce the likelihood of embezzlement, firms install internal control systems, which are an integral part of the firm's control system. Internal and external auditors' first responsibility is to test the integrity of the firm's internal controls. Fraud and theft are prevented not just by having security guards and door locks but also by having procedures that require checks above a certain amount to be authorized by two people. Internal control systems include internal procedures, codes of conduct, and policies that prohibit corruption, bribery, and kickbacks. Finally, internal control systems should prevent intentional (or accidental) financial misrepresentation by managers.

Concept Questions		
	Q1–6	Define *economic Darwinism.*
	Q1–7	Describe the major functions of the chief financial officer.

E. Evolution of Management Accounting: A Framework for Change

Management accounting has evolved with the nature of organizations. Prior to 1800, most businesses were small, family-operated organizations. Management accounting was less important for these small firms. It was not critical for planning decisions and control reasons because the owner could directly observe the organization's entire environment. The owner, who made all of the decisions, delegated little decision-making authority and had no need to devise elaborate formal systems to motivate employees. The owner observing slacking employees simply replaced them. Only as organizations grew larger with remote operations would management accounting become more important.

Most of today's modern management accounting techniques were developed in the period from 1825 to 1925 with the growth of large organizations.[9] Textile mills in the early nineteenth century grew by combining the multiple processes (spinning the thread, dying, weaving, etc.) of making cloth. These large firms developed systems to measure the cost per yard or per pound for the separate manufacturing processes. The cost data allowed managers to compare the cost of conducting a process inside the firm versus purchasing the process from external vendors. Similarly, the railroads of the 1850s to 1870s developed cost systems that reported cost per ton-mile and operating expenses per dollar of revenue. These measures allowed managers to increase their operating efficiencies. In the early 1900s, Andrew Carnegie (at what was to become U.S. Steel) devised a cost system that reported detailed unit cost figures for material and labor on a daily and weekly basis. This system allowed senior managers to maintain very tight controls on operations and gave them accurate and timely information on marginal costs for pricing decisions. Merchandising firms such as Marshall Field's and Sears, Roebuck developed gross margin (revenues less cost of goods sold) and stock-turn ratios (sales divided by inventory) to measure and evaluate performance. Manufacturing companies such as Du Pont Powder Company and General Motors were also active in developing performance measures to control their growing organizations.

In the period from 1925 to 1975, management accounting was heavily influenced by external considerations. Income taxes and financial accounting requirements (e.g., those of the Financial Accounting Standards Board) were the major factors affecting management accounting.

Since 1975, two major environmental forces have changed organizations and caused managers to question whether traditional management accounting procedures (pre-1975) are still appropriate. These environmental forces are (1) factory automation and computer/information technology and (2) global competition. To adapt to these environmental forces, organizations must reconsider their organizational structure and their management accounting procedures.

Information technology advances such as the Internet, intranets, wireless communications, and faster microprocessors have had a big impact on internal accounting processes.

[9] P Garner, *Evolution of Cost Accounting to 1925* (Montgomery, AL: University of Alabama Press, 1954); and A Chandler, *The Visible Hand* (Cambridge, MA: Harvard University Press, 1977).

More data are now available faster than ever before. Electronic data interchange, XHTML, e-mail, B2B e-commerce, bar codes, data warehousing, and online analytical processing (OLAP) are just a few examples of new technology impacting management accounting. For example, managers now have access to daily sales and operating costs in real time, as opposed to having to wait two weeks after the end of the calendar quarter for this information. Firms have cut the time needed to prepare budgets for the next fiscal year by several months because the information is transmitted electronically in standardized formats.

The brief history of management accounting from 1825 to the present illustrates how management accounting has evolved in parallel with organizations' structure. Management accounting provides information for planning decisions and control. It is useful for assigning decision-making authority, measuring performance, and determining rewards for individuals within the organization. Because management accounting is part of the organizational structure, it is not surprising that management accounting evolves in a parallel and consistent fashion with other parts of the organizational structure.

Figure 1–3 is a framework for understanding the role of accounting systems within firms and the forces that cause accounting systems to change. As described more fully in Chapter 14, environmental forces such as technological innovation and global competition change the organization's business strategies. For example, the Internet has allowed banks to offer electronic, online banking services. To implement these new strategies, organizations must adapt their organizational structure or architecture, which includes management accounting. An organization's architecture (the topic of Chapter 4) is composed of three related processes: (1) the assignment of decision-making responsibilities, (2) the measurement of performance, and (3) the rewarding of individuals within the organization.

The first component of the organizational architecture is assigning responsibilities to the different members of the organization. Decision rights define the duties each member of an organization is expected to perform. The decision rights of a particular individual within an organization are specified by that person's job description. Checkout clerks in grocery stores have the decision rights to collect cash from customers but don't have the decision rights to accept certain types of checks. A manager must be called for that decision. A division manager may have the right to set prices on products but not the right to borrow money by

FIGURE 1–3
Framework for organizational change and management accounting

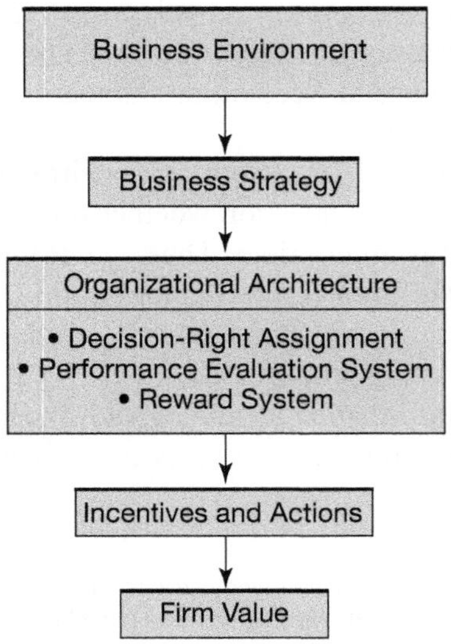

issuing debt. The president or the board of directors usually retains the right to issue debt, subject to board of directors' approval.

The next two parts of the organizational architecture are the performance evaluation and reward systems. To motivate individuals within the organization, organizations must have a system for measuring their performance and rewarding them. Performance measures for a salesperson could include total sales and customer satisfaction based on a survey of customers. Performance measures for a manufacturing unit might be number of units produced, total costs, and percentage of defective units. The internal accounting system is often an important part of the performance evaluation system.

Performance measures are extremely important because rewards are generally based on these measures. Rewards for individuals within organizations include wages and bonuses, prestige and greater decision rights, promotions, and job security. Because rewards are based on performance measures, individuals and groups are motivated to act to influence the performance measures. Therefore, the performance measures chosen influence individual and group efforts within the organization. A poor choice of performance measures can lead to conflicts within the organization and derail efforts to achieve organizational goals. For example, measuring the performance of a college president based on the number of students attending the college encourages the president to allow ill-prepared students to enter the college and reduces the quality of the educational experience for other students.

As illustrated in Figure 1–3, changes in the business environment lead to new strategies and ultimately to changes in the firm's organizational architecture, including changes in the accounting system to better align the interests of the employees with the objectives of the organization. The new organizational architecture provides incentives for members of the organization to make decisions, which leads to a change in the value of the organization. Within this framework, accounting assists in the control of the organization through the organization's architecture and provides information for decision making. This framework for change will be referred to throughout the book.

F. Vortec Medical Probe Example

To illustrate some of the basic concepts developed in this text, suppose you have been asked to evaluate the following decision. Vortec Inc. manufactures a single product, a medical probe. Vortec sells the probes to wholesalers who then market them to physicians. Vortec has two divisions. The manufacturing division produces the probes; the marketing division sells them to wholesalers. The marketing division is rewarded on the basis of sales revenues. The manufacturing division is evaluated and rewarded on the basis of the average unit cost of making the probes. The plant's current volume is 100,000 probes per month. The following income statement summarizes last month's operating results.

VORTEC MANUFACTURING
Income Statement
Last Month

Sales revenue (100,000 units @ $5.00)	$500,000
Cost of sales (100,000 units @ $4.50)	450,000
Operating margin	$ 50,000
Less: Administrative expenses	27,500
Net income before taxes	$ 22,500

Medsupplies is one of Vortec's best customers. Vortec sells 10,000 probes per month to Medsupplies at $5 per unit. Last week Medsupplies asked Vortec's marketing division to increase its monthly shipment to 12,000 units, provided that Vortec would sell the additional 2,000 units at $4 each. Medsupplies would continue to pay $5 for the original 10,000 units. Medsupplies argued that because this would be extra business for Vortec, no overhead should be charged on the additional 2,000 units. In this case, a $4 price should be adequate.

Vortec's finance department estimates that with 102,000 probes the average cost is $4.47 per unit, and hence the $4 price offered by Medsupplies is too low. The current administrative expenses of $27,500 consist of office rent, property taxes, and interest and will not change if this special order is accepted. Should Vortec accept the Medsupplies offer?

Before examining whether the marketing and manufacturing divisions will accept the order, consider Medsupplies's offer from the perspective of Vortec's owners, who are interested in maximizing profits. The decision hinges on the cost to Vortec of selling an additional 2,000 units to Medsupplies. If the cost is more than $4 per unit, Vortec should reject the special order.

It is tempting to reject the offer because the $4 price does not cover the average total cost of $4.47. But will it cost Vortec $4.47 per unit for the 2,000-unit special order? Is $4.47 the cost per unit for each of the next 2,000 units?

To begin the analysis, two simplifying assumptions are made that are relaxed later:

- Vortec has excess capacity to produce the additional 2,000 probes.
- Past historical costs are unbiased estimates of the future cash flows for producing the special order.

Based on these assumptions, we can compare the incremental revenue from the additional 2,000 units with its incremental cost:

Incremental revenue (2,000 units × $4.00)		$8,000
Total cost @ 102,000 units (102,000 × $4.47)	$455,940	
Total cost @ 100,000 units (100,000 × $4.50)	450,000	
Incremental cost of 2,000 units		5,940
Incremental profit of 2,000 units		$2,060

The estimated incremental cost per unit of the 2,000 units is then

$$\frac{\text{Change in total cost}}{\text{Change in volume}} = \frac{\$455{,}940 - \$450{,}000}{2{,}000} = \$2.97$$

The estimated cost per incremental unit is $2.97. Therefore, $2.97 is the average per-unit cost of the extra 2,000 probes. The $4.47 cost is the average cost of producing 102,000 units, which is more than the $2.97 incremental cost per unit of producing the extra 2,000 probes.

Based on the $2.97 estimated cost, Vortec should take the order. Is this the right decision? Not necessarily. There are some other considerations:

1. Will these 2,000 additional units affect the $5 price of the 100,000 probes? Will Vortec's other customers continue to pay $5 if Medsupplies buys 2,000 units at $4? What prevents Medsupplies from reselling the probes to Vortec's other customers at less than $5 per unit but above $4 per unit? Answering these questions requires management to acquire knowledge of the market for the probes.

2. What is the alternative use of the excess capacity consumed by the additional 2,000 probes? As plant utilization increases, congestion costs rise, production becomes less efficient, and the cost per unit rises. Congestion costs include the wages of the additional production employees and supervisors required to move, store, expedite, and rework products as plant volume increases. The $2.97 incremental cost computed from the average cost data on page 16 might not include the higher congestion costs as capacity is approached. This suggests that the $4.47 average cost estimate is wrong. Who provides this cost estimate and how accurate is it? Management must acquire knowledge of how costs behave at a higher volume. If Vortec accepts the Medsupplies offer, will Vortec be forced at some later date to forgo using this capacity for a more profitable project?

3. What costs will Vortec incur if the Medsupplies offer is rejected? Will Vortec lose the normal 10,000-unit Medsupplies order? If so, can this order be replaced?

4. Does the Robinson-Patman Act apply? The **Robinson-Patman Act** is a U.S. federal law prohibiting charging customers different prices if doing so is injurious to competition. Thus, it may be illegal to sell an additional 2,000 units to Medsupplies at less than $5 per unit. Knowledge of U.S. antitrust laws must be acquired. Moreover, if Vortec sells internationally, it will have to research the antitrust laws of the various jurisdictions that might review the Medsupplies transaction.

We have analyzed the question of whether Medsupplies's 2,000-unit special order maximizes the owners' profit. The next question to address is whether the marketing and manufacturing divisions will accept Medsupplies' offer. Recall that marketing is evaluated based on total revenues, and manufacturing is evaluated based on average unit costs. Therefore, marketing will want to accept the order as long as Medsupplies does not resell the probes to other Vortec customers and as long as other Vortec customers do not expect similar price concessions. Manufacturing will want to accept the order as long as it believes average unit costs will fall. Increasing production lowers average unit costs and makes it appear as though manufacturing has achieved cost reductions.

Suppose that accepting the Medsupplies offer will not adversely affect Vortec's other sales, but the incremental cost of producing the 2,000 extra probes is really $4.08, not $2.97, because there will be overtime charges and additional factory congestion costs. Under these conditions, both marketing and manufacturing will want to accept the offer. Marketing increases total revenue and thus appears to have improved its performance. Manufacturing still lowers average unit costs from $4.50 to $4.4918 per unit:

$$\frac{(\$4.50 \times 100{,}000) + (\$4.08 \times 2{,}000)}{102{,}000} = \$4.4918$$

However, the shareholders are worse off. Vortec's cash flows are lower by $160 [or 2,000 units × ($4.00 − $4.08)]. The problem is not that the marketing and manufacturing managers are "making a mistake." The problem is that the measures of performance are creating the wrong incentives. In particular, rewarding marketing for increasing total revenues and manufacturing for reducing average unit costs means there is no mechanism to ensure that the incremental revenues from the order ($8,000 = $4 × 2,000) are greater than the incremental costs ($8,160 = $4.08 × 2,000). Both marketing and manufacturing are doing what they were told to do (increase revenues and reduce average costs), but the value of the firm falls because the incentive systems are poorly designed.

Four key points emerge from this example:

1. *Beware of average costs.* The $4.50 unit cost tells us little about how costs will vary with changes in volume. Just because a cost is stated in dollars per unit does not mean that producing one more unit will add that amount of incremental cost.

2. *Use opportunity costs.* Opportunity costs measure what the firm forgoes when it chooses a specific action. The notion of opportunity cost is crucial in decision making. The opportunity cost of the Medsupplies order is what Vortec forgoes by accepting the special order. What is the best alternative use of the plant capacity consumed by the Medsupplies special order? (More on this in Chapter 2.)
3. *Supplement accounting data with other information.* The accounting system contains important data relevant for estimating the cost of this special order from Medsupplies. But other knowledge that the accounting system cannot capture must be assembled, such as what Medsupplies will do if Vortec rejects its offer. Managers usually augment accounting data with other knowledge such as customer demands, competitors' plans, future technology, and government regulations.
4. *Use accounting numbers as performance measures cautiously.* Accounting numbers such as revenues or average unit manufacturing costs are often used to evaluate managers' performance. Just because managers are maximizing particular performance measures tailored for each manager does not necessarily cause firm profits to be maximized.

The Vortec example illustrates the importance of understanding how accounting numbers are constructed, what they mean, and how they are used in decision making and control. The accounting system is a very important source of information to managers, but it is not the sole source of all knowledge. Also, in the overly simplified context of the Vortec example, the problems with the incentive systems and with using unit costs are easy to detect. In a complex company with hundreds or thousands of products, however, such errors are very difficult to detect. Finally, for the sake of simplicity, the Vortec illustration ignores the use of the accounting system for external reporting.

G. Outline of the Text

Internal accounting systems provide data for both decision making and control. The organization of this book follows this dichotomy. The first part of the text (Chapters 2 through 5) describes how accounting systems are used in decision making and providing incentives in organizations. These chapters provide the conceptual framework for the remainder of the book. The next set of chapters (Chapters 6 through 8) describes basic topics in managerial accounting, budgeting, and cost allocations. Budgets not only are a mechanism for communicating knowledge within the firm for decision making but also serve as a control device and as a way to partition decision-making responsibility among the managers. Likewise, cost allocations serve decision-making and control functions. In analyzing the role of budgeting and cost allocations, these chapters draw on the first part of the text.

The next section of the text (Chapters 9 through 13) describes the prevalent accounting system used in firms: absorption costing. Absorption cost systems are built around cost allocations. The systems used in manufacturing and service settings generate product costs built up from direct labor, direct material, and allocated overheads. After first describing these systems, we critically analyze them. A common criticism of absorption cost systems is that they produce inaccurate unit cost information, which can lead to dysfunctional decision making. Two alternative accounting systems (variable cost systems and activity-based cost systems) are compared and evaluated against a traditional absorption cost system. The next topic describes the use of standard costs as extensions of absorption cost systems. Standard costs provide benchmarks to calculate accounting variances: the difference between the actual costs and standard costs. These variances are performance measures and thus are part of the firm's motivation and control system described earlier.

The last chapter (Chapter 14) expands the integrative approach summarized in section E of this chapter. This approach is then used to analyze three modifications of internal cost systems: quality measurement systems, just-in-time production, and balanced scorecards. These recent modifications are evaluated within a broad historical context. Just because these systems are new does not suggest they are better. Some have stood the test of time, while others have not.

H. Summary

This book provides a framework for the analysis, use, and design of internal accounting systems. It explains how these systems are used for decision making and motivating people in organizations. Employees care about their self-interest, not the owners' self-interest. Hence, owners must devise incentive systems. Accounting numbers are used as measures of managers' performance and hence are part of the control system used to motivate managers. Most firms use a single internal accounting system as the primary data source for external reporting and internal uses. The fact that managers rely heavily on accounting numbers is not fully understood. Applying the economic Darwinism principle, the costs of multiple systems likely outweigh the benefits for most firms. The costs are not only the direct costs of operating the system but also the indirect costs from dysfunctional decisions resulting from faulty information and poor performance evaluation systems. The remainder of this book addresses the costs and benefits of internal accounting systems.

Problems

P 1–1: MBA Students

One MBA student was overheard saying to another, "Accounting is baloney. I worked for a genetic engineering company and we never looked at the accounting numbers and our stock price was always growing."

"I agree," said the other. "I worked in a rust bucket company that managed everything by the numbers and we never improved our stock price very much."

Evaluate these comments.

SOURCE: K Gartrell.

P 1–2: One Cost System Isn't Enough

Robert S. Kaplan in "One Cost System Isn't Enough" (*Harvard Business Review,* January–February 1988, pp. 61–66) states,

> No single system can adequately answer the demands made by diverse functions of cost systems. While companies can use one method to capture all their detailed transactions data, the processing of this information for diverse purposes and audiences demands separate, customized development. Companies that try to satisfy all the needs for cost information with a single system have discovered they can't perform important managerial functions adequately. Moreover, systems that work well for one company may fail in a different environment. Each company has to design methods that make sense for its particular products and processes.
>
> Of course, an argument for expanding the number of cost systems conflicts with a strongly ingrained financial culture to have only one measurement system for everyone.

Critically evaluate the preceding quote.

P 1–3: U.S. and Japanese Tax Laws

Tax laws in Japan tie taxable income directly to the financial statements' reported income. That is, to compute a Japanese firm's tax liability, multiply the net income as reported to shareholders by the appropriate tax rate to derive the firm's tax liability. In contrast, U.S. firms typically have more discretion in choosing different accounting procedures for calculating net income for shareholders (financial reporting) and taxes.

What effect would you expect these institutional differences in tax laws between the United States and Japan to have on internal accounting and reporting?

P 1–4: Managers Need Accounting Information

The opening paragraph of an accounting textbook says, "Managers need accounting information and need to know how to use it."[10] Critically evaluate this statement.

P 1–5: Using Accounting for Planning

The owner of a small software company felt his accounting system was useless. He stated, "Accounting systems only generate historical costs. Historical costs are useless in my business because everything changes so rapidly."

Required:

a. Are historical costs useless in rapidly changing environments?

b. Should accounting systems be limited to historical costs?

P 1–6: Goals of a Corporation

A finance professor and a marketing professor were recently comparing notes on their perceptions of corporations. The finance professor claimed that the goal of a corporation should be to maximize the value to the shareholders. The marketing professor claimed that the goal of a corporation should be to satisfy customers.

What are the similarities and differences in these two goals?

P 1–7: Budgeting

Salespeople at a particular firm forecast what they expect to sell next period. Their supervisors then review the forecasts and make revisions. These forecasts are used to set production and purchasing plans. In addition, salespeople receive a fixed bonus of 20 percent of their salary if they exceed their forecasts.

Discuss the incentives of the salespeople to forecast next-period sales accurately. Discuss the trade-off between using the budget for decision making versus using it as a control device.

P 1-8: Golf Specialties

Golf Specialties (GS), a Belgian company, manufactures a variety of golf paraphernalia, such as head covers for woods, embroidered golf towels, and umbrellas. GS sells all its products exclusively in Europe through independent distributors. Given the popularity of Tiger Woods, one of GS's more popular items is a head cover in the shape of a tiger.

GS is currently making 500 tiger head covers a week at a per unit cost of 3.50 euros, which includes both variable costs and allocated fixed costs. GS sells the tiger head covers to distributors for 4.25 euros. A distributor in Japan, Kojo Imports, wants to purchase 100 tiger head covers per week from GS and sell them in Japan. Kojo offers to pay GS 2 euros per head cover. GS has enough capacity to produce the additional 100 tiger head covers and estimates that if it accepts Kojo's offer, the per unit cost of all 600 tiger head covers will be 3.10 euros. Assume the cost data provided (3.50 euros and 3.10 euros) are accurate estimates of GS's costs of producing the tiger head covers. Further assume that GS's variable cost per head cover does not vary with the number of head covers manufactured.

[10] D Hansen and M Mowen, *Management Accounting,* 3rd ed. (Cincinnati: South-Western Publishing Co., 1994), p. 3.

Required:

a. To maximize firm value, should GS accept Kojo's offer? Explain why or why not.

b. Given the data in the problem, what is GS's weekly fixed cost of producing the tiger head covers?

c. Besides the data provided above, what other factors should GS consider before making a decision to accept Kojo's offer?

P 1–9: Parkview Hospital

Parkview Hospital, a regional hospital, serves a population of 400,000 people. The next closest hospital is 50 miles away. Parkview's accounting system is adequate for patient billing. The system reports revenues generated per department but does not break down revenues by unit within departments. For example, Parkview knows patient revenue for the entire psychiatric department but does not know revenues in the child and adolescent unit, the chemical dependence unit, or the neuropsychiatric unit.

Parkview receives its revenues from three principal sources: the federal government (Medicare), the state government (Medicaid), and private insurance companies (Blue Cross Blue Shield). Until recently, the private insurance companies continued to pay Parkview's increasing costs and passed these on to the firms through higher premiums for their employees' health insurance.

Last year Trans Insurance (TI) entered the market and began offering lower-cost health insurance to local firms. TI cut benefits offered and told Parkview that it would pay only a fixed dollar amount per patient. A typical firm could cut its health insurance premium 20 percent by switching to TI. TI was successful at taking 45 percent of the Blue Cross–Blue Shield customers. These firms faced stiff competition and sought to cut their health care costs.

Parkview management estimated that its revenues would fall 6 percent, or $3.2 million, next year because of TI's lower reimbursements. Struggling with how to cope with lower revenues, Parkview began the complex process of deciding what programs to cut, how to shift the delivery of services from inpatient to outpatient clinics, and what programs to open to offset the revenue loss (for example, open an outpatient depression clinic). Management can forecast some of the costs of the proposed changes, but many of its costs and revenues (such as the cost of the admissions office) have never been tracked to the individual clinical unit.

Required:

a. Was Parkview's accounting system adequate 10 years ago?

b. Is Parkview's accounting system adequate today?

c. What changes should Parkview make in its accounting system?

P 1–10: Montana Pen Company

Montana Pen Company manufactures a full line of premium writing instruments. It has 12 different styles and within each style, it offers ball point pens, fountain pens, mechanical pencils, and a roller ball pen. Most models also come in three finishes—gold, silver, and black matte. Montana Pen's Bangkok, Thailand, plant manufactures four of the styles. The plant is currently producing the gold clip for the top of one of its pen styles, no. 872. Current production is 1,200 gold no. 872 pens each month at an average cost of 185 baht per gold clip. (One U.S. dollar currently buys 35 baht.) A Chinese manufacturer has offered to produce the same gold clip for 136 baht. This manufacturer will sell Montana Pen 400 clips per month. If it accepts the Chinese offer and cuts the production of the clips from 1,200 to 800, Montana Pen estimates that the cost of each clip it continues to produce will rise from 185 baht to 212.5 baht per gold clip.

Required:

a. Should Montana Pen outsource 400 gold clips for pen style no. 872 to the Chinese firm? Provide a written justification of your answer.

b. Given your answer in part (*a*), what additional information would you seek before deciding to outsource 400 gold clips per month to the Chinese firm?

Chapter Four

Organizational Architecture

Chapter Outline

A. Basic Building Blocks

1. Self-Interested Behavior, Team Production, and Agency Costs
2. Decision Rights and Rights Systems
3. Role of Knowledge and Decision Making
4. Markets versus Firms
5. Influence Costs

B. Organizational Architecture

1. Three-Legged Stool
2. Decision Management versus Decision Control

C. Accounting's Role in the Organization's Architecture

D. Example of Accounting's Role: Executive Compensation Contracts

E. Summary

Chapter 2 described the important concept of opportunity cost and its relation to other costing terms. Understanding the nature of costs is critical to making decisions. Internal accounting systems are used not only in decision making but also for influencing the behavior of individuals within organizations.

This chapter addresses the general problem of controlling behavior and describes how the firm's organizational architecture can influence behavior. Individuals working in firms will maximize their welfare, sometimes to the detriment of the organization's objectives, unless provided incentives to do otherwise. Accounting systems are often used to provide these incentives. For example, incentive bonuses are often based on accounting earnings. Section A presents some building blocks underlying the analysis. Section B describes how the firm's organizational architecture creates incentives for employees to maximize the organization's objectives. Sections C and D describe how accounting controls conflicts of interest inside the organization. The next chapter discusses two more accounting tools that are used to resolve organizational problems: responsibility accounting and transfer pricing.

A. Basic Building Blocks[1]

Before describing the general problem of how to motivate and control behavior in organizations (the economics of organizations), this section first describes some underlying concepts:

1. Self-interested behavior, team production, and agency costs.
2. Decision rights and rights systems.
3. Role of knowledge and decision making.
4. Markets versus firms.
5. Influence costs.

1. Self-Interested Behavior, Team Production, and Agency Costs

One of the fundamental tenets of economics is that individuals act in their self-interest to maximize their utility. Employees, managers, and owners are assumed to be rational, utility-maximizing people. Individuals have preferences for a wide variety of not only goods and services but also intangibles such as prestige, love, and respect, and they are willing to trade one thing they value for another. People evaluate the opportunities they face and select those that they perceive will make them better off. Moreover, individuals are not generally able to satisfy all their preferences. Limited resources (time, money, or skills) force people to make choices. When confronted with constraints or a limited set of alternatives, individuals will use their resourcefulness to relax the constraints and generate a larger opportunity set. For example, when the highway speed limit was reduced to 55 miles per hour, the CB radio and radar detector industries emerged to help resourceful, self-interested people circumvent the new law.[2]

Individuals coalesce to form a firm because it can (1) presumably produce more goods or services collectively than individuals are capable of producing alone and (2) thus generate a larger opportunity set. Team production is the key reason that firms exist. Firms are contracting intermediaries. They facilitate exchanges among resource owners who voluntarily

---

[1] Much of the next two sections is based on M Jensen and W Meckling, "Specific and General Knowledge and Organizational Structure," *Contract Economics,* ed. L Werin and H Wijkander (Oxford: Blackwell, 1992), pp. 251–74. Also see J Brickley, C Smith, and J Zimmerman, *Managerial Economics and Organizational Architecture*, 5th ed. (Boston: McGraw-Hill, 2009).

[2] W Meckling, "Values and the Choice of the Model of the Individual in the Social Sciences," *Schweizerische Zeitschrift für Volkswirtschaft und Statistik,* December 1976.

Academic Application: Alternative Models of Behavior

Economists assume that individuals are self-interested and have preferences over a wide variety of things. This is not the only model of behavior. Psychologists offer another set of assumptions about how individuals make choices. Like economists, Maslow (1954) assumes that individuals are self-interested and have their own goals. He describes these goals in terms of satisfying different levels of needs. According to Maslow, an individual first seeks to satisfy physiological needs (food and shelter), followed by safety needs (security), love and belonging (a place within a group), esteem (self-respect), and self-actualization (creative expression).

No single model perfectly describes all behavior. Choosing among models of human behavior involves trading off predictive ability and complexity. Usually, the more complex the model, is the more it can explain. The advantage of using a simple economic model as presented here is its ease of exposition. While it is not literally correct and ignores many important complicating issues, its simplicity allows the essential elements to be communicated easily.

SOURCE: A Maslow, *Motivation and Personality* (New York: Harper & Row, 1954). For an excellent review of alternative models of behavior, including a critique of the economic theories, see C Perrow, *Complex Organizations: A Critical Essay*, 3rd ed. (New York: Random House, 1986).

contract among themselves to benefit each party.[3] People choose to enter contracts because they are made better off by the exchange; there are gains to each party in contracting.

Team production implies that the productivity of any one resource owner is affected by the productivity of all the other team members, because output is a joint product of all the inputs. Suppose Sally and Terry can produce more working together than working separately because they assist each other. Hence, Sally can increase Terry's output and vice versa. This interdependency has important implications for organizations and internal accounting. For one thing, measuring the productivity of one team member requires observing the inputs of all the other team members. However, inputs (such as effort) are typically difficult to observe. If two people are carrying a large, awkward box and it slips and falls, which employee do you blame? Did one of them let it go? Or did it slip out of one employee's hands because the other employee tripped?

In most cases, a resource owner's input cannot be directly observed. Hence, team members have incentives to shirk their responsibilities. If it is difficult to observe Sally's effort, she has incentives to shirk when working with Terry. She can always blame either Terry or random uncontrollable events such as bad weather or missing parts as the reason for low joint output. If Sally and Terry are paid based on their joint output, each still has an incentive to shirk because each bears only half the cost of the reduced output. As the team size is increased, the incentive to shirk becomes greater because the reduced output is spread over more team members. The incentive to shirk in team production is called the *free-rider problem.* Teams try to overcome the free-rider problem through the use of team loyalty—pressure from other team members—and through monitoring. Team production clearly has advantages, but it also causes a variety of organizational problems, in particular the free-rider problem.[4]

---

[3] C Barnard, *The Functions of the Executive* (Cambridge, MA: Harvard University Press, 1938), p. viii defines organizations as "a system of consciously coordinated activities or forces of two or more persons." See also M Jensen and W Meckling, "Theory of the Firm: Managerial Behavior, Agency Costs and Ownership Structure," *Journal of Financial Economics* 3 (1976), pp. 305–60.

[4] A Alchian and H Demsetz, "Production, Information Costs, and Economic Organization," *American Economic Review* 62 (1972), pp. 777–95.

Managerial Application: Agency Problems at General Electric

General Electric's (GE) former CEO Jack Welch received a lavish retirement package that attracted considerable public attention when the details became public. The package promised Welch lifetime access to such perks as use of a luxury Manhattan apartment, office space in New York and Connecticut, and access to GE aircraft and a chauffeured limousine. Mr. Welch received lifetime use of a $15 million apartment facing Central Park, floor-level seats to New York Knicks basketball games, Yankees tickets, a box at the Metropolitan Opera, use of the corporate Boeing 737, free flowers, free toiletries, and free satellite TV at his four homes. The exact details of Mr. Welch's retirement perks came to light when his wife filed for divorce. The perks, valued at $2.5 million a year, were a fraction of Welch's total retirement package, estimated at $20 million to $50 million. After an investigation by securities industry regulators and public outcry, GE revoked some of Welch's privileges, and he said he would pay for the rest.

SOURCE: L Browning, "Executive Pay: A Special Report; The Perks Still Flow (But With Less Fizz)," *The New York Times*, April 6, 2003, and A Borrus, "Exposing Execs' 'Stealth' Compensation," *BusinessWeek*, September 12, 2004, http://www.businessweek.com/bwdaily/dnflash/sep2004/nf20040924_8648_db016.htm.

Another organizational problem arises when principals hire agents to perform tasks for them. For example, the chief executive officer (CEO) is the agent of the board of directors, who are in turn the elected agents of the shareholders. Vice presidents of the firm are agents of the president, managers are agents of vice presidents, and employees are agents of supervisors. Most employees in a chain of command are both principals to those who report to them and agents to those to whom they report. These principal-agent relationships pervade all organizations: profit and nonprofit firms, the military, and other government units.

When hired to do a task, agents maximize their utility, which may or may not maximize the principal's utility. Agents' pursuit of their self-interest instead of the principal's is called the *principal-agent problem* or simply the *agency problem.*[5] The extreme example of an agency problem is employee theft of firm property. If undetected, such theft benefits the agent at the expense of the principal. The agent would prefer to see firm resources directed into activities that improve the agent's welfare even if these expenditures do not benefit the principal to the same degree. For example, agents prefer excessive perquisites such as gourmet company-provided lunches and on-the-job leisure. Differences among employees' risk tolerances, working horizons, and desired levels of job perks generate **agency costs**—the decline in firm value that results from agents pursuing their own interests to the detriment of the principal's interest. Agency costs can also arise when agents seek larger organizations to manage (empire building) for the sole purpose of increasing either their job security or their pay. (Many firms base pay on the number of employees reporting to the manager.)

In general, agency problems arise because of information asymmetries. The principal possesses less information than the agent. In the classic principal-agent problem, the principal hires the agent to perform some task, such as managing the principal's investment portfolio. If the agent works hard, the portfolio grows more than if the agent shirks. But the principal cannot observe how hard the agent is working (information asymmetry). Moreover,

[5] M Jensen and W Meckling (1976); H Simon, "A Formal Theory of the Employment Relationship," *Econometrica* 19 (1951), pp. 293–305; S Ross, "The Economic Theory of Agency: The Principal's Problem," *American Economic Review* 63 (1973), pp. 134–39; and O Williamson, *The Economic Institutions of Capitalism* (New York: The Free Press, 1985).

Managerial Application: Agency Problems at Société Générale

Société Générale was founded in the 1860s and in 2008 was France's second largest bank. It pioneered some of the most complex international finance instruments, earned billions of dollars, and gained the respect of bankers throughout the world. In January 2008 the bank discovered fraudulent securities trading by one of its low-level traders, Jérôme Kerviel. The fraud was estimated to cost a staggering $7.14 billion, making it one of the largest financial frauds in history. The bank asserted that the fraud was the result of one employee's illegal activities, did not involve other employees at the bank, and represented the aberrant and unexplainable actions of one "rogue trader."

Kerviel's job involved arbitraging small differences between various stock market indexes, such as the CAC in France and the DAX in Germany, by selling a security on the exchange with the higher price and simultaneously buying an equivalent instrument on the exchange with the lower price. Small prices differences on the two exchanges can produce a substantial profit when done in sufficient volume. Purchasing and selling equal amounts on the two exchanges should produce little net exposure to price changes. However, Kerviel had bought securities on both markets, betting that European stock prices would increase. When they fell, the bank incurred a substantial loss. Kerviel told investigators that all he wanted was to be respected and to earn a large bonus. One of his primary goals was to have his supervisors recognize his "financial genius."

Prior to becoming a trader, Kerviel had worked in the bank's trading accounting office, where he gained knowledge of the bank's risk-management system. This allowed him to conceal the trades and bypass the firm's control system. An investigation of this incident concluded that Société Générale "allowed a culture of risk to flourish, creating major flaws in its operations" that enabled Kerviel's actions to proceed. Traders were rewarded for making risky investments with the bank's money. Top executives at the bank received large bonuses because of the bank's successful trading operations.

This example illustrates that agency problems (including fraud) can impose enormous costs on firms.

Source: Adapted from J Brickley, C Smith, and J Zimmerman (2009), p. 13.

the investment portfolio's performance depends not just on how hard the agent works, but also on random events, such as general market movements or embezzlement by managers in a company in the investment portfolio. If the principal were able to observe the agent's effort, then a simple contract that pays the agent for effort expended could be used to force the agent to work hard. But since the agent's effort is not observable by the principal, the principal must contract on some other basis. One such contract could pay the agent a fraction of the portfolio's growth. But since part of the portfolio's performance depends on random factors, the agent could work hard, but adverse random events outside the agent's control could negate that hard work. While this contract induces hard work, it also imposes risk on the agent for which he or she must be compensated. Hence, most agency problems involve balancing stronger incentives for the agent to work hard against the higher risk premium required by the agent to compensate for the additional risk involved.

Consider another example of an agency problem, that of senior executives paid a fixed salary. Because executives have less incentive to maximize shareholder value than if they owned the entire firm themselves, incentive compensation plans are introduced to tie the executive's welfare more closely to shareholder welfare. The agent may have a lower tolerance for risk than the principal and therefore will choose more conservative actions. Principal–agent problems can also arise because most supervisors find it personally unpleasant to discipline or dismiss poorly performing subordinates. Instead of taking these unpopular actions, supervisors

Managerial Application: Agency Problems with Corporate Jet Pilots

Corporate jets often have to refuel on intercontinental flights, usually in Kansas or Nebraska. Refuelers at the same airport compete by offering pilots frozen steaks, wine, or top-of-the-line golf gear. These freebies are usually offered only if the pilot forgoes discounts on fuel, and they are almost always given in a covert manner—so that the corporation owning the plane never knows why the pilot has chosen that particular refueler. Suppose the pilot chooses a refueler who charges $150 more than the least-cost option because the pilot gets $80 worth of gifts. This wealth transfer from the owners of the jet to the pilot is an example of an agency problem.

SOURCE: S McCartney, "We'll Be Landing So the Crew Can Grab a Steak," *The Wall Street Journal*, September 8, 1998, p. A1.

TABLE 4–1 **Example of the Horizon Problem**

Year	*Outlay*	*Cost Savings*	*Effect on Henry Metz's Bonus Compensation*
1	$100,000	—	−$5,000
2	100,000	—	− 5,000
3	0	$150,000	+ 7,500
4	0	150,000	0
5	0	150,000	0
6	0	150,000	0

allow underperforming subordinates to remain in their positions, which reduces firm value. The difference between the value of the firm with and without the poorly performing subordinate is the agency cost imposed on the owners of the firm by the shirking supervisor.

If the agent expects to leave the organization before the principal, the agent will tend to focus on short-run actions. This leads to the *horizon problem:* Managers expecting to leave the firm in the near future place less weight than the principal on those consequences that may occur after they leave. As an example of the horizon problem, consider the case of a divisional manager, Henry Metz, who expects to retire in three years. Henry is paid a fixed salary plus 5 percent of his division's profits. To simplify the example, make the unrealistic assumption that Henry cares only about cash compensation. He can spend $100,000 on process improvements this year and next year that will yield $150,000 of cost savings for each of the following four years. Table 4–1 illustrates the cash flows.

The process improvements are clearly profitable, so they should be accepted.[6] But Henry, who has a three-year horizon, rejects the project because it reduces his total bonus. He bears much of the cost while his successor receives most of the benefits in years 4, 5, and 6. Nonpecuniary interests of the manager, such as peer pressure, tend to reduce the horizon problem. However, the basic point remains: Agents facing a known departure date place less weight on events that occur after they leave than on events that occur while they are still there; the short-term consequences of current decisions will matter far more to them than the long-term consequences.

To reduce agency costs such as employee theft and the free-rider and horizon problems, firms incur costs. These costs include hiring security guards to prevent theft, hiring supervisors to monitor employees, installing accounting and reporting systems to measure

[6] These process improvements have a positive net present value unless the discount rate is greater than 45 percent. Hence, under most market discount rates, they are profitable.

Academic Application: Adverse Selection and Moral Hazard Problems

Two types of agency problems have been given specific names. *Adverse selection* refers to the tendency of individuals with private information about something that benefits them to make offers that are detrimental to the trading partner. For example, individuals have more information regarding their health than do life insurance companies. If unconstrained, people who buy life insurance are likely to have more severe health problems than the average person assumed by the insurance company when setting its rates. After the insurance company sets its rates based on an average person, an adverse group of individuals will buy the insurance and the insurance company will lose money. To protect itself from adverse selection, insurance companies require medical exams to exclude the overly ill or to charge them higher prices (e.g., smokers).

Moral hazard problems arise when an individual has an incentive to deviate from the contract and take self-interested actions because the other party has insufficient information to know if the contract was honored. An example of a moral hazard problem often occurs in automobile accident claims. The insured may claim that the door was dented in the accident when in fact it was already damaged. To reduce moral hazard problems a variety of solutions exist, including inspections and monitoring.

and reward output, and paying legal fees to enforce compliance with contracts. However, as long as it is costly to monitor agents' actions, some divergence of interests between agents and principals will remain. It is usually not cost-efficient to eliminate all divergent acts.

Agency costs are also limited by the existence of a job market for managers, the market for corporate control, and competition from other firms. The job market for managers causes managers to limit their divergent actions to avoid being replaced by other (outside) managers.[7] Replacements will occur if the board of directors has access to these job markets and incentives to replace the managers. If the board fails to reduce the firm's agency costs, the firm's stock price declines. Low stock prices encourage takeovers. The market for corporate control will then limit the agency costs of existing management via unfriendly takeovers. Finally, if both the job and corporate control markets fail, other firms in the same product market will supply better products at lower prices and eventually force firms with high agency costs out of business. However, to the extent that there are transactions costs in all these markets, it will not be cost-beneficial to drive agency costs to zero. For example, if the transaction costs of a corporate takeover, including legal, accounting, and underwriting fees, are 3 percent of the value of the firm, then it will not pay outsiders to acquire the firm if the magnitude of the agency costs they hope to eliminate are less than 3 percent. Thus, this level of agency costs will persist.

Agents maximize their utility, not the principal's. This problem is commonly referred to as **goal incongruence**, which simply means that individual agents have different goals from their principal. The term is misleading, because it suggests that the firm can secure congruence by changing personal preferences (i.e., utility functions) so that all individuals in the organization adopt the principal's goal. However, self-interested individuals' preferences are not easily altered. The firm can reduce the agency problem, if not goal incongruence, by structuring agents' incentives so that when agents maximize their utility (primarily incentive-based compensation), the principal's utility (or wealth) is also maximized. In other words, the agents' and principals' goals become congruent through the agents' incentive scheme, not through a change in the agents' underlying preferences.

[7] E Fama, "Agency Problems and the Theory of the Firm," *Journal of Political Economy,* April 1980, pp. 288–307.

Managerial Application: Use of Specific Knowledge at Apple Computer

Apple's PowerBook was among the first portable Macs. It had so many bells and whistles that it weighed 17 pounds. It did not do well in the market. In 1990, Apple began completely reworking the design of the computer from the consumer's viewpoint. The entire product-development team of software designers, industrial engineers, marketing people, and industrial designers was sent into the field to observe potential customers using other products. The team discovered that people used laptops on airplanes, in cars, and at home in bed. People wanted mobile computers, not just small computers. In response, Apple redesigned the PowerBook as a new product that was easy to use and distinctive. Sales improved.

The knowledge of what customers really wanted in a laptop computer was acquired by a team who interacted closely with customers. The team also had important knowledge that allowed them to take this information and use it to design a marketable product. Finally, they had the authority to modify the product based on their findings. It is less likely that this specific knowledge would have been incorporated in product design in a large centrally planned firm—in which a central office is in charge of making literally thousands of decisions.

SOURCE: "Hot Products, Smart Design Is the Common Thread," *BusinessWeek,* June 7, 1993, pp. 54–57.

2. Decision Rights and Rights Systems

All economic resources or assets are bundles of decision rights with respect to how they can or cannot be used. For example, ownership of a car includes a bundle of decision rights over its use, although not unrestricted use. The car owner can drive, sell, paint, or even destroy the car, but it is illegal to drive the car over the speed limit. The police powers of the state enforce private decision rights over assets; the threat of legal sanctions is brought to bear against someone interfering with another's rights. If someone prevents you from driving your car by stealing it, the thief can be imprisoned. Our system of private property rights, including the courts and the police, enforces and limits individual decision rights.

Decision rights over the firm's assets are assigned to various people within the firm who are then held accountable for the results. If an individual is given decision-making authority over some decision (such as setting the price of a particular product), we say that person has the *decision right* for that product's price. Throughout the remainder of the book, we describe the importance of assigning decision rights to various individuals within the organization and the role of accounting in the assignment process. Who or what group of individuals has the decision rights to set the price, hire employees, accept a new order, or sell an asset? A key decision for many managers is whether to retain the right to make a particular decision or delegate the right to someone else. The question of whether the organization is centrally managed or decentralized is an issue of decision right assignment. **Employee empowerment** is a term that means assigning more decision rights to employees (i.e., decentralization). Accounting-based budgets assign decision rights to make expenditures to specific employees.

3. Role of Knowledge and Decision Making

Although they are rational and self-interested, individuals have limited capacities to gather and process knowledge. Since information (knowledge) is costly to acquire, store, and process, individual decision-making capacities are limited. Steve Jobs cannot make all of the decisions at Apple because he lacks the time to acquire the knowledge necessary for decision making. The process of generating the knowledge necessary to make a decision and then transferring that knowledge within the firm drives the assignment of decision rights.[8]

[8] M Jensen and W Meckling, *Contract Economics,* ed. L Werin and H Wijkander (Oxford: Blackwell, 1992), pp. 251–74.

Managerial Application: Skoda

The large Czech automaker, Skoda, has some of its suppliers actually located physically inside Skoda's assembly plants. To improve quality and costs, an independent supplier that provides dashboards is in the Skoda assembly plant. While this is an example of two separate firms producing across markets, the two firms are closely linked physically.

SOURCE: H Noori and W Lee, "Fractal Manufacturing Partnership," *Logistics Information Management*, 2000, pp. 301–11.

Because knowledge is valuable in decision making, knowledge and decision making are generally linked; the right to make the decision and the knowledge to make it usually reside within the same person. In fact, a key organizational architecture issue is *whether and how to link knowledge and decision rights.* Some knowledge, such as price and quantity, is easy (inexpensive) to transfer. In these cases, the knowledge is transferred to the person with the right to make the decision. Other knowledge is more difficult and hence costlier to transfer. Technical knowledge, such as how to design a computer chip, is costly to transfer. Knowledge that changes quickly, such as whether a machine is idle for the next hour, is costly to transfer in time to be useful; therefore, the decision right to schedule the machine is transferred to the person with the knowledge.

Ideally, knowledge and decision rights are linked, but they do not always reside with the same person. Suppose it is very difficult to transfer knowledge and very difficult to monitor the person with the knowledge. Moreover, suppose large agency costs arise if the person with the knowledge has the decision rights. Firm value might be higher if another manager with less knowledge makes the decision. This will occur if the costs from the inferior decisions made by the manager with less knowledge are smaller than the agency costs that result from giving the decision rights to the person with the better knowledge. For example, in many firms, salespeople do not have the decision right to negotiate prices directly with the customer, even though they have specialized knowledge of the customer's demand curve. Pricing is determined centrally by managers with less information, perhaps to reduce the likelihood that the salesperson will offer a low price and receive a kickback from the customer.

Within all organizations, decision rights and knowledge must be linked. As we will see, accounting systems, especially budgets (Chapter 6) and standard costs (Chapter 12), are important devices for transferring knowledge to the individuals with the decision rights or giving the decision rights to individuals with the knowledge.

4. Markets versus Firms

Production occurs either within a firm or across markets. For example, some computer software is produced by computer hardware companies and bundled with the computer, while other software is produced and sold separately. As another example, stereos can be purchased as entire systems. Here, the manufacturer designs, assembles, and ships complete units composed of a tuner-amplifier, CD player, speakers, and tape deck. Alternatively, the consumer can purchase the components separately and assemble a complete system.

Nobel Prize winner in economics Ronald Coase argued that firms lower certain transactions costs below what it would cost to acquire equivalent goods or services in a series of market transactions.[9] He conjectured that firms exist when they have lower costs than markets. Team production, discussed earlier, is one way firms can have lower costs than markets. When a firm can substitute one transaction that occurs inside the firm for a series of external market contracts, total contracting costs usually are lower.

[9] R Coase, "The Nature of the Firm," *Economica* 4 (1937), pp. 386–405. Also, see R Watts, "Accounting Choice Theory and Market-Based Research in Accounting," *British Accounting Journal* 24 (1992), pp. 242–46 for a summary of the arguments for the types of costs that are lowered by firms. These arguments include economies of scale in contracting, team production and monitoring, postcontractual opportunism, and knowledge costs.

Historical Application: Firms versus Markets When Markets Ruled

Much of the world's economic activity is conducted within firms. In fact, it is hard to envision a world where large firms do not play an important role in the production and distribution of products. The importance of firms, however, is a relatively recent phenomenon. Prior to the middle of the nineteenth century, there were almost no large firms. Most production was conducted by small owner-managed operations. The activities of these operations were coordinated almost entirely through market transactions and prices.

> The traditional American business (before 1950) was a single-unit business enterprise. In such an enterprise an individual or a small number of owners operated a shop, factory, bank, or transportation line out of a single office. Normally, this type of firm handled only a single economic function, dealt in a single product line, and operated in one geographic area. Before the rise of the modern firm, the activities of one of these small personally owned and managed enterprises were coordinated and monitored by market and price mechanisms.

The large firm became feasible only with the development of improved energy sources, transportation, and communications. In particular, coal provided a source of energy that made it possible for the factory to replace artisans and small mill owners, while railroads enabled firms to ship large quantities of goods to newly emerging urban centers. The telegraph allowed firms to coordinate activities of employees over larger geographic areas. These developments made it less expensive to coordinate production and distribution using administrative controls, rather than relying on numerous market transactions among numerous small firms.

SOURCE: A Chandler, *The Visible Hand: The Managerial Revolution in American Business* (Cambridge, MA: Harvard University Press, 1977).

The longer the term of a contract, the more difficult and costly it is to negotiate and to specify the respective parties' tasks. Firms eliminate a series of short-term market contracts and replace them with a single long-term contract. For example, if the firm has a long-term project to develop a sophisticated piece of computer software, it is likely that such software will be developed inside the firm as opposed to being purchased from an outside firm.

The costs of acquiring knowledge and enforcing contracts drive some production to occur within firms and other production to occur in markets. If knowledge were costless to acquire and process and there were no transactions costs, there would be no multiperson firms. To purchase an automobile, the consumer would enter into thousands of separate contracts with individual assemblers. If knowledge were free, these contracts would be costless. But knowledge is not free; our ability to acquire and process it is limited. Firms emerge because they economize on repetitive contracting. For example, individuals usually hire general contractors to build custom homes. The general contractor has specialized knowledge of the various skilled tradespeople (plumbers, carpenters, and electricians) and can monitor these subcontractors more cheaply (including transaction costs) than the individual home owner.

Coase's analysis has led to an important proposition in economics. Firms that survive in competition must have a comparative advantage in constructing contracts for internal production. Surviving firms have lower transactions costs than the market. This is an application of economic Darwinism (discussed in Chapter 1).

Nonetheless, markets perform certain functions far better than firms. Ultimately, markets exist because of the right to transfer ownership of an asset and receive the proceeds. As noted earlier, individuals or firms have decision rights with respect to resources that they own, including the right to use those resources as they see fit (within the limits of the law), the right

Managerial Application: Markets versus Firms: Taxicabs

To illustrate how markets help to control human behavior, consider the example of privately owned and operated cabs versus cabs owned by a taxi company and driven by different-salaried drivers. Which cabs will have a higher market value after being driven 50,000 miles? The owners of privately owned cabs have a greater incentive to maintain their cabs than the drivers of company-owned cabs. The resale price of each cab reflects wear and tear and maintenance. Since private cab drivers, as the sole drivers, bear all the financial consequences of their actions, they have an incentive to provide the correct amount of maintenance and generally drive the cab in such a way as to maximize the market value of the cab at resale. Drivers for the taxi company do not bear the consequences of any abusive driving and/or poor maintenance, unless the taxi company implements costly procedures to monitor the condition of the cabs after each driver's shift. To provide incentives for the cabbies not to damage the cabs, the taxi company must install monitoring devices, but it is prohibitively costly to detect all abuse (such as transmission damage).

to sell the resources, and the right to the sales proceeds. Markets discipline those who have the resources to use them in their highest-valued way. If owners lower the value of their assets by not properly maintaining them, markets punish them by lowering the resale price. Thus, markets not only measure decision makers' performance but also reward or punish that behavior. In fact, markets do three things automatically that organizations (firms) can accomplish only through elaborate administrative devices: (1) measure performance, (2) reward performance, and (3) partition rights to their highest-valued use. When Adam Smith described the invisible hand of the market and how the market allocates resources to their most highly valued use, he was describing how the market influences behavior and assigns decision rights.[10]

Because an asset's current price reflects the future cash flows associated with it, decision rights over how assets will be used in the future tend to be assigned to those who value them the highest. In markets, decision rights are linked with knowledge. Individuals or firms with "better" knowledge in using the asset will be willing to pay a higher price for the asset, thereby linking knowledge with decision rights.

5. Influence Costs

To this point, we have assumed that when decision-making authority is granted to an individual or a team within the firm, that agent or team is then actively involved in decision making (subject to ratification and monitoring from others). Sometimes, however, firms use bureaucratic rules that purposely limit active decision making. For example, airlines allocate routes to flight attendants based on seniority—there is no supervisor deciding who gets which route. Similarly, some firms base promotions solely on years worked with the firm.

One potential benefit of limiting discretion in making decisions is that it reduces the resources consumed by individuals in trying to influence decisions. Employees are often very concerned about the personal effects of decisions made within the firm. For example, flight attendants care about which routes they fly. Employees are not indifferent to which colleagues are laid off in an economic downturn. These concerns motivate politicking and other potentially nonproductive activities. For instance, employees might waste valuable time trying to influence decision makers. In vying for promotions, employees might take dysfunctional actions to make other employees look bad.

By not assigning the decision right to a specific individual, influence costs are lowe-red because there is no one to lobby. This policy, however, can impose costs on an organization. For example, consider individuals who are competing for a promotion. Each of these individuals

[10] A Smith, *The Wealth of Nations,* 1776, Cannan edition (New York: Modern Library, 1937).

has an incentive to provide evidence to the supervisor that he or she is the most qualified person for the promotion. Such information is often useful in making better promotion decisions. However, the information comes at a cost—employees spend time trying to convince the supervisor that they are the most qualified candidate rather than performing some other activity such as selling products.

In some cases, the firm's profits are largely unaffected by decisions that greatly affect individual employee welfare. For example, firm profits might be invariant as to which flight attendant gets the Hawaii route versus the Sioux Falls route. It is in this setting that bureaucratic rules for decision making are most likely. The firm benefits from a reduction in influence costs but is little affected by the particular outcome of the decision process.

Concept Questions

Q4–1	What generates agency costs?
Q4–2	How are agency costs reduced, and what limits them?
Q4–3	Define *goal incongruence.*
Q4–4	How does one achieve goal congruence?
Q4–5	Why are knowledge and decision making linked within a firm?
Q4–6	Name three things markets do automatically that must be replaced with elaborate administrative systems in the firm.
Q4–7	What are influence costs?
Q4–8	Why do firms exist?

B. Organizational Architecture

When firms undertake certain repetitive transactions instead of contracting for them in outside markets, market prices for resources used inside the firm no longer exist. For example, the firm can be thought of as a bundle of resources used jointly to produce a product. Suppose one of the many jointly used resources is a machine used in manufacturing. There is not a specific market price for the machine used inside the firm. There is not a price for an hour of time on the machine because the firm does not engage in selling time on this machine. There may be market prices for leasing time on other firms' machine, but if buying outside machine firm was cheaper than using the internal machine, the machine would not exist inside the time.[11] The cost of buying outside services includes the external price and the transactions costs of using the market. Even if prices for seemingly equivalent transactions occurring in markets exist, they are unlikely to represent the opportunity cost for transactions within the firm. The transaction exists within the firm, not in the market, because the firm can perform the transaction more cheaply than the market. Hence, the external market price for the machine, while indicative of what the firm can charge for time on its machine, does not capture the opportunity cost of using the machine inside the firm. The market price does not entirely capture the transactions cost savings of owning the machine.[12]

[11] R Ball, "The Firm as a Specialist Contracting Intermediary: Applications to Accounting and Auditing," manuscript (Rochester, NY: William E. Simon Graduate School of Business Administration, University of Rochester, 1989).

[12] "Observed market prices cannot directly guide the owner of the input to perform in the same manner as if every activity he performs were measured and priced." S Cheung, "The Contractual Nature of the Firm," *Journal of Law & Economics* 26 (April 1983), p. 5.

Managerial Application: Gaming Objective Performance-Evaluation Systems

This example illustrates how members of one local management team who did not want to lose their jobs successfully gamed the performance-evaluation system their company used in deciding when to close unprofitable mines.

> In this particular company, mines were shut down after the yield per ton of ore dropped below a certain level. One old marginal mine managed to stay open for several years because of the strategic behavior of its management. It happened that the mine contained one very rich pocket of ore. Instead of mining this all at once, the management used it as its reserve. Every time the yield of the ore it was mining fell below an acceptable level, it would mix in a little high-grade ore so the mine would remain open.

SOURCE: E Lawler and J Rhode, *Information and Control in Organizations* (Santa Monica, CA: Goodyear Publishing, 1976), pp. 87–88.

1. Three-Legged Stool

The firm cannot always use the external market's price (even if available) to guide internal transactions. More important, in the absence of the discipline of the market, the parties to the firm must design administrative devices to (1) measure performance, (2) reward performance, and (3) partition decision rights. These three activities (called **organizational architecture**) are performed automatically by markets but must be performed by (costly) administrative devices inside the firm.[13]

Performance evaluation can involve either objective or subjective performance measures or combinations of both. Objective criteria include explicit, verifiable measures such as paying employees on piece rates or sales. Subjective criteria focus on multiple hard-to-measure factors. For example, subjective performance measures of a manager include a variety of factors such as improving team spirit, getting along with peers, meeting budgets and schedules, and affirmative action hiring. Firms use implicit, subjective performance measures because jobs typically have multiple dimensions. If a few explicit characteristics are chosen to reward performance, employees will ignore the hard-to-quantify aspects of their work. Although firms must measure and reward performance, the performance measure need not be objective. Firms that use objective performance measures supplement them with subjective measures to ensure that employees do not focus entirely on the objective criteria to the detriment of their other responsibilities.

Besides measuring performance, organizations must reward favorable performance and in some cases punish unwanted behaviors (sometimes by firing employees). Agents meeting or exceeding performance expectations are rewarded with pay increases, bonuses, promotions, and perquisites. Superior performance is rewarded with both monetary and nonmonetary compensation. Monetary rewards involve salary, bonus, and retirement benefits. Nonmonetary rewards include prestigious job titles, better office location and furnishings, reserved parking spaces, and country club memberships.

Another administrative device in firms is partitioning decision rights. Within organizations, all decision rights initially reside with the board of directors. The vast majority of these rights are assigned to the chief executive officer (CEO), with the exception of the right to replace the CEO and set his or her pay. The CEO retains some rights and reassigns the rest to subordinates. This downward cascading of decision rights within an organization gives rise to the familiar pyramid of hierarchies. Centralization and decentralization revolve around the issues of partitioning decision rights between higher versus lower levels of the organization and linking knowledge and decision rights.

[13] Jensen and Meckling (1992), p. 265.

Managerial Application: Objective and Subjective Performance Criteria at Lincoln Electric Company

Lincoln Electric manufactures electric arc welding machines and welding disposables (electrodes). At the heart of Lincoln Electric's success is a strategy of building quality products at a lower cost than its competitors and passing the savings on to customers. Lincoln has been able to implement this strategy, in part, through an employee incentive system that fosters labor-productivity increases arising from a pay-for-performance compensation plan.

The two components of Lincoln's performance evaluation scheme are pieces produced and merit rating. The first component is an objective, readily quantifiable performance measure for each production employee (i.e., the number of good units produced). The employee's wage is equal to the piece rate times the number of good units produced. (Employees are not paid for defects.) By working hard, in some cases even through lunch and breaks, employees can double and sometimes triple their pay.

The second component of Lincoln's evaluation scheme is the employee's merit rating. These ratings are used to determine the employee's share of the bonus pool. The size of the bonus pool approximately equals wages and is about twice Lincoln's net income after taxes, although there is substantial annual variation in the size of the pool. Each employee's merit evaluation is based on employee dependability, quality, output, and ideas and cooperation, assessed primarily by the employee's immediate supervisor.

Two important observations emerge from Lincoln Electric. First, the output from the performance evaluation system is used as an input by the performance reward system; the two systems are linked. Second, Lincoln uses highly objective, explicit measures of performance (piecework) as well as subjective measures (ideas and cooperation).

SOURCE: www.lincolnelectric.com

Managerial Application: Performance Evaluation and Rewards at the Haier Group

Haier, one of China's fastest growing firms, stresses customer service, product quality, efficiency, and speed to market. It is one of the 100 most recognizable brands in the world and manufactures more than 15,000 different home appliances such as refrigerators, air conditioners, microwaves, and washing machines that are sold in 160 countries through 59,000 sales outlets. In the 1980s it was near bankruptcy. What explains Haier's phenomenal success?

Haier utilizes advanced information technology in operating its employee performance measurement and reward systems. Each day every factory worker receives a detailed report card outlining his or her production quantity, quality, defects, technology level, equipment use, and safety record. Each employee is expected to improve 1 percent over the previous day. Realizing these improvements results in higher wages, bonuses, more job training, and additional social benefits. People not achieving their targets are demoted and eventually fired. Managers are reviewed weekly based on their achieving both qualitative and quantitative goals such as process improvement and innovation. Managers, like factory workers, are rewarded with additional pay and promotions for meeting their targets or they are demoted or even fired for poor performance. Dozens of Haier employees are fired every month. "Whoever tarnishes the brand of the company will be dismissed by the company."

SOURCE: T Lin, "Lessons from China," *Strategic Finance*, October 2006, pp. 48–55; http://www.haier.com.pk/.

Managerial Application: Use of Financial and Nonfinancial Performance Measures

One study found that nonfinancial physical measures such as labor headcounts, units of output, units in inventory, and units scrapped are used to run day-to-day operations. The nonfinancial data chosen are highly correlated with the financial reports of the manager's performance and are readily available on a daily or even hourly basis. Also, the nonfinancial data tend to be variables that the manager can control. Yet when asked about their "most valuable report in general," respondents said it was the monthly income or expense statement.

SOURCE: S McKinnon and W Bruns, *The Information Mosaic* (Boston: Harvard Business School Press, 1992).

Ultimately, all organizations must construct three systems:

1. A system that measures performance.
2. A system that rewards and punishes performance.
3. A system that assigns decision rights.

These three systems make up the firm's organizational architecture. They are like the legs of a three-legged stool. For the stool to remain level, all three legs must balance. Similarly, each of the three systems that compose the organization's architecture must be coordinated with the other two. The performance measurement system must measure the agent's performance in areas over which he or she has been assigned the decision rights. Likewise, the reward system must be matched to those areas over which performance is being measured. A person should not be assigned decision rights if the exercise of these rights cannot be measured and rewarded. Though this sounds obvious, changing one system often requires changing the other two systems.

The internal accounting system is a significant part of the performance measurement system. Changes are often made to this system without regard to their impact on the performance-reward and decision-assignment systems. Managers making changes to the accounting system are surprised when the stool is no longer level because one leg is now a different length than the other two.

Performance measurement systems generally use financial and nonfinancial measures of performance. Nonfinancial metrics include: percentage of on-time deliveries, order completeness, factory ability to meet production schedules, excess inventory, employee turnover, manufacturing quality, percentage of defects and units of scrap, schedule performance, and customer complaints.

Financial indicators are collected and audited by the firm's accountants, whereas nonfinancial measures are more likely to be self-reported. Therefore, financial measures are usually more objective and less subject to managerial discretion. Nonfinancial indicators usually relate to important strategic factors. For example, airline profitability is very sensitive to the fraction of airline seats occupied. Thus, load factors are an important strategic measure in airlines. Nonfinancial measures provide information for decision making. Financial measures of performance tend to be for control.

One problem with using nonfinancial measures is that they tend to proliferate to the point that managers can no longer jointly maximize multiple measures. Numerous performance measures dilute attention. If several key indicators are used, senior managers must implicitly specify the relative weights for each indicator for performance evaluation. Which indicator is really the most important in assessing performance? If senior management does not specify the weights, subordinates are uncertain which specific goal should receive the most attention. Chapter 14 describes the Balanced Score Card, and specifically the problem of using multiple performance measures.

Managerial Application: Bonuses Abused at the VA

Most federal agencies pay executive bonuses to increase accountability in government by tying pay closely to performance. Federal bonuses are designed to retain and reward knowledgeable and professional career public servants. While bonuses can help retain key employees, nonperformance-based bonuses can be counter-productive.

In 2007, top officials at the Department of Veterans Affairs (VA), the agency charged with caring for military veterans, received an average bonus of $16,700, and a deputy assistant secretary and several regional directors each received $33,000, about 20 percent of their salaries. The heads of the VA's various divisions supposedly determine the bonuses, based in part on performance evaluations.

These bonuses came to light and proved politically embarrassing after stories appeared about a $1 billion shortfall that put veterans' health care in peril and substandard care at Walter Reed Hospital in Washington, D.C.

Senator Daniel Akaka, chairman of the Senate Veterans' Affairs Committee, said the payments pointed to an improper "entitlement for the most centrally placed or well-connected staff, and awards should be determined according to performance."

Steve Ellis, vice president of Taxpayers for Common Sense, said that "while the VA bonuses were designed to increase accountability in government by tying raises more closely to performance, damage can be done when payments turn into an automatic handout regardless of performance."

This example illustrates how pay-for-performance systems, in this case bonuses, can be gamed and, in the end, produce dysfunctional results.

SOURCE: "VA Officials' Bonuses Raise Eyebrows," May 3, 2007, http://www.cbsnews.com/stories/2007/05/03/national/main2757717.shtml.

Managerial Application: When the Legs of the Stool Don't Balance

This example illustrates how dysfunctional decisions can result when the three legs of the stool do not match. A plane was grounded for repairs at an airport. The nearest qualified mechanic was stationed at another airport. The decision right to allow the mechanic to work on the airplane was held by the manager of the second airport. The manager's compensation, however, was tied to meeting his own budget rather than to the profits of the overall organization. The manager refused to send the mechanic to fix the plane immediately, because the mechanic would have had to stay overnight and the hotel bill would have been charged to the manager's budget. The mechanic was dispatched the next morning so that he could return the same day. A multimillion-dollar aircraft was grounded, costing the airline thousands of dollars. The manager, however, avoided a $100 hotel bill. The mechanic would probably have been dispatched immediately had the manager been rewarded on the overall profit of the company or had the decision right been held by someone else with this objective.

SOURCE: M Hammer and J Champy, *Reengineering the Corporation* (New York: Harper Business, 1993).

2. Decision Management versus Decision Control

Markets automatically control behavior and partition decision rights. The firm must design administrative devices to do what the market does. These mechanisms include hierarchies to separate decision management from control, budgeting systems, periodic performance evaluation systems, standard operating rules and policy manuals, bonus plans and executive compensation schemes, and accounting systems. Some of these administrative devices, such as hierarchies and performance evaluation systems, are described in greater detail below. Budgeting systems and accounting systems are deferred to later chapters. (Standard operating rules and policy manuals are not addressed.)

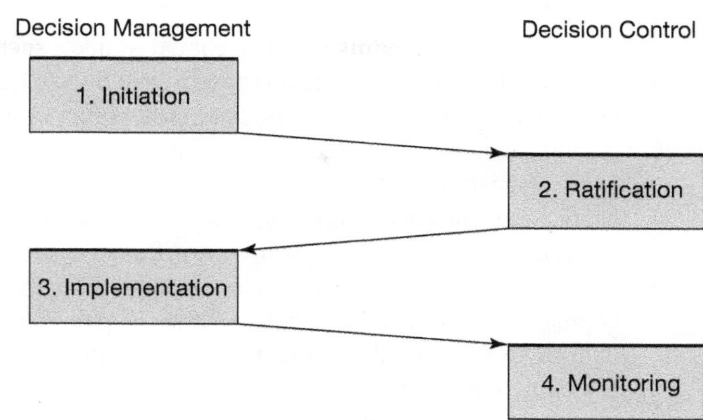

FIGURE 4–1
Steps in the decision-making process: Decision management versus decision control

Perhaps the most important mechanism for resolving agency problems is a hierarchical structure that separates decision management from decision control.[14] All organizations have hierarchies with higher-level managers supervising lower-level employees. **Decision management** refers to those aspects of the decision process in which the manager either *initiates* or *implements* a decision. **Decision control** refers to those aspects of the decision process whereby managers either *ratify* or *monitor* decisions. See Figure 4–1. Managers rarely are given all the decision rights to make a particular decision. Rather, an elaborate system of approvals and monitoring exists. Consider a typical decision to hire a new employee. First, a manager requests authorization to add a new position. This request is reviewed by higher-level managers. Once the position is authorized, the manager making the request usually begins the recruiting and interviewing process. Eventually a new employee is hired. After a certain period, the employee's performance is evaluated. In general, the following steps in the decision process occur (categorized according to decision management or decision control): (1) initiation (management), (2) ratification (control), (3) implementation (management), and (4) monitoring (control). *Initiation* is the request to hire a new employee. *Ratification* is the approval of the request. *Implementation* is hiring the employee. *Monitoring* involves assessing the performance of the hired employee at periodic intervals to evaluate the person who hires the employee.

Individual managers typically do not have the authority to undertake all four steps in this decision process. The manager requesting a new position does not have the decision right to ratify (approve) the request. There is a *separation of decision management from control.* The same principle in the U.S. Constitution separates the powers of the various branches of government. The executive branch requests spending, which is approved by the legislature. The executive branch is then charged with making the expenditures. The judicial branch ultimately monitors both the executive and legislative branches.

As another example of how knowledge is linked with initiation rights and how hierarchies separate decision management from decision control, consider the decision to acquire capital assets. The decision to build a new plant usually begins with division managers who make a formal proposal to senior management. This is decision *initiation.* The initiating managers have specialized knowledge of their production process and product demand. The formal proposal usually takes the form of a capital budget request. Senior managers then ask the finance department to evaluate the discounted cash flow assumptions in the capital budget request. The finance department possesses specialized knowledge to judge risk-and-return assumptions in the discount rate and the analysis of the cash flows in the plan. Senior management assembles other knowledge from the human resource, real estate, and legal departments in the *ratification*

[14] See E Fama and M Jensen, "Separation of Ownership and Control," *Journal of Political Economy,* June 1983, pp. 301–25.

Managerial Application: Capital Project Monitoring at Caterpillar

Caterpillar Inc. monitors strategic capital projects such as a new plant over the life of each project. Once a capital project is approved and installed, a monitoring team reviews it every six months. Only large strategic projects (often composed of several individual capital assets), such as an axle factory or an assembly line, are evaluated. The project monitoring team consists of representatives from industrial engineering, manufacturing, materials acquisition, and cost accounting. They prepare a report that compares the actual results with the budgeted results. Reasons for any differences are listed, including a detailed report that reconciles why the project's current results differ from what was expected at the time the capital project was approved. In addition, the monitoring team issues a list of recommendations to improve the performance of the project. The monitoring team's findings are distributed to the manager of the project being evaluated, the building superintendent, the plant manager, the group presidents, and the corporate board of directors.

SOURCE: J Hendricks, R Bastian, and T Sexton, "Bundle Monitoring of Strategic Projects," *Management Accounting*, February 1992, pp. 31–35.

process. Construction of the project—*implementation*—is the responsibility of the proposing managers or a separate facilities department within the firm. After construction is completed, accountants prepare monthly, quarterly, and annual reports on the division requesting and operating the capital project. This is part of the *monitoring* process.

Organizations separate decision management from decision control. Before implementing a decision, someone higher up in the organization must ratify it. Management and control are not separated, however, when it is too costly to separate them. For example, managers are often assigned the decision rights to make small purchases (perhaps under $500) without ratification because the cost of separating management from control exceeds the benefits. Since it takes time to receive ratification, lost opportunities or other adverse consequences can occur. The most vivid illustration of delay costs is in the military. Fighter pilots flying in noncombat situations do not have the decision rights to fire at unauthorized or potential enemy planes. They first must notify their superiors and seek authority to shoot. But in combat situations, decision management and decision control are not separated because to do so would hamper the pilots' ability to respond in situations when delays can be catastrophic. In combat, pilots have the authority to fire at enemy aircraft. An example of avoiding a delay that could possibly be deadly: In some states paramedics can administer certain drugs in life-threatening situations without first getting a physician's approval.

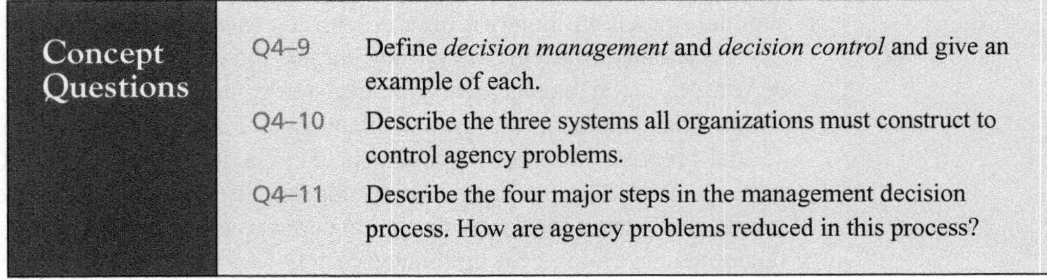

Concept Questions

Q4–9 Define *decision management* and *decision control* and give an example of each.

Q4–10 Describe the three systems all organizations must construct to control agency problems.

Q4–11 Describe the four major steps in the management decision process. How are agency problems reduced in this process?

C. Accounting's Role in the Organization's Architecture

The preceding section described the separation of decision management from decision control. One way to limit agency costs is to separate the decision rights to initiate and implement decisions (decision management) from the ratifying and monitoring functions (decision

Historical Application: Performance Measures in Retailing

Large department stores with multiple lines of goods such as clothing, furniture, jewelry, and glassware began to appear in the United States in the latter half of the 1800s (Lord & Taylor in 1858 and Macy's in 1870). These stores were in big cities that could support the large inventories they carried. These successful retailers had high volume and high inventory turnover by selling at low prices and low margins. They marked down slow-moving lines and did extensive local advertising.

In rural areas, mass marketing was done by mail-order houses. Montgomery Ward began in 1872; Sears and Roebuck began in 1887. The 1887 Montgomery Ward mail-order catalog was 540 pages long and contained 24,000 items. The success of the mail-order houses, like the department stores, was due to low prices and high volumes. Mail-order houses could process 100,000 orders per day.

At the heart of both the department stores and mail-order houses were the operating departments (such as women's and children's clothing, furniture, and housewares) and their buyers. The buyers had to acquire specialized knowledge of their customers' preferences. They committed their departments to purchase millions of dollars of goods before they knew whether the items could be sold.

Two types of information generated by the accounting department were used to evaluate the operating managers and their buyers: gross margin and stock turn. *Gross margin* is income (sales less cost) divided by sales. *Stock turn* or *inventory turnover* is sales divided by average inventory; it measures the number of times stock on hand is sold and replaced during the year. Departments with higher stock turns are using their capital invested in inventories more efficiently. For example, the large Chicago merchandiser Marshall Field's had a stock turn of around five in the 1880s. The development of gross margin and stock turn illustrates how accounting-based performance-evaluation measures develop to match the decision rights partitioned to particular managers. Critical to the success of large mass distributors was partitioning decision rights to the buyers with the specialized knowledge and then evaluating and rewarding them based on their decision rights.

SOURCE: A Chandler, *The Visible Hand: The Managerial Revolution in American Business* (Cambridge, MA: Harvard University Press, 1977), pp. 223–36.

control). Accounting systems play a very important role in monitoring as part of the performance evaluation system. Accounting numbers are probably more useful in decision monitoring and often least useful in decision initiation and implementation. For decision management, managers want opportunity costs (described in Chapter 2). Accounting data are often criticized as not being useful for decision management, but their usefulness for decision control is frequently overlooked.

As a monitoring device, the accounting function is usually independent of operating managers whose performance the accounting report is measuring. The reason for this separation is obvious. Accounting, as part of the firm's monitoring technology, is designed to reduce agency costs, including theft and embezzlement. Since accounting reports bring subordinates' performance to the attention of their superiors, the reports should not be under the control of the subordinates. Internal accounting reports provide an overall review of subordinates' performance by giving senior managers reasonably objective and independent information. Shareholders and the board of directors use the accounting system to check on the performance of the chief executive officer (CEO) and senior managers. The CEO often has substantial influence over the accounting system since the corporate controller usually reports ultimately to the CEO. Some firms have the controller report to the independent audit committee of the board of directors.

To use the accounting system for control of the CEO and senior management, the shareholders and outside directors on the board insist on an external, third-party audit of the financial results.[15]

To the extent financial measures are used for decision control and nonfinancial measures are used for decision management, the following implications arise:

1. Financial measures are not under the complete control of the people being monitored (i.e., the operating managers).
2. Nonaccounting measures, such as customer complaints and defect rates, are often more timely than accounting measures. Nonfinancial data can be reported more frequently than quarterly or monthly, as is usually the case for accounting data.
3. Not every decision requires ratification or monitoring. Decision control can be based on aggregate data to average out random fluctuations. Instead of monitoring every machine setup, it is usually cost-efficient to aggregate all setups occurring over the week and make sure the average setup time or cost is within acceptable levels.
4. Operating managers tend to be dissatisfied with financial measures for making operating decisions. The accounting numbers are not especially timely for operating decisions. They often are at too aggregate a level and do not provide sufficient detail for the particular decision. In response, these operating managers develop their own, often nonfinancial, information systems to provide the more timely knowledge they require for decision management. But at the same time, they rely on accounting data to monitor the managers who report to them.

A number of specific internal accounting procedures, such as standard costs, budgeting, and cost allocations (described in later chapters), help reduce agency problems. Many accounting procedures are better understood as control mechanisms than as aids in decision management. For example, economists have long cautioned against using accountants' allocation of fixed costs to compute "average" unit costs in making short-term decisions. These unit costs bear little relation to short-term variable cost, which is necessary for determining the short-term profit-maximizing level of output. However, average unit accounting costs can be useful as a control mechanism for detecting changes in a subunit's cost performance.

Applying the economic Darwinism principle (marmots and bears) suggests that these seemingly irrational accounting procedures must be yielding benefits in excess of their costs. Economists describe the dysfunctional output/pricing decision that can result when accounting average costs are used instead of variable costs. These dysfunctional decisions are the indirect costs of using the accounting procedures. Reducing the firm's agency problems provides the necessary offsetting benefits to explain the preponderance of so-called irrational accounting procedures. In addition to the benefits provided via organizational reasons, such procedures can provide benefits (or costs) via external reporting, tax reporting, and/or as a cost control device (see Figure 1–1).

The next section provides a specific example of how accounting earnings are used in executive compensation plans to better align managers' and shareholders' interests.

---

[15] R Watts and J Zimmerman, "Agency Problems, Auditing and the Theory of the Firm: Some Evidence," *Journal of Law & Economics,* October 1983, pp. 613–33.

Managerial Application: General Electric's Executive Compensation Contract

General Electric defines its 2007 bonus formula as follows:

> The Plan Authorizes the Board of Directors to appropriate to an incentive compensation reserve each year up to 10% of the amount by which the company's consolidated net earnings exceeds 5% of the Company's average consolidated capital investment.

In General Electric's plan, the executives do not receive a bonus unless the firm earns at least 5 percent on capital. This is a lower bound. Some businesses also place an upper bound on the bonus payout. A typical upper limit to a bonus payout might be stated as, "The incentive compensation reserve shall not exceed 10 percent of the total amount of the dividends paid on the corporation's stock." This upper bound, which is tied to dividends, helps reduce the overretention of cash in the firm. If the business is very profitable, the only way executives can increase their bonus payouts is by increasing dividends paid out to the shareholders.

SOURCE: General Electric Co. Proxy Statement (February 28, 2007).

D. Example of Accounting's Role: Executive Compensation Contracts

Executive compensation contracts illustrate how accounting numbers help reduce agency costs. To better align the interests of shareholders and senior managers, most large U.S. corporations have incentive compensation contracts. This section briefly describes the design of these contracts and their reliance on accounting numbers. It illustrates how accounting performance measures are used to reduce agency problems.

Senior executives in large U.S. firms typically are paid a salary plus an annual bonus; the bonus is often 100 percent of the salary. The compensation committee of the board of directors, which usually consists of outside nonmanagement directors, administers the annual bonus and the annual salary adjustment. The committee annually sets performance goals for each senior executive and establishes how large a bonus each will receive if the goals are achieved. The goals often consist of earnings growth targets, market share, new product introduction schedules, affirmative action hiring targets, and other strategic measures appropriate for the particular manager. If executives meet their targets, they receive some combination of cash, stock options, restricted stock, or deferred compensation.

To protect shareholders from excessive payouts to senior executives and to give senior executives a sense of the whole organization rather than just their own part, the total bonus payout to all eligible managers is limited to some fraction of accounting earnings. Executive compensation contracts usually must be approved by the shareholders every three years. Besides defining who is eligible for awards and how they are administered and paid, these contracts constrain the total annual bonus payments to be paid out of an annual fund.

Accounting numbers enter executive compensation in two ways. First, accounting earnings are often used as individual performance measures (such as divisional profits). Second, accounting earnings constrain the total amount of compensation paid out to executives.

Surveys of compensation practices in publicly traded firms find that almost all of them rely on some measure of accounting profit to measure and reward the performance of senior executives.[16] Large-scale empirical studies routinely find a strong positive association between changes in accounting profits and changes in executive pay. Executive pay is usually measured as salary plus bonus paid to the chief executive officer. In these studies,

[16] K Murphy, "Executive Compensation," in *Handbook of Labor Economics* 3, ed. O Ashenfelter and D Card (Amsterdam: North Holland, 1999).

Academic Application: Executives Manage Accounting Earnings

A research study examining Fortune 250 firms with bonus plans (some dating back to 1930) provides evidence that executives manage earnings. Using 1,527 observations from 94 firms, the study finds that managers are more likely to take accounting actions that increase earnings when earnings are between the two bonus plan bounds and to take accounting actions that decrease earnings when earnings are outside the bounds. While the evidence suggests that managers manage reported earnings to increase executive bonuses, the prevalence of accounting-based executive bonus plans indicates that these plans are useful in resolving agency problems.

Accounting earnings are also used to measure the performance of lower-level managers. A study of 54 profit centers in 12 publicly traded U.S. corporations finds that all 12 firms link bonuses to profit center accounting performance. The profit center manager's annual bonus depends on achieving a budgeted target. The size of the bonus for achieving the target varies from 20 to 100 percent of the base salary, with the most common being about 25 percent.

SOURCE: P Healy, "The Effect of Bonus Schemes on Accounting Decisions," *Journal of Accounting & Economics* 7 (April 1985), pp. 85–107. For later evidence, see J Gaver, K Gaver, and J Austin, "Additional Evidence on Bonus Plans and Income Management," *Journal of Accounting & Economics* 19 (February 1995); R Holthausen, D Larcker, and R Sloan, "Annual Bonus Schemes and the Manipulation of Earnings," *Journal of Accounting & Economics* 19 (February 1995); A Leone, F Guidry, and S Rock, "Earnings-Based Bonus Plans and Earnings Management by Business-Unit Managers," *Journal of Accounting & Economics* 26 (January 1999), pp. 113–42.

FIGURE 4–2
Typical executive bonus pool

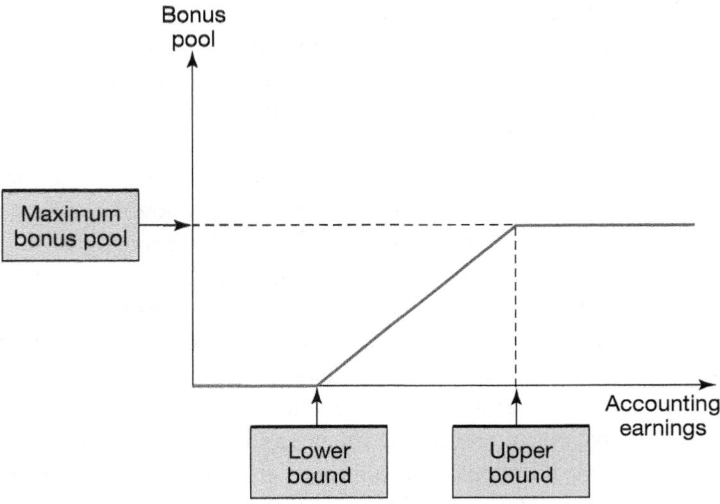

accounting profits are usually one of the most important explanatory variables of executive pay among firm size, stock returns, and industry classification. Thus, it appears as if accounting profits either are used directly in setting executive compensation or are highly correlated with performance measures used in setting pay.

All executive bonus plans have a lower bound and some have upper bounds. Figure 4–2 shows how the bonus pool varies with firmwide accounting earnings. If accounting earnings are below the lower bound, the pool is zero and no bonuses are paid. Between the lower and upper bounds, the pool increases with earnings. Above the upper bound, the pool stops increasing with earnings. Bonus plans with upper and lower bounds create incentives for management to increase accounting earnings if earnings are between the lower and upper bounds. Earnings can be increased by increasing net cash flows or by selecting income-increasing accounting methods. For example, reducing bad debt expense raises net income. If earnings are below Figure 4–2's lower bound or above the upper bound, managers have incentives to choose income-decreasing accounting accruals, such as writing off obsolete inventories and plant and equipment. These types of accounting charges remove assets from the balance sheet that would have been expensed in future accounting periods, thereby lowering income in this period but raising income in future years.

E. Summary

Besides providing information for making operating decisions, accounting numbers are also used in controlling conflicts of interest between owners (principals) and employees (agents). Agency problems arise because self-interested employees maximize their welfare, not the principal's welfare, and principals cannot directly observe the agents' actions.

The free-rider problem, one specific agency problem, arises because, for agents working in teams, the incentive to shirk increases with team size. Usually it is more difficult to monitor individual agents as team size increases. Also, each agent bears a smaller fraction of the reduced output from his or her shirking. The horizon problem, another agency problem, arises when employees expecting to leave the firm in the future place less weight than the principal does on those consequences occurring after they leave.

Transactions that occur across markets have fewer agency problems because the existence of markets and market prices gives owners of an asset the incentive to maximize its value by linking knowledge with decision rights. But once transactions occur within firms, administrative devices must replace market-induced incentives. In particular, firms try to link decision rights with knowledge and then provide incentives for people with the knowledge and decision rights to maximize firm value.

To maximize firm value, which involves minimizing agency costs, managers design the organization's architecture—three interrelated and coordinated systems that measure and reward performance and assign decision rights. The analogy of the three-legged stool illustrates how important it is that the three legs be matched to one another. Changing one leg usually requires changing the other two to keep the stool level.

The internal accounting system, used to measure agents' performance, provides an important monitoring function. Hence, the accounting system usually is not under the control of those agents whose performance is being monitored. Primarily a control device, accounting is not necessarily as useful for decision making as managers would like.

The performance evaluation system, one leg of the stool, consists of both financial and nonfinancial measures of performance. Executive compensation plans routinely use accounting earnings as a performance measure both to evaluate managers and to reduce agency costs by constraining the total bonus payouts to managers. Chapter 5 describes two more accounting tools that are used to reduce agency problems: responsibility accounting and transfer pricing.

Self-Study Problem

Span of Control

Span of control is defined as "the number of subordinates whom a superior directly controls."[17] Whether the span of control is large or small depends on several factors, including training. "(I)f a person was well trained, he or she would need little supervision. The span of control would be wide. If

[17] C Perrow, *Complex Organizations: A Critical Essay,* 3rd ed. (New York: Random House, 1986), p. 30.

personnel were not well trained, they would need more supervision, and the span of control would be narrow and the hierarchy higher." But the evidence shows "the more qualified the people, the less the span of control" and the higher the hierarchy.[18]

In some situations, we observe a span of control of 40 or 50 (e.g., the faculty in a business school). In other situations, we observe spans of control of two to five (e.g., card dealers in a casino). What factors would you expect to be important in determining the optimum span of control? Give examples where appropriate.

Solution:

Span of control (or the height/shape of the organization chart) is a central feature of the control problem faced by organizations. The amount of monitoring required by each individual in the firm affects the span of control. High levels of monitoring decrease the span of control because supervisors have limited processing capacities.

A number of factors will affect the span of control:

1. Knowledge—it is useful to try to link knowledge and decision rights. If decision management rights are delegated, decision control rights are usually retained, thereby decreasing the span of control.
2. If monitoring costs are reduced, span of control increases, other things being equal. A case of reduced monitoring costs is grouping subordinates close to the supervisor. Performance evaluation and reward systems that reduce agency costs (including monitoring costs) increase the span of control. If agency costs are high because the residual loss is large (e.g., bank tellers or card dealers in casinos), the span of control is smaller, other things being equal.
3. Perrow argues that one can change behavior via training to induce people to behave in the organization's interest. This is inconsistent with the view that people are self-interested, rational maximizers.

Problems

P 4–1: Empowerment

It is frequently argued that for empowerment to work, managers must "let go of control" and learn to live with decisions that are made by their subordinates. Evaluate this argument.

P 4–2: Pay for Performance

Communities are frequently concerned about whether or not police are vigilant in carrying out their responsibilities. Several communities have experimented with incentive compensation for police. In particular, some cities have paid members of the police force based on the number of arrests that they personally make. Discuss the likely effects of this compensation policy.

P 4–3: Course Packets

Faculty members at a leading business school receive a budget to cover research expenditures, software and hardware purchases, travel expenses, photocopying for classroom use, and so forth. The budget is increased $250 for each class taught (independent of the number of students enrolled). For example, a faculty member receives a base budget of $14,000 for this year and teaches three courses—hence, the faculty's total budget is $14,750.

Finance professors teach much larger classes than any other functional area (e.g., accounting) and they tend to have larger course packets per student. Faculty can photocopy their course packets and have their budgets reduced by the photocopying charges. Or the faculty can distribute course materials via the school's network where students can download them and print them on their personal printers.

[18] Perrow (1986), p. 31.

Required:

a. Which faculty members are more likely to put course packets and lecture notes on their Web pages and which faculty are more likely to photocopy the material and distribute it to their students?

b. Is this partitioning of faculty members distributing materials electronically versus making paper copies efficient?

P 4–4: Allied Van Lines

Why are drivers for long-haul (cross-country) moving companies (e.g., Allied Van Lines) often franchised, while moving companies that move households within the same city hire drivers as employees? Franchised drivers own their own trucks. They are not paid a fixed salary but rather receive the profits from each move after paying the franchiser a fee.

P 4–5: Voluntary Financial Disclosure

Prior to the Securities Acts of 1933 and 1934, corporations with publicly traded stock were not required to issue financial statements, yet many voluntarily issued income statements and balance sheets. Discuss the advantages and disadvantages of such voluntary disclosures.

P 4–6: University Physician Compensation

Physicians practicing in Eastern University's hospital have the following compensation agreement. Each doctor bills the patient (or Blue Cross Blue Shield) for his or her services. The doctor pays for all direct expenses incurred in the clinic, including nurses, medical malpractice insurance, secretaries, supplies, and equipment. Each doctor has a stated salary target (e.g., $100,000). For patient fees collected over the salary target, less expenses, the doctor retains 30 percent of the additional net fees. For example, if $150,000 is billed and collected from patients and expenses of $40,000 are paid, then the doctor retains $3,000 of the excess net fees [30 percent of ($150,000 − $40,000 − $100,000)] and Eastern University receives $7,000. If $120,000 of fees are collected and $40,000 of expenses are incurred, the physician's net cash flow is $80,000 and Eastern University receives none of the fees.

Required:

Critically evaluate the existing compensation plan and recommend any changes.

P 4–7: Desert Storm Mail Deliveries

Mail delivery during the Christmas holidays of 1990 to U.S. troops stationed in Saudi Arabia for Operation Desert Storm was haphazard. So many letters and packages were mailed during the holidays, that warehouse space in Germany, which was the intermediate staging area for mail to Saudi Arabia, became full. Letters were often delivered weeks late, while packages were delivered with less delay. Airplanes flying between Germany and the Middle East have both a physical volume capacity and a weight capacity. A cubic foot of letters weighs more than a cubic foot of packages.

Required:

Analyze the mail delivery system and offer a plausible explanation as to why letters were treated differently than packages.

SOURCE: N O'Connor, Capt., 2nd Marine Division.

P 4–8: American InterConnect I

Employee satisfaction is a major performance measure used at American Inter Connect (AI), a large communications firm. All employees receive some bonus compensation. The lower-level employees receive a bonus that averages 20 percent of their base pay whereas senior corporate officers receive bonus pay that averages 80 percent of their base salary. Bonus payments for all employees are linked to their immediate work group's performance on the following criteria: income, revenue growth, customer satisfaction, and employee satisfaction. Managers can have these criteria supplemented with additional specific measures including hiring targets and some other specific objective for each manager such as meeting a new product introduction deadline or a market share target.

Employee satisfaction usually has a weight of between 15 and 20 percent in determining most employees' overall bonus. To measure employee satisfaction, all employees in the group complete a two-page survey each quarter. The survey asks a variety of questions regarding employee satisfaction. One question in particular asks employees to rate how satisfied they are with their job using a seven-point scale (where 7 is very satisfied and 1 is very dissatisfied). The average score on this question for all employees in the group is used to calculate the group's overall employee satisfaction score.

Required:

Describe what behaviors you would expect to observe at AI.

P 4–9: Raises

A company recently raised the pay of employees by 20 percent. The productivity of the employees, however, remained the same. The CEO of the company was quoted as saying, "It just goes to show that money does not motivate people." Provide a critical evaluation of this statement.

P 4–10: Decentralization

Some economists (e.g., Hayek) argue that decentralization of economic decisions in the economy leads to efficient resource allocation. What differences exist within the firm that make the link between decentralization and efficiency less clear?

P 4–11: Vanderschmidt's

Jan Vanderschmidt was the founder of a successful chain of restaurants located throughout Europe. He died unexpectedly last week at the age of 55. Jan was sole owner of the company's common stock and was known for being very authoritarian. He made most of the company's personnel decisions himself. He also made most of the decisions on the menu selection, food suppliers, advertising programs, and so on. Employees throughout the firm are paid fixed salaries and have been heavily monitored by Mr. Vanderschmidt. Jan's son, Joop, spent his youth driving BMWs around the Netherlands and Germany at high speeds. He spent little time working with his dad in the restaurant business. Nevertheless, Joop is highly intelligent and just received his MBA degree from a prestigious school. Joop has decided to follow his father as the chief operating officer of the restaurant chain. Explain how the organization's architecture might optimally change now that Joop has taken over.

P 4–12: Sales Commissions

Sue Koehler manages a revenue center of a large national manufacturer that sells office furniture to local businesses in Detroit. She has decision rights over pricing. Her compensation is a fixed wage of $23,000 per year plus 2 percent of her office's total sales. Critically evaluate the organizational architecture of Koehler's revenue center.

P 4–13: Formula 409

"I used to run the company that made Formula 409, the spray cleaner. From modest entrepreneurial beginnings, we'd gone national and shipped the hell out of P&G, Colgate, Drackett, and every other giant that raised its head. From the beginning, I'd employed a simple incentive plan based on 'case sales': Every month, every salesman and executive received a bonus check based on how many cases of 409 he'd sold. Even bonuses for the support staff were based on monthly case sales. It was a happy time, with everyone making a lot of money, including me.

"We abandoned our monthly case-sales bonus plan and installed an *annual* profit-sharing plan, based on personnel evaluations. It didn't take long for the new plan to produce results."

SOURCE: Wilson Harrell, "Inspire Action: What Really Motivates Your People to Excel?" *Success,* September 1995.

Required:

What do you think happened at this company after it started the annual profit-sharing plan?

P 4–14: Pratt & Whitney

A *Wall Street Journal* article (December 26, 1996) describes a series of changes at the Pratt & Whitney plant in Maine that manufactures parts for jet engines. In 1993 it was about to be closed because of high operating costs and inefficiencies. A new plant manager overhauled operations. He broadened job descriptions so inspectors do 15 percent more work than they did five years ago. A "results-sharing" plan pays hourly employees if the plant exceeds targets such as cost cutting and on-time delivery. Now, everyone is looking to cut costs.

Hourly employees also helped design a new pay scheme that is linked to the amount of training, not seniority, that an employee has. This was after the plant manager drafted 22 factory-floor employees, gave them a conference room, and told them to draft a new pay plan linked to learning.

Shop-floor wages vary between $9 and $19 per hour with the most money going to people running special cost studies or quality projects, tasks previously held by managers.

This text emphasizes the importance of keeping all three legs of the stool in balance. Identify the changes Pratt & Whitney made to all three legs of the stool at its Maine plant.

P 4–15: Theory X–Theory Y

A textbook on organization theory says:

> Drawing upon the writings of Maslow, McGregor presented his Theory X–Theory Y dichotomy to describe two differing conceptions of human behavior. Theory X assumptions held that people are inherently lazy, they dislike work, and that they will avoid it whenever possible. Leaders who act on Theory X premises are prone to controlling their subordinates through coercion, punishment, and the use of financial rewards; the use of external controls is necessary, as most human beings are thought to be incapable of self-direction and assuming responsibility. In contrast, Theory Y is based on the assumption that work can be enjoyable and that people will work hard and assume responsibility if they are given the opportunity to achieve personal goals at the same time.[19]

Using the framework presented in the text, critically analyze Theory X–Theory Y.

P 4–16: American InterConnect II

Employee bonuses at American InterConnect (AI), a large communications firm, depend on meeting a number of targets, one of which is a revenue target. Some bonus is awarded to the group if it meets or exceeds its target revenue for the year. The bonus is also tied to meeting targets for earnings, employee satisfaction, hiring goals, and other specific objectives tailored to the group or manager.

AI has several product development groups within the firm. Each is assigned the task of developing new products for specific divisions within the firm. Product developers, primarily engineers and marketing people, are assigned to a new product development team to develop a specific new product. Afterward, they are assigned to new development teams for a different division or are reassigned back to their former departments. Sometimes they become product managers for the new product. Product development teams take roughly 18 months to develop and design the product. For example, Network Solutions is one group of products AI sells. The employees in the product development group for Network Solutions receive part of their bonus based on whether Network Solutions achieves its revenue target for that year.

It typically takes AI three years from the time a product development team is formed until the product reaches the market. Once a new product idea is identified and researched, a prototype must be built and tested. Finally it is introduced. Another 18 months is required for approval, manufacturing design, further testing, and marketing. These functions are performed after the product development team has been reassigned.

Required:

Analyze the incentives created by basing a portion of each current product developer's bonus on revenues for products now being sold.

---

[19] V K Narayanan and R Nath, *Organization Theory: A Strategic Approach* (Burr Ridge, IL: Richard D. Irwin, 1993), p. 403.

P 4–17: Private Country Clubs

It is often argued that private country clubs tend to have low-quality food operations because the members do not join or frequent their clubs for the food but rather for the golf and fellowship.

(Note: A private country club charges an initiation fee and monthly dues. Members pay for food and drink they consume. The members own the club and frequently pay annual assessments. When members resign or die, some clubs allow the members or their estate to resell the membership, subject to board approval of the new member. Other clubs resell the membership and retain the new initiation fee.)

Critically evaluate the first paragraph.

P 4–18: Tipping

One of the main tenets of economic analysis is that people act in their narrow self-interest. Why then do people leave tips in restaurants? If a study were to compare the size of tips earned by servers in restaurants on interstate highways with those in restaurants near residential neighborhoods, what would you expect to find? Why?

P 4–19: White's Department Store

Employees at White's Department Store are observed engaging in the following behavior: (1) They hide items that are on sale from the customers and (2) they fail to expend appropriate effort in designing merchandise displays. They are also uncooperative with one another. What do you think might be causing this behavior and what might you do to improve the situation?

P 4–20: Coase Farm

Coase Farm grows soybeans near property owned by Taggart Railroad. Taggart can build zero, one, or two railroad tracks adjacent to Coase Farm, yielding a net present value of $0, $9 million, or $12 million.

Value of Taggart Railroad (in millions) as a Function of the Number of Train Tracks (before any damages)

Zero tracks	$ 0
One track	9
Two tracks	12

Coase Farm can grow soybeans on zero, one, or two fields, yielding a net present value of $0, $15 million, or $18 million before any environmental damages inflicted by Taggart trains. Environmental damages inflicted by Taggart's trains are $4 million per field per track. Coase Farm's payoffs as a function of the number of fields it uses to grow soybeans and the number of tracks that Taggart builds are shown below.

Value of Coase Farm (in millions) as a Function of the Number of Fields Planted and the Number of Train Tracks

	Zero fields	*One field*	*Two fields*
Zero tracks	$0	$15	$18
One track	0	11	10
Two tracks	0	7	2

It is prohibitively expensive for Taggart Railroad and Coase Farm to enter into a long-term contract regarding either party's use of its land.

Required:

a. Suppose Taggart Railroad cannot be held liable for the damages its tracks inflict on Coase Farm. Show that Taggart Railroad will build two tracks and Coase Farm will plant soybeans on one field.

b. Suppose Taggart Railroad can be held fully liable for the damages that its tracks inflict on Coase Farm. Show that Taggart Railroad will build one track and Coase Farm will plant soybeans on two fields.

c. Now suppose Taggart Railroad and Coase Farm merge. Show that the merged firm will build one track and plant soybeans on one field.

d. What are the implications of the merger for the organizational architecture of the newly merged firm in terms of decision rights, performance measurement, and employee compensation?

SOURCE: R Sansing.

P 4–21: Rothwell Inc.

Rothwell Inc. is the leader in computer-integrated manufacturing and factory automation products and services. The Rothwell product offering is segmented into 15 product categories, based on product function and primary manufacturing location.

Rothwell's sales division sells all 15 product categories and is composed of 25 district offices located throughout the United States. The company is highly decentralized, with district offices responsible for setting sales price, product mix, and other variables.

District offices are rewarded based on sales. Some large customers have plants in more than one of Rothwell's sales districts. In cases where sales are made to these customers, the district offices participate jointly and sales credits are shared by each district involved.

The sales division compensation plan designed by L. L. Rothwell, founder of the firm, was structured so that the staff would pursue sales in each of the 15 product categories. The selling program has the following features:

- Each sales representative receives a commission based on a percentage of the sales revenue generated.
- Each district (approximately 160 sales reps) is assigned a quota for each product line, defined in terms of dollar sales.
- In addition to commission, sales reps are eligible for an annual bonus. The company calculates individual bonuses by multiplying the number of bonus points earned by the individual target bonus amount. Points are credited at the district level.
- In order for all sales reps in a district to qualify for a bonus, the district must achieve 50 percent of quota in all 15 product groups and 85 percent of quota in at least 13 groups.
- Bonus points are awarded for sales greater than 85 percent of quota.
- Five product groups have been identified as strategic to Rothwell. These "pride-level" products are weighted more heavily in bonus point calculations.

Over the past three years, Rothwell generated exceptionally high sales—and awarded record bonuses. Profits, however, were lackluster. L. L. was befuddled!

Required:

a. Evaluate the compensation situation at Rothwell.

b. Identify the types of behavior the existing system promotes and explain how such behavior may be contributing to the firm's declining profitability. Suggest improvements.

P 4–22: Gong-Fen

"It was in Deyang in 1969 that I came to know how China's peasants really lived. Each day started with the production team leader allocating jobs. All the peasants had to work, and they each earned a fixed number of 'work points' (*gong-fen*) for their day's work. The number of work points accumulated was an important element in the distribution at the end of the year. The peasants got food, fuel, and other daily necessities, plus a tiny sum of cash, from the production team. After the harvest, the production team paid part of it over as tax to the state. Then the rest was divided up. First, a basic quantity was meted out equally to every male, and about a quarter less to every female. Children under three received a half portion.

"The remainder of the crop was then distributed according to how many work points each person had earned. Twice a year, the peasants would all assemble to fix the daily work points for each person. No one missed these meetings. In the end, most young and middle-aged men would be allocated 10 points a day, and women 8. One or two whom the whole village acknowledged to be exceptionally strong got an extra point. 'Class enemies' like the former village landlord and his family got a couple of points less than the others, in spite of the fact that they worked no less hard and were usually given the toughest jobs.

"Since there was little variation from individual to individual of the same gender in terms of daily points, the number of work points accumulated depended mainly on how many days one worked, rather than how one worked."

SOURCE: J Chang, *Wild Swans: Three Daughters of China* (New York: Anchor Books, 1991), pp. 414–15.

Required:

What predictable behavior do you expect the Chinese agricultural system will generate?

P 4–23: International Computer Company

International Computer Company (ICC) has annual revenues of $2 billion primarily from selling and leasing large networked workstation systems to businesses and universities. The manufacturing division produces the hardware that is sold or leased by the marketing division. After the expiration of the lease, leased equipment is returned to ICC, where it is either disassembled for parts by the field service organization or sold by the international division. Internal studies have shown that equipment leased for four years is worth 36⅔ percent of its original manufacturing cost as parts or sold overseas. About half of ICC's systems are leased and half are sold, but the fraction being leased by ICC is a falling proportion of total sales.

The leasing department is evaluated on profits. Its annual profits are based on the present value of the lease payments from new leases signed during the year, less

1. The unit manufacturing cost of the equipment.
2. Direct selling, shipping, and installation costs.
3. The present value of the service agreement costs.

Each leased piece of equipment will be serviced over its life by ICC's field service organization. The leasing division arranges a service contract for each piece of leased equipment from the field service organization. The field service organization commits to servicing the leased equipment at a fixed annual cost, determined at the time the lease is signed. The leasing department then builds the service cost into the annual lease payment.

The leasing department negotiates the lease terms individually for each customer. In general, the leasing division sets the annual lease terms to recover all three cost components plus a 25 percent markup (before taxes). The 25 percent markup for setting the annual lease payment seemed to work well in the past and provided the firm with a reasonable return on its investment when ICC had dominance in the workstation market niche. However, in recent years new entrants have forced the ICC leasing department to reduce its markup to as low as 10 percent to sign leases. At this small margin, senior management is considering getting out of the lease business and just selling the systems.

The following lease to Gene Science is being priced by the leasing department. A four-year lease of a small network of three workstations is being negotiated. The unit manufacturing cost of the network is $30,000. The service costs, which are payable to the field service department at the beginning of each year, are $2,000 (payable at installation), $3,000, $4,000, and $5,000 (payable at the beginning of each of the next three years, respectively). Selling, shipping, and installation costs are $7,000. The leasing department has an 8 percent cost of capital.

To simplify the analysis, ignore all tax considerations.

Required:

a. Using a 25 percent markup on costs and an 8 percent discount rate, calculate the fixed annual lease payment for the four-year lease to Gene Science.

b. Comment on some likely reasons why a 25 percent markup on leased equipment is proving more difficult to sustain. Should ICC abandon the lease market? What are some alternative courses of action?

P 4–24: Repro Corporation

Repro Corporation is the leading manufacturer and seller of office equipment. Its most profitable business segment is the production and sale of large copiers. The company is currently organized into two divisions: manufacturing and sales. Manufacturing produces all products; sales is responsible for the distribution of all finished products to the final customers. Each division is evaluated on profits. Market research shows an existing demand for a facilities management service whereby Repro installs its equipment and personnel at a client's site and operates the client's copy center. To meet this demand, Repro is considering a proposal to expand its operations to include a service division responsible for contracting with firms to install Repro's equipment in a copy service agreement. This copy service is named Facilities Management (FM).

A contract for FM includes the leasing of a complete copy center from the service division, including all necessary equipment and personnel. The client provides space for FM on site.

The value offered by the service division is threefold. The service division will be organized so that a base center in each city covered will be responsible for acting as both an independent copy center and a backup to the FMs contracted in the local area. Any FM processing shortfalls due to equipment failure or shop overflows would result in a transfer of copy needs to the center. Additionally, since the equipment used in FM contracts is leased and not purchased, contracting companies are not strapped with showing a return on assets for this equipment (allowing the flexibility of adjusting the lease as company needs vary). Nor are they responsible for equipment maintenance. Finally, the personnel to run the equipment in the FM sites are service division employees, not employees of the client. Thus, no additional headcount is needed by the client. For this complete value-added service, firms are charged based on projected monthly copy volume, with an agreed-upon surcharge for copies processed in excess of the contracted volume.

With the introduction of this new division, Repro would reorganize itself into three divisions: *manufacturing, products,* and *service.* The responsibility of selling business equipment (copiers, fax machines, etc.) would be assigned to the products division, and the service division would become responsible for the sale of FM sites (products and services would utilize separate sales forces). Both divisions would buy hardware from manufacturing at similar costs.

Currently, Repro's sales comprise approximately 80 percent repeat-purchase customers (who are either replacing existing equipment with similar equipment or upgrading to new Repro products) and 20 percent new customers. It has been estimated that 30 percent of the current market base would, given the opportunity, choose a Facilities Management contract rather than purchase equipment outright.

Repro's current sales force compensation is a function of a fixed salary plus a commission based on a percentage of sales. The average salesperson's compensation consists of a $25,000 base salary and a 2 percent sales commission. Over the last four years, the average piece of copy equipment from Repro sold for $80,000 and the average salesperson sold $1 million of equipment (adjusted for inflation). If the proposal for a service division is undertaken, this compensation scheme will be applied to both the products and service divisions' sales force.

Required:

a. Discuss the conflict that will result if the service division is introduced.

b. Propose a solution to solve this conflict.

SOURCE: D Holahan, D Lee, W Reidy, A Tom, and E Tufekcioglu.

Cases

Case 4–1: Christian Children's Fund

Christian Children's Fund, Inc. (CCF), established in 1938, is an international, nonsectarian, nonprofit organization dedicated to assisting children. With program offices around the world, it provides health and educational assistance to more than 4.6 million children and families through over 1,000 projects in 30 countries, including the United States. CCF's programs promote long-term development designed to help break the cycle of poverty by improved access to health care, safe water, immunizations, better nutrition, educational assistance, literacy courses, skills training, and other services specific to improving children's welfare.

Most of CCF's revenues come from individual donors who are linked with a specific child. About 75 percent of the sponsors are in the United States, and in 2003, CCF had total revenues of about $143 million. (See Exhibit 1.)

In 1995 CCF began developing an evaluation system, nicknamed AIMES (Annual Impact Monitoring and Evaluation System), to assess the performance of its programs and whether they are making a positive, measurable difference in children's lives. A working group of national directors, program managers, CCF finance and audit managers, and outside consultants developed a series of metrics that allowed CCF to be more accountable to its sponsors as well as an evaluation tool to continually assess the impact of its programs on children. The working group wanted metrics that (1) captured critical success factors for CCF's projects; (2) focused on a program's impact, not its activities; (3) measured the program's impact on children; and (4) could be measured and tracked.

The following indicators were chosen:

Under 5-year old mortality rate

Under 5-year old moderate and severe malnutrition rate

Adult literacy

One-to-two-year-old immunizations

Tetanus vaccine-protected live births

Families that correctly know how to manage a case of diarrhea

Families that correctly know how to manage acute respiratory infection

Families that have access to safe water

Families that practice safe sanitation

Children enrolled in a formal or informal educational program

Each family in a community with a CCF program is given a family card that tracks each of the preceding 10 indicators for that family. In 1997, the first year of implementation, AIMES captured the health status of about 1.9 million children in approximately 850 projects in 18 countries. Annual visits by project staff or volunteers update each family's card. The family cards are aggregated at the community level, national level, and then in total for CCF, and provide a reporting system. CCF managers then track trends and compare performance at the community, national, and organizational levels.

It took CCF two years to develop these metrics, test them, and train the staff in all the national offices in how to use the system. AIMES does not prescribe the strategy each community should adopt but rather allows each community to design programs that promote the well-being of children in that community. Program directors can use the AIMES data as a tool to monitor and manage their programs. If child mortality is high, local program directors decide how best to reduce the rate. The 10 AIMES metrics have made project managers more focused and better able to concentrate resources in those areas that make a measurable difference in children's health. CCF uses the information to make program and resource allocation decisions at the community level. The family card has promoted better nutrition via appropriate feeding and child care practices because there is now more direct contact between CCF staff and volunteers and families.

Required:

Using this chapter's organizational architecture framework, discuss the strengths and weaknesses of CCF's AIMES project.

SOURCE: D Henderson, B Chase, and B Woodson, "Performance Measures for NPOs," *Journal of Accountancy* (January 2002), pp. 63–68, and www.christianchildrensfund.org.

EXHIBIT 1
CHRISTIAN CHILDREN'S FUND, INC.
Consolidated Statements of Activities and Changes in Net Assets
For the Years Ended June 30, 2003, and 2002

	Total	
	2003	*2002*
Public Support		
Sponsorships:		
U.S. sponsors	$ 76,838,477	$ 74,077,556
International sponsors	22,086,375	18,151,969
Special gifts from sponsors for children	12,351,284	11,838,912
Total sponsorships	$111,276,136	$104,068,437
Contributions:		
General contributions	$ 13,657,676	$ 13,642,476
Major gifts and bequests	4,712,032	4,751,059
Gifts in kind	804,247	637,977
Total contributions	$ 19,173,955	$ 19,031,512
Grants:		
Grants and contracts	$ 10,164,264	$ 7,768,755
Total public support	$140,614,355	$130,868,704
Revenue		
Investment and currency transactions	$ 264,893	$ 350,841
Service fees and other	1,636,717	1,522,652
Total revenue	$ 1,901,610	$ 1,873,493
Net Assets Released from Restrictions		
Satisfaction of program and time restrictions	—	—
Total public support and revenue	$142,515,965	$132,742,197
Expenses		
Program:		
Basic education	$ 41,263,708	$ 40,964,478
Health and sanitation	28,767,904	29,442,196
Nutrition	13,824,871	15,635,046
Early childhood development	11,850,954	10,717,133
Micro enterprise	14,555,029	9,183,004
Emergencies	2,802,575	2,861,528
Total program expenses	$113,032,041	$108,803,385
Supporting Services		
Fund raising	$ 16,777,149	$ 15,484,634
Management and general	12,651,014	11,156,134
Total supporting services	29,428,163	26,640,768
Total expenses from operations	142,493,204	135,444,153
Change in net assets from operations	$ 22,761	$ (2,701,956)
Non-Operating Revenues (Expenses)		
Realized (loss) gain on investments	$ (602,619)	$ 387,223
Unrealized gain (loss) on investments	696,584	(1,967,114)
Total non-operating revenues (expenses)	93,965	(1,579,891)
Change in net assets	$ 116,726	$ (4,281,847)

Case 4–2: Woodhaven Service

Background

Woodhaven Service is a small, independent filling station located in the Woodhaven section of Queens. The station has three gasoline pumps and two service bays. The repair facility specializes in automotive maintenance (oil changes, tune-ups, etc.) and minor repairs (mufflers, shock absorbers, etc.). Woodhaven generally refers customers who require major work such as transmission rebuilds and electronics to shops that are better equipped to handle such repairs. Major repairs are done in-house only when both the customer and mechanic agree that this is the best course of action.

During the 20 years that he has owned Woodhaven Service, Harold Mateen's competence and fairness have built a loyal customer base of neighborhood residents. In fact, demand for his services has been more than he can reasonably meet, yet the repair end of his business is not especially profitable. Most of his competitors earn the lion's share of their profits through repairs, but Harold is making almost all of his money by selling gasoline. If he could make more money on repairs, Woodhaven would be the most successful service station in the area. Harold believes that Woodhaven's weakness in repair profitability is due to the inefficiency of his mechanics, who are paid the industry average of $500 per week. While Harold does not think he overpays them, he feels he is not getting his money's worth.

Harold's son, Andrew, is a student at the university, where he has learned the Socratic dictum, "To know the Good is to do the Good." Andrew provided his father with a classic text on employee morality, Dr. Weisbrotten's *Work Hard and Follow the Righteous Way.* Every morning for two months, Harold, Andrew, and the mechanics devoted one hour to studying this text. Despite many lively and fascinating discussions on the rights and responsibilities of the employee, productivity did not improve one bit. Harold figured he would just have to go out and hire harder-working mechanics.

The failure of the Weisbrotten method did not surprise Lisa, Harold's daughter. She knew that Andrew's methods were bunk. As anyone serious about business knows, the true science of productivity and management of human resources resides in Professor von Drekken's masterful *Modifying Organizational Behavior through Employee Commitment.* Yes, employee commitment was the answer to everything! Harold followed the scientific methods to the letter. Yet, despite giving out gold stars, blowing up balloons, and wearing a smiley face button, he found Lisa's approach no more successful than Andrew's.

Compensation Plans

Harold thinks that his neighbor Jack Myers, owner of Honest Jack's Pre-Enjoyed Autorama, might be helpful. After all, one does not become as successful as Jack without a lot of practical knowledge. Or maybe it is Jack's great radio jingle that does it. Jack tells Harold,

> It's not the jingle, you idiot! It's the way I pay my guys. Your mechanics make $500 a week no matter what. Why should they put out for you? Because of those stupid buttons? My guys—my guys get paid straight commission and nothing more. They do good by me and I do good by them. Otherwise, let 'em starve.
>
> Look, it's real simple. Pay 'em a percent of the sales for the work they do. If you need to be a nice guy about it, make that percent so that if sales are average, then they make their usual $500. But if sales are better, they get that percent extra. This way they don't get hurt but got real reason to help you out.

This hurt Harold. He really liked those buttons. Still, Jack did have a point. Straight commission, however, seemed a little radical. What if sales were bad for a week? That would hurt the mechanics.

Harold figured that it would be better to pay each mechanic a guaranteed $300 a week plus a commission rate that would, given an average volume of business, pay them the extra $200 that would bring their wage back to $500. Under this system, the mechanics would be insulated from a bad week, would not be penalized for an average week, and would still have the incentive to attempt to improve sales. Yes, this seemed more fair.

On the other hand, maybe Jack knows only about the used car business, not about business in general. Harold figured that he should look for an incentive pay method more in line with the way things are done in the auto repair business. Perhaps he should pay his mechanics as he is paid by his customers—by the job. It is standard practice for service stations to charge customers a flat rate for the labor associated with any job. The number of labor hours for which the customer is charged is generally taken from a manual that outlines expected labor times for specific jobs on specific vehicles. The customer pays for these expected hours regardless of how many actual labor hours are expended on the job. Many shops also pay their mechanics by the job. Harold thinks that this approach makes sense because it links the mechanic's pay to the labor charges paid by the customer.

Required:

a. This case presents some popular approaches to alleviating agency costs. Although certain aspects of each of these methods are consistent with the views presented in the text, none of these methods is likely to succeed. Discuss the similarities and differences between the ideas of the chapter and
   (i) Dr. Weisbrotten's approach.
   (ii) Harold Mateen's idea of hiring "harder-working" mechanics.

b. Discuss the expected general effect on agency costs at Woodhaven Service of the new incentive compensation plans. How might they help Woodhaven? Assuming that Harold wants his business to be successful for a long time to come, what major divergent behaviors would be expected under the new compensation proposals? How damaging would you expect these new behaviors to be to a business such as Woodhaven Service? Also, present a defense of the following propositions:
   (i) Harold's plan offers less incentive for divergent behavior than Honest Jack's.
   (ii) Limiting a mechanic's pay by placing an upper bound of $750 per week on his or her earnings reduces the incentive for divergent behavior.

c. Suppose Harold owned a large auto repair franchise located in a department store in a popular suburban shopping mall. Suppose also that this department store is a heavily promoted, well-known national chain that is famous for its good values and easy credit. How should Harold's thinking on incentive compensation change? What if Harold did not own the franchise but was only the manager of a company-owned outlet?

d. In this problem, it is assumed that knowledge and decision rights are linked. The mechanic who services the car decides what services are warranted. Discuss the costs and benefits of this fact for Woodhaven Service and the independently owned chain-store repair shop.

e. Suppose that Woodhaven's problems are not due to agency costs. Briefly describe a likely problem that is apparent from the background description in this problem.

Chapter Six

Budgeting

Chapter Outline

A. Generic Budgeting Systems

1. Country Club
2. Private University
3. Large Corporation

B. Trade-Off between Decision Management and Decision Control

1. Communicating Specialized Knowledge versus Performance Evaluation
2. Budget Ratcheting
3. Participative Budgeting
4. New Approaches to Budgeting
5. Managing the Trade-Off

C. Resolving Organizational Problems

1. Short-Run versus Long-Run Budgets
2. Line-Item Budgets
3. Budget Lapsing
4. Static versus Flexible Budgets
5. Incremental versus Zero-Based Budgets

D. Summary

Appendix: Comprehensive Master Budget Illustration

Chapter 4 described the firm's organizational architecture as consisting of three integrated systems: assigning decision rights, measuring performance, and rewarding performance. The firm's organizational architecture reduces conflicts of interest among the various parties contracting with the firm. This chapter describes how budgeting is used for decision making and to control conflicts of interest. A **budget** is management's formal quantification of the operations of an organization for a future period. It is an aggregate forecast of all transactions expected to occur.

Giving a manager an advertising budget of $8 million authorizes that manager to consume $8 million of firm resources on advertising. Put another way, the advertising budget authorizes the manager to spend $8 million on advertising by assigning these decision rights to the manager. At the end of the year, actual spending on advertising can be compared with the budget; any difference is a measure of the manager's performance and can be used in determining the manager's performance rewards. Budgets are thus part of the firm's organizational architecture; they partition decision rights and control behavior.

Dwight D. Eisenhower, Supreme Commander of the Allied Forces in Europe during World War II and the 34th president of the United States, is quoted as saying, "In preparing for battle, I have always found that plans are useless but planning is indispensable."[1] Budgets are a form of planning. And as expressed by Eisenhower, in many cases their value lies more in the process of planning than in the actual budgets produced. Many times budgets are obsolete before they can be implemented because the world has changed in some unexpected manner. However, the process of budgeting remains vital.

Budgets are an integral part of decision making by assembling knowledge and communicating it to the managers with the decision rights. Budgets are developed using key planning assumptions or basic estimating factors that are widely accepted forecasts of strategic elements faced by the firm. Typical planning assumptions are product prices, unit sales, foreign currency exchange rates, and external prices of key inputs. Budgets help assemble and then communicate these key planning assumptions. Various managers throughout the firm must accept these planning assumptions as reasonable and likely. Key planning assumptions represent those factors that are, to some extent, beyond management control and that set a limit on the overall activities of the firm.

Each key planning assumption must be forecast using past experience, field estimates, and/or statistical analysis. Making these forecasts usually involves accumulating the collective knowledge of numerous individuals in the firm. No single manager has detailed knowledge of total expected unit sales, but individual salespeople have knowledge of likely unit sales in their districts. Because salespersons have specific knowledge of their customer's future purchases, the firm develops an accurate estimate of the planning assumption (firmwide sales) by adding sales forecasts from all the salespeople. From these key planning assumptions, a complete set of management plans is developed regarding raw materials acquisition, labor requirements, financing plans, and distribution and marketing budgets.

Figure 6–1 summarizes the various functions performed by budgets. James McKinsey, founder of the consulting firm McKinsey & Co., describes budgetary control as involving the following:

1. The statement of the plans of all departments of the business for a certain period of time in the form of estimates.
2. The coordination of these estimates into a well-balanced program for the business as a whole.

[1] Quoted by Richard Nixon in *Six Crises* (Garden City, NY: Doubleday, 1962), http://en.wikipedia.org/wiki/Dwight_D._Eisenhower#_note-34.

Managerial Application: Budgeting at General Electric

General Electric has grown by global acquisition. Once it acquires a company, GE installs its management system. Nuovo Pignone (NP) of Italy illustrates the process. NP manufactures machinery and equipment for the oil and gas industry. Following acquisition by GE, NP underwent a massive cultural transformation with the installation of performance measurement systems built around the budgeting process. The first three GE executives to arrive at NP were the chief financial officer, the financial planning manager, and the corporate auditor. These managers installed a new budgeting and performance evaluation system that aligned business goals with timely and accurate financial information as well as linking NP with GE's global environment. The integration process at NP involved a major change in performance measurement. Very early in the integration process, significant effort was put into creating financial budgets that tied NP and GE's strategy to metrics for specific departments. Before NP initiates a new project, the project's benefits and costs are quantified in a budget, and this information is used to select and prioritize projects. But more important, the GE systems in NP are driven by the language of measurement, communication, and accountability.

SOURCE: C Busco, M Frigo, E Giovannoni, A Riccaboni, and R Scapens, "Integrating Global Organizations through Performance Measurement Systems," *Strategic Finance*, January 2006, pp. 31–35.

FIGURE 6–1
Functions of budgets

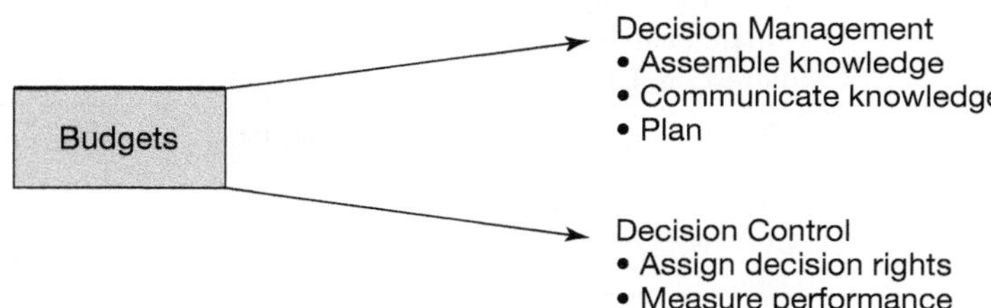

3. The preparation of reports showing a comparison between the actual and the estimated performance, and the revision of the original plans when these reports show that such revision is necessary.[2]

Because budgeting performs such critical functions involving decision management and decision control, it is ubiquitous—virtually all organizations prepare budgets. This chapter first describes some generic budgeting systems used by different organizations (section A). It then discusses how budgeting involves the trade-off between decision management and decision control (section B). Section C describes how budgets help reduce conflicts of interest between owners and managers. A comprehensive budget example is provided in the appendix.

A. Generic Budgeting Systems

The following discussion illustrates the essential aspects of budgeting using a simple organizational form (a hypothetical private country club), a more complicated organization (a university), and a large corporation. In all three examples, budgeting is part of the system whereby decision rights are partitioned and performance is measured and rewarded.

1. Country Club

This example illustrates the use of budgets to assign decision rights and create incentives for employees to act in the owners' interests.

[2] J McKinsey, *Budgetary Control* (New York: Ronald Press, 1922), p. 8.

TABLE 6–1

BAY VIEW COUNTRY CLUB
Operating Results
September 2011

	Actual September	*Budget September*	*Favorable (Unfavorable) Variance*	*Last Year*
Revenues				
Dues	$133,350	$134,750	$(1,400)	$129,600
Guest fees	2,900	2,500	400	2,200
Food and bar	46,000	44,500	1,500	45,000
Golf carts	2,200	1,900	300	2,100
Miscellaneous	1,600	1,800	(200)	1,700
Total revenue	$186,050	$185,450	$ 600	$180,600
Expenses				
Food & bar	$ 57,000	$ 51,300	$(5,700)	$ 49,700
Golf course	79,500	80,000	500	75,000
Administration & maintenance	47,050	45,350	(1,700)	45,600
Interest on debt	8,500	8,500	0	9,000
Total expenses	$192,050	$185,150	$(6,900)	$179,300
Net operating surplus (deficit)	$ (6,000)	$ 300	$(6,300)	$ 1,300

Bay View Country Club is a private club with 350 members. Members pay a one-time initiation fee of $45,000 and dues of $385 per month. They have access to the golf course, pool, tennis courts, and restaurant.

Bay View Country Club has three departments (each managed by a full-time employee): the restaurant, the golf course, and the pro shop. The restaurant is managed by the club manager; the maintenance of the golf course is supervised by the golf course superintendent; and the pro shop is operated by the golf professional. The restaurant is treated as a profit center and the golf course and pro shop are treated as cost centers. The club manager is responsible for revenues and expenses in operating the restaurant, whereas the golf course superintendent and golf professional are responsible primarily for controlling expenses in their operations.

Table 6–1 is the operating statement for the club. Bay View Country Club is essentially a cash business. All of the members pay their dues on time and there are negligible inventories of food and liquor. Because it is a cash business, revenues are equivalent to cash receipts, while expenses are equivalent to cash disbursements. Table 6–1 lists the revenues and expenses for September 2011 and September 2010, and the budget for September 2011, including variances from budget. Parentheses denote negative numbers and unfavorable variances from budget. An unfavorable budget variance occurs when actual expenses exceed budgeted expenses or when actual revenues are less than budgeted revenues. The annual operating budget and monthly operating statement are the principal control devices used in most organizations, including Bay View Country Club.

At the beginning of the operating year, the board of directors submits an operating budget to the general membership for approval. This plan shows projected revenues (including

TABLE 6–2

BAY VIEW COUNTRY CLUB Food and Bar Operations September 2011				
	Actual September	*Budget September*	*Favorable (Unfavorable) Variance*	*Last Year*
Revenues				
Parties	$ 8,300	$11,500	$(3,200)	$11,000
Food	24,000	22,000	2,000	21,500
Bar	12,700	10,500	2,200	10,500
Miscellaneous	1,000	500	500	2,000
Total revenue	$ 46,000	$44,500	$ 1,500	$45,000
Expenses				
Parties	$ 9,000	$ 4,000	$(5,000)	$ 5,000
Food	44,000	43,000	(1,000)	40,000
Bar	4,000	4,300	300	4,700
Total expenses	$ 57,000	$51,300	$(5,700)	$49,700
Net operating surplus (deficit)	$(11,000)	$(6,800)	$(4,200)	$(4,700)

dues) and projected expenses. To prepare the budget, management and the board examine each revenue and expense item for the previous year and adjust it for expected inflation and any change in operating plans. For example, the golf course superintendent reviews last year's spending on labor and supplies. The superintendent decides how to change the golf course maintenance schedule and forecasts how these changes, adjusted for price changes, translate into a total operating budget for the year. Knowing the maintenance program for each month, the superintendent estimates how the annual amount will be spent each month.

The annual budget, after approval by the members, authorizes the board and club management to operate the club for the next year under the limits it specifies. For example, the budgeted amount to be spent on the golf course in September 2011 is $80,000. The members (who are the owners of the club) control the operations by authorizing the board of directors and hence the management to spend club resources according to the plan. If there is a major unanticipated cost during the year (e.g., the swimming pool heater breaks), the board of directors can either pay for this out of cash generated from prior years' accumulated surpluses or call a special meeting of the membership and propose an assessment from each member.

Table 6–1 reports the actual amounts received and spent in September 2011. The club had a net operating deficit of $6,000 in September. The budget projected a surplus of $300. Thus, September's operations were $6,300 below budget. Last year in September, actual revenue exceeded actual expenses by $1,300. Comparing budget with actual for individual line items indicates that most of this September's $6,300 unfavorable variance is from food and bar expenses, which were $5,700 over budget. At this point, additional information is needed to determine the reasons for the unfavorable variance in food and bar expenses. The operating statement merely identifies a budget variance. Additional analysis is required to identify its causes and any corrective action needed to solve the problem.

Table 6–2 provides additional information on the food and bar operations. It indicates that actual expenses exceeded actual revenues by $11,000. The budget called for only a

$6,800 deficit. Thus, there was an unfavorable budget variance of $4,200 in the net operating deficit. September's unfavorable variances occurred because party revenue was $3,200 under budget and party expenses were $5,000 over budget. Further investigation reveals that the assistant manager in charge of parties quit in August. A large party was canceled in September, but no one at the club canceled the additional staff, food, and flower orders. The board criticized the club manager for not supervising these parties more closely during the absence of the assistant manager. A new assistant manager for parties was hired, and these problems were solved.[3]

Chapter 4 described organizational architecture as consisting of administrative systems that assign decision rights and evaluate and reward performance. Bay View Country Club's budgeting system illustrates how each of these three administrative systems is used to reduce agency problems at Bay View. *Decision rights,* which are initially held by the members, are assigned to the board of directors. The board hires professional managers who have the specialized knowledge to operate the various club functions: the club manager, the golf course superintendent, and the golf professional. These individuals submit their operating plans for the upcoming year via the budget.

Their budgets translate the plans for the next year into financial terms—the dollars of revenue and expenses that are expected to occur when their plans are implemented. The board reviews and modifies these plans to reflect member preferences and to ensure that monies are available to implement the plans. Once the membership approves the budget, the three managers have the decision rights to spend monies as specified in the budget. Decision rights are linked with knowledge. For example, the golf course superintendent has the specialized knowledge of the golf course as well as the available chemicals and maintenance procedures to maintain the course. The budget assigns to the superintendent the decision rights to implement a specific set of actions.

Notice the bottom-up nature of the budgeting process. The operating managers submit their budgets to the board of directors, who adjust the budgeted figures and recommend the budget to the membership. The members then have final approval rights over the budget.

Budgets are also a *performance measurement system.* Monthly operating statements for each manager are prepared. Table 6–2 is the operating statement for the club manager's food and bar operation. This statement is only one component of the club manager's performance. It shows whether the club manager met revenue and expense targets. Another indication of the manager's performance is the level of member satisfaction with the food and bar operation. Member satisfaction will ultimately show up in revenues and expenses if quality falls and members stop using the restaurant. Similarly, it does little good for the golf course superintendent to meet financial targets if the golf course condition deteriorates. Also, the condition of the course relative to other courses in the area is an important consideration in evaluating the superintendent's performance.

Budget variances are indicators of whether managers are meeting expectations and they are used in the *performance reward system* to determine pay increases or, in the case of extremely unfavorable variances, the need to terminate the responsible

[3] A well-known agency problem with private clubs (and other nonprofit organizations) is that the board of directors has little financial incentive to oversee the club. Board members receive no cash compensation for serving on the board. Thus, firing the manager imposes costs on them because they have to spend their time replacing the manager. All the members gain from the improved operations with the new (better) manager. Each board member receives 1/350th of the benefit (if there are 350 members) but incurs 1/15th of the cost (if there are 15 board members). This free-rider problem is one of the reasons member-owned country clubs usually are run less efficiently than owner-managed, for-profit clubs. Members are willing to bear these higher agency costs because of the prestige and exclusivity of belonging to the club and because of social interactions from associating with a stable membership.

Managerial Application: Most Large Corporations Review Budgets Monthly

Most organizations compare actual operations with budget on a monthly basis. This comparison is usually made by the chief executive officer (CEO). A survey of 120 large publicly traded firms inquired how frequently budgeted and actual results are compared. The study reports that 90 percent of the line managers reporting to the CEO compare monthly, 4 percent compare weekly or biweekly, and 6 percent compare quarterly. CEOs compare actual and budgeted results monthly in 83 percent of the firms and quarterly in 15 percent of the firms.

SOURCE: A Christie, M Joye, and R Watts, "Decentralization of the Firm: Theory and Evidence," *Journal of Corporate Finance* 118 (2001).

manager. The large unfavorable variance in party operations caused the board of directors to search for reasons for the variance, which led to the discovery that the manager did not supervise the parties. The lack of supervision caused the board to criticize the club manager. If unfavorable variances continue and the board determines that they are the fault of the manager, they may be grounds for dismissal or for not granting a pay increase. On the other hand, favorable budget variances need not indicate superior performance. If less was spent than was budgeted, quality may have been sacrificed.

One danger inherent in annual budgets such as the Bay View Country Club example is their tendency to focus managers' attention on next year's operations only, ignoring the long-term well-being of the organization. For example, if budgeted expenses exceed budgeted revenues, there is pressure to reduce maintenance expenditures. Reducing maintenance and repairs brings the one-year budget into line, but the long-term goals of the organization are compromised. To reduce the tendency of short-term budgets to focus managers too narrowly on short-term performance, many organizations prepare long-term budgets of three- to five-year duration at the same time as the short-run budgets. A budget for five years is more likely to reveal the effects of reducing short-run maintenance than a one-year budget. Section C discusses short-run versus long-run budgets in greater detail.

Bay View Country Club's budget separates decision management (decision initiation and implementation) from decision control (decision ratification and monitoring):

1. *Decision initiation* (budget preparation) is done by the operating managers.
2. *Decision ratification* (budget approval) is done by the board and the members.
3. *Decision implementation* (operating decisions) is done by the managers.
4. *Decision monitoring* (reviewing monthly operating statements) is done directly by the board and indirectly by the members.

The managers prepare the budget and make day-to-day operating decisions in their area (decision management rights). The board of directors approves budget requests and monitors operations (decision control rights). The board not only examines financial operating variances (the favorable and unfavorable variances on the operating statements) but also monitors member satisfaction with the club's food and golf operations.

In the country club example, the budget and the monthly operating statements are an integral part of the various administrative mechanisms that reduce the club's organizational problems. We now turn to a larger, more complex organization—namely, a private university. Again, the budget is a key device in resolving organizational problems.

FIGURE 6–2
Organization of Eastern University

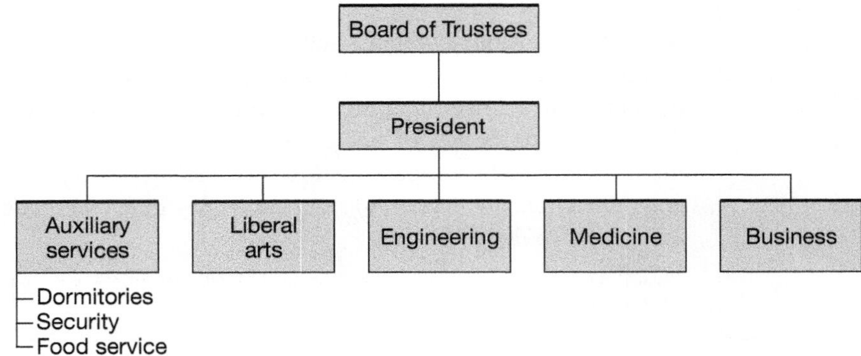

2. Private University

The private university example illustrates how budgets are used to assign decision rights to operating managers and then hold those managers responsible for their actions. Figure 6–2 is the organization chart for Eastern University, a nonprofit organization. The university has four separate colleges: liberal arts, engineering, medicine, and business. Liberal arts and engineering have both undergraduate and graduate programs. Engineering undergraduates take the first two years in liberal arts and the last two years in engineering. Medicine and business have only graduate programs. The auxiliary services department of the university provides dormitories, security, and food services.

The budgeting process begins with the chief financial officer (CFO) predicting general inflation and other key parameters for next year based on specialized knowledge of local markets. The managers of food service, dormitories, and security use this information and their specialized knowledge to prepare their budgets for the next year.

The deans of the colleges have specialized knowledge of faculty salaries in their areas and knowledge about the demand curve relating tuition to enrollments. Not all faculty markets have the same salary inflation. Each education program faces its own demand curve. Supply and demand for students vary across educational markets, thereby differentially affecting the cost of faculty and the tuition that can be charged in different disciplines.

At this university, liberal arts and engineering are treated as *cost centers.* That is, the deans have decision rights over expenditures, not revenues. This is because most of their revenues are from undergraduates who enter liberal arts and either stay in liberal arts or shift to engineering. The university administration believes neither the liberal arts nor the engineering deans are totally responsible for undergraduate enrollment and it is too complicated to account for the tuition revenue generated by undergraduates. Medicine and business are evaluated as *profit centers* in the sense that they are expected to generate revenues to cover their expenditures, where revenues include grants, annual alumni giving, fees, and tuition revenues.[4]

As profit centers, medicine and business must forecast revenues in addition to costs. Likewise, the CFO must forecast liberal arts and engineering revenues. Forecasting revenues requires estimates of the number of students enrolled, the tuition rate, and the financial aid budget. Net revenue received is the number of students enrolled times the stated tuition rate less financial aid awarded. Before the academic year begins, each school announces its tuition for next year. Half of the business school's total enrollment next year

[4] Nonprofit institutions, such as private universities invent terminology like *tubs on their own bottoms* to avoid using the term *profit centers.* In reality, all organizations must avoid generating negative cash flows or else they will not survive in a competitive environment. Their operating budgets can be subsidized through gifts and endowments, but these are just other services being provided by the nonprofit institution. Nonprofit institutions seek to make profits and hence to grow and survive, but legally they cannot distribute these profits to their "owners." There are no legal owners of the residual cash flow streams in nonprofit firms.

is reasonably easy to forecast based on the number of first-year students currently enrolled who are expected to return next year. The size of this group will not change much based on the tuition increase. However, the new entering class is more price sensitive than the class already enrolled. A large tuition increase may require an increase in the financial aid budget if the school is to maintain both the quantity and quality of entering students. Thus, estimating revenue requires trading off total revenue net of financial aid for student quality. Lowering student quality reduces the demand for the school's programs by high-quality students in the future.

Once the deans prepare their budgets for next year, they are sent to the CFO, who ensures that total projected revenues cover total projected expenditures. The CFO and the president also must ensure that the plans of each college are consistent with the overall strategy of the university. For example, if the president sees the university as primarily a graduate research institution, college budgets that put substantial additional resources into undergraduate education are inconsistent with that mission. The president would cut back these undergraduate resource requests. Through this back-and-forth negotiating process between the president, who has specialized knowledge of the university's mission, and the managers and deans of the various units, a consensus is reached and an overall budget for the university is prepared.

The budget is then sent to the board of trustees for approval. The board of trustees at this private institution consists of alumni, local leaders, and donors. Trustees do not receive any cash compensation from the university. They are appointed to the board for fixed terms and usually have a strong commitment to the preservation and improvement of the institution. The board of trustees examines the budget to ensure that it meets the university's mission and that it is fiscally prudent, meaning that the university will survive in the long run.

After the budget is approved, managers and deans have the decision rights to operate their units. Faculty are hired, food is purchased, and dormitory maintenance is provided consistent with the amounts in the budget. Monthly and annual reports, similar to Tables 6–1 and 6–2, are prepared to show each unit's compliance with the budget. These reports are part of the *decision-monitoring* process. This example again illustrates the linking of knowledge and decision rights and the separation of decision management and decision control via the use of the hierarchy. Like most budgeting systems, it is bottom up; lower levels in the organization prepare the initial budgets because they have much of the specialized knowledge. As the budget moves through the *decision ratification* process, higher levels review the budget and bring to bear their specialized knowledge.

Two points emerge from this example. First, managers and deans have an incentive to request "too large" a budget. The dean of liberal arts is under pressure from students and faculty in liberal arts to add more courses, more programs, and more student services, which can be done only by requesting more money. The dean of medicine is under pressure to provide more medical services in the hospital and more medical education. Even though medicine is treated as a profit center, the dean of medicine has an incentive to prepare a budget that shows a deficit (where expenditures exceed revenues) in hopes that the president will finance this deficit out of surpluses generated in other divisions. That is, the medical school dean hopes for *cross subsidization.*

The second point is that the deans of liberal arts and engineering have different incentives from the deans of medicine and business. Liberal arts and engineering are treated as cost centers, so they receive little benefit from additional revenues generated by adding more students. These deans have less incentive than the medicine and business deans to innovate cash-generating new programs because they do not directly capture the additional tuition. The liberal arts and engineering deans have incentives to lobby for more resources for new programs. But since these deans do not bear the full consequences of adding programs

Managerial Application: "Budgeting for Curve Balls"

The Chicago White Sox baseball team has an annual budget of over $200 million. Budget assumptions are set in August/September, and by October the new budget is prepared for the next year. The team owner first sets guidelines for the total player salary budget; this is the largest single expense category. Department heads assemble assumption sheets, books of 1,500–2,000 pages, one for every account. These sheets contain details—such as the number of security people for each game based on expected attendance levels, their pay rates, and union contracts—and explain any recommended changes from last year. Then the vice president of finance, the accounting manager, and the controller review the budgets with each department head. These meetings ensure consistent assumptions are being made across departments and that the budget requests are realistic. The team owner then reviews the budget requests. Once the budget is set, department heads must explain cost overruns and underruns.

SOURCE: A Dennis, "Budgeting for Curve Balls," *Journal of Accountancy,* September 1998, pp. 89–92; www.usatoday.com/sports/baseball/salaries.

that cost more than they bring in, they are more likely to add unprofitable programs than are the business and medicine deans.

One problem the president faces with the medicine and business deans is their incentives to free ride on the university's reputation by offering lower-quality programs. For example, suppose the university has a reputation for high quality. The dean of medicine can generate additional revenues by starting low-quality programs, but this will debase the overall university reputation. The dean's incentive to reduce quality is controlled by presidential monitoring of faculty appointments and academic programs.

3. Large Corporation

The two previous examples described budgeting primarily as a process by which knowledge is assembled *vertically,* from both lower levels and higher levels in the organization's hierarchy. But budgeting is also an important device for assembling specialized knowledge *horizontally* within the firm. In a large, complex corporation, it is a major challenge to disseminate specific knowledge. Getting managers to share their knowledge among superiors and subordinates (vertically) as well as among peers in other parts of the organization (horizontally) and giving managers incentives to acquire valuable knowledge are important aspects of the budgeting system. Consider the case of Xerox Corporation.

Xerox produces, sells, leases, and services a wide range of copiers with different copy output rates, features, and sales and rental plans. The field organization consists of branch offices with sales, service, and administrative personnel. The manufacturing organization produces copiers at sites around the world and is treated as a cost center. Besides manufacturing copiers, Xerox also sells supplies, such as toner. The field offices that are part of marketing are cost centers; the supplies division is a profit center.

Each year Xerox must plan how many new copiers of each type will be placed in service and how many old copiers will be returned. These numbers drive the manufacturing plans for the year. The number of various types of copiers currently in the field, which is called the *installed base,* affects the number of service personnel in the field, the training programs they require, and the stock of spare parts needed to service the base. The installed base also affects the amount of supplies Xerox sells.

Each part of Xerox must communicate with the other parts of the firm. Manufacturing wants to know how many of each type of copier marketing expects to sell. Marketing wants to know what prices will be charged for each type of copier. Copier placements depend on the market's expectation of new product introductions. In setting their forecasts, manufacturing

Managerial Application: Budgeting at Nestlé Waters Division

The Nestlé Waters Division was created to manage the two Nestlé water businesses: the French brands of Perrier, Vittel, and Contrex, and the Italian brands of Pellegrino and Acqua Panna. These brands are sold worldwide through the Nestlé Waters distribution system. The French and Italian units start the budgeting process by developing a multiyear, long-term global brand strategy that includes positioning, pricing, and brand development. Next, the Nestlé Waters headquarters approves the global strategy. This strategy then generates a plan for each Nestlé distributor that defines market priorities, volumes, and price targets, as well as budgets to implement the plan. Each distributor prepares a budget for achieving its piece of the global strategy and discusses it with the French and Italian Nestlé Waters producers until all parties are in agreement. Once approved by the French and Italian units and distributors, the first year of the plan becomes the operating plan (budget).

Monthly, quarterly, and annual reports provide actual sales statistics, outlook by brand, actual profits by brand, and variances from budget. Prior to implementing the new organization and budgeting system, very limited information flowed laterally among the French and Italian producers and distributors, and there was no integrated international brand strategy. The new structure and budgeting system forces Nestlé Waters producers and distributors to think strategically in terms of joint profitability as equal partners belonging to the same global organization. A Pellegrino finance manager said, "The new performance measurement and accountability . . . has brought a new end-to-end mentality, fostering the (business unit) integration through shared goals between the producer and the distributor. On the one hand, it improved the producer's control over the distributors' activities. On the other hand, it links the distributors and the producer to a common faith as they have a shared goal to achieve, and, in so doing, it favors identification around a global brand commitment."

SOURCE: C Busco, M Frigo, E Giovannoni, A Riccaboni, and R Scapens, "Integrating Global Organizations through Performance Measurement Systems," *Strategic Finance,* January 2006, pp. 31–35.

and marketing managers want to know about new products. Likewise, the toner division needs to know the size of the installed base and its composition so it can plan the production of supplies for the year.

Not only must the various parts of Xerox share their specialized knowledge, but they must have incentives to acquire it. The sales force must acquire the knowledge, about the forecasted quantities and prices of particular copiers to be sold (or leased). These sales estimates must be transmitted to manufacturing with enough lead time to build the projected quantities of new copiers.

An important part of the budgeting process is sharing and assembling knowledge about such key planning assumptions as unit placements, prices, and copier returns. Knowledge of these numbers is widely dispersed throughout the firm. In the process of assembling the knowledge, people will change their expectations of the key planning assumptions. In addition, all managers affected by a key planning assumption are usually required to approve it and then build their budgets using it. Each manager's approval helps ensure that expectations are consistent throughout the firm.

The corporate budgeting system is also a communication device through which some of the specialized knowledge and key planning assumptions are transmitted. It also involves a process by which various individuals arranged vertically and horizontally in the organization negotiate the terms of trade among the various parts of the organization. For example, for a given price schedule, the marketing organization estimates the quantity of each type of copier placed. Manufacturing agrees to produce this quantity of copiers and estimates the cost at

Managerial Application: Budgeting Continuous Improvements

A number of Japanese car companies use an elaborate system of continuous cost improvement called Kaizen costing. Toyota defines Kaizen as the work process and ethic that involves continuous search for improvement, constantly taking measures to improve work procedures and equipment. Kaizen often involves utilizing teams of employees who revise their work procedures and standards round-the-clock to achieve improvements in efficiency, quality, and working conditions. Kaizen systems employ a variety of planning documents, including production, distribution, and sales plan; unit sales and contribution margins; capital projects; and fixed expenses. Kaizen also requires a variable cost reduction goal for each plant and each department within the plant. Monthly variance reports document differences between actual and budgeted cost reductions and managers in each department are held responsible for the variances.

SOURCE: J Liker, *The Toyota Way Field Book* (New York: McGraw-Hill, 2006).

which they will be produced. Usually, price schedules are adjusted to bring manufacturing (supply) in line with marketing (demand). In principle, when sales forecasts and production plans are produced, knowledge of cost (from manufacturing) and revenue (from marketing) is transferred to those agents with the decision rights to set prices, who ideally set the price for each product to maximize profits. Likewise, the supplies and service organizations accept their targets. Senior management ensures that all parts of the budget are consistent: Marketing and manufacturing are in agreement, the financing is in place, the parts inventory is adequate to meet service requirements, and so on. Moreover, senior management likely has specialized knowledge to forecast some assumptions such as interest rates and salary levels and to arbitrate disputes that arise between departments during the budgeting process.

Exercise 6–1:

Shocker Company's sales budget shows quarterly sales for next year as follows:

Quarter 1	10,000 units
Quarter 2	8,000 units
Quarter 3	12,000 units
Quarter 4	14,000 units

Company policy is to have a finished goods inventory at the end of each quarter equal to 20 percent of the next quarter's sales.

Required:

Compute budgeted production for the second quarter of next year.

Solution:

Quarter 2 sales	8,000 units
+ Ending Inventory: 20% of Quarter 3 sales (12,000 × 20%)	2,400 units
– Beginning Inventory: 20% of Quarter 2 sales (8,000 × 20%)	(1,600) units
Budgeted production	8,800 units

Many budgeting systems involve a bottom-up, top-down approach. Usually, some key planning assumptions are announced. Then, the lowest levels in the decision hierarchy submit budgets for the next year. For example, product prices or the general inflation rate for next year is announced by a budget officer at the beginning of the budget process. These first-round, lowest-level projections are accumulated at the next level up in the organization, revised and submitted again to the next level, and so on up the hierarchy. At each level, managers ensure that the budget assumptions are consistent across their departments and that each department's forecast is reasonable. Each manager also modifies subordinates' plans with any specialized knowledge the manager has acquired. In most firms, lower-level managers have a significant role in both the initial and revision stages of the budget's preparation.

As the budget is passed from one level of the organization up to a higher level, potential bottlenecks are uncovered before they occur. For example, if one department's budget calls for 10,000 units of a part and the parts fabrication department can produce only 7,500 units, this bottleneck is identified before production actually begins. At some point, the key assumptions may be challenged by managers with better specialized knowledge. On occasion, the assumptions are revised and the budgets updated.

The budget is revised at the top and passed back down through the organization. Either lower-level managers with specialized knowledge will agree with the changes and adapt to the new strategy or they will disagree. If there is enough disagreement and it is made known to senior management, another round of budget revisions will occur.

Large corporations use budgets to

1. Assign decision rights.
2. Communicate information both vertically and horizontally.
3. Set goals through negotiation and internal contracting.
4. Measure performance.

Concept Questions

Q6–1	How are budgets developed?
Q6–2	How are key planning assumptions derived?
Q6–3	Define *budget variance.*
Q6–4	Are budgets part of the performance measurement system or the performance reward system?
Q6–5	What are some of the synergies that budgets provide within a large corporation?
Q6–6	How do budgets partition decision rights within a firm?
Q6–7	What purposes are served by the budgeting process in a large firm?

B. Trade-Off between Decision Management and Decision Control

The budgeting process plays an important role in both decision management and decision control in organizations. In one survey, over 50 percent of managers agreed that budgets are indispensable in running their business.[5]

[5] T Libby and M Lindsay, "Beyond Budgeting or Better Budgeting," *Strategic Finance,* August 2007, pp. 47–51.

1. Communicating Specialized Knowledge versus Performance Evaluation

As the earlier examples describe, budgeting systems perform several functions within firms, including decision management and decision control. In decision management, budgets serve to communicate specialized knowledge about one part of the organization to another part. In decision control, budgets are part of the performance measurement system. Because budgets serve several purposes, trade-offs must be made when a budgeting system is designed or changed. The budget becomes the benchmark against which to judge actual performance. If too much emphasis is placed on the budget as a performance benchmark, then managers with the specialized knowledge will stop disclosing unbiased forecasts of future events and will report conservative budget figures that enhance their performance measure.

The trade-off between decision management and decision control is best illustrated in marketing. Salespeople usually have specialized knowledge of future sales. This information is important in setting production plans. But if budgeted sales are used to evaluate sales reps at the end of the year (i.e., actual sales are compared with budget), then sales reps have an incentive to ex ante underforecast future sales, thus improving their ex post performance evaluation. However, production plans will then be too low and the firm will not be able to plan the most efficient production schedules.[6] For example, suppose the salespeople underforecast sales by 20 percent. When actual sales are higher than the plant expects, overtime must be paid to produce the extra units. It would have been cheaper to expand the plant's permanent work force.

An important lesson from this chapter is that whenever budgets are used to evaluate managers' performance and then to compensate (or promote) them based on their performance relative to the budget target, strong incentives are created for these managers to game the system. Even subjective performance evaluations based on meeting or exceeding the budget create dysfunctional behavior. Gaming occurs in both the budget-setting process and in the actions managers take during the year to achieve the budgeted targets. Most companies report that budgeting induces dysfunctional behaviors, including negotiating easier targets to help ensure they will receive bonuses ("sandbagging"), spending money at the end of the year to avoid losing it in the next budget period, deferring needed spending (maintenance and advertising) to meet the budget, accelerating sales near the end of the period to achieve the budget, and taking a "big bath" when budgets cannot be achieved in order to lower next year's budgets. In rare cases, trying to achieve budget targets has induced managers to commit fraud by recording fictitious revenues or misclassifying expenses as assets.[7]

2. Budget Ratcheting

Using historical data on past performance is a common mechanism for setting next year's budget. Unfortunately, it often leads to a perverse incentive called the *ratchet effect.* The ratchet effect refers to basing next year's standard of performance on this year's actual performance. However, performance targets are usually adjusted in only one direction—upward. A bad year usually does not cause subsequent years' targets to fall. For example, if this year's sales budget is $1 million and the salesperson sells $1.3 million, next year's sales budget becomes $1.3 million. However, if actual sales are only $0.9 million, next year's budget is not cut back to $0.9 million.

[6] In some cases, it is possible to structure an incentive contract that induces managers to disclose their private information in an unbiased fashion. See J Gonik, "Tie Salesmen's Bonuses to Their Forecasts," *Harvard Business Review,* 1978, pp. 116–23; M Weitzman, "The New Soviet Incentive Model," *Bell Journal of Economics,* Spring 1976, pp. 251–57; and A Kirby, S Reichelstein, P Sen, and Y Paik, "Participation, Slack, and Budget-Based Performance Evaluation," *Journal of Accounting Research,* Spring 1991, pp. 109–28.

[7] T Libby and M Lindsay, "Beyond Budgeting or Better Budgeting," *Strategic Finance,* August 2007, p. 50.

Managerial Application: Budgets Used for Decision Management and Control

A survey of British financial managers asked them to evaluate the importance of their firm's budgets for planning, control, and evaluation. The table below summarizes the results.

	Not very Important Almost or Irrelevant (%)	*Important or Extremely Important (%)*
Overall	5.1	94.9
Planning	2.5	97.5
Control	5.0	95.0
Co-ordination	17.5	82.5
Communication	17.5	82.5
Authorisation	10.0	90.0
Motivation	37.5	62.5
Performance evaluation	12.5	87.5

There are three interesting insights from this survey:

- Budgets are important overall.
- Budgets are important for decision management (planning and coordination) and control (control, motivation, and performance evaluation).
- While 87.5 percent of the managers believe budgets are important for performance evaluation, only 62.5 percent report they are important for motivation. This seems to suggest problems exist in using budgets to motivate people. One possible explanation is that managers game their budgets and this reduces the budget's usefulness as a motivational tool.

SOURCE: CIMA and ICAEW, "Better Budgeting: A Report on the Better Budgeting Forum," July 2004.

H. J. Heinz, a producer of processed food (best known for its catsup) sets next year's profit center budgets at the greater of 115 percent of either last year's budget or last year's actual results. For example, if last year's budgeted earnings were \$10 million and actual earnings were \$11 million in a particular profit center, next year's profit for this center would be budgeted at \$12.65 million (\$11 million × 115%). However, if earnings last year were only \$9 million, next year's budget would be \$11.5 million (\$10 million × 115%). Thus, at Heinz budgeted earnings only increase. One study of a large international conglomerate found that when the actual earnings of a subsidiary exceed budgeted earnings by, say, \$100,000, the next year's budget is increased by \$90,000. However, if actual earnings fall short of the budget by \$100,000, next year's budget is only reduced by \$40,000.[8] Hence, favorable budget variances are more likely to lead to larger increases than unfavorable variances are to lead to decreases.

This "ratcheting up" of budgets causes employees to temper this year's better-than-budgeted performance to avoid being held to a higher standard in future periods. Many illustrations of dysfunctional behavior induced by the ratchet effect exist:

- In the former Soviet Union, central planners would set a plant's production quota based on past experience. Plant managers meeting their targets received various

[8] A Leone and S Rock, "Empirical Tests of Budget Ratcheting and Its Effect on Managers' Discretionary Accrual Choices," *Journal of Accounting and Economics*, February 2002.

Managerial Application: Budgeting at Best Buy

At Best Buy, with more than 1,100 retail stores across the United States, Canada, and China selling consumer electronics, home-office products, entertainment software, appliances, and related services, budgeting was a nightmare. It was time consuming and was not helpful at assembling knowledge. Corporate-level planners made broad assumptions about what each store would sell and the resources needed to meet their targets. Best Buy spent four years revamping its budgeting and planning system. First, Best Buy pushed the planning down to the district managers, and then to the stores. The districts and the stores have firsthand knowledge of what the customers want and where the opportunities for cost savings lie. A senior finance analyst at Best Buy states, "There is a gap between what the store managers know about their operations and what corporate knows."

SOURCE: D Durfee, "The Last Mile," *CFO,* January 2007, pp. 49–55.

rewards and those missing the target were punished. This created incentives for managers to just barely exceed their quota.

- Companies often base a salesperson's bonus on meeting a sales target that is based on last year's sales. If salespeople expect an unusually good year, they will try to defer some sales into the next fiscal year. They may take a customer's order but delay processing it until the next fiscal year.
- In one company, each department's target was based in part on last year's performance plus an increase. This created incentives for managers to defer making big productivity improvements in any one year, preferring instead to spread them over several years.[9]

Why do firms ratchet up their budgets given the perverse incentives induced? One possible reason is that even more perverse incentives might arise if they don't. For example, one simple solution to the dysfunctional incentives arising from the ratchet effect is to eliminate budget targets completely and simply base salespeople's salary on actual sales. Assume that budgeted sales next year are $1 million. Instead of paying a commission of 10 percent on all sales of more than $1 million, pay a commission of 2 percent on total sales. Suppose that both commission schemes have the same expected compensation. The 10 percent commission gives the employee five times the incentive (10 percent versus 2 percent) to make an additional sale. Thus, eliminating the $1 million target reduces the commission rate and hence the employee's marginal incentives.

Asking the salespeople to estimate next year's sales instead of ratcheting up next year's target based on this year's actual sales eliminates the perverse incentives of the ratchet effect. However, this alternative creates another problem. In particular, salespeople will forecast next year's sales far below what they expect to sell, thereby increasing their expected compensation and communicating too low an expected sales forecast to manufacturing.

Or, instead of ratcheting up to set next year's budget, a central planning group can prepare top-down budgets by using past sales and cost patterns, macroeconomic trends, and customer surveys. But this central forecasting group might be more expensive than a simple ratcheting-up budget algorithm. The direct costs of preparing budgets centrally (personnel and occupancy costs) could exceed the indirect costs from dysfunctional decision making induced by the ratchet effect.

[9] R Kaplan and A Sweeney, "Peoria Engine Plant (A)," Harvard Business School Case 9-193-082.

Managerial Application: Improving Budgeting

Budgeting is the bane of many executives. About 55 percent of executives say budgeting is too time consuming, 65 percent believe budgets are slow to detect problems, 50 percent think they quickly get out of date, and 35 percent see budgets as disrupting cooperation within their firms. At Nortel, budgets contained up to 100 line items for each unit and took four to five months to prepare. After streamlining the process by better tying the budget to strategic objectives, Nortel now reports only eight line items on a rolling quarterly basis.

Technology is improving budgeting. Web-based software is replacing numerous nonstandard spreadsheets submitted by operating divisions that often have to be reentered and consolidated with other divisions' spreadsheets. For example, within one company each of 28 operating units would e-mail or send on diskette its own spreadsheet, which corporate would have to rekey or upload to create a consolidated budget. Just making simple changes delayed the process and maintaining all the spreadsheets cost $100,000 a year. Browser-based budgeting software now allows divisions to enter and revise data remotely using a standard format and allows corporate managers access to the consolidated numbers instantly. Conexant Systems Inc., a supplier of semiconductor products, uses a Web-based budgeting tool to manage 1,200 cost centers that each use up to 500 accounts. Cost center managers enter their own budget data with less help from financial analysts.

SOURCE: T Reason, "Building Better Budgets," *CFO*, December 2000, pp. 91–98; D Dufee, "Alternative Budgeting," *CFO*, June 2006, p. 28; and T Libby and M Lindsay, 2007, p. 49.

Another way to reduce the problems caused by ratcheting up each year's performance targets is more frequent job rotation. If you know that next year someone else has to meet the sales figures you achieve this year, you will sell more now. However, job rotation destroys job-specific human capital such as customer-specific relationships.

In summary, while the ratchet effect creates dysfunctional behavior, the alternatives might prove more costly. In essence, one agency problem is replaced with another one. Depending on the particular situation, senior managers must choose the lesser of the two evils.

3. Participative Budgeting

The trade-off between decision management and decision control is often viewed as a trade-off between bottom-up and top-down budgeting. Bottom-up budgets are those submitted by lower levels of the organization to higher levels and usually imply greater decision management. An example of a bottom-up budget is the field sales offices' submission of their forecasts for next year to the marketing department. A top-down budget would be the marketing department's use of aggregate data on sales trends to forecast sales for the entire firm and then its disaggregation of this firmwide budget into field office targets. This top-down budget provides greater decision control. Bottom-up budgeting, in which the person ultimately being held responsible for meeting the target makes the initial budget forecast, is called *participative budgeting.*

Participative budgeting supposedly enhances the motivation of the lower-level participants by getting them to accept the targets. Whether budgeting is bottom-up or top-down ultimately depends in part on where the knowledge is located. If the field salespeople have the knowledge, this would tend to favor a bottom-up approach to link the knowledge and decision rights. If the central marketing organization has better knowledge, a top-down budget is likely to prove better. Which budgeting scheme provides better motivation ultimately depends on how the performance measurement and performance reward systems are designed.

A survey of 98 Standard & Poor's 500 U.S. companies found that these firms use participative budgeting more frequently when lower-level managers have more knowledge than central management.[10] Participative budgeting is more frequently observed when managers' rewards are based on the performance against the budget. Likewise, the use of budget-based incentives and the extent of specialized knowledge held by lower-level managers are positively correlated. This evidence is consistent with budgets and performance reward systems' being designed to link decision-making rights and specialized knowledge.

Once the budget is set, it becomes the target by which performance is evaluated and rewarded. Some experts argue the budget should be "tight" but achievable. If budgets are too easily achieved, they provide little incentive to expend extra effort. If budgets are unachievable, they provide little motivation. As discussed earlier, most budgets are set in a negotiation process involving lower- and higher-level managers. Lower-level managers have incentives to set a loose target to guarantee they will meet the budget and be favorably rewarded. Higher-level managers have incentives to set a tight target to motivate the lower-level managers to exert additional effort. A study of 54 profit center managers in 12 corporations found that budgeted profits were set so that they were achieved 8 or 9 years out of 10.[11] These managers reported that these loose budgets improved resource planning, control, and motivation.

4. New Approaches to Budgeting

The trade-off between decision management and decision control in budgeting creates tension between the two roles, and these tensions lead to criticism. Budgets are criticized often because they:

- Are time consuming to construct.
- Add little value.
- Are developed and updated too infrequently.
- Are based on unsupported assumptions and guesswork.
- Constrain responsiveness and act as a barrier to change.
- Are rarely strategically focused and often contradictory.
- Strengthen vertical command and control.
- Concentrate on cost reduction.
- Encourage gaming and perverse behaviors.
- Do not reflect emerging network structures organizations are adopting.
- Reinforce departmental barriers rather than encourage knowledge-sharing.
- Make people feel undervalued.

The widespread dissatisfaction with budgeting arises, in part, because budgets are so ubiquitous. If budgeting wasn't as pervasive, fewer complaints would arise. Many firms are seeking to improve their budgeting process, while others are abandoning it altogether. One reason firms retain their budgets is because budgets often remain the only central coordinating mechanism within the firm.

Two different approaches are proposed to improve the budgeting process.[12] One method involves building the budget in two distinct steps. The first step, which involves the lowest levels of the organization, is to construct budgets in operational, not financial terms.

---

[10] M Shields and S Young, "Antecedents and Consequences of Participative Budgeting: Evidence on the Effects of Asymmetrical Information," *Journal of Management Accounting Research,* 1993, pp. 265–80.

[11] K Merchant and J Manzoni, "The Achievability of Budget Targets in Profit Centers: A Field Study," *Accounting Review* 64 (July 1989), pp. 539–58.

[12] S Hansen, D Otley, and W Van der Stede, "Practice Developments in Budgeting: An Overview and Research Perspective," *Journal of Management Accounting Research* 15 (2003), pp. 95–116.

Managerial Application: Microsoft's New Budgeting System

Microsoft Corp., with 60,000 employees in 99 countries, was reorganized into seven distinct businesses. The budgeting system also changed. Prior to the change, Microsoft's centralized management proved too unwieldy, and its software engineering groups had little responsibility for sales. After the reorganization, each business group had its own CFO responsible for that group's strategy, budgeting, and analysis of market performance and operating expenses. Each of the seven businesses has a budget based on its own product-development strategy and on the firmwide corporate strategy.

The budget process consists of the following steps:

1. Each business reviews its strategy, proposed changes, and investments at the end of June with the CEO.
2. July involves a "deep midyear review" that examines operational trends by geography, business lines, and channels. Based on this evaluation the corporate office begins setting targets for each group.
3. Once preliminary targets are set by the corporate office, the CEO meets with each business group about the "ambition" for the next year. "Ambition" is the Microsoft CEO's expectation for that business group in terms of revenue growth, earnings, and product development.
4. After the CEO and each business group reach a consensus on the overall targets, then the detailed budgeting begins—roughly an eight-week effort.

SOURCE: T Reason, "Budgeting in the Real World," *CFO,* July 2005, pp. 43–48.

At this step, budgeting requires data about estimated demand for resources and outputs stated in nonfinancial terms such as units of output, hours of various types of labor, and consumption rates of resources. Operational budgets are in balance when resource consumption requirements equal the resources available for each resource required to operate the firm. The second step develops a financial plan based on the operational plans developed in step one. This two-step process makes the budgeting process more representative of how the organization actually operates by balancing operational requirements. The first step provides a more sophisticated model for balancing capacity. Lower-level managers more easily understand and communicate information in operational rather than financial terms. Lower-level managers' specific knowledge is usually couched in nonfinancial terms, and the first step of the process utilizes their specific knowledge directly.

However, this approach is more costly than traditional budgets (which are stated in financial terms only) because the additional detailed information about individual resources must be collected and managed. Also, this approach, at least as described by its proponents, does not involve a third step whereby the organization iterates between steps one and two until all the various inconsistencies are resolved. For example, consider a package delivery company. Assume that a particular resource such as the number of delivery vans and the number of orders expected to be delivered are in balance. During budget construction, senior marketing executives learn that the average size of each shipment is expected to increase. This increase in the average shipment size must be communicated to the executive responsible for managing the fleet. With a larger average package size, the firm might not have enough capacity to deliver the same number of packages. The firm has to decide whether to increase fleet size, acquire larger trucks, raise the price of deliveries (to reduce the quantity shipped), or some combination of the three. A cost-benefit trade-off must be made somewhere in the firm. Exactly how and

Managerial Application: Why Budgets Are Bad for Business

Budgets are often criticized for controlling the wrong things, like head count, and for missing the right things, such as quality and customer service. Often they erect walls between various parts of the company. Moreover, because a budget was not overspent does not mean it was well spent. Budgets are good at tracking spending. But big problems arise when the budget becomes management's main tool for gauging performance and for compensating managers.

When managers' pay is based on meeting their budget, they start doing dumb things. First, they have strong incentives to distort their budgets to make them easier to achieve. These distortions bias the transmission of information needed to coordinate the disparate parts of the firm. Second, managers game their actual performance to meet the current targets or to set more favorable future budgets.

These criticisms fail to recognize that budgeting systems are almost universally used and have survived. Thus, they must be yielding benefits at least as large as their costs. The question is whether even more dysfunctional behavior arises when budgets are not used. The fact that so many firms use budgets suggests that forgoing budgets is an unlikely formula for success.

Budgeting critics rarely address the benefits such systems provide that allow these systems to survive. Moreover, most of the dysfunctional behaviors created by budgets can be resolved by not tying pay to meeting the budget.

SOURCE: M Jensen, "Paying People to Lie: The Truth about the Budgeting Process," *European Financial Management* 9 (September 2003), pp. 379–406.

where this analysis and decision occurs is not specified by the proponents of the two-step approach to improving budgeting.

A second approach to improve budgeting involves breaking the so-called "annual performance trap." This approach does not use budgets as performance targets. Budgets are still constructed for financial planning (decision management), but they are not used for performance evaluation. Rather, firms use relative performance targets of other units or firms and compare these peer-units' performance to the actual performance achieved by the unit being judged. First a peer benchmark group is set for each budget unit. The benchmarks are either different units in the same firm or their leading competitors. Then the unit's actual achieved performance is compared to the actual performance achieved by the benchmark. Actual rewards are then determined subjectively, taking into account not just the benchmark's performance but other financial and nonfinancial performance measures. This approach to improving the budget process decouples financial planning, information communication, and coordination (decision management) from performance evaluation and performance rewards (decision control). Proponents of this approach claim that by decoupling decision management and decision control, decision management is improved because executives have less incentive to game the initial budget estimates. However, the use of relative performance evaluations and subjective evaluations are not without problems. Managers still have incentives to game how the benchmarks are chosen. There are no guarantees that the managers making the subjective evaluations will do so in an unbiased way, and therefore there is no guarantee that the person being evaluated based in part on the performance of some peer group will accept such an assessment without undue griping or without exerting undue influence costs.

No simple "one-size-fits-all" panacea exists for resolving the conflict between decision management versus decision control when it comes to budgeting. Nor is such a solution ever likely to be found. Budgets perform both decision management and decision control roles, and each firm must find the solution that best fits its unique circumstances at that point in time. Budgeting processes (and associated compensation schemes) will evolve as the firm's circumstances change.

5. Managing the Trade-Off

To manage the trade-off between decision management and decision control, many organizations put the chief executive officer in charge of the budgeting process. While the actual collection of data and preparation of the budget are formal responsibilities of the chief financial officer or controller, the president or CEO has the final decision rights. There are several reasons for the chief executive to have ultimate control. First, it signals the importance of the budgeting process. Second, the CEO has the specialized knowledge and the overall view of the entire firm to make the trade-offs needed to resolve disagreements among departments regarding key planning assumptions or coordination of activities. McKinsey writes,

> [T]he sales department may desire to sell more than the production department thinks it can produce profitably, or the production department may desire to produce articles which the sales department does not think it can sell, or both the sales and production departments may desire to increase their activities beyond what the financial department thinks can be financed. Obviously the only authority who can decide these questions is the chief executive who is superior to all executives interested in the controversy.[13]

In addition to placing the chief executive in charge of the budgeting process, many firms use a budget committee consisting of the major functional executives (vice presidents of sales, manufacturing, finance, and personnel), with the CEO as chair. This committee seeks to facilitate the exchange of specialized knowledge and reach consensus on the key planning assumptions. In essence, no budget or estimate is accepted until the budget committee approves. Then all the various parts of the organization agree to the inherent exchanges among the various parts of the organization. The budget is the informal set of contracts between the various units of the organization.

Concept Questions		
	Q6–8	Why would managers bias their forecasts when preparing a budget?
	Q6–9	What is a bottom-up budgeting system?
	Q6–10	What is the *ratchet effect?*
	Q6–11	Describe participative budgeting.

C. Resolving Organizational Problems

As the three examples in section A illustrate, budgeting systems are an administrative device used to resolve organizational problems. In particular, these systems help (1) link knowledge with the decision rights and (2) measure and reward performance. The Bay View Country Club example illustrates how budgets provide performance measurements. The Eastern University example illustrates the concepts of cost centers and profit centers and how budgets assign decision rights. The Xerox Corporation example illustrates the linking of knowledge and decision rights. This section further describes various budgeting devices, such as short-run versus long-run budgets, line-item budgets, budget lapsing, flexible budgets, and incremental versus zero-based budgets.

[13] McKinsey (1922), pp. 44–45.

Managerial Application: Lenders Want Five-Year Budgets

Firms prepare long-run budgets for a variety of reasons. One reason is that their bankers demand to see budgets that cover the period of the loans extended to the company. Many bank loans are for three to five years. Bank of America often requires borrowers to produce forecasts that cover the duration of nearly any loan request: "We're looking for the cash-flow perspective and how we're getting paid. We build our loan agreements and covenants on that information. We're obviously asking so we understand the risk of a deal."

One company CFO who finds the process very useful says, "We do five-year plans to give ourselves a longer-term view to achieve long-term growth goals."

SOURCE: K Frieswick, "The Five-Year Itch," *CFO,* February 2003, pp. 68–70.

1. Short-Run versus Long-Run Budgets

The budgeting examples in section A described annual budgeting processes. Starting in the prior year, firms develop detailed plans of how many units of each product they expect to sell at what prices, the cost of such sales, and the financing necessary for operations. These budgets then become the internal "contracts" for each responsibility center (cost, profit, and investment center) within the firm. These annual budgets are short-run in the sense that they project only one year at a time. But most firms also project 2, 5, and sometimes 10 years in advance. These long-run budgets are a key feature of the organization's strategic planning process.

Strategic planning refers to the process whereby managers select the firm's overall objectives and the tactics to achieve them. It involves deciding what markets to be in, what products to produce, and what price-quality combinations to offer. For example, Time Warner faces the strategic question of whether to provide local telephone service in its cable markets. Making this decision requires specialized knowledge of the various technologies Time Warner and its competitors face, in addition to knowledge of the demand for various future products. Strategic planning also addresses questions of what the organization's future structure must be to support the strategy, including future R&D and capital spending and the financial structure.

Like short-run budgets, long-run budgets force managers with specialized knowledge to communicate their forecasts of future expected events under various scenarios. Long-run budgets contain future capital budgeting forecasts (and thus financing plans) required to implement the strategy. R&D budgets are long-run plans of the multiyear spending required to acquire and develop the technologies to implement the strategies.

In short-run budgets, the key planning assumptions involve quantities and prices. All parts of the organization must accept these annual key assumptions. In long-run budgets, the key planning assumptions involve what markets to be in and what technologies to acquire.

Chapter 3 described capital budgeting. Before accepting a new investment, the future cash flows from that investment are projected. Capital budgets are long-run budgets for each project.

A typical firm integrates short-run and long-run budgeting into a single process. As next year's budget is being developed, a five-year budget is also produced. Year 1 of the five-year plan is next year's budget. Years 2 and 3 are fairly detailed and year 2 becomes the base to establish next year's one-year budget. Years 4 and 5 are less detailed but begin to look at new market opportunities. Each year, the five-year budget is rolled forward one year and the process begins anew.

The short-run (annual) budget involves both decision management and decision control functions, and as discussed earlier a trade-off arises between these two functions. Long-run budgets are hardly ever used as a decision control (performance evaluation) device. Rather,

Managerial Application: Rolling Budgets

Many companies, such as Cisco, are replacing their static annual budgets with rolling 18-month budgets. Static annual budgets often become out of date. At the end of the fiscal year, when sales targets are missed, massive price discounts are offered to boost sales. Instead of preparing an annual budget that remains static for the year, companies such as Cisco produce an 18-month budget and then update the projections every month. So at the end of January, the monthly budgets for the next 17 months are revised and July of next year is added. In effect, the whole budget for the remainder of the year and the first five months of next year is recalculated and a new month 18 is added. Unlike static annual budgets, managers are encouraged to react more quickly to changing economic or business conditions. Rolling budgets force managers to better integrate planning and execution.

SOURCE: R Myers, "Budgets on a Roll," *Journal of Accountancy,* December 2001, pp. 41–46; and M Astley, "Intranet Budgeting," *Strategic Finance,* May 2003, pp. 30–33.

Exercise 6–2

Two Internet-based, e-commerce companies were started about two years ago and both went public last month. They have about the same number of employees, but they offer different services (i.e., they are not competitors). Both firms use a one-year budgeting process, but only one firm supplements its annual budget with a three-year budget.

Required:

Offer some plausible reasons why one firm uses only an annual budget and the other firm uses both an annual and a three-year budget.

Solution:

One-year (or short-term) budgets are used as both decision management and decision control mechanisms. They help assemble knowledge for decision making and are also used as benchmarks in performance evaluation. Obviously, these two functions involve trade-offs. Three-year budgets are used almost exclusively as planning documents to help assemble information for decision making. The executives in the company using both one- and three-year budgets must believe first that they (and their colleagues) have substantial specialized knowledge of long-term (three-year) cash flows and trends and second that the benefits of assembling this knowledge outweighs the costs of preparing the three-year budget. The nature of the knowledge held by the managers in the other company must be of shorter duration.

Also, the company with the three-year budget might be worried that only using a one-year budget creates short-run incentives for managers to cut spending on R&D and advertising.

long-run budgets are used primarily for decision management. Five- and 10-year budgets force managers to think strategically and to communicate the specialized knowledge of their future markets and technologies. Thus, long-run budgets emphasize decision management more than decision control because less reliance is placed on using them as a performance measurement tool.

Long-run budgets also reduce managers' focus on short-term performance. Without long-term budgets, managers have an incentive to cut expenditures such as maintenance, advertising, and R&D to improve short-run performance or to balance short-term budgets

TABLE 6–3 **Line-Item Budget Example**

Line Item	*Amount*
Salaries	$185,000
Office supplies	12,000
Office equipment	3,000
Postage	1,900
Maintenance	350
Utilities	1,200
Rent	900
Total	$204,350

at the expense of the long-term viability of the organization. Budgets that span five years help alert top management and/or the board of directors to the long-term trade-offs being taken to accomplish short-run goals.

Some firms use rolling budgets. A rolling budget covers a fixed time period, such as one or two years. A future period is added as the current period concludes. For example, suppose a two-year rolling budget is used with quarterly intervals. When the current quarter is concluded, a new quarter (two years ahead) is added. In this way, management is always looking at a two-year planning horizon.

2. Line-Item Budgets

Line-item budgets refer to budgets that authorize the manager to spend only up to the specified amount on each line item. For example, consider Table 6–3. In this budget, the manager is authorized to spend $12,000 on office supplies for the year. If the supplies can be purchased for $11,000, the manager with a line-item budget cannot spend the $1,000 savings on any other category such as additional office equipment. Because the manager cannot spend savings from one line item on another line item without prior approval, the manager has less incentive to look for savings. If next year's line item is reduced by the amount of the savings, managers have even less incentive to search for savings.

Line-item budgets reduce agency problems. Managers responsible for the line-item budgets cannot reduce spending on one item and divert the savings to items that enhance their own welfare. By maintaining tighter control over how much is spent on particular items, the organization reduces possible managerial opportunism.

Line-item budgets are quite prevalent in governments. They also are used in some corporations, but with fewer restrictions. Line-item budgets provide more control. The manager does not have the decision rights to substitute resources among line items as circumstances change. To make such changes during the year requires approval from a higher level in the organization.

Line-item budgets illustrate how the budgeting system partitions decision rights, thereby controlling behavior. In particular, a manager given the decision rights to spend up to $3,000 on office equipment does not have the decision rights to substitute office equipment for postage.

A survey of large publicly traded firms found that among units reporting directly to the CEO, 23 percent cannot substitute among line items, 24 percent can substitute if they receive authorization, 26 percent can make substitutions within specified limits, and 27 percent can substitute among line items to improve the unit's financial objective.[14] These findings suggest that line-item budgets are prevalent even at fairly high levels in for-profit firms.

[14] A Christie, M Joye, and R Watts (2001).

Governments use **encumbrance accounting** in addition to line-item budgets. When contracts for purchases are signed or purchase orders are issued, even though no legal liability for the goods or services exists until delivery occurs, encumbrance accounting requires the dollar amounts of such goods and services to be recorded in special encumbrance accounts. When the goods and services are delivered, the encumbrance entry is reversed and the purchase is charged to the appropriate line-item expenditure. By adding the actual purchases to the outstanding encumbrance, those responsible for monitoring the integrity of the budget can ensure that line-item spending authority is maintained.[15]

3. Budget Lapsing

Another common feature is **budget lapsing**, in which unspent funds do not carry over to the next year. Budget lapsing creates incentives for managers to spend all their budget. Otherwise, not only do managers lose the benefits from the unspent funds, but next year's budget may be reduced by the amount of the underspending.

Budgets that lapse provide tighter controls on managers than budgets that do not lapse. However, the opportunity cost of lapsing budgets can be less-efficient operations. Managers devote substantial time at the end of the year spending their remaining budget, even if it means buying items that have lower value (and a higher cost) than they would purchase if they could carry the remaining budget over to the next fiscal year. Often the firm incurs substantial warehousing costs to hold the extra end-of-year purchases. In one example, a Navy ship officer purchased an 18-month supply of paper to spend his remaining budget. The paper weighed so much that it had to be stored evenly around the ship to ensure the ship did not list to one side.

In addition, budgets that lapse reduce managers' flexibility to adjust to changing operating conditions. For example, if managers have expended all of their budget authority and the opportunity to make a bargain purchase arises, they cannot borrow against next year's budget without getting special permission.

Without budget lapsing, managers could build up substantial balances in their budgets. Toward the end of their careers or before taking a new job in the same firm, these managers would then be tempted to make very large expenditures on perquisites. For example, they could take their staff to Hawaii for a "training retreat." Budget lapsing also prevents risk-averse managers from saving their budget for a rainy day. If it is optimum for a manager to spend a certain amount of money on a particular activity, then saving part of that amount as a contingency fund is not optimum. One way to prevent these agency problems is for budgets to lapse.

As in the case of budget ratcheting, the use of budget lapsing (or not) involves a choice between two evils. Agency costs can not be driven to zero; they can only be minimized.

4. Static versus Flexible Budgets

All of the examples in this chapter so far have presented **static budgets**, which do not vary with volume. Each line item is a fixed amount. In contrast, a **flexible budget** is stated as a function of some volume measure and is adjusted for changes in volume. Flexible budgets provide different incentives than do static budgets.

As an example of flexible budgeting, consider a concert where a band is hired for $20,000 plus 15 percent of the gate receipts. The auditorium is rented for $5,000 plus 5 percent of the gate receipts. Security guards costing $80 apiece are hired, one for every 200 people. Advertising, insurance, and other fixed costs are $28,000. Ticket prices are $18 each. A flexible budget for the concert is presented in Table 6–4.

Each line item in the budget is stated in terms of how it varies with volume (ticket sales in this case). Budgets are then prepared at different volume levels. At ticket sales of 3,000, an $11,000 loss is projected. At sales of 4,000 and 5,000 tickets, $3,000 and $17,000 of profits are forecasted, respectively.

[15] S Sunder, *Theory of Accounting and Control* (Cincinnati, OH: South-Western Publishing, 1997), pp. 196–97.

TABLE 6–4 Concert Operating Results

	Formula	Ticket Sales 3,000	4,000	5,000
Revenues	$18N*	$ 54,000	$ 72,000	$ 90,000
Band	$20,000 + 0.15(18N)	(28,100)	(30,800)	(33,500)
Auditorium	$5,000 + 0.05(18N)	(7,700)	(8,600)	(9,500)
Security	$80(N/200)	(1,200)	(1,600)	(2,000)
Other costs	$28,000	(28,000)	(28,000)	(28,000)
Profit/(loss)		$ (11,000)	$ 3,000	$ 17,000

*N is the number of tickets sold.

TABLE 6–5 Concert Operating Results

	Flexible Budget at 5,000 Tickets	*Actual Results*	*Favorable (Unfavorable) Variance*
Revenues	$90,000	$87,000	$(3,000)
Band	(33,500)	(33,500)	0
Auditorium	(9,500)	(9,900)	(400)
Security	(2,000)	(2,000)	0
Other costs	(28,000)	(28,700)	(700)
Profit/(loss)	$17,000	$12,900	$(4,100)

Flexible budgets are better than static budgets for gauging the actual performance of a person or venture *after controlling for volume effects*—assuming, of course, that the individual being evaluated is not responsible for the volume changes. For example, 5,000 people attended the concert. Table 6–5 compares actual results with the flexible budget for 5,000 tickets. Total profits were $4,100 less than expected. Most of the difference—$3,000—resulted from not being able to sell all 5,000 tickets at $18 each. To sell 5,000 tickets, some were sold at a discount. The actual cost of the auditorium was $9,900 instead of the $9,500 estimated by the flexible budget. The additional $400 was for damage. The budget for the auditorium is automatically increased to $9,500 due to the 5,000 ticket sales, and the manager is not held responsible for volume changes. However, the manager is held responsible for the $400 difference that resulted from damage. Finally, "other costs" were higher by $700 because the promoters underestimated the cost of the rented sound system.

The key question is, Should managers be held responsible for volume changes if the factors that cause the volume changes are outside their control? The initial reaction is no. Managers should be held responsible for volume effects only if they have some control over volume. However, this reasoning is incomplete. Recall the discussion of the controllability principle in Chapter 5. If the manager's actions influence the effects of volume changes, then the manager should not be insulated from the volume effects. For example, if managers can reduce inventory holdings of perishable inventories during economic downturns, they should be held accountable for the entire inventory amount. This creates an incentive to take actions that mitigate or enhance the effect on the organization of the uncontrollable volume.

Exercise 6–3

August Company's budget for the month just ended called for producing and selling 5,000 units at $8 each. Actual units produced and sold were 5,200, yielding revenue of $42,120. Variable costs were budgeted at $3 per unit and fixed costs were budgeted at $2 per unit. Actual variable costs were $3.30 and fixed costs were $12,000.

Required:

a. Prepare a performance report for the current month's operation.

b. Write a short memo analyzing the current month's performance.

Solution:

a. The performance report for the month is given below:

AUGUST COMPANY
Performance Report
Current Month

	I *Static Budget*	*II* *Actual*	*III* *Variance (II − I)*	*IV* *Flexible Budget (at 5,200)*	*V* *Variance (II − IV)*
Revenue	$40,000	$42,120	$2,120F	$41,600*	$ 520F
Less:					
Variable costs	15,000	17,160	2,160U	15,600†	1,560U
Contribution margin	$25,000	$24,960	$ 40U	$26,000	$1,040U
Less:					
Fixed costs	10,000	12,000	2,000U	10,000	2,000U
Profits	$15,000	$12,960	$2,040U	$16,000	$3,040U

NOTE: F = Favorable; U = Unfavorable.
* 5,200 × $8
† 5,200 × $3

b. The question to address is whether performance should be gauged against a static budget or a flexible budget. Column III in the above report benchmarks current performance against the static budget and shows that while revenues were better than planned, variable costs more than consumed the favorable revenue variance. When the unfavorable variance in fixed costs is considered, profits were $2,040 (13.6 percent) below budget.

The last two columns in the table take a different perspective. Here the benchmark is not the static budget at 5,000 units but rather what the results should have been given the volume of 5,200 units. In this case, profits fell $3,040 (19 percent) short of the flexible plan. If our cost structure stayed the same, then a volume of 5,200 units should have generated profits of $16,000. But variable costs per unit rose more than prices, causing an unfavorable contribution margin variance of $1,040. When the $2,000 unfavorable fixed cost variance is included, there is an unfavorable variance in profits from the flexible budget of $3,040.

Therefore, the question is: Should the managers be held accountable for the volume changes or not?

Managerial Application: Budgeting during a Global Economic Crisis

The economic meltdown that started in 2008 with the U.S. subprime mortgage and housing markets quickly spread to virtually all sectors of the global economy. When asked why the Federal Reserve did not foresee the pending problems, Alan Greenspan, the former chairman of the Fed, remarked, "We're not smart enough as people. We just cannot see events that far in advance." Greenspan's comments capture the sentiment of CFOs and their ability to prepare accurate forecasts. A survey found that during the 2008–09 recession, 39 percent of finance executives said they can't forecast more than one quarter out, 15 percent said they can't forecast more than two weeks ahead, and an equal number said, "We are in the dark."

Because preparing accurate one-year-ahead budgets is so difficult, some firms incorporate scenario modeling, sensitivity analysis, and contingency planning to identify a wide range of potential situations. Scenario planning creates a set of stories that help managers think about plausible, challenging events and how they might respond if blowups occur. As one executive stated, "Plan for the worst and hope for the better."

The Principal Financial Group, a life and health insurer, uses a comprehensive forecasting process that includes short- and long-term components with stochastic modeling that generates various random scenarios. It develops 5-quarter, 5-year, and 10-year forecasts and then introduces variances to these forecasts to understand the impact on earnings, sales, and assets.

Generating timely, reliable financial forecasts via scenario planning requires managers to identify the key drivers of their business. These drivers consist of those operational measures (such as hours of temporary labor required and associated labor rates in a manufacturing plant) that capture how changes in the environment affect the firm. Identifying these drivers helps executives implement decisions quickly when unexpected events occur. While identifying these drivers sounds simple, it can be quite complicated, because it requires the management team to really understand their firm's business model. For example, the most important driver of satellite service provider Hughes Communication's profitability is new consumer subscriptions. Profit and loss and cash flow forecasts depend critically on new consumer subscriptions. Forecasted new subscriptions affect whether Hughes launches its own satellite (a $400 million project) or continues to lease transponders on other satellites.

While it is very important for managers to identify and understand the key drivers of their business in order to respond to unforeseen events, the problem still remains of how to identify all plausible, yet unforeseen scenarios. Computer simulations and scenario planning cannot predict totally unexpected events such as the 9/11 terrorist attacks or the 2008 subprime meltdown.

SOURCE: V Ryan, "Future Tense," *CFO*, December 2008, pp. 36–42; and N Taleb, *The Black Swan: The Impact of the Highly Improbable* (New York: Random House, 2007).

When should a firm or department use a static budget and when should it use a flexible budget? Since static budgets do not adjust for volume effects, volume fluctuations are passed through and show up in the variances. Thus, static budgets force managers to be responsible for volume fluctuations. If the manager has some control over volume or the consequences of volume, then static budgets should be used as the benchmark to gauge performance. Since flexible budgets do adjust for volume effects, volume fluctuations are not passed through and do not show up in the variances. Flexible budgets do not hold managers responsible for volume fluctuations. Therefore, if the manager does not have any control over either volume or the consequences of volume, then flexible budgets should be used as the benchmark to gauge performance. Flexible budgets reduce the risk of volume changes borne by managers.

Flexible budgets are more widely used in manufacturing departments than in distribution, marketing, or administration. Flexible budgets are more widely used in manufacturing than other parts of the firm, because volume measures are readily available.

The preceding examples illustrate how budgets can be adjusted for different levels of volume, but flexible budgeting is more general. Budgets can be adjusted for variables other than volume levels, such as market share, foreign currency fluctuations, different rates of inflation, or any other variable outside of the manager's control that can cause the budget to vary.

5. Incremental versus Zero-Based Budgets

Most organizations construct next year's budget by starting with the current year's budget and adjusting each line item for expected price and volume changes. Since most budgeting processes are bottom up, where the detailed specialized knowledge resides, lower-level managers submit a budget for next year by making incremental changes in each line item. For example, the manager calculates the line item in next year's budget for "purchases" by increasing last year's purchases for inflation and including any incremental expenditures for volume changes and new programs. Only detailed explanations justifying the increments are submitted as part of the budget process. These incremental budgets are reviewed and changed at higher levels in the organization, but usually only the incremental changes are examined in detail. The core budget (i.e., last year's base budget) is taken as given.

Under **zero-based budgeting** (ZBB), each line item in total must be justified and reviewed annually. Each line item is reset to zero annually and must be justified in total. Departments must defend the entire expenditure (or program expenditure) each year, not just the changes. In a zero-based budget review, the following questions are usually asked: Should this activity be provided? What will happen if the activity is eliminated? At what quality and quantity level should the activity be provided? Can the activity be achieved in some other way, such as hiring an outside firm to provide the goods or service (outsourcing)? How much are similar companies spending on this activity?

In principle, zero-based budgeting causes managers to maximize firm value by identifying and eliminating those expenditures whose total cost exceeds total benefits. Under incremental budgeting, in which incremental changes are added to the base budget, incremental expenditures are deleted when their costs exceed their benefits. But inefficient base budgets can continue to exist.

In practice, ZBB is infrequently used. It is supposed to overcome traditional incremental budgeting, but it often deteriorates into incremental budgeting. Under ZBB, the same rationales and justifications as last year's are submitted and adjusted for incremental changes. Because the volume of detailed reports is substantially larger under ZBB than under incremental budgeting, higher-level managers tend to focus on the changes from last year. Moreover, firms usually promote people from within the firm rather than hiring from outside. Promotions tend to be vertical within the same department or division. Internally promoted managers bring with them specific knowledge of their previous job, including knowledge of previous budgets. Thus, managers reviewing detailed lower-level budgets have substantial knowledge of those operations, having earlier had decision management rights over at least some of the operations. These managers often already know the base budgets and now want to know the changes from the base level.

ZBB is most useful in organizations in which considerable turnover exists in middle- and senior-level ranks. Management turnover destroys specialized knowledge. Also, ZBB is useful in cases where there has been substantial strategic change or high uncertainty. For example, a defense contractor shifting into civilian markets might want to use ZBB. In these cases, rejustifying each line item annually helps to inform managers with decision control rights of the total costs and benefits of each department or program. However, ZBB is significantly more costly to perform than incremental budgeting.

ZBB is often used in government budgets. President Carter used it both in Georgia when he was governor and in the federal government during the 1970s. In government, managers with decision management rights tend to be career civil servants in the departments and agencies. Decision control rights are vested in elected officials in the executive and legislative branches. Elected officials have short tenures in monitoring a specific agency and therefore lack detailed specialized knowledge of the department's functions. Zero-based budgets are useful in helping these elected officials make trade-offs between programs, as opposed to just making trade-offs among increments to programs.

Concept Questions

Q6–12	What are short-run and long-run budgets?
Q6–13	What are the advantages and disadvantages of line-item budgets?
Q6–14	Why do some organizations practice budget lapsing? What are the disadvantages?
Q6–15	Define *static* and *flexible budgets.* Discuss their advantages and weaknesses.
Q6–16	Define *incremental* and *zero-based budgeting.* Discuss their advantages and weaknesses.

D. Summary

Budgets are an important mechanism for resolving firms' organizational problems. Budgets help partition decision rights and provide a benchmark against which performance can be measured. By preparing a budget, each unit in the organization implicitly recognizes the decision rights it has authority to exercise.

The advantages of budgeting consist of

1. Coordination of sales, production, marketing, finance, and so forth.
2. Formulation of a profitable sales and production program.
3. Coordination of sales and production with finances.
4. Proper control of expenditures.
5. Formulation of a financial program including investment and financing.
6. Coordination of all the activities of the business.

The process of building a budget via a bottom-up, top-down iterative procedure involves assembling specialized knowledge. Budgeting is a negotiation and consensus-building exercise. Thus, budgeting is part of the decision management process. Budgets are also used in decision control. In practice, budgeting involves a trade-off between decision making and control. Ideally, the budget system helps link specialized knowledge and decision rights, thus improving decision making. But if the budget is also used for control and incentives are provided for meeting it, then managers will bias their forecasts during budget preparation to enhance their reported performance relative to their forecast. Again, designers of the budgeting and performance evaluation systems must trade off more accurate forecasts (transfers of specialized knowledge) for incentive effects (control). We return to these incentive effects of budgeting and variance analysis again in Chapters 12 and 13.

One way to prevent managers from biasing their budgets is to set the budgets at the top, and one top-down method is referred to as the ratchet effect. Here, next year's budget is set based on last year's deviation of actual from budget. When last year's actual results are better than budget, next year's budget increases by more than it would fall were last year's actual results to fall short of last year's budget. This simple ratcheting up of budgets means that managers no longer need to set their own budgets, but it creates incentives for them to hold back effort when they are having a good year to prevent next year's budget from being too challenging.

Short-run budgets involve both decision management and decision control. Long-run budgets (3 to 10 years) place less emphasis on decision control. Managers are less likely to be held responsible for meeting long-term budget targets than short-term budget goals because long-term budgets are used for information sharing.

Line-item budgeting and budget lapsing are devices that constrain managers' decision rights. Line-item budgets prevent managers from shifting resources across different line items in the budget. Budgets that lapse prevent managers from shifting unspent funds from the current year into future years. Both line-item budgeting and budget lapsing reduce managers' incentives to search for cost savings because it is less likely that the manager can spend the savings.

Static budgets hold managers responsible for changes in volume, whereas flexible budgets do not. Even though they might not be able to control volume, managers evaluated under flexible budgets have less incentive to control the consequences of volume changes.

Finally, most budgeting processes are incremental in the sense that managers need only justify changes from last year's budgets. Under zero-based budgeting, managers must justify the entire budget. ZBB is most useful when those managers with decision ratification and monitoring rights over the budget do not have the specific knowledge of the operations. If managers with decision control rights have the knowledge because they have been promoted from within the organization, ZBB usually becomes incremental budgeting.

Appendix: Comprehensive Master Budget Illustration

Chapter 6 discussed the important conceptual issues of budgeting. This appendix illustrates how the various departments of a firm communicate their specialized knowledge via a firmwide master budget. This example demonstrates how various parts of the organization develop their budgets, the importance of coordinating the volume of activity across the different parts of the organization, and how budgets are then combined for the firm as a whole.

1. Description of the Firm: NaturApples

NaturApples is an upstate New York apple processor with two products, applesauce and apple pie filling. The applesauce is eaten as is, and the pie filling is used to make apple pies. Two types of apples are purchased from local growers, McCouns and Grannys. They are processed and packed in tin cans as either apple sauce or pie filling. Principal markets are institutional buyers, such as hospitals, public schools, military bases, and universities. NaturApples is a small processor. Its market is regional and is serviced by four sales reps who call on customers in a four-state area. A fifth salesperson markets the products to food distributors, who then sell them directly to restaurants.

The firm is organized into two departments: processing and marketing. Each is headed by a vice president who reports directly to the president. The vice president of finance is responsible for all financial aspects of the firm, including preparing budgets. The three vice presidents and the president make up NaturApples's executive committee, which oversees the budgeting process.

Apples are harvested in the fall of each year. The firm has long-term contracts with a number of local apple growers for their crops. If the local harvest is smaller than expected, additional apples can be purchased in the spot market. Likewise, if more apples are delivered than NaturApples wants to process, the extra apples can be sold in the spot market. Long-term contracts with local farmers and spot-market purchases and sales are the responsibility of the president and the vice president of finance.

Once harvested, the apples are stored either in coolers at NaturApples or in third-party warehouses until NaturApples processes them. Processing takes nine months. In October, the plant starts up after a three-month shutdown. Workers first thoroughly clean and inspect all equipment. The apples begin arriving in the middle of October. By the end of November, the apple harvest is in warehouses or started in production. By June, all of the apples have been processed and the plant shuts down for July, August, and September. NaturApples has a fiscal year starting October 1 and ending September 30.

Each of the two products (applesauce and pie filling) uses a combination of the two types of apples (McCouns and Grannys). The production process consists of inspection, washing, peeling, and coring. The apples are either mashed for applesauce or diced for pie filling and then are combined with other ingredients such as spices and chemical stabilizers and cooked in vats. Both products are immediately canned on a single canning line in five-pound tins and packed in cases of 12 cans per case. The product has a two-year shelf life and is inventoried until ordered by the customer. Independent truckers deliver apples to NaturApples and deliver finished product to customers.

FIGURE 6–3
Logical flow of components of the master budget

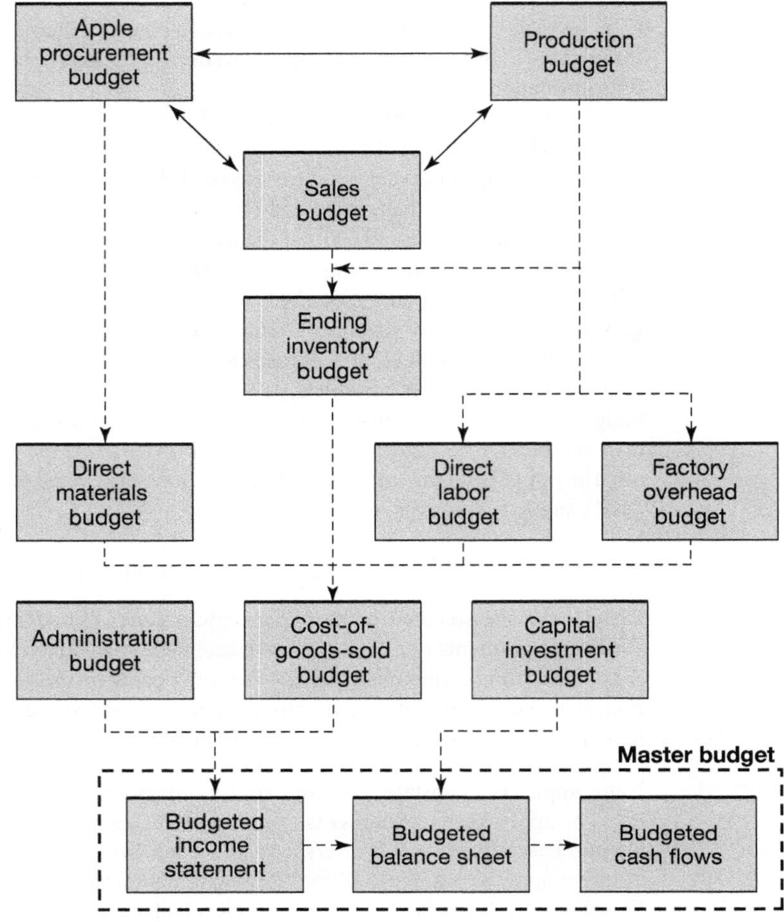

2. Overview of the Budgeting Process

The budgeting process begins in August for the next fiscal year's budget, which will begin in 14 months. That is, even though the current fiscal year beginning in October has not yet started, the preparation of next year's budget begins in August. In August, the coming fall harvest is reasonably well known. The president and the vice president of finance forecast the following year's crop harvest under long-term contract. The vice president of marketing begins forecasting sales that will be made from the harvest a year from this fall. Likewise, the processing vice president forecasts production costs and capacity. Every 2 months for the next 14 months, these budgets are revised with regard to marketing, processing, and apple procurement in light of any new information, and all three vice presidents and the president meet for a morning to discuss their revisions. In June of each year, the final master budget for the next fiscal year, which begins October 1, is adopted by the executive committee and approved by the board of directors. The executive committee also meets weekly to review current-year operations as compared with budget and to discuss other operational issues.

Figure 6–3 is a schematic diagram that illustrates the relations among component budgets and the NaturApples master budget. The master budget encompasses the budgeted income statement, budgeted balance sheet, and budgeted cash flows at the bottom of Figure 6–3. All the other budgets provide the supporting detail, including the various key planning assumptions underlying the master budget.

Three key pieces in NaturApples's budgeting process include apple procurement, sales, and production. These three components must be internally consistent with respect to the amount of each type of apple purchased and the volume of each product produced and sold. Once these three component budgets are determined, the budgeted ending inventory can be calculated. Given the production budget, the direct labor and factory overhead budgets can be generated. These last two budgets and the direct

TABLE 6–6 **NaturApples**
Basic Data for Budgeting Example for Fiscal Year Beginning 10/1/11

	Cases	*Cost/Case*	*Total*
Beginning Inventory			
Sauce	13,500	$57.96	$782,460
Pie filling	2,300	$48.81	$112,263
	McCoun	*Granny*	
Pounds of Apples/Case			
Sauce	60	40	
Pie filling	50	30	

materials budget (from the apple procurement estimates) determine the cost-of-goods-sold budget. The budgeted income statement can then be prepared using these budgets and the budget for administration, which includes senior officer salaries and other administrative expenses not included elsewhere.

Toward the bottom of Figure 6–3 is the capital investment budget, which is based on an analysis of investment proposals. All profitable projects are in the capital investment budget, including those projects started in previous years but not yet completed. The capital investment budget and budgeted income statement are used to prepare NaturApples's budgeted balance sheet and then the cash flow budget. The remainder of this appendix illustrates the preparation of these various component budgets.

NaturApples uses the following accounting conventions:

1. FIFO is used for inventory accounting.
2. Factory overhead is estimated using a flexible budget.

Variable overhead varies with the number of direct labor hours in the plant. Total overhead is then assigned to product costs using the number of hours of direct labor in the product. Chapter 9 further explains how overhead is assigned to products.

Table 6–6 provides the basic data for the budgeting illustration. This table contains some primary operating data, such as the beginning inventory figures. The bottom half of the table also shows the amount of each type of apple required to make a case of applesauce and a case of pie filling.

By June, the executive committee has agreed on next year's volumes. The sales budget for the next fiscal year is given in Table 6–7. These data are examples of the *key planning assumptions* described in the chapter. The executive committee agrees that the firm should be able to sell 140,000 cases of sauce at $68.95 per case and 60,000 cases of pie filling at $53.95 per case. These quantities and prices were derived after exploring alternative price-quantity combinations. In particular, these price-quantity points represent the managers' best judgment of where profits are maximized. Presumably, higher prices (and thus lower sales) or lower prices (and higher sales) would both result in lower profits than the combinations in Table 6–7.

TABLE 6–7 **NaturApples**
Sales Budget for Fiscal Year Beginning 10/1/11

	Budgeted Cases	*Budgeted Price/Case*	*Budgeted Revenue*
Sauce	140,000	$68.95	$ 9,653,000
Pie filling	60,000	53.95	3,237,000
Total			$12,890,000

TABLE 6–8 **NaturApples**
Apple Procurement Budget for Fiscal Year Beginning 10/1/11

	Pounds (in 000s)		Price		Cost ($ in 000s)		
	McCoun	*Granny*	*McCoun*	*Granny*	*McCoun*	*Granny*	*Total*
Long-term contracts	10,900	8,000	$380	$310	$4,142.0	$2,480.0	$6,622.0
Market purchases (sales)	50	(910)	450	330	22.5	(300.3)	(277.8)
Total	10,950	7,090			$4,164.5	$2,179.7	$6,344.2
Pounds used					10,950	7,090	
Cost per thousand pounds					$380.32	$307.43	

TABLE 6–9 **NaturApples**
Production Budget for Fiscal Year Beginning 10/1/11

	Budgeted Cases	*Pounds of McCouns*	*Pounds of Grannys*
Sauce	130,000	7,800,000	5,200,000
Pie filling	63,000	3,150,000	1,890,000
Total		10,950,000	7,090,000

3. Departmental Budgets

Table 6–8 presents the apple procurement budget. Given the harvest projections and the production plans, NaturApples plans to purchase an additional 50,000 pounds of McCoun apples and sell 910,000 pounds of Granny apples. The total cost of apples is projected to be $6,344,200. The average cost per thousand pounds is $380.32 for McCoun apples and $307.43 for Granny apples. These average cost figures are used later in Table 6–12 to calculate the cost of applesauce and pie filling.

The third major budget component is the production budget presented in Table 6–9. The production budget, the apple procurement budget, and the sales budget must satisfy the following inventory-production-sales identity:

$$\text{Beginning inventory} + \text{Production} = \text{Sales} + \text{Ending inventory}$$

The total units in beginning inventory and this period's production must be either sold or in ending inventory. The beginning inventory numbers are known in advance. Choosing two of the remaining three parameters uniquely determines the third. Given the number of apples purchased, the sales budget, and minimum inventory levels, the production budget is derived from the inventory-production-sales identity as long as the processing department has the capacity.

In the production budget in Table 6–9, notice first that the number of cases budgeted for production is different from the number of cases budgeted for sales in Table 6–7. Ten thousand fewer cases of sauce are planned to be produced than sold. Management has decided to reduce the applesauce inventory. On the other hand, the inventory of pie filling is being increased by 3,000 cases. The last two columns in Table 6–9 display the number of pounds of McCoun and Granny apples needed to produce the budgeted cases. The total pounds of each type of apple (10.95 million of McCouns and 7.09 million of Grannys) is the same as in the procurement budget in Table 6–8, reflecting the coordination process involved in budgeting. All the various parts of the organization end up agreeing on the volume of production.

Tables 6–7, 6–8, and 6–9 correspond to the top three boxes in Figure 6–3. Given these three key component budgets, the remainder of the master budget can be prepared. The next budget to compute

TABLE 6–10 **NaturApples**
Ending Inventory Budget for Fiscal Year Beginning 10/1/11 (Cases)

	Sauce	*Pie Filling*
Beginning inventory	13,500	2,300
Plus: Production	130,000	63,000
Available for sale	143,500	65,300
Less: Cases sold	140,000	60,000
Ending inventory	3,500	5,300

TABLE 6–11 **NaturApples**
Direct Labor Budget for Fiscal Year Beginning 10/1/11

	Direct Labor Hours/Case	
	Sauce	*Pie Filling*
Inspection, washing, peeling, coring	0.30	0.24
Saucing	0.10	0.00
Dicing	0.00	0.04
Cooking	0.10	0.16
Canning	0.10	0.10
Total hours per case	0.60	0.54
× Budgeted cases	130,000	63,000
Budgeted labor hours	78,000	34,020
× Budgeted labor rate	$8.75	$8.75
Budgeted labor cost	$682,500	$297,675

is the ending inventory budget. This is presented in Table 6–10. The ending inventory of sauce is budgeted to be 3,500 cases and the ending inventory of pie filling is budgeted at 5,300 cases.

Next is the set of direct labor, direct materials, and factory overhead budgets. These budgets are presented in Tables 6–11, 6–12, and 6–13, respectively. Direct labor, as opposed to indirect labor, represents the time employees are actually working to produce a particular product. Indirect labor represents the time workers are maintaining machines or are idle. (Chapter 9 explains these distinctions in greater detail.) Table 6–11 provides the number of direct labor hours needed to perform each of the processing functions to produce sauce and pie filling. Sauce requires 0.60 direct labor hours (36 minutes) per case and pie filling requires 0.54 labor hours (32.4 minutes). Multiplying these hours per case times budgeted cases determines the total number of direct labor hours for each product for next year (78,000 for sauce and 34,020 for pie filling).

The direct materials budget in Table 6–12 is a straightforward extension of the procurement budget for apples and includes the spices and other ingredients that are added to the sauce and pie filling. The average cost of 1,000 pounds of each type of apple from Table 6–8 is used to cost the quantity of each type of apple in sauce and pie filling. To the cost of apples is added the cost of other ingredients: $0.45 per case for sauce and $0.33 per case for pie filling. Management estimates these costs by taking the known quantities of these other ingredients from the recipes and forecasting any price changes. The total cost of direct materials for sauce is budgeted at $4,623,632, and the total cost of direct materials for pie filling is budgeted at $1,799,841.

TABLE 6–12 **NaturApples**
Direct Materials Budget for Fiscal Year Beginning 10/1/11

	Sauce		Pie Filling	
Cost of Apples				
Thousands of pounds of McCouns	7,800		3,150	
× Average cost of McCouns	$ 380.32	$2,966,496	$380.32	$1,198,008
Thousands of pounds of Grannys	5,200		1,890	
× Average cost of Grannys	$ 307.43	$1,598,636	$307.43	$ 581,043
Total cost of apples		$4,565,132		$1,779,051
Cost of Other Ingredients				
Cost per case	$ 0.45		$ 0.33	
× Number of cases	130,000	$ 58,500	63,000	$ 20,790
Total direct materials cost		$4,623,632		$1,799,841

TABLE 6–13 **NaturApples**
Factory Overhead Budget for Fiscal Year Beginning 10/1/11

A. Factory Overhead Flexible Budget			
Fixed factory overhead			$1,300,000
Variable overhead per direct labor hour		$13	
Direct labor hours			
Sauce	78,000		
Pie filling	34,020		
× Budgeted direct labor hours		112,020	
Budgeted variable overhead			$1,456,260
Budgeted factory overhead			$2,756,260
÷ Budgeted direct labor hours			112,020
Budgeted overhead rate per direct labor hour			$ 24.61

B. Factory Overhead	Sauce		Pie Filling	
Direct labor hours	78,000		34,020	
Overhead rate per labor hour	× $24.61		× $24.61	
Factory overhead cost		$1,919,580		$ 837,232

Table 6–13 presents the factory overhead budget for each product. The top part of Table 6–13 provides the flexible budget for factory overhead. Fixed factory overhead, which contains $650,000 of depreciation, is budgeted to be $1.3 million and variable overhead is budgeted at $13 per direct labor hour. Chapter 9 expands on how these parameters are forecasted. Given these forecasts and the number of direct labor hours from Table 6–11, management calculates the budgeted factory overhead as $2,756,260. This quantity is then divided by the budgeted direct labor hours (112,020 hours) to compute the budgeted overhead rate per hour of direct labor ($24.61). The $24.61 represents the average overhead cost assigned to sauce and pie filling per direct labor hour.

TABLE 6–14 **NaturApples**
Cost-of-Goods-Sold Budget for Fiscal Year Beginning 10/1/11

	Sauce		*Pie Filling*	
Beginning inventory		$ 782,460		$ 112,263
Cost of goods processed:				
Direct labor cost	$ 682,500		$ 297,675	
Direct materials cost	4,623,632		1,799,841	
Canning ($1.20/case)	156,000		75,600	
Factory overhead cost	1,919,580		837,232	
Total cost of processing		7,381,712		3,010,348
Available for sale		$8,164,172		$3,122,611
Less: Ending inventory*		(198,738)		(253,251)
Cost of goods sold		$7,965,434		$2,869,360

*Calculation of ending inventory (costs per case are not rounded for calculating ending inventories):

	Sauce	*Pie Filling*
Total cost of processing	$7,381,712	$3,010,348
÷ Cases produced	130,000	63,000
Cost per case	$ 56.78	$ 47.78
× Cases in ending inventory	3,500	5,300
Ending inventory	$ 198,730	$ 253,251

Panel B of Table 6–13 calculates the factory overhead for sauce and pie filling. Since sauce is budgeted to use 78,000 direct labor hours, sauce is allocated $1,919,580 of factory overhead ($24.61 × 78,000 direct labor hours) and pie filling is assigned $837,232 (or $24.61 × 34,020).

Refer to Figure 6–3. Given the direct labor, direct materials, factory overhead, ending inventory budgets, and beginning inventory levels, management can now prepare the budget for cost of goods sold, as shown in Table 6–14. The beginning inventory cost is from Table 6–6. The direct labor and material and factory overhead costs are taken directly from Tables 6–11, 6–12, and 6–13. Added to these previous data is the cost of cans and packaging materials, $1.20 per case (see Table 6–14). The sum of the beginning inventory and the cost of goods processed is the amount available for sale. From this is deducted the ending inventory to arrive at the cost of goods sold. Since the firm uses FIFO, the ending inventory is valued at the cost of the current units processed. The current processing cost is the total cost of units processed divided by the units processed. The footnote to Table 6–14 indicates that the average cost to process a case of sauce is budgeted at $56.78 and the average cost to process a case of pie filling is budgeted at $47.78. These unit cost figures are used to value the ending inventory.

The administration budget in Table 6–15 contains the remaining operating expenses, including the marketing and finance departments' expenses, trucking costs, and the costs of the president's office. The total of all these administrative costs is $1.19 million.

4. Master Firmwide Budget

The budgeted income statement in Table 6–16 assembles the various pieces from all the earlier statements. The only additional data in Table 6–16 are interest on debt ($380,000) and the provision for corporate income taxes (a 42 percent combined state and federal rate is used). It projects net income after taxes to be $281,420. Clearly, an important question to ask is whether this budgeted profit is high or low, acceptable or unacceptable. To answer this question requires a benchmark for comparison. As we have seen, last year's budget and actuals can provide such a benchmark.

Some managers end their budgeting process with the budgeted income statement as in Table 6–16. But this statement does not address the firm's cash needs. Just because the firm forecasts positive

TABLE 6–15 **NaturApples**
Administration Budget for Fiscal Year Beginning 10/1/11

	Administrative Cost
Marketing	$ 470,000
Finance	160,000
Trucking	380,000
President's office	180,000
Total administration	$1,190,000

TABLE 6–16 **NaturApples**
Budgeted Income Statement for Fiscal Year Beginning 10/1/11

	Sauce	*Pie Filling*	*Total*
Revenue	$9,653,000	$3,237,000	$12,890,000
Less:			
Cost of goods sold	(7,965,434)	(2,869,359)	(10,834,793)
Gross margin	$1,687,566	$ 367,641	$ 2,055,207
Less:			
Administration costs			(1,190,000)
Interest on debt			(380,000)
Net income before taxes			$ 485,207
Taxes (42%)			(203,787)
Net income			$ 281,420

profits does not mean there will be sufficient cash flow to finance operations. In NaturApples's case, the cost of apples represents about half of total revenues. The apples are harvested and paid for in the fall, but the revenue from selling the processed apples is received over the next 12 months. Therefore, NaturApples must find a source of operating cash to finance its apple procurement.

Table 6–17 presents the budgeted statement of cash flows by quarter. NaturApples must borrow $3,385,722 in the first quarter to finance operations, including the apple purchases. Its beginning cash balance of $1.5 million is insufficient to finance all the apple purchases and production costs. Of this $1.5 million, $400,000 must be kept as minimum cash reserves, leaving only $1.1 million to finance operations. In quarter 2, NaturApples repays $1,872,978 of the loan, leaving a balance of $1,512,744 to be repaid in quarter 3. Interest of 3 percent per quarter is paid in quarter 3 on the outstanding balances in quarters 1 and 2 ($101,572 + $45,382). In quarter 4, capital expenditures of $900,000 are budgeted. The budgeted ending cash balance is $2,424,834. The notes to Table 6–17 explain the quarterly timing of the various cash flows.

Having completed the budgeted statement of cash flows, NaturApples can prepare the budgeted statement of financial position (balance sheet) listing all the assets, liabilities, and equities (see Table 6–18). Cash is budgeted to increase from $1,500,000 to $2,424,834. There is no provision at this time to budget a dividend to shareholders, which would decrease the budgeted cash amount and the ending balance in shareholder equity. Budgeted fixed assets are increased by budgeted capital expenditures ($900,000) and decreased by depreciation ($650,000), for a net increase of $250,000. Accounts payable is budgeted to increase from $1,300,000 to $1,765,180. Shareholder equity is budgeted to increase by budgeted net income of $281,420.

TABLE 6–17

NATURAPPLES
Budgeted Statement of Cash Flows
For Fiscal Year Beginning 10/1/11

	Quarter 1	*Quarter 2*	*Quarter 3*	*Quarter 4*	*Annual*
Sales in the quarter	$ 3,222,500	$3,222,500	$3,222,500	$3,222,500	$12,890,000
80% collected in this quarter	2,578,000	2,578,000	2,578,000	2,578,000	10,312,000
20% collected from last quarter	630,000	644,500	644,500	644,500	2,563,500
Cash from sales	$ 3,208,000	$3,222,500	$3,222,500	$3,222,500	$12,875,500
Less:					
Apple purchases	$ 6,344,200	$ 0	$ 0	$ 0	$ 6,344,200
Direct labor	326,725	326,725	326,725	0	980,175
Other ingredients	26,430	26,430	26,430	0	79,290
Variable overhead	485,420	485,420	485,420	0	1,456,260
Fixed factory overhead	162,500	162,500	162,500	162,500	650,000
Administrative costs	297,500	297,500	297,500	297,500	1,190,000
Income taxes	50,947	50,947	50,947	50,947	203,787
Total cash expenses before interest	$ 7,693,722	$1,349,522	$1,349,522	$ 510,947	$10,903,712
Cash flows from operations	$(4,485,722)	$1,872,978	$1,872,978	$2,711,553	$ 1,971,788
Beginning cash balance	$ 1,500,000	$ 400,000	$ 400,000	$ 613,290	
Less: minimum cash reserves	400,000	400,000	400,000	400,000	
Cash available for operations	$ 1,100,000	$ 0	$ 0	$ 213,280	
New short-term borrowings	$ 3,385,722	$ 0	$ 0	$ 0	
Repayment of loan and interest	0	1,872,978	1,659,698	0	
Outstanding loan balance	$ 3,385,722	$1,512,744	$ 0	$ 0	
Interest at 3% per quarter	$ 101,572	$ 45,382	$ 0	$ 0	
Capital expenditures	$ 0	$ 0	$ 0	$ 900,000	
Ending cash balance	$ 400,000	$ 400,000	$ 613,280	$2,424,833	

NOTES:

1. Sales, fixed factory overhead, administrative costs, and income taxes are incurred uniformly over four quarters.
2. Apple purchases are paid in quarter 1.
3. Direct labor, other ingredients, and variable overhead are incurred uniformly over the first three quarters.
4. One-half of the fixed factory overhead is depreciation.
5. 80% of sales are collected in the quarter; the other 20% are collected in the next quarter.
6. There are no uncollectible accounts.
7. $630,000 of accounts receivable from last year, quarter 4, are collected in quarter 1.
8. All interest in the first two quarters is paid in the third quarter.
9. Minimum cash reserves are $400,000.
10. Beginning cash balance is $1.5 million.
11. Interest on short-term borrowing is 3% per quarter.
12. Capital expenditures of $900,000 are paid in quarter 4.
13. Interest expense of $380,000 in Table 6–16 includes interest on short-term borrowing and long-term debt.

TABLE 6–18

NATURAPPLES Statement of Financial Position Years Ending 9/30/11 and 9/30/12	*Year Ending 9/30/11*	*Year Ending 9/30/12*
Cash	$1,500,000	$2,424,834
Accounts receivable	630,000	644,500
Inventory:		
Sauce	782,460	198,738
Pie filling	112,263	253,251
Total inventory	894,723	451,989
Fixed assets	2,755,000	3,005,000
Total assets	$5,779,723	$6,526,323
Accounts payable	$1,300,000	$1,765,180
Long-term debt	1,950,000	1,950,000
Shareholder equity	2,529,723	2,811,143
Total liabilities	$5,779,723	$6,526,323

Self-Study Problems

Self-Study Problem 1: GAMESS Inc.

GAMESS Inc. develops, markets, packages, and distributes multimedia computer games. GAMESS has outsourced production since it does not believe it can manufacture the games competitively. Its most recent development is an interactive adventure game. Since its multimedia games are different from other computer games in both physical size of the package and price, GAMESS established a new profit center for the adventure game and future CD computer games.

GAMESS is in the process of selecting the profit-maximizing price for the new adventure game. Management estimates demand for the new game at various wholesale prices. The retail stores then set the retail price of the game sold to the public. Estimated demand is shown in Table 1.

The manufacturer of the CDs charges GAMESS $9 per CD produced (assume CDs produced equal CDs sold). Packaging expense is $5 per unit sold. Distribution, which includes the amount paid to distributors for selling the game to retailers, is $3 per unit sold.

Note that although packaging and distribution are estimated to be $5 and $3, respectively, management is not sure how retailers will treat the different packaging size. Advertising contains fixed and variable elements. The fixed portion is $1 million. The variable portion is computed using the ratio of $1 advertising expense for each $500 of expected sales. Fixed overhead, which includes administration and management salaries, is projected at $2.5 million.

Required:

a. Compute the production, packaging, distribution, advertising, and fixed overhead expenses for the various sales prices and quantities in Table 1. Explain why GAMESS would not consider selling its adventure game for any price other than $44.

b. Actual data for the year are shown in Table 2. Calculate the budget variances.

c. Provide a possible interpretation for the variances.

TABLE 1 **Price and Quantity Demanded for Adventure Game**

Wholesale sales price	$40	$44	$48	$52
Sales volume (units)	435,000	389,000	336,000	281,000

TABLE 2 **First-Year Operating Results for Adventure Game**

Sales price	$ 44
Sales volume (units)	389,000
Revenues	$17,116,000
Production costs	3,501,000
Packaging	1,798,700
Distribution	1,633,800
Advertising	1,148,232
Fixed overhead	2,506,200
Net income	$ 6,528,068

Solution:

a. $44 is the profit-maximizing price, as seen in Table 3.

b. The variances from the flexible budget are computed as follows:

Sales price	$44		
Sales volume (units)	389,000		
	Actual	*Budgeted*	*Variance*
Sales	$17,116,000	$17,116,000	$ 0
Production	3,501,000	3,501,000	0
Packaging	1,798,700	1,945,000	146,300
Distribution	1,633,800	1,167,000	(466,800)
Advertising	1,148,232	1,034,232	(114,000)
Fixed overhead	2,506,200	2,500,000	(6,200)
Net income	$ 6,528,068	$ 6,968,768	$(440,700)

c. As displayed in the table above, packaging has a moderately large favorable variance, while distribution and advertising have large unfavorable variances and fixed overhead has a small unfavorable variance. One possible reason for this pattern of variances is that management cut corners on the packaging of the game. This change in package, combined with the difference in the packaging size between CD games and other computer games, resulted in higher shipping and distribution costs when stores insisted on smaller shipments since their shelf space was not designed for GAMESS CDs. The increase in advertising helped prevent lost sales because of the distribution problems. The fixed overhead variance is less than 1 percent of budgeted fixed overhead and is likely because of random fluctuations.

TABLE 3 **Sales Price**

	$40	*$44*	*$48*	*$52*
Sales volume (units)	435,000	389,000	336,000	281,000
Sales	$17,400,000	$17,116,000	$16,128,000	$14,612,000
Production	3,915,000	3,501,000	3,024,000	2,529,000
Packaging	2,175,000	1,945,000	1,680,000	1,405,000
Distribution	1,305,000	1,167,000	1,008,000	843,000
Advertising	1,034,800	1,034,232	1,032,256	1,029,224
Fixed overhead	2,500,000	2,500,000	2,500,000	2,500,000
Net income	$ 6,470,200	$ 6,968,768	$ 6,883,744	$ 6,305,776

Self-Study Problem 2: Sandy Cove Bank

Sandy Cove is a new small commercial bank operating in Sandy Cove, Michigan. The bank limits interest rate risk by matching the maturity of its assets to the maturity of its liabilities. By maintaining a spread between interest rates charged and interest rates paid, the bank plans to earn a small income. Management establishes a flexible budget based on interest rates for each department.

The Boat and Car Loan Department offers five-year loans. It matches certificates of deposit (CDs) against car and boat loans. Given all the uncertainty about interest rates, management believes that five-year savings interest rates could vary between 2 percent and 16 percent for the coming year. The savings rate is the rate paid on CD savings accounts. The loan rate is the rate charged on auto and boat loans. Table 1 shows the expected new demand for fixed-rate, five-year loans and new supply of fixed-rate, five-year savings accounts at various interest rates. There are no loans from previous years. Note that the department maintains a 4 percent spread between loan and savings rates to cover processing, loan default, and overhead.

The amount of new loans granted is always the lesser of the loan demand and loan supply. For simplicity, this bank may lend 100 percent of deposits. Although rates are set nationally, the bank may pay or charge slightly different rates to limit demand or boost supply as needed in its local market.

The Boat and Car Loan Department incurs processing, loan default, and overhead expenses related to these accounts. The first two expenses vary, depending on the dollar amount of the accounts. The annual processing expense is budgeted to be 1.5 percent of the loan accounts. Default expense is budgeted at 1 percent of the amount loaned per year. Again, loans and savings would ideally be the same. Overhead expenses are estimated to be $30,000 for the year, regardless of the amount loaned.

TABLE 1 **Demand and Supply of Five-Year Funds**

Loan Rate	*Loan Demand*	*Savings Rate*	*Savings Supply*
6%	$12,100,000	2%	$ 4,700,000
7	10,000,000	3	5,420,000
8	8,070,000	4	8,630,000
9	6,030,000	5	9,830,000
10	4,420,000	6	11,800,000

TABLE 2 Actual Income Statement of the Boat and Car Loan Department

Interest income	$ 645,766
Interest expense	314,360
Net interest income	$ 331,406
Fixed overhead	30,200
Processing expense	130,522
Default expense	77,800
Net income	$ 92,884
Loans	$8,062,000
Deposits	$8,123,000

Required:

a. Calculate the processing, loan default, and overhead expenses for each possible interest rate.

b. Create an annual budgeted income statement for five-year loans and deposits for the Boat and Car Loan Department given a savings interest rate of 4 percent. Remember to match supply and demand.

c. Table 2 shows the actual income statement for the Boat and Car Loan Department. Included are the actual loans and savings for the same period. Calculate the variances and provide a possible explanation.

Solution:

a. Flexible budget for the Boat and Car Loan Department:

	($ in Millions)					
Savings Rate	*Loan Demand*	*Savings Supply*	*New Business*	*Loan Processing*	*Default Expense*	*Overhead Expense*
2%	$12.10	$ 4.70	$4.70	$ 70,500	$47,000	$30,000
3	10.00	5.42	5.42	81,300	54,200	30,000
4	8.07	8.63	8.07	121,050	80,700	30,000
5	6.03	9.83	6.03	90,450	60,300	30,000
6	4.42	11.80	4.42	66,300	44,200	30,000

b. Budgeted income statement, 4 percent savings rate for the Boat and Car Loan Department:

Interest income	$645,600*
Interest expense	322,800†
Net interest income	$322,800
Fixed overhead	30,000
Processing expense	121,050
Default expense	80,700
Net income	$ 91,050

*$645,600 = $8,070,000 × 8%

†$322,800 = $8,070,000 × 4%

c. Variance report:

	Actual	Budgeted @ 4%	Fav. (Unfav.) Variance
Interest income	$ 645,766	$ 645,600	$ 166
Interest expense	314,360	322,800	8,440
Net interest income	$ 331,406	$ 322,800	$ 8,606
Fixed overhead	30,200	30,000	(200)
Processing expense	130,522	121,050	(9,472)
Default expense	77,800	80,700	2,900
Net income	$ 92,884	$ 91,050	$ 1,834
Loans	$8,062,000	$8,070,000	$ (8,000)
Deposits	$8,123,000	$8,070,000	$(53,000)

Even though loans were lower and deposits were higher than expected, interest income was higher and interest expense was lower than expected. The answer can be obtained by calculating the average interest rates earned and paid. On $8,062,000 worth of loans, Sandy Cove earned $645,766 interest, or 8.01 percent (0.01 percent more than expected). Similarly, it paid only 3.87 percent (0.13 percent less) on deposits. Therefore, the net interest income variance of $8,606 is a combination of two effects: the variance in the actual loans and deposits (quantity) and the variance in the interest rates (price). The combined effects are a favorable interest income variance, a favorable interest expense variance, and an overall favorable net interest income variance.

At a savings interest rate of 4 percent, there is an excess supply of deposits over demand for loans. The Boat and Car Loan Department lowered the interest rate on deposits to stem additional deposits. The increase in the interest rate on loans can be attributed only to an increase in the demand for loans, which resulted in the department charging a slightly higher average interest rate.

The higher processing expense could be related to the higher number of accounts processed and improvements in the default rate. That is, the favorable default expense could be attributed to an improved screening process—related to spending more on processing.

Problems

P 6–1: G. Bennett Stewart on Management Incentives

I've given a good deal of thought to this issue of how companies . . . go about negotiating objectives with their different business units. The typical process in such cases is that once the parent negotiates a budget with a unit, the budget then becomes the basis for the bonus. And they are also typically structured such that the bonus kicks in when, say, 80 percent of the budgeted performance is achieved; and the maximum bonus is earned when management reaches, say, 120 percent of the budgeted level. There is thus virtually no downside and very limited upside.

Now, because the budget is negotiated between management and headquarters, there is a circularity about the whole process that makes the resulting standards almost meaningless. Because the budget is intended to reflect what management thinks it can accomplish—presumably without extraordinary effort and major changes in the status quo—the adoption of the budget as a standard is unlikely to motivate exceptional performance, especially since the upside is so limited. Instead it is likely to produce cautious budgets and mediocre performance.

So, because of the perverse incentives built into the budgeting process itself, I think it's important for a company to break the connection between the budget and planning process on the one hand and the bonus systems on the other hand. The bonuses should be based upon absolute performance standards that are not subject to negotiation.

Required:

Critically evaluate this quotation.

SOURCE: B Stewart, "CEO Roundtable on Corporate Structure and Management Incentives," *Journal of Applied Corporate Finance,* Fall 1990, p. 27.

P 6–2: Investment Banks

Rogers Petersen and Cabots are two of the five largest investment banks in the United States. Last year there was a major scandal at Cabots involving manipulation of some auctions for government bonds. A number of senior partners at Cabots were charged with price fixing in the government bond market. The ensuing investigation led four of the eight managing directors (the highest-ranking officials at Cabots) to resign. A new senior managing director was brought in from outside to run the firm. This individual recruited three outside managing directors to replace the ones who resigned. There was then a thorough housecleaning. In the following six months, 15 additional partners and over 40 senior managers left Cabots and were replaced, usually with people from outside the firm.

Rogers Petersen has had no such scandal, and almost all of its senior executives have been with the firm for all of their careers.

Required:

a. Describe zero-based budgeting.

b. Which firm, Rogers Petersen or Cabots, is most likely to be using ZBB? Why?

P 6–3: Ice Storm

In March, a devastating ice storm struck Monroe County, New York, causing millions of dollars of damage. Mathews & Peat (M&P), a large horticultural nursery, was hit hard. As a result of the storm, $653,000 of additional labor and maintenance costs were incurred to clean up the nursery, remove and replace damaged plants, repair fencing, and replace glass broken when nearby tree limbs fell on some of the greenhouses.

Mathews & Peat is a wholly owned subsidiary of Agro Inc., an international agricultural conglomerate. The manager of Mathews & Peat, R. Dye, is reviewing the operating performance of the subsidiary for the year. Here are the results for the year as compared with budget:

MATHEWS & PEAT

Summary of Operating Results for the Current Year ($000s)

	Actual Results	*Budgeted Results*	*Actual as % of Budget*
Revenues	$32,149	$31,682	101%
Less			
Labor	13,152	12,621	104
Materials	8,631	8,139	106
Occupancy costs*	4,234	4,236	100
Depreciation	2,687	2,675	100
Interest	1,875	1,895	99
Total expenses	$30,579	$29,566	103%
Operating profits	$ 1,570	$ 2,116	74%

*Includes property taxes, utilities, maintenance and repairs of buildings, and so on.

After thinking about how to present the performance of M&P for the year, Dye decides to break out the costs of the ice storm from the individual items affected by it and report the storm separately. The total cost of the ice storm, $653,000, consists of additional labor costs of $320,000, additional materials of $220,000, and additional occupancy costs of $113,000. These amounts are net of the insurance payments received due to the storm. The alternative performance statement follows:

MATHEWS & PEAT
Summary of Operating Results for the Current Year ($000s)

	Actual Results	*Budgeted Results*	*Actual as % of Budget*
Revenues	$32,149	$31,682	101%
Less			
Labor	12,832	12,621	102
Materials	8,411	8,139	103
Occupancy costs	4,121	4,236	97
Depreciation	2,687	2,675	100
Interest	1,875	1,895	99
Total expenses	29,926	29,566	101%
Operating profits before ice storm costs	2,223	2,116	105%
Ice storm costs	653	0	
Operating profits after ice storm costs	$ 1,570	$ 2,116	74%

Required:

a. Put yourself in Dye's position and write a short, concise cover memo for the second operating statement summarizing the essential points you want to communicate to your superiors.

b. Critically evaluate the differences between the two performance reports as presented.

P 6–4: Budget Lapsing versus Line-Item Budgets

a. What is the difference between budget lapsing and line-item budgets?

b. What types of organizations would you expect to use budget lapsing?

c. What types of organizations would you expect to use line-item budgets?

P 6–5: DMP Consultants

You work in the finance department of a telecommunications firm with a large direct sales force selling high-speed fiber optics access lines to companies wanting telephone and Internet access. Your firm uses a top-down budget that sets the sales quota for each of its 180 salespeople. The salespeople are compensated based on a commission as well as a bonus whenever actual sales exceed their individual budgeted sales quota. Each salesperson's quota is estimated by senior marketing managers in the corporate office based on the size of each customer in that salesperson's geographic territory and projected growth of business in that territory.

DMP Consultants specializes in redesigning antiquated budgeting systems. DMP has made a presentation to your finance department after conducting a thorough analysis of your firm's sales force budgeting system. DMP Consultants has emphasized that your current budgeting system does not take advantage of what your salespeople know about future sales to their customer regions. By ignoring this information, your firm does not effectively plan for this growth, and you are at a competitive disadvantage when deciding to add capacity to your fiber optic network in a timely and efficient way. Moreover, DMP points to extensive research documenting that when people participate in setting budgets that are used to evaluate their performance, these people more readily accept the budgets and there is an increase in employee morale. That is, "participative budgeting" (where employees who are judged against the budget participate in setting the budget) results in happier, more motivated employees. DMP Consultants has made a proposal to implement a bottom-up, participative budgeting scheme to replace your top-down system.

You have been asked to write a short memo to the head of the finance department that analyzes the pros and cons of DMP's proposal.

P 6–6: Federal Insurance

Two years ago Federal Insurance was charged with making misleading marketing claims about the way it was selling its insurance products. In response to these allegations and subsequent investigations, Federal's board of directors fired the chief executive officer (CEO), the chief financial officer (CFO), and the senior vice presidents of marketing and underwriting. They replaced these managers last year with other managers from within the insurance industry, but from firms other than Federal.

A similar insurance firm, Northeast, is about the same size as Federal, operates in the same states, and writes the same lines of insurance (home, auto, life). Both firms prepare detailed annual budgets.

Which of the two firms, Federal or Northeast, is more likely to use zero-based budgeting and why?

P 6–7: Golf World

Golf World is a 1,000-room luxury resort with swimming pools, tennis courts, three golf courses, and many other resort amenities.

The head golf course superintendent, Sandy Green, is responsible for all golf course maintenance and conditioning. Green also has the final say as to whether a particular course is open or closed due to weather conditions and whether players can rent motorized riding golf carts for use on a particular course. If the course is very wet, the golf carts will damage the turf, which Green's maintenance crew will have to repair. Since she is out on the courses every morning supervising the maintenance crews, she knows the condition of the courses.

Wiley Grimes is in charge of the golf cart rentals. His crew maintains the golf cart fleet of over 200 cars, cleans them, puts oil and gas in them, and repairs minor damage. He also is responsible for leasing the carts from the manufacturer, including the terms of the lease, the number of carts to lease, and the choice of cart vendor. When guests arrive at the golf course to play, they pay greens fees to play and a cart fee if they wish to use a cart. If they do not wish to rent a cart, they pay only the greens fee and walk the course.

Grimes and Green manage separate profit centers. The golf cart profit center's revenue is composed of the fees collected from the carts. The golf course profit center's revenue is from the greens fees collected. When the results from April were reviewed, golf cart operating profits were only 49 percent of budget. Wiley argued that the poor results were due to the unusually heavy rains in April. He complained that there were several days when, though only a few areas of the course were wet, the entire course was closed to carts because the grounds crew was too busy to rope off these areas.

To better analyze the performance of the golf cart profit center, the controller's office recently implemented a flexible budget based on the number of cart rentals:

GOLF WORLD
Golf Cart Profit Center
Operating Results—April

	Static Budget	*Actual Results*	*Variance from Static Budget*	*Flexible Budget*	*Variance from Flexible Budget*
Number of cart rentals	6,000	4,000	2,000	4,000	0
Revenues (@ $25/cart)	$150,000	$100,000	$50,000U	$100,000	0
Labor (fixed cost)	7,000	7,200	200U	7,000	200U
Gas and oil					
(@ $1/rental)	6,000	4,900	1,100F	4,000	900U
Cart lease (fixed cost)	40,000	40,000	0	40,000	0
Operating profit	$ 97,000	$ 47,900	$49,100U	$ 49,000	$1,100U

Note: F = Favorable; U = Unfavorable.

Required:

a. Evaluate the performance of the golf cart profit center for the month of April.

b. What are the advantages and disadvantages of the controller's new budgeting system?

c. What additional recommendations would you make regarding the operations of Golf World?

P 6–8: Coating Department

The coating department of a parts manufacturing department coats various parts with an antirust, zinc-based material. The parts to be processed are loaded into baskets; the baskets are passed through a coating machine that dips the parts into the zinc solution. The machine then heats the parts to ensure that the coating bonds properly. All parts being coated are assigned a cost for the coating department based on the number of hours the parts spend in the coating machine. Prior to the beginning of the year, cost categories are accumulated by department (including the coating department). These cost categories are classified as either fixed or variable and then a flexible budget for the department is constructed. Given an estimate of machine hours for the next year, the coating department's projected cost per machine hour is computed.

Here are data for the last three operating years. Expected coating machine hours for 2012 are 16,000 hours.

COATING DEPARTMENT
Operating Data

	2009	*2010*	*2011*
Machine hours	12,500	8,400	15,200
Coating materials	$ 51,375	$ 34,440	$ 62,624
Engineering support	27,962	34,295	31,300
Maintenance	35,850	35,930	36,200
Occupancy costs (square footage)	27,502	28,904	27,105
Operator labor	115,750	78,372	147,288
Supervision	46,500	47,430	49,327
Utilities	12,875	8,820	16,112
Total costs	$317,814	$268,191	$369,956

Required:

a. Estimate the coating department's flexible budget for 2012. Explicitly state and justify the assumptions used in deriving your estimates.

b. Calculate the coating department's cost per machine hour for 2012.

P 6–9: Marketing Plan

Robin Jensen, manager of market planning for Viral Products of the IDP Pharmaceutical Co., is responsible for advertising a class of products. She has designed a three-year marketing plan to increase the market share of her product class. Her plan involves a major increase in magazine advertising. She has met with an advertising agency that has designed a three-year ad campaign involving 12 separate ads that build on a common theme. Each ad will run in three consecutive monthly medi276cal magazines and then be followed by the next ad in the sequence. Up to five medical journals will carry the ad campaign. Direct mail campaigns and direct sales promotional material will be designed to follow the theme of the ad currently appearing. The accompanying table summarizes the cost of the campaign:

	Year 1	*Year 2*	*Year 3*	*Year 4*
Number of ads	4	4	4	12
Number of magazines	5	5	4	
Cost per ad	$ 6,000	$ 6,200	$ 6,500	
Advertising cost	$120,000	$124,000	$104,000	$348,000

The firm's normal policy is to budget each year as a separate entity without carrying forward unspent monies. Jensen is requesting that, instead of just approving the budget for next year (Year 1 above), the firm approve and budget the entire three-year project. This would allow her to move forward with her campaign and give her the freedom to apply any unspent funds in one year to the next year or to use them in another part of the campaign. She argues that the ad campaign is an integrated project stretching over three years and should be either approved or rejected in its entirety.

Required:

Critically evaluate Jensen's request and make a recommendation as to whether a three-year budget should be approved per her proposal. (Assume that the advertising campaign is expected to be a profitable project.)

P 6–10: Potter-Bowen

Potter-Bowen (PB) manufactures and sells postage meters throughout the world. Postage meters print the necessary postage on envelopes, eliminating the need to affix stamps. The meter keeps track of the postage, the user takes the meter's counter to a post office and pays money, and the post office initializes the meter to print postage totaling that amount. The firm offers about 30 different postage systems, ranging from small manual systems (costing a few hundred dollars) to large automated ones (costing up to $75,000).

PB is organized into Research and Development, Manufacturing, and Marketing. Marketing is further subdivided into four sectors: North America, South America, Europe, and Asia. The North American marketing sector has a sales force organized into 32 regions with approximately 75 to 200 salespeople per region.

The budgeting process begins with the chief financial officer (CFO) and the vice president of marketing jointly projecting the total sales for the next year. Their staffs look at trends of the various PB models and project total unit sales by model within each marketing sector. Price increases are forecast and dollar sales per model are calculated. The North American sector is then given a target number of units and a target revenue by model for the year. The manager of the North American sector, Helen Neumann, and her staff then allocate the division's target units and target revenue by region.

The target unit sales for each model per region are derived by taking the region's historical percentage sales for that machine times North America's target for that model. For example, model 6103 has North American target unit sales of 18,500 for next year. The Utah region last year sold 4.1 percent of all model 6103s sold in North America. Therefore, Utah's target of 6103s for next year is 758 units (4.1% × 18,500). The average sales price of the 6103 is set at $11,000. Thus, Utah's revenue budget for 6103s is $8,338,000. Given the total forecasted unit sales, average selling prices, and historical sales of each model in all regions, each region is assigned a unit target and revenue budget by model. The region's total revenue budget is the sum of the individual models' revenue targets.

Each salesperson in the region is given a unit and revenue target by model using a similar procedure. If Gary Lindenmeyer (a salesperson in Utah) sold 6 percent of Utah's 6103s last year, his unit sales target of 6103s next year is 45 units (6% × 758). His total revenue target for 6103s is $495,000 (or 45 × $11,000). Totaling all the models gives each salesperson's total revenue budget. Salespeople are paid a fixed salary plus a bonus. The bonus is calculated based on the following table:

% of Total Revenue Target Achieved	*Bonus*
< 90%	No bonus
90–100%	5% of salary
101–110	10% of salary
111–120	20% of salary
121–130	30% of salary
131–140	40% of salary
141–150	50% of salary
>150%	60% of salary

Required:

Critically evaluate PB's sales budgeting system and sales force compensation system. Describe any potential dysfunctional behaviors that PB's systems are likely to generate.

P 6–11: Feder Purchasing Department

The purchasing department at Feder buys all of its raw materials, supplies, and parts. This department is a cost center. It uses a flexible budget based on the number of different items purchased each month to forecast spending and as a control mechanism.

At the beginning of February, the purchasing department expected to purchase 8,200 different items. Given this expected number of purchased items, purchasing calculated its flexible budget for February to be $1,076,400. In reviewing actual spending in February, the purchasing department was over its flexible budget by $41,400 (unfavorable) when calculated using the actual number of items purchased. Actual spending in February was $1,175,000, and the department purchased 9,300 units.

Budgeted fixed cost and budgeted variable cost per item purchased remained the same in the flexible budgets calculated at the beginning and end of February.

Required:

Calculate the fixed cost and the variable cost per item purchased used in the purchasing department's flexible budget in February.

P 6–12: Access.Com

Access.Com produces and sells software to libraries and schools to block access to Web sites deemed inappropriate by the customer. In addition, the software also tracks and reports on Web sites visited and advises the customer of other Web sites the customer might choose to block. Access.Com's software sells for between $15,000 and $20,000.

Three account managers (V. J. Singh, A. C. Chen, and P. J. Martinez) sell the software and are paid a fixed salary plus a percentage of all sales in excess of targeted (budgeted) sales. Vice President of Marketing S. B. Ro sets the budgeted sales amount for each account manager. The following table reports actual and budgeted sales for the three account managers for the past five years.

	A. C. Chen		V. J. Singh		P. J. Martinez	
	Actual	*Budget*	*Actual*	*Budget*	*Actual*	*Budget*
2003	$1.630	$1.470	$2.240	$2.400	$2.775	$2.695
2004	1.804	1.614	2.586	2.384	2.995	2.767
2005	1.685	1.785	2.406	2.566	2.876	2.972
2006	1.665	1.775	2.600	2.550	2.698	2.963
2007	1.924	1.764	2.385	2.595	3.107	2.936

Required:

a. Based on the data in the table, describe the process used by Ro to set sales quotas for each account manager.

b. Discuss the pros and cons of Access.Com's budgeting process for setting account managers' sales targets.

P 6–13: Videx

Videx is the premier firm in the security systems industry. Martha Rameriz is an account manager at Videx responsible for selling residential systems. She is compensated based on beating a predetermined sales budget. The last seven years' sales budgets and actual sales data follow. Videx sets its sales budgets centrally in a top-down fashion.

Year	*Budget*	*Actual*	*Difference*
1	$850,000	$865,000	$15,000
2	862,000	888,800	26,800
3	884,000	852,000	−32,000
4	884,000	895,000	11,000
5	893,000	878,000	−15,000
6	893,000	902,000	9,000
7	901,000		
Average	881,000	880,133	2,467
Standard deviation	18,385	18,970	21,715
Median	884,000	883,400	10,000

Required:

a. Martha Rameriz sells $908,000 in year 7. What budget will she be assigned for year 8?

b. Suppose Rameriz sells $900,000 of systems in year 7. What budget will she be assigned in year 8?

P 6–14: New York Fashions

New York Fashions owns 87 women's clothing stores in shopping malls. Corporate headquarters of New York Fashions uses flexible budgets to control the operations of each of the stores. The following table presents the August flexible budget for the New York Fashions store located in the Crystal Lakes Mall:

NEW YORK FASHIONS—CRYSTAL LAKES MALL STORE
Flexible Budget
August

Expense	*Fixed*	*Variable*
Cost of goods sold		45%
Management	$ 7,000	1
Salespersons	2,000	8
Rent	12,000	5
Utilities	900	
Other	1,500	

Variable costs are based on a percentage of revenues.

Required:

a. Revenues for August were $80,000. Calculate budgeted profits for August.

b. Actual results for August are summarized in the following table:

NEW YORK FASHIONS—CRYSTAL LAKES MALL STORE
Actual Results from Operations
August

Revenues	$80,000
Cost of goods sold	38,000
Management	7,600
Salespersons	9,800
Rent	16,000
Utilities	875
Other	1,400

Prepare a report for the New York Fashions—Crystal Lakes Mall store for the month of August comparing actual results to the budget.

c. Analyze the performance of the Crystal Lakes Mall store in August.

d. How does a flexible budget change the incentives of managers held responsible for meeting the flexible budget as compared to the incentives created by meeting a static (fixed) budget?

P 6–15: International Telecon

You are working in the office of the vice president of administration at International Telecon (IT) as a senior financial planner. IT is a Fortune 500 firm with sales approaching $1 billion. IT provides long-distance satellite communications around the world. Deregulation of telecommunications in Europe has intensified worldwide competition and has increased pressures inside IT to reduce costs so it can lower prices without cutting profit margins.

IT is divided into several profit and cost centers. Each profit center is further organized as a series of cost centers. Each profit and cost center submits a budget to IT's vice president of administration and then is held responsible for meeting that budget. The VP of administration described IT's financial control, budgeting, and reporting system as "pretty much a standard, state-of-the-art approach where we hold our people accountable for producing what they forecast."

Your boss has assigned you the task of analyzing firmwide supplies expenditures, with the goal of reducing waste and lowering expenditures. Supplies include all consumables ranging from pencils and paper to electronic subcomponents and parts costing less than \$1,000. Long-lived assets that cost under \$1,000 (or the equivalent dollar amount in the domestic currency for foreign purchases) are not capitalized (and then depreciated) but are categorized as supplies and written off as expenses in the month purchased.

You first gather the last 36 months of operating data for both supplies and payroll for the entire firm. The payroll data help you benchmark the supplies data. You divide each month's payroll and supplies amount by revenues in that month to control for volume and seasonal fluctuations. The accompanying graph plots the two data series.

Payroll fluctuates from 35 to 48 percent of sales, and supplies fluctuate from 13 to 34 percent of sales. The graph contains the last three fiscal years of supplies and payroll, divided by the vertical lines. For financial and budgeting purposes, IT is on a calendar (January–December) fiscal year.

International Telecon monthly payroll and supply expenses, last 36 months

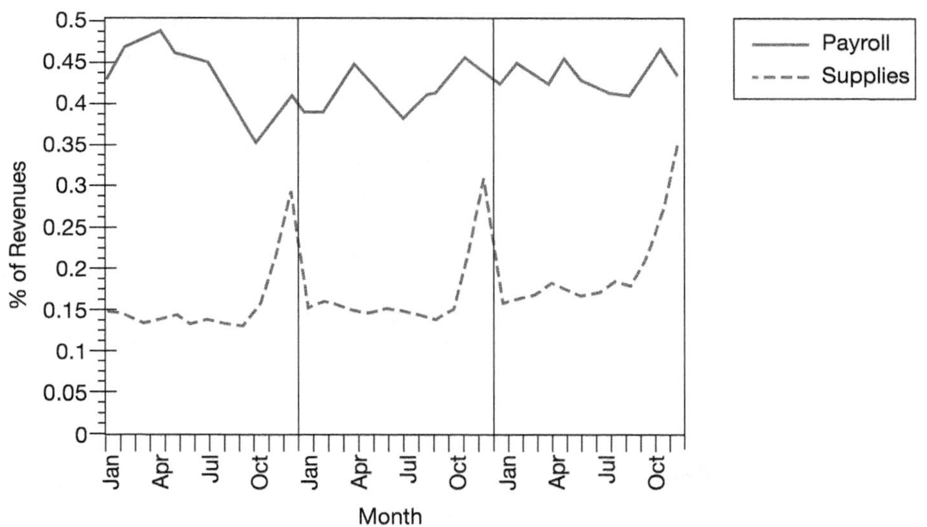

Besides focusing on consolidated firmwide spending, you prepare disaggregated graphs like the one shown, but at the cost and profit center levels. The general patterns observed in the consolidated graphs are repeated in general in the disaggregated graphs.

Required:

a. Analyze the time-series behavior of supplies expenditures for IT. What is the likely reason for the observed patterns in supplies?

b. Given your analysis in (*a*), what corrective action might you consider proposing? What are its costs and benefits?

P 6–16: Adrian Power

Adrian Power manufactures small power supplies for car stereos. The company uses flexible budgeting techniques to deal with the seasonal and cyclical nature of the business. The accounting department provided the accompanying data on budgeted manufacturing costs for the month of January:

ADRIAN POWER
Planned Level of Production for January

Budgeted production (in units)	14,000
Variable costs (vary with production)	
Direct materials	$140,000
Direct labor	224,000
Indirect labor	21,000
Indirect materials	10,500
Maintenance	6,300
Fixed costs	
Supervision	24,700
Other (depreciation, taxes, etc.)	83,500
Total plant costs	$510,000

Actual operations for January are summarized as

ADRIAN POWER
Actual Operations for January

Actual production (in units)	15,400
Actual costs incurred	
Direct materials	$142,400
Direct labor	259,800
Indirect labor	27,900
Indirect materials	12,200
Maintenance	9,800
Supervision	28,000
Other costs (depreciation, taxes, etc.)	83,500
Total plant costs	$563,600

Required:

a. Prepare a report comparing the actual operating results with the flexible budget at actual production.

b. Write a short memo analyzing the report prepared in (*a*). What likely managerial implications do you draw from this report? What are the numbers telling you?

P 6–17: Panarude Airfreight

Panarude Airfreight is an international air freight hauler with more than 45 jet aircraft operating in the United States and the Pacific Rim. The firm is headquartered in Melbourne, Australia, and is organized into five geographic areas: Australia, Japan, Taiwan, Korea, and the United States. Supporting these areas are several centralized corporate function services (cost centers): human resources, data processing, fleet acquisition and maintenance, and telecommunications. Each responsibility center has a budget, negotiated at the beginning of the year with the vice president of finance. Funds unspent at the end of the year do not carry over to the next fiscal year. The firm is on a January-to-December fiscal year.

After reviewing the month-to-month variances, Panarude senior management became concerned about the increased spending occurring in the last three months of each fiscal year. In particular, in the first nine months of the year, expenditure accounts typically show favorable variances (actual spending is less than budget), but in the last three months, unfavorable variances are the norm. In an attempt to smooth out these spending patterns, each responsibility center is reviewed at the end of each calendar quarter and any unspent funds can be deleted from the budget for the remainder of the year. The accompanying table shows the budget and actual spending in the telecommunications department for the first quarter of this year.

PANARUDE AIRFREIGHT
Telecommunications Department: First Quarter
Budget and Actual Spending (Australian Dollars)

	Monthly Budget	*Cumulative Budget*	*Actual Spending*	*Cumulative Spending*	*Monthly Variance**	*Cumulative Variance**
Jan.	$110,000	$110,000	$104,000	$104,000	$6,000 F	$6,000 F
Feb.	95,000	205,000	97,000	201,000	2,000 U	4,000 F
Mar.	115,000	320,000	112,000	313,000	3,000 F	7,000 F

*F = Favorable; U = Unfavorable.

At the end of the first quarter, telecommunications' total annual budget for this year can be reduced by $7,000, the total budget underrun in the first quarter. In addition, the remaining nine monthly budgets for telecommunications are reduced by $778 (or $7,000 ÷ 9). If, at the end of the second quarter, telecommunications' budget shows an unfavorable variance of, say, $8,000 (after the original budget is reduced for the first-quarter underrun), management of telecommunications is held responsible for the entire $8,000 unfavorable variance. The first-quarter underrun is not restored. If the second-quarter budget variance is also favorable, the remaining six monthly budgets are each reduced further by one-sixth of the second-quarter favorable budget variance.

Required:

a. What behavior would this budgeting scheme engender in the responsibility center managers?

b. Compare the advantages and disadvantages of the previous budget regime, where any end-of-year budget surpluses do not carry over to the next fiscal year, with the system of quarterly budget adjustments just described.

P 6–18: Veriplex

Veriplex manufactures process control equipment. This 100-year-old German company has recently acquired another firm that has a design for a new proprietary process control system. A key component of the new system to be manufactured by Veriplex is called the VTrap, a new line of precision air-flow gauges.

Veriplex uses tight financial budgets linked to annual bonuses to control its manufacturing departments. Each manufacturing department is a cost center. The VTrap gauge is being manufactured in Veriplex's gauge department, which also manufactures an existing line of gauges. The gauge department's budget for the current year consists of two parts: €6.60 million for manufacturing the existing line of gauges and €0.92 million to develop and manufacture VTrap.

The gauge department is responsible for introducing VTrap, which has been in development in the gauge department since the beginning of the year. The new gauge will be manufactured using much of the same equipment and personnel as the existing gauges. VTrap is an integral part of the proprietary process control system that Veriplex hopes will give it a sustainable competitive advantage. Senior management is heavily committed to this strategy. Senior engineering staff members are always in the gauge department working with the manufacturing personnel to modify and refine both the gauges' design and the production processes to produce them. (Note: Engineering department costs are not assigned to the gauge department.)

By the end of the fiscal year, the gauge department had spent €1.30 million on the VTrap program and €6.39 million on existing gauge production. Both the new and existing gauge lines achieved their target production quotas and quality goals for the year.

Required:

a. Prepare a financial statement for the gauge department that details its financial performance for the fiscal year just completed.

b. Upon further investigation of previous new product introductions, you discover the same patterns in other departments between new and existing products and their budgets and actual costs. What are some possible reasons why the pattern in the gauge department is not an isolated occurrence but has occurred with other new product introductions and is likely to occur with future new product introductions?

P 6–19: Madigan Modems

Madigan produces a single high-speed modem. The following table summarizes the current month's budget for Madigan's modem production:

Projected production and sales	4,000 units
Variable costs	$ 640,000
Fixed costs	$ 480,000
Total production budget	$1,120,000

Actual production and sales for the month were 3,900 units. Total production costs were $1,114,800, of which $631,800 were variable costs.

Required:

a. Prepare an end-of-month variance report for the production department using the beginning-of-month static budget.

b. Prepare an end-of-month variance report for the production department using the beginning-of-month flexible budget.

c. Write a short memo evaluating the performance of the production manager based on the variance report in (*a*).

d. Write a short memo evaluating the performance of the production manager based on the variance report in (*b*).

e. Which variance report—the one in (*a*) or (*b*)—best reflects the performance of the production manager? Why?

P 6–20: Webb & Drye

Webb & Drye (WD) is a New York City law firm with over 200 attorneys. WD has a sophisticated set of information technologies—including intranets and extranets, e-mail servers, the firm's accounting, payroll, and client billing software, and document management systems—that allows WD attorneys and their expert witnesses access to millions of pages of scanned documents that often accompany large class action lawsuits. Bev Piccaretto was hired at the beginning of last year to manage WD's IT department. She and her staff maintain these various systems, but they also act as an internal consulting group to WD's professional staff. They help the staff connect to and use the various IT systems and troubleshoot problems the staff may encounter.

The IT department is a cost center. Piccaretto receives an annual operating budget and believes she is accountable for not exceeding the budget while simultaneously providing high-quality IT services to WD. Piccaretto reports to Marge Malone, WD's chief operating officer. Malone is responsible for IT, accounting, marketing, human resources, and finance functions for Webb & Drye. She reports directly to WD's managing partner, who is the firm's chief executive officer.

The fiscal year has just ended. The following table contains IT's annual budget, actual amounts spent, and variances from the budget.

WEBB & DRYE
IT Department
Budgeted and Actual Expenditures and Variances from Budget Last Year

	Budget	*Actual*	*Variance*	*Fav./Unfav.*
Salaries	$ 350,000	$ 336,000	$14,000	F
Benefits*	140,000	134,400	5,600	F
Software site licenses	143,000	168,000	(25,000)	U
Hardware leases	630,000	635,000	(5,000)	U
Travel	59,000	57,000	2,000	F
Supplies	112,000	110,000	2,000	F
Training	28,000	20,000	8,000	F
Occupancy costs	195,000	198,000	(3,000)	U
Total	$1,657,000	$1,658,400	$ (1,400)	U

*40% of salaries

Malone expresses her concern that the IT department had substantial deviations from the original budgeted amounts for software licenses and salaries, and that Piccaretto should have informed Malone of these actions before they were implemented. Piccaretto argues that since total spending within the IT department was in line with the total budget of $1,657,000 she managed her budget well. Furthermore, Piccaretto points out that she had to buy more sophisticated antivirus software to protect the firm from hacker attacks and that, in paying for these software upgrades, she did not replace a staff person who left in the fourth quarter of the year. Malone counters that this open position adversely affected a large lawsuit because the attorneys working on the case had trouble downloading the scanned documents in the document management system that IT is responsible for maintaining.

Required:

Write a short memo analyzing the disagreement between Malone and Piccaretto. What issues underlie the disagreement? Who is right and who is wrong? What corrective actions (if any) do you recommend?

P 6–21: Spa Ariana

Spa Ariana promotes itself as an upscale spa offering a variety of treatments, including massages, facials, and manicures, performed in a luxurious setting by qualified therapists. The owners of Spa Ariana invested close to $450,000 of their own money three years ago in building and decorating the interior of their new spa (six treatment rooms, relaxation rooms, showers, and waiting area). Located on the main street in a ski resort, the spa has a five-year renewable lease from the building owner. The owners hire a manager to run the spa.

The average one-hour treatment is priced at $100. Ariana has the following cost structure:

	Variable Cost/ Treatment	Fixed Cost/ Month
Therapist	$40	
Supplies/laundry	4	
Management		$ 5,500
Utilities		1,600
Rent	7	6,000
Repairs/upkeep/cleaning	6	1,500
Total	$57	$14,600

Assume that all treatments have the same variable cost structure depicted in the table.

Required:

a. Calculate the number of treatments Spa Ariana must perform each month in order to break even.

b. In April, the owners of Ariana expect to perform 550 treatments. Prepare a budget for April assuming 550 treatments are given.

c. In April Spa Ariana performs 530 treatments and incurs the following actual costs. Prepare a performance report for April comparing actual performance to the static budget in part (*b*) based on 550 treatments.

Actual Operating Results for April

Revenue		$53,000
Therapists	$21,280	
Supplies/laundry	1,795	
Management	5,125	
Utilities	1,725	
Rent	9,710	
Repairs/upkeep/cleaning	5,080	$44,715
Actual profit		$ 8,285

d. Prepare a performance report for April comparing actual performance to a flexible budget based on the actual number of treatments performed in April of 530.

e. Which of the two performance reports you prepared in parts (*c*) and (*d*) best reflect the true performance of the Spa Ariana in April? Explain your reasoning.

f. Do the break-even calculation you performed in part (*a*) and the budgeted and actual profits computed in parts (*a*)–(*d*) accurately capture the true economics of the Ariana Spa? Explain why or why not.

P 6–22: Picture Maker

Picture Maker is a freestanding photo kiosk consumers use to download their digital photos and make prints. Shashi Sharma has a small business that leases several Picture Makers from the manufacturer for $120 per month per kiosk, and she places them in high-traffic retail locations. Customers pay $0.18 per print. (The kiosk only makes six- by eight-inch prints.) Sharma has one kiosk located in the

Sanchez Drug Store, for which Sharma pays Sanchez $80 per month rent. Sharma checks each of her kiosks every few days, refilling the photographic paper and chemicals, and collects the money. Sharma hires a service company that cleans the machine, replaces any worn or defective parts, and resets the kiosk's settings to ensure the kiosk continues to provide high-quality prints. This maintenance is performed monthly and is independent of the number of prints made during the month. The average cost of the service runs about $90 per month, but it can vary depending on the extent of repairs and parts required to maintain the equipment.

Paper and chemicals are variable costs, and maintenance, equipment lease, and store rent are fixed costs. If the kiosk is malfunctioning and the print quality deteriorates, Sanchez refunds the customer's money and then gets his money back from Sharma when she comes by to check the paper and chemical supplies. These occasional refunds cause her variable costs *per print* for paper and chemicals to vary over time.

The following table reports the results from operating the kiosk at the Sanchez Drug Store last month. Budget variances are computed as the difference between actual and budgeted amounts. An unfavorable variance (U) exists when actual revenues fall short of budget or when actual expenses exceed the budget. Last month, the kiosk had a net loss of $23, which was $87 more than budgeted.

Sanchez Drug Store Kiosk
Last Month

	Actual Results	*Variance from Budget*	*(U = unfavorable F = favorable)*
Revenue	$360	$108	U
Expenses:			
Paper	$ 65	$ 13	F
Chemicals	28	2	U
Maintenance	90	10	F
Equipment lease	120	0	
Store rent	80	0	
Total expenses	$383	$ 21	F
Net income (loss)	($23)	($87)	U

Required:

a. Prepare a schedule that shows the budget Sharma used in calculating the variances in the preceding report.

b. How many good prints were made last month at the Sanchez Drug Store kiosk?

c. Prepare a flexible budget for the Sanchez Drug Store kiosk based on a volume of 2,000 prints.

P 6–23: City Hospital Nursing

City Hospital is a city government-owned and -operated hospital providing basic health care to low-income people. Most of the hospital's revenues are from federal, state, county, and city governments. Some patients covered by private insurance are also admitted, but most of the patients are covered by government assistance programs (Medicare and Medicaid).

Maxine Jones is the director of nursing for the 40-bed pediatrics unit at City Hospital. She is responsible for recruiting nurses, scheduling when they work (days, evenings, weekends), and preparing the nursing budget for the pediatrics unit. A variety of different nursing skills is needed to staff the unit: There are nursing aides, nurse practitioners, registered nurses, nursing supervisors, and clinical nurses. Each type of nurse provides different patient care services (care and feeding, drawing blood samples, giving injections, changing dressings, supervising, etc.). Not all types of nurses can provide all services, and each type of nurse has a different wage rate. Minimum nurse staffing levels per patient must be maintained. If the minimums are violated, new patients cannot be admitted.

Over 45 full-time nurses are required to staff the pediatrics unit. The number of each type of nurse is set in the budget (8 nurses aides, 12 nurse practitioners, 14 registered nurses, etc.). To change the mix of nurse types or their wage rates during the year requires time-consuming approval from the nursing administration, the hospital administration, and finally the city council. The director can change the staffing mix and pay scales in the next budget year by submitting a budget with the revised staffing levels and wage rates and having the budget approved through a lengthy review process that ultimately requires the city council's agreement.

In selecting where to work, nurses evaluate working conditions, pay, and amenities, as all employees do. A key working condition for nurses is flexibility in choosing their schedule. Because of the shortage of nurses in the community, all hospitals have become competitive in terms of work schedules and hours. Some private hospitals allow nurses to schedule when they want to work and how many hours a week they are willing to work. City Hospital often finds its nurses being hired away by private hospitals. If a nurse practitioner is hired away, Jones must replace her or him with another nurse practitioner. The private hospitals do not have such a constraint. If a nurse practitioner position is open, a private hospital will temporarily move a registered nurse with a higher level of skills into the position until a nurse practitioner can be found.

Required:

a. What type of specialized knowledge does Maxine Jones acquire in preparing the nursing schedule for the upcoming month?

b. What are some of the consequences of the constraints Jones must operate under?

c. Explain why City Hospital does not allow Jones as much freedom in her staffing decisions as her counterparts in private hospitals.

P 6–24: Madden International

Madden International is a large ($7 billion sales), successful international pharmaceuticals firm operating in 23 countries with 15 autonomous subsidiaries. The corporate office consists of five vice presidents who oversee the operations of the subsidiaries. These five vice presidents report to two executive vice presidents, who in turn report to the president of the firm.

The 15 subsidiaries specialize by pharmaceutical type and in some cases by country. The pace of innovation in this industry is very fast. In addition, each country has its own elaborate regulatory environment that controls new drug introduction, pricing, and distribution. Each market has its own peculiarities concerning hospital drug purchases. It is an understatement to say that Madden International operates in a very complex world that changes daily.

The corporate office requires each subsidiary to maintain an elaborate, detailed budget and control system. The following points summarize the budget and control system in each subsidiary:

- One-, three-, and five-year budgets are prepared each year.
- The vice president overseeing the subsidiary looks for three- and five-year budgets that stretch the subsidiary's capabilities. That is, subsidiaries are pushed to devise programs that increase value.
- These budgets are developed and approved first at the subsidiary level, then by corporate headquarters.
- Every three months the subsidiaries must reconcile actual performance to budget and write detailed reports to the corporate office explaining variances and corrective actions to be taken.

- The corporate vice president assigned to the subsidiary makes quarterly visits for three days of meetings that involve extensive reviews of the budgets and operating results. These meetings involve all the senior managers in the subsidiary.
- Subsidiary senior managers are not compensated or rewarded for meeting budget targets. Rather, they are evaluated on their ability to develop new markets, solve short-run problems, add value to their organization and to Madden International, and manage and motivate their subordinates. These performance evaluation criteria are quite subjective. But the corporate vice presidents have a great deal of in-depth personal contact with each of the senior people in their subsidiaries and are able to arrive at suitable performance evaluations.
- Preparing for these meetings with the corporate vice president and developing the budgets requires the involvement of all the senior managers in the subsidiary. One manager remarked, "I'd hate to see how much more money we could be making if we didn't have to spend so much time in budget and financial review meetings."

It turns out that Madden International is not unique in the amount of senior management time spent on budgeting and financial reviews. A survey of large, publicly traded U.S. firms supports the Madden system. Researchers found that innovative firms in complex environments characterized by high uncertainty and change used much more elaborate formal financial control (budgeting) systems than did firms in more stable, mature industries. Innovative firms seem to employ more financial controls than less-innovative firms.

Required:

a. List the strengths and weaknesses of the budgeting and control system at Madden International.

b. Why might you expect firms like Madden International to rely so heavily on formal financial control systems?

P 6–25: Brehm Vineyards

Brehm Vineyards grows a unique white pinot noir grape that they use to produce a white wine that is in high demand. Brehm uses all the grapes they can grow to produce their own white pinot noir wine. Brehm pinot noir wine contains 100 percent Brehm-grown grapes. The company neither buys nor sells grapes. Because of the uniqueness and difficulty of growing white pinot grapes, Brehm can only produce 8,000 cases (12 bottles per case) in a normal year. A good growing season might yield 10,000 cases, whereas bad weather can cut production to 5,000 cases. In a normal year Brehm expects to sells its wine to wholesalers for $120 per case.

The following table summarizes how Brehm managers expect their costs to vary with the number of cases produced.

	Fixed Cost (per year)	*Variable Cost (per case)*
Grape costs	$240,000	$2.10
Labor	75,000	2.15
Packaging		14.00
Selling and administrative costs	36,000	
Utilities	4,000	0.75

Required:

a. Prepare a flexible budget (including budgeted net income) assuming Brehm produces and sells 8,000 cases of wine.

b. Calculate the breakeven number of cases.

c. How many cases does Brehm have to produce if they want an after-tax profit of $300,000 and the income tax rate is 40 percent?

d. Bad weather this year cut Brehm's production and sales to only 6,000 cases. The low yield drove up wholesale prices of the white pinot wine from $120 to $140 per case. Brehm's actual expenses for the year were:

Actual Costs for the Year

Grape costs	$260,000
Labor	98,000
Packaging	83,000
Selling and administrative costs	39,000
Utilities	8,800

Design and prepare a table that reports the performance of Brehm for the year.

e. Write a short memo summarizing Brehm's performance during the past year. Did management do a good or bad job?

P 6–26: Republic Insurance

Republic Insurance has a direct sales force that sells life insurance policies. All salespeople at the beginning of the year forecast the number of policies they expect to sell that year. At the end of the year, they are evaluated based on how many policies they actually sell. The compensation scheme is based on the following formula:

$$\text{Total compensation} = \$20{,}000 + \$100B + \$20(S - B) \quad \text{if } S \geq B$$

$$\$20{,}000 + \$100\text{B} - \$400(B - S) \quad \text{if } S < B$$

where

B = Budgeted number of policies reported by the manager
S = Actual number of policies sold

Required:

a. Suppose a particular salesperson expects to sell 100 policies. This salesperson is considering reporting budgeted policies of 90, 99, 100, 101, 102, and 110. What level of budgeted policy sales should this person report at the beginning of the year?

b. Critically analyze the Republic Insurance compensation scheme.

P 6–27: Old Rosebud Farms

Old Rosebud is a Kentucky horse farm that specializes in boarding thoroughbred breeding mares and their foals. Customers bring their breeding mares to Old Rosebud for delivery of their foals and after-birth care of the mare and foal. Recent changes in the tax laws brought about a substantial decline in thoroughbred breeding. As a result, profits declined in the thoroughbred boarding industry.

Old Rosebud prepared a master budget for the current year by splitting costs into variable costs and fixed costs. The budget was prepared before the extent of the downturn was fully recognized. Table 1 above compares actual with budget for the current year.

Required:

Prepare an analysis of the operating performance of Old Rosebud Farms. Supporting tables or calculations should be clearly labeled.

TABLE 1

OLD ROSEBUD FARMS
Income Statement for Year Ended 12/31

	Budget Formula (per Mare per Day)	*Actual*	*Master Budget*	*Variance**
Number of mares		52	60	8
Number of boarding days		18,980	21,900	2,920
Revenues	$25.00	$379,600	$547,500	$167,900 U
Less variable expenses				
Feed & supplies	5.00	104,390	109,500	5,110 F
Veterinary fees	3.00	58,838	65,700	6,862 F
Blacksmith fees	.30	6,074	6,570	496 F
Total variable expenses	8.30	169,302	181,770	12,468 F
Contribution margin	$16.70	$210,298	$365,730	$155,432 U
Less fixed expenses				
Depreciation & insurance		$ 56,000	$ 56,000	$ 0
Utilities		12,000	14,000	2,000 F
Repairs & maintenance		10,000	11,000	1,000 F
Labor		88,000	96,000	8,000 F
Total fixed expenses		166,000	177,000	11,000 F
Net income		$ 44,298	$188,730	$144,432 U

*F = Favorable; U = Unfavorable.

P 6–28: Troika Toys

Adrian and Pells (AP) is an advertising agency that uses flexible budgeting for both planning and control. One of its clients, Troika Toys, asked AP to prepare an ad campaign for a new toy. AP's contract with Troika calls for paying AP $120 per design hour for between 150 and 200 hours.

AP has a staff of ad campaign designers who prepare the ad campaigns. Customers are billed only for the time designers work on their project. Partner time is not billed directly to the customer. As part of the planning process, Sue Bent, partner-in-charge of the Troika account, prepared the following flexible budget. "Authorized Design Hours" is the estimated range of time AP expects the job to require and what the client agrees to authorize.

TROIKA TOYS
Flexible Budget

	Fixed Component	*Variable Component*	**Authorized Design Hours** *150*	*175*	*200*
Revenues		$120	$18,000	$21,000	$24,000
Design labor	$ 0	45	6,750	7,875	9,000
Artwork	1,700	11	3,350	3,625	3,900
Office and occupancy costs*	0	6	900	1,050	1,200
Total costs	$1,700	$ 62	$11,000	$12,550	$14,100
Budgeted profits			$ 7,000	$ 8,450	$ 9,900

*Consists of rent, phone charges, fax costs, overnight delivery, and so on.

AP's executive committee reviewed Bent's budget and approved it and the Troika contract. After some preliminary work, Troika liked the ideas so much it expanded the authorized time range to be between 175 and 250 hours.

Bent and her design team finished the Troika project. Two hundred and twenty design hours were logged and billed to Troika at the contract price ($120 per hour). Upon completion of the Troika campaign, the following revenues and costs had been accumulated:

TROIKA TOYS
Actual Costs Incurred

Revenue ($120 × 220)	$26,400
Design labor	10,320
Artwork	4,350
Office and occupancy costs	1,690
Total costs	$16,360
Profits	$10,040

AP's accounting manager keeps track of actual costs incurred by AP on each account. AP employs a staff of designers. Their average salary is $45 per hour. New designers earn less than the average; those with more experience earn more. The actual design labor costs charged to each project are the actual hours times the designer's actual hourly cost. Artwork consists of both in-house and out-of-house artists who draw up the art for the ads designed by the designers. Office and occupancy costs consist of a charge per designer hour to cover rent, photocopying, and phones, plus actual long-distance calls, faxes, and overnight delivery services.

Required:

Prepare a table that reports on Sue Bent's performance on the Troika Toys account and write a short memo to the executive committee that summarizes her performance on this project.

P 6–29: Cellular First

The sales department of a cellular phone company pays its salespeople $1,500 per month plus 25 percent of each new subscriber's first month's billings. A new subscriber's first-month bill averages $80. Salespeople work 160 hours a month (four weeks at 40 hours per week). If salespeople work more than 160 hours per month, they receive $12 per hour for hours in excess of 160.

Sales leads for the sales department are generated in a variety of ways—direct mailings to potential customers who then call to speak to a salesperson, lists of prospective customers purchased from outside marketing firms, and so forth. The manager of the sales department reviews potential leads and assigns them to particular salespeople who contact them. The manager of the sales department is expected to oversee the time spent by each salesperson per assigned lead and to approve overtime requests to work beyond the 40 hours per week. Each new customer added requires on average 2 hours of salesperson time to make the sale.

Last month, the sales department was budgeted for eight full-time salespeople. However, because of a new ad campaign, an additional salesperson was hired and overtime was approved, bringing actual hours worked up to 1,580. The department added 725 new customers.

Required:

a. Prepare a performance report comparing actual performance to budgeted performance using a static budget based on eight salespeople and no budgeted overtime.

b. Prepare a performance report comparing actual performance to budgeted performance using a flexible budget based on nine salespeople selling 725 new accounts.

c. Discuss when you would expect to see the report prepared in (*a*) used and when you would expect to see the report in (*b*) used.

P 6–30: Magee Inc.

Magee Inc. pays its sales manager a bonus of $10,000 if the manager meets the sales quota. The sales manager can exert either high effort or low effort. The additional disutility of the manager in exerting high effort relative to low effort to meet the sales quota is $1,500. Management can set a tight quota that is extremely difficult to achieve even with a great deal of effort, a loose quota that is achieved easily, or a medium-tight quota. The probability of achieving the sales figure under each quota is summarized in the accompanying table.

Probability of Achieving Quota

	Loose Quota	*Medium-Tight Quota*	*Tight Quota*
High effort	0.90	0.60	0.30
Low effort	0.60	0.40	0.25

The sales manager can either achieve the sales quota or not. Because each quota affects the total number of units sold and thus the gross margin earned by the firm, the following table outlines the gross margin earned by the firm when each quota is reached and is not reached.

Gross Margin of Achieving Quota

	Loose Quota	*Medium-Tight Quota*	*Tight Quota*
Quota achieved	$50,000	$70,000	$73,000
Quota not achieved	20,000	40,000	43,000

Should management set a loose, medium-tight, or tight quota?

SOURCE: R Magee, *Advanced Managerial Accounting* (New York: Harper & Row, 1986), pp. 286–87.

P 6–31: James Marketing Campaign

James, Inc., a large mail-order catalog firm, is thinking of expanding into Canada. The Buffalo district office would manage the expansion and must decide how much to spend on the advertising campaign. The expansion project will be either successful (S) or unsuccessful (U). The probability of success depends on the amount spent on the advertising campaign. If the project is successful, the gross profit (before advertising) is $1.4 million. If the project is unsuccessful, the gross profit (before advertising) is $100,000. The accompanying table lists how the probability of success varies with the amount of spending on the Canadian venture.

Amount of Advertising (000s)	*Probability of Success (S)*	**Gross Profit (000s)**	
		If Successful	*If Unsuccessful*
$ 10	0.20	$1,400	$100
25	0.21	1,400	100
40	0.22	1,400	100
55	0.23	1,400	100
70	0.24	1,400	100
85	0.25	1,400	100
100	0.26	1,400	100
115	0.27	1,400	100
130	0.28	1,400	100
145	0.29	1,400	100

James, Inc., is a publicly traded firm and its senior managers and shareholders wish to maximize expected net cash flows from this venture. The Buffalo manager receives a bonus of 10 percent of the net profit (gross profit less advertising).

The bonus is paid only if the firm has gross profit net of advertising. If gross profit less advertising is negative, no bonus is paid. The manager wants to maximize her bonus and has private knowledge of how the probability of success varies with advertising.

Required:

a. What advertising level would senior managers choose if they had access to the Buffalo manager's specialized knowledge?

b. What advertising level will the Buffalo manager select, knowing that senior managers do not have the specialized knowledge of the payoffs?

c. If the advertising levels in (*a*) and (*b*) differ, explain why.

Cases

Case 6–1: Artisans Shirtcraft

Background

Artisans Shirtcraft manufactures and sells hand-painted shirts of original design. The company was founded in 1999 by three sisters: Cathy, Linda, and Valerie Montgomery. Shirtcraft started out as a means of financing a hobby; profits from shirt sales were used to pay the cost of supplies. However, word of the sisters' appealing products spread quickly, eventually creating strong and widespread demand for Shirtcraft shirts. By 2003, the year of Shirtcraft's incorporation, the company no longer relied on selling at the occasional crafts fair. It now earned almost all of its revenues through sales to upscale boutiques and department stores. Shirtcraft had grown into a legitimate business, but the hobby mentality remained. The company retained a simple approach that had served it well: Buy quality materials when available at a bargain price and produce them into shirts. At this time, the sisters had a ready market for whatever they could produce.

In 2004, the sisters loosely organized Shirtcraft into three functional areas, each based around a talent at which one of them excelled. Cathy would hunt high and low for the best prices, Linda would oversee the painting of the original designs, and Valerie would sell the shirts and deal with the general annoyances of business administration. No separate departmental financial records were kept.

Demand for Shirtcraft shirts continued to grow. To finance additional production, the company had become increasingly dependent upon debt. By 2007, bankers had become an integral part of life at Shirtcraft. The sisters were devoting themselves primarily to executive administration, leaving most day-to-day operations to hired managers.

By the end of 2009, more than 75 employees were on the payroll. However, some of Shirtcraft's creditors began to get cold feet. Given the sluggish economy, some felt that continued investment in a company such as Shirtcraft would be foolish. In light of the scrutiny under which their industry presently operated, the bankers wondered about the prudence of increased and continued commitment to a company that was virtually devoid of financial controls. The bankers were particularly concerned by Shirtcraft's continuing reliance on the bargain purchase strategy. They thought the company would inevitably vacillate between periods of incurring excessive inventory holding costs for overpurchased materials and periods of lost sales due to underpurchasing. If Shirtcraft wanted the banks to commit long term to a rapidly growing credit line, the sisters would have to demonstrate their willingness to establish organizational structures and controls such as those found in larger companies.

Plan

In April 2010, a plan was established. Three functional areas were organized: purchasing, production, and sales and administration. Purchasing and production would be cost centers, each monitored by comparisons of actual costs to budgeted costs. Compensation for key personnel of the cost centers would be tied to the results of this comparison. The sisters would officially be employees of the sales and administrative department, which would hold final responsibility for all executive and corporate decisions. Key employees of sales and administration would be judged and compensated based on overall firm profitability.

For the 12 months beginning in September 2010, the sisters expected to sell 192,000 shirts at an average price of $23 per shirt. Expenses for the sales and administrative department are estimated at $750,000 for the year. Interest expenses for the period are estimated at $550,000. Incentive pay to the various departments is expected to amount to $75,000 per functional area. Under the plan, all expenses are charged to the individual department that incurs them, except for interest expenses, taxes, and incentive pay. These are treated as corporate profit and loss items. Taxes are expected to be 40 percent of corporate pretax income.

After considerable negotiations between the sisters and the purchasing manager, it was agreed that direct materials costs should average about $7 per shirt if purchases are made based on production department demand. Although this approach results in higher direct materials costs than a bargain purchase strategy, the demand-based purchase strategy is cheaper when opportunity costs such as inventory holding costs and contribution margin forgone due to lost sales are considered. Salaries and other overhead for the purchasing department are expected to amount to $150,000 for the year.

Discussions with the production manager led to estimates that production will use fixed overhead costing $240,000. Production's variable overhead consists wholly of direct labor. An average of 1/2 hour of direct labor, at a cost of $6 per hour, is needed for each shirt.

Previously, financial records were kept only on a corporate level. Under the new plan, cost records, both budgeted and actual, will be kept for each department. Of Shirtcraft's sales, 40 percent are expected to occur during September, October, November, and December. Sales are divided equally between months within each group of months. All costs that do not vary with shirt production are divided equally throughout the year. All monthly purchasing and production are based on that month's orders and are assumed to be completely sold during that month. Only negligible inventory is held.

Required:

a. Considering only costs, prepare budgeted annual and monthly financial statements for purchasing and production. (Assume that production is not responsible for any costs already assigned to purchasing.) Prepare an annual budgeted income statement for Artisans Shirtcraft for the period September 2010 through August 2011. Annual costs for income statement purposes consist of the following:

    Cost of goods sold
    Administrative expenses
    Interest
    Taxes

  All salaries and overhead for purchasing and production are treated as product costs and assigned to individual units. Therefore, these costs should be included in Shirtcraft's annual income statement under cost of goods sold.

b. In general terms, consider the changes in Shirtcraft due to growth. How is the company different from an organizational standpoint? What role do budgeting and cost centers have in attempting to meet the challenges presented by this growth?

SOURCE: G Hurst.

Case 6–2: Scion Corp.

Scion Corp. manufactures earth-moving equipment. Department A303 produces a number of small metal parts for the equipment, including specialized screw products, rods, frame fittings, and some engine parts. Scion uses flexible budgeting. The budget for each line item is based on an estimate of the

TABLE 1 Part Number UAV 672
Budgeting Standards per 100 Parts per Batch

Raw materials	$26.72
Direct labor, salaried	2.5 hours
Direct labor, hourly	3.2 hours
Machine hours	6.3 hours

fixed costs and variable costs per unit of volume for that item. The volume measure chosen for each line item is the one with the greatest cause-and-effect relation to the item. For example, the volume measure for utilities is machine hours, whereas the volume measure for supervision is direct labor hours of hourly employees.

At the beginning of the year, the plant is given an annual production quota consisting of the number of each piece of earth-moving equipment to produce. These equipment quotas are exploded into the total number of parts each department must produce, using data about what parts are required for each unit of equipment. Each department has a detailed set of standards, developed over a number of years, that translate each part produced into the number of machine hours, direct labor hours, raw materials, and so on. Table 1 summarizes the operating results of department A303—specifically, the budgeted cost per batch of 100 parts for part number UAV 672.

Given the production quotas and the detailed set of quantities of each input required to produce a particular part, Department A303's financial budget for the year can be developed. At the end of the year, the actual number of each type of part produced times the budgeting standards for each part can be used to calculate the flexible budget for that line item in the budget. That is, given the actual list of parts produced in Department A303, the flexible budget in Table 2 reports how much should have been spent on each line item. Price fluctuations in raw materials are not charged to the production managers. If low-quality materials are purchased and cause the production departments to incur higher costs, these variances are not charged to the production departments.

The manager of Department A303 does not have any say over which parts to produce. The manager's major responsibilities include delivering the required number of good parts at the specified time while meeting or bettering the cost targets. The two most important components of the manager's compensation and bonus depend on meeting delivery schedules and the favorable cost variances from the flexible budget.

Senior management of the plant is debating the process used each year to update the various budgeting standards. Productivity increases for labor would cause the amount of direct labor per part to fall over time. One updating scheme would be to take the budgeting standards from last year (e.g., Table 1) and reduce each part's direct labor standard by an average productivity improvement factor estimated by senior plant management to apply across all departments in the plant. The productivity improvement factor is a single plantwide number. For example, if the average productivity factor is forecast to be 5 percent, then for part UAV 672 the budgeting standard for "Direct labor, salaried" becomes 2.375 hours (95 percent of 2.5 hours). This is termed "adjusting the budget."

An alternative scheme, called "adjusting the actual," takes the actual number of direct labor hours used for each part and applies the productivity improvement factor. For example, suppose part UAV 672 used an average of 2.6 hours of salaried direct labor last year for all batches of the part manufactured. The budgeting standard for "Direct labor, salaried" for next year then becomes 2.47 hours (95 percent of 2.6 hours).

Under both schemes, last year's actual numbers and last year's budgeted numbers are known before this year's budget is set.

Required:

Discuss the advantages and disadvantages of the two alternative schemes (adjusting the budget versus adjusting the actual).

TABLE 2 Scion Corporation
Machining Department A303 Operating Results for Last Year

	Actual Last Year	Budget* Last Year	Favorable (Unfavorable) Variance
Volume Measures			
Machine hours	238,654	265,000	
Direct labor hours	146,400	152,000	
Parts machined	33,565,268	35,759,000	
Departmental Financial Performance			
Raw materials	$ 8,326,875	$ 8,150,000	$(176,875)
Direct labor, salaried	1,546,729	1,643,000	96,271
Direct labor, hourly	1,465,623	1,375,000	(90,623)
Supervision	451,597	460,000	8,403
Maintenance	315,864	325,000	9,136
Engineering	279,780	285,000	5,220
Utilities	69,539	82,000	12,461
Training	85,750	53,000	(32,750)
Factory overhead	188,500	210,000	21,500
Total operating expenses	$12,730,257	$12,583,000	$(147,257)

*Budget reflects expected fixed costs plus variable costs per unit volume times actual volume.

Case 6–3: LaserFlo

Marti Meyers, vice president of marketing for LaserFlo, was concerned as she reviewed the costs for the AP2000 laser printer she was planning to launch next month. The AP2000 is a new commercial printer that LaserFlo designed for medium-size direct mail businesses. The basic system price was set at $74,500; the unit manufacturing cost of the AP2000 is $46,295, and selling and administrative cost is budgeted at 33 percent of the selling price. The maintenance price she planned to announce was $85 per hour of LaserFlo technician time. While the $74,500 base price is competitive, $85 per hour is a bit higher than the industry average of $82 per hour. However, Meyers believed she could live with the $85 price. She is concerned because she has just received a memo from the Field Service organization stating that it was increasing its projected hourly charge for service from $35.05 to $38.25.

The $85 price Meyers was prepared to charge for service was based on last year's $35.05 service cost. She thought that using last year's cost was conservative since Field Service had been downsizing and she expected the cost to go down, not up. The $35.05 cost still did not yield the 60 percent margin on service that was the standard for other LaserFlo printers, but Meyers had difficulty justifying a higher maintenance price given the competition. With a service cost of $38.25, Meyers knows she cannot raise the price to the customer enough to cover the higher costs without significantly reducing sales. Given the higher cost of the LaserFlo field technicians and the prices charged for maintenance by the competition, she will not be able to make the profit target in her plan.

Background

LaserFlo manufactures, sells, and services its printers throughout the United States using direct sales and service forces. It has been in business for 22 years and is the largest of three manufacturers of high-speed laser printers for direct mailers in the United States. LaserFlo maintains its market leadership by innovating new technology. Direct mail marketing firms produce customized letters of solicitation for bank credit cards, real estate offers, life insurance, colleges and universities, and magazine giveaway contests. Personalized letters are printed on high-speed printers attached to computers that have the mailing information. The printers print either the entire letter or the address and salutation ("Dear Mrs. Jeremy McConnell") on preprinted forms. Direct mail firms have computer systems to manage their address lists and mailings, and LaserFlo printers are attached to the client's computer system.

Direct mail laser printers process very high volumes; a single printer commonly addresses 75,000 letters a day. Hence, LaserFlo printers for direct mail marketers differ from general-purpose high-speed printers. In particular, they have specialized paper transfer mechanisms to handle the often custom, heavy paper; varying paper sizes; and high-speed paper flows. With such high paper flow rates, these printers require regular adjustments to prevent paper jams and misalignments. LaserFlo's nationwide field service organization of about 500 employees maintains these printers.

The standard LaserFlo sales contract contains two parts: the purchase price of the equipment and a maintenance contract for the equipment. All LaserFlo printers are maintained by LaserFlo field service personnel, and the maintenance contract specifies the price per hour charged for routine and unscheduled maintenance. Most of LaserFlo's profits come from printer maintenance. Printers have about a 5 to 10 percent markup over manufacturing and selling cost, but the markup on maintenance has historically averaged about 60 percent.

LaserFlo printers have a substantial amount of built-in intelligence to control the printing and for self-diagnostics. Each printer has its own microcomputer with memory to hold the data to be printed. These internal microcomputers also keep track of printing statistics and can alert the operator to impending problems (low toner, paper alignment problems, form breaks). When customers change their operating system or computer, this often necessitates a LaserFlo service call to ensure that the new system is compatible with the printer. The standard service contract calls for normal maintenance after a fixed number of impressions (pages); for example, the AP2000 requires service after every 500,000 pages are printed. Its microcomputer is programmed to call LaserFlo's central computer to schedule maintenance whenever the machine has produced 375,000 pages since the last servicing.

LaserFlo organization

LaserFlo is organized into engineering, manufacturing, marketing, field service, and administration divisions. Engineering designs the new printers and provides consulting services to marketing and field service regarding system installation and maintenance. Engineering is evaluated as a cost center.

Manufacturing produces the printers, which are assembled from purchased parts and subassemblies. LaserFlo's comparative advantage is quality control and design. Manufacturing also provides parts for field service maintenance. Manufacturing is treated as a cost center and evaluated based on meeting cost targets and delivery schedules. Manufacturing's unit cost is charged to marketing for each printer sold.

Marketing, a profit center, is responsible for designing the marketing campaigns, pricing the printers, and managing the field sales staff. LaserFlo sells six different printers; each has a separate marketing program manager. The six marketing program managers report to Marti Meyers, vice president of marketing, who also manages field sales.

Field sales is organized around four regional managers responsible for the sales offices in their region. Each of the 27 sales offices has a direct sales force that contacts potential customers and sells the six programs. Salespeople receive a salary and a commission depending on the printer and options sold. The salesperson continues to receive commissions from ongoing revenues paid by the account for service. Since ongoing maintenance forms a significant amount of a printer's total profit, the salesperson has an incentive to keep the customer with LaserFlo.

Field service contains the technical people who install and maintain the printers. Headed by Phil Hansen, vice president of field service, field service usually shares office space with field sales in the cities where they operate. Field service is a cost center, and its direct and indirect costs are charged to programs when the printers are serviced. The price charged is based on the budgeted rate set at the beginning of the year. Any difference between the actual amount charged to the programs and the total cost incurred by the field service group is charged to a corporate overhead account, not to the marketing programs.

Administration manages human resources, finance, accounting, and field office leases. It handles customer billing and collections, payroll, and negotiating office space for the field sales and field service people. Administration is evaluated as a cost center. While local office space is managed by administration, the cost of the office space is allocated to the field sales and service groups and included in their budgets and monthly operating statements.

Service contracts

Each LaserFlo printer sold requires a service contract. The AP2000's service contract calls for normal maintenance every 500,000 pages at a price of $0.51 per 1,000 pages. Normal maintenance requires three hours. The typical AP2000 prints 12 million pages per year. Besides normal maintenance (sometimes called *preventive maintenance*), unscheduled maintenance occurs due to improper operator setups, paper jams, system upgrades, and harsh usage of the equipment. Past statistical studies have shown that each normal maintenance hour generates 0.50 unscheduled maintenance hours. Unscheduled maintenance is billed to the customer at the service contract rate of $85 per hour.

When maintenance is performed on a particular machine, the service revenues less field service costs are credited to the marketing manager for that program. All the programs' actual service profits are compared with the plan; they form part of Meyers's performance evaluation. The field salesperson receives a commission based on the total service revenue generated by the account. In evaluating each new printer program, LaserFlo uses the following procedure. Profits from service are expected to create an annuity that will last for five years at 18 percent interest. To evaluate a proposed new printer, the one-year maintenance profits are multiplied by 3.127 to reflect the present value of the future service profits each printer is expected to generate over its life (about five years).

Parts

Any parts used during service are charged directly to the customer and do not flow through field service budgets or operating statements. LaserFlo purchases most of the printers' parts from outside suppliers, and the customer pays only a token markup. Marketing does not receive any revenue, nor is it charged any costs when customers use parts in the service process. The reason for not charging customers a larger markup on parts stems from an antitrust case filed against LaserFlo and other printer companies six years ago. A third-party service company, Servwell, sued the printer manufacturers for restraint of trade, claiming they prevented Servwell from maintaining the printers by only selling replacement parts at very high prices. To prevent other such claims, LaserFlo sells parts at a small markup over costs. Yet Servwell and other third-party service firms have never been able to penetrate LaserFlo's service markets because laser printing technology changes rapidly, and an outside company cannot keep a work force trained to fix the latest products. Besides, each printer usually has at least two engineering modifications each year to fix problems or upgrade the printer or its microcomputer hardware and/or software. An outside service company cannot learn of these changes and provide the same level of service as LaserFlo.

Recent changes in field service

LaserFlo field service had two types of technicians: Tech1 and Tech2. Both were trained to repair electromechanical problems, but Tech2s had more training in electronics and computers to work on the latest, most sophisticated printers.

Field service had been trying to reduce the size of the service force the last few years through voluntary retirements and attrition. As the printers became more sophisticated, they became more reliable. The newer systems had self-diagnosing software that allowed a service technician to call up a customer's printer and run a diagnostic program. Often the problem was solved over the phone line by having a LaserFlo technician make the repair in the software. If a mechanical problem was detected, the technician dispatched a repair person (often a Tech1) with the right part. Also, past customers replaced their older printers with newer ones that required less maintenance. The result was excess capacity in the field staff.

The voluntary retirements over the past few years did not produce the reductions necessary to eliminate the excess capacity. In 2010, field service went through a very large involuntary reduction of its workforce. Through attrition, early retirements, and terminations, LaserFlo reduced the number of technicians by 75, down to 500 budgeted for 2011. The company simultaneously improved the skill level of its remaining field force substantially.

AP2000 sales plan for 2011

Marti Meyers's 2011 sales plan for the AP2000 calls for 120 placements this year and a program profit projection of about $2.5 million based on capitalizing the service income using the 3.127 annuity factor. If she were to raise the service price much above $0.51 per 1,000 pages, LaserFlo would lose sales, which are already ambitious. She called Phil Hansen and raised her concerns with him.

"Phil," she began, "explain to me how you downsized your field personnel, cut some office locations, consolidated inventories, and reduced other fixed costs, yet the price I'm being charged for service increased from $35.05 per hour to $38.25. I thought the whole purpose of the field service reorganization was to streamline and make us more cost competitive. You know that our service costs were out of line with our competitors'. We were planning to charge $85 an hour for the AP2000 service contract. Even at $85 per hour, I would be violating the corporate policy of maintaining a 60 percent markup on service. If I were to follow the 60 percent rule, I would have to charge $87.63 per hour if you had kept your cost to me at $35.05. But with your cost of $38.25 and my price at $85, the margin falls to 55 percent. I already had to get special permission to lower the margin to 59 percent with $35.05."

TABLE 1 **Field Service Projected Hourly Rate for 2011**

Variable Costs		
Tech1*		
Salary & benefits	$ 42,800	
Number	× 175	
Total direct cost of Tech1		$ 7,490,000
Tech2†		
Salary & benefits	$ 54,800	
Number	× 325	
Total direct cost of Tech2		$17,810,000
Total variable cost		$25,300,000
Fixed Costs		
Supervision	$1,475,000	
Occupancy costs	1,864,000	
Utilities	772,000	
Insurance	368,000	
Other	56,000	
Total fixed cost		$ 4,535,000
Total cost		$29,835,000
Number of Tech1	175	
Number of Tech2	325	
Total technicians	500	
Number of technician months	6,000	
Average number of billable hours per month per technician‡	130	
Protected number of billable hours		780,000
Cost per hour projected for 2011		$38.25
Note: Cost per hour in 2010		$35.05

*300 Tech1s in 2010 with salary & benefits of $40,100.

†275 Tech2s in 2010 with salary & benefits of $52,900.

‡Same in 2010.

Hansen replied, "Well, there are a number of issues that you've just raised. Let me respond to a few over the phone now and suggest we meet to discuss this more fully next week when I'm back in the office. In the meantime, I'll send you our projected budget for next year that derived the $38.25 rate. Regarding the key question as to how our hourly rate could go up after downsizing, it's really quite simple. We had a lot of idle time being built into the numbers. People just pretended to be busy. Had we not downsized, the hourly charge would have gone up even more than it did. For example, on the AP2000 that you mentioned, we would have used 3.25 hours per normal servicing had we kept our labor force mix of Tech1s and 2s the same as in 2010. Had we not downsized, our fixed costs in 2011 would have remained the same as they were in 2010, and our variable costs for Tech1s and 2s would have increased to the 2011 amounts because of wage increases and inflation. Let me get you our numbers so you can see for yourself how much progress we've been making."

That afternoon, Meyers received a fax from Hansen's office (see Table 1). In trying to decide how to proceed, Meyers would like you to address the following questions:

a. Calculate the projected five-year profits of an AP2000 using first the $35.05 and then the $38.25 service cost.

b. Why did the field service hourly cost increase? What caused the hourly rate to go from $35.05 to $38.25?

c. Did the reorganization of field service reduce the cost of servicing the AP2000? Calculate what the total annual service cost of the AP2000 would have been had the reorganization not occurred.

d. Identify the various options Meyers has for dealing with the service cost increase and analyze them.

e. Why does LaserFlo make more money on servicing printers than selling them? Does such a policy make sense?

Chapter Seven

Cost Allocation: Theory

Chapter Outline

A central issue in all internal accounting systems is **cost allocation**, the assignment of indirect, common, or joint costs to different departments, processes, or products. The major problem in product costing is whether and how indirect costs (overheads) are allocated to products. The allocation of corporate headquarters costs and service department costs, such as information technology and human resources, is in fact a form of transfer pricing within the firm and is thus an integral part of the organization's architecture described in Chapter 4. This chapter presents a general framework for analyzing cost allocations in all organizations, using the earlier framework of costing for decision making (Chapter 2) and costing for control (Chapter 4).

Consider the following two examples. In the first example, a patient with abdominal pain is admitted to the hospital. After five days, a series of tests, and an operation to remove an ulcer, the patient is discharged. During the patient's stay, she used a variety of services: physicians, nurses, laboratory technicians, food workers, and laundry services. Indirect services include the hospital's admitting and billing offices, building maintenance and security, information technology, and senior hospital administrators.What was the cost of this patient's stay in the hospital? One could just examine the incremental (or marginal) cost of the patient's stay or the "full" cost, including all the indirect services. Calculating the full cost of the patient's stay requires allocating the costs of food workers, laundry services, hospital administrators, and so forth to patients.

In the second example, the drilling department in a manufacturing plant drills holes in the sheet-metal chassis that forms the base for a fax machine. Several types of fax machine chassis are drilled in the department, each with its own configuration and sizes of holes. The drilling department costs consist of labor, tools, supplies, space occupancy (utilities, maintenance, accounting, and plant administration), and accounting depreciation of the drilling machines. Last month, the department drilled 2,100 units of a particular chassis model. What was the "full" cost of drilling holes in this particular type of chassis? Answering this question requires allocating the drilling department costs to each chassis model produced.

Despite different organizational settings, both organizations face a similar problem: allocating a set of costs to a **cost object**. A cost object is a product, process, department, or program that managers wish to cost. In the two examples, a patient and a chassis are the cost objects. Corporate-level R&D expenses are allocated to the Chevrolet division of General Motors because senior executives at General Motors want to assess the total profitability of Chevrolet net of corporate R&D. The Chevrolet division is the cost object. Managers allocate common costs to cost objects for several reasons, including decision making and/or control. The framework developed in Chapters 2 and 4 will be used to illustrate the trade-off between decision management and decision control in designing cost allocations. Since cost allocations are used for multiple purposes, we will again see that no single way of allocating costs is always right or always wrong. Trade-offs must be made in choosing whether and how to allocate a given common cost. As we will see later, exactly how the cost allocation is performed depends on what purposes the allocation serves.

Section A in this chapter describes several different institutional settings and organizations in which cost allocation takes place. Costs are allocated for a variety of reasons, including taxes, financial reporting, cost-based reimbursement, decision making, and control. The various reasons for allocating costs, including organizational control reasons, are described in section B. The incentive effects of cost allocations are further examined in section C. Allocated costs are intended as proxies for certain hard-to-observe opportunity costs. While allocated costs measure the opportunity cost with error, they are much less expensive to compute than opportunity costs.

A. Pervasiveness of Cost Allocations

The vast majority of organizations allocate common costs. A **common cost** arises when a resource is shared by several users. For example, human resource department costs are a common cost because all employees in the firm utilize its services. Hospitals allocate the common costs of shared medical equipment to departments that use it. Telecommunications costs are allocated to users. Purchasing department costs are allocated to products.

Common costs are sometimes called **indirect costs** because they cannot be directly traced to units produced or cost objects precisely because such costs are incurred in providing benefits to several different cost objects. Likewise, "overhead" refers to indirect, common costs. Following general practice, we will use the terms *common costs, indirect costs,* and *overhead* interchangeably.

The terms *cost allocation, cost assignment, cost apportionment,* and *cost distribution* are synonyms. All describe the process of taking a given common cost and dividing it between various cost objects (patients or fax machine chassis). Direct costs do not have to be allocated because they can be directly traced to the cost object. For example, if the firm's intranet is used only by the sales department, then the intranet costs are a direct cost of the sales department. However, if both the sales and the manufacturing departments share the same intranet, the intranet costs are not a direct cost of either department but rather a common cost that must be allocated to the cost objects—the two departments.

Cost allocation requires the following steps:

1. *Define the cost objects.* The organization must decide what departments, products, or processes to cost. For example, intranet users may be defined as cost objects. The cost object is often a subunit of the organization, such as a cost or profit center. Costs are often allocated to subunits to better evaluate the subunit's performance and to assess product-line profitability. Or costs are allocated as a control device.
2. *Accumulate the common costs to be assigned to the cost objects.* Suppose intranet costs are to be assigned to the intranet users. This step requires the identification and accumulation of the common costs such as the cost of the hardware, personnel expenditures, utilities, and software costs of the intranet that will be distributed to the users.
3. *Choose a method for allocating common costs accumulated in step 2 to the cost objects defined in step 1.* An **allocation base**, a measure of activity associated with the pool of common costs being distributed to the cost objects, must be selected. The allocation base to distribute intranet center costs to users can be time used, computer memory, or some combination of these. As discussed later in this chapter, common costs usually are allocated to cost objects using an allocation base that approximates how the cost objects consume the common resources.

For example, to provide e-mail services for its employees a firm incurs expenses of \$575,000 per year consisting of a computer lease (\$273,000), labor (\$195,000), software (\$78,000), and other costs (\$29,000). Four departments use various amounts of disk space for e-mail messages measured in terabytes (trillion characters). Table 7–1 shows disk space usage for the four departments.

Terabytes of storage are used as the allocation base to distribute the annual e-mail cost of \$575,000 to the departments. The allocation rate is \$2,875 per terabyte per year (\$575,000 ÷ 200). Table 7–2 displays the resulting allocated costs to each user.

Most U.S. corporations allocate a significant amount of corporate overhead back to their profit centers. Frequently allocated costs include research and development, distribution expense, income taxes, and finance and accounting costs.

TABLE 7–1 **E-Mail Users of Disk Space**
(in Terabytes of Memory)

Users	*Terabytes of Memory*
Manufacturing	40
Sales	80
Research and development	20
Administration	60
Total	200

TABLE 7–2 **Allocation of Annual E-Mail Cost to User Departments**

Users	*Cost per Terabyte*	*Terabytes of Memory*	*Allocated Cost*
Manufacturing	$2,875	40	$115,000
Sales	2,875	80	230,000
Research and development	2,875	20	57,500
Administration	2,875	60	172,500
Total		200	$575,000

In a survey of large Canadian firms, 70 percent indicated they allocate costs.[1] Of those allocating costs, the primary objective of cost allocation was:

Decision control	42%
Decision making	32
Other purposes:	
Cost determination	19
Overhead recovery	5
Equity or fairness	2

These findings reinforce the relative importance of cost allocations in decision management and control. In fact, in this survey, decision control is more important than decision making. The next three examples illustrate the prevalence of cost allocations in both profit and nonprofit organizations and another role of cost allocations: cost-based reimbursement.

1. Manufacturing Organizations

Cost allocations are quite prevalent in manufacturing. Manufacturers cannot deduct all their manufacturing costs for financial reporting and tax purposes. Rather, they must trace their direct manufacturing costs and allocate their indirect manufacturing costs between units sold and units remaining in inventory. Hence, for calculating cost of goods sold, net income, and inventories, financial reporting and taxes often mandate that indirect manufacturing costs be

[1] A Atkinson, *Intra-Firm Cost and Resource Allocations: Theory and Practice* (Toronto: Canadian Academic Accounting Association, 1987), p. 5.

allocated. Cost allocations also arise whenever the firm has a cost-based reimbursable contract. In this case, the firm's revenues depend on reported costs, including allocated costs. For example, certain government defense contracts are cost based. The contractor's revenues are contractually tied to reported costs. In these circumstances, the contractor has an incentive to allocate as much cost to the government work as is permitted under the terms of the contract. Suppose an aircraft company manufactures both military and commercial aircraft. Military aircraft are produced under a cost-based contract. Subject to the contractual stipulations, the firm has an incentive to find the allocation basis that maximizes the fraction of the president's salary allocated to the military contract.

2. Hospitals

Hospitals rely on reimbursement by the government and by private medical insurance companies. At one time in the United States, these payments depended on the costs reported by the hospital. In some states, nursing home reimbursement under Medicaid is still based on reported costs. Under cost-based reimbursements, cost allocation becomes an important determinant of revenue. For example, suppose a hospital serves two patient populations: poor elderly cases and affluent maternity cases. Suppose the medical costs for the elderly are paid by the government at a fixed amount per case, whereas private insurance companies reimburse the hospital for maternity cases at "cost." Given these patient populations and reimbursement rules, the hospital administrator has an incentive to choose a cost allocation method that loads as much cost as permitted onto the maternity cases in order to maximize revenues. For example, laundry costs can be assigned using various allocation bases: patient days, floor space, nursing hours, and so on. The hospital administrator wants to use the allocation base that allocates as much laundry cost as possible to maternity because this maximizes hospital revenue.

Today, hospital reimbursement in the United States is less tied to reported costs than previously. Hospitals basically are reimbursed at a flat amount for a given medical procedure (diagnostic-related groups, or DRGs). This change in hospital reimbursement rules has reduced the opportunity to maximize hospital revenues using cost allocations.[2]

3. Universities

Universities also allocate costs. A recurring debate at most campuses concerns *indirect cost pools.* Research-oriented universities derive significant revenues from government contracts and grants. Grants from organizations such as the National Science Foundation and the National Institutes of Health pay for basic research. University scientists submit research proposals to a government funding agency describing their experiments, anticipated contribution, and costs of the project. Besides the direct cost of the experiment, the research grant is expected to pay for the indirect costs of research such as building occupancy, library facilities, administration, and security. University research proposals include a reimbursable cost item for such indirect costs. The university estimates the total cost of all indirect expenses attributable to government-sponsored research as well as the total direct costs of government-sponsored research. The ratio of these estimates is the *indirect cost rate,* which varies from 40 to 75 percent across universities. If a cancer researcher seeks \$250,000 of direct cost support for laboratory staff, supplies, and salaries, and the university has a 50 percent indirect cost rate, the grant proposal includes an additional \$125,000 of indirect cost recovery.

---

[2] Many states regulate hospitals by limiting the total revenues a hospital can receive in a given year. For example, the state of Washington places a cap on each hospital's total revenues based on its projected costs for the year and adjusted for actual volume. Such a method has been shown to provide hospital administrators with incentives to bias their forecasted costs in order to increase their budget. See G Blanchard, C Chow, and E Noreen, "Information Asymmetry, Incentive Schemes, and Information Biasing: The Case of Hospital Budgeting under Rate Regulations," *Accounting Review* 61 (January 1986), pp. 1–15.

Managerial Application: The Legacy of the $7 Aspirin

Hospitals routinely justify the prices they charge for services and procedures based on costs. For example, a hospital explains the $7 price for two aspirin tablets as follows:

Two aspirin tablets	$0.012
Direct labor	
Physician	0.500
Pharmacist	0.603
Nurse	0.111
Indirect labor (recordkeeping and orderly)	0.400
Cup	0.020
Shared and shifted costs	
Unreimbursed Medicare	0.200
Indigent care	0.223
Malpractice insurance and uncollectible receivables	0.152
Excess bed capacity	0.169
Other administrative and operating costs	0.242
Product cost	$2.632
Hospital overhead costs @ 32.98%	0.868
Full cost (incl. overhead)	$3.500
Profit	3.500
Price (per dose)	$7.000

While the $7 price of the aspirin might at first appear ridiculous, this is the amount necessary to recover both the direct and indirect costs of prescribing the aspirin, costs that the hospital cannot recover from its other patients, and to provide a profit.

SOURCE: D McFadden, "The Legacy of the $7 Aspirin," *Management Accounting,* April 1990, pp. 38–41.

Universities have an incentive to recover as much indirect cost as possible. Stanford University received about $400 million to support research in 1988, which included about $91 million of overhead costs. A September 14, 1990, *Wall Street Journal* article reported that the federal government claims that Stanford "officials may have engaged in 'fraudulent acts' and made 'false claims' in its billing practices including 'excessive library cost reimbursement' amounting to $30 million to $40 million from 1983 to 1986." In 1991, the president, provost, and chief financial officer of Stanford resigned. The U.S. government reduced Stanford's indirect cost recovery rate from 78 percent to 55.5 percent, which reduced government payments to Stanford by $22 million per year. This Stanford example, while an isolated case, illustrates that cost allocations can at times have serious consequences for organizations and their leaders.

Cost allocations also affect the resources available to the various colleges and departments. Chapter 6 described a university budget system. If each college within the university is treated as a profit center, then cost allocations become relevant. If the business school must operate within a balanced budget, in which revenues equal expenditures plus allocated costs, then the amount of central administration, library, security, or human resource department costs allocated to the business school affects its other spending. A college within the university with positive net cash flows can be "taxed" and these cash flows used to subsidize colleges within the university with negative net cash flows. This is

Historical Application: The Allocation of Overhead Has Been Contentious for Decades

The allocation of overhead has received more attention than any other cost accounting topic and has been a hotly debated problem ever since accountants began recording indirect expenses. One commentator writing in 1916 described the situation as follows:

> Indirect expense is one of the most important of all the accounts appearing on the books of the manufacturer. Methods of handling its [allocation] have given rise to more arguments than the problem of the descent of man. It is the rock upon which many a ship of industry has been wrecked.

SOURCE: C Thompson, *How to Find Factory Costs* (Chicago, IL: A. W. Shaw Co., 1916), p. 105. Quoted by P Garner, *Evolution of Cost Accounting to 1925* (Montgomery, AL: University of Alabama Press, 1954), pp. 170–71.

accomplished by allocating more university overhead to the positive cash-flow colleges and less overhead to the negative cash-flow colleges. These overhead allocations absorb some of the positive cash flows, allowing the president to use other funds that would otherwise have been used to pay the overheads to subsidize the negative cash-flow colleges. Cost allocations are no longer an idle academic speculation in such settings; they often consume a considerable amount of the deans' and central administration's time.

This discussion is not a thorough listing of all cost allocation situations, but it illustrates that cost allocations are important in many types of organizations. Cost allocations can affect real resource utilization and cash flows.

B. Reasons to Allocate Costs

Most organizations allocate costs. However, some responsibility accounting proponents argue that managers should only be allocated a cost if they have some control over that cost. For example, the maintenance department is a cost center. Its budget contains allocated costs such as a charge for office space over which the maintenance manager has no control. Why give the budget center manager a budget and then take some of it back via a cost allocation? Why not just give the manager a smaller budget?

This section describes three possible reasons why organizations allocate costs: external reporting (including taxes), cost-based reimbursements, and decision making and control.

1. External Reporting/Taxes

External financial reports and tax accounting rules require that inventory be stated at cost, including indirect manufacturing costs. For example, inventory includes not only direct labor and direct material but also a fraction of factory depreciation, property taxes, and the salaries of security guards at the factory. Overhead costs, including indirect costs, must be allocated to products. This does not require the firm to use cost allocations for internal reports. To avoid the extra bookkeeping costs of a second set of accounts that exclude the allocated costs, firms use the same accounts internally as externally. However, additional bookkeeping costs would likely be small and offset by the costs of dysfunctional decisions from using the external system for internal operating decisions. Thus, external reporting requirements are not likely to explain the widespread use of cost allocations for internal reporting, such as divisional performance evaluation.

Exercise 7–1

Network Systems (NS) offers telecommunications design and consulting services to organizations. The firm offers two types of contracts to its clients: a cost-plus 25 percent contract and a fixed-fee contract where NS offers a fixed price for the job. For cost-plus contracts, total cost includes both direct costs and indirect overheads. NS completes 10 cost-plus contracts at a

continued

total direct cost of $450,000 and 15 fixed-fee contracts. Revenues collected from the fixed-fee contracts totaled $2,400,000. The total direct cost of the fixed-fee contracts amounted to 75 percent of the collected revenues. NS has indirect overheads of $350,000.

Required:

a. Allocate the indirect overhead of $350,000 to the fixed-fee and cost-plus 25 percent contracts using direct cost as the overhead allocation base.

b. Allocate the indirect overhead of $350,000 to the fixed-fee and cost-plus 25 percent contracts using number of contracts as the overhead allocation base.

c. Should NS allocate overhead using direct cost or number of contracts? Explain why.

Solution:

a. Indirect overhead allocated using direct cost as the overhead allocation base.

	Fixed Fee	*Cost-Plus*	*Total*
Direct cost	$1,800,000*	$450,000	$2,250,000
% of direct cost	80%	20%	100%
Allocated overhead based on direct cost	$280,000	$70,000	$350,000

* 75% × $2,400,000.

b. Indirect overhead allocated using contracts as the overhead allocation base.

	Fixed Fee	*Cost-Plus*	*Total*
Number of contracts	15	10	25
% of contracts	60%	40%	100%
Allocated overhead based on number of contracts	$210,000	$140,000	$350,000

c. Assuming that (1) the only use of overhead allocations is the computation of total cost for pricing cost-plus contracts and (2) the total number of cost-plus contracts is insensitive to the final price, NS should allocate overhead using number of contracts. Using number of contracts leads to $70,000 ($140,000 − $70,000) more indirect costs allocated to the cost-plus contracts and hence to $87,500 (1.25 × $70,000) of additional revenues on these contracts.

2. Cost-Based Reimbursement

Cost-based reimbursement is another reason for cost allocations. Government cost-based contracts and medical reimbursements for cost give rise to cost allocations. The U.S. Department of Defense purchases billions of dollars of goods a year under cost-plus contracts. Most new weapons systems are procured under negotiated contracts in which the producer's revenues are in part a function of reported costs. To help regulate the cost allocations contractors use in government contracts, the federal government established the Cost Accounting Standards Board (CASB). The CASB has issued standards covering the cost accounting period, capitalization of tangible assets, accounting for insurance and pension costs, and the allocation of direct and indirect costs.

The revenues of public utilities such as electric and gas companies are also tied to reported costs. States often grant public utilities exclusive monopolies over service territories.

Managerial Application: Federal Reserve Banks: Reallocating Costs Due to Cost-Based Reimbursements

The Federal Reserve banks in the United States provide several services to their member banks: check-clearing, wire transfers, currency processing, and so forth. The Federal Reserve banks are an agency of the U.S. government, and they are required by law to charge private banks fees for their services. Moreover, the law mandates that these fees be based on all direct and allocated costs. Some of the services provided by the Federal Reserve Banks (check-clearing) are also provided by private, for-profit competitors. Other Fed services (electronic transfer) face little outside competition.

A study found that the Fed shifted the allocation of costs from competitive services and markets to less competitive services. Because the prices charged by the Fed had to be documented based on costs (both direct and indirect), this reallocation of costs from more to less competitive services allowed the Fed to justify charging lower prices in its competitive services and higher prices in its less competitive services. This is an example of how cost-based reimbursement contracts create incentives for managers to design cost allocation schemes that maximize total revenues.

SOURCE: K Cavalluzo, C Ittner, D Larcker, "Competition, Efficiency and Cost Allocation in Government Agencies: Evidence on the Federal Reserve System," *Journal of Accounting Research* (Spring 1998), pp. 1–32.

Historical Application: Incentive Effects of Cost Allocations

James McKinsey, founder of the consulting firm bearing his name, wrote

> [O]ne of the largest items of expense to be allocated in a department store is advertising. The usual method of allocating this to the various departments of the store is on the basis of sales. This practice leads to two undesirable results. First, some departments profit more than others by advertising, since it is devoted to articles sold by some departments much more than to articles sold by other departments. . . . This gives inaccurate (departmental profit) figures. . . . Secondly, if advertising is distributed on the basis of sales, each department head will try to secure as much advertising as possible, since he will feel that each of the other departments must pay part of its cost which results in his department's paying only a small part of the total. He naturally concludes that he must certainly get more benefit from the advertising than it costs him; therefore he will request and urge it. He will be more apt to do this because he knows every other department is seeking advertising, for which his department must pay its proportionate part.

After discussing the allocation of expenses, McKinsey concludes

> [C]are should be exercised to allocate (costs) in such a manner as to attain two results:
>
> 1. Greatest possible accuracy.
> 2. The fixing of responsibility in such a manner that those responsible for the expense will desire to decrease and not to increase it.

McKinsey recognized that cost allocations affect managers' incentives.

SOURCE: J McKinsey, *Budgetary Control* (New York: Ronald Press, 1922), pp. 283–84.

In return, the state regulates the rates the utility can charge customers. In many cases, the regulated prices are based on reported costs, including allocated costs. In public utility regulation, the major issue is deciding how to allocate the common costs of capacity, such as the electricity-generating plant, among the different classes of users (residential versus business customers). In many public utility rate-setting cases, cost allocation is the preeminent issue.

In firms whose revenues depend on reported costs, cost allocations can have a large impact on cash flows. But relatively few firms have revenues contractually based on costs, and cost allocations are prevalent in firms without cost-based revenues. Therefore, the widespread use of cost allocations cannot be explained by the existence of cost-based reimbursement contracts.

3. Decision Making and Control

Decision making and control are the most likely explanation for the prevalence of cost allocations. Cost allocations are an important part of the organization's budget system (by which resources are allocated within the firm) and an important part of the organization's performance evaluation system. Cost allocations change the way decision rights are partitioned within the firm.

Cost allocations change managers' incentives and thus their behavior. For instance, in the university example discussed earlier, the university president constrains the deans of the cash-rich colleges by allocating more costs to them; they receive fewer resources and, therefore, fewer decision rights. Hence, the allocation of more costs to one school and less to another transfers decision rights over the amount of other spending each school can do. Or consider the following example. You are at an expensive restaurant with four friends. Before ordering it is agreed that you will split the bill evenly—equal cost allocations. What are your incentives under this cost allocation method? Overconsumption. With equal cost allocation, you only bear $0.20 of each additional dollar you eat and drink. The other $0.80 of your incremental consumption is paid by your colleagues. Likewise, you pay 20 percent for each of your friends' bill. Hence, each of you has an incentive to spend more than you would had you agreed upon separate checks. The simple solution is for everyone to pay for only what they consume. But this requires either separate bills (which servers dislike) or one of you to calculate each person's actual cost. This illustrates that how the bill is allocated affects how the parties will order. Cost allocations affect behavior.

Consider another example. Suppose a firm is studying installing an expensive information system that managers throughout the firm will use to help them make better decisions and provide better customer service. Neither senior management nor the system designers have the specialized knowledge of each user's demand or the value to be derived from using the proposed system. The users must reveal this knowledge during the design phase. If users know that before the system is installed they will not be charged for it, they will request too large a system and overutilize it once it is built.

Once the system is installed and users are allocated the cost of the system based on usage, they will tend to underutilize the system if it has excess capacity. (Allocated cost is an average cost transfer price that is likely above the marginal cost.) So the transfer price that elicits the efficient use of the system (marginal cost) is less than what the users are charged. Therefore, in deciding whether to use cost allocations for the new information system, managers must balance the efficiency of system acquisition against the efficiency of system utilization.[3]

The next section elaborates on the various organizational reasons for allocating costs.

Concept Questions		
	Q7–1	What are some of the reasons for allocating costs?
	Q7–2	Describe some ways cost allocations can affect cash flows.

[3] S Sunder, *Theory of Accounting and Control* (Cincinnati, OH: South-Western Publishing 1997), pp. 55–56.

C. Incentive/Organizational Reasons for Cost Allocations[4]

1. Cost Allocations Are a Tax System

Cost allocations act as an internal tax system. Like a tax system, they change behavior. For example, consider a computer company with 38 branch offices around the world. Each branch is treated as a profit center and is thus evaluated on total sales less expenses. The branch manager chooses the number of salespeople and the local advertising and promotion budget. The firm incurs substantial R&D, distribution, and administration expenses. Should these costs be allocated to the 38 sales offices?

To understand how cost allocations act as a tax, suppose the branch manager's decision is simplified to choosing how much to spend on salespeople and how much to spend on local advertising. Table 7–3 summarizes the various combinations of salespeople required to sell \$10 million of computers per month. Salespeople cost \$4,000 per month, and a standard ad costs \$2,000. To sell \$10 million of computers a month, the manager can hire 30 salespeople and buy 182.57 ads or can hire 31 salespeople and buy 179.61 ads. More salespeople require fewer ads to produce the same level of sales. Likewise, more ads require fewer salespeople to yield the same sales.

To select the combination of salespeople and advertising, the branch manager will choose the one that minimizes total costs. Therefore the cost of the first combination is

$$30 \times \$4{,}000 + 182.57 \times \$2{,}000 = \$485{,}140$$

Likewise, the cost of the second combination is

$$31 \times \$4{,}000 + 179.61 \times \$2{,}000 = \$483{,}220$$

The cost of the second allocation is less than the first combination, so it is preferred. From Table 7–3, we see that 40 salespeople and 158.11 ads is the lowest cost combination needed to produce \$10 million of sales per month. The calculations so far do not involve any cost allocations.

Suppose corporate expense is allocated based on the number of salespeople. In particular, for each salesperson in the branch, that branch is allocated \$1,000 of corporate overhead. The branch manager's reported costs for the first combination now becomes

$$30 \times \$4{,}000 + 182.57 \times \$2{,}000 + 30 \times \$1{,}000 = \$515{,}140$$

The first combination is \$30,000 more expensive than the earlier one before cost allocations.

The "price" the branch manager now "pays" for salespeople includes both the wage (\$4,000) and the overhead rate (\$1,000). The last column in Table 7–3 calculates the total cost of each combination including the \$1,000 cost allocation per salesperson. With cost allocations, the lowest cost combination consists of 34 salespeople and 171.5 ads. This combination has six fewer people but 13.39 more ads. With cost allocations, the branch manager uses more advertising and fewer salespeople than when there was no overhead allocation. The branch manager uses less of the now relatively more expensive input, salespeople, and more of the relatively cheaper input, advertising.

The overhead rate, \$1,000, is a tax on salespeople (labor). Like all taxes on consumption items (such as beer, gasoline, and cigarettes), the tax discourages use of the item levied with the tax. Overhead rates and cost allocations are de facto tax systems in firms. The factor input used as the allocation base is being taxed (salespeople in the example). The tax also "distorts" the price of the factor input. Instead of viewing the price of labor as

[4] This section is based on J Zimmerman, "The Costs and Benefits of Cost Allocations," *Accounting Review* 54 (July 1979), pp. 504–21.

TABLE 7–3 **Number of Salespeople and Amount of Advertising before Cost Allocation Required to Sell $10 Million of Computers per Month**

Number of Salespeople	*Number of Standard Advertisements*	*Total Cost (before allocations)*	*Total Cost (after allocations)*
30	182.57	$485,140	$515,140
31	179.61	483,220	514,220
32	176.78	481,560	513,560
33	174.08	480,160	513,160
34	171.50	479,000	513,000
35	169.03	478,060	513,060
36	166.67	477,340	513,340
37	164.40	476,800	513,800
38	162.22	476,440	514,440
39	160.13	476,260	515,260
40	158.11	476,220	516,220
41	156.17	476,340	517,340
42	154.30	476,600	518,600

$4,000 per month, the branch manager sees the price for salespeople as $5,000 ($4,000 + $1,000) per month. If the opportunity cost of salespeople is $4,000, but the branch manager is charged $5,000 (including the $1,000 of overhead), the manager will employ too few salespeople.

There are two important lessons from this example. Compared with no allocations, cost allocations

- Reduce the manager's reported profits.
- Change the mix of factor inputs; less of the input taxed by the overhead is used (salespeople), and more of the untaxed factor inputs are used (advertising).

Senior managers and their accountants want to distort the price of salespeople by allocating costs if the price of salespeople is not the total cost to the firm of salespersons. Taxing salespeople induces operating managers to use fewer salespeople. Cost allocations also change the pattern of other incentives within the firm. Each of these reasons is explored in more detail below.

2. Taxing an Externality

One reason for taxing the use of salespeople in the computer company example is that the cost of another salesperson is really not $4,000 per month, but something larger: $4,000 includes all the direct costs of the salesperson: wages, medical benefits, payroll taxes, pensions, and the like. But it does not include the indirect costs of the human resource office, which hires the person, maintains records, and administers benefits. It does not include the legal costs the firm incurs when employees are injured on the job or sue the firm for other reasons. Nor does $4,000 per month include the data processing costs, security costs, and other overhead costs required to support the additional salesperson. It does not include the **externalities** the sales department imposes on other parts of the organization by hiring an additional salesperson.

Externalities in economics are costs or benefits imposed on other individuals without their participation in the decision and without compensation for the costs or benefits imposed on them. The price of an apple compensates the growers and distributors for providing the apple; there are no externalities. But the apple's price does not pay for the refuse

FIGURE 7–1
Total cost of human resource department

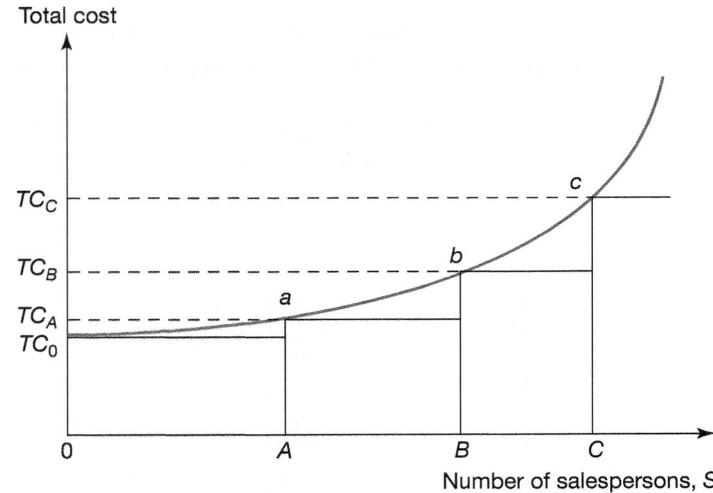

collection if the apple core is discarded on the street and someone else has to pay to cart it away. Similarly, the price paid for a lawnmower does not reflect the annoyance to the neighborhood of the noise it makes when in use. Discarding an apple core on the street and using a lawnmower cause externalities. If the apple's purchase price includes a sales tax that helps pay the municipality's cost of street cleaning and refuse collection, then the apple's disposal cost has been paid for.

Externalities can be positive or negative. Pollution is a **negative externality**. Automobile exhaust pollutes the air, yet car drivers do not pay for the costs they impose on others by their pollution (except via gasoline taxes). The consumers of polluted air are not compensated directly for the pollution they consume. Education contains a **positive externality** in that people derive benefits from having more educated citizens with whom to interact. Well-manicured lawns of private homes create positive externalities as people pass and enjoy the sight and property values of neighboring homes are increased.

When the computer company branch manager hires an additional salesperson, a negative externality is imposed on the firm. More human resources, security, and legal services will be demanded. Buying another personal computer that sits on a desk imposes few significant externalities. But adding an additional employee who consumes human resource and security services and who can sue the firm and steal property imposes externalities that are not captured in the direct cost (or price) of this newly hired person. Employees' direct cost consists of wages, payroll taxes, and benefits. The opportunity cost externalities are very difficult to estimate, especially when the employee is hired. But one way to handle this externality is to tax it via a cost allocation, like the sales tax on the apple.

Cost allocation can be used to approximate these hard-to-observe externalities. Consider the case of the human resource department of a sales division. The human resource department maintains the records and answers employee questions regarding retirement and medical benefits. The human resource department is represented by the step function in Figure 7–1. Total human resource department costs behave as a step function that depends on the number of salespeople, *S*, employed in the sales division. The scale of the human resource department is added in fixed increments rather than in a smooth, continuous curve.

When the firm is small, it is spending TC_0 on the human resource function. This spending remains constant until the number of salespeople reaches *A*. Then a larger human resource department is required and spending is increased. The human resource department is expanded at *A* because as salespeople are added between 0 and *A*, the service provided to

Managerial Application: Examples of Externalities within Organizations

Positive Externalities

- Customer purchases of particular items are entered into a database by point-of-sale terminals. These data allow market research into customer buying habits and better-designed marketing programs.
- If the group at Microsoft responsible for Vista improves the software, this has a positive effect on the demand for other Microsoft products.

Negative Externalities

- The purchasing department, trying to reduce costs, purchases substandard raw materials. More manufacturing labor is required to produce acceptable final products.
- Suppose some managers wish to use Macintosh computers, while others wish to use Microsoft vista PCs. The lack of a uniform standard imposes a series of costs on the firm: File exchange is more difficult, helping each other learn to operate new software/hardware is impeded, and technical service is more costly since consultants must know both operating systems.
- In a law firm, if the lawyer handling a client's divorce does a poor job, this lowers the client's perceived quality of the entire law firm. This negative quality externality reduces this client's demand for other law services of this firm (e.g., taxes, wills, and estates) and lowers the demand for the law firm by other clients if the dissatisfied client complains to friends.

each employee is degraded. More employees are sharing a fixed amount of service. The firm acquires additional human resource department capacity when the cost of the degraded service exceeds the cost of the additional capacity.

The total cost of the human resource department is the smooth curve. The cost reported by the accounting system is the step function. The difference is the opportunity cost of the degraded service. This service degradation in the human resource department is an exterality created by hiring an additional employee. For example, suppose the human resource department is responsible for advertising openings and screening job applicants. The department is spending $500,000 a year on these functions, and on average it takes two weeks to place an ad and identify potential employees. The firm has grown and more position openings now occur. These additional openings cause the average delay to increase to three weeks. If the additional week's delay is imposing opportunity costs on the firm in excess of the cost of hiring another person to process job openings, another human resource employee should be hired. Before hiring the new human resource person, the total cost of the human resource department is the reported cost plus the cost of the additional week's delay in staffing positions in the firm.

The shape of the total cost varies across departments. The particular shape of the curve drawn in Figure 7–1 is chosen to illustrate the general analysis and is not intended to represent how overhead costs vary in general.

Focusing only on the accounting costs (the step function in Figure 7–1) would lead to the conclusion that the opportunity cost in the human resource department of an additional salesperson was zero, unless the salesperson just happened to be at a step. But the opportunity cost in the human resource department of an additional salesperson is the slope of the smooth

FIGURE 7–2
Total cost of human resource department: Relation between overhead rate and marginal cost (overhead allocation dominates no allocation)

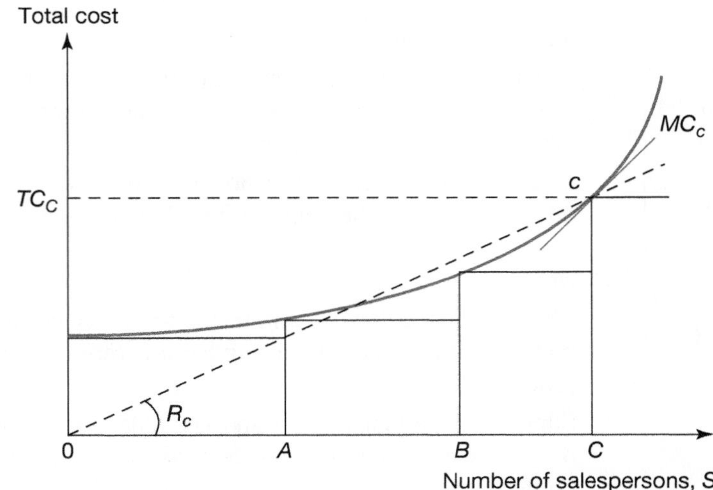

curve. The slope of the smooth curve represents the incremental delay cost in the human resource department imposed on the rest of the firm by adding one more salesperson.

Should human resource department costs be allocated back to the branch manager to tax the manager for the externality of degraded service in the human resource department caused by the branch manager's hiring an additional salesperson? It depends on the exact shape of the total cost curve and where the firm happens to be on the curve. There are three cases to consider.

Case 1 (Figure 7–2)
At point *c*, the overhead rate, R_c, is

$$R_c = \frac{TC_C}{C} < MC_c$$

MC denotes the marginal cost in the human resource department and is the slope of the smooth curve. The slope of the line from the origin through point *c* is the overhead rate at point *c*, R_c. The slope of this line, R_c, is the average cost of the human resource department when there are *C* salespeople. The slope of this line is not as steep as the marginal cost line at point *c* (solid line). At point *c*, or whenever $R < MC$, the cost allocation rate, which is the average cost, understates the marginal cost of the externality. Whenever the average cost (the cost allocation rate) is less than the marginal cost of the human resource department, using a cost allocation to tax the externality is better than no allocation. With no allocation, the branch manager will not attach any cost to the externality imposed on other parts of the firm when salespeople are hired. Since $R_c < MC_c$, the branch manager does not "pay" the entire marginal cost of the externality. Nonetheless, some tax is better than no tax. Whenever a service department's average cost is less than its marginal cost, allocating the service department costs strictly dominates not allocating them. Each user should be charged the marginal cost, *MC*, but the firm does not know this number without special studies. However, average cost is easily approximated as the ratio of accounting cost divided by salespeople.

Case 2 (Figure 7–3)
At point *b*, the overhead rate, R_b, is

$$R_b = \frac{TC_B}{B} = MC_b$$

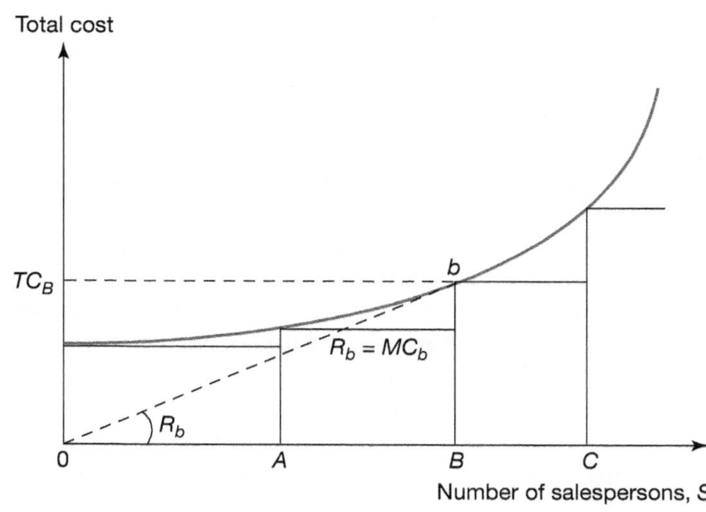

FIGURE 7–3
Total cost of human resource department: Relation between overhead rate and marginal cost (cost allocation equals marginal cost)

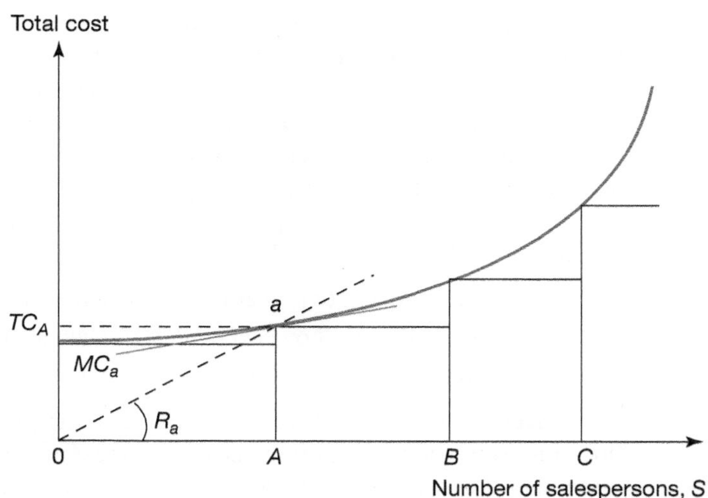

FIGURE 7–4
Total cost of human resource department: Relation between overhead rate and marginal cost (no allocation may dominate cost allocation)

The slope of the line from the origin through point b is the average cost of the service department when B salespeople are employed. The slope of this line also happens to be the marginal cost of adding one more employee. At this point the cost allocation rate (the average cost) and the marginal cost are equal. It is highly unlikely that the firm will be operating at this point. But if it is, cost allocations perfectly mimic the correct opportunity cost. Clearly, if the firm happens to be at point b, it should allocate overhead, because the overhead rate is exactly equal to the marginal cost in the human resource department of hiring one more salesperson. Unfortunately, there is no guarantee that the firm will be at point b.

Case 3 (Figure 7–4)

At point a, the overhead rate, R_a, is

$$R_a = \frac{TC_A}{A} > MC_a$$

The slope of the line from the origin through point a is the overhead rate at point a, R_a. Again, R_a is the average cost of the human resource department when there are A salespeople.

The slope of this line is steeper than the marginal cost at point *a* (solid line). At point *a*, or wherever $R > MC$, the cost allocation rate overstates the marginal cost of the externality. Taxing the branch manager R_a might cause too large a reduction in salespeople. Whenever $R > MC$, cost allocations might do more harm than good. For example, suppose the overhead rate, R, on an additional salesperson is \$2,000, yet the externality from degraded service of hiring the person is \$100. Suppose the additional profit from hiring the salesperson is \$55,500 and her wages and benefits are \$55,000. The profit-maximizing sales manager will not hire the person because the additional profit of \$55,500 is less than the reported accounting costs of \$57,000 (or \$55,000 + \$2,000). However, the actual opportunity cost of \$55,100 is less than the benefits. Therefore (unlike in Case 1, in which the firm should always allocate overhead), we cannot unambiguously demonstrate that human resource costs should be allocated in Case 3.

The analysis presented in Figures 7–1 through 7–4 demonstrates that situations do exist where allocating overhead is better than not allocating. Whenever average cost is less than marginal cost, the costs allocated are less than the marginal cost incurred by the firm. Although the firm is not allocating enough cost, it is probably better to impose some tax than no tax on the managers who cause human resource department costs to rise. Unfortunately, a simple rule such as "always allocate" or "never allocate" does not exist. The allocation decision depends on the exact shape of the cost curve of the overhead department and where the firm is on the curve. It also depends on whether other inputs are allocated and the relation among inputs. The only guidance, without more knowledge of the cost structure, is to consider allocating whenever marginal cost is above average cost; if marginal cost is below average cost, allocating may not be a good idea.

While knowledge of marginal costs is often difficult to obtain without special studies, the following facts hold for all cost curves:

1. Marginal cost equals average cost when average cost is at a minimum (point *b*).
2. Marginal cost is above average cost when average cost is increasing (point *c*).
3. Marginal cost is below average cost when average cost is decreasing (point *a*).[5]

Given these relations between average and marginal costs, the firm should consider allocating overhead when average cost is increasing, because in this case we also know that marginal cost is always above average cost. Hence, the decision to allocate or not does not require knowledge of marginal costs, but of whether the average cost is falling or rising as output expands.

To summarize, cost allocations are average costs and are a proxy for difficult-to-observe marginal costs. This is an example of using cost allocations to improve decision making. However, some care should be exercised in using cost allocations as internal taxes. In some situations, the cost allocation rate can be significantly larger than the marginal cost of the externality (Case 3). Allocating costs in this case might cause managers to reduce consumption of the allocation base (say, direct labor) by too much. Firm profits might fall more if they underutilize salespeople than if they overutilize salespeople when there is no allocation of human resource department costs.

The allocation base chosen often determines whether firm value is enhanced or harmed by cost allocation. Suppose a service department's output can be directly metered to the user

[5]Consider average and marginal baseball batting averages. If a professional baseball player has a season batting average of .300 and has two at-bats and gets one hit and one strike-out, his marginal batting average that day is .500 and his season's batting average rises. If he strikes out both times at bat, his marginal batting average for the day is .000 and his seasonal average falls.

in the same way that a power department measures electric consumption using electric meters. A reasonably accurate "cost" per unit of service can be established. However, the more indirect the measure of consumption, the less useful is the cost allocation because the allocated cost bears less relation to opportunity cost. For example, if power consumption is allocated based on floor space instead of on meter readings, the consuming departments have no incentive to conserve electricity, only to reduce square footage.

Often allocation bases are chosen that have the greatest association with the cost being allocated. Rent is allocated based on square footage. Advertising and data processing are allocated using the time spent on the responsibility center. Allocating advertising and marketing expense using the time marketing personnel spend on the marketing for the responsibility center reminds the manager of the responsibility center that marketing is not free. Cost allocations also affect managers' incentives in other ways, which are discussed next.

3. Insulating versus Noninsulating Cost Allocations

As discussed at the beginning of this chapter, a common cost arises when some resource—and hence its cost—is shared by several users; human resource department costs are a common cost. Suppose two distinct manufacturing divisions share a common plant location and share common costs, including property taxes, security costs, grounds and building maintenance, and human resource department costs. One division manufactures computer modems and the other assembles computer disk drives. Although the two divisions share a common building, each is treated as a separate profit center.

Two questions arise:

1. Should the common costs be allocated to the two divisions?
2. If so, how should they be allocated?

The following discussion assumes that both profit center managers' compensation is based on accounting profits, which have deducted any allocated common cost. That is, cost allocations affect the managers' welfare. If common costs are not allocated, the managers in the two divisions have less incentive to invest in the specialized knowledge necessary to determine the optimum level of the common costs. If the decision rights over the level of common costs do not reside with the managers of the two divisions and the common costs are not allocated back to the two divisions, the division managers will always be demanding more common resources. If these managers individually or collectively have the decision rights over the common resources but are not charged for the common costs, these costs will grow rapidly as the managers invent ways to substitute off-budget common costs for currently consumed factor inputs that are included in their budget. For example, security guards are a common cost. Suppose security costs are not charged to either division. The division managers have an incentive to use security guards to perform maintenance or even operate machines, thereby reducing the amount of direct labor charged to each division's budget.

Most firms allocate common costs, presumably to prevent individual divisions from overconsuming the common resource. The next task is choosing an allocation base. Choosing an allocation base causes it to be taxed and, as demonstrated earlier, managers will reduce their consumption of the taxed item. But this creates other incentives. Consider the following illustration.

Suppose our two manufacturing divisions have a significant amount of interaction: They hire from a common local workforce, they use common shippers, and they deal with the same set of government officials for building permits, air quality standards, and safety standards. Ideally, the two division managers should cooperate with each other. However, within their firm, they are probably competitors, vying for the same promotion. If one division does poorly, it might enhance the other manager's chances when a promotion opportunity arises.

TABLE 7–4 Noninsulating and Insulating Cost Allocation Methods ($000s)

	January		February	
	Modem Division	*Disk Drive Division*	*Modem Division*	*Disk Drive Division*
A. Noninsulating Method				
Division profits before allocation	$8,000	$8,000	$8,000	$2,000
Allocated common costs*	(500)	(500)	(800)	(200)
Net income	$7,500	$7,500	$7,200	$1,800
B. Insulating Method				
Division profits before allocation	$8,000	$8,000	$8,000	$2,000
Allocated common costs†	(600)	(400)	(600)	(400)
Net income	$7,400	$7,600	$7,400	$1,600

*Common costs are allocated based on actual division profits before allocated costs.

†Common costs are allocated based on square footage. The modem division has 60 percent of the square footage.

Cost allocations can promote or discourage cooperation between the two managers, depending on the type of allocation method. With an **insulating allocation**, the costs allocated to one division do not depend on the operating performance of the other division. With a **noninsulating allocation**, the allocated costs of one division do depend on the other division's operating performance. For example, our two divisions share the same factory building and both are profit centers. Assume that the common costs of the shared factory space are $1 million per month. In January and February, the computer modem division has profits of $8 million before allocations. The disk drive division has profits of $8 million in January and $2 million in February. If common costs are allocated using actual profits, then profits after cost allocations for one division depend on the performance of the other division, as illustrated in Table 7–4. This is a noninsulating cost allocation.

In part A of Table 7–4, common costs of $1 million per month are allocated based on actual profits. The modem division has the same level of division profits before allocation each month: $8 million. Yet its profits after cost allocation are smaller by $300,000 in February. This reduction occurs because the modem division is allocated more common costs when the disk drive division's profits fall; at the same time, the disk drive division receives lower allocated costs.

In Table 7–4, part A's allocation method is noninsulating because each division's allocation depends on the performance of the other. An insulating allocation method is presented in part B of Table 7–4 in which common costs are allocated using floor space. The modem division has 60 percent of the floor space and is therefore allocated $600,000 of common costs. To the extent that floor space does not vary with performance, at least in the short run, the performance of one division is not affected by the other division's performance. In the long run, if one division expands floor space relative to the other, it will receive a larger fraction of the common costs. Using floor space to allocate the common costs insulates each division's profits from the performance of the other division.

Noninsulating systems can use sales or head count (employment) instead of profits. Either of these allocation bases will cause one division's profits to vary with the actual results of the other division. Insulating allocation systems use predetermined allocation rates that do not vary with actual results.

Both insulating and noninsulating methods give the division managers an incentive to economize on common costs. The noninsulating method (Table 7–4, part A) provides each division manager with incentives to increase the other division's profitability, thereby increasing the other division's share of the common costs. In this sense, noninsulating allocations create incentives for mutual monitoring and cooperation by managers. Noninsulating cost allocations are examples of cost allocations used for control purposes.

The disadvantage of a noninsulating method is that it distorts the performance measure of one division by tying it to another division's performance. Some argue that managers should be held responsible for only those cost items over which they have decision rights and hence control. (This controllability principle was discussed in Chapter 5.) In the above example, the common costs are jointly controllable by both managers. If there is a large interaction effect between the two managers in that one can significantly affect the other's performance, then each manager is held responsible for the other's performance through a noninsulating allocation method.

While noninsulating allocations distort the performance measure by basing one division's share of overhead on another division's performance, they can reduce the risk managers bear. Suppose two divisions are affected by random events outside their control. Moreover, suppose these random events affecting the two divisions are not perfectly positively correlated. If one division has an unusually unfavorable random shock, the other division is unlikely to have such an adverse shock and will absorb more overhead in that period. The division with the adverse shock will absorb less overhead and will show a larger profit after common costs are allocated than it would if an insulating allocation method were used. Likewise, a highly favorable random event in one division is likely to occur when the other division does not have such a good period. The division with the good fortune will absorb more overhead, and its performance measure will not be as large as it would if overhead were allocated using an insulating method.

Noninsulating methods act like shock absorbers for random events and reduce the variability of all managers' performance measures. If managers were risk-neutral, such risk sharing would not matter. Variations in allocated costs due to noninsulating allocations wash out over time. And since a risk-neutral manager does not care about variability, the lower risk imposed by noninsulating cost allocation does not matter. But decreased variability does matter to risk-averse managers. Noninsulating methods reduce the variability of their performance measures.[6]

In the previous example, the two divisions shared common factory resources and controlled the level of common costs. Now consider corporate headquarters expenses, such as the president's staff expenditures. The divisions do not have decision rights over the level of corporate headquarters expenses, but noninsulating allocations still create incentives for mutual monitoring. Although they cannot directly control the level of the costs being allocated, subordinate managers can pressure senior management to control staff growth.

To summarize the discussion,

1. Common costs should be allocated for decision making and control whenever the marginal cost of a common resource, such as the human resource department, is equal to or greater than the resource's reported average cost.

---

[6]As long as the random events are not perfectly positively correlated, then noninsulating methods diversify some of the risk managers bear. The analysis is a straightforward application of portfolio theory as to why risk-averse investors want to hold a diversified portfolio of securities.

2. Common costs should be allocated using an allocation base that does not insulate subunits whenever interactions among the subunits are high and cooperation is important. If interaction is unimportant, an allocation base should be chosen that does not fluctuate with other subunits' performance.
3. Noninsulating cost allocations can reduce the risk managers bear by diversifying that risk across other managers.

Concept Questions

Q7–3	How do cost allocations act as a tax system?
Q7–4	Define *externality* and give an example of one.
Q7–5	What is the difference between a positive and a negative externality?
Q7–6	How are externalities reduced within a firm?
Q7–7	Describe the three cases to consider when determining if a cost allocation is beneficial.
Q7–8	Should common costs be allocated?
Q7–9	Describe how a noninsulating allocation promotes cooperation among managers and encourages mutual monitoring.
Q7–10	Why would senior managers want to distort factor prices by using cost allocations?

D. Summary

Cost allocations pervade all organizations. Managers allocate costs for a variety of reasons, including: financial reporting, taxes, cost-reimbursement contracts, and government regulation. But it appears that many organizations allocate costs for decision making and control. The important lessons from this chapter are

1. Cost allocations act as an internal tax on the factor input being used as the allocation base. And, like taxes in general, cost allocations change managers' incentives and hence the decisions they make.
2. Certain inputs, used to produce the firm's goods or services, notably labor, impose externalities on the firm in the sense that when more of that input is used, other costs in the firm also rise. Managers and their accountants will want to tax that input if its reported cost does not fully reflect its cost plus the externality it generates. The way to tax the input is to use it as the allocation base for allocating some other cost to the manager with the decision rights over the taxed input. For example, labor can be taxed by allocating corporate overhead to departments based on the number of employees in each department.
3. Costs can be allocated in ways that increase or decrease managers' mutual monitoring and cooperation with each other. Noninsulating cost allocations increase mutual monitoring and coordination; insulating methods do the opposite.
4. Noninsulating cost allocations can reduce the risk managers face. For example, if a division's profits are unusually low, fewer costs are allocated to this division, thereby softening the full impact of the lower profits. Hence, noninsulating allocations induce risk-sharing among managers and can diversify the risk borne by managers.

Self-Study Problem

Fitzhugh Investors

Fitzhugh Investors sells, manages, and operates three mutual funds: Money Market, Blue Chip, and Fixed Income. Each fund's prospectus specifies a schedule of fees payable to Fitzhugh Investors for its services. The company derives all of its revenue from two fees. The first fee Fitzhugh receives from each fund is based on the net assets in the fund. The second fee is based on the number of accounts. Table 1 itemizes the fee structure for each fund.

Each fund is operated as a separate line of business, incurring avoidable direct expenses for sales and administration, fund management, and transfer agency functions (brokerage fees, maintaining customer accounts, and safekeeping securities). Additionally, the funds employ several common corporate resources, such as a Web site, computer facilities, telephone representatives, security analysts, and corporate staff. Fitzhugh Investors allocates these corporate expenses to the respective funds based on the number of accounts. Corporate expenses total $2,595,000. Management estimates that closing any one fund could avoid $125,000 and any two funds $200,000 of the corporate expenses. Table 2 presents the direct expenses for each fund.

Required:

a. Prepare an income statement that shows the direct expenses and the allocated corporate expenses by mutual fund for Fitzhugh.

b. Fitzhugh's managers are reviewing the income statement prepared in part (*a*). Some of the funds are reporting a loss. What actions should management take?

Solution:

a. Revenues of each fund are composed of the asset-based fee times the net assets plus the per-account fee times the number of accounts. Corporate expenses are allocated based on the number of accounts.

TABLE 1 **Fitzhugh Investors Product Line Summary Data**

	Money Market	*Blue Chip*	*Fixed Income*	*Total Funds*
Asset-based fees	0.75%	1.75%	1.25%	—
Per-account fee	$25	$8	$9	—
Net assets (millions)	$1,050	$1,150	$1,824	$4,024
Accounts (thousands)	275	110	185	570

TABLE 2 **Fitzhugh Investors Direct Expenses by Fund**

	Money Market	*Blue Chip*	*Fixed Income*
Sales and administration	$ 2,696,000	$2,332,000	$ 6,838,000
Fund management	1,400,000	2,750,000	1,800,000
Transfer agency	10,465,000	7,224,000	18,911,000

FITZHUGH INVESTORS
Net Income by Fund Both Before and After
Allocated Corporate Expenses

	Money Market	*Blue Chip*	*Fixed Income*	*Total Funds*
Revenues				
Asset-based fees	$ 7,875,000	$20,125,000	$22,800,000	$50,800,000
Per-account fees	6,875,000	880,000	1,665,000	9,420,000
Direct Expenses				
Sales and administration	2,696,000	2,332,000	6,838,000	11,866,000
Fund management	1,400,000	2,750,000	1,800,000	5,950,000
Transfer agency	10,465,000	7,224,000	18,911,000	36,600,000
Gross profit	$ 189,000	$ 8,699,000	$ (3,084,000)	$ 5,804,000
Corporate expense	1,252,000	501,000	842,000	2,595,000
Net income (loss)	$(1,063,000)	$8,198,000	$(3,926,000)	$ 3,209,000

b. Based on the current accounting system, the money market and fixed income funds are reporting losses after allocating corporate expenses. If the money fund is closed, Fitzhugh does not avoid losing $1,063,000 because this includes allocated corporate expense. Only $125,000 of corporate expense is avoided by closing one fund. The money fund is generating $189,000 of gross profit before corporate expenses. If this fund is eliminated, Fitzhugh forgoes $189,000 of cash flow but saves only $125,000. Thus it should not eliminate the money fund.

The fixed income fund is losing over $3 million before any corporate expense is allocated. Therefore it appears that if this fund is closed, Fitzhugh would save this loss plus corporate expenses of $125,000.

However, the preceding analysis fails to account for the positive externalities associated with having related funds. Exchange privileges between the funds—specifically, the ability to shift money across funds—are valued by investors. Before dropping the fixed income fund, Fitzhugh must consider how many blue chip and money market accounts such action would sacrifice now and in the future. An accounting system such as Fitzhugh's offers no real way of assessing the impact of such externalities.

Problems

P 7–1: MRI

Magnetic resonance imaging (MRI) is a noninvasive medical diagnostic device that uses magnets and radio waves to produce a picture of an area under investigation inside the body. A patient is positioned in the MRI and a series of images of the area (say, the knee or abdomen) is generated. Radiologists then read the resulting image to diagnose cancers and internal injuries. The MRI at Memorial Hospital has the following projected operating data for next year.

	Fixed Cost	*Variable Cost*	*Total Cost*
Equipment lease	$350,000		$350,000
Supplies		$ 97,000	97,000
Labor	145,000	182,000	327,000
Hospital administration	63,000		63,000
Occupancy	48,000		48,000
Total projected costs	$606,000	$279,000	$885,000
Number of images			33,600
Number of hours			2,800

Memorial Hospital serves two types of patients: elderly, whose hospital bills are covered by governments (state and federal reimbursement), and other patients who are covered by private insurance (such as Blue Cross and Blue Shield). About one-third of Memorial's patients are elderly. Elderly patients using MRI services normally require more time per MRI image. The typical elderly patient requires one hour of MRI time to produce the 10 MRI images needed for the radiologist. Other patients only require about 45 minutes per patient to generate the 10 MRI images.

Governments reimburse MRI imaging based on the reported cost by the hospital. Reimbursable costs include both the fixed and variable costs of providing MRIs. Private insurers reimburse MRI imaging based on a standard fee schedule set by the insurance company. These fee schedules are independent of the hospitals' cost of providing MRI services.

Required:

a. Calculate Memorial Hospital's projected cost per MRI image.

b. Calculate Memorial Hospital's projected cost per hour of MRI time.

c. Suppose a typical elderly patient at Memorial Hospital requires 10 MRI images and takes one hour of MRI time. Calculate the cost of providing this service if Memorial Hospital calculates MRI costs based on cost per image.

d. Suppose a typical elderly patient at Memorial Hospital requires 10 MRI images and takes one hour of MRI time. Calculate the cost of providing this service if Memorial Hospital calculates MRI costs based on cost per hour of MRI time.

e. Should Memorial Hospital calculate the cost of MRI services based on the cost per image or the cost per MRI hour? Explain why.

P 7–2: Slawson

Slawson is a publicly traded Argentine company with three operating companies located in Argentina, the United States, and Germany. Slawson's corporate headquarters in Buenos Aires oversees the three operating companies. The annual cost of the corporate headquarters, including office expenses, salaries, and legal and accounting fees, is 2.4 million pesos. The following table summarizes operating details of each of the three operating companies.

	Argentina	*United States*	*Germany*
Number of employees	1,500	300	200
Net income (loss) in pesos (millions)	(100)	400	500

Required:

a. Allocate the 2.4 million pesos corporate headquarters cost to the three operating companies using number of employees in each operating company.

b. Allocate the 2.4 million pesos corporate headquarters cost to the three operating companies using net income of each operating company as the allocation base.

c. Discuss the advantages and disadvantages of allocating corporate headquarters costs using (1) employees and (2) net income.

P 7–3: The Corporate Jet

A large corporation maintains a fleet of three 30-passenger corporate jets that provide (weather permitting) daily scheduled service between Detroit and several cities that are home to its production facilities. The jets are used for business, not personal, travel. Corporate executives book reservations through a centralized transportation office. Because of the limited number of seats available, the planes almost always fly full, at least in the nonwinter months. Excess demand for seats is assigned by executive rank within the firm. The executive's budget is charged for the flight at the end of the month. The charge is based on the jet's total operating expenses during the month (including fuel, pilot's salary and fringes, maintenance, licensing fees, landing fees, and 1/12 of the annual accounting depreciation) divided by the actual passenger miles logged in the month. This rate per passenger mile is multiplied by each passenger's mileage flown in the month.

Required:

a. Describe the formula being used to calculate the cost per passenger mile flown.

b. As passenger miles flown increases, what happens to the cost per passenger mile?

c. Describe what causes the monthly charge per passenger mile flown to fluctuate.

d. What other problems are present in the current system and what improvements do you suggest making?

P 7–4: Massey Electronics

Massey Electronics manufactures heat sinks. Heat sinks are small devices attached to solid-state circuit boards that dissipate the heat from the circuit board components. Made of aluminum, the devices consist of many small fins cut in the metal to increase its surface area and hence its ability to dissipate the heat. For example, Intel Pentium and Celeron processors are first mounted onto heat sinks and then attached to circuit boards. These processors generate heat that will ultimately destroy the processor and other components on the circuit board without a heat sink to disperse the heat.

Massey has two production facilities, one in Texas and the other in Mexico. Both produce a wide range of heat sinks that are sold by the three Massey lines of business: laptops and PCs, servers, and telecommunications. The three lines of business are profit centers, whereas the two plants are cost centers. Products produced by each plant are charged to the lines of business selling the heat sinks at full absorption cost, including all manufacturing overheads. Both plants supply heat sinks to each line of business.

The Texas plant produces more complicated heat sinks that require tighter engineering tolerances. The Texas workforce is more skilled, but also more expensive. The Mexico plant is larger and employs more people. Both facilities utilize a set of shared manufacturing resources: a common manufacturing IT system that schedules and controls the manufacturing process, inventory control, and cost accounting, industrial engineers, payroll processing, and quality control. These shared manufacturing overhead resources cost Massey $9.5 million annually.

Massey is considering four ways to allocate this $9.5 million manufacturing overhead cost pool: direct labor hours, direct labor dollars, direct material dollars, or square footage of the two plants. The following table summarizes the operations of the two plants:

	Texas	*Mexico*
Direct labor hours	3,000,000	4,000,000
Direct labor dollars	$60,000,000	$40,000,000
Direct material dollars	$180,000,000	$200,000,000
Square footage	200,000	300,000

Massey has significant tax loss carryforwards due to prior losses and hence expects no income tax liability in any tax jurisdiction where it operates for the next five years.

Required:

a. Prepare a table showing how the $9.5 million would be allocated using each of the four proposed allocation schemes (direct labor hours, direct labor dollars, direct material dollars, and square footage of the two plants).

b. Discuss the advantages and disadvantages of each of the four proposed allocation methods (direct labor hours, direct labor dollars, direct material dollars, and square footage of the two plants).

P 7–5: Avid Pharmaceuticals

Avid, a small, privately held biotech pharmaceutical manufacturing firm, specializes in developing and producing a set of drugs for rare classes of cancers. Avid has two divisions that share the same manufacturing and research facility. The two divisions, while producing and selling two different classes of products to different market segments, share a common underlying science and related manufacturing processes. It is not unusual for the divisions to exchange technical know-how, personnel, and equipment. The following table summarizes their most current year's operating performance:

	Division A	*Division B*
Number of employees	80	20
Plant square footage (000)	80	120
Revenues (000)	$2,000	$1,000
Operating expenses (000)	600	500
Operating profits (000)	$1,400	$ 500

Avid's corporate overhead amounts to $900,000 per year. Management is debating various ways to allocate the corporate overhead to the two divisions. Allocation bases under consideration include: number of employees, plant square footage, revenues, operating expenses, and operating profits. Each division is treated as a separate profit center with each manager receiving a bonus based on his or her division's net income (operating profits less allocated corporate overhead).

Required:

a. For each of the five proposed allocation bases, compute Division A's and Division B's net income (operating income less allocated corporate overhead).

b. Recommend one of the five methods (or no allocation of corporate overhead) to allocate corporate overhead to the two divisions. Be sure to justify your recommendation.

P 7–6: Wasley

Wasley has three operating divisions. Each manager of a division is evaluated on that division's total operating income. Managers are paid 10 percent of operating income as a bonus.

The AB division makes products A and B. The C division makes product C. The D division makes product D. All four products use only direct labor and direct materials. However, a fixed (unavoidable) $1,784 corporate overhead is applied to each division (or product) based on direct labor dollars. In the following operating income statement for the first quarter of the year all numbers are in 000s.

	Income Statement			
	Product A	*Product B*	*Product C*	*Product D*
Net sales	$1,250	$850	$1,250	$1,650
Direct labor	450	600	540	640
Direct materials	250	0	125	160
Corporate overhead				

Required:

a. Allocate the corporate overhead and compute divisional operating income (after allocating corporate overhead) for each of the three divisions.

b. One day the manager of the AB division, Shirley Chen, announces that starting in the second quarter she will be discontinuing product B (replacing it with nothing and letting the labor go, cutting all direct costs attributable to the product). She reasons that product B is losing money for her division and the company. Recompute first-quarter operating income for both division AB and the corporation without division AB's product B (as though the manager had already dropped product B).

c. Is Shirley Chen, the manager of the AB division, better off this way? Why or why not?

d. Is the corporation better off this way? Why or why not?

e. What problems do you see with the reporting/evaluation/incentive system currently in place?

SOURCE: Charles Kile.

P 7-7: Hallsite Imaging

Hallsite Imaging produces hardware and software for imaging the structures of the human eye and the optic nerve. Hallsite systems are in most major medical centers and leading ophthalmology clinics. Hallsite has three divisions: Hardware, Software, and Marketing. All three are profit centers, and the three divisional presidents are compensated based on their division's profits. The Hardware Division produces the equipment that captures the images, which are then viewed on desktop PCs. The Software Division produces the software that runs on both Hallsite imaging equipment and the users' PCs to view, manipulate, and manage the images. Hallsite hardware only works with the Hallsite software, and the software can only be used for images captured by Hallsite hardware.

The Marketing Division produces the marketing materials and has a direct sales force of 1,000 Hallsite people that sells both the hardware and software in the United States (Hallsite operates only in the United States). To assess the profits of the Hardware and Software Divisions, the costs of the Marketing Division are allocated back to the Hardware and Software Divisions based on the revenues of the two divisions. The following table summarizes the divisional sales and divisional expenses (before allocation of Marketing Division costs) for the Hardware and Software Divisions for last quarter and this quarter. (All figures are in millions of dollars.)

	Last Quarter		**This Quarter**	
	Hardware Division	*Software Division*	*Hardware Division*	*Software Division*
Revenue	$500.00	$700.00	$510.00	$400.00
Division expenses	315.00	308.00	321.30	176.00

The Marketing Division reported divisional costs of $320 million last quarter and $370 million this quarter.

Required:

a. Allocate the Marketing Division's costs to the Hardware and Software Divisions for last quarter and this quarter.

b. Calculate the Hardware and Software Divisions' profits for this quarter and last quarter after allocating the Marketing Division's expenses to each division.

c. After receiving her division's profit report for this quarter (which included the Hardware Division's share of the Marketing Division's costs), the president of the Hardware Division called Hallsite's chief financial officer (whose office prepared the report) and said, "There must be something wrong with my division's profit report. Hardware's sales rose and our expenses were in line with what they should have been given last quarter's operating margins. But my profits tanked. Now I know that there was a major problem with Software's new version 7.0 that hurt new sales of upgrades to version 7.0 and required more Marketing resources to address our customers' concerns with this new software. But why am I getting hammered? I didn't cause the software problems. My hardware continues to sell well because version 6.8 of the software still works great. This is really very unfair."

Write a memo from Hallsite's chief financial offer to the Hardware Division president explaining that the Hardware Division's current quarter profit report (which includes the Division's share of the Marketing expenses) is in fact correct and outlining the various rationales as to why Hallsite allocates the Marketing Division's expenses to the other two divisions.

P 7–8: Jolsen International

Jim Shoe, chief executive officer of Jolsen International, a multinational textile conglomerate, has recently been evaluating the profitability of one of the company's subsidiaries, Pride Fashions, Inc., located in Rochester, New York. The Rochester facility consists of a dress division and a casual wear division. Daneille's Dresses produces women's fine apparel, while the other division, Tesoro's Casuals, produces comfortable cotton casual clothing.

Jolsen's chief financial officer, Pete Moss, has recommended that the casual wear division be closed. The year-end financials Shoe just received show that Tesoro's Casuals has been operating at a loss for the past year, while Daneille's Dresses continues to show a respectable profit. Shoe is puzzled by this fact because he considers both managers to be very capable.

The Rochester site consists of a 140,000-square-foot building where Tesoro's Casuals and Daneille's Dresses utilize 70 percent and 30 percent of the floor space, respectively. Fixed overhead costs consist of the annual lease payment, fire insurance, security, and the common costs of the purchasing department's staff. Fixed overhead is allocated based on percentage of floor space. Housing both divisions in this facility seemed like an ideal situation to Shoe because both divisions purchase from many of the same suppliers and have the potential to combine materials ordering to take advantage of quality discounts. Furthermore, each division is serviced by the same maintenance department. However, the two managers have been plagued by an inability to cooperate due to disagreements over the selection of suppliers as well as the quantities to purchase from common suppliers. This is of serious concern to Shoe as he turns his attention to the report in front of him.

	Tesoro's Casuals ($000s)	*Daneille's Dresses ($000s)*
Sales revenue	$ 500	$1,000
Expenses:		
Direct materials	$(200)	$ (465)
Direct labor	(70)	(130)
Selling expenses (all variable)	(100)	(200)
Overhead expenses:		
Fixed overhead	(98)	(42)
Variable overhead	(40)	(45)
Net income before taxes	$ (8)	$ 118

Required:

a. Evaluate Pete Moss's recommendation to close Tesoro's Casuals.

b. Should the overhead costs be allocated based on floor space or some other measure? Justify your answer.

SOURCE: R Drake, J Olsen, and J Tesoro.

P 7–9: Winterton Group

The Winterton Group is an investment advisory firm specializing in high-income investors in upstate New York. Winterton has offices in Rochester, Syracuse, and Buffalo. Operating as a profit center, each office receives central services, including information technology, marketing, accounting, and payroll. Winterton has 20 investment advisors, 7 each in Syracuse and Rochester, and 6 in Buffalo. Each investment advisor is paid a fixed salary, a commission based on the revenue generated from clients, plus 2 percent of regional office profits and 1 percent of firm profits. One of the senior investment advisors in each office is designated as the office manager and is responsible for running the office. The office manager receives 8 percent of the regional office profits instead of 2 percent.

Regional office expenses include commissions paid to investment advisors. The following regional profits are calculated before the 2 percent profit sharing. Firm profits are the sum of the three regional office profits.

This table summarizes the current profits per office after allocating central service costs based on office revenues.

WINTERTON GROUP
Profits by Office
Current Year (Millions)

	Rochester	*Syracuse*	*Buffalo*
Revenue	$16.00	$14.00	$20.00
Operating expenses	(12.67)	(11.20)	(16.30)
Central services*	(1.92)	(1.68)	(2.40)
	$ 1.41	$ 1.12	$ 1.30

*Allocated on the basis of revenue.

The manager of the Buffalo office sent the following e-mail to the other office managers, the president, and the chief financial officer:

> One of the primary criteria by which all cost allocation schemes are to be judged is fairness. The costs allocated to those bearing them should view the system as fair. Our current system, which allocates central services using office revenues, fails this important test of fairness. Receiving more allocated costs penalizes those offices generating more revenues. A fairer, and hence more defensible, system would be to allocate these central services based on the number of investment advisors in each office.

Required:

a. Recalculate each office's profits before any profit sharing assuming the Buffalo manager's proposal is adopted.

b. Do you believe the Buffalo manager's proposal results in a fairer allocation scheme than the current one? Why or why not?

c. Why is the Buffalo manager concerned about fairness?

P 7–10: National Training Institute

Five departments of National Training Institute, a nonprofit organization, share a rented building. Four of the departments provide services to educational agencies and have little or no competition for their services. The fifth department, Technical Training, provides educational services to the business community in a competitive market with other nonprofit and private organizations. Each department is a cost center. Revenues received by Technical Training are based on a fee for services, identified as tuition.

All five departments have dedicated space as listed in the accompanying table. Common shared space, including hallways, restrooms, meeting rooms, and dining areas, is not included in these allocations. National Training Institute rents space at $10 per square foot.

Allocation Table

Department	*Square Footage*	*Percentage of Space*	*Revenue*
Administration	13,500	9.0%	$ 3,600,000
Support services	46,500	31.0	11,000,000
Computer services	12,000	8.0	8,800,000
Technical training	6,000	4.0	1,900,000
Transportation	72,000	48.0	4,700,000
Total allocated	150,000	100.0%	$30,000,000
Common space	50,000		

In addition to its assigned space, the technical training department offers training during off-hours using many of the areas allocated to other departments. Technical Training also uses off-site facilities for the same purpose. About 50 percent of its training activities are in off-site facilities, which have excess capacity, charge no rent, and are available only during off-hours.

John Daniels, the administration department's business manager, proposed a rental allocation plan based on each department's percentage of dedicated square footage plus the same percentage of the common space. The technical training department would be charged an additional amount for the space it uses during off-hours that is dedicated to other departments. This additional amount would be based on planned usage per year.

Jane Richards, director of technical training, claims this allocation method will cause her to increase the price of services. As a result, she will lose business to competition. She would rather see the allocation method use the percentage of department revenue in relation to total revenue.

Required:

Comment on Daniels's and Richards's proposed rent allocation plans. Make appropriate recommendations.

SOURCE: C Lewis, M Dohm, R Bakel, M Mucci, and R Stern.

P 7–11: Encryption, Inc.

Encryption, Inc. (EI), sells and maintains fax encryption hardware and software. EI hardware and software are attached to both sending and receiving fax machines that encode/decode data, preventing anyone from wiretapping the phone line to receive a copy of the fax.

Two EI product groups (Federal Systems and International) manufacture and sell the hardware and software in different markets. Both are profit centers. Federal Systems contracts with federal government agencies to manufacture, install, and service EI products. Existing contracts call for revenues of $1 million per quarter for the next eight quarters.

International is currently seeking foreign buyers. Expected quarterly revenues will be $1 million, but with equal likelihood revenues can be $1.5 or $0.5 million in any given quarter.

Federal Systems and International each have their own products that differ in some ways but share a common underlying technology. Fax encryption is a new technology and offers new markets. Transferring manufacturing and marketing ideas across products and customers provides important synergies.

The variable cost of Federal Systems and International is 50 percent of revenues. The only fixed cost in EI is its Engineering Design group.

Engineering Design is EI's R&D group. It designs new hardware and software that Federal Systems and International sell. Quarterly expenses for Engineering Design will be $0.60 million for the next two years. These expenses do not vary with revenues or production costs.

Engineering Design costs are to be included in calculating profits for the Federal Systems and International groups. Two ways of assigning the Engineering Design costs to Federal Systems and International are (1) group revenues, and (2) an even 50–50 split.

Required:

a. Prepare financial statements for Federal Systems and International illustrating the effects of the alternative ways of handling Engineering Design costs.

b. Which method of assigning Engineering Design costs do you favor? Why?

P 7–12: Ball Brothers Purchasing Department

The purchasing department of Ball Brothers purchases raw materials and supplies for the various divisions in the firm. Most of the purchasing department's costs are labor costs. The costs of the purchasing department depend on the number of items purchased. The manager of the purchasing department estimates how her department's costs will vary with different levels of demand by the divisions. The following table provides her estimates of how the costs of purchasing vary with the aggregate number of items purchased by all divisions.

Number of Items Purchased per Week	*Total Cost per Week*
100–199	$1,000
200–299	1,100
300–399	1,200
400–499	1,400
500–599	1,700
600–699	2,100
700–799	2,600
800–999	3,200

In deriving this table, the manager of purchasing projects expanding the size of the department in order to keep roughly constant the time to purchase an item and the quality of the purchasing department's services at all levels of demand placed on the department. That is, if the department is processing 750 items per week, it will provide the same quality of services given a budget of $2,600 as it would processing 250 items per week given a budget of $1,100.

Required:

a. Suppose the purchasing department is currently purchasing 610 items per week. Should the department's costs of $2,100 per week be allocated back to the divisions, making the purchases at a charge of $3.44 per item purchased ($2,100 ÷ 610)? Explain why or why not.

b. Suppose the purchasing department is currently purchasing 210 items per week. Should the department's costs of $1,100 per week be allocated back to the divisions, making the purchases at a charge of $5.23 per item purchased ($1,100 ÷ 210)? Explain why or why not.

c. Reconcile (explain) why your answers to (*a*) and (*b*) are either the same or different.

P 7–13: Telstar Electronics

Telstar Electronics manufactures and imports a wide variety of consumer and industrial electronics, including stereos, televisions, camcorders, telephones, and VCRs. Each line of business (LOB) handles a single product group (e.g., televisions) and is organized as a profit center. The delivery of the product to the wholesaler or retailer is handled by Telstar's distribution division, a cost center. Previously, Telstar was organized functionally, with manufacturing, marketing, and distribution as separate cost centers. Two years ago, it reorganized to the present arrangement.

Distribution assembles products from the various LOBs into larger shipments to the same geographic area to capture economies of scale. The division is also responsible for inbound shipments and storage of imported products. It has its own fleet of trucks, which handles about two-thirds of the shipments, and uses common carriers for the remainder. Currently, the costs of the distribution division are not allocated to the LOBs, but LOBs do pay the cost for any special rush shipment using an overnight or fast delivery service, such as Federal Express or UPS. For example, if a customer must have overnight delivery, the LOB ships directly without using Telstar's distribution center and the LOB is charged for the special delivery.

The corporate controller is mulling over the issue of allocating the costs of distribution. Several allocation schemes are possible:

1. Allocate all distribution division costs based on gross sales of the LOBs.
2. Allocate all distribution division costs based on LOB profits.
3. Allocate the direct costs of each shipment (driver, fuel, truck depreciation, tolls) using the gross weight of each LOB's product in the shipment. Then allocate the other costs of the distribution division (schedulers, management, telephones, etc.) using the total direct shipping costs assigned to each LOB.

One argument against allocating is that it will distort relative profitability. The controller says, "Because allocations are arbitrary, the resulting LOB profitabilities become arbitrary." Another argument is that it is not fair to charge managers for costs they cannot control. LOBs cannot control shipping costs. For example, there are savings when two small separate shipments are combined into a single large shipment. LOBs will tend to avoid opening up new sales territories when other Telstar products are not being shipped to that area.

Required:

Write a memo addressing the controller's concerns. Should Telstar begin allocating distribution costs to the LOBs? If so, which allocation scheme should it use?

P 7–14: Diagnostic Imaging Software

Diagnostic Imaging Software (DIS) is the leading producer of imaging software for the health sciences. DIS develops, writes, produces, and sells its software through two direct selling organizations: North America and South America. Each of these direct selling forces is evaluated and rewarded as profit centers. The remaining world sales of DIS software are handled through independent distributors in Europe, Asia, and Africa. DIS has a software development group that designs, writes, and debugs the software before turning it over to the direct sales organizations (North and South America) and the independent distributors who then sell the software. The cost of designing, writing, and debugging the software is $12 million this year.

The following table presents the income statements of the two divisions (millions of $) for this year:

	North America	*South America*
Revenues	$17.800	$6.700
Operating expenses*	5.340	3.015
Profit before software development cost	$12.460	$3.685

*Does not include any costs of developing, writing, or debugging the software.

Senior management of DIS wants to allocate the software costs to the two direct-selling forces in order to evaluate and reward their performance.

Required:

a. Calculate the profits of the two direct selling organizations (North and South America) after allocating the software costs of $12 million based on the relative revenues of the two organizations. (Round all decimals to 3 significant digits.)

b. Calculate the profits of the two direct selling organizations (North and South America) after allocating the software cost of $12 million based on the relative profits before software development cost of the two organizations. (Round all decimals to 3 significant digits.)

c. Calculate the profits of the two direct selling organizations (North and South America) after allocating the software cost of $12 million where 75 percent of the cost is assigned to North America and 25 percent to South America. (Round all decimals to 3 significant digits.)

d. Discuss the advantages and disadvantages of each of the three allocation methods used in parts (*a*), (*b*), and (*c*) above.

P 7–15: Fuentes Systems

Fuentes Systems provides security software to law enforcement agencies. It has a sales force of 70 and has plans to add another 10–15 salespeople. Fuentes allocates corporate administrative costs based on the number of salespeople. The current total administrative cost of $2,184,000 comprises the costs of the human resources, payroll, accounting, and information technology departments.

You manage the western region of Fuentes Systems with 18 salespeople and you plan to add one or two more salespersons. Each salesperson you hire costs $120,000, which includes salary, benefits, and payroll taxes. If you hire one additional salesperson, you expect that person will generate $185,000 of net operating margin for your region. Net operating margin is revenues less cost of sales and less travel and entertainment expenses associated with that salesperson. Net operating margin does *not* include the salary, benefits, and payroll taxes of the salesperson. If you hire two salespeople, the combined additional net operating margin added to your region is expected to be $323,000. You are evaluated and rewarded as a profit center, where profits are calculated as net operating margin less the total salaries, benefits, and payroll taxes of all salespeople employed in the region, plus allocated corporate administrative costs.

Required:

a. What is the current allocated administrative cost per salesperson?

b. Assuming that your hiring of additional salespeople does not alter the allocated cost per salesperson, how many salespersons will you hire in the western region?

c. Suppose that Fuentes hires an additional 10 salespeople, and the total corporate administrative cost rises from $2,184,000 to $2,640,000. Should Fuentes continue to allocate corporate administrative costs to the regions? Explain why or why not.

d. Now suppose that Fuentes hires an additional 10 salespeople and the total corporate administrative cost rises from $2,184,000 to $2,200,000. Should Fuentes continue to allocate corporate administrative costs to the regions? Explain why or why not.

P 7–16: Vorma

Vorma manufactures two proprietary all-natural fruit antioxidant food additives that are approved by the U.S. Food and Drug Administration. One is for liquid vitamins (LiqVita) and the other is used by dry cereal producers (Dry). Both of these products are sold only in the United States, and although they both share common chemistry and manufacturing, their end markets are completely separated. Both are produced in the same plant and share common manufacturing processes, such as purchasing, quality control, human resources, and so forth. These common fixed overhead costs amount to $1,500,000 per month. Each product also has its own directly traceable fixed costs, such as dedicated equipment leases used only by one of the two products, dedicated product engineers, and so forth. The following table summarizes the operations of Vorma for a typical month.

	LiqVita	*Dry*
Units	200,000	75,000
Price per unit	$10	$21
Variable cost per unit	$6	$11
Own fixed costs per month	$90,000	$110,000

Again, the "Own fixed costs" consist of all fixed costs that can be traced directly to one of the two products (LiqVita and Dry), and these costs do not vary with the number of units produced.

Required:

a. Prepare a typical monthly income statement for LiqVita and Dry after allocating the common fixed overhead costs of $1,500,000 per month to the two product lines based on the relative proportions of total variable costs generated by each product.

b. Which of the two products in part (*a*) is the most profitable and which is the least profitable? NOTE: you are not being asked to analyze or explain the relative profitablities of LiqVita and Dry.

c. Vorma is planning to introduce a tablet version of its vitamin into China, with a selling price of $9 and a variable cost per unit of $7. At a price of $9, Vorma managers believe they will sell 950,000 units per month in China. Introducing the new product (called China) will require additional "Own fixed costs" (just for China) of $800,000. As in part (*a*), prepare monthly income statements, computing the monthly net income for the three products (LiqVita, Dry, and China). Allocate the common fixed overhead of $1,500,000 based on the relative proportions of total variable costs generated by each product.

d. As in part (*b*), list the order of the most profitable to least profitable products. Do not do any analysis.

e. Compare the relative profitability of the two products (LiqVita and Dry) before introducing China (part *b*) and after introducing China (part *d*). Analyze and discuss why the relative profitability of the two preexisting products (LiqVita and Dry) does or does not change with the introduction of the new product (China).

P 7–17: Bio Labs

Bio Labs is a genetic engineering firm manufacturing a variety of gene-spliced, agricultural-based seed products. The firm has five separate laboratories producing different product lines. Each lab is treated as a profit center and all five labs are located in the same facility. The wheat seed lab and corn seed lab manufacture two of the five product lines. These two labs are located next to each other and are of roughly equal size in terms of sales. The two departments have close interaction, often sharing equipment and lab technicians. Both use very similar technology and science and usually attend the same scientific meetings.

Recent discoveries have shown how low-power lasers can be used to significantly improve product quality. The wheat seed and corn seed managers are proposing the creation of a laser testing department to employ this new technology. Leasing the equipment and hiring the personnel cost $350,000 per year. Supplies, power, and other variable costs are $25 per testing hour. The testing department is expected to provide 2,000 testing hours per year. The wheat seed manager expects to use 700 testing hours per year of the laser testing department and the corn seed manager expects to use 800 testing hours. The remaining 500 hours of testing capacity can be used by the other three labs if the technology applies or can be left idle for future expected growth of the two departments. Initially, only wheat and corn are expected to use laser testing.

The executive committee of Bio Labs has approved the proposal but is now grappling with how to treat the costs of the laser testing department. The committee wants to charge the costs to the wheat seed and corn seed labs but is unsure of how to proceed.

At the end of the first year of operating the laser, wheat seed used 650 testing hours, corn seed used 900 hours, and 450 hours were idle.

Required:

a. Design two alternative cost allocation systems.

b. Give numerical illustrations of the charges the corn and wheat seed labs will incur in the first year of operations under your two alternatives.

c. Discuss the advantages and disadvantages of each.

P 7–18: World Imports

World Imports buys products from around the world for import into the United States. The firm is organized into a number of separate regional sales districts that sell the imported goods to retail stores. The eastern sales district is responsible for selling the imports in the northeastern region of the country. Sales districts are evaluated as profit centers and have authority over what products they wish to sell and the price they charge retailers. Each sales district employs a full-time direct sales force. Salespeople are paid a fixed salary plus a commission of 20 percent of revenues on what they sell to the retailers.

The eastern district sales manager, J. Krupsak, is considering selling an Australian T-shirt that the firm can import. Krupsak has prepared the following table of his estimated unit sales at various prices and costs. The cost data of the imported T-shirts were provided by World Imports's corporate offices.

WORLD IMPORTS
Eastern Sales District
Proposed Australian T-Shirt
Estimated Demand and Cost Schedules

Quantity (000s)	*Wholesale Price*	*T-Shirt Imported Cost*
10	$6.50	$2.00
20	5.50	2.20
30	5.00	2.50
40	4.75	3.00

The unit cost of the imported shirts rises because the Australian manufacturer has limited capacity and will have to add overtime shifts to produce higher volumes. Corporate headquarters of World Imports is considering allocating corporate expenses (advertising, legal, interest, taxes, and administrative salaries) back to the regional sales districts based on the sales commissions paid in the districts. It estimates that the corporate overhead allocation rate will be 30 percent of the commissions (for every $1 of commissions paid in the districts, $0.30 of corporate overhead will be allocated). District sales managers receive a bonus based on net profits in their district. Net profits are revenues less costs of imports sold, sales commissions, other costs of operating the districts, and corporate overhead allocations.

The corporate controller, who is proposing that headquarters costs be allocated to the sales regions and included in bonus calculations, argues that all of these costs must ultimately be covered by the profits of the sales districts. Therefore, the districts should be aware of these costs and must price their products to cover the corporate overhead.

Required:

a. Before the corporate expenses are allocated to the sales districts, what wholesale price will Krupsak pick for the Australian T-shirts and how many T-shirts will he sell? Show how you derived these numbers.

b. Does the imposition of a corporate overhead allocation affect Krupsak's pricing decision on the Australian T-shirts? If so, how? Show calculations.

c. What are the arguments for and against the controller's specific proposal for allocating corporate overhead to the sales districts?

P 7–19: Painting Department

You are manager of a painting department of a large office complex. The painting department is responsible for painting the buildings' exteriors and interiors. Your performance is judged in part on minimizing your department's operating costs, which consist of paint and labor, while providing a high-quality and timely service.

The job of painting the halls of a particular building is being evaluated. Paint and labor are substitutes. To provide the quality job demanded, you can use less paint and more labor, or more paint and less labor. The accompanying table summarizes this trade-off. Paint costs $10 per gallon and labor costs $6.40 per hour.

Paint (Gallons)	*Labor (Hours)*
50	200
80	125
100	100
125	80
200	50

Required:

a. How much paint and how much labor do you choose in order to minimize the total cost of the hall painting job? (Show calculations in a neatly labeled exhibit.)

b. The accounting department institutes an overhead allocation on labor. For every dollar spent on labor, $0.5625 of overhead is allocated to the paint department to cover corporate overhead items, including payroll, human resource, security, legal costs, and so forth. Now how much labor and paint do you choose to minimize the total accounting cost of the hall painting job? (Show calculations in a neatly labeled exhibit.)

c. Explain why your decisions differ between parts (*a*) and (*b*).

d. Explain why the accounting department might want to allocate corporate overhead based on direct labor to your painting department.

P 7–20: Scanners Plus

Scanners Plus manufactures and sells two types of scanners for personal computers, the Home Scanner and the Pro Scanner. The Home model is a low resolution model for small office applications. The Pro model is a high resolution model for professional use. The two models are manufactured in separate facilities and each model is treated as a profit center. This table summarizes the prices and costs of each model.

	Home Scanner	*Pro Scanner*
Selling price to retailers	$ 1,600	$ 8,800
Variable cost	600	2,800
Fixed cost (annual)	800,000	2,400,000

Both models are sold through large office supply and computer stores and through computer catalogs. The marketing department of Scanners Plus sells both models. It has a direct sales force that sells to retail stores and an advertising group that prepares and places ads in computer magazines and computer catalogs. The annual operating budget of the marketing group is $1,000,000.

The marketing costs can be allocated to the two profit centers in one of two ways: either on the basis of total revenues or on the basis of 24 percent to the Home model and 76 percent to the Pro model.

At a selling price of $1,600, the Home model division projects the number of units it expects to sell next year to be either 1,000 units or 1,400 units, each equally likely. Similarly, at $8,800, either 600 or 800 units of the Pro model are equally likely to be sold. The demand for Pro scanners is independent of the demand for Home scanners. That is, one can be in high demand while the other one can be in either low or high demand.

Required:

a. Calculate total revenues under various scenarios for the Home model.

b. Calculate total revenues under various scenarios for the Pro model.

c. Suppose the marketing department costs of $1 million are allocated to Home and Pro models using the predetermined, fixed proportions of 24 percent to Home and 76 percent to Pro. Prepare a table projecting all the various total profits of Home and Pro after allocating marketing costs using these predetermined rates.

d. Calculate all the possible overhead proportions that can result from allocating the marketing department costs using the revenues in each profit center as the allocation base. (Round all overhead proportions to two significant digits, e.g., 44.67 percent rounds to 45 percent.)

e. Same as in (*c*), except calculate profits for the two profit centers using the overhead rates computed in (*d*).

f. Parts (*c*) and (*e*) asked you to compute divisional profits for the Home and Pro models using two different methods for allocating marketing costs. Comment on the relative advantages and disadvantages of the two methods.

P 7–21: Giza Farms

Giza Farms in Cairo, Egypt, has a corporate headquarters staff and three operating divisions: consulting services, chemicals, and agricultural products. Giza is considering allocating 160 million Egyptian pounds of corporate overhead (which includes salaries and benefits of corporate headquarters staff, advertising, human resources, legal, and so forth) to the three divisions using either divisional revenues or divisional earnings before corporate overhead allocations as the allocation base. (One Egyptian pound is worth about $0.30.) The following table describes the revenues and earnings before corporate overhead allocations for each of the three operating divisions.

GIZA FARMS
Divisional Revenues and Earnings before Corporate Overhead Allocations
(Millions of Egyptian pounds)

	Consulting Services	*Chemicals*	*Agricultural Products*	*Total*
Revenue	250	250	500	1,000
Earnings before corporate overhead allocations	80	50	70	200

Required:

a. Calculate divisional earnings after corporate overhead allocations using divisional revenues as the allocation base.

b. Calculate divisional earnings after corporate overhead allocations using divisional earnings before corporate overhead allocations as the allocation base.

c. Given that overhead will be allocated to the division, should revenue or earnings be the allocation base? Why?

d. After reviewing the data from parts (*a*) and (*b*), all three divisional managers were critical of the decision to allocate corporate overhead, but the manager of agricultural products was particularly outspoken. She said, "This is just another hair-brained scheme of the [expletive deleted]. They have nothing better to do with their time than to push numbers around. We in the divisions have no control over corporate spending and all these allocations do is create dissension among the divisional managers and distort the true relative profitability of the divisions." Respond to the agricultural products manager's remarks.

P 7–22: Allied Adhesives

Allied Adhesives (AA) manufactures specialty bonding agents for very specialized applications (electronic circuit boards, aerospace, health care, etc.). AA operates a number of small plants around the world, each one specializing in particular products for its niche market. AA has a small plant in St. Louis that manufactures aerospace epoxy resins and a larger plant in Atlanta that manufactures epoxies for electronics. Each produces somewhat similar epoxy resins that are sold to different customers. The manufacturing processes of the aerospace and electronic adhesives are quite similar, but the selling processes and the types of customers are very different across the two divisions. The St. Louis plant is being closed and moved to Atlanta to economize on duplicative selling, general, and administrative costs (SGA). Aerospace and Electronics will continue to operate as separate divisions. The following table summarizes the current operations of the two plants:

	Aerospace (St. Louis)	*Electronics (Atlanta)*
Revenue	$16.800	$42.100
Manufacturing cost	8.568	23.155
Manufacturing margin	$ 8.232	$18.945
SGA–variable	5.376	12.630
SGA–fixed	1.900	2.500
Net income	$ 0.956	$ 3.815
Return on sales	5.69%	9.06%

NOTE: Costs in millions.

After Aerospace moves to the Atlanta facility, each division continues to operate as a separate profit center, and neither Aerospace nor Electronics is expected to have its revenues, manufacturing cost, or variable SGA impacted. The only change projected from moving Aerospace to Atlanta is the total fixed SGA will fall from $4.4 million to $3.0 million through elimination of redundant occupancy, administrative, and human resource expenses.

AA evaluates its divisional managers based on return on sales (net income divided by sales).

Required:

a. Prepare separate financial statements reporting *net income* and *return on sales* for Aerospace and Electronics after the move where the expected lower fixed SGA of $3 million is allocated to the two divisions using:
   (1) Revenues as the allocation base.
   (2) Manufacturing cost as the allocation base.
   (3) Manufacturing margin as the allocation base.
   (Round all allocations to the nearest $1,000.)

b. Discuss how moving Aerospace into Atlanta affects the relative profitability of the Aerospace and Electronics divisions.

c. Which of the three possible allocation schemes in part (*a*) will each division manager (Aerospace and Electronics) prefer? Why?

d. Which allocation scheme should AA adopt? Explain why.

e. Should AA be using return on sales as the performance measure for its divisional managers?

P 7–23: Chicago Omni Hotel

The Chicago Omni Hotel is a 750-room luxury hotel offering guests the finest facilities in downtown Chicago. The hotel is organized into four departments: lodging, dining, catering, and retail stores. Each of these departments is treated as a profit center. Lodging is the largest profit center and is responsible for room rental, maids, reservations, main lobby, and bell captains. Dining operates the coffee shop, room service, and three restaurants out of a single kitchen. Catering services is separate from the dining operations. It offers banquet services to large parties, weddings, and business meetings through its own kitchen and staff separate from the dining department's kitchen. However, dining and catering coordinate purchasing and staff scheduling. Retail is responsible for leasing space off the lobby to independent store owners (gift shop, car rental agencies, airline ticket counters, jewelry, flowers, toys, liquor, etc.). There are currently 14 independent stores operating in the hotel. Profit center managers are paid a salary and a bonus. The annual bonus depends on a number of factors, including their unit's profits, customer satisfaction, and employee retention.

The following table presents budgeted operating data for the first year:

	Lodging	*Dining*	*Catering*	*Retail Stores*	*Total*
Revenues ($ millions)	$39.20	$9.80	$5.80	$1.90	$56.70
Separable operating expenses	$31.10	$6.20	$3.50	$0.30	$41.10
Square footage (1,000s)	625	50	125	80	880
Number of employees	1,000	140	35	4	1,179

Besides the separable expenses traced directly to each profit center, the hotel incurs the following additional expenses:

Occupancy costs (interest, taxes, insurance)	$5.6 million
Marketing costs	1.4 million
Administration (accounting, human resource, security, maintenance, and senior management)	1.1 million
Total	$8.1 million

Profit center performance is part of each profit center manager's annual bonus. Also, to evaluate how each department of the hotel is performing, senior management desires a statement calculating a performance measure.

Required:

a. Design a performance report for the Chicago Omni Hotel. Provide a statement calculating the performance of each unit using your performance report format. This statement should calculate for each unit a bottom-line profit/loss, which will be used as part of the performance evaluation and reward systems.

b. Discuss the rationale underlying the design of the performance report you chose.

c. Using your report, discuss the relative performance of each profit center. Which ones are the best and which are the worst?

P 7–24: Plastic Chairs

Plastic Chairs manufactures plastic lawn chairs using a combination of new and recycled plastic. Varying amounts of each type of plastic can be used to produce a batch of 100 chairs. The table below lists the various combinations of recycled and new plastic required to produce one batch of 100 chairs.

Pounds of New and Recycled Plastic Required to Manufacture One Batch of 100 Chairs

Pounds of New Plastic	*Pounds of Recycled Plastic*
20	72
24	60
30	48
32	45
36	40
40	36
45	32
48	30
60	24
72	20

New plastic costs $16 per pound and recycled plastic costs $10 per pound. The manager of the chair manufacturing department receives a bonus based on minimizing the cost per batch of 100 chairs.

Required:

a. What combination of new and recycled plastic will the manager of the chair manufacturing department choose?

b. Overhead (including plant administration, utilities, property taxes, and insurance) is allocated to the chair manufacturing department based on the number of pounds of recycled plastic used in each batch. For each pound of recycled plastic used, the chair manufacturing department is charged $30 of plant overhead. What combination of new and recycled plastic will the manager of the chair manufacturing department select if the manager's bonus is based on minimizing the total cost per batch, which includes new and recycled plastic and plant overhead?

c. Why are your answers to (*a*) and (*b*) either the same or different?

d. Should the plastic chairs manufacturing manager's bonus be based on minimizing only the plastic costs or should it also be based on minimizing plastic costs plus allocated plant overhead?

P 7–25: Woodley Furniture

Woodley Furniture is a small boutique manufacturer of high quality contemporary wood tables. They make two models: end tables and coffee tables in a variety of different woods and finishes. Current annual production of end tables is 8,000 units that sell for $250 and have variable cost of $120 each. Current annual production of coffee tables is 6,000 units that sell for $475 and have variable cost of $285 each. Woodley has fixed costs of $2.4 million. Woodley sells all the tables they produce each year.

Required:

a. Calculate total firmwide profits and product-line profits for the end tables and coffee tables after allocating the fixed costs to the two product lines using sales revenues as the allocation base.

b. Which of the two products is the most profitable based on total profits (after allocating fixed costs)? Is Woodley making an adequate profit?

c. Woodley management decides to add a dining table to its product offerings. The plant currently has excess capacity, so no additional fixed costs are required to produce the dining tables. The new dining table will not affect the number of units sold or prices of the existing coffee and end tables. They expect to sell 4,000 dining tables at a price of $620 each, and variable cost per table is $500. Calculate total firmwide profits and product-line profits for the end tables, coffee tables, and dining tables after allocating the fixed costs to the three product lines using sales revenues as the allocation base.

d. Analyze the profitability of the three products and firm-wide profits calculated in part (*c*) compared to the profitability of the two products alone and firmwide profits in part (*a*).

e. Recalculate your answers to parts (*a*) and (*c*), but, instead of allocating the $2.4 million of fixed costs using sales revenues as in parts (*a*) and (*c*), allocate the $2.4 million of fixed costs using the total contribution margin of each product (total sales revenue less total variable cost).

f. Discuss the relative advantages and disadvantages of using total contribution margin to allocate the fixed costs in part (*e*) relative to using sales revenues to allocate the fixed costs, as in parts (*a*) and (*c*).

P 7–26: Transmation

Transmation, with sales of over $2.2 billion, builds and markets several of the world's leading brands of construction and agricultural equipment. Transmation has three operating divisions that are decentralized investment centers. While the three divisions produce and sell different lines of equipment to different customers, they do share a common R&D platform, corporate brand name, and many of the same marketing strategies, and operate in many of the same international jurisdictions. Currently, each division president is evaluated and rewarded based on the division's return on assets, defined as net income divided by total assets invested in the division. Net income is revenues generated by the division less operating expenses incurred by the division. The table below summarizes Transmation's annual operating results by division ($ millions).

	DIV A	*DIV B*	*DIV C*
Operating expenses	$300	$ 900	$800
Total divisional assets	$500	$ 500	$400
Revenues	$370	$1,050	$950

Required:

a. Calculate each division's ROA.

b. Each of the three Transmation divisions utilizes substantial corporate office resources. These include legal, marketing, information technology, human resources, and research and development. In addition to these corporate level services, Transmation incurs expenses for being a publicly traded firm (accounting, taxes, and the cost of corporate officers and director). These annual corporate-level expenses amount to $270 million, and currently each division is not being charged for these corporate expenses. The divisional operating expenses in the above table do not include any allocation of the $270 million corporate expenses. The corporate chief financial officer (CFO) argues that because each division has roughly equal amounts of total assets, each division should be allocated one-third of the $270 million corporate expenses. Calculate each division's ROA after allocating the corporate expenses using the CFO's proposed scheme.

c. Transmation's chief executive officer (CEO) likes the CFO's idea of allocating the corporate expenses to the divisions, but argues that each division does not consume equal corporate resources. Rather, each division's consumption of the various corporate resources is more likely proportional to the division's operating expenses. The CFO and CEO rule out more elaborate metering systems whereby each corporate resource, such as

HR or IT, would keep track of the time they devote to each division. The CEO and CFO are convinced that such direct metering would be costly and generate much ill will between the divisions and the corporate departments. Calculate each division's ROA after allocating the corporate expenses using the CEO's proposed scheme.

d. Briefly describe how the relative profitability of the three divisions changes across the three scenarios calculated in parts (*a*), (*b*), and (*c*). Do NOT discuss the pros and cons of the various scenarios. Just describe how the numbers change.

e. Now describe the pros and cons of the three allocation scenarios [including part (*a*), where there are no allocations].

f. Which of the three allocation schemes would you recommend, or would you propose an alternative allocation scheme?

P 7–27: BFR Ship Building

BFR is a ship-building firm that has just won a government contract to build 10 high-speed patrol boats for the Coast Guard for drug interdiction and surveillance. Besides building ships for the government, BFR has a commercial vessel division that designs and manufactures commercial fishing and commuting ships. The commercial division and the government division are the only two divisions of BFR, and the Coast Guard contract is the only work in the government division.

The Coast Guard contract is a cost-plus contract. BFR will be paid its costs plus 5 percent of total costs to cover profits. Total costs include all direct materials, direct labor, purchased subassemblies (engines, radars, radios, etc.), and overhead. Overhead is allocated to the Coast Guard contract based on the ratio of direct labor expense on the contract to firmwide direct labor.

BFR can either purchase the engines from an outside source or build them internally. The following table describes the costs of the commercial division and the Coast Guard contract if the engines are built by BFR versus purchased outside.

BFR
Cost Structure
($ in Millions)

	Commercial Division	*Coast Guard Contract (Engines Manufactured Internally)*	*Coast Guard Contract (Engines Purchased Externally)*
Direct labor	$14.600	$22.800	$18.200
Direct material		32.900	25.900
Purchased engines		0.000	17.000

Overhead for BFR is $83.5 million and does not vary if the engines are purchased outside or manufactured inside BFR. Overhead consists of corporate-level salaries, building depreciation, property taxes, insurance, and factory administration costs.

Required:

a. How much overhead is allocated to the Coast Guard contract if
  (1) The engines are manufactured internally?
  (2) The engines are purchased outside?

b. Based on the total contract payment to BFR, will the Coast Guard prefer BFR to manufacture or purchase the engines?

c. What is the difference in net cash flows to BFR of manufacturing versus purchasing the engines?

d. Explain how cost-plus reimbursement contracts in the defense industry affect the make–buy decision for subassemblies.

Cases

Case 7–1: Phonetex

Phonetex is a medium-size manufacturer of telephone sets and switching equipment. Its primary business is government contracts, especially defense contracts, which are very profitable. The company has two plants: Southern and Westbury. The larger plant, Southern, is running at capacity producing a phone system for a new missile installation. Existing government contracts will require Southern to operate at capacity for the next nine months. The missile contract is a firm, fixed-price contract. Part of the contract specifies that 3,000 phones will be produced to meet government specifications. The price paid per phone is $300.

The second Phonetex plant, Westbury, is a small, old facility acquired two years ago to produce residential phone systems. Phonetex feared that defense work was cyclical, so to stabilize earnings, a line of residential systems was developed at the small plant. In the event that defense work deteriorated, the excess capacity at Southern could be used to produce residential systems. However, just the opposite has happened. The current recession has temporarily depressed the residential business. Although Westbury is losing money ($10,000 per month), top management considers this an investment. Westbury has developed a line of systems that are reasonably well received. Part of its workforce has already been laid off. It has a very good workforce remaining, with many specialized and competent supervisors, engineers, and skilled craftspeople. Another 20 percent of Westbury's workforce could be cut without affecting output. Current operations are meeting the reduced demand. If demand does not increase in the next three months, this 20 percent will have to be cut.

The plant manager at Westbury has tried to convince top management to shift the missile contract phones over to his plant. Even though his total cost to manufacture the phones is higher than at Southern, he argues that this will free up some excess capacity at Southern to add more government work. The unit cost data for the 3,000 phones are as follows:

	Southern	*Westbury*
Direct labor cost	$ 70	$ 95
Direct materials cost	40	55
Variable factory overhead*	35	45
Fixed factory overhead*	40	80
General burden†	10	20
Total unit cost	$195	$295

*Based on direct labor costs.

†Allocated corporate headquarters expense based on direct labor cost.

Westbury cannot do other government work, because it does not have the required security clearances. But Westbury can do the work involving the 3,000 phones. And it can complete this project in three months. "Besides," Westbury's manager argues, "my labor costs are not going to be $95 per phone. We are committed to maintaining employment at Westbury at least for the next three months. I can utilize most of my existing people who have slack. I will have to hire back about 20 production workers I laid off. For the three months, we are talking about $120,000 of additional direct labor."

Phonetex is considering another defense contract with an expected price of $1.1 million and an expected profit of $85,000. The work would have to be completed over the next three months, but Southern does not have the capacity to do the work and Westbury does not have the security clearances or capital equipment required by the contract.

Southern's manager says it isn't fair to make him carry Westbury. He points out that Westbury's variable cost, ignoring labor, is 33 percent greater than Southern's variable costs. Southern's manager also argues, "Adding another government contract will not replace the profit that we will be forgoing if Westbury does the telephone manufacturing. See my schedule."

Profits from Southern ($300 − 195)3,000		$ 315,000
Less: Profits from Westbury ($300 − 295)3,000		(15,000)
Forgone profits		$ 300,000
Profit in the next best government contract:		
Expected price		$1,100,000
Less:		
Direct labor	260,000	
Direct material	435,000	
Variable overhead	130,000	
Fixed factory overhead	150,000	
General burden	40,000	1,015,000
Expected profit		$ 85,000

Required:

Top management has reviewed the Southern manager's data and believes his cost estimates on the new contract to be accurate. Should Phonetex shift the 3,000 phones to Westbury and take the new contract or not? Prepare an analysis supporting your conclusions.

Case 7–2: Durango Plastics

SCX is a $2 billion chemical company with a plastics plant located in Durango, Colorado. The Durango plastics plant of SCX was started 30 years ago to produce a particular plastic film for snack food packages. The Durango plant is a profit center that markets its product to film producers. It is the only SCX facility that produces this plastic.

A few years ago, worldwide excess capacity for this plastic developed as a number of new plants were opened and some food companies began shifting to a more environmentally safe plastic that cannot be produced with the Durango plant technology.

Last year, with Durango's plant utilization down to 60 percent, senior management of SCX began investigating alternative uses of the Durango plant. The Durango plant's current annual operating statement appears in the accompanying table.

DURANGO PLANT
Income Statement, 2008
(Millions)

Revenue		$36
Variable costs	$21	
Fixed costs		
Plant administration (salaries and other out-of-pocket expenses)	17	
Deprecation	5	43
Net loss before taxes		$(7)

One alternative use of the Durango plant's excess capacity is a new high-strength plastic used by the auto industry to reduce the weight of cars. Additional equipment required to produce the automotive plastic at the Durango plant can be leased for $3 million per year. Automotive plastic revenues are projected to be $28 million and variable costs are $11 million. Additional fixed costs for marketing, distribution, and plant overhead attributable solely to auto plastics are expected to be $4 million.

All of SCX's divisions are evaluated on a before-tax basis.

Required:

a. Evaluate the auto industry plastic proposal. Compare the three alternatives: (1) close Durango, (2) produce only film plastic at Durango, and (3) produce both film and auto plastic at Durango. Which of the three do you suggest accepting? (If Durango is closed, additional one-time plant closing costs just offset the proceeds from selling the plant.)

b. Suppose the Durango plant begins manufacturing both film and auto plastic. Prepare a performance report for the two divisions for the first year, assuming that the initial projections are realized and the film division's 2009 revenue and expenses are the same as in 2008. Plant administration ($17 million) and depreciation ($5 million) are common costs to both the film and auto plastics divisions. For performance evaluation purposes, these costs are assigned to the two divisions based on sales revenue. All costs incurred for the Auto Plastics division should be charged to that division.

c. Does the performance report in (*b*) accurately reflect the relative performance of the two divisions? Why or why not?

d. In the year 2010, the Durango plant is able to negotiate a $1 million reduction in property taxes. Property taxes are included in the "plant administration account." In addition, the Film Division is able to add $3 million in additional revenues (with $2.1 of additional variable cost) by selling film to European food packagers. Assuming that these are the only changes at the Durango plant between 2009 and 2010, how does the Auto Plastics Division's performance change between these two years? Allocate the common costs using the method described in (*b*).

e. Write a short memo evaluating the performance of the Auto Plastics Division in light of the events in the year 2010 and describing how these events affect the reported performance of the Auto Plastics Division.

Contents

Hilton: *Managerial Accounting,* 9/e,
ISBN: 0-07-811091-2

Note: Entries printed in blue denote topics that emphasize contemporary issues in managerial accounting and cost management.

MILK

FOCUS COMPANY >>>

THIS CHAPTER'S FOCUS COMPANY is the Patio Grill Company, which manufactures high-end gas barbeque grills in its Denver plant. The company has recently experienced intense competition in its two high-volume product lines, forcing management to drop these products' prices below their target levels. A careful study of this situation revealed that Patio Grill Company's traditional product-costing system distorted product costs by assigning too much cost to the high-volume gas-grill lines and not enough cost to the low-volume, complex line of grills. Management then implemented a new costing system, called activity-based costing, or ABC, which assigns product costs more accurately than traditional product-costing systems. Armed with the cost insights from the ABC system, management was able to change its pricing structure to compete more effectively in the gas-grill market.

5 Activity-Based Costing and Management

IN CONTRAST >>>

In contrast to the manufacturing setting of the Patio Grill Company, we explore the use of activity-based costing by the Delaware Medical Center's Primary Care Unit. ABC is used in this health care services setting to assign treatment costs to categories of patient visits, such as routine, extended, and complex visits, as well as new and continuing patients.

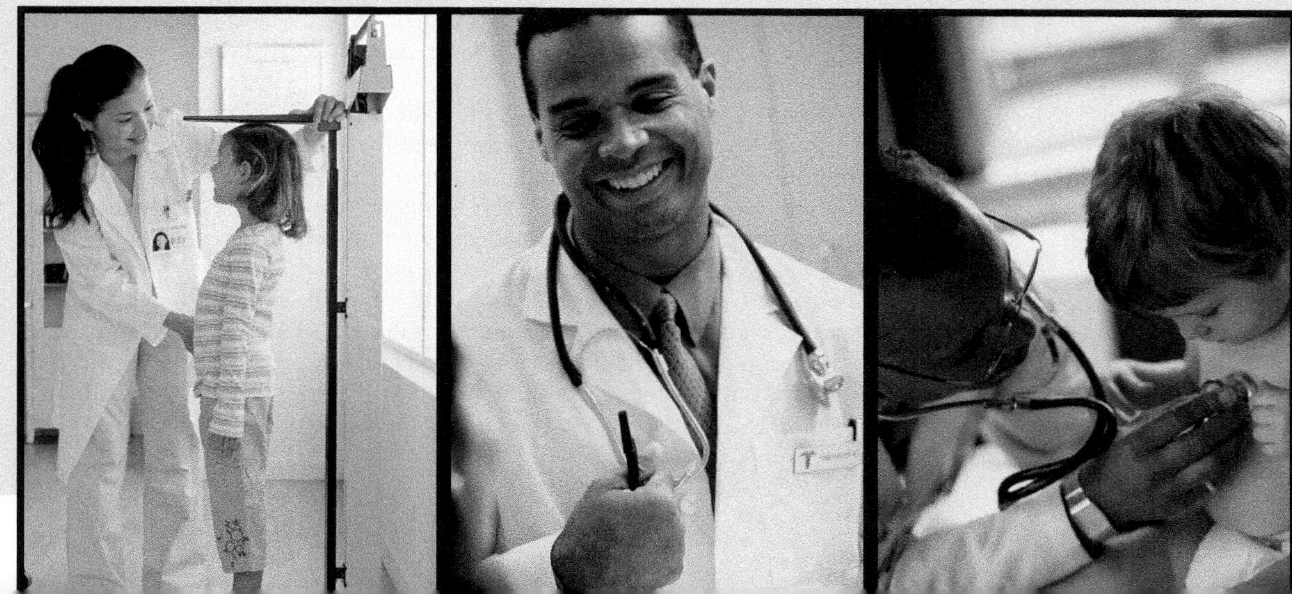

AFTER COMPLETING THIS CHAPTER, YOU SHOULD BE ABLE TO:

1. Compute product costs under a traditional, volume-based product-costing system.
2. Explain how an activity-based costing system operates, including the use of a two-stage procedure for cost assignment, the identification of activity cost pools, and the selection of cost drivers.
3. Explain the concept of cost levels, including unit-level, batch-level, product-sustaining-level, and facility-level costs.
4. Compute product costs under an activity-based costing system.
5. Explain why traditional, volume-based costing systems tend to distort product costs.
6. Explain three criteria for selecting cost drivers.
7. Discuss several key issues in activity-based costing, including data collection and storyboarding.
8. Explain the concepts of activity-based management and two-dimensional ABC.
9. Explain and execute a customer-profitability analysis.
10. Understand and discuss how activity-based costing is used in service-industry organizations.
11. List and explain eight important features of just-in-time inventory and production management systems (Appendix).

A revolution is transforming the world of business. Not since the mid-19th century have we seen changes as sweeping and dramatic. The growth of international competition, the breakneck pace of technological innovation, and startling advances in computerized systems have created a new playing field for manufacturers around the globe. Some manufacturers have emerged as world-class producers, while others have fallen by the wayside. World-class companies such as Caterpillar, Coca-Cola, Johnson & Johnson, and Pfizer are among the many manufacturers that have changed key business processes to compete effectively in the 21st century.

The service industry also is undergoing dramatic transformation. The growth of the Internet, the trend toward a service economy, and the willingness of businesses to outsource many critical service functions have caused many service organizations to reinvent the way they do business. Among the many service-industry firms that have adapted most successfully to the changing business environment are American Express, Bank of America, FedEx, Google, and Southwest Airlines.

What is the role of managerial accounting in this rapidly changing environment? To explore this issue, we will review recent events in the life of Patio Grill Company, a manufacturer of barbeque grills and accessories. The company's Denver plant manufactures three product lines, all high-end gas barbeque grills. The plant's three gas grill lines are the Patio Standard (STD), the Deluxe (DEL), and the Ultimate (ULT).

Traditional, Volume-Based Product-Costing System

Learning Objective 1

Compute product costs under a traditional, volume-based product-costing system.

Until recently, Patio Grill Company's Denver plant used a job-order product-costing system similar to the one described in Chapter 3 for Adirondack Outfitters. The cost of each product was the sum of its actual direct-material cost, actual direct-labor cost, and applied manufacturing overhead. Overhead was applied using a predetermined overhead rate based on direct-labor hours. Exhibit 5–1 provides the basic data upon which the traditional costing system was based.

The Excel spreadsheet in Exhibit 5–2 shows the calculation of the product cost for each of three gas-grill lines (STD, DEL, and ULT). Overhead is applied to the products at the rate of $24 per direct-labor hour. Notice that all of the Denver plant's budgeted manufacturing overhead costs are lumped together in a single cost pool. This total budgeted overhead amount ($4,896,000) then is divided by the plant's total budgeted direct-labor hours (204,000 hours). The 204,000 direct labor hours is also equal to the plant's practical capacity for production, as expressed in terms of direct-labor hours.

Patio Grill Company's labor-hour-based product-costing system is typical of many manufacturing companies. Labor hours are related closely to the volume of activity in the factory, which sometimes is referred to as *throughput.* Consequently, these traditional product-costing systems often are said to be **volume-based** (or **throughput-based) costing systems.**

Trouble in Denver

The profitability of Patio Grill Company's Denver operation has been faltering in recent years. The company's pricing policy has been to set a target price for each grill equal to 120 percent of the full product cost. Thus, the prices were determined as shown in Exhibit 5–3. Also shown are the actual prices that Patio Grill Company has been obtaining for its products.

Due to price competition from other grill manufacturers, Patio Standard (STD) grills were selling at $585, approximately $10 below their target price of $595.20. Moreover, Patio Grill Company's competition had forced management to reduce the price of the Deluxe grill (DEL) to $705, almost $20 below its target price of $724.80. Even at this lower price, the sales team was having difficulty getting orders for its planned volume of Deluxe grill production. Fortunately, the disappointing profitability of the Patio Standard and Deluxe model grills was partially offset by greater-than expected profits on the Ultimate (ULT) line of grills. Patio Grill Company's sales personnel had discovered that the company was swamped with orders when the Ultimate grill's target price of $902.40 was charged. Consequently, management had raised the price on the Ultimate grills several times, and eventually the product was selling for $940. Even at this price, Patio Grill Company's customers did not seem to hesitate to place orders. Moreover, the company's

Exhibit 5–1

Basic Production and Cost Data: Patio Grill Company

	Patio Standard Grill STD	Deluxe Grill DEL	Ultimate Grill ULT
Planned annual production:			
Volume in units	10,000	8,000	2,000
Production runs	80 runs of 125 units each	80 runs of 100 units each	40 runs of 50 units each
Direct material	$100	$120	$180
Direct labor (not including setup time)	$180 (9 hours @ $20 per hour)	$220 (11 hours @ $20 per hour)	$260 (13 hours @ $20 per hour)
Machine hours (MH) per product unit	10 MH	12 MH	17 MH
Total machine hours consumed by product line	100,000 (10 MH × 10,000 units)	96,000 (12 MH × 8,000 units)	34,000 (17 MH × 2,000 units)

Exhibit 5–2
Product Costs from Traditional, Volume-Based Product-Costing System: Patio Grill Company

Microsoft Excel - Product Costs from Traditional, Volume-Based Product-Costing System

G7 =SUM(G3:G6)

	A	B	C	D	E	F	G	H
1			STD		DEL		ULT	
2								
3	Direct material		$100.00		$120.00		$180.00	
4	Direct labor							
5	(not including set-up time)		180.00	(9 hr. @ $20)	220.00	(11 hr. @ $20)	260.00	(13 hr. @ $20)
6	Manufacturing overhead*		216.00	(9 hr. @ $24)	264.00	(11 hr. @ $24)	312.00	(13 hr. @ $24)
7	Total		$496.00		$604.00		$752.00	
8								
9								
10	*Calculation of predetermined-overhead rate:							
11								
12	Budgeted manufacturing overhead			$4,896,000				
13								
14	Direct labor, budgeted hours:							
15	STD: 10,000 units x 9 hours			90,000				
16	DEL: 8,000 units x 11 hours			88,000				
17	ULT: 2,000 units x 13 hours			26,000				
18	Total direct-labor hours			204,000	hours			
19								
20	Predetermined overhead rate:							
21	(Budgeted manufacturing overhead / Budgeted direct-labor hours) = $4,896,000 / 204,000 = $24 per hour							

competitors did not mount a challenge in the market for the Ultimate line of grills. Patio's management was pleased to have a niche for the Ultimate grill market, which appeared to be a highly profitable, low-volume specialty product. Nevertheless, concern continued to mount in Denver about the difficulty in the Patio Standard and Deluxe grill markets. After all, these were the Denver plant's bread-and-butter products, with projected annual sales of 10,000 Patio Standard grills and 8,000 Deluxe grills.

Activity-Based Costing System

Learning Objective 2

Explain how an activity-based costing system operates, including the use of a two-stage procedure for cost assignment, the identification of activity cost pools, and the selection of cost drivers.

Patio Grill Company's director of cost management, Hamilton Burger, had been thinking for some time about a refinement in the Denver plant's product-costing system. He wondered if the traditional, volume-based system was providing management with accurate data about product costs. Burger had read about **activity-based costing (ABC) systems,** which follow a two-stage procedure to assign overhead costs to products. The first stage identifies significant activities in the production of the three products and assigns overhead costs to each activity in accordance with the cost of the organization's resources used by the activity. The overhead costs assigned to each activity comprise an **activity cost pool.**

After assigning overhead costs to activity cost pools in stage one, cost drivers appropriate for each cost pool are identified in stage two. Then the overhead costs are allocated from each activity cost pool to each product line in proportion to the amount of the cost driver consumed by the product line.

Exhibit 5–3
Target and Actual Selling Prices: Patio Grill Company

	Patio Standard Grill STD	Deluxe Grill DEL	Ultimate Grill ULT
Production cost under traditional, volume-based system (Exhibit 5–2)	$496.00	$604.00	$752.00
Target selling price (cost × 120%)	595.20	724.80	902.40
Actual current selling price	585.00	705.00	940.00

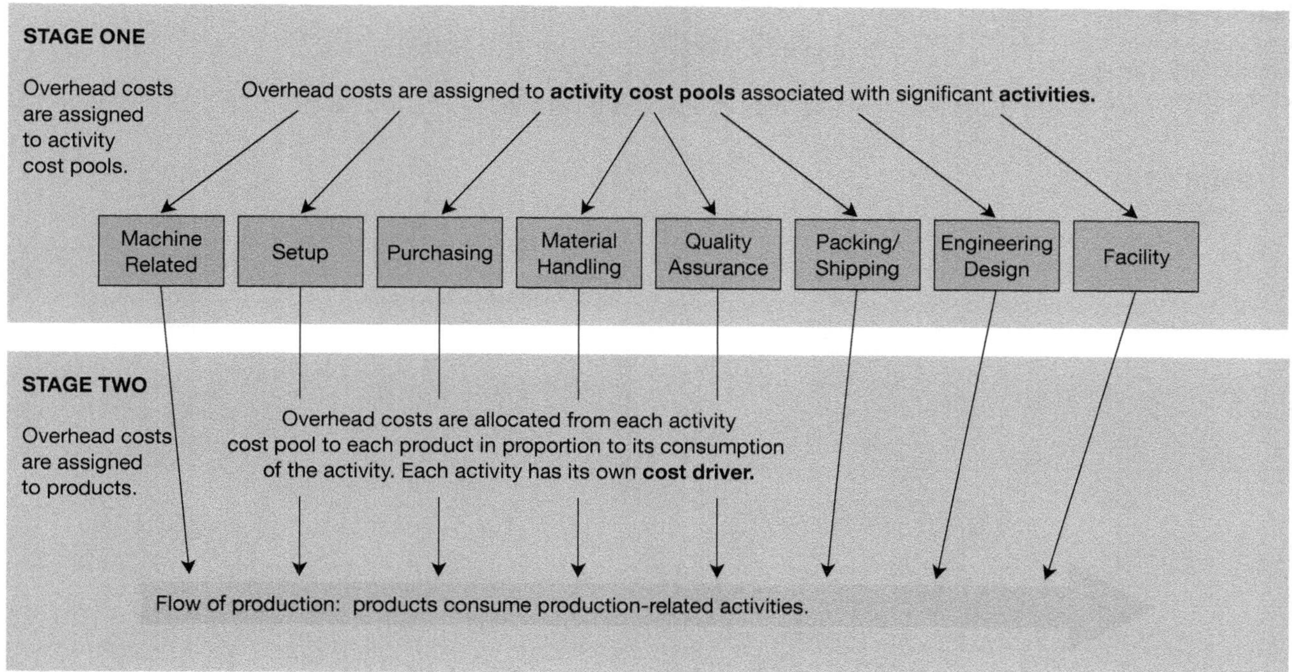
STAGE ONE
Overhead costs are assigned to activity cost pools.
Overhead costs are assigned to **activity cost pools** associated with significant **activities.**
Machine Related
Setup
Purchasing
Material Handling
Quality Assurance
Packing/ Shipping
Engineering Design
Facility
STAGE TWO
Overhead costs are assigned to products.
Overhead costs are allocated from each activity cost pool to each product in proportion to its consumption of the activity. Each activity has its own **cost driver.**
Flow of production: products consume production-related activities.

Exhibit 5–4
Activity-Based Costing System

The two-stage cost-assignment process of activity-based costing is depicted in Exhibit 5–4.

Burger discussed activity-based costing with Patty Cook, the assistant director of cost management. Together they met with all of Patio Grill Company's department supervisors to discuss development of an ABC system. After initial discussion, an ABC proposal was made to the company's top management. Approval was obtained, and an ABC project team was formed, which included Burger, Cook, and representatives of various functional departments. Through several months of painstaking data collection and analysis, the project team was able to gather the data necessary to implement an ABC system.

ABC Stage One

Patio Grill Company's ABC project team identified eight activity cost pools, which fall into four broad categories.

Learning Objective 3

Explain the concept of cost levels, including unit-level, batch-level, product-sustaining-level, and facility-level costs.

1. *Unit level.* This type of activity must be done for each unit of production. The machine-related activity cost pool represents a **unit-level activity** since every product unit requires machine time.
2. *Batch level.* These activities must be performed for each batch of products, rather than each unit. Patio Grill Company's **batch-level activities** include the setup, purchasing, material handling, quality assurance, and packing/shipping activity cost pools.
3. *Product-sustaining level.* This category includes activities that are needed to support an entire product line but are not performed every time a new unit or batch of products is produced. Patio Grill Company's project team identified engineering design costs as a **product-sustaining-level activity** cost pool.
4. *Facility (or general operations) level.* **Facility-level activities** are required in order for the entire production process to occur. Examples of such activity costs include plant management salaries, plant depreciation, property taxes, plant maintenance, and insurance.

This classification of activities into unit-level, batch-level, product-sustaining-level, and facility-level activities is called a **cost hierarchy.**

Exhibit 5–5
Stage One of Activity-Based Costing: Identification of Activity Cost Pools

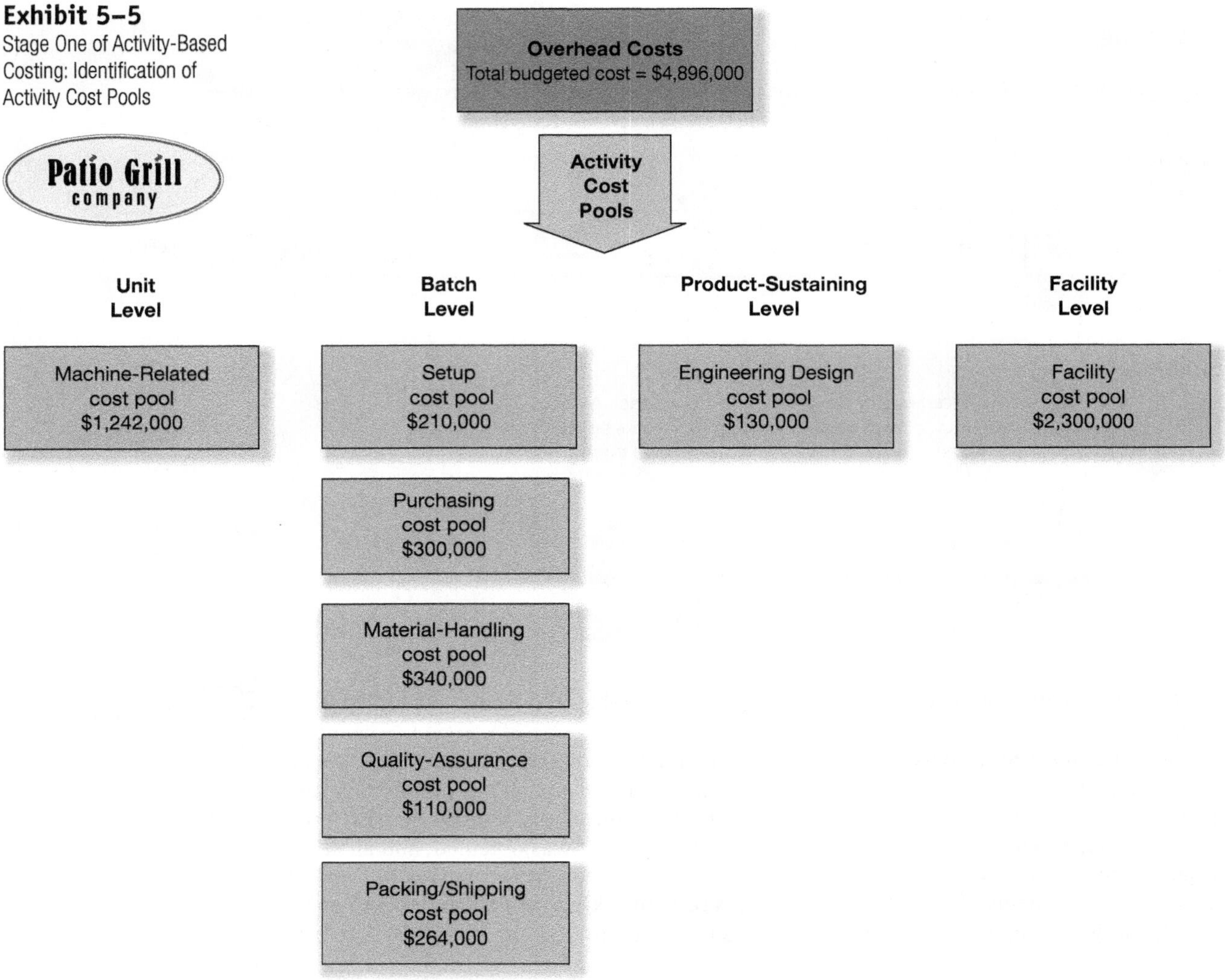

Patio Grill company

Overhead Costs
Total budgeted cost = $4,896,000

Activity Cost Pools

Unit Level	Batch Level	Product-Sustaining Level	Facility Level
Machine-Related cost pool $1,242,000	Setup cost pool $210,000	Engineering Design cost pool $130,000	Facility cost pool $2,300,000
	Purchasing cost pool $300,000		
	Material-Handling cost pool $340,000		
	Quality-Assurance cost pool $110,000		
	Packing/Shipping cost pool $264,000		

Patio Grill Company's eight activity cost pools are depicted in Exhibit 5–5. Notice that the total overhead cost for all eight activity cost pools, $4,896,000, is shown at the top of Exhibit 5–5. This amount is the same as the total overhead cost shown in Exhibit 5–2, which shows the details of the product costs calculated under Patio Grill Company's traditional product-costing system.

ABC Stage Two

Learning Objective 4

Compute product costs under an activity-based costing system.

In stage two of the activity-based costing project, Burger and Cook identified cost drivers for each activity cost pool. Then they used a three-step process to compute unit activity costs for each of Patio Grill Company's three product lines, and for each of the eight activity cost pools. In the following sections, we will discuss in detail how stage two of the ABC project was carried out for the various activity cost pools identified in stage one. Then we will complete the ABC project by developing new product costs for each of the company's gas-grill product lines.

Machine-Related Cost Pool Let's begin by focusing on only one of the eight activity cost pools. The machine-related cost pool, a unit-level activity, totals $1,242,000 and includes the costs of machine maintenance, depreciation, computer support, lubrication, electricity, and calibration. Burger and Cook selected machine hours for the cost driver, since a product that uses more machine hours should bear a larger share of machine-related costs. Exhibit 5–6 shows how machinery costs are assigned to products in stage two of the ABC analysis. Notice that Exhibit 5–6 includes just a portion of a larger spreadsheet that we will examine in due course. The spreadsheet rows shown in Exhibit 5–6 focus just on the machine-related activity cost pool. Most of the columns in Exhibit 5–6 contain ABC data that were collected by the ABC project team. We will learn more later in this chapter about how that information is collected. For now, though, let's just take this ABC information as a given. As noted in Exhibit 5–6, the following columns contain *data collected by the ABC project team.*

Data Collected by ABC Project Team (Exhibit 5–6)

Column A	Activity: machine related
Column B	Activity cost pool: $1,242,000 (from Exhibit 5–5)
Column C	Cost driver: machine hours
Column D	Cost driver quantity: 230,000 machine hours (total of machine hours for the three product lines in column G)[1]
Column F	Product lines: STD, DEL, ULT
Column G	Cost driver quantity for each product line: STD, 100,000 machine hours (from Exhibit 5–1) DEL, 96,000 machine hours (from Exhibit 5–1) ULT, 34,000 machine hours (from Exhibit 5–1)
Column I	Product line production volume: STD, 10,000 units (from Exhibit 5–1) DEL, 8,000 units (from Exhibit 5–1) ULT, 2,000 units (from Exhibit 5–1)

Notice that only three columns in Exhibit 5–6 remain: columns E, H, and J. These columns contain the *amounts that are computed* during the ABC calculations, and they appear in red in Exhibit 5–6.

Amounts Computed During ABC Calculations (Exhibit 5–6)

Column E	Pool rate
Column H	Activity cost for each product line
Column J	Activity cost per unit of product for each product line

Exhibit 5–6, below the spreadsheet excerpt, shows in detail how each of these amounts (shown in red) is computed. Take time now to examine Exhibit 5–6 carefully, in order to understand how these amounts are computed in the ABC calculations.

A key number computed in Exhibit 5–6 (column E) is the **pool rate,** which is defined as the cost per unit of the *cost driver* for a particular activity cost pool. The pool rate for the machine-related cost pool is $5.40, which means that Patio Grill Company's machine-related cost is $5.40 per machine hour. Each activity cost pool will have its own pool rate.

Now we have seen the type of data that the ABC project team must supply for the machine-related cost pool. In addition, we have studied how the ABC calculations are carried out in order to determine the machine-related activity cost per unit of each type of product (STD, DEL, and ULT). The final conclusion of the ABC analysis *for the machine-related cost pool only* is given in column J of Exhibit 5–6. Thus, under activity-based costing, the following machine-related costs per product unit should be assigned to each of the three product lines.

STD: $54.00 of machine-related cost per grill
DEL: $64.80 of machine-related cost per grill
ULT: $91.80 of machine-related cost per grill

[1]The 230,000 machine hours used to compute the pool rate for the machine-related cost pool is also equal to management's estimate of the company's practical capacity of production, as expressed in terms of machine hours.

Exhibit 5–6
ABC Data and Calculations for the Machine-Related Cost Pool: Patio Grill Company

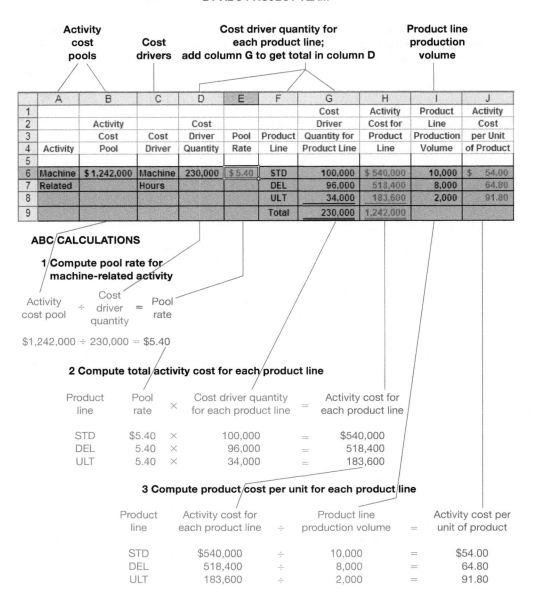

INFORMATION SUPPLIED BY ABC PROJECT TEAM

Activity cost pools | Cost drivers | Cost driver quantity for each product line; add column G to get total in column D | Product line production volume

	A	B	C	D	E	F	G	H	I	J
1							Cost	Activity	Product	Activity
2		Activity		Cost			Driver	Cost for	Line	Cost
3		Cost	Cost	Driver	Pool	Product	Quantity for	Product	Production	per Unit
4	Activity	Pool	Driver	Quantity	Rate	Line	Product Line	Line	Volume	of Product
5										
6	Machine	$1,242,000	Machine	230,000	$5.40	STD	100,000	$540,000	10,000	$54.00
7	Related		Hours			DEL	96,000	518,400	8,000	64.80
8						ULT	34,000	183,600	2,000	91.80
9						Total	230,000	1,242,000		

ABC CALCULATIONS

1 Compute pool rate for machine-related activity

Activity cost pool ÷ Cost driver quantity = Pool rate

$1,242,000 ÷ 230,000 = $5.40

2 Compute total activity cost for each product line

Product line	Pool rate	×	Cost driver quantity for each product line	=	Activity cost for each product line
STD	$5.40	×	100,000	=	$540,000
DEL	5.40	×	96,000	=	518,400
ULT	5.40	×	34,000	=	183,600

3 Compute product cost per unit for each product line

Product line	Activity cost for each product line	÷	Product line production volume	=	Activity cost per unit of product
STD	$540,000	÷	10,000	=	$54.00
DEL	518,400	÷	8,000	=	64.80
ULT	183,600	÷	2,000	=	91.80

Learning Objective 4

Compute product costs under an activity-based costing system.

Completing the ABC Calculations Now that we have studied the ABC data requirements and calculations for the machine-related cost pool (Exhibit 5–6), we can complete the ABC calculations by including all eight of the activity cost pools. These eight cost pools were given in Exhibit 5–5. The entire Excel spreadsheet for Patio Grill Company's activity-based costing project is displayed in Exhibit 5–7. As the cliché goes, there is good news and bad news. The bad news is that the spreadsheet in Exhibit 5–7 contains eight times as many rows as the one we just examined in detail for the machine-related cost pool. The good news, though, is that the ABC data requirements and calculations are conceptually *identical* for each of the eight activity cost pools. In other words, the same type of ABC data is supplied for each activity cost pool, and the three steps of ABC computations are performed for each activity cost pool in exactly the same manner as they were for the machine-related cost pool. So if we understand the computations in Exhibit 5–6 (for the machine-related costs), then we will understand

Microsoft Excel - Activity-Based Costing Data and Calculations

E6 =B6/D6

	A	B	C	D	E	F	G	H	I	J
1							Cost	Activity	Product	Activity
2		Activity		Cost			Driver	Cost for	Line	Cost
3		Cost	Cost	Driver	Pool	Product	Quantity for	Product	Production	per Unit
4	Activity	Pool	Driver	Quantity	Rate	Line	Product Line	Line	Volume	of Product
5										
6	Machine	$ 1,242,000	Machine	230,000	$ 5.40	STD	100,000	$ 540,000	10,000	$ 54.00
7	Related		Hours			DEL	96,000	518,400	8,000	64.80
8						ULT	34,000	183,600	2,000	91.80
9						Total	230,000	1,242,000		
10	Setup	210,000	Production	200	1,050.00	STD	80	84,000	10,000	8.40
11			Runs			DEL	80	84,000	8,000	10.50
12						ULT	40	42,000	2,000	21.00
13						Total	200	210,000		
14	Purchasing	300,000	Purchase	600	500.00	STD	200	100,000	10,000	10.00
15			Orders			DEL	192	96,000	8,000	12.00
16						ULT	208	104,000	2,000	52.00
17						Total	600	300,000		
18	Material	340,000	Production	200	1,700.00	STD	80	136,000	10,000	13.60
19	Handling		Runs			DEL	80	136,000	8,000	17.00
20						ULT	40	68,000	2,000	34.00
21						Total	200	340,000		
22	Quality	110,000	Inspection	2,200	50.00	STD	800	40,000	10,000	4.00
23	Assurance		Hours			DEL	800	40,000	8,000	5.00
24						ULT	600	30,000	2,000	15.00
25						Total	2,200	110,000		
26	Packing/	264,000	Shipments	2,200	120.00	STD	1,000	120,000	10,000	12.00
27	Shipping					DEL	800	96,000	8,000	12.00
28						ULT	400	48,000	2,000	24.00
29						Total	2,200	264,000		
30	Engineering	130,000	Engineering	1,300	100.00	STD	500	50,000	10,000	5.00
31	Design		Hours			DEL	400	40,000	8,000	5.00
32						ULT	400	40,000	2,000	20.00
33						Total	1,300	130,000		
34	Facility	2,300,000	Machine	230,000	10.00	STD	100,000	1,000,000	10,000	100.00
35			Hours			DEL	96,000	960,000	8,000	120.00
36						ULT	34,000	340,000	2,000	170.00
37						Total	230,000	2,300,000		
38										
39	Grand Total	$ 4,896,000				Grand Total		$ 4,896,000		

Sheet1 / Sheet2 / Sheet3

Ready

Exhibit 5–7

Activity-Based Costing Data and Calculations: Patio Grill Company

the computations in Exhibit 5–7 for all eight activity cost pools. (The amounts that are *computed* in Exhibit 5–7 are shown in red.)

Pause here and take a few moments to examine Exhibit 5–7. Select an activity other than the machine-related activity we studied earlier. Try to verify the computations of the pool rate in column E, the activity cost for each product line in column H, and the ABC overhead cost per unit of product in column J.

Now that we have the activity cost per unit of product for each activity cost pool and each product line, it is straightforward to compute the total unit product cost for each type of grill. To do so, we need only add the direct-material and direct-labor costs for each grill type (given in Exhibit 5–1) to the ABC activity costs calculated in Exhibit 5–7. We do this in the Excel spreadsheet displayed as Exhibit 5–8.

Exhibit 5–8
Product Costs from Activity-Based Costing System: Patio Grill Company

Microsoft Excel - Product Costs from Activity-Based Costing System

G17 =SUM(G9:G16)

	A	B	C	D	E	F	G	H
1			STD		DEL		ULT	
2								
3	Direct material		$100.00		$120.00		$180.00	
4	Direct labor							
5	(not including set-up time)		180.00	(9 hr. @ $20)	220.00	(11 hr. @ $20)	260.00	(13 hr. @ $20)
6	Total direct costs per unit		$280.00		$340.00		$440.00	
7								
8	Manufacturing overhead (based on ABC):*							
9	Machine-related		$ 54.00		$ 64.80		$ 91.80	
10	Setup		8.40		10.50		21.00	
11	Purchasing		10.00		12.00		52.00	
12	Material handling		13.60		17.00		34.00	
13	Quality assurance		4.00		5.00		15.00	
14	Packing/shipping		12.00		12.00		24.00	
15	Engineering design		5.00		5.00		20.00	
16	Facility		100.00		120.00		170.00	
17	Total ABC overhead cost per unit		$207.00		$246.30		$427.80	
18	Total product cost per unit		$487.00		$586.30		$867.80	
19								
20	*ABC overhead costs from Exhibit 5-7							

Sheet1 / Sheet2 / Sheet3

Interpreting the ABC Product Costs

Hamilton Burger was amazed to see the product costs reported under the activity-based costing system. Both the STD and DEL grills exhibited lower product costs under the ABC system than under the traditional system. This could explain the price competition Patio Grill Company faced on its STD and DEL grills. Patio Grill Company's competitors could sell their comparable standard and deluxe grills at a lower price because they realized it cost less to produce these grills than Patio Grill Company's traditional costing system had indicated. However, as Burger scanned the new product costs shown in Exhibit 5–8, he was alarmed by the substantial increase in the reported cost of an ULT grill. The cost of an ULT grill had risen by more than $100 above the company's original estimate. The complexity of the ULT grills, and its impact on costs, was hidden by the traditional, volume-based costing system. To compare the results of the two alternative costing systems, Burger prepared Exhibit 5–9.

As shown in Exhibit 5–9, the STD grills emerged as a profitable product, selling for approximately 120 percent of their reported cost under the activity-based costing system ($585 ÷ $487). The DEL grills also were selling at approximately 120 percent of their new reported product cost ($705 ÷ $586.30). "No wonder we couldn't sell the deluxe

This forklift operator is engaged in material handling, which is usually a batch-level activity in an ABC system. The engineer using this computer-aided design (CAD) system is engaged in the product-sustaining-level activity of product design.

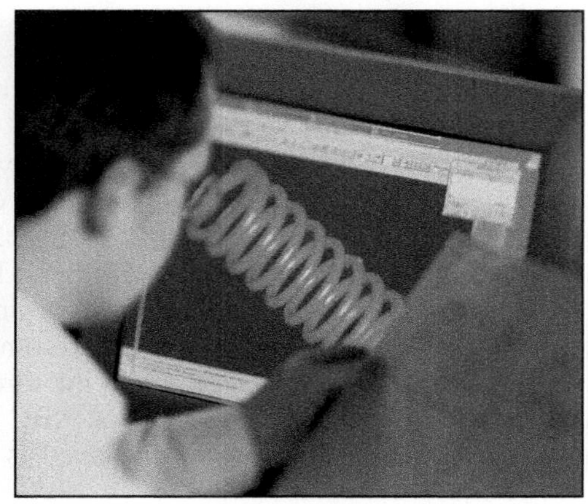

	STD	DEL	ULT
Reported unit *overhead* cost:			
Traditional, volume-based costing system (Exhibit 5–2)	$216.00	$264.00	$ 312.00
Activity-based costing system (Exhibit 5–8)	207.00	246.30	427.80
Reported unit *product* cost (direct material, direct labor, and overhead):			
Traditional, volume-based costing system (Exhibit 5–2)	496.00	604.00	752.00
Activity-based costing system (Exhibit 5–8)	487.00	586.30	867.80
Sales price data:			
Original target price (120% of product cost based on traditional, volume-based costing system (Exhibit 5–3)	595.20	724.80	902.40
New target price (120% of product cost based on activity-based costing system	584.40	703.56	1,041.36
Actual current selling price (Exhibit 5–3)	585.00	705.00	940.00

Exhibit 5–9

Comparison of Product Costs and Target Prices from Alternative Product-Costing Systems: Patio Grill Company

grills at the old target price of $724.80," said Burger to Cook, as they looked over the data. "Our competitors probably knew their deluxe grills cost around $586, and they priced them accordingly." When he got to the ULT column in Exhibit 5–9, Burger was appalled. "We thought those ultimate grills were a winner," lamented Burger, "but we've been selling them at a price that is just about 8 percent over their cost!" (Burger had made this calculation: actual current selling price of $940 ÷ ABC product cost of $867.80.) "And worse yet," Burger continued, "we've been selling the ultimate grills for $940, which is more than a hundred dollars below the new target price of $1,041.36." After looking over the data, Burger made a beeline for the president's office. "We've got to get this operation straightened out," he thought.

Burger also realized that the comparison of the two product-costing systems was even more striking when he focused on just the reported *overhead* costs. He commented to Cook, "The direct-material and direct-labor costs for each product line don't change under ABC. They're the same under both costing systems. Since these are direct costs, it's straightforward to trace these costs to each product with considerable accuracy. It's the overhead costs that cause the problem." To see what Burger was getting at, look again at Exhibit 5–9 and focus on the top two rows. The overhead cost of a STD grill dropped from the old reported cost of $216 to $207 under ABC. Similarly, the overhead cost of a DEL grill dropped from the old reported cost of $264 to $246.30 under ABC. Now look at the ULT column, though. Here the overhead cost rose from the old reported cost of $312 to $427.80 under ABC! This represents an increase of more than a third. ($427.80 ÷ $312.00 is a little over 137 percent, which yields an *increase* of over 37 percent.)

The Punch Line

Learning Objective 5

Explain why traditional, volume-based costing systems tend to distort product costs.

What has happened at Patio Grill Company's Denver plant? The essence of the problem is that the traditional, volume-based costing system was overcosting the high-volume product lines (STD and DEL) and undercosting the complex, relatively low-volume product line (ULT). The high-volume products basically subsidized the low-volume line. The activity-based costing system revealed this problem by more accurately assigning overhead costs to the three product lines.

Exhibit 5–10 summarizes the effects of the cost distortion under the traditional product-costing system. Patio Grill Company's traditional system *overcosted* each STD grill by $9.00, for a total of $90,000 for the STD product line on a volume of 10,000 units. Each DEL grill was *overcosted* by $17.70, for a total of $141,600 on a volume of 8,000 units for the DEL product line. These excess costs had to come from somewhere, and that place was the ULT product line. Each ULT grill was *undercosted* by $115.80, for a total of $231,600 for the ULT product line on a volume of 2,000 units. Notice that the *total* amount by which the STD and DEL grill lines were overcosted equals the *total* amount by which the ULT grill line was undercosted.

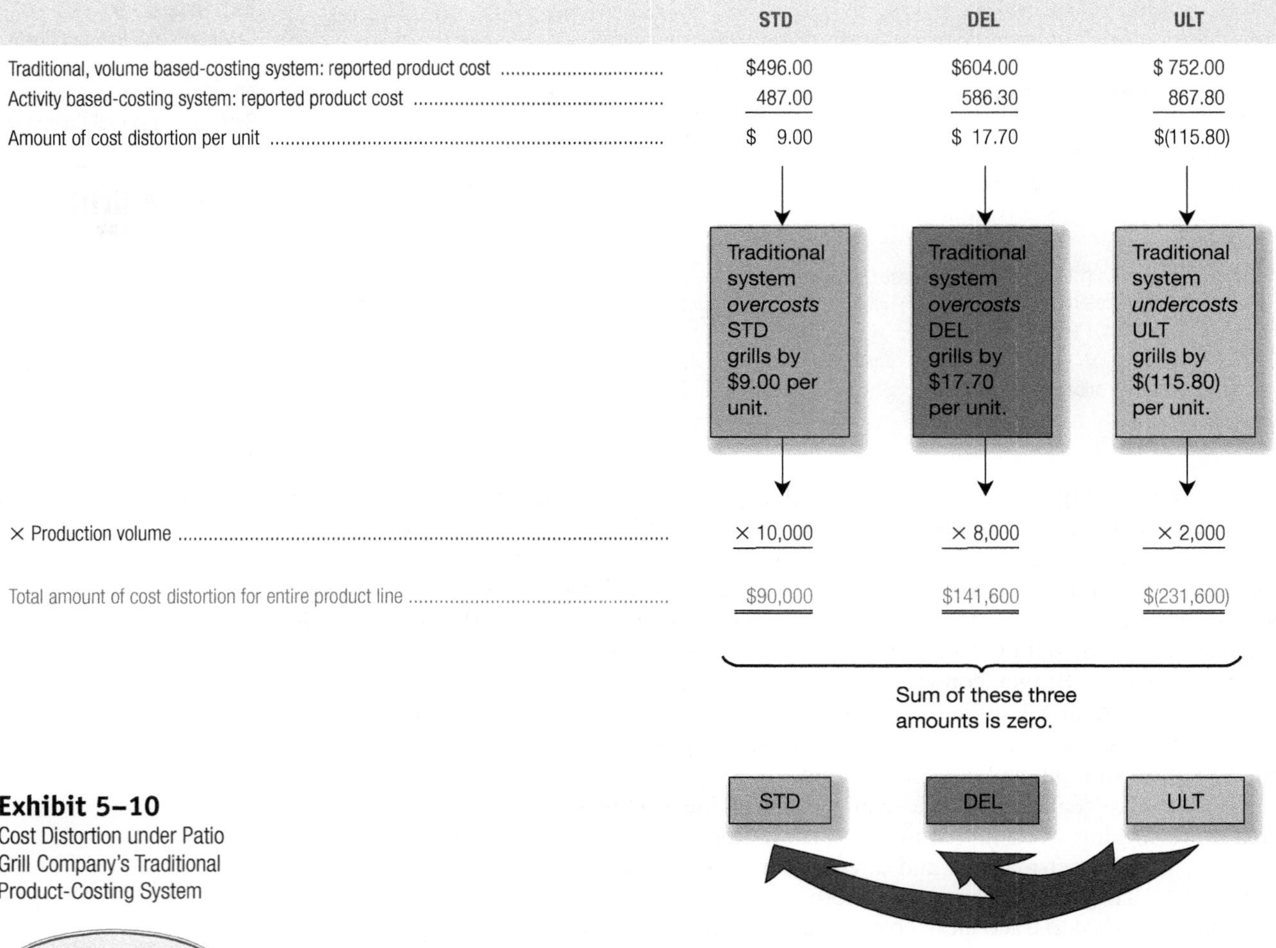

	STD	DEL	ULT
Traditional, volume based-costing system: reported product cost	$496.00	$604.00	$ 752.00
Activity based-costing system: reported product cost	487.00	586.30	867.80
Amount of cost distortion per unit	$ 9.00	$ 17.70	$(115.80)
× Production volume	× 10,000	× 8,000	× 2,000
Total amount of cost distortion for entire product line	$90,000	$141,600	$(231,600)

Traditional system *overcosts* STD grills by $9.00 per unit.
Traditional system *overcosts* DEL grills by $17.70 per unit.
Traditional system *undercosts* ULT grills by $(115.80) per unit.
Sum of these three amounts is zero.
STD
DEL
ULT
Traditional system shifts costs from ULT product line to STD and DEL product lines.

Exhibit 5–10
Cost Distortion under Patio Grill Company's Traditional Product-Costing System

Patio Grill company

Why Traditional, Volume-Based Systems Distort Product Costs

Why did Patio Grill Company's traditional product-costing system distort its product costs? The answer lies in the use of a single, volume-based cost driver. The company's old costing system assigned overhead to products on the basis of their relative usage of direct labor. Since the STD and DEL grill lines use substantially more direct labor than the ULT grill line, *in total,* the traditional system assigned them more overhead costs.

The problem with this result is that for every one of Patio Grill Company's overhead activities, the proportion of the activity actually consumed by the ULT grill line is far greater than its low volume would suggest. The ULT grill line has a budgeted production volume of just 2,000 units, which is only 10 percent of Patio Grill Company's total budgeted production volume of 20,000 units. (20,000 units = 10,000 STD units + 8,000 DEL units + 2,000 ULT units.) Now examine the ABC calculations in Exhibit 5–7. Focus on column G, which details the consumption of the cost driver by each product line for each activity cost pool. Notice that for every one of the overhead activities, the ULT grill line consumes much more than a 10 percent share of the activity, even though the ULT line accounts for only 10 percent of budgeted production volume. The relatively heavy consumption of overhead activities by the ULT product line is due to its greater complexity and small production runs. We must conclude, therefore, that direct labor is not a suitable cost driver for Patio Grill Company's overhead costs. Usage of direct labor does not drive most overhead costs in this company.

There are actually two factors working against Patio Grill Company's old product-costing system. First, many of the activities that result in the company's overhead costs are *not unit-level activities.* Second, the company manufactures a *diverse set of products.*

Non-Unit-Level Overhead Costs When Patio Grill Company's ABC project team designed the activity-based costing system, only the machine-related overhead cost pool was classified as a unit-level activity. All of the other activities were classified as batch-level, product-sustaining-level, or facility-level activities. This means that many of the company's overhead costs are not incurred every time a unit is produced. Instead, many of these overhead costs are related to starting new production batches, supporting an entire product line, or running the entire operation. Since direct labor is a unit-level cost driver, it fails to capture the forces that drive these other types of costs. In Patio Grill Company's new ABC system, cost drivers were chosen that were appropriate for each activity cost pool. For example, since setting up machinery for a new production run is a batch-level activity, the number of production runs is an appropriate batch-level cost driver.

Product Diversity Patio Grill Company manufactures three different products. Although all three are gas barbeque grills, the three grills are quite different. The STD and DEL grills are high-volume, relatively simple products. The ULT grills constitute a considerably more complex, and relatively low-volume, product line. As a result of this *product line diversity,* Patio Grill Company's three product lines consume overhead activities in different proportions. For example, compare the *consumption ratios* for the purchasing and material-handling activity cost pools shown below. The **consumption ratio** is the proportion of an activity consumed by a particular product.

	Consumption Ratios*		
Activity Cost Pool	**STD**	**DEL**	**ULT**
Purchasing activity (cost driver is purchase orders, or POs)	200 POs (33%)	192 POs (32%)	208 POs (35%)
Material-handling activity (cost driver is production runs)	80 runs (40%)	80 runs (40%)	40 runs (20%)

*The purchase order and production run data come from Exhibit 5–7.

These widely varying consumption ratios result from Patio Grill Company's product line diversity. A single cost driver will not capture the widely differing usage of these activities by the three products. The activity-based costing system uses two different cost drivers to assign these costs to the company's diverse products.

Two Key Points To summarize, each of the following characteristics will undermine the ability of a volume-based product-costing system to assign overhead costs accurately.

- *A large proportion of non-unit-level activities.* A unit-level cost driver, such as direct labor, machine hours, or throughput, will not be able to assign the costs of non-unit-level activities accurately.
- *Product diversity.* When the consumption ratios differ widely between activities, no single cost driver will accurately assign the resulting overhead costs.

When either of these characteristics is present, a volume-based product-costing system is likely to distort product costs.

Does the sort of product-cost distortion experienced by Patio Grill Company occur in other companies? The answer is yes, as illustrated by the following examples from Rockwell International and DHL express transport service. (See tops of next two pages.)

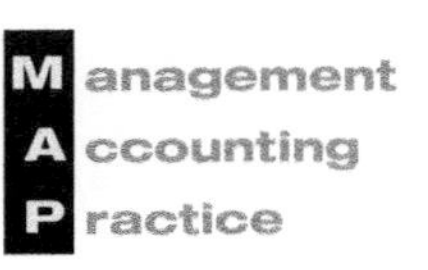

Rockwell International

COST DISTORTION AT ROCKWELL INTERNATIONAL

When managers at Rockwell International noticed erratic sales in one of the company's lines of truck axles, they investigated. One of the company's best axle products was losing market share. A special cost study revealed that the firm's costing system, which applied costs to products in proportion to direct-labor costs, had resulted in major distortions. The reported product costs for high-volume axles were approximately 20 percent too high, and the low-volume axles were being undercosted by roughly 40 percent. The firm's practice of basing prices on reported product costs resulted in the overpricing of the high-volume axles. As a consequence, Rockwell's competitors entered the market for the high-volume axle business.[2]

Activity-Based Costing: Some Key Issues

"Before the industry really became wide open in long-distance competition [as the result of deregulation], you could get by with knowing less. You could get by with having price structures that were not based on the underlying activities and the costs associated with those activities, but were instead based on broad averages. It was okay. It worked. It's not good enough anymore. We have to get more precise in our costs. We have to deliver the kinds of prices to our customers that they're willing to pay." (5a)

TELUS

Patio Grill Company's movement toward activity-based costing is typical of changes currently underway in many companies. Added domestic and foreign competition is forcing manufacturers to strive for a better understanding of their cost structures. Moreover, the cost structures of many manufacturers have changed significantly over the past decade. Years ago, a typical manufacturer produced a relatively small number of products that did not differ much in the amount and types of manufacturing support they required. Labor was the dominant element in such a firm's cost structure. Nowadays, it's a different ball game. Products are more numerous, are more complicated, and vary more in their production requirements. Perhaps most important, labor is becoming an ever-smaller component of total production costs. All these factors mean manufacturers must take a close look at their traditional, volume-based costing systems and consider a move toward activity-based costing. Among the many well-known manufacturers that have benefited from ABC are Boise Cascade, Caterpillar, Coca-Cola, Chrysler, Hewlett-Packard, John Deere, Johnson & Johnson, Pennzoil, and Pfizer to name only a few.

The service sector also has undergone dynamic change in recent years. Increasing competition, outsourcing of key business processes, and the growth of the Internet have changed many service companies' business models. As their business environment changes, many service-industry firms have made use of activity-based costing. Service companies benefiting from ABC include American Airlines, American Express, AT&T, Blue Cross/Blue Shield, DHL, FedEx, Gemico (GE Capital Mortgage Insurance Company), and Summit Bank, among many others. Governmental units also have implemented activity-based costing. Among the governmental units that have benefited from ABC are such diverse organizations as the British Navy, the California Department of Taxation, the City of Indianapolis, and several agencies of the U.S. government, including the Immigration and Naturalization Service, the Internal Revenue Service, the Veterans Affairs Department, and the U.S. Postal Service.

An important factor in the move toward ABC systems is related to the information requirements of such systems. The data required for activity-based costing are more readily available than in the past. Increasing automation, coupled with sophisticated real-time information systems, provides the kind of data necessary to implement highly accurate product-costing systems. Some key issues related to activity-based costing systems are discussed in the following sections.

[2]Ford S. Worthy, "Accounting Bores You? Wake Up," *Fortune* 116, no. 8, pp. 43–53. For another example of cost distortion, see S. L. Mintz, "Compaq's Secret Weapon," *CFO* 10, no. 10, pp. 93–97.

DHL

COST DISTORTION AT DHL

DHL, the express transport company, ships packages to 220 countries and territories throughout the world. Management at DHL found that its cost accounting system had distorted costs between the various types of express transport services the firm provided. Before implementation of a full activity-based costing system at DHL, express transport services provided to banks appeared to be unprofitable, whereas transport services provided to heavy manufacturers appeared to be highly profitable. "This was bad news because we (DHL) had a lot more banking customers than heavy manufacturing customers." After fully implementing ABC, however, management found that the previous costing system had used cost drivers that failed to account for package weights, thereby distorting costs between services to banks and services to heavy manufacturers. The ABC analysis revealed that express transport services to banks were actually quite profitable after all.[3]

Cost Drivers

Learning Objective 6

Explain three criteria for selecting cost drivers.

A **cost driver** is a characteristic of an event or activity that results in the incurrence of costs. In activity-based costing systems, the most significant cost drivers are identified. Then a database is created, which shows how these cost drivers are distributed across products. Three factors are important in selecting appropriate cost drivers.

1. *Degree of correlation.* The central concept of an activity-based costing system is to assign the costs of each activity to product lines on the basis of how each product line consumes the cost driver identified for that activity. The idea is to *infer* how each product line consumes the activity by *observing* how each product line consumes the cost driver. Therefore, the accuracy of the resulting cost assignments depends on the *degree of correlation* between consumption of the activity and consumption of the cost driver.

   Say that inspection cost is selected as an activity cost pool. The objective of the ABC system is to assign inspection costs to product lines on the basis of their consumption of the inspection activity. Two potential cost drivers come to mind: number of inspections and hours of inspection time. If every inspection requires the same amount of time for all products, then the number of inspections on a product line will be highly correlated with the consumption of inspection activity by that product line. On the other hand, if inspections vary significantly in the time required, then simply recording the number of inspections will not adequately portray the consumption of inspection activity. In this case, hours of inspection time would be more highly correlated with the actual consumption of the inspection activity.

2. *Cost of measurement.* Designing any information system entails cost-benefit trade-offs. The more activity cost pools there are in an activity-based costing system, the greater will be the accuracy of the cost assignments. However, more activity cost pools also entail more cost drivers, which results in greater costs of implementing and maintaining the system.

   Similarly, the higher the correlation between a cost driver and the actual consumption of the associated activity, the greater the accuracy of

"ABC is not a magic bullet, but it is a tool to help you understand your business better." (5b)
Braas Company

[3]See DHL Web site; S. Kranz, "Sitting Pretty in Prague: DHL's Tech Triumph," *BusinessWeek,* December 12, 2005, p. 56; and S. Player and C. Cobble, *Cornerstones of Decision Making: Profiles of Enterprise ABM* (Greensboro, NC: Oakhill Press, 1999), pp. 131–44.

"After the initial run-through, we completed a separate analysis detailing how many times a [cost] driver was used. We performed a sort of cost-benefit analysis. We gave each [cost] driver a grade, such as how easy would the driver be to collect." (5c)

John Deere Health Care, Inc.

the cost assignments. However, it also may be more costly to measure the more highly correlated cost driver. Returning to our example of the inspection activity, it may be that inspection hours make a more accurate cost driver than the number of inspections. It is likely, however, that inspection hours also will be more costly to measure and track over time.

3. *Behavioral effects.* Information systems have the potential not only to facilitate decisions but also to influence the behavior of decision makers. This can be good or bad, depending on the behavioral effects. In identifying cost drivers, an ABC analyst should consider the possible behavioral consequences. For example, in a just-in-time (JIT) production environment, a key goal is to reduce inventories and material-handling activities to the absolute minimum level possible. The number of material moves may be the most accurate measure of the consumption of the material-handling activity for cost assignment purposes. It also may have a desirable behavioral effect of inducing managers to reduce the number of times materials are moved, thereby reducing material-handling costs.

   Dysfunctional behavioral effects are also possible. For example, the number of vendor contacts may be a cost driver for the purchasing activity of vendor selection. This could induce purchasing managers to contact fewer vendors, which could result in the failure to identify the lowest-cost or highest-quality vendor.

Collecting ABC Data

Learning Objective 7

Discuss several key issues in activity-based costing including data collection and storyboarding.

The output of an organization's various departments consists of the activities performed by personnel or machines in those departments. Activities usually result in paperwork or the generation of computer documents. For example, engineering departments typically deal with documents such as specification sheets and engineering change orders. Purchasing departments handle requisitions and orders, which may be either hard-copy or computer documents. In an ABC system, analysis of documents such as these can be used to assign the costs of activities to product lines on the basis of the amount of activity generated by each product.

"We were negotiating fees, and the customer was under the impression that they were paying more than they should . . . . To make this customer comfortable with the pricing, we needed a [more accurate] costing system." (5d)

Dana Commercial Credit Corporation

Interviews and Paper Trails The information used in Patio Grill Company's ABC system came initially from extensive interviews with key employees in each of the organization's support departments and a careful review of each department's records. In the engineering area, for example, ABC project team members interviewed each engineer to determine the breakdown of time spent on each of the three products. They also examined every engineering change order completed in the past two years. The team concluded that engineering costs were driven largely by engineering hours and that the breakdown was 500 hours for the STD grill line, 400 hours for the DEL grill line, and 400 hours for the ULT grill line.

Storyboarding As Patio Grill Company's project team delved further into the ABC analysis, they made considerable use of another technique for collecting activity data. **Storyboarding** is a procedure used to develop a detailed process flowchart, which visually represents activities and the relationships among the activities. A storyboarding session involves all or most of the employees who participate in the activities oriented toward achieving a specific objective. A facilitator helps the employees identify the key activities involved in their jobs. These activities are written on small cards and placed on a large board in the order they are accomplished. Relationships among the activities are shown by the order and proximity of the cards. Other information about the activities is recorded on the cards, such as the amount of time and other resources that are expended on each activity and the events that trigger the activity. After several storyboarding sessions, a completed storyboard emerges, recording key activity information vital to the ABC project. Historically, storyboards have been used by Walt Disney and other film producers in the development of plots for animated films. More recently, storyboarding has been used by advertising agencies in developing event sequences for TV commercials.

Interviews with department personnel and storyboarding sessions are often used by activity-based costing project teams to accumulate the data needed for an ABC study. In the interview sessions, an ABC project team member asks departmental employees to detail their activities, as well as the time and other resources consumed by the activities. Storyboards, like the one depicted here, visually show the relationships between the activities performed in an organization.

Storyboarding provides a powerful tool for collecting and organizing the data needed in an ABC project. Patio Grill Company's ABC project team used storyboarding very effectively to study each of the firm's activity cost pools. The team concluded that purchasing costs were driven by the number of purchase orders. Material-handling costs were driven by the number of production runs. Quality-assurance costs were driven by the number of inspection hours devoted to each product line. Packaging and shipping costs were driven by the number of shipments made.

In summary, the ABC project team conducted a painstaking and lengthy analysis involving many employee interviews, the examination of hundreds of documents, and storyboarding sessions. The final result was the data used in the ABC calculations displayed in Exhibits 5–7 and 5–8.

Multidisciplinary ABC Project Teams In order to gather information from all facets of an organization's operations, it is essential to involve personnel from a variety of functional areas. A typical ABC project team includes accounting and finance people as well as engineers, marketing personnel, production and operations managers, and so forth. A multidisciplinary project team not only designs a better ABC system but also helps in gaining credibility for the new system throughout the organization.

Activity Dictionary and Bill of Activities

Many organizations' ABC teams compile an **activity dictionary,** which is a complete listing of the activities identified and used in the ABC analysis. An activity dictionary helps in the implementation of activity-based costing across several divisions of an organization, because it provides for consistency in the ABC system terminology and the complexity of the ABC analyses in the various divisions.

A **bill of activities** is another commonly used element in an ABC analysis. A bill of activities for a product or service is a complete listing of the activities required for the product or service to be produced. As a familiar analogy, think about a recipe for chocolate chip cookies. The *bill of materials* for the cookies is the list of ingredients provided

"Having a plant-level activity dictionary allows the plant to manage its activities locally and serves as a standard reference that employees can use to see which activities roll up into which processes." (5e)

Navistar International Corporation

in the recipe. The *bill of activities* is the list of steps given in the recipe for making the cookies (e.g., combine ingredients in a bowl, stir in chocolate chips, place spoon-size globs of dough on greased cookie sheet, bake at 375° for 10 minutes or until done).

Activity-Based Management

Learning Objective 8

Explain the concepts of activity-based management and two-dimensional ABC.

Using activity-based costing (ABC) information to support organizational strategy, improve operations, and manage costs is called **activity-based management** or **ABM.** We have already caught a glimpse of activity-based management earlier in this chapter, where the management of Patio Grill Company used ABC information to better understand its product-pricing decisions. The company's management discovered through the ABC analysis that some products were overcosted and some products were undercosted by their traditional product-costing system. This important insight presented management with the opportunity to revise its product pricing in order to reflect the more accurate product costs provided by the ABC analysis. When management followed up on this product-pricing opportunity, it was engaging in activity-based management. However, ABM is a much broader concept than this. Activity-based management involves any use of ABC information to support the organization's strategy, improve operations, or manage activities and their resulting costs.

Two-Dimensional ABC

One way of picturing the relationship between ABC and ABM is in terms of the **two-dimensional ABC model** depicted in Exhibit 5–11.[4] The vertical dimension of the model depicts the cost assignment view of an ABC system. From the *cost assignment viewpoint,* the ABC system uses two-stage cost allocation to *assign* the costs of resources to the firm's cost objects. These cost objects could be products manufactured, services produced, or customers served.

Now focus on the horizontal dimension of the model. Depicted here is the *process view* of an ABC system. The emphasis now is on the activities themselves, the various processes by which work is accomplished in the organization. The left-hand side of Exhibit 5–11 depicts **activity analysis,** which is the detailed identification and description of the activities conducted in the enterprise. Activity analysis entails identification not only of the activities but also of their *root causes,* the events that *trigger* activities, and the *linkages* among activities. The right-hand side of Exhibit 5–11 depicts the evaluation of activities through performance measures. It is these processes of *activity analysis and evaluation* that comprise activity-based management. Notice that the *activities,* which appear in the center of both dimensions in Exhibit 5–11, are the focal point of ABC and ABM.

Using ABM to Identify Non-Value-Added Activities and Costs

An important goal of activity-based management is to identify and eliminate non-value-added activities and costs. **Non-value-added activities** are operations that are either (1) unnecessary and dispensable or (2) necessary, but inefficient and improvable.[5] **Non-value-added costs,** which result from such activities, are the costs of activities that can be eliminated without deterioration of product quality, performance, or perceived value.

---

[4]This section draws on Lewis J. Soloway, "Using Activity-Based Management in Aerospace and Defense Companies," *Journal of Cost Management* 6, no. 4 (Winter 1993), pp. 56–66; and Peter B. B. Turney, "What an Activity-Based Cost Model Looks Like," *Journal of Cost Management* 5, no. 4 (Winter 1992), pp. 54–60.

[5]This definition, as well as other material in this section, is drawn from James A. Brimson, "Improvement and Elimination of Non-Value-Added Costs," *Journal of Cost Management* 2, no. 2 (Summer 1988), pp. 62–65.

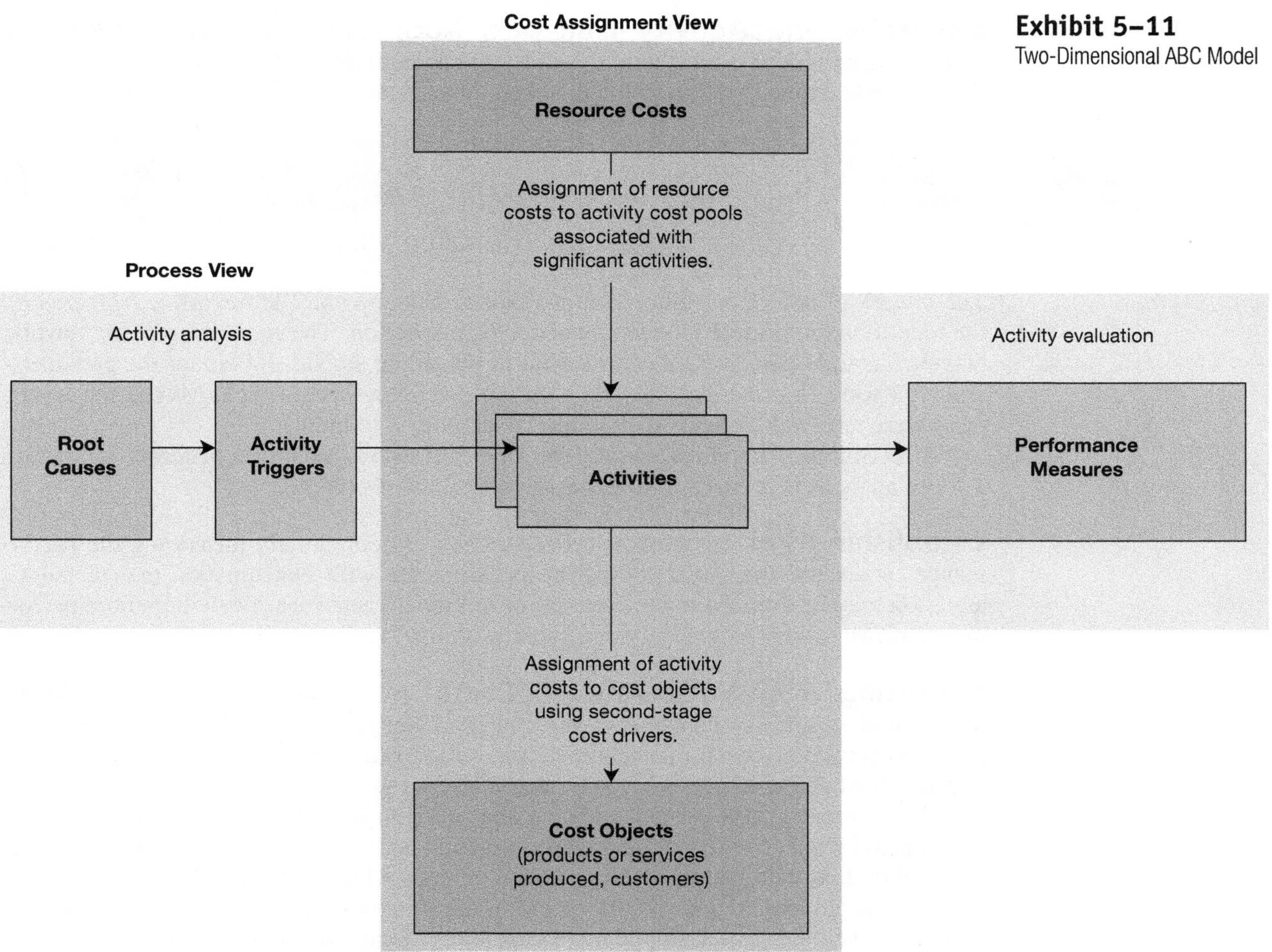

Exhibit 5–11
Two-Dimensional ABC Model

The following five steps provide a strategy for eliminating non-value-added costs in both manufacturing and service industry firms.

Identifying Activities The first step is activity analysis, which identifies all of the organization's significant activities. The resulting activity list should be broken down to the most fundamental level practical. For example, rather than listing purchasing as an activity, the list should break down the purchasing operation into its component activities, such as obtaining part specifications, compiling vendor lists, selecting vendors, negotiating prices, ordering, and expediting.

Identifying Non-Value-Added Activities Three criteria for determining whether an activity adds value are as follows:

- *Is the activity necessary?* If it's a duplicate or nonessential operation, it is non-value-added.
- *Is the activity efficiently performed?* In answering this question, it is helpful to compare the actual performance of the activity to a value-added baseline established using budgets, targets, or external benchmarks.
- *Is an activity sometimes value-added and sometimes non-value-added?* For example, it may be necessary to move work-in-process units between production operations, but unnecessary to move raw materials around while in storage.

> "Putting a spotlight on non-value-added activities, such as [correcting] errors in procurement, provided the focus for ultimately implementing process improvements." (5f)
>
> **GTE Supply** (currently a part of Verizon)

Understanding Activity Linkages, Root Causes, and Triggers In identifying non-value-added activities, it is critical to understand the ways in which activities are linked together. The following chain of activities provides an example:

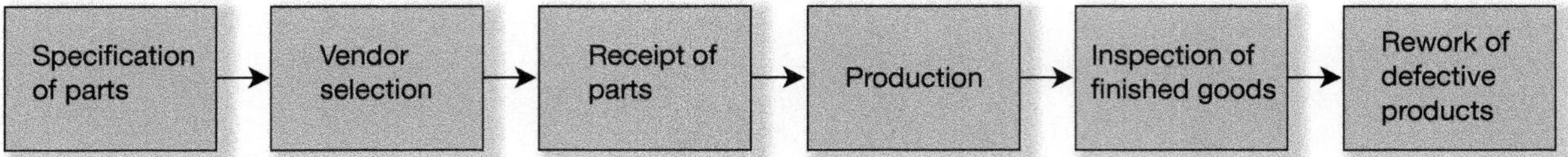

The rework of defective units is a non-value-added activity. The rework is *triggered* by the identification of defective products during inspection. The *root cause* of the rework, however, could lie in any one of a number of preceding activities. Perhaps the part specifications were in error. Possibly an unreliable vendor was selected. Maybe the wrong parts were received. Perhaps the production activity is to blame.

A set of linked activities (such as that depicted above) is called a **process.** Sometimes activity analysis is referred to as **process value analysis (PVA).**

Establishing Performance Measures By continually measuring the performance of all activities, and comparing performance with benchmarks, management's attention may be directed to unnecessary or inefficient activities. We will explore performance measurement extensively in Chapters 10 and 11.

Reporting Non-Value-Added Costs Non-value-added costs should be highlighted in activity center cost reports. By identifying non-value-added activities, and reporting their costs, management can strive toward the ongoing goals of process improvement and elimination of non-value-added costs.

One approach that cost-management analysts find helpful in identifying non-value-added activities is to categorize the ways in which time is spent in a production process. Let's return to our illustration of Patio Grill Company's Denver plant, where gas barbeque grills are manufactured. How is time spent in the plant from the time raw material arrives until a finished gas grill is shipped to a customer? As in most manufacturing operations, time is spent in the following five ways.

1. *Process time.* The time during which a product is undergoing conversion activity.
2. *Inspection time.* The amount of time spent ensuring that the product is of high quality.
3. *Move time.* The time spent moving raw materials, work in process, or finished goods between operations.
4. *Waiting time.* The amount of time that raw materials or work in process spend waiting for the next operation.
5. *Storage time.* The time during which materials, partially completed products, or finished goods are held in stock before further processing or shipment to customers.

Thinking about the production operation in these terms allows management to ask the questions, "Does the time spent in all of these activities add value to the product? Will the customer pay for it? Can the time spent on inspection be reduced without diminishing product quality? Can production efficiency be improved by reducing the number of times materials, work-in-process, or finished goods are moved from one place to another? Can production be scheduled so that partially completed products spend less time just waiting for the next operation? Can storage time be reduced by ordering raw material and producing products only as they are needed?" Many companies have implemented just-in-time (JIT) inventory and production management systems to reduce move, waiting, and storage time. JIT systems are covered in the appendix to this chapter.

If reductions can be made in any of these time-consuming activities, without diminishing product quality or functionality, management has a real opportunity to reduce non-value-added costs.

Some companies have begun making a distinction between *customer-value-added activities* and *business-value-added activities.* For example, the addition of a 24/7 customer-service hotline to assist customers in maximizing their benefits from the products or services they have purchased would likely be an activity that customers would value. In contrast, most customers would not value a company's expenditures on information technology (IT) or accounting, whereas these activities are likely to be critical to the success of the company's business model.

Customer-Profitability Analysis

Learning Objective 9

Explain and execute a customer-profitability analysis.

It is quite possible for a company to have profitable products and, at the same time, incur customer-related costs that make certain customer relationships unprofitable. **Customer-profitability analysis** uses activity-based costing to determine the activities, costs, and profit associated with serving particular customers. Suppose, for example, that customer X frequently changes its orders after they are placed, but customer Y typically does not. Then the costs incurred in updating sales orders for changes should be recorded in a manner that reflects the fact that customer X is more responsible for those activities and costs than is customer Y. An effective cost management system should allow managers to derive such cost details.

Many factors can result in some customers being more profitable than others. Customers that order in small quantities, order frequently, often change their orders, require special packaging or handling, demand faster delivery, or need special parts or engineering design generally are less profitable than customers who demand less in terms of customized services. If managers have a good understanding of which customers are generating the greatest profit, they can make more-informed decisions about customer service. Moreover, this allows customers to be educated as to the costs they are causing when demanding special services. In many cases, customers' behavior can be changed in a way that reduces costs to the supplier. Then these cost savings can be shared by the supplier and the customer.

The task of assigning costs to customers is a challenge. A system must be in place that enables the company to identify which customers are using customer support services and how frequently they do so. How much time must the company spend on a customer to make the sale and to provide ongoing support services? These costs are in addition to the cost of manufacturing the product or initially providing a service for the customer.

Illustration of Customer-Profitability Analysis

To illustrate customer-profitability analysis, let's focus again on Patio Grill Company. Two more years have passed, and the company has successfully implemented its activity-based costing system in its Denver plant. At a recent strategy meeting with her senior management team, Patio Grill Company's president and CEO expressed interest in assessing the profitability of the entire company's various customer relationships. She found support for the idea from the director of cost management, who had been reading about customer-profitability analysis in some of his professional journals. The company's marketing manager also expressed interest in customer-profitability analysis, since he was concerned about the profitability of a couple of Patio Grill Company's customers in particular. "We have a few customers who seem to want the moon and the stars when it comes to customer service," he complained. "I know the customer is always right and all, but you really have to wonder if we're making any money from a couple of these customers, what with all the extra design and packaging they demand. And some of our other customers seem to require an awful lot of extra attention in sales calls, order processing, and billing. If we had a better idea of each customer's profitability, it would help our marketing and sales staffs to focus their efforts."

The controller soon had his cost management staff attacking the customer-profitability analysis that the president had requested. The first step required an activity-based costing analysis of certain *customer-related costs* that could seriously

Exhibit 5–12
ABC Analysis for Customer-Related Costs: Patio Grill Company

Customer-Related Activities	Cost Driver Base	Cost Driver Rate
Order processing	Purchase orders	$ 150
Sales contacts (phone calls, faxes, etc.)	Contacts	100
Sales visits	Visits	1,000
Shipment processing	Shipments	200
Billing and collection	Invoices	160
Design/engineering change orders	Engineering/design changes	4,000
Special packaging	Units packaged	40
Special handling	Units handled	60

"When we saw what some of our customers were costing us, we were quite surprised. We shared this information with them, and they were also surprised to see how much work went into servicing them. At this point, we negotiated with them to eliminate certain discounts they were receiving." (5g)
Pfizer
(formerly Warner Lambert)

affect a customer's profitability. Recall that ABC analysis relies on a cost hierarchy with cost levels, such as unit-level, batch-level, product-line-level, customer-level, and facility- or general-operations-level costs. In this use of activity-based costing, the cost management team is focusing on the customer-related costs. After an extensive analysis and several interviews with personnel throughout Patio Grill Company, the cost management team came up with the ABC analysis in Exhibit 5–12.[6]

Based on the activity-based costing information, the cost management team assessed the profitability of each of Patio Grill Company's customer relationships. Detailed information from that analysis for five of these customers appears in the Excel spreadsheet in Exhibit 5–13. These five customers were singled out because three of them are key customers (i.e., customers 106, 112, and 113), and two of them (107 and 119) were suspected by the marketing manager to be at best marginally profitable. As it turned out, suspicions about customers 107 and 119 were well founded. Both customers were found to be unprofitable; in fact, customer 119 had caused a loss of almost $120,000 during the year.

[6]An important point that could be overlooked here is that activity-based costing analysis can be used in a very specific, targeted manner to address a particular management problem. In this case, the ABC focus is customer-profitability analysis. This is the essence of activity-based management, using the results of an ABC analysis to manage an enterprise more effectively.

Exhibit 5–13
Customer-Profitability Analysis for Five Designated Customers: Patio Grill Company

Microsoft Excel - Customer-Profitability Analysis for Five Designated Customers

F20 =F6-F19

	A	B	C	D	E	F
1		Designated Customers (By 3-Digit Customer Code)				
2		Customer 106	Customer 107	Customer 112	Customer 113	Customer 119
3						
4	Sales revenue	$ 4,320,000	$ 3,480,000	$ 6,500,000	$ 4,490,000	$ 1,960,000
5	Cost of goods sold	3,220,000	2,810,000	4,890,000	3,380,000	1,480,000
6	Gross margin	$ 1,100,000	$ 670,000	$ 1,610,000	$ 1,110,000	$ 480,000
7	Selling and administrative costs:					
8	General selling costs	$ 362,000	$ 220,000	$ 530,000	$ 366,000	$ 160,000
9	General administrative costs	181,000	110,000	265,000	183,000	80,000
10	Customer-related costs					
11	Order processing	11,100	80,250	16,050	22,200	38,400
12	Sales contacts	22,000	13,400	32,000	24,100	28,800
13	Sales visits	44,000	20,000	47,000	38,000	32,000
14	Shipment processing	33,000	27,800	64,200	44,600	19,200
15	Billing and collection	33,600	14,000	80,480	22,400	9,600
16	Design/engineering changes	93,000	96,000	84,000	112,000	68,000
17	Special packaging	88,000	27,200	64,440	44,480	76,800
18	Special handling	33,000	80,400	48,300	33,300	86,400
19	Total selling and administrative cost	$ 900,700	$ 689,050	$ 1,231,470	$ 890,080	$ 599,200
20	Operating income	$ 199,300	$ (19,050)	$ 378,530	$ 219,920	$ (119,200)

Sheet1 / Sheet2 / Sheet3

Ready

Bank One Corp.

CUSTOMER PROFITABILITY ANALYSIS AT BANK ONE CORP.

The Wall Street Journal described how Bank One Corp. (now part of JPMorgan Chase Bank) has used customer-profitability analysis to guide decisions about customer service.

At Bank One Corp., at the time one of the largest banks, "the line in the sand between preferred and nonpreferred customers has become strikingly obvious." The bank is redesigning its 218 branches in Louisiana so its "Premier One" customers can be whisked away to a special teller window with no wait or to the desk of an appropriate bank officer. "Customers qualify by keeping at least $2,500 in a checking account or a total of $25,000 in a combination of certain bank accounts," or by paying a $17 monthly fee. "Management estimates that the extra attention will go only to the top 20 percent of its customers."[7]

A complete customer-profitability analysis for all of Patio Grill Company's customers appears in the spreadsheet in Exhibit 5–14. This exhibit reveals several interesting aspects of the customer-profitability scenario. Seventeen of 20 customers are profitable. The three unprofitable customers (107, 134, and 119) resulted in losses of over $240,000 in operating income for Patio Grill Company in a single year! Notice that over 25 percent of the company's profit is generated by its top three customers. Almost half the company's profit comes from its top six customers, and fully three-quarters of its

"Almost any person in any organization that implements ABM has some real surprises when they start seeing the data about customer profitability and product profitability." (5h)
Shiloh Industries, Inc.

[7]"Alienating Customers Isn't Always a Bad Idea Many Firms Discover," *The Wall Street Journal,* January 7, 1999.

Exhibit 5–14
Customer-Profitability Analysis with Customers Ranked by Operating Income: Patio Grill Company

Microsoft Excel - Customer-Profitability Analysis - Customers Ranked by Operating Income

E25 =SUM(D6:D25)

	A	B	C	D	E	F
1						Cumulative Operating
2	3-Digit	Customer	Customer	Customer	Cumulative	Income as a
3	Customer	Sales	Gross	Operating	Operating	Percentage of Total
4	Code	Revenue	Margin	Income	Income	Operating Income
5						
6	112	$ 6,500,000	$ 1,610,000	$ 378,530	$ 378,530	8.8%
7	108	6,964,000	1,570,000	370,000	748,530	17.3%
8	114	6,694,000	1,484,300	351,000	1,099,530	25.5%
9	116	5,846,000	1,461,600	340,000	1,439,530	33.4%
10	110	5,602,000	1,430,000	336,070	1,775,600	41.1%
11	121	5,400,000	1,413,000	331,000	2,106,600	48.8%
12	124	5,601,000	1,405,520	330,000	2,436,600	56.5%
13	127	5,090,000	1,280,020	300,000	2,736,600	63.4%
14	128	4,760,000	1,160,200	281,400	3,018,000	69.9%
15	125	5,000,200	1,181,000	276,000	3,294,000	76.3%
16	135	4,431,000	1,150,000	270,000	3,564,000	82.6%
17	133	4,008,000	1,059,800	251,400	3,815,400	88.4%
18	113	4,490,000	1,110,000	219,920	4,035,320	93.5%
19	111	4,200,000	875,220	205,000	4,240,320	98.2%
20	106	4,320,000	1,100,000	199,300	4,439,620	102.9%
21	136	1,920,000	351,200	82,000	4,521,620	104.8%
22	137	1,641,000	139,400	35,600	4,557,220	105.6%
23	107	3,480,000	670,000	(19,050)	4,538,170	105.1%
24	134	2,820,000	582,000	(102,600)	4,435,570	102.8%
25	119	1,960,000	480,000	(119,200)	4,316,370	100.0%

Chart1 | Sheet1 | Sheet2 | Sheet3

Ready

Exhibit 5–15
Customer-Profitability Profile in Terms of Cumulative Operating Income as a Percentage of Total Operating Income: Patio Grill Company

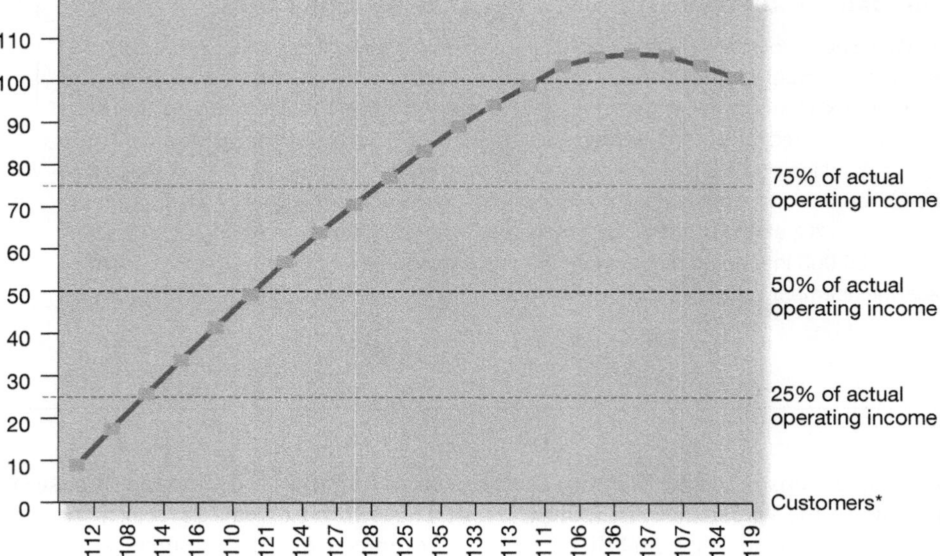

*Customers ranked by operating income.

profit is generated by half its customers. This sort of customer-profitability scenario is quite typical for manufacturers. The lion's share of most companies' profits comes from a handful of their customers. Such an insight is important for management as it determines where to devote the company's resources in serving customers.[8]

A graphical portrayal of Patio Grill Company's complete customer-profitability analysis is given in Exhibit 5–15. This graph is called a **customer-profitability profile,** and it is a common and useful way of presenting a customer-profitability analysis to management.

Activity-Based Costing in the Service Industry

Learning Objective 10

Understand and discuss how activity-based costing is used in service-industry organizations.

We conclude this chapter with the important point that activity-based costing has found widespread usage in the service industry as well as in manufacturing. There have been many ABC success stories in such diverse organizations as airlines, insurance companies, banks, hospitals, financial services firms, hotels, railroads, and government agencies. Among the service organizations that used activity-based costing are Air France, American Airlines, American Express, Bank of America, Cambridge Hospital Community Health Care Network, City of Indianapolis, FedEx, Owens & Minor, Telus, Union Pacific, U.S. Naval Supply Center, and the U.S. Postal Service.

"As bankers become more familiar with the [ABC] numbers and start to embrace them, their decision making improves, their profitability increases, and the growth of the business improves." (5i)
Summit Bancorp

The overall objectives of ABC in service firms are no different than they are in manufacturing companies. Managers want more accurate information about the cost of producing the services they are selling. Moreover, they want to use this information to improve operations and to better meet the needs of their customers in a more cost-effective manner. The general approach of identifying activities, activity cost pools, and cost drivers is used in the service industry as well as in manufacturing. The classification of activities into unit-level, batch-level, product-sustaining-level, and facility-level activities

[8]In a conversation with a vice president from a large consumer-products manufacturer, the author was struck by the executive's statement that, "You can bet we pay a lot of attention to the needs and desires of the 'Mart Brothers,' K and Wal."

Management **A**ccounting **P**ractice

Best Buy

CUSTOMER PROFITABILITY ANALYSIS AT BEST BUY

After Circuit City's recent liquidation, Best Buy, with over $45 billion in annual revenue, became the country's last major consumer electronics retailer.[9] Best Buy's CEO "is embracing a heretical notion for a retailer. He wants to separate the best customers among the 1.5 million people who visit Best Buy's stores every day from the worst customers." Best Buy's preferred customers "boost profits at the consumer-electronics giant by snapping up high-definition televisions, portable electronics, and newly released DVDs without waiting for markdowns or rebates."[10] The retailer's worst customers, on the other hand, "buy products, apply for rebates, return the purchases, and then buy them back at returned-merchandise discounts. They load up on loss-leaders, severely discounted merchandise designed to boost store traffic, then "flip" the goods at a profit on eBay. They slap down rock-bottom price quotes from Web sites and demand that Best Buy make good on its lowest-price pledge." According to Best Buy's CEO, these customers "can wreak enormous economic havoc." The company estimates "that as many as 100 million of its 500 million customer visits each year are undesirable." And Best Buy's CEO "wants to be rid of these customers." The company's new approach "upends what has long been standard practice for mass merchants. Most chains use their advertising budgets chiefly to maximize customer traffic." Best Buy's new plan is to "rate its customers according to profitability, and then dump the up to 20 percent that are unprofitable." Best Buy rolled out its new strategy in about 100 of its 670 stores. Best Buy "is examining its sales records and demographic data and sleuthing through computer databases to identify good and bad customers. To lure the high spenders, it is stocking more merchandise and providing more appealing service. To deter the undesirables, it is cutting back on promotions and sales tactics that tend to draw them, and culling them from the marketing lists."[11]

also applies in service industry settings. For example, Pennsylvania Blue Shield used these activity classifications in its ABC system.[12] Examples from the Blue Shield system are as follows:

- *Unit level:* Entering initial claim data into the computer (for each claim received).
- *Batch level:* Moving a batch of claims from one processing step to the next.
- *Product-sustaining level:* Maintenance of the medical-services provider network (i.e., maintaining relationships with physicians and hospitals providing medical care to claimants).
- *Facility (general operations) level:* General administration of the claims business unit.

---

[9] "Why Tech Bows to Best Buy," *BusinessWeek,* December 21, 2009, and recent Best Buy annual reports.

[10] G. McWilliams, "Analyzing Customers, Best Buy Decides Not All Are Welcome," *The Wall Street Journal,* November 8, 2004.

[11] Ibid.

[12] Angela Norkiewicz, "Nine Steps to Implementing ABC," *Management Accounting* 75, no. 10 (April 1994), pp. 28–33.

Activity-Based Costing at Delaware Medical Center

To see how management can use activity-based costing in a service-industry setting, let's explore how ABC is used at Delaware Medical Center's Primary Care Unit.[13] Delaware Medical Center serves patients in Wilmington, Delaware, and several surrounding counties. The Primary Care Unit is the medical center's outpatient clinic and provides nearly 25,000 patient appointments in a typical year. The Primary Care Unit's administration implemented activity-based costing in order to determine how much it costs to serve patients in various categories. The Primary Care Unit classifies patient appointments as routine, extended, or complex, depending on the appointment length and complexity. In addition, each appointment is classified as either a new-patient appointment or a continuing-patient appointment. Thus, every patient appointment is one of the following six types.

	Routine	**Extended**	**Complex**
New patient	New patient; routine appointment	New patient; extended appointment	New patient; complex appointment
Continuing patient	Continuing patient; routine appointment	Continuing patient; extended appointment	Continuing patient; complex appointment

Every patient appointment involves a registered nurse (or RN), who takes vital signs and prepares the patient for the primary health care professional. Then, every patient is seen by one primary health care professional, which can be a physician, a nurse practitioner, an intern, or a resident. No appointment involves more than one of these types of primary health care professionals.

The Primary Care Unit's ABC project team designated the following activities and cost drivers.

Activity	**Cost Driver**
Physician time	Physician minutes with patient
Nurse practitioner time	Nurse practitioner minutes with patient
Intern or resident time	Intern or resident minutes with patient
Registered nurse time	Registered nurse minutes with patient
Clerical time: new patients	New patient visits
Clerical time: continuing patients	Continuing patient visits
Billing	Billing lines (i.e., number of line items on bill)
Facility	Patient visits (both new and continuing)

The activity-based costing analysis is displayed in the Excel spreadsheet in Exhibit 5–16. Notice that this ABC spreadsheet for Delaware Medical Center's Primary Care Unit has a format that is identical to the ABC spreadsheet prepared for Patio Grill Company (Exhibit 5–7 on page 177). The column headings are different, because the Primary Care Unit provides medical services to patients, whereas Patio Grill Company manufactures barbeque grills. Conceptually and computationally, however, the two Excel spreadsheets are identical.

The *information supplied by the primary care unit's ABC project team* is located in the following columns.

Column A: Activity
Column B: Activity cost pool
Column C: Cost driver
Column D: Cost driver quantity

[13]For a more elaborate example of activity-based costing in a hospital's primary care unit, see V. G. Narayanan, R. Moore, and L. Brem, "Cambridge Hospital Community Health Care Network—The Primary Care Unit" (Boston: The President and Fellows of Harvard College, 2000). In this case, minutes of time with a health care professional is a key cost driver.

Column F: Patient visit type (routine, extended, or complex)
Column G: Cost driver quantity for each type of patient visit
Column I: Patient volume for each type of visit

The *ABC computations* are in columns E, H, and J and are shown in red.

Column E: Pool rate

Pool rate (column E) = Activity cost pool (column B) ÷ Cost driver quantity (column D)

For example, the pool rate for physician time (cell E6) is calculated as follows:

\$4.00 per physician minute = \$960,000 ÷ 240,000 minutes of physician time

Column H: Activity cost for patient type

Activity cost for patient type (column H) = Pool rate (column E) × Cost driver quantity for patient type (column G)

For example, the physician activity cost for a routine visit (cell H6) is calculated as follows:

\$320,000 = \$4.00 per physician minute × 80,000 physician minutes on routine visits

Column J: Activity cost per patient of each type

Activity cost per patient of each type (column J) = Activity cost for patient type (column H) ÷ Patient type volume (column I)

For example, the physician activity cost per routine patient visit (cell J6) is calculated as follows:

\$40 per routine visit attended by a physician = \$320,000 ÷ 8,000 routine visits attended by a physician

Interpreting the Primary Care Unit's ABC Information

The Primary Care Unit's administration can use the ABC information in Exhibit 5–16 to determine the cost of each of the six types of patient appointments discussed earlier. Notice, though, that there is an important conceptual difference in the interpretation of the Primary Care Unit's ABC data (Exhibit 5–16) versus the interpretation of Patio Grill Company's ABC data (Exhibit 5–7 on page 177). In the Patio Grill Company manufacturing illustration, *all eight of the activities* identified in the ABC analysis were required by each line of barbeque grills manufactured. However, that is not true in the Primary Care Unit example. In this health care services setting, each patient sees *either* a physician, *or* a nurse practitioner, *or* an intern, *or* a resident—not all four. Moreover, each patient is *either* a new patient *or* a continuing patient—not both. Therefore, to compute the cost of a particular type of appointment, we must *select only one of the primary health care professionals,* which are highlighted by the red bar on the right-hand side of Exhibit 5–16. Moreover, we select *just one of the two categories for clerical time,* new patient or continuing patient, which are highlighted by the green bar on the right-hand side of Exhibit 5–16. Finally, since every patient appointment involves a registered nurse, *and* billing, *and* use of the primary care unit facility, *all* of these activities must be included in the cost calculation. (These activities are highlighted by the yellow bars on the right-hand side of Exhibit 5–16.)

Let's compute the cost of an extended appointment in which a new patient sees a nurse practitioner.

Exhibit 5–16
Activity-Based Costing Analysis: Delaware Medical Center

Microsoft Excel - Activity-Based Costing Analysis - Delaware Medical Center

E6 =B6/D6

	A	B	C	D	E	F	G	H	I	J
1							Cost Driver	Activity	Patient	Activity
2		Activity		Cost		Patient	Quantity for	Cost for	Type	Cost per
3		Cost	Cost	Driver	Pool	Visit	Patient	Patient	Visit	Patient of
4	Activity	Pool	Driver	Quantity	Rate	Type	Visit Type	Type	Volume	Each Type
5										
6	Physician	$ 960,000	Physician	240,000	$4.00	Routine	80,000	$ 320,000	8,000	$ 40.00
7	Time		Minutes			Extended	100,000	400,000	5,000	80.00
8			With Patient			Complex	60,000	240,000	2,000	120.00
9						Total	240,000	960,000		
10	Nurse	90,000	NP	30,000	3.00	Routine	12,000	36,000	1,200	30.00
11	Practitioner		Minutes			Extended	10,000	30,000	500	60.00
12	(NP) Time		With Patient			Complex	8,000	24,000	320	75.00
13						Total	30,000	90,000		
14	Intern or	412,500	I/R	125,000	3.30	Routine	40,000	132,000	4,000	33.00
15	Resident		Minutes			Extended	50,000	165,000	2,500	66.00
16	(I/R) Time		With Patient			Complex	35,000	115,500	1,000	115.50
17						Total	125,000	412,500		
18	Registered	281,980	RN	245,200	1.15	Routine	132,000	151,800	13,200	11.50
19	Nurse		Minutes			Extended	80,000	92,000	8,000	11.50
20	(RN) Time		With Patient			Complex	33,200	38,180	3,320	11.50
21						Total	245,200	281,980		
22	Clerical Tim	135,300	New	12,300	11.00	Routine	7,200	79,200	7,200	11.00
23	New		Patient			Extended	3,000	33,000	3,000	11.00
24	Patients		Visits			Complex	2,100	23,100	2,100	11.00
25						Total	12,300	135,300		
26	Clerical Tim	61,100	Continuing	12,220	5.00	Routine	6,000	30,000	6,000	5.00
27	Continuing		Patient			Extended	5,000	25,000	5,000	5.00
28	Patients		Visits			Complex	1,220	6,100	1,220	5.00
29						Total	12,220	61,100		
30	Billing	38,480	Billing	76,960	0.50	Routine	26,400	13,200	13,200	1.00
31			Lines			Extended	24,000	12,000	8,000	1.50
32						Complex	26,560	13,280	3,320	4.00
33						Total	76,960	38,480		
34	Facility	245,200	Patient	24,520	10.00	Routine	13,200	132,000	13,200	10.00
35			Visits			Extended	8,000	80,000	8,000	10.00
36			(Both New &			Complex	3,320	33,200	3,320	10.00
37			Continuing)			Total	24,520	245,200		
38										
39	Grand Total	$2,224,560				Grand Total		$2,224,560		

Sheet1 / Sheet2 / Sheet3

Ready

Activity	Cost (spreadsheet cell)
Nurse practitioner time	$60.00 (cell J11 in Exhibit 5–16)
Registered nurse time	11.50 (cell J19 in Exhibit 5–16)
Clerical time: new patients	11.00 (cell J23 in Exhibit 5–16)
Billing	1.50 (cell J31 in Exhibit 5–16)
Facility	10.00 (cell J35 in Exhibit 5–16)
Total	$94.00

Now let's compute the cost of a routine appointment in which a continuing patient sees a physician.

Activity	Cost (spreadsheet cell)
Physician time	$40.00 (cell J6 in Exhibit 5–16)
Registered nurse time	11.50 (cell J18 in Exhibit 5–16)
Clerical time: continuing patients	5.00 (cell J26 in Exhibit 5–16)
Billing	1.00 (cell J30 in Exhibit 5–16)
Facility	10.00 (cell J34 in Exhibit 5–16)
Total	$67.50

With a good understanding of how much it costs the Primary Care Unit to provide various types of patient appointments, the clinic's administration is in a much better position to make decisions. Determining appropriate charges for appointments, justifying third-party reimbursements from insurance companies and government agencies, and adding or discontinuing services are among the types of decisions that will be enhanced by the ABC information.

Focus on Ethics

ETHICAL ISSUES SURROUNDING ACTIVITY-BASED COSTING

Xavier Auto Parts, Inc. manufactures a wide range of auto parts, which it sells to auto manufacturers, primarily in the United States and Canada.* The company's Engine Parts Division operated three plants in South Carolina and specialized in engine parts. The division's Charlotte plant manufactured some 6,500 different parts.

Trouble Brewing

Both the Engine Parts Division, as well as the Charlotte plant in particular, had shown satisfactory profitability for the past 20 years. In 2009, however, the Charlotte plant's profitability took a sharp downward turn, in spite of rising sales. The trend continued through the next several years. Management at both the division and plant levels took note of the plant's declining profits and held several strategy meetings as a result.

Division Strategy

The Engine Parts Division had always positioned itself as the industry's full-line producer. If a customer wanted a product, the division would make it. Although occasionally very-low-volume products were discontinued due to lack of consistent orders, the division's product line remained a full line of engine parts. As part of its strategy review, division management did two things. First, an activity-based costing study was initiated in the Charlotte plant in order to give management a better picture of each product line's profitability. Second, a high-level review was undertaken to determine whether the full-line-producer strategy continued to make sense.

Activity-based Costing

An ABC project team was formed, and a successful pilot study was conducted on two of the Charlotte plant's product lines. Then the ABC project was extended to the entire Charlotte operation. Management was astonished to find that fully a quarter of the plant's products were selling at a loss. Moreover, the ABC project highlighted the extent of the product-line proliferation at the Charlotte plant. It turned out that in many instances, unprofitable products had been dropped only to creep back into the product line-up after a customer requested it and a salesperson acquiesced. It became a joke around the plant that the only way to be sure a dropped product was really gone was to burn the engineering drawings and destroy the special tools required to make it.

ABC Team Recommendations

The ABC project team made sweeping recommendations to division management, which suggested that the Charlotte plant's product lines be pruned and that roughly 20 percent of its products be dropped. New emphasis would then be devoted to increasing the profitability of the remaining 80 percent of the Charlotte plant's products. Attention would be given to identifying inefficient processes, and process improvements would be evaluated.

Top Management Response

Top management balked at the recommendations of the ABC project team. Some top managers did not believe the ABC results. It just seemed impossible to them that so many of the Charlotte plant's products were losers. Other members of the management team largely accepted the validity of the ABC study, but they, too, hesitated to drop so many products. To do so would most likely have meant massive layoffs and even the possibility of closing the Charlotte plant altogether, while shifting its remaining production to the division's other two plants. Some members of the ABC project team quietly speculated that some of the division's managers were more concerned about their own pay and perks than they were about the well-being of the division. In the final analysis, only a handful of products were dropped, and then only if they were suspected to be unprofitable before the ABC study was undertaken.

*The scenario described here, while fictitious, is based on several real-world events described in the ABC literature. Anecdotes in various ABC cases and other sources, as well as the author's research, form the basis for the events described. A key source is the well-known "Schrader-Bellows" case, by R. Cooper (Boston: President and Fellows of Harvard College), which remains a classic case describing issues surrounding activity-based costing.

Aftermath

The Charlotte plant's profits continued to deteriorate, as did the Engine Parts Division's profitability. Eventually, Xavier's corporate management cut its losses by selling off the Engine Parts Division to a competitor at bargain-basement prices. The division's new owners closed the Charlotte plant and changed the division's focus to be a boutique producer of high-quality engine parts, which was more in line with its own corporate strategy.

Ethical Issues

What ethical issues do you see in this scenario? How would you resolve them?

Chapter Summary

LO1 Compute product costs under a traditional, volume-based product-costing system. Traditional product-costing systems are structured on single, volume-based cost drivers, such as direct labor or machine hours. Overhead is applied to production jobs using a predetermined overhead rate, which is based on estimates of manufacturing overhead (in the numerator) and the level of some cost driver (in the denominator).

LO2 Explain how an activity-based costing system operates, including the use of a two-stage procedure for cost assignment, the identification of activity cost pools, and the selection of cost drivers. In the first stage of ABC, resource costs are identified and divided into activity cost pools. In the second stage, a cost driver is selected for each activity cost pool, and the costs in each pool are assigned to cost objects, such as products, services, product lines, customers, and so forth.

LO3 Explain the concept of cost levels, including unit-level, batch-level, product-sustaining-level, and facility-level costs. Unit-level costs are incurred for each unit produced. Batch-level costs are incurred once for each batch of products (i.e., one production run). Product-sustaining-level costs are incurred once for each product line. Facility-level costs are incurred to keep the overall facility in operation.

LO4 Compute product costs under an activity-based costing system. A product's cost is the sum of its direct-material cost, its direct-labor cost, and its overhead cost, which is the accumulation of all the resource costs driven to the product by the various cost drivers selected for the ABC system.

LO5 Explain why traditional, volume-based costing systems tend to distort product costs. Traditional, volume-based costing systems tend to distort product costs because of two factors: (1) product-line diversity and (2) non-unit-level overhead costs. No single cost driver can capture the complex relationships between products and the myriad activities necessary to produce and sell them.

LO6 Explain three criteria for selecting cost drivers. Three criteria for selecting cost drivers are: (1) the degree of correlation between the cost driver and the incurrence of costs in the activity cost pool associated with the cost driver; (2) the cost of measurement of the cost driver; and (3) the behavioral effects that might result from the selection of a cost driver.

LO7 Discuss several key issues in activity-based costing, including data collection and storyboarding. Collecting ABC data is difficult and costly. Techniques for data collection include interviews, examination of work product and other documentation, and sometimes storyboarding, which is a detailed map of the processes used in the organization.

LO8 Explain the concepts of activity-based management and two-dimensional ABC. Activity-based management (ABM) is the use of activity-based costing information to improve operations and eliminate non-value-added costs. One way of depicting ABM is the two-dimensional ABC model. This model combines the cost assignment role of ABC with the process and activity evaluation view of an ABC system.

LO9 Explain and execute a customer-profitability analysis. Customer profitability analysis is an application of ABM in which management determines the cost drivers for customer-related costs. The resulting ABC information is then used to assess the profitability of key customer relationships.

LO10 Understand and discuss how activity-based costing is used in service-industry organizations. Activity-based costing has found widespread successful implementation in the service industry. The application of ABC in the service industry is similar to that in manufacturing, wherein a two-stage costing model is used that first assigns resource costs to activity cost pools and then uses cost drivers to assign the costs in these pools to the various services provided and customers served. Many service-industry firms are implementing ABC and ABM systems to better meet the needs of management.

LO11 List and explain eight important features of just-in-time inventory and production management systems (Appendix). The key features of JIT systems are: (1) a smooth, uniform production rate; (2) a pull method of coordinating steps in the production process; (3) purchase and manufacturing in small lot sizes; (4) quick and inexpensive machine setups; (5) high quality levels for raw materials and finished products; (6) effective preventive maintenance of equipment; (7) an atmosphere of teamwork to improve the production process; and (8) multiskilled workers and flexible facilities.

Review Problem on Cost Drivers and Product-Cost Distortion

Edgeworth Box Corporation manufactures a variety of special packaging boxes used in the pharmaceutical industry. The company's Dallas plant is semiautomated, but the special nature of the boxes requires some manual labor. The controller has chosen the following activity cost pools, cost drivers, and pool rates for the Dallas plant's product-costing system.

Activity Cost Pool	Overhead Cost	Cost Driver	Budgeted Level for Cost Driver	Pool Rate
Purchasing, storage, and material handling	$ 200,000	Raw-material costs	$ 1,000,000	20% of material cost
Engineering and product design	100,000	Hours in design department	5,000 hrs.	$20 per hour
Machine setup costs	70,000	Production runs	1,000 runs	$70 per run
Machine depreciation and maintenance	300,000	Machine hours	100,000 hrs.	$3 per hour
Factory depreciation, taxes, insurance, and utilities	200,000	Machine hours	100,000 hrs.	$2 per hour
Other manufacturing-overhead costs	150,000	Machine hours	100,000 hrs.	$1.50 per hour
Total	$1,020,000			

Two recent production orders had the following requirements.

	20,000 Units of Box C52	10,000 Units of Box W29
Direct-labor hours	42 hr.	21 hr.
Raw-material cost	$40,000	$35,000
Hours in design department	10	25
Production runs	2	4
Machine hours	24	20

Required:

1. Compute the total overhead that should be assigned to each of the two production orders, C52 and W29.
2. Compute the overhead cost per box in each order.

3. Suppose the Dallas plant were to use a single predetermined overhead rate based on direct-labor hours. The direct-labor budget calls for 4,000 hours.
   a. Compute the predetermined overhead rate per direct-labor hour.
   b. Compute the total overhead cost that would be assigned to the order for box C52 and the order for box W29.
   c. Compute the overhead cost per box in each order.
4. Why do the two product-costing systems yield such widely differing overhead costs per box?

Solution to Review Problem

1.

	Box C52	Box W29
Purchasing, storage, and material handling	$8,000 (20% × $40,000)	$7,000 (20% × $35,000)
Engineering and product design	200 (10 × $20/hr.)	500 (25 × $20/hr.)
Machine setup costs	140 (2 × $70/run)	280 (4 × $70/run)
Machine depreciation and maintenance	72 (24 × $3/hr.)	60 (20 × $3/hr.)
Factory depreciation, taxes, insurance, and utilities	48 (24 × $2/hr.)	40 (20 × $2/hr.)
Other manufacturing overhead costs	36 (24 × $1.50/hr.)	30 (20 × $1.50/hr.)
Total overhead assigned to production order	$8,496	$7,910

2. Overhead cost per box: $.4248 per box $\left(\frac{\$8{,}496}{20{,}000}\right)$ $.791 per box $\left(\frac{\$7{,}910}{10{,}000}\right)$

3. Computations based on a single predetermined overhead rate based on direct-labor hours:

   a. $\frac{\text{Total budgeted overhead}}{\text{Total budgeted direct-labor hours}} = \frac{\$1{,}020{,}000}{4{,}000} = \$255/\text{hr.}$

   b. Total overhead assigned to each order:
   Box C52 order: 42 direct-labor hours × $255/hr. = $10,710
   Box W29 order: 21 direct-labor hours × $255/hr. = $5,355

   c. Overhead cost per box:
   Box C52: $10,710 ÷ 20,000 = $.5355 per box
   Box W29: $5,355 ÷ 10,000 = $.5355 per box

4. The widely differing overhead costs are assigned as a result of the inherent inaccuracy of the single, volume-based overhead rate. The relative usage of direct labor by the two production orders does not reflect their relative usage of other manufacturing support services.

Key Terms

For each term's definition refer to the indicated page, or turn to the glossary at the end of the text.

activity analysis, 186
activity-based costing (ABC) system, 172
activity-based management (ABM), 186
activity cost pool, 172
activity dictionary, 185
batch-level activity, 173
bill of activities, 185
consumption ratio, 181
cost driver, 183
cost hierarchy, 173
customer-profitability analysis, 189
customer profitability profile, 192
facility- (or general-operations) level activity, 173
just-in-time (JIT) inventory and production management system,* 201
just-in-time (JIT) purchasing,* 202
non-value-added activities, 186
non-value-added costs, 186
pool rate, 175
process, 188
process value analysis (PVA), 188
production Kanban,* 201
product-sustaining-level activity, 173
pull method,* 201
storyboarding, 184
total quality control (TQC),* 202
two-dimensional ABC model, 186
unit-level activity, 173
volume-based (or throughput-based) costing system, 171
withdrawal Kanban,* 201

*Term appears in appendix.

APPENDIX TO CHAPTER 5

Just-in-Time Inventory and Production Management

Learning Objective 11

List and explain eight important features of just-in-time inventory and production management systems.

A cost management tool that is widely used in manufacturing is the *just-in-time* (or *JIT*) system. A **just-in-time (JIT) inventory and production management system** is a comprehensive inventory and manufacturing control system in which no materials are purchased and no products are manufactured until they are needed. Raw materials and parts are purchased only as they are needed in some phase of the production process. Component parts and subassemblies are not manufactured in any stage of production until they are required in the next stage. Finished goods are manufactured only as they are needed to fill customer orders. A primary goal of a JIT production system is to *reduce or eliminate inventories* at every stage of production, from raw materials to finished goods. The JIT philosophy, made famous by Toyota, has been credited with the success of many of the world's leading manufacturers. Tremendous cost savings have been realized by many companies that have adopted the JIT approach.

How does a JIT system achieve its vast reductions in inventory and associated cost savings? A production-systems expert lists the following key features of the JIT approach.[14]

1. *A smooth, uniform production rate.* An important goal of a JIT system is to establish a smooth production flow, beginning with the arrival of materials from suppliers and ending with the delivery of goods to customers.
2. *A pull method of coordinating steps in the production process.* Most manufacturing processes occur in multiple stages. Under the **pull method,** goods are produced in each manufacturing stage only as they are needed at the next stage. This approach reduces or eliminates work-in-process inventory between production steps. The result is a reduction in waiting time and its associated non-value-added cost.

   The pull method of production begins at the last stage of the manufacturing process.[15] When additional materials and parts are needed for final assembly, a message is sent to the immediately preceding work center to send the amount of materials and parts that will be needed over the next few hours. Often this message is in the form of a **withdrawal Kanban,** a card indicating the number and type of parts requested from the preceding work center. The receipt of the withdrawal Kanban in the preceding work center triggers the release of a **production Kanban,** which is another card specifying the number of parts to be manufactured in that work center. Thus, the parts are "pulled" from a particular work center by a need for parts in the subsequent work center. This *pull approach* to production is repeated all the way back through the manufacturing sequence toward the beginning. Nothing is manufactured at any stage until its need is signaled from the subsequent process via a Kanban.[16]
3. *Purchase of materials and manufacture of subassemblies and products in small lot sizes.* This is an outgrowth of the pull method of production planning. Materials are purchased and goods are produced only as required, rather than for the sake of building up stocks.
4. *Quick and inexpensive setups of production machinery.* In order to produce in small lot sizes, a manufacturer must be able to set up production runs quickly. Advanced manufacturing technology aids in this process, as more and more machines are computer-controlled.
5. *High quality levels for raw material and finished products.* If raw materials and parts are to arrive "just in time" for production, they must be "just right" for their intended purpose. Otherwise, the production line will be shut down and significant non-value-added costs of waiting will result. Moreover, if very small stocks of finished goods are to be maintained, then finished

---

[14]James B. Dilworth, *Production and Operations Management,* 3rd ed. (New York: Random House, 1996), pp. 354–61.

[15]You may find it helpful to review Exhibit 1–5 on page 24, which depicts the pull method of the JIT system.

[16]Toyota's ground-breaking JIT system originally was referred to as *Kanban,* a Japanese word meaning "signboard." See Takeo Tanaka, "Kaizen Budgeting: Toyota's Cost Control System under TQC," *Journal of Cost Management* 8, no. 3 (Fall 1994), p. 57.

products must be of uniform high quality. For this reason, a **total quality control (TQC)** program often accompanies a just-in-time production environment.

6. *Effective preventive maintenance of equipment.* If goods are to be manufactured just in time to meet customer orders, a manufacturer cannot afford significant production delays. By strictly adhering to routine maintenance schedules, the firm can avoid costly down time from machine breakdowns.
7. *An atmosphere of teamwork to improve the production system.* A company can maintain a competitive edge in today's worldwide market only if it is constantly seeking ways to improve its product or service, achieve more efficient operations, and eliminate non-value-added costs. My favorite football coach often says that a team must improve from one week to the next. Otherwise the team will get worse, because it rarely will stay at the same level. So it goes in business as well. If a company's employees are not constantly seeking ways to improve the firm's performance, before long its competitors will pass it by.
8. *Multiskilled workers and flexible facilities.* To facilitate just-in-time production, manufacturing equipment must be flexible enough to produce a variety of components and products. Otherwise, if a particular production line can produce only one item, bottlenecks may result. A bottleneck can hold up production in subsequent manufacturing stages and result in the non-value-added costs associated with waiting time.

JIT Purchasing Along with a JIT production approach, many companies implement *JIT purchasing.* Under this approach, materials and parts are purchased from outside vendors only as they are needed. This avoids the costly and wasteful buildup of raw-material inventories. The following are five key features of **JIT purchasing.**

1. *Only a few suppliers.* This results in less time spent on vendor relations. Only highly reliable vendors, who can invariably deliver high-quality goods on time, are used.
2. *Long-term contracts negotiated with suppliers.* This eliminates costly paperwork and negotiations with each individual transaction. The need for delivery can be communicated via a telephone call or computer message. The long-term contracts state the price, quality, and delivery terms of the goods.
3. *Materials and parts delivered in small lot sizes immediately before they are needed.* This is the essence of the just-in-time approach. Costly inventories are avoided by having supplies arrive "just-in-time" to be placed into production.
4. *Only minimal inspection of delivered materials and parts.* The long-term contracts clearly state the quality of material required. Vendors are selected on the basis of their reliability in meeting these stringent standards and in delivering the correct amount of materials on time.
5. *Grouped payments to each vendor.* Instead of paying for each delivery, payments are made for batches of deliveries according to the terms of the contract. This reduces costly paperwork for both the vendor and the purchaser.

JIT purchasing is widely used in a variety of organizations. In manufacturing firms, it goes hand in hand with JIT production. In retail and service industry firms, JIT purchasing reduces costly warehouse inventories and streamlines the purchasing function.

Review Questions

5–1. Briefly explain how a traditional, volume-based product-costing system operates.

5–2. Why was Patio Grill Company's management being misled by the traditional product-costing system? What mistakes were being made?

5–3. Explain how an activity-based costing system operates.

5–4. What are cost drivers? What is their role in an activity-based costing system?

5–5. List and briefly describe the four broad categories of activities identified in stage one of an activity-based costing system.

5–6. How can an activity-based costing system alleviate the problems Patio Grill Company's management was having under its traditional, volume-based product-costing system?

5–7. Why do product-costing systems based on a single, volume-based cost driver tend to overcost high-volume products? What undesirable strategic effects can such distortion of product costs have?

5–8. How is the distinction between direct and indirect costs handled differently under volume-based versus activity-based costing systems?

5–9. Explain the concept of a *pool rate* in activity-based costing. (Refer to Exhibit 5–6.)

5–10. Briefly explain two factors that tend to result in product cost distortion under traditional, volume-based product-costing systems.

5–11. List three factors that are important in selecting cost drivers for an ABC system.

5–12. What is the role of *activity dictionary* in an ABC project?

5–13. Explain why a new product-costing system may be needed when line managers suggest that an apparently profitable product be dropped.

5–14. Explain why a manufacturer with diverse product lines may benefit from an ABC system.

5–15. Are activity-based costing systems appropriate for the service industry? Explain.

5–16. Explain why the maintenance of the medical-services provider network is treated as a product-sustaining-level activity by Pennsylvania Blue Shield.

5–17. How could the administration at Delaware Medical Center's Primary Care Unit use the activity-based costing information developed by the ABC project team?

5–18. Explain a key difference in the interpretation of the ABC data in Exhibit 5–7 (Patio Grill Company) and Exhibit 5–16 (Delaware Medical Center).

5–19. Explain the concept of *two-dimensional ABC.* Support your explanation with a diagram.

5–20. What is meant by the term *activity analysis?* Give three criteria for determining whether an activity adds value.

5–21. Distinguish between an activity's *trigger* and its *root cause.* Give an example of each.

5–22. What is meant by *customer-profitability analysis?* Give an example of an activity that might be performed more commonly for one customer than for another.

5–23. Explain the relationship between customer profitability analysis and activity-based costing.

5–24. What is a customer profitability profile?

5–25. (Appendix) Explain in words and then draw a diagram depicting the pull method of coordinating steps in a JIT system. (Refer to the JIT discussion in this chapter and to the JIT exhibit in Chapter 1.)

Exercises

Exercise 5–26
Volume-Based Cost Driver versus ABC
(LO 1, 2, 4)

Tioga Company manufactures sophisticated lenses and mirrors used in large optical telescopes. The company is now preparing its annual profit plan. As part of its analysis of the profitability of individual products, the controller estimates the amount of overhead that should be allocated to the individual product lines from the following information.

	Lenses	Mirrors
Units produced	25	25
Material moves per product line	5	15
Direct-labor hours per unit	200	200

The total budgeted material-handling cost is $50,000.

Required:

1. Under a costing system that allocates overhead on the basis of direct-labor hours, the material-handling costs allocated to one lens would be what amount?
2. Answer the same question as in requirement (1), but for mirrors.
3. Under activity-based costing (ABC), the material-handling costs allocated to one lens would be what amount? The cost driver for the material-handling activity is the number of material moves.
4. Answer the same question as in requirement (3), but for mirrors.

(CMA, adapted)

Exercise 5–27
Activity-Based Costing; Quality Control Costs
(LO 1, 2, 4)

Urban Elite Cosmetics has used a traditional cost accounting system to apply quality-control costs uniformly to all products at a rate of 14.5 percent of direct-labor cost. Monthly direct-labor cost for Satin Sheen makeup is $27,500. In an attempt to more equitably distribute quality-control costs, management is considering activity-based costing. The monthly data shown in the following chart have been gathered for Satin Sheen makeup.

Activity Cost Pool	Cost Driver	Pool Rates	Quantity of Driver for Satin Sheen
Incoming material inspection	Type of material	$11.50 per type	12 types
In-process inspection	Number of units	.14 per unit	17,500 units
Product certification	Per order	77.00 per order	25 orders

Required:

1. Calculate the monthly quality-control cost to be assigned to the Satin Sheen product line under each of the following product-costing systems. (Round to the nearest dollar.)
   a. Traditional system, which assigns overhead on the basis of direct-labor cost.
   b. Activity-based costing.
2. Does the traditional product-costing system overcost or undercost the Satin Sheen product line with respect to quality-control costs? By what amount?

(CMA, adapted)

Exercise 5–28
Cost Drivers; Activity Cost Pools
(LO 2, 3, 6)

Kentaro Corporation manufactures VCRs in its Tokyo plant. The following costs are budgeted for January. (Yen is the Japanese monetary unit.)

Raw materials and components	2,950,000 *yen*
Insurance, plant	600,000
Electricity, machinery	120,000
Electricity, light	60,000
Engineering design	610,000
Depreciation, plant	700,000
Depreciation, machinery	1,400,000
Custodial wages, plant	40,000
Equipment maintenance, wages	150,000
Equipment maintenance, parts	30,000
Setup wages	40,000
Inspection of finished goods	30,000
Property taxes	120,000
Natural gas, heating	30,000

Required: Divide these costs into activity cost pools, and identify a cost driver for assigning each pool of costs to products. Calculate the total cost in each activity cost pool.

Exercise 5–29
Categorizing Activity Cost Pools
(LO 2, 3)

Refer to the information given in the preceding exercise. For each of the activity cost pools identified, indicate whether it represents a unit-level, batch-level, product-sustaining-level, or facility-level activity.

Exercise 5–30
Activity-Based Costing in a Government Agency; Use of Internet
(LO 2, 7, 10)

Visit the Web site of a city, state, or Canadian province of your choosing (e.g., the City of Charlotte, N.C., www.charmeck.org).

Required: Read about the services offered to the public by this governmental unit. Then discuss how activity-based costing could be used effectively by the governmental unit to determine the cost of providing these services.

Exercise 5–31
Distortion of Product Costs
(LO 2, 5)

Wheelco, Inc. manufactures automobile and truck wheels. The company produces four basic, high-volume wheels used by each of the large automobile and pickup truck manufacturers. Wheelco also has two specialty wheel lines. These are fancy, complicated wheels used in expensive sports cars.

Lately, Wheelco's profits have been declining. Foreign competitors have been undercutting Wheelco's prices in three of its bread-and-butter product lines, and Wheelco's sales volume and market share have declined. In contrast, Wheelco's specialty wheels have been selling steadily, although in relatively small numbers, in spite of three recent price increases. At a recent staff meeting. Wheelco's president made the following remarks: "Our profits are going down the tubes, folks. It costs us 29 dollars to manufacture our A22 wheel. That's our best seller, with a volume last year of 17,000 units. But our chief competitor is selling basically the same wheel for 27 bucks. I don't see how they can do it. I think it's just one more example of foreign dumping. I'm going to write my senator about it! Thank goodness for our specialty wheels. I think we've got to get our salespeople to push those wheels more and more.

Take the D52 model, for example. It's a complicated thing to make, and we don't sell many. But look at the profit margin. Those wheels cost us 49 dollars to make, and we're selling them for 105 bucks each."

Required: What do you think is behind the problems faced by Wheelco? Comment on the president's remarks. Do you think his strategy is a good one? What do you recommend, and why?

Exercise 5–32
Key Features of Activity-Based Costing
(LO 2, 5, 7)

Refer to the description given for Wheelco, Inc. in the preceding exercise. Suppose the firm's president has decided to implement an activity-based costing system.

Required:

1. List and briefly describe the key features that Wheelco's new product-costing system should have.
2. What impact will the new system be likely to have on the company's situation?
3. What strategic options would you expect to be suggested by the product-costing results from the new system?

Exercise 5–33
Winery; Classification of Activities
(LO 2, 3, 7)

Finger Lakes Winery is a small, family-run operation in upstate New York. The winery produces two varieties of wine: riesling and chardonnay. Among the activities engaged in by the winery are the following:

1. Trimming:	At the end of a growing season, the vines are trimmed, which helps prepare them for the next harvest.
2. Tying:	The vines are tied onto wires to help protect them from the cold. (This also occurs at the end of the season.)
3. Hilling:	Dirt is piled up around the roots to help protect them from frost.
4. Conditioning:	After the snow melts in the spring, dirt is leveled back from the roots.
5. Untying:	The vines are untied from the wires to allow them freedom to grow during the spring and summer months.
6. Chemical spraying:	The vines are sprayed in the spring to protect them from disease and insects.
7. Harvesting:	All of the grapes of both varieties are picked by hand to minimize damage.
8. Stemming and crushing:	Batches of grapes are hand-loaded into a machine, which gently removes the stems and mildly crushes them.
9. Pressing:	After removal from the stemmer/crusher, the juice runs freely from the grapes.
10. Filtering:	The grapes are crushed mechanically to render more juice from them.
11. Fermentation:	The riesling grape juice is placed in stainless steel tanks for fermentation. The chardonnay grape juice undergoes a two-stage fermentation process in oak barrels.
12. Aging:	The riesling wines are aged in the stainless steel tanks for approximately a year. The chardonnays are aged in the oak barrels for about two years.
13. Bottling:	A machine bottles the wine and corks the bottles.
14. Labeling:	Each bottle is manually labeled with the name of the vintner, vintage, and variety.
15. Packing:	The bottles are manually packed in 12-bottle cases.
16. Case labeling:	The cases are hand-stamped with the same information that the bottles received.
17. Shipping:	The wine is shipped to wine distributors and retailers, mainly in central New York. Generally, about 100 cases are shipped at a time.
18. Maintenance on buildings:	This is done during the slow winter months.
19. Maintenance on equipment:	This is done when needed, and on a routine basis for preventive maintenance.

Required: Classify each of the activities listed as a unit-, batch-, product-sustaining-, or facility-level activity.

Exercise 5–34
United Technologies; Classification of Activities
(LO 2, 3, 7)

United Technologies Corporation is using activity-based costing in two of its subsidiaries: Otis Elevator Company and Carrier Corporation. The following table shows 27 activities and eight accounts identified at Carrier, along with the classification determined by the ABC project team.[17]

Name of Activity or Account	Classification by Activity level
Acquiring material	Batch
Inspecting incoming materials	Batch
Moving materials	Batch
Planning production	Batch
Processing special orders	Batch
Processing supplier invoices	Batch
Receiving material	Batch
Scheduling production	Batch
Inspecting production processes	Batch
Processing purchase orders	Batch
Building occupancy	Facility
Depreciation	Facility
General management	Facility
Maintaining facilities	Facility
Managing the environment	Facility
Assuring quality	Sustaining
Expediting	Sustaining
Maintaining tools and dies	Sustaining
Maintaining/improving production processes	Sustaining
Managing human resources	Sustaining
Managing waste disposal	Sustaining
Processing payroll	Sustaining
Processing production information	Sustaining
Providing product cost	Sustaining
Setting manufacturing methods	Sustaining
Supervising production	Sustaining
Sustaining accounting	Sustaining
Maintaining production equipment	Sustaining
Direct-labor allowances	Unit
Direct-labor fringes	Unit
Utilities (equipment)	Unit
Overtime (hourly)	Unit
Rework	Unit
Shift differential	Unit
Spoilage	Unit

Required: Choose two activities or accounts from each of the four classifications and explain why you agree or disagree with the ABC project team's classification.

Exercise 5–35
ABC; Selling Costs
(LO 2, 4)

Redwood Company sells craft kits and supplies to retail outlets and through its catalog. Some of the items are manufactured by Redwood, while others are purchased for resale. For the products it manufactures, the company currently bases its selling prices on a product-costing system that accounts for direct material, direct labor, and the associated overhead costs. In addition to these product costs, Redwood incurs substantial selling costs, and Roger Jackson, controller, has suggested that these selling costs should be included in the product pricing structure.

[17]Robert Adams and Ray Carter, "United Technologies' Activity-Based Accounting Is a Catalyst for Success," *As Easy as ABC* 18, p 4. United Technologies uses the term "*structural*-level activity." instead of "*facility*-level activity" as we have done in the chapter and in the table presented here.

After studying the costs incurred over the past two years for one of its products, skeins of knitting yarn, Jackson has selected four categories of selling costs and chosen cost drivers for each of these costs. The selling costs actually incurred during the past year and the cost drivers are as follows:

Cost Category	Amount	Cost Driver
Sales commissions	$ 675,000	Boxes of yarn sold to retail stores
Catalogs	295,400	Catalogs distributed
Cost of catalog sales	105,000	Skeins sold through catalog
Credit and collection	60,000	Number of retail orders
Total selling costs	$1,135,400	

The knitting yarn is sold to retail outlets in boxes, each containing 12 skeins of yarn. The sale of partial boxes is not permitted. Commissions are paid on sales to retail outlets but not on catalog sales. The cost of catalog sales includes telephone costs and the wages of personnel who take the catalog orders. Jackson believes that the selling costs vary significantly with the size of the order. Order sizes are divided into three categories as follows:

Order Size	Catalog Sales	Retail Sales
Small	1–10 skeins	1–10 boxes
Medium	11–20 skeins	11–20 boxes
Large	Over 20 skeins	Over 20 boxes

An analysis of the previous year's records produced the following statistics.

	Order Size			
	Small	Medium	Large	Total
Retail sales in boxes (12 skeins per box)	2,000	45,000	178,000	225,000
Catalog sales in skeins	79,000	52,000	44,000	175,000
Number of retail orders	485	2,415	3,100	6,000
Catalogs distributed	254,300	211,300	125,200	590,800

Required:

1. Prepare a schedule showing Redwood Company's total selling cost for each order size and the per-skein selling cost within each order size.
2. Explain how the analysis of the selling costs for skeins of knitting yarn is likely to impact future pricing and product decisions at Redwood Company.

(CMA, adapted)

Exercise 5–36
Classification of Activities in a University; Cost Drivers
(LO 2, 3, 6, 7, 10)

As a group, discuss the activities of your college or university (e.g., admission, registration, etc.). List as many activities as you can.

Required: Make a presentation to your class that includes the following:

1. Your list of activities.
2. The classification of each activity (e.g., unit level).
3. An appropriate cost driver for each activity.

Exercise 5–37
Non-Value-Added Costs
(LO 8)

Non-value-added costs occur in nonmanufacturing organizations, just as they do in manufacturing firms.

Required: Identify four potential non-value-added costs in (1) an airline, (2) a bank, and (3) a hotel.

Exercise 5–38
Design Your Own Production Process; Non-Value-Added Costs
(LO 8)

Since you have always wanted to be an industrial baron, invent your own product and describe at least five steps used in its production.

Required: Explain how you would go about identifying non-value-added costs in the production process.

Exercise 5–39
Performance Measures in Two-Dimensional ABC; ABM
(LO 8, 10)

List five activities performed by the employees of an airline *on the ground.*

Required: For each of these activities, suggest a performance measure that could be used in activity-based management.

Exercise 5–40
Activity Analysis; Non-Value-Added Activities
(LO 8, 10)

Visit a restaurant for a meal or think carefully about a recent visit to a restaurant. List as many activities as you can think of that would be performed by the restaurant's employees for its customers.

Required: For each activity on your list, indicate the following:

1. Value-added or non-value-added.
2. The trigger of the activity.
3. The possible root causes of the activity.

Exercise 5–41
College Registration; Activity Analysis
(LO 8, 10)

As a group, think carefully about the various activities and steps involved in the course registration process at your college or university.

Required:

1. List the steps in the registration process in the sequence in which they occur.
2. Prepare an activity analysis of the registration process. Discuss the activity linkages, triggers, and root causes.
3. Redesign your institution's course registration process with these goals in mind:
   a. Improve the convenience and effectiveness of the process for a student registering.
   b. Improve the effectiveness and cost efficiency of the process from the standpoint of the institution.

Exercise 5–42
Customer Profitability Analysis; Customers Ranked by Sales Revenue
(LO 9)

The customer-profitability analysis for Patio Grill Company, which is displayed in Exhibit 5–14, ranks customers by operating income. An alternative, often-used approach is to rank customers by sales revenue.

Required:

1. List the customer numbers in the left-hand column of Exhibit 5–14 by sales revenue, from highest to lowest. Is the ranking different from that in Exhibit 5–14?
2. Patio Grill Company's smallest customers, in terms of sales revenue, are last in the listing prepared for requirement (1). Are these customers the company's least profitable?
3. Would the customer-profitability profile in Exhibit 5–15 be different if the customers were ranked by sales revenue instead of operating income? Explain.
4. What factors could cause a larger customer (in terms of sales revenue) to be less profitable than a smaller customer?

Exercise 5–43
Customer-Profitability Graph
(LO 9)

Big Apple Design Company specializes in designing commercial office space in Chicago. The firm's president recently reviewed the following income statement and noticed that operating profits were below her expectations. She had a hunch that certain customers were not profitable for the company and asked the controller to perform a customer-profitability analysis showing profitability by customer for the month of March.

BIG APPLE DESIGN COMPANY
Income Statement
For the Month Ended March 31

Sales revenue	$300,000
Cost of services billed	255,000
Gross margin	$ 45,000
Marketing and administrative costs	30,000
Operating profit	$ 15,000

The controller provided the following customer-profitability graph:

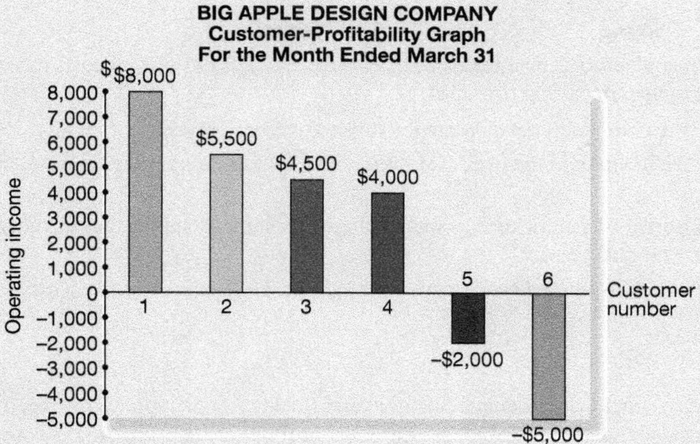

Required: Put yourself in the position of Big Apple's controller and write a memo to the president to accompany the customer-profitability graph. Comment on the implications of the customer-profitability analysis and raise four or more questions that should be addressed by the firm's management team.

Exercise 5–44
Activity-Based Costing
(LO 2, 3, 10)

Service-industry firms can make effective use of ABC systems as well as manufacturers. For each of the following businesses, list five key activities that are important in the provision of the firm's service. For each activity cost pool, suggest an appropriate cost driver to use in assigning costs from the activity cost pool to the services provided to customers.

1. Southwest Airlines
2. Burger King
3. Island Health & Fitness Club
4. Bank of America branch bank
5. Marriott Hotels
6. Massachusetts General Hospital

Problems

All applicable Problems are available with McGraw-Hill's *Connect Accounting*™. 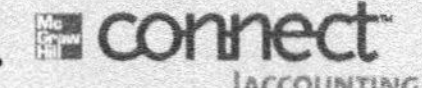

Problem 5–45
Overhead Application; Activity-Based Costing
(LO 1, 2, 7)

Borealis Manufacturing has just completed a major change in its quality control (QC) process. Previously, products had been reviewed by QC inspectors at the end of each major process, and the company's 10 QC inspectors were charged as direct labor to the operation or job. In an effort to improve efficiency and quality, a computerized video QC system was purchased for $250,000. The system consists of a minicomputer, 15 video cameras, other peripheral hardware, and software. The new system uses cameras stationed by QC engineers at key points in the production process. Each time an operation changes or there is a new operation, the cameras are moved, and a new master picture is loaded into the computer by a QC engineer. The camera takes pictures of the units in process, and the computer compares them to the picture of a "good" unit. Any differences are sent to a QC engineer, who removes the bad units and discusses the flaws with the production supervisors. The new system has replaced the 10 QC inspectors with two QC engineers.

The operating costs of the new QC system, including the salaries of the QC engineers, have been included as factory overhead in calculating the company's plantwide manufacturing-overhead rate, which is based on direct-labor dollars. The company's president is confused. His vice president of production has told him how efficient the new system is. Yet there is a large increase in the overhead rate. The computation of the rate before and after automation is as follows:

	Before	After
Budgeted manufacturing overhead	$1,900,000	$2,100,000
Budgeted direct-labor cost	1,000,000	700,000
Budgeted overhead rate	190%	300%

"Three hundred percent," lamented the president. "How can we compete with such a high overhead rate?"

Required:

1. *a.* Define "manufacturing overhead," and cite three examples of typical costs that would be included in manufacturing overhead.

   b. Explain why companies develop predetermined overhead rates.
2. Explain why the increase in the overhead rate should not have a negative financial impact on Borealis Manufacturing.
3. Explain how Borealis Manufacturing could change its overhead application system to eliminate confusion over product costs.
4. Discuss how an activity-based costing system might benefit Borealis Manufacturing.

(CMA, adapted)

Problem 5–46
Activity-Based Costing; Cost Analysis
(LO 1, 2, 4, 5, 7)

1. Total cost, standard: $157
2. Manufactured cost, standard unit: $181

Ontario, Inc. manufactures two products, Standard and Enhanced, and applies overhead on the basis of direct-labor hours. Anticipated overhead and direct-labor time for the upcoming accounting period are $800,000 and 25,000 hours, respectively. Information about the company's products follows.

Standard:

Estimated production volume, 3,000 units
Direct-material cost, $25 per unit
Direct labor per unit, 3 hours at $12 per hour

Enhanced:

Estimated production volume, 4,000 units
Direct-material cost, $40 per unit
Direct labor per unit, 4 hours at $12 per hour

Ontario's overhead of $800,000 can be identified with three major activities: order processing ($150,000), machine processing ($560,000), and product inspection ($90,000). These activities are driven by number of orders processed, machine hours worked, and inspection hours, respectively. Data relevant to these activities follow.

	Orders Processed	Machine Hours Worked	Inspection Hours
Standard	300	18,000	2,000
Enhanced	200	22,000	8,000
Total	500	40,000	10,000

Top management is very concerned about declining profitability despite a healthy increase in sales volume. The decrease in income is especially puzzling because the company recently undertook a massive plant renovation during which new, highly automated machinery was installed—machinery that was expected to produce significant operating efficiencies.

Required:

1. Assuming use of direct-labor hours to apply overhead to production, compute the unit manufacturing costs of the Standard and Enhanced products if the expected manufacturing volume is attained.
2. Assuming use of activity-based costing, compute the unit manufacturing costs of the Standard and Enhanced products if the expected manufacturing volume is attained.
3. Ontario's selling prices are based heavily on cost.

   a. By using direct-labor hours as an application base, which product is overcosted and which product is undercosted? Calculate the amount of the cost distortion for each product.

   b. Is it possible that overcosting and undercosting (i.e., cost distortion) and the subsequent determination of selling prices are contributing to the company's profit woes? Explain.
4. *Build a spreadsheet:* Construct an Excel spreadsheet to solve requirements 1, 2, and 3(*a*) above. Show how the solution will change if the following data change: the overhead associated with order processing is $300,000 and the overhead associated with product inspection is $270,000.

Problem 5–47
Straightforward ABC calculations
(LO 1, 2, 4, 5)

2. Machine-related cost, REG line: $135,000
3. Total cost per unit, under ABC, GMT line: $663.90
4. Cost distortion per unit, ADV line: overcosted by $8.85

Kitchen King's Toledo plant manufactures three product lines, all multi-burner, ceramic cook tops. The plant's three product models are the Regular (REG), the Advanced (ADV), and the Gourmet (GMT). Until recently, the plant used a job-order product-costing system, with manufacturing overhead applied on the basis of direct-labor hours. The following table displays the basic data upon which the traditional costing system was based.

	REG	ADV	GMT
Planned annual production:			
Volume in units	5,000	4,000	1,000
Production runs	40 runs of 125 units	40 runs of 100 units	20 runs of 50 units
Direct material	$129	$151	$203
Direct labor: (not including setup)	$171 (9 hrs. @ $19 per hr.)	$209 (11 hrs. @ $19 per hr.)	$247 (13 hrs. @ $19 per hr.)
Machine hours (MH) per product unit	10 MH	12 MH	17 MH
Total machine hours consumed by product line in a year	50,000 (10 MH × 5,000)	48,000 (12 MH × 4,000)	17,000 (17 MH × 1,000)

The annual budgeted overhead is $1,224,000, and the company's predetermined overhead rate is $12 per direct-labor hour. The product costs for the three product models, as reported under the plant's traditional costing system, are shown in the following table.

	REG	ADV	GMT
Direct material	$129.00	$151.00	$203.00
Direct labor (not including set-up time)	171.00 (9 hr. @ $19)	209.00 (11 hr. @ $19)	247.00 (13 hr. @ $19)
Manufacturing overhead	108.00 (9 hr. @ $12)	132.00 (11 hr. @ $12)	156.00 (13 hr. @ $12)
Total	$408.00	$492.00	$606.00

Kitchen King's pricing policy is to set a target price for each product equal to 130 percent of the full product cost. Due to price competition from other appliance manufacturers, REG units were selling at $525, and ADV units were selling for $628. These prices were somewhat below the firm's target prices. However, these results were partially offset by greater-than-expected profits on the GMT product line. Management had raised the price on the GMT model to $800, which was higher than the original target price. Even at this price, Kitchen King's customers did not seem to hesitate to place orders, Moreover, the company's competitiors did not mount a challenge in the market for the GMT product line. Neverthless, concern continued to mount in Toledo about the difficulty in the REG and ADV markets. After all, these were the plant's bread-and-butter products, with projected annual sales of 5,000 REG units and 4,000 ADV units.

Kitchen King's director of cost management, Angela Ramirez, had been thinking for some time about a refinement in the Toledo plant's product-costing system. Ramirez wondered if the traditional, volume-based system was providing management with accurate data about product costs. She had read about activity-based costing, and wondered if ABC would be an improvement to the plant's product-costing system. After some discussion, an ABC proposal was made to the company's top management, and approval was obtained. The data collected for the new ABC system is displayed in the following table.

Activity	Activity Cost Pool	Cost Driver	Product Line	Cost Driver Quantity for Product Line
Machine related	$310,500	Machine Hours	REG	50,000
			ADV	48,000
			GMT	17,000
			Total	115,000
Material handling	52,500	Production Runs	REG	40
			ADV	40
			GMT	20
			Total	100

(continues)

Activity	Activity Cost Pool	Cost Driver	Product Line	Cost Driver Quantity for Product Line
Purchasing	$ 75,000	Purchase Orders	REG	100
			ADV	96
			GMT	104
			Total	300
Setup	85,000	Production Runs	REG	40
			ADV	40
			GMT	20
			Total	100
Inspection	27,500	Inspection Hours	REG	400
			ADV	400
			GMT	300
			Total	1,100
Shipping	66,000	Shipments	REG	500
			ADV	400
			GMT	200
			Total	1,100
Engineering	32,500	Engineering Hours	REG	250
			ADV	200
			GMT	200
			Total	650
Facility	575,000	Machine Hours	REG	50,000
			ADV	48,000
			GMT	17,000
			Total	115,000

Required:

1. Show how the company's overhead rate of $12 per direct-labor hour was calculated.
2. Complete an activity-based costing analysis for Kitchen King's three product lines. Display the results of your ABC analysis in a table similar to Exhibit 5–7 in the text.
3. Prepare a table similar to Exhibit 5–8, which computes the new product cost for each product line under ABC.
4. Prepare a table similar to Exhibit 5–9, which compares the overhead cost, total product cost, and target price for each product line under the two alternative costing systems.
5. Was each of Kitchen King's three product lines overcosted or undercosted? By how much per unit?
6. *Build a spreadsheet:* Construct an Excel spreadsheet to solve requirement (2) above. Show how the solution would change if the machine-related cost pool was $621,000, and the facility cost pool was $1,150,000.

Problem 5–48
Continuation of Preceding Problem; Explaining ABC
(LO 2, 4)

Refer to your solution to requirement (2) of the preceding problem.

Required: Prepare an exhibit similar to Exhibit 5–6 in the text to explain the ABC calculations for the material-handling activity. Use your exhibit to explain ABC to a friend who is not a business major.

Problem 5–49
Activity-Based Costing; Product Promotion
(LO 1, 2, 4, 5)

1. Type A manufacturing overhead cost: $160 per unit
2. Manufactured cost of type A cabinet: $243.50

Maxey & Sons manufactures two types of storage cabinets—Type A and Type B—and applies manufacturing overhead to all units at the rate of $80 per machine hour. Production information follows.

	Type A	Type B
Anticipated volume (units)	8,000	15,000
Direct-material cost per unit	$ 35	$ 60
Direct-labor cost per unit	20	20

The controller, who is studying the use of activity-based costing, has determined that the firm's overhead can be identified with three activities: manufacturing setups, machine processing, and product shipping. Data on the number of setups, machine hours, and outgoing shipments, which are the activities' three respective cost drivers, follow.

	Type A	Type B	Total
Setups	50	30	80
Machine hours	16,000	22,500	38,500
Outgoing shipments	100	75	175

The firm's total overhead of $3,080,000 is subdivided as follows: manufacturing setups, $672,000; machine processing, $1,848,000; and product shipping, $560,000.

Required:

1. Compute the unit manufacturing cost of Type A and Type B storage cabinets by using the company's current overhead costing procedures.
2. Compute the unit manufacturing cost of Type A and Type B storage cabinets by using activity-based costing.
3. Is the cost of the Type A storage cabinet overstated or understated (i.e., distorted) by the use of machine hours to allocate total manufacturing overhead to production? By how much?
4. Assume that the current selling price of a Type A storage cabinet is $260 and the marketing manager is contemplating a $30 discount to stimulate volume. Is this discount advisable? Briefly discuss.

Problem 5–50
Activity-Based Costing; Analysis of Operations
(LO 1, 2, 4, 7, 10)

2. E-commerce consulting, income: $22,040
3. Activity-based application rate, staff support: $720 per client
Billings, information systems services: $387,500

Grady and Associates performs a variety of activities related to information systems and e-commerce consulting in Toronto, Canada. The firm, which bills $125 per hour for services performed, is in a very tight local labor market and is having difficulty finding quality help for its overworked professional staff. The cost per hour for professional staff time is $45. Selected information follows.

- Billable hours to clients for the year totaled 5,000, consisting of information systems services, 3,100; e-commerce consulting, 1,900.
- Administrative cost of $342,000 was (and continues to be) allocated to both services based on billable hours. These costs consist of staff support, $180,000; in-house computing, $136,400; and miscellaneous office charges, $25,600.

A recent analysis of staff support costs found a correlation with the number of clients served. In-house computing and miscellaneous office charges varied directly with the number of computer hours logged and number of client transactions, respectively. A tabulation revealed the following data:

	Information Systems Services	E-Commerce Consulting	Total
Number of clients	200	50	250
Number of computer hours	2,600	1,800	4,400
Number of client transactions	400	600	1,000

Required:

1. Activity-based costing (ABC) is said to result in improved costing accuracy when compared with traditional costing procedures. Briefly explain how this improved accuracy is attained.
2. Assume that the firm uses traditional costing procedures, allocating total costs on the basis of billable hours. Determine the profitability of the firm's information systems and e-commerce activities, expressing your answer both in dollars and as a percentage of activity revenue.
3. Repeat requirement (2), using activity-based costing.

4. Jeffrey Grady, one of the firm's partners, doesn't care where his professionals spend their time because, as he notes, "many clients have come to expect both services and we need both to stay in business. Also, information systems and e-commerce professionals are paid the same hourly rate." Should Grady's attitude change? Explain.
5. Is an aggressive expansion of either service currently desirable? Briefly discuss.

Problem 5–51
Automation; Robotics; Overhead Application; Activity-Based Costing
(LO 1, 2, 5, 8)

John Patrick has recently been hired as controller of Valdosta Vinyl Company (VVC), a manufacturer of vinyl siding used in residential construction. VVC has been in the vinyl siding business for many years and is currently investigating ways to modernize its manufacturing process. At the first staff meeting Patrick attended, Jack Kielshesky, chief engineer, presented a proposal for automating the Molding Department. Kielshesky recommended that the company purchase two robots that would have the capability of replacing the eight direct-labor employees in the department. The cost savings outlined in the proposal include the elimination of direct-labor cost in the Molding Department plus a reduction of manufacturing overhead cost in the department to zero, because VVC charges manufacturing overhead on the basis of direct-labor dollars using a plantwide rate. The president of VVC was puzzled by Kielshesky's explanation: "This just doesn't make any sense. How can a department's overhead rate drop to zero by adding expensive, high-tech manufacturing equipment? If anything, it seems like the rate ought to go up."

Kielshesky responded by saying "I'm an engineer, not an accountant. But if we're charging overhead on the basis of direct labor, and we eliminate the labor, then we eliminate the overhead."

Patrick agreed with the president. He explained that as firms become more automated, they should rethink their product-costing systems. The president then asked Patrick to look into the matter and prepare a report for the next staff meeting. Patrick gathered the following data on the manufacturing-overhead rates experienced by VVC over the years. Patrick also wanted to have some departmental data to present at the meeting and, by using VVC's accounting records, he was able to estimate the following annual averages for each manufacturing department over the five decades since VVC's formation.

Historical Plantwide Data

Decade	Average Annual Manufacturing-Overhead Cost	Average Annual Direct-Labor Cost	Average Manufacturing-Overhead Application Rate
1st	$ 2,200,000	$2,000,000	110%
2nd	6,240,000	2,400,000	260
3rd	13,600,000	4,000,000	340
4th	24,600,000	6,000,000	410
5th	38,710,000	7,900,000	490

Annual Averages during Recent Years

	Cutting Department	Finishing Department	Molding Department
Manufacturing overhead	$22,000,000	$14,000,000	$4,000,000
Direct labor	4,000,000	3,500,000	500,000

Required:

1. Disregarding the proposed use of robots in the Molding Department, describe the shortcomings of the system for applying overhead that is currently used by Valdosta Vinyl Company.
2. Explain the misconceptions underlying Kielshesky's statement that the manufacturing-overhead cost in the Molding Department will be reduced to zero if the automation proposal is implemented.
3. Recommend ways to improve VVC's method for applying overhead by describing how it should revise its product-costing system for each of the following departments:
   a. In the Cutting and Finishing Departments.
   b. To accommodate automation in the Molding Department.

(CMA, adapted)

Problem 5–52
Activity Cost Pools; Cost Drivers; Pool Rates
(LO 1, 2, 3, 4, 5, 7)

3. Predetermined overhead rate: $31.25 per machine hr.

The controller for Tulsa Photographic Supply Company has established the following activity cost pools and cost drivers.

Activity Cost Pool	Budgeted Overhead Cost	Cost Driver	Budgeted Level for Cost Driver	Pool Rate
Machine setups	$250,000	Number of setups	125	$2,000 per setup
Material handling	75,000	Weight of raw material	37,500 lb.	$2 per pound
Hazardous waste control	25,000	Weight of hazardous chemicals used	5,000 lb.	$5 per pound
Quality control	75,000	Number of inspections	1,000	$75 per inspection
Other overhead costs	200,000	Machine hours	20,000	$10 per machine hour
Total	$625,000			

An order for 1,000 boxes of film development chemicals has the following production requirements.

Machine setups	5 setups
Raw material	10,000 pounds
Hazardous materials	2,000 pounds
Inspections	10 inspections
Machine hours	500 machine hours

Required:

1. Compute the total overhead that should be assigned to the development-chemical order.
2. What is the overhead cost per box of chemicals?
3. Suppose Tulsa Photographic Supply Company were to use a single predetermined overhead rate based on machine hours. Compute the rate per hour.
4. Under the approach in requirement (3), how much overhead would be assigned to the development-chemical order?
   a. In total.
   b. Per box of chemicals.
5. Explain why these two product-costing systems result in such widely differing costs. Which system do you recommend? Why?
6. *Build a spreadsheet:* Construct an Excel spreadsheet to solve requirements (1), (2), (3), and (4) above. Show how the solution will change if the following data change. The overhead associated with machine setups is $375,000, and there are 500 inspections budgeted.

Problem 5–53
Overhead Cost Drivers
(LO 2, 3, 4)

1. Unit cost per plate: $260.25

Refer to the original data given in the preceding problem for Tulsa Photographic Supply Company.

Required:

1. Calculate the unit cost of a production order for 100 specially coated plates used in film development. In addition to direct material costing $120 per plate and direct labor costing $40 per plate, the order requires the following:

Machine setups	3
Raw material	900 pounds
Hazardous materials	300 pounds
Inspections	3
Machine hours	50

2. *Build a spreadsheet:* Construct an Excel spreadsheet to solve the preceding requirement. (This will be an extension of the spreadsheet constructed for the preceding problem.) Show how the solution will change if the data *given in the preceding problem* change as follows: the overhead associated with machine setups is $375,000, and there are 500 inspections budgeted.

■ **Problem 5–54**
Activity-Based Costing; Activity-Based Management
(LO 2, 3, 4, 5, 7)

2. Total cost, royal: $4,431,900

Montreal Electronics Company manufactures two large-screen television models: the Nova, which has been produced for 10 years and sells for $900, and the Royal, a new model introduced in early 20x0, which sells for $1,140. Based on the following income statement for 20x1, a decision has been made to concentrate Montreal's marketing resources on the Royal model and to begin to phase out the Nova model.

MONTREAL ELECTRONICS COMPANY
Income Statement
For the Year Ended December 31, 20x1

	Royal	Nova	Total
Sales	$4,560,000	$19,800,000	$24,360,000
Cost of goods sold	3,192,000	12,540,000	15,732,000
Gross margin	$1,368,000	$ 7,260,000	$ 8,628,000
Selling and administrative expense	978,000	5,830,000	6,808,000
Net income	$ 390,000	$ 1,430,000	$ 1,820,000
Units produced and sold	4,000	22,000	
Net income per unit sold	$ 97.50	$ 65.00	

The standard unit costs for the Royal and Nova models are as follows:

	Royal	Nova
Direct material	$584	$208
Direct labor:		
Royal (3.5 hr. × $12)	42	
Nova (1.5 hr. × $12)		18
Machine usage:		
Royal (4 hr. × $18)	72	
Nova (8 hr. × $18)		144
Manufacturing overhead*	100	200
Standard cost	$798	$570

*Manufacturing overhead was applied on the basis of machine hours at a predetermined rate of $25 per hour.

Montreal Electronics Company's controller is advocating the use of activity-based costing and activity-based management and has gathered the following information about the company's manufacturing-overhead costs for 20x1.

		Number of Events		
Activity Center (cost driver)	**Traceable Costs**	**Royal**	**Nova**	**Total**
Soldering (number of solder joints)	$ 942,000	385,000	1,185,000	1,570,000
Shipments (number of shipments)	860,000	3,800	16,200	20,000
Quality control (number of inspections)	1,240,000	21,300	56,200	77,500
Purchase orders (number of orders)	950,400	109,980	80,100	190,080
Machine power (machine hours)	57,600	16,000	176,000	192,000
Machine setups (number of setups)	750,000	14,000	16,000	30,000
Total traceable costs	$4,800,000			

Required:

1. Briefly explain how an activity-based costing system operates.
2. Using activity-based costing, determine if Montreal Electronics should continue to emphasize the Royal model and phase out the Nova model.

(CMA, adapted)

Problem 5–55
Activity-Based Costing
(LO 1, 2, 4, 5)

2. Total contribution margin from PC board: $2,360,000
3. Using ABC, total contribution margin from TV board: $2,557,100

Manchester Technology, Inc. manufactures several different types of printed circuit boards; however, two of the boards account for the majority of the company's sales. The first of these boards, a television circuit board, has been a standard in the industry for several years. The market for this type of board is competitive and price-sensitive. Manchester plans to sell 65,000 of the TV boards in 20x1 at a price of $150 per unit. The second high-volume product, a personal computer circuit board, is a recent addition to Manchester's product line. Because the PC board incorporates the latest technology, it can be sold at a premium price. The 20x1 plans include the sale of 40,000 PC boards at $300 per unit.

Manchester's management group is meeting to discuss how to spend the sales and promotion dollars for 20x1. The sales manager believes that the market share for the TV board could be expanded by concentrating Manchester's promotional efforts in this area. In response to this suggestion, the production manager said, "Why don't you go after a bigger market for the PC board? The cost sheets that I get show that the contribution from the PC board is more than double the contribution from the TV board. I know we get a premium price for the PC board. Selling it should help overall profitability."

The cost-accounting system shows that the following costs apply to the PC and TV boards.

	PC Board	TV Board
Direct material	$140	$80
Direct labor	4 hr.	1.5 hr.
Machine time	1.5 hr.	.5 hr.

Variable manufacturing overhead is applied on the basis of direct-labor hours. For 20x1, variable overhead is budgeted at $1,120,000, and direct-labor hours are estimated at 280,000. The hourly rates for machine time and direct labor are $10 and $14, respectively. The company applies a material-handling charge at 10 percent of material cost. This material-handling charge is not included in variable manufacturing overhead. Total 20x1 expenditures for direct material are budgeted at $10,800,000.

Andrew Fulton, Manchester's controller, believes that before the management group proceeds with the discussion about allocating sales and promotional dollars to individual products, it might be worthwhile to look at these products on the basis of the activities involved in their production. Fulton has prepared the following schedule to help the management group understand this concept.

"Using this information," Fulton explained, "we can calculate an activity-based cost for each TV board and each PC board and then compare it to the standard cost we have been using. The only cost that remains the same for both cost methods is the cost of direct material. The cost drivers will replace the direct labor, machine time, and overhead costs in the old standard cost figures."

Budgeted Cost		Cost Driver	Budgeted Annual Activity for Cost Driver
Procurement	$ 400,000	Number of parts	4,000,000 parts
Production scheduling	220,000	Number of boards	110,000 boards
Packaging and shipping	440,000	Number of boards	110,000 boards
Total	$ 1,060,000		
Machine setup	$ 446,000	Number of setups	278,750 setups
Hazardous waste disposal	48,000	Pounds of waste	16,000 pounds
Quality control	560,000	Number of inspections	160,000 inspections
General supplies	66,000	Number of boards	110,000 boards
Total	$ 1,120,000		
Machine insertion	$ 1,200,000	Number of parts	3,000,000 parts
Manual insertion	4,000,000	Number of parts	1,000,000 parts
Wave-soldering	132,000	Number of boards	110,000 boards
Total	$ 5,332,000		

Required per Unit	PC Board	TV Board
Parts:	55	25
Machine insertions	35	24
Manual insertions	20	1
Machine setups	3	2
Hazardous waste disposal	.35 lb.	.02 lb.
Inspections	2	1

Required:

1. Identify at least four general advantages associated with activity-based costing.
2. On the basis of Manchester's unit cost data given in the problem, calculate the total amount that each of the two product lines will contribute toward covering fixed costs and profit in 20x1. (In other words, for each product line, calculate the total sales revenue minus the total *variable* costs. This amount is often referred to as a product's total *contribution margin.*)
3. Repeat requirement (2) but now use the cost data from the activity-based costing system.
4. Explain how a comparison of the results of the two costing methods may impact the decisions made by Manchester's management group.

(CMA, adapted)

Problem 5–56
Activity-Based Costing
(LO 1, 2, 4, 5, 7)

2. New product cost, under ABC: $7.46 per pound of Kona

World Gourmet Coffee Company (WGCC) is a distributor and processor of different blends of coffee. The company buys coffee beans from around the world and roasts, blends, and packages them for resale. WGCC currently has 15 different coffees that it offers to gourmet shops in one-pound bags. The major cost is raw materials; however, there is a substantial amount of manufacturing overhead in the predominantly automated roasting and packing process. The company uses relatively little direct labor.

Some of the coffees are very popular and sell in large volumes, while a few of the newer blends have very low volumes. WGCC prices its coffee at full product cost, including allocated overhead, plus a markup of 30 percent. If prices for certain coffees are significantly higher than market, adjustments are made. The company competes primarily on the quality of its products, but customers are price-conscious as well.

Data for the 20x1 budget include manufacturing overhead of $3,000,000, which has been allocated on the basis of each product's direct-labor cost. The budgeted direct-labor cost for 20x1 totals $600,000. Based on the sales budget and raw-material budget, purchases and use of raw materials (mostly coffee beans) will total $6,000,000.

The expected prime costs for one-pound bags of two of the company's products are as follows:

	Kona	Malaysian
Direct material	$3.20	$4.20
Direct labor	.30	.30

WGCC's controller believes the traditional product-costing system may be providing misleading cost information. She has developed an analysis of the 20x1 budgeted manufacturing-overhead costs shown in the following chart.

Activity	Cost Driver	Budgeted Activity	Budgeted Cost
Purchasing	Purchase orders	1,158	$ 579,000
Material handling	Setups	1,800	720,000
Quality control	Batches	720	144,000
Roasting	Roasting hours	96,100	961,000
Blending	Blending hours	33,600	336,000
Packaging	Packaging hours	26,000	260,000
Total manufacturing-overhead cost			$3,000,000

Data regarding the 20x1 production of Kona and Malaysian coffee are shown in the following table. There will be no raw-material inventory for either of these coffees at the beginning of the year.

	Kona	Malaysian
Budgeted sales	2,000 lb.	100,000 lb.
Batch size	500 lb.	10,000 lb.
Setups	3 per batch	3 per batch
Purchase order size	500 lb.	25,000 lb.
Roasting time	1 hr. per 100 lb.	1 hr. per 100 lb.
Blending time	.5 hr. per 100 lb.	.5 hr. per 100 lb.
Packaging time	.1 hr. per 100 lb.	.1 hr. per 100 lb.

Required:

1. Using WGCC's current product-costing system:
   a. Determine the company's predetermined overhead rate using direct-labor cost as the single cost driver.
   b. Determine the full product costs and selling prices of one pound of Kona coffee and one pound of Malaysian coffee.
2. Develop a new product cost, using an activity-based costing approach, for one pound of Kona coffee and one pound of Malaysian coffee.
3. What are the implications of the activity-based costing system with respect to
   a. The use of direct labor as a basis for applying overhead to products?
   b. The use of the existing product-costing system as the basis for pricing?

(CMA, adapted)

Problem 5–57
Activity-Based Costing; Activity Cost Pools; Pool Rates; Calculation of Product Costs; Cost Distortion
(LO 1, 2, 3, 4, 5)

2. Pool rate, plant-related costs: $50 per sq. ft.
5. New target price, odds: $605.16

Knickknack, Inc. manufactures two products: odds and ends. The firm uses a single, plantwide overhead rate based on direct-labor hours. Production and product-costing data are as follows:

	Odds	Ends
Production quantity	1,000 units	5,000 units
Direct material	$ 40	$ 60
Direct labor (not including setup time)	30 (2 hr. at $15)	45 (3 hr. at $15)
Manufacturing overhead*	96 (2 hr. at $48)	144 (3 hr. at $48)
Total cost per unit	$ 166	$ 249

*Calculation of predetermined overhead rate:

Manufacturing overhead budget:	
Machine-related costs	$450,000
Setup and inspection	180,000
Engineering	90,000
Plant-related costs	96,000
Total	$816,000

Predetermined overhead rate:

$$\frac{\text{Budgeted manufacturing overhead}}{\text{Budgeted direct-labor hours}} = \frac{\$816{,}000}{(1{,}000)(2) + (5{,}000)(3)} = \$48 \text{ per direct-labor hour}$$

Knickknack, Inc. prices its products at 120 percent of cost, which yields target prices of $199.20 for odds and $298.80 for ends. Recently, however, Knickknack has been challenged in the market for ends by a European competitor, Bricabrac Corporation. A new entrant in this market, Bricabrac has been selling ends for $220 each. Knickknack's president is puzzled by Bricabrac's ability to sell ends at such a low cost. She has asked you (the controller) to look into the matter. You have decided that Knickknack's traditional, volume-based product-costing system may be causing cost distortion between the firm's two products. Ends are a high-volume, relatively simple product. Odds, on the other hand, are quite complex and exhibit a much lower volume. As a result, you have begun work on an activity-based costing system.

Required:

1. Let each of the overhead categories in the budget represent an activity cost pool. Categorize each in terms of the type of activity (e.g., unit-level activity).
2. The following cost drivers have been identified for the four activity cost pools.

Activity Cost Pool	Cost Driver	Budgeted Level of Cost Driver
Machine-related costs	Machine hours	9,000 hr.
Setup and inspection	Number of production runs	40 runs
Engineering	Engineering change orders	100 change orders
Plant-related costs	Square footage of space	1,920 sq. ft.

You have gathered the following additional information:

- Each odd requires 4 machine hours, whereas each end requires 1 machine hour.
- Odds are manufactured in production runs of 50 units each. Ends are manufactured in 250-unit batches.
- Three-quarters of the engineering activity, as measured in terms of change orders, is related to odds.
- The plant has 1,920 square feet of space, 80 percent of which is used in the production of odds.

For each activity cost pool, compute a pool rate. (*Hint:* Regarding the pool rate refer to Exhibit 5–6.)

3. Determine the unit cost, for each activity cost pool, for odds and ends.
4. Compute the new product cost per unit for odds and ends, using the ABC system.
5. Using the same pricing policy as in the past, compute prices for odds and ends. Use the product costs determined by the ABC system.
6. Show that the ABC system fully assigns the total budgeted manufacturing overhead costs of $816,000.
7. Show how Knickknack's traditional, volume-based costing system distorted its product costs. (Refer to Exhibit 5–10 for guidance.)

Problem 5–58
Activity-Based Costing; Forecasting; Ethics
(LO 1, 2, 4, 5)

1. Total Material-Handling Department costs: $288,000
3. Reduction in material-handling costs allocated to government contracts: $74,600
4. Cumulative impact of recommended change in allocating Material-Handling Department costs: $234,346

Northwest Aircraft Industries (NAI) was founded 45 years ago by Jay Preston as a small machine shop producing machined parts for the aircraft industry, which is prominent in the Seattle/Tacoma area of Washington. By the end of its first decade, NAI's annual sales had reached $15 million, almost exclusively under government contracts. The next 30 years brought slow but steady growth as cost-reimbursement government contracts continued to be the main source of revenue. Realizing that NAI could not depend on government contracts for long-term growth and stability, Drew Preston, son of the founder and now president of the company, began planning for diversified commercial growth. As a result of these efforts, three years ago NAI had succeeded in reducing the ratio of government contract sales to 50 percent of total sales.

Traditionally, the costs of the Material-Handling Department have been allocated to direct material as a percentage of direct-material dollar value. This was adequate when the majority of the manufacturing was homogeneous and related to government contracts. Recently, however, government auditors have rejected some proposals, stating that "the amount of Material-Handling Department costs allocated to these proposals is disproportionate to the total effort involved."

Kara Lindley, the newly hired cost-accounting manager, was asked by the manager of the Government Contracts Unit, Paul Anderson, to find a more equitable method of allocating Material-Handling Department costs to the user departments. Her review has revealed the following information.

- The majority of the direct-material purchases for government contracts are high-dollar, low-volume purchases, while commercial materials represent low-dollar, high-volume purchases.
- Administrative departments such as marketing, finance and administration, human resources, and maintenance also use the services of the Material-Handling Department on a limited basis but have never been charged in the past for material-handling costs.
- One purchasing agent with a direct phone line is assigned exclusively to purchasing high-dollar, low-volume material for government contracts at an annual salary of $36,000. Employee benefits are estimated to be 20 percent of the annual salary. The annual dedicated phone line costs are $2,800.

The components of the Material-Handling Department's budget for 20x1, as proposed by Lindley's predecessor, are as follows:

Payroll	$ 180,000
Employee benefits	36,000
Telephone	38,000
Other utilities	22,000
Materials and supplies	6,000
Depreciation	6,000
Direct-material budget:	
Government contracts	2,006,000
Commercial products	874,000

Lindley has estimated the number of purchase orders to be processed in 20x1 to be as follows:

Government contracts*	80,000
Commercial products	156,000
Marketing	1,800
Finance and administration	2,700
Human resources	500
Maintenance	1,000
Total	242,000

*Exclusive of high-dollar, low-volume materials.

Lindley recommended to Anderson that material-handling costs be allocated on a per-purchase-order basis. Anderson realizes and accepts that the company has been allocating to government contracts more material-handling costs than can be justified. However, the implication of Lindley's analysis could be a decrease in his unit's earnings and, consequently, a cut in his annual bonus. Anderson told Lindley to "adjust" her numbers and modify her recommendation so that the results will be more favorable to the Government Contracts Unit.

Being new in her position, Lindley is not sure how to proceed. She feels ambivalent about Anderson's instructions and suspects his motivation. To complicate matters for Lindley, Preston has asked her to prepare a three-year forecast of the Government Contracts Unit's results, and she believes that the newly recommended allocation method would provide the most accurate data. However, this would put her in direct opposition to Anderson's directives.

Lindley has assembled the following data to project the material-handling costs.

- Total direct-material costs increase 2.5 percent per year.
- Material-handling costs remain the same percentage of direct-material costs.
- Direct government costs (payroll, employee benefits, and direct phone line) remain constant.
- The number of purchase orders increases 5 percent per year.
- The ratio of government purchase orders to total purchase orders remains at 33 percent.
- In addition, she has assumed that government material in the future will be 70 percent of total material.

Required:

1. Calculate the material-handling rate that would have been used by Kara Lindley's predecessor at Northwest Aircraft Industries.
2. *a.* Calculate the revised material-handling costs to be allocated on a per-purchase-order basis.
   b. Discuss why purchase orders might be a more reliable cost driver than the dollar amount of direct material.
3. Calculate the difference due to the change to the new method of allocating material-handling costs to government contracts.
4. Prepare a forecast of the cumulative dollar impact over a three-year period from 20x1 through 20x3 of Kara Lindley's recommended change for allocating Material-Handling Department costs to the Government Contracts Unit. Round all calculations to the nearest whole number.
5. Referring to the standards of ethical conduct for management accountants:
   a. Discuss why Kara Lindley has an ethical conflict.
   b. Identify several steps that Lindley could take to resolve the ethical conflict.

(CMA, adapted)

Problem 5–59
Activity-Based Costing; Production and Pricing Decisions
(LO 1, 2, 3, 4, 5)

1(b). Tuff Stuff unit cost: $28.00
3. Fabricating cost per unit, Tuff Stuff: $4.93 per unit (rounded)

Marconi Manufacturing produces two items in its Trumbull Plant: Tuff Stuff and Ruff Stuff. Since inception, Marconi has used only one manufacturing-overhead cost pool to accumulate costs. Overhead has been allocated to products based on direct-labor hours. Until recently, Marconi was the sole producer of Ruff Stuff and was able to dictate the selling price. However, last year Marvella Products began marketing a comparable product at a price below the cost assigned by Marconi. Market share has declined rapidly, and Marconi must now decide whether to meet the competitive price or to discontinue the product line. Recognizing that discontinuing the product line would place an additional burden on its remaining product, Tuff Stuff, management is using activity-based costing to determine if it would show a different cost structure for the two products.

The two major indirect costs for manufacturing the products are power usage and setup costs. Most of the power is used in fabricating, while most of the setup costs are required in assembly. The setup costs are predominantly related to the Tuff Stuff product line.

A decision was made to separate the Manufacturing Department costs into two activity cost pools as follows:

Fabricating: machine hours will be the cost driver.

Assembly: number of setups will be the cost driver.

The controller has gathered the following information.

MANUFACTURING DEPARTMENT
Annual Budget before Separation of Overhead

	Total	Product Line	
		Tuff Stuff	Ruff Stuff
Number of units		20,000	20,000
Direct-labor hours*		2 hours per unit	3 hours per unit
Total direct-labor cost	$800,000		
Direct material		$5.00 per unit	$3.00 per unit
Budgeted overhead:			
Indirect labor	24,000		
Fringe benefits	5,000		
Indirect material	31,000		
Power	180,000		
Setup	75,000		
Quality assurance	10,000		
Other utilities	10,000		
Depreciation	15,000		

*Direct-labor hourly rate is the same in both departments.

MANUFACTURING DEPARTMENT
Cost Structure after Separation of Overhead into Activity Cost Pools

	Fabrication	Assembly
Direct-labor cost	75%	25%
Direct material (no change)	100%	0%
Indirect labor	75%	25%
Fringe benefits	80%	20%
Indirect material	$ 20,000	$11,000
Power	$160,000	$20,000
Setup	$ 5,000	$70,000
Quality assurance	80%	20%
Other utilities	50%	50%
Depreciation	80%	20%

Cost driver:

	Product Line	
	Tuff Stuff	Ruff Stuff
Machine-hours per unit	4.4	6.0
Setups	1,000	272

Required:

1. Assigning overhead based on direct-labor hours, calculate the following:
   a. Total budgeted cost of the Manufacturing Department.
   b. Unit cost of Tuff Stuff and Ruff Stuff.
2. After separation of overhead into activity cost pools, compute the total budgeted cost of each department: fabricating and assembly.

3. Using activity-based costing, calculate the unit costs for each product. (In computing the pool rates for the fabricating and assembly activity cost pools, round to the nearest cent. Then, in computing unit product costs, round to the nearest cent.)
4. Discuss how a decision regarding the production and pricing of Ruff Stuff will be affected by the results of your calculations in the preceding requirements.

(CMA, adapted)

Problem 5–60
Traditional versus Activity-Based Costing Systems
(LO 1, 2, 3, 4, 5)

5. Reported product costs with ABC, product G: $141.67
6. Reported product costs with ABC, product T: $163.74

Gigabyte, Inc. manufactures three products for the computer industry:

Gismos (product G): annual sales, 8,000 units
Thingamajigs (product T): annual sales, 15,000 units
Whatchamacallits (product W): annual sales, 4,000 units

The company uses a traditional, volume-based product-costing system with manufacturing overhead applied on the basis of direct-labor dollars. The product costs have been computed as follows:

	Product G	Product T	Product W
Raw material	$ 35.00	$ 52.50	$17.50
Direct labor	16.00 (.8 hr. at $20)	12.00 (.6 hr. at $20)	8.00 (.4 hr. at $20)
Manufacturing overhead*	140.00	105.00	70.00
Total product cost	$191.00	$169.50	$95.50

*Calculation of predetermined overhead rate:

Manufacturing overhead budget:	
Machine setup	$ 5,250
Machinery	1,225,000
Inspection	525,000
Material handling	875,000
Engineering	344,750
Total	$2,975,000

Direct-labor budget (based on budgeted annual sales):			
Product G:	8,000 × $16.00	=	$128,000
Product T:	15,000 × $12.00	=	180,000
Product W:	4,000 × $8.00	=	32,000
Total			$340,000

$$\text{Predetermined overhead rate} = \frac{\text{Budgeted overhead}}{\text{Budgeted direct labor}} = 875\%$$

Gigabyte's pricing method has been to set a target price equal to 150 percent of full product cost. However, only the thingamajigs have been selling at their target price. The target and actual current prices for all three products are the following:

	Product G	Product T	Product W
Product cost	$191.00	$169.50	$ 95.50
Target price	286.50	254.25	143.25
Actual current selling price	213.00	254.25	200.00

Gigabyte has been forced to lower the price of gismos in order to get orders. In contrast, Gigabyte has raised the price of whatchamacallits several times, but there has been no apparent loss of sales. Gigabyte, Inc. has been under increasing pressure to reduce the price even further on gismos. In contrast, Gigabyte's competitors do not seem to be interested in the market for whatchamacallits. Gigabyte apparently has this market to itself.

Required:

1. Is product G the company's least profitable product?
2. Is product W a profitable product for Gigabyte, Inc.?
3. Comment on the reactions of Gigabyte's competitors to the firm's pricing strategy. What dangers does Gigabyte, Inc. face?
4. Gigabyte's controller, Nan O'Second, recently attended a conference at which activity-based costing systems were discussed. She became convinced that such a system would help Gigabyte's management to understand its product costs better. She got top management's approval to design an activity-based costing system, and an ABC project team was formed. In stage one of the ABC project, each of the overhead items listed in the overhead budget was placed into its own activity cost pool. Then a cost driver was identified for each activity cost pool. Finally, the ABC project team compiled data showing the percentage of each cost driver that was consumed by each of Gigabyte's product lines. These data are summarized as follows:

Activity Cost Pool	Cost Driver	Product G	Product T	Product W
Machine setup	Number of setups	20%	30%	50%
Machinery	Machine hours	25%	50%	25%
Inspection	Number of inspections	15%	45%	40%
Material handling	Raw-material costs	25%	69%	6%
Engineering	Number of change orders	35%	10%	55%

Show how the controller determined the percentages given above for raw-material costs. (Round to the nearest whole percent.)

5. Develop product costs for the three products on the basis of an activity-based costing system. (Round to the nearest cent.)
6. Calculate a target price for each product, using Gigabyte's pricing formula. Compare the new target prices with the current actual selling prices and previously reported product costs.
7. *Build a spreadsheet:* Construct an Excel spreadsheet to solve requirements (5) and (6) above. Show how the solution will change if the inspection activity was divided among the three products in the following manner: product G, 20%; product T, 40%, and product W, 40%.

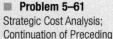

Problem 5–61
Strategic Cost Analysis; Continuation of Preceding Problem
(LO 2, 5, 7)

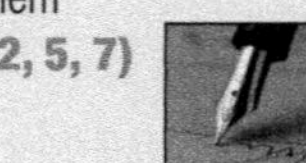

Refer to the new target prices for Gigabyte's three products, based on the new activity-based costing system calculated in the preceding problem.

Required: Write a memo to the company president commenting on the situation Gigabyte, Inc. has been facing regarding the market for its products and the actions of its competitors. Discuss the strategic options available to management. What do you recommend, and why?

Problem 5–62
Cost Distortion; Continuation of Problem 5–60
(LO 2, 5)

Traditional system undercosts product W by $120.25 per unit

Refer to the product costs developed in requirement (5) of Problem 5–60. Prepare a table showing how Gigabyte's traditional, volume-based product-costing system distorts the product costs of gismos, thingamajigs, and whatchamacallits. (You may wish to refer to Exhibit 5–10 for guidance. Because of rounding in the calculation of the product costs, there will be a small rounding error in this cost distortion analysis as well.)

Problem 5–63
Basic Elements of a Production Process; Non-Value-Added Costs
(LO 7, 8, 10)

Better Bagels, Inc. manufactures a variety of bagels, which are frozen and sold in grocery stores. The production process consists of the following steps.

1. Ingredients, such as flour and raisins, are received and inspected. Then they are stored until needed.
2. Ingredients are carried on hand carts to the mixing room.
3. Dough is mixed in 40-pound batches in four heavy-duty mixers.
4. Dough is stored on large boards in the mixing room until a bagel machine is free.
5. A board of dough is carried into the bagel room. The board is tipped, and the dough slides into the hopper of a bagel machine. This machine pulls off a small piece of dough, rolls it into a cylindrical shape, and then squeezes it into a doughnut shape. The bagel machines can be adjusted in a setup

procedure to accommodate different sizes and styles of bagels. Workers remove the uncooked bagels and place them on a tray, where they are kept until a boiling vat is free.

6. Next the trays of uncooked bagels are carried into an adjoining room, which houses three 50-gallon vats of boiling water. The bagels are boiled for approximately one minute.
7. Bagels are removed from the vats with a long-handled strainer and placed on a wooden board. The boards full of bagels are carried to the oven room, where they are kept until an oven rack is free. The two ovens contain eight racks which rotate but remain upright, much like the seats on a Ferris wheel. A rack full of bagels is finished baking after one complete revolution in the oven. When a rack full of bagels is removed from the oven, a fresh rack replaces it. The oven door is opened and closed as each rack completes a revolution in the oven.
8. After the bagels are removed from the oven, they are placed in baskets for cooling.
9. While the bagels are cooling, they are inspected. Misshapen bagels are removed and set aside. (Most are eaten by the staff.)
10. After the bagels are cool, the wire baskets are carried to the packaging department. Here the bagels are dumped into the hopper on a bagging machine. This machine packages a half-dozen bagels in each bag and seals the bag with a twist tie.
11. Then the packaged bagels are placed in cardboard boxes, each holding 24 bags. The boxes are placed on a forklift and are driven to the freezer, where the bagels are frozen and stored for shipment.

Required:

1. Identify the steps in the bagel-production process that fall into each of the following categories: process time, inspection time, move time, waiting time, storage time.
2. List the steps in the production process that could be candidates for non-value-added activities.

Problem 5–64
Key Features of JIT Production Systems (Appendix)
(LO 11)

Refer to the information given in the preceding problem for Better Bagels, Inc.

Required: Redesign the bagel production process so that it adheres to the JIT philosophy. Explain how the eight key features of JIT systems would be present in the new production process. What new equipment would the company need to purchase in order to implement the JIT approach fully?

Problem 5–65
Two-Dimensional Activity-Based Costing; Activity Analysis; ABM
(LO 8)

Midwest Home Furnishings Corporation (MHFC) manufactures a variety of housewares for the consumer market in the midwest. The company's three major product lines are cooking utensils, tableware, and flatware. MHFC implemented activity-based costing four years ago and now has a well-developed ABC system in place for determining product costs. Only recently, however, has the ABC system been systematically used for the purposes of activity-based management. As a pilot project, MHFC's controller asked the ABC project team to do a detailed activity analysis of the purchasing activity. The following specific activities were identified.

1. Receipt of parts specifications from the Design Engineering Department.
2. Follow-up with design engineers to answer any questions.
3. Vendor (supplier) identification.
4. Vendor consultations (by phone or in person).
5. Price negotiation.
6. Vendor selection.
7. Ordering (by phone or mail).
8. Order follow-up.
9. Expediting (attempting to speed up delivery).
10. Order receiving.
11. Inspection of parts.
12. Return of parts not meeting specifications.
13. Consultation with design engineers and production personnel if parts do not satisfy intended purpose.
14. Further consultation and/or negotiation with vendor if necessary.
15. Ship parts back to vendor if necessary.
16. If satisfactory, move parts to storage.

Required:

1. Draw a diagram to depict MHFC's two-dimensional activity-based costing efforts. The diagram should include the following:
   a. The cost assignment role of ABC, with the cost pools, activities, and product lines represented.
   b. The process view of ABC, with the purchasing activities displayed. Also indicated here will be the linkages among the activities. (To save space, indicate the activities by their numbers.)
   c. The activity evaluation phase of two-dimensional ABC.
2. Identify the triggers for each of the following activities in MHFC's purchasing activity analysis:
   Follow-up with design engineers (activity 2)
   Expediting (activity 9)
   Inspection of parts (activity 11)
   Return of parts (activity 12)
   Consultation with design engineers and production personnel (activity 13)
3. For each of the activities listed in requirement (2), identify the possible root causes.
4. Choose four activities in MHFC's purchasing function, and suggest a performance measure for each of these activities.

Problem 5–66
Customer-Profitability Analysis; Activity-Based Costing
(LO 9)

1. Operating income, Trace Telecom: $7,000

Fresno Fiber Optics, Inc. manufactures fiber optic cables for the computer and telecommunications industries. At the request of the company vice president of marketing, the cost management staff has recently completed a customer-profitability study. The following activity-based costing information was the basis for the analysis.

Customer-Related Activities	Cost Driver Base	Cost Driver Rate
Sales activity	Sales visits	$1,000
Order taking	Purchase orders	200
Special handling	Units handled	50
Special shipping	Shipments	500

Cost-driver data for two of Fresno's customers for the most recent year are

Customer-Related Activities	Trace Telecom	Caltex Computer
Sales activity	8 visits	6 visits
Order taking	15 orders	20 orders
Special handling	800 units handled	600 units handled
Special shipping	18 shipments	20 shipments

The following additional information has been compiled for Fresno Fiber Optics for two of its customers, Trace Telecom and Caltex Computer, for the most recent year:

	Trace Telecom	Caltex Computer
Sales revenue	$190,000	$123,800
Cost of goods sold	80,000	62,000
General selling costs	24,000	18,000
General administrative costs	19,000	16,000

Required:

1. Prepare a customer profitability analysis for Trace Telecom and Caltex Computer. (*Hint:* Refer to Exhibit 5–13 for guidance.)
2. *Build a spreadsheet:* Construct an Excel spreadsheet to solve requirement (1) above. Show how the solution will change if the following information changes: Trace Telecom's sales revenue was $185,000 and Caltex Computer's cost of goods sold was $59,000.

Problem 5–67
Customer-Profitability Profile; Continuation of Preceding Problem
(LO 9)

Tele-Install, operating profit: $(18,000)

Refer to the information given in the preceding problem for Fresno Fiber Optics and two of its customers, Trace Telecom and Caltex Computer. Additional information for six of Fresno's other customers for the most recent year follows:

Customer	Operating Income
Golden Gate Service Associates	$71,000
Tele-Install, Inc	(18,000)
Graydon Computer Company	60,000
Mid-State Computing Company	42,000
Network-All, Inc	93,000
The California Group	6,000

Required:

1. Prepare Fresno Fiber Optics' customer profitability profile for the most recent year.
2. As Fresno Fiber Optics' director of cost management, write a memo to the company's vice president of marketing that will accompany the customer profitability profile. Include a brief explanation of the methodology used and comment on the results.

Cases

Case 5–68
Activity-Based Costing; Budgeted Operating Margin
(LO 1, 2, 4, 5, 7)

3. Total cost, JR-14, estimated 20x2 product cost: $1,540,000
4. Gross margin, RM-13: $(113,000)

Whitestone Company produces two subassemblies, JR-14 and RM-13, used in manufacturing trucks. The company is currently using an absorption costing system that applies overhead based on direct-labor hours. The budget for the current year ending December 31, 20x1, is as follows:

WHITESTONE COMPANY
Budgeted Statement of Gross Margin for 20x1

	JR-14	RM-13	Total
Sales in units	5,000	5,000	10,000
Sales revenue	$1,700,000	$2,200,000	$3,900,000
Cost of goods manufactured and sold:			
Beginning finished-goods inventory	$ 240,000	$ 300,000	$ 540,000
Add: Direct material	1,000,000	1,750,000	2,750,000
Direct labor	185,185	92,593	277,778
Applied manufacturing overhead*	544,025	272,013	816,038
Cost of goods available for sale	$1,969,210	$2,414,606	$4,383,816
Less: Ending finished-goods inventory	240,000	300,000	540,000
Cost of goods sold	$1,729,210	$2,114,606	$3,843,816
Gross margin	$ (29,210)	$ 85,394	$ 56,184

*Applied on the basis of direct-labor hours:

Machining	$ 424,528
Assembly	216,981
Material handling	56,604
Inspection	117,925
Total	$ 816,038

Mark Ward, Whitestone's president, has been reading about a product-costing method called activity-based costing. Ward is convinced that activity-based costing will cast a new light on future profits. As a result, Brian Walters, Whitestone's director of cost management, has accumulated cost pool information for this year shown on the following chart. This information is based on a product mix of 5,000 units of JR-14 and 5,000 units of RM-13.

Cost Pool Information for 20x1

Cost Pool	Activity	JR-14	RM-13
Direct labor	Direct-labor hours	10,000	5,000
Machining	Machine hours	15,000	30,000
Assembly	Assembly hours	6,000	5,500
Material handling	Number of parts	5	10
Inspection	Inspection hours	5,000	7,500

In addition, the following information is projected for the next calendar year, 20x2.

	JR-14	RM-13
Beginning inventory, finished goods (in units)	800	600
Ending inventory, finished goods (in units)	700	700
Sales (in units)	5,100	4,900

On January 1, 20x2, Whitestone is planning to increase the prices of JR-14 to $355 and RM-13 to $455. Material costs are not expected to increase in 20x2, but direct labor will increase by 8 percent, and all manufacturing overhead costs will increase by 6 percent. Due to the nature of the manufacturing process, the company does not have any beginning or ending work-in-process inventories.

Whitestone uses a just-in-time inventory system and has materials delivered to the production facility directly from the vendors. The raw-material inventory at both the beginning and the end of the month is immaterial and can be ignored for the purposes of a budgeted income statement. The company uses the first-in, first-out (FIFO) inventory method.

Required:

1. Explain how activity-based costing differs from traditional product-costing methods.
2. Using activity-based costing, calculate the total cost for the following activity cost pools: machining, assembly, material handling, and inspection. (Round to the nearest dollar.) Then, calculate the pool rate per unit of the appropriate cost driver for each of the four activities. (*Hint:* Refer to Exhibit 5–6, regarding calculation of the pool rate.)
3. Prepare a table showing for each product line the estimated 20x2 cost for each of the following cost elements: direct material, direct labor, machining, assembly, material handling, and inspection. (Round to the nearest dollar.)
4. Prepare a budgeted statement showing the gross margin for Whitestone Company for 20x2, using activity-based costing. The statement should show each product and a total for the company. Be sure to include detailed calculations for the cost of goods manufactured and sold. (Round each amount in the statement to the nearest dollar.)

(CMA, adapted)

Case 5–69
Traditional versus Activity-Based Costing Systems
(LO 1, 2, 3, 4, 5)

2. Product costs with ABC, Standard Model: $437.75
3. New target price, Heavy-Duty Model: $248.73

Morelli Electric Motor Corporation manufactures electric motors for commercial use. The company produces three models, designated as standard, deluxe, and heavy-duty. The company uses a job-order cost-accounting system with manufacturing overhead applied on the basis of direct-labor hours. The system has been in place with little change for 25 years. Product costs and annual sales data are as follows:

	Standard Model	Deluxe Model	Heavy-Duty Model
Annual sales (units)	20,000	1,000	10,000
Product costs:			
Raw material	$ 10	$ 25	$ 42
Direct labor	10 (.5 hr. at $20)	20 (1 hr. at $20)	20 (1 hr. at $20)
Manufacturing overhead*	85	170	170
Total product cost	$105	$215	$232

*Calculation of predetermined overhead rate:

Manufacturing-overhead budget:

Depreciation, machinery	$1,480,000
Maintenance, machinery	120,000
Depreciation, taxes, and insurance for factory	300,000
Engineering	350,000
Purchasing, receiving and shipping	250,000
Inspection and repair of defects	375,000
Material handling	400,000
Miscellaneous manufacturing overhead costs	295,000
Total	$3,570,000

Direct-labor budget:

Standard model:	10,000 hours
Deluxe model:	1,000 hours
Heavy-duty model:	10,000 hours
Total	21,000 hours

$$\text{Predetermined overhead rate: } \frac{\text{Budgeted overhead}}{\text{Budgeted direct-labor hours}} = \frac{\$3,570,000}{21,000 \text{ hours}} = \$170 \text{ per hour}$$

For the past 10 years, the company's pricing formula has been to set each product's target price at 110 percent of its full product cost. Recently, however, the standard-model motor has come under increasing price pressure from offshore competitors. The result was that the price on the standard model has been lowered to $110.

The company president recently asked the controller, "Why can't we compete with these other companies? They're selling motors just like our standard model for 106 dollars. That's only a buck more than our production cost. Are we really that inefficient? What gives?"

The controller responded by saying, "I think this is due to an outmoded product-costing system. As you may remember, I raised a red flag about our system when I came on board last year. But the decision was to keep our current system in place. In my judgment, our product-costing system is distorting our product costs. Let me run a few numbers to demonstrate what I mean."

Getting the president's go-ahead, the controller compiled the basic data needed to implement an activity-based costing system. These data are displayed in the following table. The percentages are the proportion of each cost driver consumed by each product line.

		Product Lines		
Activity Cost Pool	**Cost Driver**	**Standard Model**	**Deluxe Model**	**Heavy-Duty Model**
I: Depreciation, machinery Maintenance, machinery	Machine time	40%	13%	47%
II: Engineering Inspection and repair of defects	Engineering hours	47%	6%	47%
III: Purchasing, receiving, and shipping Material handling	Number of material orders	47%	8%	45%
IV: Depreciation, taxes, and insurance for factory Miscellaneous manufacturing overhead	Factory space usage	42%	15%	43%

Required:

1. Compute the target prices for the three models, based on the traditional, volume-based product-costing system.
2. Compute new product costs for the three products, based on the new data collected by the controller. Round to the nearest cent.
3. Calculate a new target price for the three products, based on the activity-based costing system. Compare the new target price with the current actual selling price for the standard-model electric motor.
4. Write a memo to the company president explaining what has been happening as a result of the firm's traditional, volume-based product-costing system.
5. What strategic options does Morelli Electric Motor Corporation have? What do you recommend, and why?

Case 5–70
Cost Distortion; Continuation of Preceding Case
(LO 2, 5)

Traditional system undercosts Deluxe Model by $222.75 per unit

Refer to the product costs developed in requirement (2) of the preceding case. Prepare a table showing how Morelli Electric Motor Corporation's traditional, volume-based product-costing system distorts the product costs of the standard, deluxe, and heavy-duty models. (You may wish to refer to Exhibit 5–10 for guidance. Because of rounding in the calculation of the product costs, there will be a small rounding error in this cost distortion analysis as well.)

Case 5–71
Ethical Issues Related to Product-Cost Distortion; Activity-Based Costing; Continuation of Case 5–69
(LO 2, 5, 7)

Morelli Electric Motor Corporation's controller, Erin Jackson, developed new product costs for the standard, deluxe, and heavy-duty models using activity-based costing. It was apparent that the firm's traditional product-costing system had been undercosting the deluxe-model electric motor by a significant amount. This was due largely to the low volume of the deluxe-model motor. Before she could report back to the president, Jackson received a phone call from her friend, Alan Tyler. He was the production manager for the deluxe-model electric motor. Tyler was upset, and he let Jackson know it. "Erin, I've gotten wind of your new product-cost analysis. There's no way the deluxe model costs anywhere near what your numbers say. For years and years, this line has been highly profitable, and its reported product cost was low. Now you're telling us it costs more than twice what we thought. I just don't buy it."

Jackson briefly explained to her friend about the principles of activity-based costing and why it resulted in more accurate product costs. "Alan, the deluxe model is really losing money. It simply has too low a volume to be manufactured efficiently."

Tyler was even more upset now. "Erin, if you report these new product costs to the president, he's going to discontinue the deluxe model. My job's on the line, Erin! How about massaging those numbers a little bit. Who's going to know?"

"I'll know, Alan. And you'll know," responded Jackson. "Look, I'll go over my analysis again, just to make sure I haven't made an error."

Required: Discuss the ethical issues involved in this scenario.

1. Is the controller, Erin Jackson, acting ethically?
2. Is the production manager, Alan Tyler, acting ethically?
3. What are Jackson's ethical obligations? To the president? To her friend?

FOCUS COMPANY >>>

THIS CHAPTER'S FOCUS COMPANY is Tasty Donuts, Inc., a Canadian chain of 10 donut shops in Toronto, Ontario. Using the Tasty Donuts illustration, we explore cost behavior, cost estimation, and cost prediction. Cost behavior refers to the relationship between cost and activity. Variable and fixed costs, which we studied in Chapter 2, are two examples of the many types of cost behavior. Cost estimation is the process of determining how a particular cost behaves, often relying on historical cost data. Cost prediction means using our knowledge of cost behavior to forecast the cost to be incurred at a particular level of activity. Cost analysis helps Tasty Donuts' management plan for the costs to be incurred at various levels of donut sales activity.

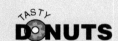

TASTY DONUTS

6 Activity Analysis, Cost Behavior, and Cost Estimation

IN CONTRAST >>>

In contrast to the service-industry setting of Tasty Donuts, we turn to a manufacturing environment to explore the effect of the learning curve on cost behavior. In many production processes, production efficiency increases with experience. As cumulative production output increases, the average labor time required per unit declines. As the labor time declines, labor cost declines as well. This phenomenon is called the learning curve. To illustrate the learning-curve concept, we explore its use by Cosmos Communications Technology (CCT), a Canadian manufacturer of sophisticated communications satellites in Vancouver, British Columbia. CCT's management has found that the learning curve applies to the labor-intensive assembly operation for each new satellite design.

AFTER COMPLETING THIS CHAPTER, YOU SHOULD BE ABLE TO:

1 Explain the relationships between cost estimation, cost behavior, and cost prediction.

2 Define and describe the behavior of the following types of costs: variable, step-variable, fixed, step-fixed, semivariable (or mixed), and curvilinear.

3 Explain the importance of the relevant range in using a cost behavior pattern for cost prediction.

4 Define and give examples of engineered costs, committed costs, and discretionary costs.

5 Describe and use the following cost estimation methods: account classification, visual fit, high-low, and least-squares regression.

6 Describe the multiple regression, engineering, and learning-curve approaches to cost estimation.

7 Describe some problems often encountered in collecting data for cost estimation.

8 Perform and interpret a least-squares regression analysis with a single independent variable (appendix).

Managers in almost any organization want to know how costs will be affected by changes in the organization's activity. The relationship between cost and activity, called **cost behavior,** is relevant to the management functions of planning, control, and decision making. In order to *plan* operations and prepare a budget, managers at Nabisco need to predict the costs that will be incurred at different levels of production and sales. To *control* the costs of providing commercial-loan services at Wachovia, executives need to have a feel for the costs that the bank should incur at various levels of commercial-loan activity. In *deciding* whether to add a new intensive care unit, a hospital's administrators need to predict the cost of operating the new unit at various levels of patient demand. In each of these situations, knowledge of *cost behavior* will help the manager to make the desired cost prediction. A **cost prediction** is a forecast of cost at a particular level of activity. In the first half of this chapter, we will study cost behavior patterns and their use in making cost predictions.

Learning Objective 1

Explain the relationships between cost estimation, cost behavior, and cost prediction.

How does a managerial accountant determine the cost behavior pattern for a particular cost item? The determination of cost behavior, which is often called **cost estimation,** can be accomplished in a number of ways. One way is to analyze historical data concerning costs and activity levels. Cost estimation is covered in the second half of this chapter.

The following diagram summarizes the key points in the preceding discussion.

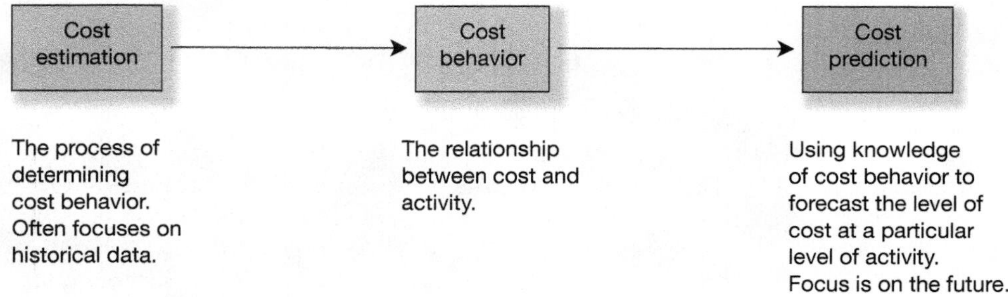
Cost estimation
Cost behavior
Cost prediction
The process of determining cost behavior. Often focuses on historical data.
The relationship between cost and activity.
Using knowledge of cost behavior to forecast the level of cost at a particular level of activity. Focus is on the future.

Cost Behavior Patterns

TASTY DONUTS

Our discussion of cost behavior patterns, also called *cost functions,* will be set in the context of a donut shop business. Tasty Donuts, Inc. operates a chain of 10 donut shops in the city of Toronto, Ontario. Each shop sells a variety of donuts, muffins, and sweet rolls as well as various beverages. Beverages, such as coffee and fruit juices, are prepared in each donut shop, but all of the company's donuts and baked products are made in a centrally located bakery. The company leases several small delivery trucks to transport the bakery items to its donut shops. Use of a central bakery is more cost-efficient. Moreover, this approach allows the firm to smooth out fluctuations in demand for each type of product. For example, the demand for glazed donuts may change from day to day in each donut shop, but these fluctuations tend to cancel each other out when the total demand is aggregated across all 10 shops.

The corporate controller for Tasty Donuts has recently completed a study of the company's cost behavior to use in preparing the firm's budget for the coming year. The controller studied the following costs.

Direct material: ingredients for donuts, muffins, and sweet rolls; beverages; paper products, such as napkins and disposable cups.

Direct labor: wages and fringe benefits of bakers, donut shop sales personnel, and delivery-truck drivers.

Overhead:

Facilities costs: property taxes; depreciation on bakery building, donut shops, and equipment; salaries and fringe benefits of maintenance personnel.

Indirect labor: salaries and fringe benefits of managers and assistant managers for bakery and donut shops.

Delivery trucks: rental payments under lease contract; costs of gasoline, oil, tires, and maintenance.

Utilities: electricity, telephone, and trash collection.

"Failure to understand costs would have left Portugal Telecom vulnerable to competition. Understanding the company's costs became essential to cost reduction efforts and to the company's long-term viability." (6a)

Accenture, regarding its client Portugal Telecom

In studying the behavior of each of these costs, the controller measured company *activity* in terms of *dozens of bakery items sold.* Thus, dozens of bakery items sold is the *cost driver* for each of the costs studied. A bakery item is one donut, muffin, or sweet roll. The costs to make each of these products are nearly identical. The number of bakery items sold each day is roughly the same as the number produced, since bakery goods are produced to keep pace with demand as reported by the company's donut shop managers.

Variable Costs

Learning Objective 2

Define and describe the behavior of the following types of costs: variable, step-variable, fixed, step-fixed, semivariable (or mixed), and curvilinear.

Variable costs were discussed briefly in Chapter 2. We will summarize that discussion here in the context of the Tasty Donuts illustration. A **variable cost** changes *in total* in direct proportion to a change in the activity level (or cost driver). Tasty Donuts' direct-material cost is a variable cost. As the company sells more donuts, muffins, and sweet rolls, the total cost of the ingredients for these goods increases in direct proportion to the number of items sold. Moreover, the quantities of beverages sold and paper products used by customers also increase in direct proportion to the number of bakery items sold. As a result, the costs of beverages and paper products are also variable costs.

Panel A of Exhibit 6–1 displays a graph of Tasty Donuts' direct-material cost. As the graph shows, *total* variable cost increases in proportion to the activity level (or cost driver). When activity triples, for example, from 50,000 dozen items to 150,000 dozen items, total direct-material costs triple, from $55,000 to $165,000. However, the variable cost *per unit* remains the same as activity changes. The total direct-material cost incurred *per dozen* items sold is constant at $1.10 per dozen. The table in panel B of Exhibit 6–1 illustrates this

Exhibit 6–1
Variable Cost: Direct-Material Cost, Tasty Donuts, Inc.

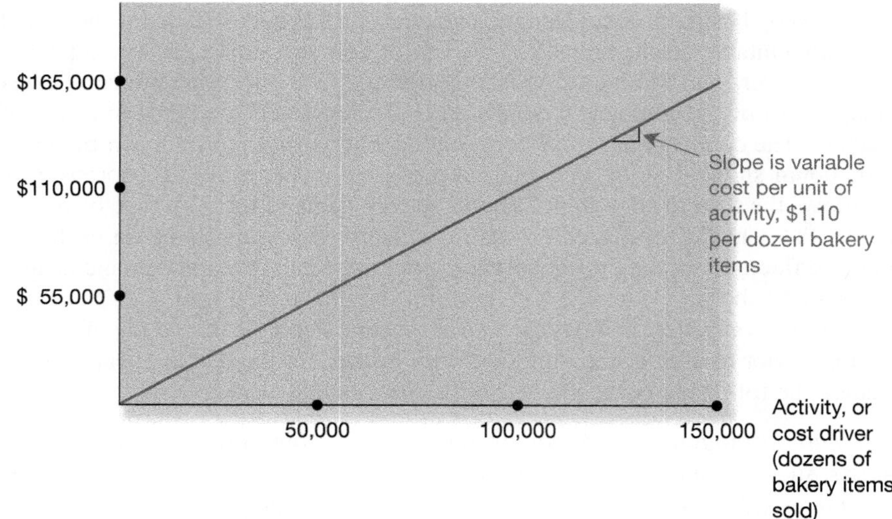

B. Tabulation of Direct-Material Cost

Activity (or cost driver)	Direct-Material Cost per Dozen Bakery Items Sold	Total Direct-Material Cost
50,000	$1.10	$ 55,000
100,000	1.10	110,000
150,000	1.10	165,000

point. The variable cost per unit also is represented in the graph in panel A of Exhibit 6–1 as the slope of the cost line.

To summarize, as activity changes, total variable cost increases in direct proportion to the change in activity level, but the variable cost per unit remains constant.

Step-Variable Costs

Some costs are nearly variable, but they increase in small steps instead of continuously. Such costs, called **step-variable costs,** usually include inputs that are purchased and used in relatively small increments. At Tasty Donuts, Inc., the direct-labor cost of bakers, counter-service personnel, and delivery-truck drivers is a step-variable cost. Many of these employees are part-time workers, called upon for relatively small increments of time, such as a few hours. On a typical day, for example, Tasty Donuts may have 35 employees at work in the bakery and the donut shops. If activity increases slightly, these employees can handle the extra work. However, if activity increases substantially, the bakery manager or various restaurant managers may call on additional help. Exhibit 6–2, a graph of Tasty Donuts' monthly direct-labor cost, shows that this cost remains constant within an activity range of about 5,000 dozen bakery items per month. When monthly activity increases beyond this narrow range, direct-labor costs increase.

Approximating a Step-Variable Cost If the steps in a step-variable cost behavior pattern are small, the step-variable cost function may be approximated by a variable cost function without much loss in accuracy. Exhibit 6–3 shows such an approximation for Tasty Donuts' direct-labor cost.

Total direct-labor cost (wages and fringe benefits of bakers, sales personnel, and delivery-truck drivers)

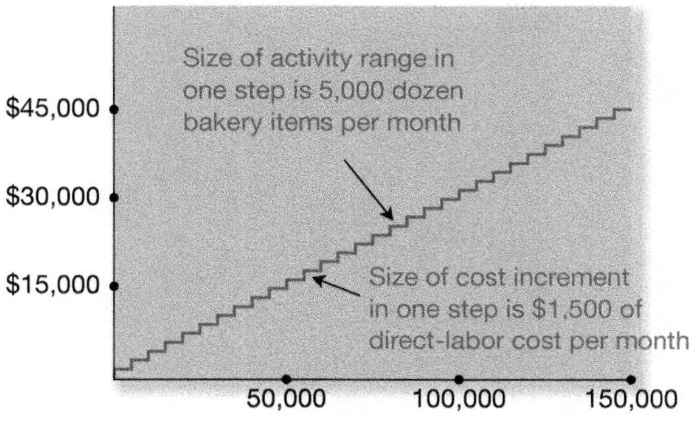

Activity, or cost driver (dozens of bakery items sold)

Exhibit 6–2
Step-Variable Cost: Direct-Labor Cost, Tasty Donuts

Total direct-labor cost (wages and fringe benefits of bakers, sales personnel, and delivery-truck drivers)

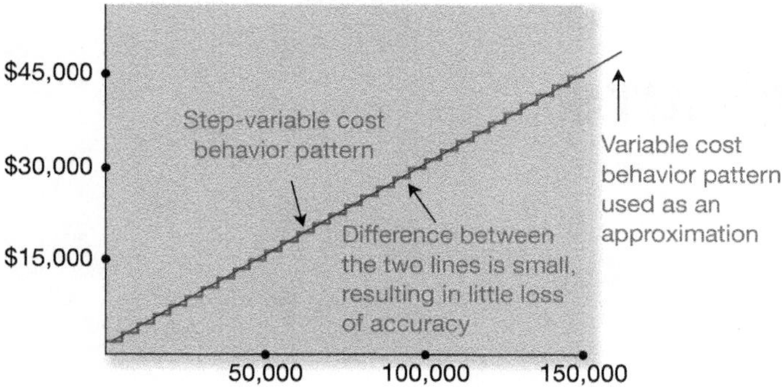

Activity, or cost driver (dozens of bakery items sold)

Exhibit 6–3
Approximating a Step-Variable Cost, Tasty Donuts

Fixed Costs

Fixed costs were covered briefly in Chapter 2. We will summarize that discussion here, using the Tasty Donuts illustration. A **fixed cost** remains unchanged *in total* as the activity level (or cost driver) varies. Facilities costs, which include property taxes, depreciation on buildings and equipment, and the salaries of maintenance personnel, are fixed costs for Tasty Donuts, Inc. These fixed costs are graphed in panel A of Exhibit 6–4. This graph shows that the *total* monthly cost of property taxes, depreciation, and maintenance personnel is $200,000 regardless of how many dozen bakery items are produced and sold during the month.

The fixed cost *per unit* does change as activity varies. Exhibit 6–4 (panel B) shows that the company's facilities cost per dozen bakery items is $4.00 when 50,000 dozen items are produced and sold. However, this unit cost declines to $2.00 when 100,000 dozen items are produced and sold. If activity increases to 150,000 dozen items, unit fixed cost will decline further, to about $1.33.

A graph provides another way of viewing the change in unit fixed cost as activity changes. Panel C of Exhibit 6–4 displays a graph of Tasty Donuts' cost of property taxes, depreciation, and maintenance personnel *per dozen bakery items.* As the graph shows, the fixed cost per dozen bakery items declines steadily as activity increases.

To summarize, as the activity level increases, total fixed cost does not change, but unit fixed cost declines. For this reason, it is preferable in any cost analysis to work with total fixed cost rather than fixed cost per unit.

Step-Fixed Costs

Some costs remain fixed over a wide range of activity but jump to a different amount for activity levels outside that range. Such costs are called **step-fixed costs.** Tasty Donuts' cost of indirect labor is a step-fixed cost. Indirect-labor cost consists of the salaries and fringe benefits for the managers and assistant managers of the company's bakery and donut shops. Tasty Donuts' monthly indirect-labor cost is graphed in Exhibit 6–5.

"By understanding the costs and workload associated with the real business activities we undertake . . . we are better positioned to understand where value is created. . . . From this information, we can then make better decisions as to the management and direction of the business." (6b)

Transco

Exhibit 6–4
Fixed Cost: Facilities Costs, Tasty Donuts, Inc.

A. Graph of Total Monthly Fixed Costs: Facilities Costs

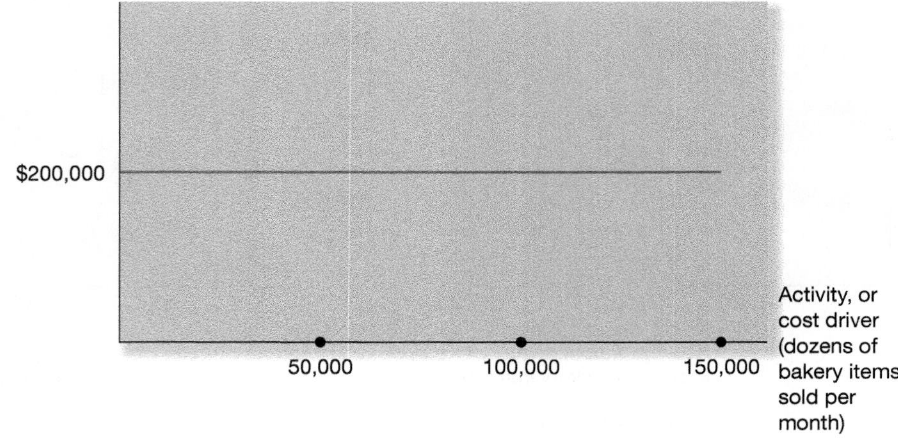

B. Tabulation of Monthly Fixed Costs: Facilities Costs

Activity (or cost driver)	Cost of Facilities per Dozen Bakery Items Sold	Total Monthly Cost of Facilities
50,000	$4.00	$200,000
100,000	2.00	200,000
150,000	1.33*	200,000

*Rounded.

C. Graph of Unit Fixed Costs: Cost of Facilities per Dozen Bakery Items Sold

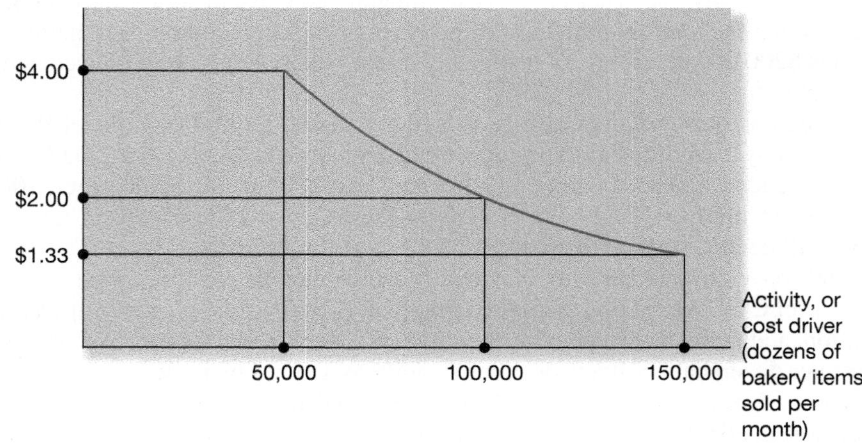

As Exhibit 6–5 shows, for activity in the range of 50,000 to 100,000 dozen bakery items per month, Tasty Donuts' monthly indirect-labor cost is $35,000. For this range of activity, the company employs a full-time manager and a full-time assistant manager in the bakery and in each donut shop. When monthly activity exceeds this range during the summer tourist season, the company employs additional part-time assistant managers in the bakery and in its busiest donut shops. The company hires college students who are majoring in restaurant management for these summer positions. Their salaries boost the monthly indirect-labor cost to $45,000. Tasty Donuts has not experienced demand of less than 50,000 dozen bakery items per month. However, the controller anticipates that if

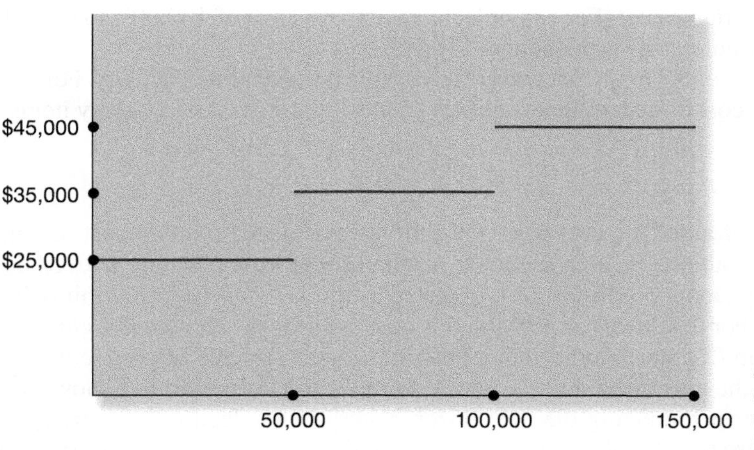

Exhibit 6–5
Step-Fixed Cost: Indirect-Labor Cost, Tasty Donuts, Inc.

such a decrease in demand were to occur, the company would reduce the daily operating hours for its donut shops. This would allow the firm to operate each donut shop with only a full-time manager and no assistant manager. As the graph in Exhibit 6–5 indicates, such a decrease in managerial personnel would reduce monthly indirect-labor cost to $25,000.

Semivariable Cost

A **semivariable** (or **mixed**) **cost** has both a fixed and a variable component. The cost of operating delivery trucks is a semivariable cost for Tasty Donuts, Inc. These costs are graphed in Exhibit 6–6. As the graph shows, the company's delivery-truck costs have two components. The fixed-cost component is $3,000 per month, which is the monthly rental payment paid under the lease contract for the delivery trucks. The monthly rental payment is constant, regardless of the level of activity (or cost driver). The variable-cost

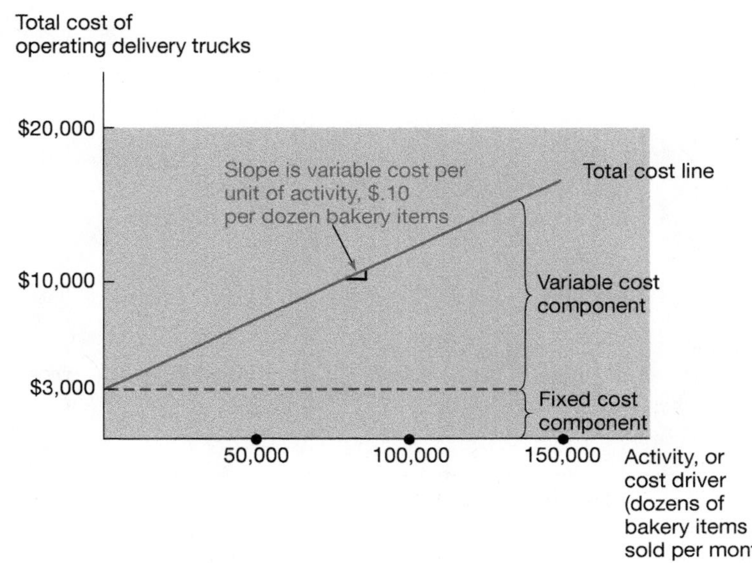

Exhibit 6–6
Semivariable Cost: Cost of Operating Delivery Trucks, Tasty Donuts, Inc.

component consists of the costs of gasoline, oil, routine maintenance, and tires. These costs vary with activity, since greater activity levels result in more deliveries. The distance between the fixed-cost line (dashed line) and the total-cost line in Exhibit 6–6 is the amount of variable cost. For example, at an activity level of 100,000 dozen bakery items, the total variable-cost component is $10,000.

The slope of the total-cost line is the variable cost per unit of activity. For Tasty Donuts, the variable cost of operating its delivery trucks is $.10 per dozen bakery items sold.

Curvilinear Cost

The graphs of all of the cost behavior patterns examined so far consist of either straight lines or several straight-line sections. A **curvilinear cost** behavior pattern has a curved graph. Tasty Donuts' utilities cost, depicted as the *solid curve* in Exhibit 6–7, is a curvilinear cost. For low levels of activity, this cost exhibits *decreasing marginal costs.* As the discussion in Chapter 2 indicated, a marginal cost is the cost of producing the next unit, in this case the next dozen bakery items. As the graph in Exhibit 6–7 shows, the marginal utilities cost of producing the next dozen bakery items declines as activity increases in the range zero to 100,000 dozen items per month. For activity greater than 100,000 dozen bakery items per month, the graph in Exhibit 6–7 exhibits *increasing marginal costs.*

Tasty Donuts' utilities cost includes electricity, telephone, and trash-collection costs. The utilities cost is curvilinear as a result of the company's pattern of electricity usage in the bakery. If the demand in a particular month is less than 100,000 dozen bakery items, the goods can be produced entirely in the modernized section of the bakery. This section

Exhibit 6–7
Curvilinear Cost: Utilities Cost, Tasty Donuts, Inc.

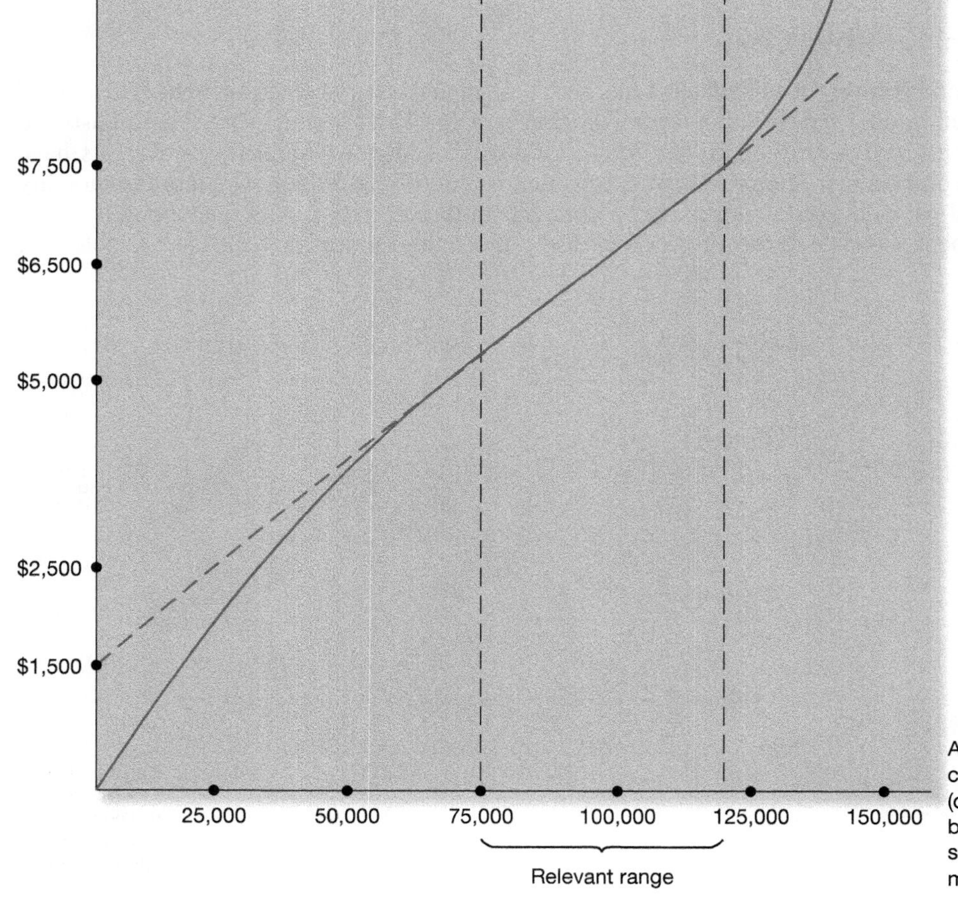

uses recently purchased deep-fat fryers and ovens that are very energy-efficient. As long as the bakery operates only the modernized section, the utilities cost per dozen items declines as production increases.

During the summer tourist months, when Tasty Donuts' sales exceed 100,000 dozen items per month, the older section of the bakery also must be used. This section uses much older cooking equipment that is less energy-efficient. As a result, the marginal utilities cost per dozen bakery items rises as monthly activity increases in the range above 100,000 dozen items per month.

Relevant Range The cost behavior graphed in Exhibit 6–7 is very different at low activity levels (below 50,000) than it is at high activity levels (above 125,000). However, management need not concern itself with these extreme levels of activity if it is unlikely that Tasty Donuts, Inc. will operate at those activity levels. Management is interested in cost behavior within the company's **relevant range,** the range of activity within which management expects the company to operate. Tasty Donuts' management believes the firm's relevant range to be 75,000 to 120,000 dozen bakery items per month. Based on past experience and sales projections, management does not expect the firm to operate outside that range of monthly activity. Tasty Donuts' relevant range is shown in Exhibit 6–7 as the section of the graph between the dashed lines.

Learning Objective 3

Explain the importance of the relevant range in using a cost behavior pattern for cost prediction.

Approximating a Curvilinear Cost within the Relevant Range The straight, dashed line in Exhibit 6–7 may be used to approximate Tasty Donuts' utilities cost. Notice that the approximation is quite accurate for activity levels within the relevant range. However, as the activity level gets further away from the boundary of the relevant range, the approximation declines in accuracy. For monthly activity levels of 25,000 or 150,000, for example, the approximation is very poor.

"Cost estimation is a critical part of our job." (6c)
Ford Motor Company

The straight, dashed line used to approximate Tasty Donuts' utilities cost *within the relevant range* represents a semivariable cost behavior pattern. This straight-line graph has a slope of $.05, which represents a unit variable-cost component of $.05 per dozen bakery items. The line intersects the vertical axis of the graph at $1,500, which represents a fixed-cost component of $1,500 per month. Managerial accountants often use a semivariable-cost behavior pattern to approximate a curvilinear cost. However, it is important to limit this approximation to the range of activity in which its accuracy is acceptable.

Using Cost Behavior Patterns to Predict Costs

How can Tasty Donuts' corporate controller use the cost behavior patterns identified in the cost study to help in the budgeting process? First, a sales forecast is made for each month during the budget year. Suppose management expects Tasty Donuts' activity level to be 110,000 dozen bakery items during the month of June. Second, a *cost prediction* is made for each of the firm's cost items. The following cost predictions are based on the cost behavior patterns discussed earlier. (Try to verify these cost predictions by referring to the graphs in Exhibits 6–1 through 6–7.)

Cost Item	Cost Prediction for June (110,000 dozen bakery items per month)
Direct material	$121,000
Direct labor	33,000
Overhead:	
Facilities costs	200,000
Indirect labor	45,000
Delivery trucks	14,000
Utilities	7,000

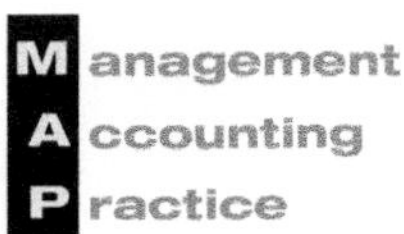

Nestlé, Lincoln Electric, and Hilton Hotels

IS DIRECT LABOR A VARIABLE OR A FIXED COST?

BusinessWeek recently published an article titled "The Disposable Worker," which explains "how companies are making the era of the 'temp' more than temporary." This raises the question: Are direct-labor costs variable or fixed? The answer, as with many questions, is "it depends." What it depends on is the ability and willingness of a company's management to continually fine-tune the size of its workforce. If labor contracts make it difficult to lay off workers during an economic downturn, or if top management adopts a policy of maintaining a stable workforce, direct-labor costs will tend to be largely fixed (or step-fixed). However, if management can *and is willing to* reduce the labor force when activity declines, then labor cost will be a variable (or step-variable) cost.

The current trend in many companies seems to be toward adjusting the workforce to conform to current needs. Here are several cases in point.

Nestlé

"Nestlé's prepared foods unit has built an in-house roster of part-time workers in Cherokee County, South Carolina, who stick by the telephone to hear if they should report on a given day to assemble frozen chicken dinners. The county job-placement office sends Nestlé lists of 'call-ins': people available to work when Nestlé phones them. The workers usually get a day's notice. Some agree to stay by the phone in the morning, in case the company is short for the afternoon shift. They typically work two to six days a week and earn slightly more than $11 an hour, which is considered good part-time pay in the area."

The head of human resources for the prepared-foods division says demand for its Lean Cuisine glazed-chicken entrees and Stouffers creamed-spinach side dishes is fairly steady. The company still hires some people full time. But the Nestlé executive says it is still hard to predict labor needs, because schedules for producing certain meals vary, and each product requires a different number of people to make. "'We don't need the same number of people every day,' he says. 'They work as we need them.'"[1]

Lincoln Electric

"In Cleveland, Lincoln Electric Co. shifts salaried workers to hourly clerical jobs, paying them a different wage for each assignment. The Cleveland-based manufacturer of welding and cutting parts says that, for nearly 60 years, it has guaranteed long-term employment for all of its workers who have worked steadily for three years in its U.S. operations. The flip side is that employees have to be willing to change their job assignments, depending on the type and volume of orders Lincoln receives.[2]

Hilton Hotels

"Many employers, wary of losing valued workers altogether, are reducing the workweek rather than the workforce. Officials of Hilton Hotels Corp. in Beverly Hills, California, boast that they have laid off relatively few workers. However, Hilton says workweek reductions are widespread among its 77,000 workers."[3]

By relying more on part-time workers and daily call-ins, cross-training and frequently moving employees to new jobs, and shortening the workweek, Nestlé, Lincoln Electric, and Hilton Hotels are moving toward direct-labor costs that are much more variable than in the past. Other companies trending toward a "just-in-time workforce" are Walmart, Taco Bell, Starbucks, and U-Haul, among others. This is "all part of the larger development in corporate America of transforming labor from a fixed to a more flexible cost."[4]

[1]P. Coy, M. Conlin, and M. Herbst, "The Disposable Worker," *BusinessWeek*, January 18, 2010, pp. 33–45; and Clare Ansberry, "In the New Workplace, Jobs Morph to Suit Rapid Change of Pace," *The Wall Street Journal*, March 3, 2002, pp. A1, A7.

[2]Ibid., pp. A1, A7.

[3]Jonathan Eig, "Do Part-Time Workers Hold Key to When the Recession Breaks?" *The Wall Street Journal*, January 3, 2002, p. A1.

[4]Michelle Conlin, "The Big Squeeze on Workers," *BusinessWeek*, May 13, 2002, pp. 96–98; and Michelle Conlin, "The Software Says You're Just Average," *BusinessWeek*, February 25, 2002, p. 126.

The preparation of a complete budget involves much more analysis and detailed planning than is shown here.[5] The point is that cost prediction is an important part of the planning process. The cost behavior patterns discussed in this chapter make those cost predictions possible.

Engineered, Committed, and Discretionary Costs

Learning Objective 4

Define and give examples of engineered costs, committed costs, and discretionary costs.

In the process of budgeting costs, it is often useful for management to make a distinction between engineered, committed, and discretionary costs. An **engineered cost** bears a definitive physical relationship to the activity measure. Tasty Donuts' direct-material cost is an engineered cost. It is impossible to produce more donuts without incurring greater material cost for food ingredients.

A **committed cost** results from an organization's ownership or use of facilities and its basic organization structure. Property taxes, depreciation on buildings and equipment, costs of renting facilities or equipment, and the salaries of management personnel are examples of committed fixed costs. Tasty Donuts' facilities cost is a committed fixed cost.

A **discretionary cost** arises as a result of a *management decision* to spend a particular amount of money for some purpose. Examples of discretionary costs include amounts spent on research and development, advertising and promotion, management development programs, and contributions to charitable organizations. For example, suppose Tasty Donuts' management decided to spend $12,400 each month on promotion and advertising.

The distinction between committed and discretionary costs is an important one. Management can change committed costs only through relatively major decisions that have long-term implications. Decisions to build a new production facility, lease a fleet of vehicles, or add more management personnel to oversee a new division are examples of such decisions. These decisions will generally influence costs incurred over a long period of time. In contrast, discretionary costs can be changed in the short run much more easily. Management can be flexible about expenditures for advertising, promotion, employee training, or research and development. This does not imply that such programs are unimportant, but simply that management can alter them over time. For example, the management of a manufacturing firm may decide to spend $100,000 on research and development in the current year, but cut back to $60,000 in the next year because of an anticipated economic downturn.

"Cost information about activities provides a benchmark to assess how we are doing against best-in-class and competitors." (6d)

BlueCross BlueShield of North Carolina

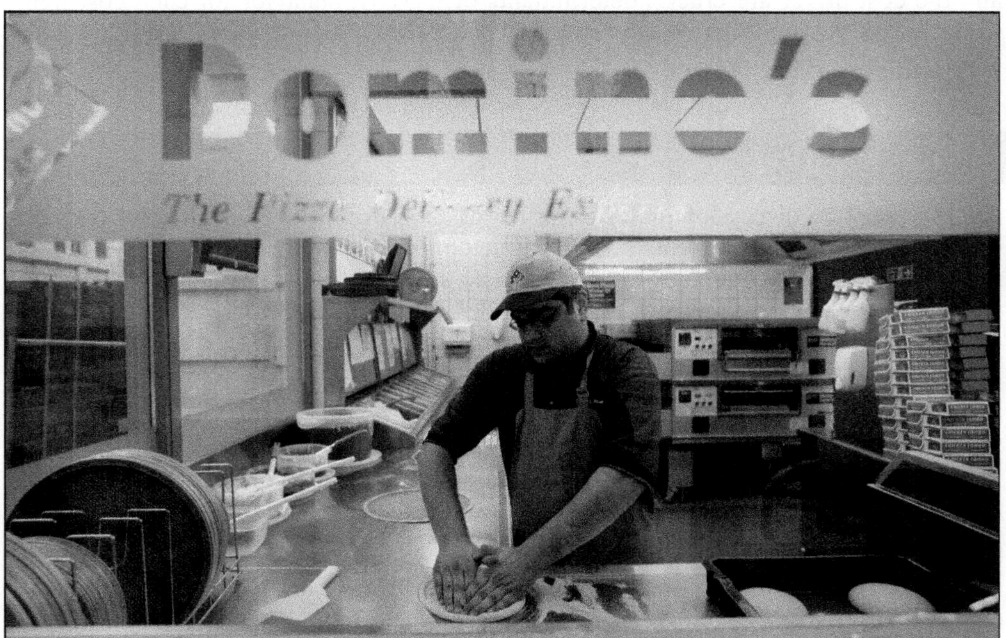

The raw material (ingredients) in these Domino's Pizzas represents an engineered cost. The depreciation on the equipment is a committed cost. Expenditures on advertising and promotion are discretionary costs.

[5]The budgeting process is covered in Chapter 9.

"In the management of a university, just like any other organization, you have to know your cost structure. We think very carefully about how student enrollment will affect faculty salary costs, computing costs, and lots of other costs students don't necessarily tend to think about." (6e)
Cornell University

Cost Behavior in Other Industries

We have illustrated a variety of cost behavior patterns for Tasty Donuts' restaurant business. The same cost behavior patterns are used in other industries. The cost behavior pattern appropriate for a particular cost item depends on the organization and the activity base (or cost driver). In manufacturing firms, production quantity, direct-labor hours, and machine hours are common cost drivers. Direct-material and direct-labor costs are usually considered variable costs. Other variable costs include some manufacturing-overhead costs, such as indirect material and indirect labor. Fixed manufacturing costs are generally the costs of creating production capacity. Examples include depreciation on plant and equipment, property taxes, and the plant manager's salary. Such overhead costs as utilities and equipment maintenance are usually semivariable or curvilinear costs. A semivariable-cost behavior pattern is generally used to approximate a curvilinear cost within the relevant range. Supervisory salaries are usually step-fixed costs, since one person can supervise production over a range of activity. When activity increases beyond that range, such as when a new shift is added, an additional supervisor is added.

In merchandising firms, such as Borders, the activity base (or cost driver) usually is sales revenue. The cost of merchandise sold is a variable cost. Most labor costs are fixed or step-fixed costs, since a particular number of sales and stock personnel can generally handle sales activity over a fairly wide range of sales. Store facility costs, such as rent, depreciation on buildings and furnishings, and property taxes, are fixed costs.

In some industries, the choice of the cost driver is not obvious, and the cost behavior pattern can depend on the cost driver selected. At Southwest Airlines, for instance, the cost driver could be air miles flown, passengers flown, or passenger miles flown. A passenger mile is the transportation of one passenger for one mile. Fuel costs are variable with respect to air miles traveled, but are not necessarily variable with respect to passenger miles flown. An airplane uses more fuel in flying from New York to Los Angeles than from New York to Chicago. However, a plane does not require significantly more fuel to fly 200 people from one city to another than to fly 190 people the same distance. In contrast, an airport landing fee is a fixed cost for a particular number of aircraft arrivals, regardless of how far the planes have flown or how many people were transported. The point of this discussion is that both the organization and the cost driver are crucial determinants of the cost behavior for each cost item. Conclusions drawn about cost behavior in one industry are not necessarily transferable to another industry.

Cost Estimation

Learning Objective 5

Describe and use the following cost estimation methods: account classification, visual fit, high-low, and least-squares regression.

As the preceding discussion indicates, different costs exhibit a variety of cost behavior patterns. Cost estimation is the process of determining how a particular cost behaves. Several methods are commonly used to estimate the relationship between cost and activity. Some of these methods are simple, while some are quite sophisticated. In some firms, managers use more than one method of cost estimation. The results of the different methods are then combined by the cost analyst on the basis of experience and judgment. We will examine five methods of cost estimation in the context of the Tasty Donuts illustration.

Account-Classification Method

The **account-classification method** of cost estimation, also called **account analysis,** involves a careful examination of the organization's ledger accounts. The cost analyst classifies each cost item in the ledger as a variable, fixed, or semivariable cost. The classification is based on the analyst's knowledge of the organization's activities and experience with the organization's costs. For example, it may be obvious to the analyst going through the ledger that direct-material cost is variable, building depreciation is fixed, and utility costs are semivariable.

Once the costs have been classified, the cost analyst estimates cost amounts by examining job-cost records, paid bills, labor time cards, or other source documents. A property-tax bill, for example, will provide the cost analyst with the information needed to estimate this fixed cost. This examination of historical source documents is combined with other knowledge that may affect costs in the future. For example, the municipal government may have recently enacted a 10 percent property-tax increase, which takes effect the following year.

For some costs, particularly those classified as semivariable, the cost analyst may use one of several more systematic methods of incorporating historical data in the cost estimate. These methods are discussed next.

Visual-Fit Method

When a cost has been classified as semivariable, or when the analyst has no clear idea about the behavior of a cost item, it is helpful to use the **visual-fit method** to plot recent observations of the cost at various activity levels. The resulting **scatter diagram** helps the analyst visualize the relationship between cost and the level of activity (or cost driver). To illustrate, suppose Tasty Donuts' controller has compiled the following historical data for the company's utility costs.

Month	Utility Cost for Month	Activity or Cost Driver (dozens of bakery items sold per month)
January	$5,100	75,000
February	5,300	78,000
March	5,650	80,000
April	6,300	92,000
May	6,400	98,000
June	6,700	108,000
July	7,035	118,000
August	7,000	112,000
September	6,200	95,000
October	6,100	90,000
November	5,600	85,000
December	5,900	90,000

The scatter diagram of these data is shown in Exhibit 6–8. The cost analyst can *visually fit a line* to these data by laying a ruler on the plotted points. The line is positioned so that roughly equal numbers of plotted points lie above and below the line. Using this method, Tasty Donuts' controller visually fit the line shown in Exhibit 6–8.

Just a glance at the visually fit cost line reveals that Tasty Donuts' utilities cost is a semivariable cost *within the relevant range.* The scatter diagram provides little or no information about the cost relationship outside the relevant range. Recall from the discussion of Tasty Donuts' utilities cost (see Exhibit 6–7) that the controller believes the cost behavior pattern to be curvilinear over the *entire range* of activity. This judgment is based on the controller's knowledge of the firm's facilities and an understanding of electricity usage by the modern bakery equipment and the older bakery equipment. As Exhibit 6–7 shows, however, the curvilinear utilities cost can be approximated closely by a semivariable cost *within the relevant range.* The data plotted in the scatter diagram lie within the relevant range. Consequently, the data provide a sound basis for the semivariable approximation that the controller has chosen to use.

Exhibit 6–8
Scatter Diagram of Cost Data with Visually Fit Cost Line, Tasty Donuts, Inc.

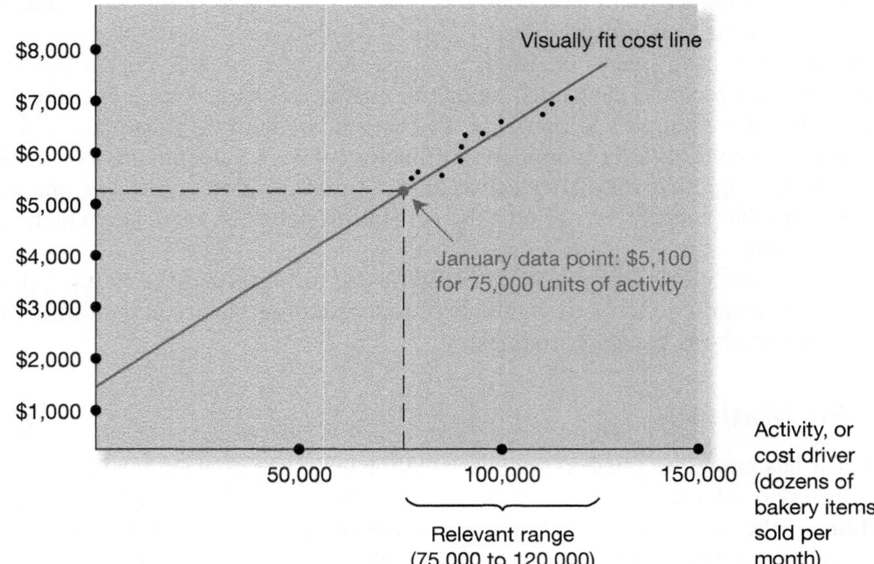

The visually fit cost line in Exhibit 6–8 intercepts the vertical axis at $1,500. Thus, $1,500 is the estimate of the fixed-cost component in the semivariable-cost approximation. To determine the variable cost per unit, subtract the fixed cost from the total cost at any activity level. The remainder is the total variable cost for that activity level. For example, the total variable cost for an activity level of 50,000 dozen items is $2,500 (total cost of $4,000 minus fixed cost of $1,500). This yields a variable cost of $.05 per dozen bakery items ($.05 = $2,500 ÷ 50,000).

These variable and fixed cost estimates were used for the semivariable-cost approximation discussed earlier in the chapter (Exhibit 6–7). These estimates are valid only *within the relevant range.*

Evaluation of Visual-Fit Method The scatter diagram and visually fit cost line provide a valuable first step in the analysis of any cost item suspected to be semivariable or curvilinear. The method is easy to use and to explain to others, and it provides a useful view of the overall cost behavior pattern.

The visual-fit method also enables an experienced cost analyst to spot *outliers* in the data. An **outlier** is a data point that falls far away from the other points in the scatter diagram and is not representative of the data. Suppose, for example, that the data point for January had been $6,000 for 75,000 units of activity. Exhibit 6–8 reveals that such a data point would be way out of line with the rest of the data. The cost analyst would follow up on such a cost observation to discover the reasons behind it. It could be that the data point is in error. Perhaps a utility bill was misread when the data were compiled, or possibly the billing itself was in error. Another possibility is that the cost observation is correct but due to unusual circumstances. Perhaps Toronto experienced a record cold wave during January that required the company's donut shops to use unusually high amounts of electric heat. Perhaps an oven in the bakery had a broken thermostat during January that caused the oven to overheat consistently until discovered and repaired. An outlier can result from many causes. If the outlier is due to an error or very unusual circumstances, the data point should be ignored in the cost analysis.

A significant drawback of the visual-fit method is its lack of objectivity. Two cost analysts may draw two different visually fit cost lines. This is not usually a serious problem, however, particularly if the visual-fit method is combined with other, more objective methods.

High-Low Method

In the **high-low method,** the semivariable-cost approximation is computed using exactly two data points. The high and low *activity levels* are chosen from the available data set. These activity levels, together with their associated cost levels, are used to compute the variable and fixed cost components as follows:

$$\text{Variable cost per dozen bakery items} = \frac{\text{Difference between the } costs \text{ corresponding to the highest and lowest activity levels}}{\text{Difference between the highest and lowest } activity \text{ levels}}$$

$$= \frac{\$7{,}035 - \$5{,}100}{118{,}000 - 75{,}000} = \frac{\$1{,}935}{43{,}000}$$

$$= \$.045 \text{ per dozen items}$$

Now we can compute the total variable cost at either the high or low activity level. At the low activity of 75,000 dozen items, the total variable cost is \$3,375 (\$.045 × 75,000). Subtracting the total variable cost from the total cost at the 75,000 dozen activity level, we obtain the fixed-cost estimate of \$1,725 (\$5,100 − \$3,375). Notice that the high and low *activity* levels are used to choose the two data points. In general, these two points need not necessarily coincide with the high and low cost levels in the data set.

Exhibit 6–9 presents a graph of Tasty Donuts' utilities cost, which is based on the high-low method of cost estimation. As in any cost estimation method, this estimate of the cost behavior pattern should be *restricted to the relevant range.*

Evaluation of High-Low Method The high-low method is more objective than the visual-fit method, since it leaves no room for the cost analyst's judgment. However, the high-low method suffers from a major weakness. Only two data points are used to estimate the cost behavior pattern; the remainder of the data points are ignored. In this regard, the visual-fit method is superior to the high-low method, since the former approach uses all of the available data.

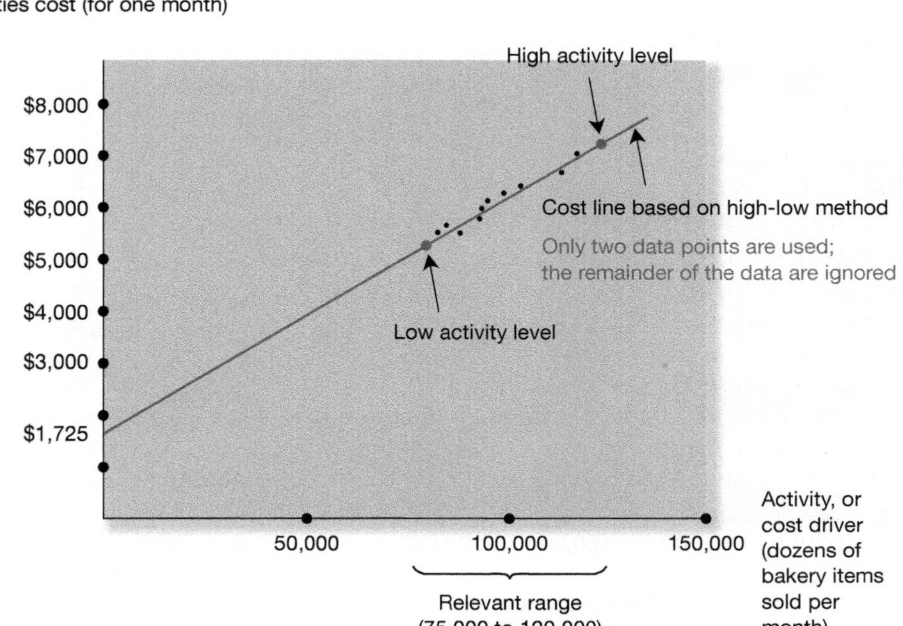

Exhibit 6–9
Graph of Utilities Cost Using High-Low Method, Tasty Donuts, Inc.

TASTY DONUTS

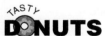

Least-Squares Regression Method

Statistical techniques may be used to estimate objectively a cost behavior pattern using all of the available data. The most common of these methods is called *least-squares regression.* To understand this method, examine Exhibit 6–10, which repeats the scatter diagram of Tasty Donuts' utilities cost data. The Exhibit also includes a cost line that has been drawn through the plotted data points. Since the data points do not lie along a perfectly straight line, any cost line drawn through this scatter diagram will miss some or most of the data points. The objective is to draw the cost line so as to make the deviations between the cost line and the data points as small as possible.

In the **least-squares regression method,** the cost line is positioned so as to *minimize* the sum of the *squared deviations* between the cost line and the data points. The inset to Exhibit 6–10 depicts this technique graphically. Note that the deviations between the cost line and the data points are measured vertically on the graph rather than perpendicular to the line. The cost line fit to the data using least-squares regression is called a *least-squares regression line* (or simply a **regression line**).

Why is the regression method based on minimizing the *squares* of the deviations between the cost line and the data points? A complete answer to this question lies in the theory of statistics. In short, statistical theorists have proved that a least-squares regression line possesses some very desirable properties for making cost predictions and drawing inferences about the estimated relationship between cost and activity. As always, the least-squares regression estimate of the cost behavior pattern should be restricted to the relevant range.

Exhibit 6–10
Graph of Utilities Cost Using Least-Squares Regression Method, Tasty Donuts, Inc.

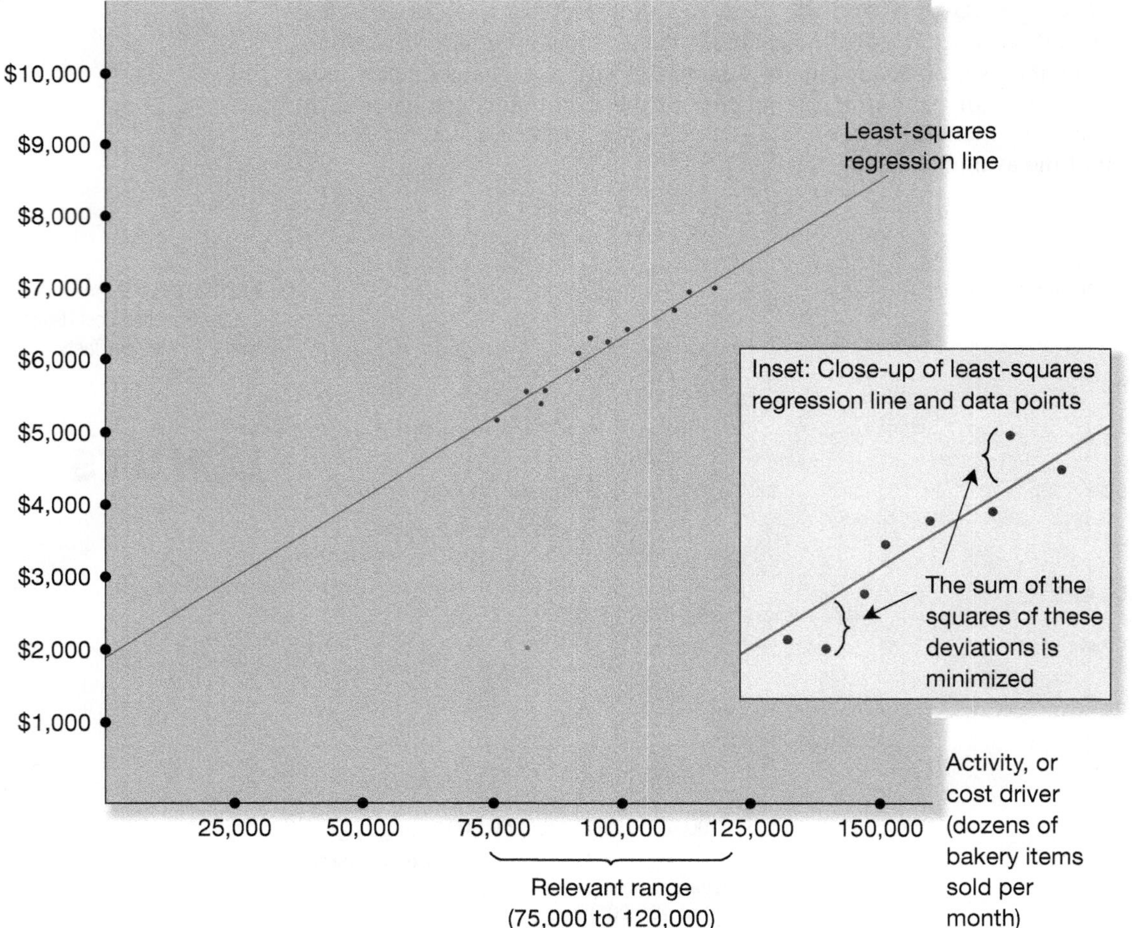

Equation Form of Least-Squares Regression Line The least-squares regression line shown in Exhibit 6–10 may be represented by the equation of a straight line. In the following equation, X denotes Tasty Donuts' activity level for a month, and Y denotes the estimated utilities cost for that level of activity. The intercept of the line on the vertical axis is denoted by a, and the slope of the line is denoted by b. *Within the relevant range,* a is interpreted as an estimate of the fixed-cost component, and b is interpreted as an estimate of the variable cost per unit of activity.

$$Y = a + bX \qquad (1)$$

In regression analysis, X is referred to as the **independent variable,** since it is the variable upon which the estimate is based. Y is called the **dependent variable,** since its estimate depends on the independent variable.

The least-squares regression line for Tasty Donuts' utilities cost is shown below in equation form.

$$Y = 1{,}920 + .0448X$$

↑ Estimated utilities cost for one month (points to Y)

↑ Activity level for one month (points to $.0448X$)

Within the relevant range of activity, the regression estimate of the fixed-cost component is \$1,920 per month, and the regression estimate of the variable-cost component is \$.0448 per dozen bakery items.

There are several statistical software packages available that do regression analysis. However, a common method of computing the least-squares regression estimates is to use a spreadsheet application such as Microsoft® Excel. This approach is covered in this chapter's appendix, which you may want to read now.

Evaluation of Least-Squares Regression Method We have seen that least-squares regression is an objective method of cost estimation that makes use of all available data. Moreover, the regression line has desirable statistical properties for making cost predictions and drawing inferences about the relationship between cost and activity. The method does require considerably more computation than either the visual-fit or high-low method. However, computer programs are readily available to perform least-squares regression.

Evaluating a Particular Least-Squares Regression Line We have seen the benefits of least-squares regression *in general.* How does a cost analyst evaluate a *particular* regression line based on a specific set of data? A number of criteria may be used, including *economic plausibility* and *goodness of fit.*

The cost analyst should always evaluate a regression line from the perspective of *economic plausibility.* Does the regression line make economic sense? Is it intuitively plausible to the cost analyst? If not, the analyst should reconsider using the regression line to make cost predictions. It may be that the chosen independent variable is not a good predictor of the cost behavior being analyzed. Perhaps another independent variable should be considered. Alternatively, there may be errors in the data upon which the regression is based. Rechecking the data will resolve this issue. It could be that fundamental assumptions that underlie the regression method have been violated. In this case, the analyst may have to resort to some other method of cost estimation.

Another criterion commonly used to evaluate a particular regression line is to assess its **goodness of fit.** Statistical methods can be used to determine objectively how well a regression line fits the data upon which it is based. If a regression line fits the data well, a large proportion of the variation in the dependent variable will be explained by the variation in the independent variable. One frequently used measure of goodness of fit is described in the appendix at the end of this chapter.[6]

Multiple Regression

Learning Objective 6

Describe the multiple regression, engineering, and learning-curve approaches to cost estimation.

In each of the cost estimation methods discussed so far, we have based the estimate on a single independent variable. Moreover, all of Tasty Donuts' cost behavior patterns were specified with respect to a single activity (or cost driver), dozens of bakery items produced and sold. However, there may be two or more independent variables that are important predictors of cost behavior.

To illustrate, we will continue our analysis of Tasty Donuts' utilities costs. The company uses electricity for two primary purposes: operating cooking equipment, such as deep-fat fryers and ovens, and heating the bakery and donut shops. The cost of electricity for food production is a function of the firm's activity, as measured in dozens of bakery items produced and sold. However, the cost of electricity for donut shop heating is related more closely to the number of customers than to the number of bakery items sold. A donut shop's heating costs go up each time the shop's door is opened, resulting in loss of heat. Two customers purchasing half a dozen donuts each result in greater heating cost than one customer buying a dozen donuts.

Suppose Tasty Donuts' controller wants to estimate a cost behavior pattern for utilities cost that is based on both units of sales and number of customers. The method of *multiple regression* may be used for this purpose. **Multiple regression** is a statistical method that estimates a linear (straight-line) relationship between one dependent variable and two or more independent variables. In Tasty Donuts' case, the following regression equation would be estimated.

$$Y = a + b_1X_1 + b_2X_2 \qquad (2)$$

where Y denotes the dependent variable, utilities cost

X_1 denotes the first independent variable, dozens of bakery items sold

X_2 denotes the second independent variable, number of customers served

In regression equation (2), a denotes the regression estimate of the fixed-cost component, b_1 denotes the regression estimate of the variable utilities cost per dozen bakery items, and b_2 denotes the regression estimate of the variable utilities cost per customer served. The multiple-regression equation will likely enable Tasty Donuts' controller to make more accurate cost predictions than could be made with the *simple regression* discussed previously. A **simple regression** is based on a single independent variable. Multiple regression is covered more extensively in cost accounting and statistics texts.

Data Collection Problems

Learning Objective 7

Describe some problems often encountered in collecting data for cost estimation.

Regardless of the method used, the resulting cost estimation will be only as good as the data upon which it is based. The collection of data appropriate for cost estimation requires a skilled and experienced cost analyst. Six problems frequently complicate the process of data collection:

1. *Missing data.* Misplaced source documents or failure to record a transaction can result in missing data.
2. *Outliers.* We have discussed these extreme observations of cost-activity relationships. If outliers are determined to represent errors or highly unusual circumstances, they should be eliminated from the data set.
3. *Mismatched time periods.* The units of time for which the dependent and independent variables are measured may not match. For example, production

[6]We have only scratched the surface of regression analysis as a tool for cost estimation. For an expanded discussion of the least-squares regression method, see any statistics text.

activity may be recorded daily, but costs may be recorded monthly. A common solution is to aggregate the production data to get monthly totals.

4. *Trade-offs in choosing the time period.* In choosing the length of the time period for which data are collected, there are conflicting objectives. One objective is to obtain as many data points as possible, which implies a short time period. Another objective is to choose a long enough time period to ensure that the accounting system has accurately associated costs with time periods. If, for example, a cost that resulted from production activity in one period is recorded in a later period, the cost and activity data will not be matched properly. Longer time periods result in fewer recording lags in the data.
5. *Allocated and discretionary costs.* Fixed costs are often *allocated* on a per-unit-of-activity basis. For example, fixed manufacturing-overhead costs such as depreciation are allocated to units of production. As a result, such costs may appear to be variable in the cost records. *Discretionary costs* often are budgeted in a manner that makes them appear variable. A cost such as advertising, for example, may be fixed once management decides on the level of advertising. If management's policy is to budget advertising on the basis of sales dollars, however, the cost will appear to be variable to the cost analyst. An experienced analyst will be wary of such costs and take steps to learn how their amounts are determined.
6. *Inflation.* During periods of inflation, historical cost data may not reflect future cost behavior. One solution is to choose historical data from a period of low inflation and then factor in the current inflation rate. Other, more sophisticated approaches are also available, and they are covered in cost accounting texts.

Engineering Method of Cost Estimation

Learning Objective 6

Describe the multiple regression, engineering, and learning-curve approaches to cost estimation.

All of the methods of cost estimation examined so far are based on historical data. Each method estimates the relationship between cost and activity by studying the relationship observed in the past. A completely different method of cost estimation is to study the process that results in cost incurrence. This approach is called the **engineering method** of cost estimation. In a manufacturing firm, for example, a detailed study is made of the production technology, materials, and labor used in the manufacturing process. Rather than asking what the cost of material was last period, the engineering approach is to ask how much material should be needed and how much it should cost. Industrial engineers sometimes perform *time and motion studies,* which determine the steps required for people to perform the manual tasks that are part of the production process. Cost behavior patterns for various types of costs are then estimated on the basis of the engineering analysis. Engineering cost studies are time-consuming and expensive, but they often provide highly accurate estimates of cost behavior. Moreover, in rapidly evolving, high-technology industries, there may not be any historical data on which to base cost estimates. Such industries as genetic engineering, superconductivity, and electronics are evolving so rapidly that historical data are often irrelevant in estimating costs.

Effect of Learning on Cost Behavior

In many production processes, production efficiency increases with experience. As cumulative production output increases, the average labor time required per unit declines. As the labor time declines, labor cost declines as well. This phenomenon is called the **learning curve.** First documented by aeronautical engineer P. T. Wright in the 1930s, the learning curve concept was popularized by the Boston Consulting Group (BCG) in the 1970s. BCG broadened the learning curve idea to include costs other than direct labor and named this phenomenon the **experience curve.** The learning-curve and experience-curve concepts have been applied primarily to complex, labor-intensive manufacturing operations, such as aircraft assembly and shipbuilding. Boeing and Airbus, for example, make extensive use of the learning and experience curve concepts when budgeting the cost for a new aircraft design. However, the learning curve also has seen limited application in the health care services industry, mainly focusing on complex surgical procedures.

To illustrate the learning curve concept, let's explore its use by Cosmos Communications Technology (CCT), a Canadian manufacturer of sophisticated communications satellites in Vancouver, British Columbia. The company's satellites transmit voice and data communications around the world. CCT's management has found that the learning curve applies to the labor-intensive assembly operation for each new satellite design. A graphical portrayal of CCT's learning curve is shown in panel A of Exhibit 6–11. On this learning curve, when cumulative output doubles, the average labor time per unit declines by 20 percent. Panel B of Exhibit 6–11 displays the total labor time and average labor time per unit for various levels of cumulative output. As cumulative output doubles from 5 to 10 units, for example, the average labor time per unit declines by 20 percent, from 100 hours per unit to 80 hours per unit. As CCT gains experience with a new satellite design, estimates of the cost of direct labor should be adjusted downward to take this learning effect into account.

When the learning-curve concept is applied to a broader set of costs than just labor costs, it is referred to as an *experience curve.* Suppose, for example, that all labor and variable overhead costs are observed to decline by 20 percent every time cumulative output doubles. Then we would change the vertical axis of Exhibit 6–11 to *labor and variable overhead costs.* The graph would then be called an *experience curve.*

Exhibit 6–11
Learning Curve

A. Graphical Presentation of Learning Curve

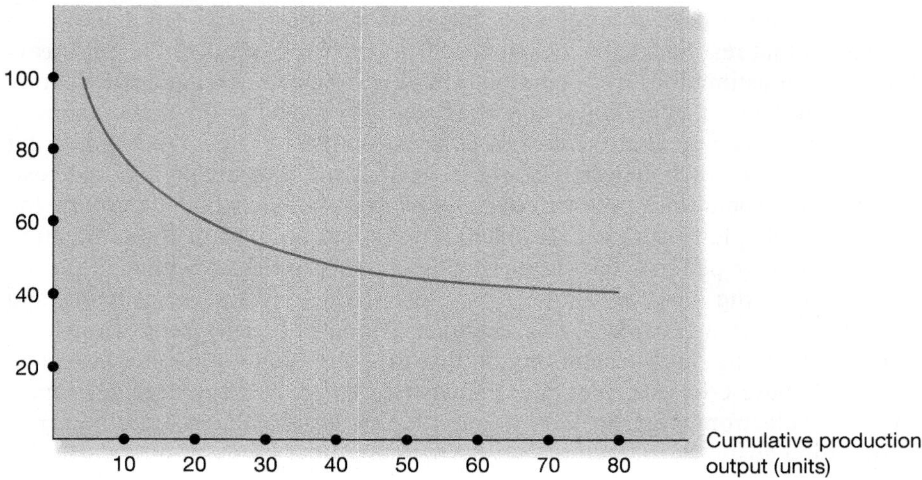

B. Tabular Presentation of Learning Curve

Cumulative Output (In units)	Average Labor Time per Unit (hours)	Total Labor Time (hours)
5	100.0	500.0
10	80.0	800.0
20	64.0	1,280.0
40	51.2	2,048.0

Focus on Ethics

CISCO SYSTEMS, WALMART, TACO BELL, STARBUCKS, U-HAUL, GENERAL DYNAMICS, AND FARMER'S INSURANCE: IS DIRECT LABOR A VARIABLE COST?

The question as to whether direct labor is a variable cost is interesting from a cost estimation perspective, but it also presents an interesting ethical issue.

Direct material is always a variable cost. At the other extreme, depreciation on fixed facilities and infrastructure typically is not. What about direct labor? Here it depends on the ability and willingness of management to adjust the labor force to current needs. If management is able *and willing* to hire workers as needed and lay them off when activity declines, direct labor would be a variable cost. The contemporary trend at many companies seems to be in this direction. "Companies are looking first to bring in contract workers that they can quickly *tap and zap* without paying any benefits or severance."* In fact, the temps have recently been the fastest-growing sector of employment. "And they aren't accounted for as regular employees. This helps companies that use a lot of them, like Cisco Systems Inc., to drive up revenue per employee."

"The growing use of the *just-in-time workforce* is not the only means by which companies are priming the productivity pump. Workers complain that many employers are taking advantage of outdated labor laws by misclassifying them as salaried-exempt so they can skirt overtime pay. Walmart, Taco Bell, Starbucks, and U-Haul, among others, have been slapped with class actions. In the case of General Dynamics Corp., this resulted in a $100 million award that is now on appeal. At Farmer's Insurance, employees got $90 million. Some employers are so worried about the issue that they are now doing wage-and-hour audits."

Is it ethical to "tap and zap" employees? What do you think? (For more on this issue, see the Management Accounting Practice inset on page 242.)

*The information and quotations in this box are from Michelle Conlin, "The Big Squeeze on Workers," *BusinessWeek,* May 13, 2002, pp. 96, 97. See also P. Coy, M. Conlin, and M. Herbst, "The Disposable Worker," *BusinessWeek,* January 18, 2010, pp. 33–39.

Learning curves have been used extensively in such industries as aircraft production, shipbuilding, and electronics to assist cost analysts in predicting labor costs. These cost predictions are then used in scheduling production, budgeting, setting product prices, and other managerial decisions.

Chapter Summary

LO1 Explain the relationships between cost estimation, cost behavior, and cost prediction. Cost behavior is the relationship between cost and activity. Cost estimation refers to the determination of a cost's behavior. A cost prediction is a forecast of a cost at a particular level of activity.

LO2 Define and describe the behavior of the following types of costs: variable, step-variable, fixed, step-fixed, semivariable (or mixed), and curvilinear. A variable cost changes in total in direct proportion to a change in the activity level (or cost driver). A step-variable cost is nearly variable, but increases in small steps instead of continuously. A fixed cost remains unchanged in total as the activity level (or cost driver) varies. A step-fixed cost remains constant over a wide range of activity but jumps to a different amount for activity levels outside that range. A semivariable (or mixed) cost has both a variable and a semivariable component. A curvilinear cost behavior pattern has a curved graph.

LO3 Explain the importance of the relevant range in using a cost behavior pattern for cost prediction. Cost predictions should be confined to the relevant range, which is the range of activity expected for the organization. If the organization operates at an activity level outside the relevant range, any cost predictions based on data from the relevant range may not be very accurate.

LO4 Define and give examples of engineered costs, committed costs, and discretionary costs. An engineered cost bears a definitive physical relationship to the activity measure. Direct material cost is an example. A committed cost results from an organization's ownership or use of facilities and its basic organization structure. Examples include property taxes and depreciation on buildings and equipment. A discretionary cost arises as a result of a management decision to spend a particular amount of money for some purpose. Examples include research and development, advertising, and promotion.

LO5 Describe and use the following cost-estimation methods: account classification, visual fit, high-low, and least-squares regression. The account-classification, visual-fit, high-low, and least-squares regression methods of cost estimation are all based on an analysis of historical cost data observed at a variety of activity levels. The account-classification method involves a careful examination of an organization's ledger accounts. In the visual-fit method, a cost analyst plots recent observations of cost at various activity levels. In the high-low method, a semivariable cost is estimated using only two data points: the high and the low activity levels. In the least-squares regression method, the cost line is estimated so as to minimize the sum of the squared deviations between the cost line and the data points.

LO6 Describe the multiple regression, engineering, and learning-curve approaches to cost estimation. Multiple regression is a statistical method that estimates a linear (straight-line) relationship between one dependent variable and two or more independent variables. The engineering method of cost estimation is based on a detailed analysis of the process that results in cost incurrence. Under the learning-curve approach, the labor cost is estimated by studying the relationship between the cumulative production quantity and the average labor time required per unit. When this approach is applied to costs other than labor, it is referred to as the experience-curve approach.

LO7 Describe some problems often encountered in collecting data for cost estimation. Some common data collection problems include missing data, outliers (highly unusual observations), mismatched time periods, and cost inflation. Allocated and discretionary costs create other challenges in data collection and cost estimation.

LO8 Perform and interpret a least-squares regression analysis with a single independent variable (Appendix). In the least-squares regression method, the cost line is estimated so as to minimize the sum of the squared deviations between the cost line and the data points. The resulting regression line has an intercept on the vertical (cost) axis and a slope, which measures how steeply the cost line rises as activity increases.

Review Problems on Cost Behavior and Estimation

Problem 1

Erie Hardware, Inc. operates a chain of four retail stores. Data on the company's maintenance costs for its store buildings and furnishings are as follows:

Month	Maintenance Cost	Sales
January	$53,000	$600,000
February	55,000	700,000
March	47,000	550,000
April	51,000	650,000
May	45,000	500,000
June	49,000	610,000

Using the high-low method, estimate and graph the cost behavior for the firm's maintenance costs.

Problem 2

The *Keystone Sentinel* is a weekly newspaper sold throughout Pennsylvania. The following costs were incurred by its publisher during a week when circulation was 100,000 newspapers: total variable costs, $40,000; total fixed costs, $66,000. Fill in your predictions for the following cost amounts.

	Circulation	
	110,000 Newspapers	120,000 Newspapers
Total variable cost	______	______
Variable cost per unit	______	______
Total fixed cost	______	______
Fixed cost per unit	______	______

Solutions to Review Problems

Problem 1

	Sales	Cost
At high activity level, February	$700,000	$55,000
At low activity level, May	500,000	45,000
Difference	$200,000	$10,000

$$\text{Variable cost per sales dollar} = \frac{\$10{,}000}{200{,}000} = \$.05 \text{ per sales dollar}$$

Total cost at $700,000 of sales	$55,000
Total variable cost at $700,000 of sales (700,000 × $.05)	35,000
Difference is total fixed cost	$20,000

The company's maintenance cost may be expressed by the following equation.

Total maintenance cost = $20,000 + $.05 (sales dollars)

Alternatively, the maintenance cost can be expressed in the following graph.

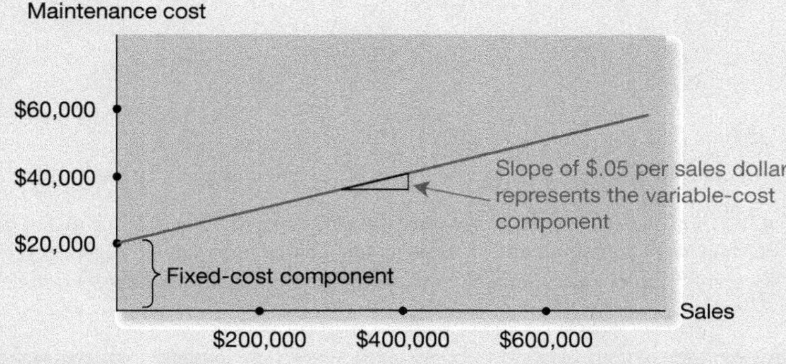

Problem 2

	Circulation	
	110,000 Newspapers	**120,000 Newspapers**
Total variable cost	$\$40{,}000 \times \left(\frac{110{,}000}{100{,}000}\right) = \$44{,}000$	$\$40{,}000 \times \left(\frac{120{,}000}{100{,}000}\right) = \$48{,}000$
Variable cost per unit	$44,000 ÷ 110,000 = $.40	$48,000 ÷ 120,000 = $.40
Total fixed cost	$66,000	$66,000
Fixed cost per unit	$66,000 ÷ 110,000 = $.60	$66,000 ÷ 120,000 = $.55

Key Terms

For each term's definition refer to the indicated page, or turn to the glossary at the end of the text.

account-classification method (also called **account analysis), 244**
coefficient of determination,* 257
committed cost, 243
cost behavior, 234
cost estimation, 234
cost prediction, 234
curvilinear cost, 240
dependent variable, 249
discretionary cost, 243
engineered cost, 243
engineering method, 251
experience curve, 251
fixed cost, 237
goodness of fit, 249
high-low method, 247
independent variable, 249
learning curve, 251
least-squares regression method, 248
multiple regression, 250
outlier, 246
regression line, 248
relevant range, 241
scatter diagram, 245
semivariable (or **mixed) cost, 239**
simple regression, 250
step-fixed costs, 237
step-variable costs, 236
variable cost, 235
visual-fit method, 245

*Term appears in the appendix.

APPENDIX TO CHAPTER 6

Least-Squares Regression Using Microsoft® Excel

The least-squares regression line, which is shown below in equation form, includes two estimates. These estimates, which are called *parameters,* are the *intercept* (denoted by a) and the *slope coefficient* (denoted by b).

$$Y = a + bX \tag{3}$$

where X denotes the independent variable (activity level for one month)
Y denotes the dependent variable (cost for one month)

Learning Objective 8

Perform and interpret a least-squares regression analysis with a single independent variable (Appendix).

Statistical theorists have shown that these parameters are defined by the following two equations.[7]

$$a = \frac{(\Sigma Y)(\Sigma X^2) - (\Sigma X)(\Sigma XY)}{n(\Sigma X^2) - (\Sigma X)(\Sigma X)} \tag{4}$$

$$b = \frac{n(\Sigma XY) - (\Sigma X)(\Sigma Y)}{n(\Sigma X^2) - (\Sigma X)(\Sigma X)} \tag{5}$$

where n denotes the number of data points
Σ denotes summation; for example, ΣY denotes the sum of the Y (cost) values in the data

Calculating the intercept (a) and the slope coefficient (b) would be very laborious to do manually. Fortunately, there are many statistical software programs available to do the regression calculations. Alternatively, Microsoft® Excel can calculate the regression estimates, as the next section demonstrates.

Using Microsoft® Excel to Calculate the Regression Parameters

A cost analyst can use commands in Microsoft® Excel to easily calculate the regression estimate for the intercept (a) and the slope (b). All the analyst needs to do is input the data in a spreadsheet. The spreadsheet in Exhibit 6–12 displays the data used to compute Tasty Donuts' utilities cost. The dependent variable (utilities cost) is in column B, and the independent variable (activity) is in column C. Then the Excel functions INTERCEPT and SLOPE are used to compute the parameters. To use each command, the analyst specifies the range of cells in the spreadsheet in which the values of the dependent variable reside and the range of cells in which the values of the independent variable reside. This is illustrated in the Excel worksheet in Exhibit 6–12 as follows:

Cell B24 contains the following formula: =INTERCEPT(B7:B18,C7:C18)
Cell B25 contains the following formula: =SLOPE(B7:B18,C7:C18)

In these formulas, B7:B18 specifies the range of cells where the values of the dependent variable reside, and C7:C18 specifies the range of cells where the values of the independent variable reside.

As the Excel calculations show in Exhibit 6–12, the regression estimates are as follows:

Intercept: $a = 1{,}920$
Slope: $b = .0448$

So the regression equation is the following:

$$Y = 1{,}920 + .0448X$$

Y ↑ Estimated utilities cost for one month
X ↑ Activity level for one month

[7]The derivation of these equations, which requires calculus, is covered in any introductory statistics text.

Goodness of Fit

The goodness of fit for Tasty Donuts' regression line may be measured by the **coefficient of determination,** commonly denoted by R^2. This measure is defined as the percentage of the variability of the dependent variable about its mean that is explained by the variability of the independent variable about its mean. The higher the R^2, the better the regression line fits the data. The interpretation for a high R^2 is that the independent variable is a good predictor of the behavior of the dependent variable. In cost estimation, a high R^2 means that the cost analyst can be relatively confident in the cost predictions based on the estimated cost behavior pattern.

Statistical theorists have shown that R^2 can be computed using the following formula:

$$R^2 = 1 - \frac{\Sigma(Y - Y')^2}{\Sigma(Y - \bar{Y})^2} \tag{6}$$

where Y denotes the observed value of the dependent variable (cost) at a particular activity level

Y' denotes the predicted value of the dependent variable (cost), based on the regression line, at a particular activity level

$\bar{Y}$ denotes the mean (average) observation of the dependent variable (cost)

Excel can be used once again to calculate the R^2. The analyst simply uses the RSQ command in Excel. As shown in cell B26 of the Excel worksheet in Exhibit 6–12, the R^2 is .949.

Cell B26 contains the following formula: =RSQ(B7:B18,C7:C18)

This is a high value for R^2, and Tasty Donuts' controller may be quite confident in the resulting cost predictions. As always, these predictions should be confined to the relevant range.

Microsoft Excel - Computation of Regression Estimates

File Edit View Insert Format Tools Data Window Help

B24 f_x =INTERCEPT(B7:B18,C7:C18)

	A	B	C	D
1		Utility		
2	Month	Cost	Activity	
3	of	for	during	
4	Preceding	Month	Month	
5	Year	Y	X	
6				
7	January	5,100	75,000	
8	February	5,300	78,000	
9	March	5,650	80,000	
10	April	6,300	92,000	
11	May	6,400	98,000	
12	June	6,700	108,000	
13	July	7,035	118,000	
14	August	7,000	112,000	
15	September	6,200	95,000	
16	October	6,100	90,000	
17	November	5,600	85,000	
18	December	5,900	90,000	
19	Total	73,285	1,121,000	
20				
21	Computation of Regression Parameters			
22	Using Spreadsheet Functions			
23				
24	Intercept	1,920		
25	Slope	0.0448		
26	R^2	0.949		

Sheet1 / Sheet2 / Sheet3

Ready

Exhibit 6–12
Using Microsoft® Excel to Compute the Least-Squares Regression Estimates

Review Questions

6–1. Describe the importance of cost behavior patterns in planning, control, and decision making.

6–2. Define the following terms, and explain the relationship between them: (*a*) cost estimation, (*b*) cost behavior, and (*c*) cost prediction.

6–3. Suggest an appropriate activity base (or cost driver) for each of the following organizations: (*a*) hotel, (*b*) hospital, (*c*) computer manufacturer, (*d*) computer sales store, (*e*) computer repair service, and (*f*) public accounting firm.

6–4. Draw a simple graph of each of the following types of cost behavior patterns: (*a*) variable, (*b*) step-variable, (*c*) fixed, (*d*) step-fixed, (*e*) semivariable, and (*f*) curvilinear.

6–5. Explain the impact of an increase in the level of activity (or cost driver) on (*a*) total fixed cost and (*b*) fixed cost per unit of activity.

6–6. Explain why a manufacturer's cost of supervising production might be a step-fixed cost.

6–7. Explain the impact of an increase in the level of activity (or cost driver) on (*a*) total variable cost and (*b*) variable cost per unit.

6–8. Using graphs, show how a semivariable (or mixed) cost behavior pattern can be used to approximate (*a*) a step-variable cost and (*b*) a curvilinear cost.

6–9. Indicate which of the following descriptions is most likely to describe each cost listed below.

Description	Costs
Engineered cost	Annual cost of maintaining an interstate highway
Committed cost	Cost of ingredients in a breakfast cereal
Discretionary cost	Cost of advertising for a credit card company
	Depreciation on an insurance company's computer
	Cost of charitable donations that are budgeted as 1 percent of sales revenue
	Research and development costs, which have been budgeted at $45,000 per year

6–10. A cost analyst showed the company president a graph that portrayed the firm's utility cost as semivariable. The president criticized the graph by saying, "This fixed-cost component doesn't look right to me. If we shut down the plant for six months, we wouldn't incur half of these costs." How should the cost analyst respond?

6–11. What is meant by a *learning curve?* Explain its role in cost estimation.

6–12. Suggest an appropriate independent variable to use in predicting the costs of the following tasks.

a. Handling materials at a loading dock.

b. Registering vehicles at a county motor vehicle office.

c. Picking oranges.

d. Inspecting computer components in an electronics firm.

6–13. What is an *outlier?* List some possible causes of outliers. How should outliers be handled in cost estimation?

6–14. Explain the cost estimation problem caused by allocated and discretionary costs.

6–15. Describe the visual-fit method of cost estimation. What are the main strengths and weaknesses of this method?

6–16. What is the chief drawback of the high-low method of cost estimation? What problem could an outlier cause if the high-low method were used?

6–17. Explain the meaning of the term *least squares* in the least-squares regression method of cost estimation.

6–18. Use an equation to express a least-squares regression line. Interpret each term in the equation.

6–19. Distinguish between *simple regression* and *multiple regression.*

6–20. List several possible cost drivers that could be used by a cruise line such as Carnival.

6–21. Briefly describe two methods that can be used to evaluate a particular least-squares regression line.

Exercises

All applicable Exercises are available with McGraw-Hill's *Connect Accounting*™. 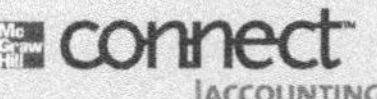

Exercise 6–22
Graphing Cost Behavior Patterns; Hospital
(LO 1, 2)

Draw a graph of the cost behavior for each of the following costs incurred by the Mountain Summit Hospital. The hospital measures monthly activity in patient days. Label both axes and the cost line in each graph.

1. The cost of food varies in proportion to the number of patient days of activity. In January, the hospital provided 3,000 patient days of care, and food costs amounted to $24,000.
2. The cost of salaries and fringe benefits for the administrative staff totals $12,000 per month.
3. The hospital's laboratory costs include two components: (*a*) $40,000 per month for compensation of personnel and depreciation on equipment and (*b*) $10 per patient day for chemicals and other materials used in performing the tests.
4. The cost of utilities depends on how many wards the hospital needs to use during a particular month. During months with activity under 2,000 patient days of care, two wards are used, resulting in utility costs of $10,000. During months with greater than 2,000 patient days of care, three wards are used, and utility costs total $15,000.

5. Many of the hospital's nurses are part-time employees. As a result, the hours of nursing care provided can be easily adjusted to the amount required at any particular time. The cost of wages and fringe benefits for nurses is approximately $2,500 for each block of 200 patient days of care provided during a month. For example, nursing costs total $2,500 for 1 to 200 patient days, $5,000 for 201 to 400 patient days, $7,500 for 401 to 600 patient days, and so forth.

Exercise 6–23
Approximating a Curvilinear Cost; Public School District
(LO 1, 2, 3)

The behavior of the annual maintenance and repair cost in the Bus Transportation Department of the Summerset Public School District is shown by the solid line in the following graph. The dashed line depicts a semivariable-cost approximation of the department's repair and maintenance cost.

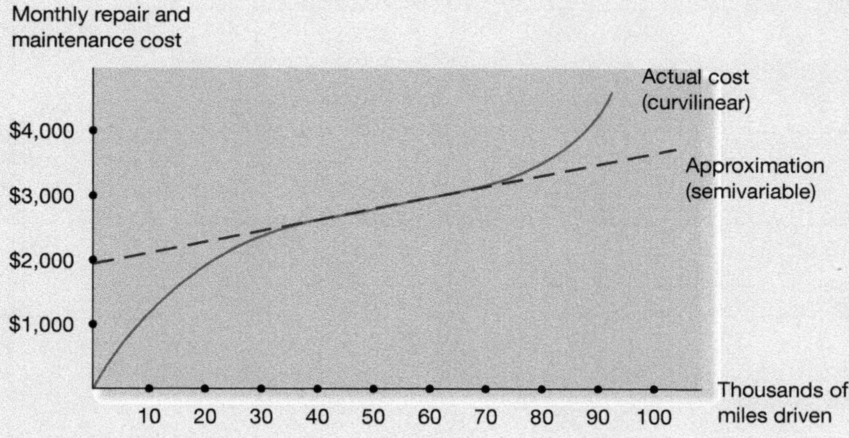

Required:

1. What is the actual (curvilinear) and estimated (semivariable) cost shown by the graph for each of the following activity levels?

	Actual	Estimated
a. 20,000 miles		
b. 40,000 miles		
c. 60,000 miles		
d. 90,000 miles		

2. How good an approximation does the semivariable-cost pattern provide if the department's relevant range is 40,000 to 60,000 miles per month? What if the relevant range is 20,000 to 90,000 miles per month?

Exercise 6–24
Behavior of Fixed and Variable Costs; Television Station
(LO 1, 2)

WMEJ is an independent television station run by a major state university. The station's broadcast hours vary during the year depending on whether the university is in session. The station's production-crew and supervisory costs are as follows for July and September.

Cost Item	Cost Behavior	Cost Amount	Broadcast Hours during Month
Production crew	Variable		
July		$4,875	390
September		8,000	640
Supervisory employees	Fixed		
July		5,000	390
September		5,000	640

Required:

1. Compute the cost per broadcast hour during July and September for each of these cost items.
2. What will be the total amount incurred for each of these costs during December, when the station's activity will be 420 broadcast hours?
3. What will be the cost per broadcast hour in December for each of the cost items?

Exercise 6–25
Estimating Cost Behavior; High-Low Method
(LO 1, 2, 5)

Jonathan Macintosh is a highly successful Pennsylvania orchardman who has formed his own company to produce and package applesauce. Apples can be stored for several months in cold storage, so applesauce production is relatively uniform throughout the year. The recently hired controller for the firm is about to apply the high-low method in estimating the company's energy cost behavior. The following costs were incurred during the past 12 months:

Month	Pints of Applesauce Produced	Energy Cost
January	35,000	$23,400
February	21,000	22,100
March	22,000	22,000
April	24,000	22,450
May	30,000	22,900
June	32,000	23,350
July	40,000	28,000
August	30,000	22,800
September	30,000	23,000
October	28,000	22,700
November	41,000	24,100
December	39,000	24,950

Required:

1. Use the high-low method to estimate the company's energy cost behavior and express it in equation form.
2. Predict the energy cost for a month in which 26,000 pints of applesauce are produced.

Exercise 6–26
Estimating Cost Behavior; Visual-Fit Method
(LO 1, 2, 5)

Refer to the data in the preceding exercise.

Required:

1. Draw a scatter diagram and graph the company's energy cost behavior using the visual-fit method.
2. Predict the energy cost for a month in which 26,000 pints of applesauce are produced.
3. What peculiarity is apparent from the scatter diagram? What should the cost analyst do?

Exercise 6–27
Cost Behavior; Use of Internet
(LO 2)

Visit the Website of one of the following companies, or a different company of your choosing.

Boeing	www.boeing.com	AOL	www.aol.com
Ford	www.ford.com/us	Hertz	www.hertz.com
Honeywell	www.honeywell.com	Lands' End	www.landsend.com
Levi Strauss	www.levi.com	McDonald's	www.mcdonalds.com
Dell Inc.	www.dell.com	Pizza Hut	www.pizzahut.com
General Electric	www.ge.com	U-Haul	www.uhaul.com

Required: Read about the company's products and operations. Then list five costs that the company would incur and explain what type of cost behavior you believe would be appropriate for each of these cost items.

Exercise 6–28
Visual-Fit Method; Veterinary Laboratory
(LO 1, 2, 5)

The Iowa City Veterinary Laboratory performs a variety of diagnostic tests on commercial and domestic animals. The lab has incurred the following costs over the past year.

Month	Diagnostic Tests Completed	Cost
January	3,050	$61,000
February	4,500	74,500
March	7,100	99,000
April	6,200	95,600
May	4,700	74,800
June	5,900	89,000
July	6,000	91,000
August	6,100	90,000
September	5,300	87,000
October	4,900	76,200
November	4,800	78,100
December	5,050	80,700

Required:

1. Plot the data above in a scatter diagram. Assign cost to the vertical axis and the number of diagnostic tests to the horizontal axis. Visually fit a line to the plotted data.
2. Using the visually fit line, estimate the monthly fixed cost and the variable cost per diagnostic test.

Exercise 6–29
Account-Classification Method; Food Processing
(LO 1, 2, 5)

Chillicothe Meat Company produces one of the best sausage products in southern Ohio. The company's controller used the account-classification method to compile the following information.

a. Depreciation schedules revealed that monthly depreciation on buildings and equipment is $19,000.
b. Inspection of several invoices from meat packers indicated that meat costs the company $1.10 per pound of sausage produced.
c. Wage records showed that compensation for production employees costs $.70 per pound of sausage produced.
d. Payroll records showed that supervisory salaries total $10,000 per month.
e. Utility bills revealed that the company incurs utility costs of $4,000 per month plus $.20 per pound of sausage produced.

Required:

1. Classify each cost item as variable, fixed, or semivariable.
2. Write a cost formula to express the cost behavior of the firm's production costs. (Use the formula $Y = a + bX$, where Y denotes production cost and X denotes quantity of sausage produced.)

Exercise 6–30
High-Low Method; Tour Company
(LO 1, 2, 5)

Rio Bus Tours has incurred the following bus maintenance costs during the recent tourist season. (The *real* is Brazil's national monetary unit. On the day this exercise was written, the *real* was equivalent in value to .5379 U.S. dollar.)

Month	Miles Traveled by Tour Buses	Cost
November	8,500	11,400 *real*
December	10,600	11,600
January	12,700	11,700
February	15,000	12,000
March	20,000	12,500
April	8,000	11,000

Required:

1. Use the high-low method to estimate the variable cost per tour mile traveled and the fixed cost per month.
2. Develop a formula to express the cost behavior exhibited by the company's maintenance cost.

3. Predict the level of maintenance cost that would be incurred during a month when 22,000 tour miles are driven. (Remember to express your answer in terms of the *real.*)
4. *Build a spreadsheet:* Construct an Excel spreadsheet to solve all of the preceding requirements. Show how the solution will change if the following information changes: in March there were 21,000 miles traveled and the cost was 12,430 *real.*

Exercise 6–31
Work Measurement; Government Agency
(LO 2, 6)

The State Department of Taxation processes and audits income-tax returns for state residents. The state tax commissioner has recently begun a program of work measurement to help in estimating the costs of running the department. The independent variable used in the program is the number of returns processed. The analysis revealed that the following variable costs are incurred in auditing a typical tax return.

Time spent by clerical employees, 10 hours at $12 per hour
Time spent by tax professional, 20 hours at $25 per hour
Computer time, $50 per audit
Telephone charges, $10 per audit
Postage, $2 per audit

In addition, the department incurs $10,000 of fixed costs each month that are associated with the process of auditing returns.

Required: Draw a graph depicting the monthly costs of auditing state tax returns. Label the horizontal axis "Tax returns audited."

Exercise 6–32
Learning Curve; High Technology
(LO 1, 6)

Weathereye, Inc. manufactures weather satellites. The final assembly and testing of the satellites is a largely manual operation involving dozens of highly trained electronics technicians. The following learning curve has been estimated for the firm's newest satellite model, which is about to enter production.

Assembly and Testing

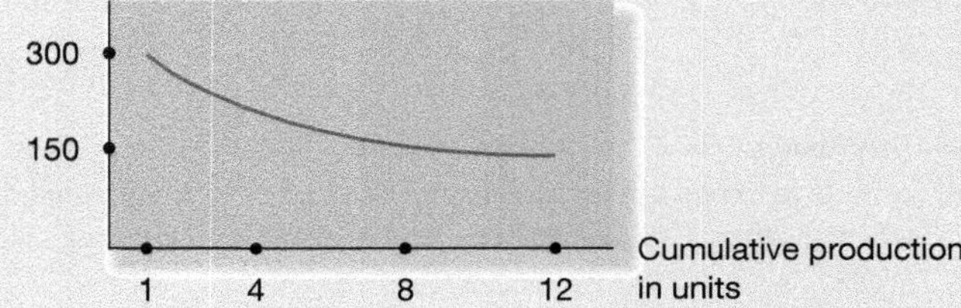

Required:

1. What will be the average labor time required to assemble and test each satellite when the company has produced four satellites? Eight satellites?
2. What will be the total labor time required to assemble and test all satellites produced if the firm manufactures only four satellites? Eight satellites?
3. How can the learning curve be used in the company's budgeting process? In setting cost standards?

Exercise 6–33
Airline; Least-Squares Regression (Appendix)
(LO 1, 2, 5, 8)

Recent monthly costs of providing on-board flight service incurred by Great Plains Airlines are shown in the following table.

Month	Number of Passengers	Cost of On-Board Flight Service
January	16,000	$18,000
February	17,000	18,000
March	16,000	19,000
April	18,000	20,000
May	15,000	18,000
June	17,000	19,000

Required:

1. *Build a spreadsheet:* Construct an Excel spreadsheet and use the Excel commands to perform a least-squares regression. Estimate the cost behavior of the airline's on-board flight service. Express the cost behavior in equation form.
2. Use Excel to calculate and interpret the R^2 value for the regression.

Exercise 6–34
Estimating Cost Behavior by Multiple Methods (Appendix)
(LO 1, 2, 5, 8)

Gator Beach Marts, a chain of convenience grocery stores in the Fort Lauderdale area, has store hours that fluctuate from month to month as the tourist trade in the community varies. The utility costs for one of the company's stores are listed below for the past six months.

Month	Total Hours of Operation	Total Utility Cost
January	550	$1,620
February	600	1,700
March	700	1,900
April	500	1,600
May	450	1,350
June	400	1,300

Required:

1. Use the high-low method to estimate the cost behavior for the store's utility costs. Express the cost behavior in formula form ($Y = a + bX$). What is the variable utility cost per hour of operation?
2. Draw a scatter diagram of the store's utility costs. Visually fit a cost line to the plotted data. Estimate the variable utility cost per hour of operation.
3. *Build a spreadsheet:* Construct an Excel spreadsheet and use the Excel commands to perform a least-squares regression. Estimate the cost behavior for the store's utility cost. Express the cost behavior in formula form. What is the variable utility cost per hour of operation?
4. During July, the store will be open 300 hours. Predict the store's total utility cost for July using each of the cost-estimation methods employed in requirements (1), (2), and (3).
5. Use your Excel sheet from requirement (3) to calculate and interpret the R^2 value for the regression.

Problems

All applicable Problems are available with McGraw-Hill's *Connect Accounting*™.

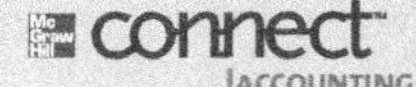

Problem 6–35
Cost Behavior Patterns in a Variety of Settings; International Issues
(LO 1, 2)

For each of the cost items described below, choose the graph (on the next page) that best represents it.

1. The salary costs of the shift supervisors at a truck depot. Each shift is eight hours. The depot operates with one, two, or three shifts at various times of the year.
2. The salaries of the security personnel at a factory. The security guards are on duty around the clock.
3. The wages of table-service personnel in a restaurant. The employees are part-time workers, who can be called upon for as little as two hours at a time.
4. The cost of electricity during peak-demand periods is based on the following schedule.

Up to 9,500 kilowatt-hours (kwh)	$.10 per kwh
Above 9,500 kilowatt-hours	$.13 per kwh

The price schedule is designed to discourage overuse of electricity during periods of peak demand.

5. The cost of sheet metal used to manufacture automobiles.
6. The cost of utilities at a university. For low student enrollments, utility costs increase with enrollment, but at a decreasing rate. For large student enrollments, utility costs increase at an increasing rate.
7. The cost of telephone service, which is based on the number of message units per month. The charge is $.08 per message unit, for up to 700 message units. Additional message units (above 700) are free.

8. The cost of the nursing staff in a hospital. The staff always has a minimum of nine nurses on duty. Additional nurses are used depending on the number of patients in the hospital. The hospital administrator estimates that this additional nursing staff costs approximately $195 per patient per day.
9. The cost of chartering a private airplane. The cost is $390 per hour for the first three hours of a flight. Then the charge drops to $280 per hour.
10. Under a licensing agreement with a South American import/export company, your firm has begun shipping machine tools to several countries. The terms of the agreement call for an annual licensing fee of $100,000 to be paid to the South American import company if total exports are under $5,000,000. For sales in excess of $5,000,000, an additional licensing fee of 10 percent of sales is due.
11. Your winery exports wine to several Pacific Rim countries. In one nation, you must pay a tariff for every case of wine brought into the country. The tariff schedule is the following:

0 to 5,500 cases per year	$12 per case
5,501 to 11,000 cases per year	$15 per case
Above 11,000 cases per year	$20 per case

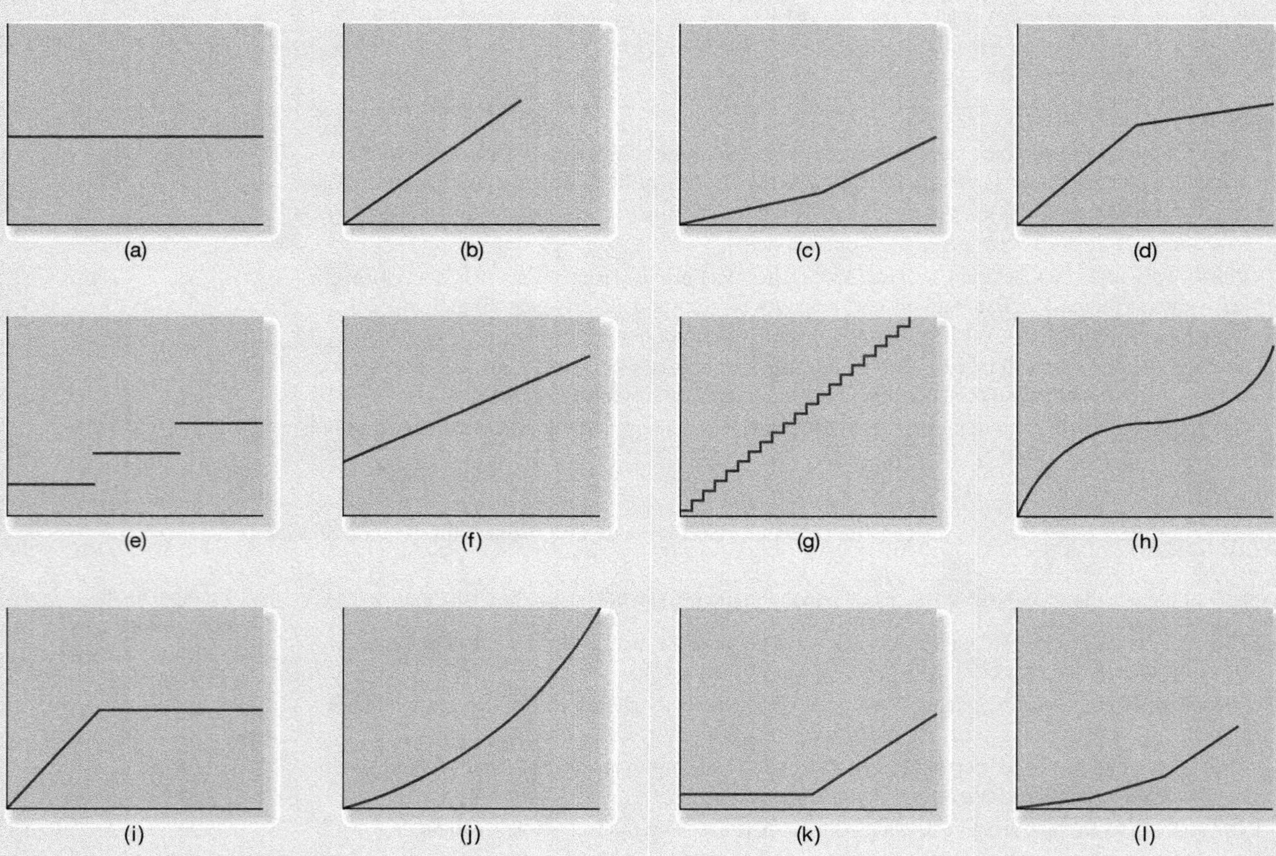

■ **Problem 6–36**
Cost Behavior and Analysis; High-Low Method
(LO 2, 5)

2. Variable maintenance cost: $9 per hour

The following selected data were taken from the accounting records of Metcalf Manufacturing. The company uses direct-labor hours as its cost driver for overhead costs.

Month	Direct-Labor Hours	Manufacturing Overhead
January	23,000	$454,000
February	30,000	517,000
March	34,000	586,000
April	26,000	499,500
May	25,000	480,000
June	28,000	515,000

March's costs consisted of machine supplies ($102,000), depreciation ($15,000), and plant maintenance ($469,000). These costs exhibit the following respective behavior: variable, fixed, and semivariable.

The manufacturing overhead figures presented in the preceding table do not include Metcalf's supervisory labor cost, which is step-fixed in nature. For volume levels of less than 15,000 hours, supervisory labor amounts to $45,000. The cost is $90,000 from 15,000–29,999 hours and $135,000 when activity reaches 30,000 hours or more.

Required:

1. Determine the machine supplies cost and depreciation for January.
2. Using the high-low method, analyze Metcalf's plant maintenance cost and calculate the monthly fixed portion and the variable cost per direct-labor hour.
3. Assume that present cost behavior patterns continue into the latter half of the year. Estimate the *total* amount of manufacturing overhead the company can expect in November if 29,500 direct-labor hours are worked.
4. Briefly explain the difference between a fixed cost and a step-fixed cost.
5. Assume that a company has a step-fixed cost. Generally speaking, where on a step should the firm attempt to operate if it desires to achieve a maximum return on its investment?

Problem 6–37
Cost Behavior and Analysis; High-Low Method
(LO 2, 4, 5)

2. Total cost for 1,650 tons: $823,500

Antioch Extraction, which mines ore in Montana, uses a calendar year for both financial-reporting and tax purposes. The following selected costs were incurred in December, the low point of activity, when 1,500 tons of ore were extracted:

Straight-line depreciation	$ 25,000	Royalties	$135,000
Charitable contributions*	11,000	Trucking and hauling	275,000
Mining labor/fringe benefits	345,000		

*Incurred only in December.

Peak activity of 2,600 tons occurred in June, resulting in mining labor/fringe benefit costs of $598,000, royalties of $201,000, and trucking and hauling outlays of $325,000. The trucking and hauling outlays exhibit the following behavior:

Less than 1,500 tons	$250,000
From 1,500–1,899 tons	275,000
From 1,900–2,299 tons	300,000
From 2,300–2,699 tons	325,000

Antioch uses the high-low method to analyze costs.

Required:

1. Classify the five costs listed in terms of their behavior: variable, step-variable, committed fixed, discretionary fixed, step-fixed, or semivariable. Show calculations to support your answers for mining labor/fringe benefits and royalties.
2. Calculate the total cost for next February when 1,650 tons are expected to be extracted.
3. Comment on the cost-effectiveness of hauling 1,500 tons with respect to Antioch's trucking/hauling cost behavior. Can the company's effectiveness be improved? How?
4. Distinguish between committed and discretionary fixed costs. If Antioch were to experience severe economic difficulties, which of the two types of fixed costs should management try to cut? Why?
5. Speculate as to why the company's charitable contribution cost arises only in December.

Problem 6–38
High-Low Method; Fitness Centers
(LO 1, 2, 5)

3. Cost prediction at 590 hours of activity, maintenance cost: $4,995

Nation's Capital Fitness, Inc. operates a chain of fitness centers in the Washington, D.C., area. The firm's controller is accumulating data to be used in preparing its annual profit plan for the coming year. The cost behavior pattern of the firm's equipment maintenance costs must be determined. The accounting staff has suggested the use of an equation, in the form of $Y = a + bX$, for maintenance costs. Data regarding the maintenance hours and costs for last year are as follows:

Month	Hours of Maintenance Service	Maintenance Costs
January	520	$ 4,470
February	490	4,260
March	300	2,820
April	500	4,350
May	310	2,960
June	480	4,200
July	320	3,000
August	400	3,600
September	470	4,050
October	350	3,300
November	340	3,160
December	320	3,030
Total	4,800	$43,200
Average	400	$ 3,600

Required:

1. Using the high-low method of cost estimation, estimate the behavior of the maintenance costs incurred by Nation's Capital Fitness, Inc. Express the cost behavior pattern in equation form.
2. Using your answer to requirement (1), what is the variable component of the maintenance cost?
3. Compute the predicted maintenance cost at 590 hours of activity.
4. Compute the variable cost per hour and the fixed cost per hour at 600 hours of activity. Explain why the fixed cost per hour could be misleading.

(CMA, adapted)

Problem 6–39
Account-Classification Method; Private School
(LO 1, 2, 5)

The Allegheny School of Music has hired you as a consultant to help in analyzing the behavior of the school's costs. Use the account-classification method of cost estimation to classify each of the following costs as variable, fixed, or semivariable. Before classifying the costs, choose an appropriate measure for the school's activity.

1. Salaries and fringe benefits of the school's full-time teachers.
2. Salaries and fringe benefits of the school's full-time administrative staff.
3. Cost of buying books, sheet music, and other academic materials that are supplied to the students by the school.
4. Repairs on musical instruments. The school employs a full-time repair technician. Repair jobs that are beyond the technician's capability are taken to a local musical-instrument dealer for repairs.
5. Fee charged by a local public accounting firm to audit the school's accounting records.
6. Wages of the school's part-time assistant recital instructors. These employees are hired on a temporary basis. For each student enrolled in the school's music programs, four hours of assistant instructor time are needed per week.
7. Depreciation on the school's musical instruments.
8. Rent for the building in which the school operates.
9. Electricity for the school. The school pays a fixed monthly charge plus $.11 per kilowatt-hour of electricity.

Problem 6–40
Approximating a StepVariable Cost; Visual-Fit Method; Golf Course
(LO 1, 2, 5)

3. Fixed-cost component: $12,010

Rolling Hills Golf Association is a nonprofit, private organization that operates three 18-hole golf courses north of Philadelphia. The organization's financial director has just analyzed the course maintenance costs incurred by the golf association during recent summers. The courses are maintained by a full-time crew of four people, who are assisted by part-time employees. These employees are typically college students on their summer vacations. The course maintenance costs vary with the number of people using the course. Since a large part of the maintenance work is done by part-time employees, the maintenance crew size can easily be adjusted to reflect current needs. The financial director's analysis revealed that the course maintenance cost includes two components:

1. A fixed component of $12,000 per month (when the courses are open).
2. A step-variable cost component. For each additional 1 to 10 people teeing off in one day, $20 in costs are incurred. Thus, if 101 to 110 people tee off, $220 of additional cost will be incurred. If 111 to 120 people tee off, $240 of additional cost will be incurred.

Required:

1. Draw a graph of Rolling Hills Golf Association's course maintenance costs. Show on the graph the fixed-cost component and the step-variable cost component. Label each clearly.
2. Use a semivariable-cost behavior pattern to approximate the golf association's course maintenance cost behavior. Visually fit the semivariable cost line to your graph.
3. Using your graph, estimate the variable- and fixed-cost components included in your semivariable approximation. Express this approximate cost behavior pattern in equation form.
4. Fill in the following table of cost predictions.

	Predicted Course Maintenance Costs	
	Using Fixed Cost Coupled with Step-Variable Cost Behavior Pattern	Using Semivariable Cost Approximation
150 people tee off	?	?
158 people tee off	?	?

Problem 6–41
Work Measurement; Cost Estimation with Different Methods; Wholesaler
(LO 1, 2, 5, 6)

3. Variable cost per unit of activity: $1.00

(*Note:* Instructors who wish to cover all three cost-estimation methods with the same data set may assign this problem in conjunction with the next one.) Martha's Vineyard Marine Supply is a wholesaler for a large variety of boating and fishing equipment. The company's controller, Mathew Knight, has recently completed a cost study of the firm's material-handling department in which he used work measurement to quantify the department's activity. The control factor unit used in the work-measurement study was hundreds of pounds of equipment unloaded or loaded at the company's loading dock. Knight compiled the following data.

Month	Units of Activity (hundreds of pounds of equipment loaded or unloaded)	Material-Handling Department Costs
January	1,400	$11,350
February	1,200	11,350
March	1,100	11,050
April	2,600	12,120
May	1,800	11,400
June	2,000	12,000
July	2,400	12,550
August	2,200	11,100
September	1,000	10,200
October	1,300	11,250
November	1,600	11,300
December	1,800	11,700

Required:

1. Draw a scatter diagram of the cost data for the material-handling department.
2. Visually fit a cost line to the scatter diagram.
3. Estimate the variable and fixed components of the department's cost behavior pattern using the visually fit cost line.
4. Using your estimate from requirement (3), specify an equation to express the department's cost behavior.
5. Estimate the material-handling department's cost behavior using the high-low method. Use an equation to express the results of this estimation method.

6. Write a brief memo to the company's president explaining why the cost estimates developed in requirements (4) and (5) differ.
7. Predict the company's material-handling costs for a month when 2,300 units of activity are recorded. Use each of your cost equations to make the prediction. Which prediction would you prefer to use? Why?

Problem 6–42
Continuation of Preceding Problem; Computing Least-Squares Regression Estimates; Comparing Multiple Methods (Appendix)
(LO 1, 2, 5, 6, 8)

2. Total monthly cost: $9,943 + $.89 per unit of activity

Refer to the orginal data in the preceding problem for Martha's Vineyard Marine Supply.

Required:

1. *Build a spreadsheet:* Construct an Excel spreadsheet and use the Excel commands to perform a least-squares regression. Estimate of the variable- and fixed-cost components in the company's material-handling department costs.
2. Write the least-squares regression equation for the department's costs.
3. Predict the firm's material-handling department's costs for a month when 2,300 units of activity are recorded.
4. Why do the three cost predictions computed in this and the preceding problem differ? Which method do you recommend? Why?
5. *Build a spreadsheet:* Use your Excel spreadsheet from requirement (1) to compute the R^2 value for the regression. Interpret the R^2 value.

Problem 6–43
Cost Estimation Methods; Cost Analysis; E-Commerce
(LO 2, 5)

4. C: $1,567,000

Shortly after being hired as an analyst with Global American Airlines, Kim Williams was asked to prepare a report that focused on passenger ticketing cost. The airline writes most of its own tickets (largely through reservations personnel), makes little use of travel agents, and has seen an ever-increasing passenger interest in e-ticketing. (i.e., electronic reservations and tickets handled over the Internet).

After some discussion, Williams thought it would be beneficial to begin her report with an overview of three different cost estimation tools: scatter diagrams, least-squares regression, and the high-low method. She would then present the results of her analysis of the past year's monthly ticketing cost, which was driven largely by the number of tickets written. These results would be presented in the form of algebraic equations that were derived by the three tools just cited. The equations follow. (C denotes ticketing cost, and PT denotes number of passenger tickets written.)

Scatter diagram: C = $320,000 + $2.15PT

Least-squares regression: C = $312,000 + $2.30PT

High-low method: C = $295,000 + $2.55PT

Williams had analyzed data over the past 12 months and built equations on these data, purposely including the slowest month of the year (February) and the busiest month (November) so that things would ". . . tend to average out." She observed that November was especially busy because of Thanksgiving, passengers purchasing tickets for upcoming holiday travel in December, and the effects of a strike by Delta Western Airlines, Global American's chief competitor. The lengthy strike resulted in many of Delta Western's passengers being rerouted on Global American flights.

Required:

1. Prepare a bullet-point list suitable for use in Williams's report that describes the features of scatter diagrams, least-squares regression, and the high-low method. Determine which of the three tools will typically produce the most accurate results.
2. Will the three cost estimation tools normally result in different equations? Why?
3. Assuming the use of least-squares regression, explain what the $312,000 and $2.30 figures represent.
4. Assuming the use of a scatter diagram, predict the cost of an upcoming month when Global American expects to write 580,000 tickets.
5. Did Williams err in constructing the equations on data of the past 12 months? Briefly explain.
6. Assume that over the next few years, more of Global American's passengers will take advantage of e-ticketing over the Internet. What will likely happen to the airline's cost structure in terms of variable and fixed cost incurred?

Problem 6–44
Comparing Regression and High-Low Estimates; Manufacturer
(LO 1, 2, 5, 7)

5. Fixed cost: $150

The controller of Chittenango Chain Company believes that the identification of the variable and fixed components of the firm's costs will enable the firm to make better planning and control decisions. Among the costs the controller is concerned about is the behavior of indirect-materials cost. She believes there is a correlation between machine hours and the amount of indirect materials used.

A member of the controller's staff has suggested that least-squares regression be used to determine the cost behavior of indirect materials. The regression equation shown below was developed from 40 pairs of observations.

$S = \$200 + \$4H$

where S = Total monthly cost of indirect materials
H = Machine hours per month

Required:

1. Explain the meaning of "200" and "4" in the regression equation $S = \$200 + \$4H$.
2. Calculate the estimated cost of indirect materials if 900 machine hours are to be used during a month.
3. To determine the validity of the cost estimate computed in requirement (2), what question would you ask the controller about the data used for the regression?
4. The high and low activity levels during the past four years, as measured by machine hours, occurred during April and August, respectively. Data concerning machine hours and indirect-material usage follow.

	April	August
Machine hours	1,100	800
Indirect supplies:		
Beginning inventory	$1,200	$ 950
Ending inventory	1,550	2,900
Purchases	6,000	6,100

   Determine the cost of indirect materials used during April and August.
5. Use the high-low method to estimate the behavior of the company's indirect-material cost. Express the cost behavior pattern in equation form.
6. Which cost estimate would you recommend to the controller, the regression estimate or the high-low estimate? Why?

(CMA, adapted)

Problem 6–45
Interpreting Regression Analysis in Cost Estimation
(LO 1, 2, 5)

3. Minimum bid for 200-person cocktail party: $4,400

Dana Rand owns a catering company that prepares banquets and parties for both individual and business functions throughout the year. Rand's business is seasonal, with a heavy schedule during the summer months and the year-end holidays and a light schedule at other times. During peak periods, there are extra costs; however, even during nonpeak periods Rand must work more to cover her expenses.

One of the major events Rand's customers request is a cocktail party. She offers a standard cocktail party and has developed the following cost structure on a per-person basis.

Food and beverages	$15
Labor (.5 hr. @ $10 per hour)	5
Overhead (.5 hr. @ $14 per hour)	7
Total cost per person	$27

When bidding on cocktail parties, Rand adds a 15 percent markup to this cost structure as a profit margin. Rand is quite certain about her estimates of the prime costs but is not as comfortable with the overhead estimate. This estimate was based on the actual data for the past 12 months presented in the following table. These data indicate that overhead expenses vary with the direct-labor hours expended. The $14 estimate was determined by dividing total overhead expended for the 12 months ($805,000) by total labor hours (57,600) and rounding to the nearest dollar.

Month	Labor Hours	Overhead Expenses
January	2,500	$ 55,000
February	2,800	59,000
March	3,000	60,000
April	4,200	64,000
May	4,500	67,000
June	5,500	71,000
July	6,500	74,000
August	7,500	77,000
September	7,000	75,000
October	4,500	68,000
November	3,100	62,000
December	6,500	73,000
Total	57,600	$805,000

Rand recently attended a meeting of the local chamber of commerce and heard a business consultant discuss regression analysis and its business applications. After the meeting, Rand decided to do a regression analysis of the overhead data she had collected. The following results were obtained.

Intercept *(a)*	48,000
Coefficient *(b)*	4

Required:

1. Explain the difference between the overhead rate originally estimated by Dana Rand and the overhead rate developed from the regression method.
2. Using data from the regression analysis, develop the following cost estimates per person for a cocktail party.
   a. Variable cost per person
   b. Absorption cost per person
   Assume that the level of activity remains within the relevant range.
3. Dana Rand has been asked to prepare a bid for a 200-person cocktail party to be given next month. Determine the minimum bid price that Rand should be willing to submit.
4. What other factors should Dana Rand consider in developing the bid price for the cocktail party?

(CMA, adapted)

Problem 6–46
Computing Least-Squares Regression Estimates; Airport Costs (Appendix)
(LO 1, 2, 5, 8)

2. Variable: $6.77 per flight
2. Fixed: $11,796 per month
4. Cost prediction, 1,600 flights: $22,628

Madison County Airport handles several daily commuter flights and many private flights. The county budget officer has compiled the following data regarding airport costs and activity over the past year.

Month	Flights Originating at Madison County Airport	Airport Costs
January	1,100	$20,000
February	800	17,000
March	1,400	19,000
April	900	18,000
May	1,000	19,000
June	1,200	20,000
July	1,100	18,000
August	1,400	24,000
September	1,000	19,000
October	1,200	21,000
November	900	17,000
December	1,500	21,000

Required:

1. Draw a scatter diagram of the airport costs shown above.
2. *Build a spreadsheet:* Construct an Excel spreadsheet and use the Excel commands to perform a least-squares regression. Estimate the variable- and fixed-cost components in the airport's cost behavior pattern.
3. Write the least-squares regression equation for the airport's costs.
4. Predict the airport's costs during a month when 1,600 flights originate at the airport.
5. Using the Excel spreadsheet prepared for requirement (2), compute the coefficient of determination (R^2) for the regression equation. Briefly interpret R^2.

Cases

Case 6–47
Interpreting Least-Squares Regression; Landscaping Service; Activity-Based Costing
(LO 1, 2, 5)

2. Total variable cost per 1,000 square feet: $496.25
5(b). Total incremental variable overhead: $3,285

Earth and Artistry, Inc. provides commercial landscaping services. Sasha Cairns, the firm's owner, wants to develop cost estimates that she can use to prepare bids on jobs. After analyzing the firm's costs, Cairns has developed the following preliminary cost estimates for each 1,000 square feet of landscaping.

Direct material	$400
Direct labor (5 direct-labor hours at $10 per hour)	50
Overhead (at $18 per direct-labor hour)	90
Total cost per 1,000 square feet	$540

Cairns is quite certain about the estimates for direct material and direct labor. However, she is not as comfortable with the overhead estimate. The estimate for overhead is based on the overhead costs that were incurred during the past 12 months as presented in the following schedule. The estimate of $18 per direct-labor hour was determined by dividing the total overhead costs for the 12-month period ($648,000) by the total direct-labor hours (36,000).

	Total Overhead	Regular Direct-Labor Hours	Overtime Direct-Labor Hours*	Total Direct-Labor Hours
January	$ 54,000	2,910	190	3,100
February	47,000	2,380	20	2,400
March	48,000	2,210	40	2,250
April	56,000	2,590	210	2,800
May	57,000	3,030	470	3,500
June	65,000	3,240	760	4,000
July	64,000	3,380	620	4,000
August	56,000	3,050	350	3,400
September	53,000	2,760	40	2,800
October	47,000	2,770	30	2,800
November	47,000	2,120	30	2,150
December	54,000	2,560	240	2,800
Total	$648,000	33,000	3,000	36,000

*The overtime premium is 50 percent of the direct-labor wage rate.

Cairns believes that overhead is affected by total monthly direct-labor hours. Cairns decided to perform a least-squares regression of overhead (OH) on total direct-labor hours (DLH). The following regression formula was obtained.

$$OH = 26{,}200 + 9.25DLH$$

Required:

1. The overhead rate developed from the least-squares regression is different from Cairns' preliminary estimate of $18 per direct-labor hour. Explain the difference in the two overhead rates.
2. Using the overhead formula that was derived from the least-squares regression, determine a total variable-cost estimate for each 1,000 square feet of landscaping.
3. Cairns has been asked to submit a bid on a landscaping project for the city government consisting of 60,000 square feet. Cairns estimates that 40 percent of the direct-labor hours required for the project

will be on overtime. Calculate the incremental costs that should be included in any bid that Cairns would submit on this project. Use the overhead formula derived from the least-squares regression.

4. Should management rely on the overhead formula derived from the least-squares regression as the basis for the variable overhead component of its cost estimate? Explain your answer.
5. After attending a seminar on activity-based costing, Cairns decided to further analyze the company's activities and costs. She discovered that a more accurate portrayal of the firm's cost behavior could be achieved by dividing overhead into three separate pools, each with its own cost driver. Separate regression equations were estimated for each of the cost pools, with the following results.

$OH_1 = 10{,}000 + 4.10DLH,$

where DLH denotes direct-labor hours

$OH_2 = 9{,}100 + 13.50SFS,$

where SFS denotes the number of square feet of turf seeded (in thousands)

$OH_3 = 8{,}000 + 6.60PL,$

where PL denotes the number of individual plantings (e.g., trees and shrubs)

Assume that 5 direct-labor hours will be needed to landscape each 1,000 square feet, regardless of the specific planting material used.

a. Suppose the landscaping project for the city will involve seeding all 60,000 square feet of turf and planting 80 trees and shrubs. Calculate the incremental *variable overhead* cost that Cairns should include in the bid.

b. Recompute the incremental variable overhead cost for the city's landscaping project assuming half of the 60,000-square-foot landscaping area will be seeded and there will be 250 individual plantings. The plantings will cover the entire 60,000-square-foot area.

c. Briefly explain, using concepts from activity-based costing, why the incremental costs differ in requirements (*a*) and (*b*).

(CMA, adapted)

Case 6–48
Approximating a Curvilinear Cost; Visual-Fit Method; Pediatrics Clinic
(LO 1, 2, 5)

6. Administrative cost = \$7,000 + \$3.00X, where X denotes number of patients

(*Note:* Instructors who wish to cover all three cost-estimation methods with the same data set may assign this case in conjunction with the following case.)

"I don't understand this cost report at all," exclaimed Jeff Mahoney, the newly appointed administrator of Mountainview General Hospital. "Our administrative costs in the new pediatrics clinic are all over the map. One month the report shows \$8,300, and the next month it's \$16,100. What's going on?"

Mahoney's question was posed to Megan McDonough, the hospital's director of Cost Management. "The main problem is that the clinic has experienced some widely varying patient loads in its first year of operation. There seems to be some confusion in the public's mind about what services we offer in the clinic. When do they come to the clinic? When do they go to the emergency room? That sort of thing. As the patient load has varied, we've frequently changed our clinic administrative staffing."

Mahoney continued to puzzle over the report. "Could you pull some data together, Megan, so we can see how this cost behaves over a range of patient loads?"

"You'll have it this afternoon," McDonough responded. Later that morning, she gathered the following data:

Month	Patient Load	Administrative Cost
January	1,400	\$13,900
February	500	7,000
March	400	6,000
April	1,000	10,000
May	1,300	11,900
June	900	9,200
July	1,100	10,200
August	300	4,100
September	700	9,400
October	1,200	11,100
November	600	8,300
December	1,500	16,100

McDonough does not believe the first year's widely fluctuating patient load will be experienced again in the future. She has estimated that the clinic's relevant range of monthly activity in the future will be 600 to 1,200 patients.

Required:

1. Draw a scatter diagram of the clinic's administrative costs during its first year of operation.
2. Visually fit a curvilinear cost line to the plotted data.
3. Mark the clinic's relevant range of activity on the scatter diagram.
4. Visually fit a semivariable-cost line to approximate the curvilinear cost behavior pattern within the clinic's relevant range.
5. Estimate the fixed- and variable-cost components of the visually fit semivariable-cost line.
6. Use an equation to express the semivariable-cost approximation of the clinic's administrative costs.
7. What is your prediction of the clinic's administrative cost during a month when 800 patients visit the clinic? When 300 patients visit? Which one of your visually fit cost lines did you use to make each of these predictions? Why?

Case 6–49
Comparing Multiple Cost Estimation Methods; Ethics (Appendix)
(LO 1, 2, 3, 5, 8)

1. High-low method, variable administrative cost per patient: $10
2. Total monthly administrative cost = $2,671 + $7.81X, where X denotes number of patients per month

Refer to the data and accompanying information in the preceding case.

Required:

1. Use the high-low method to estimate the cost behavior for the clinic's administrative costs. Express the cost behavior in formula form ($Y = a + bX$). What is the variable cost per patient?
2. *Build a spreadsheet:* Construct an Excel spreadsheet and use the Excel commands to perform a least-squares regression and estimate the administrative cost behavior. Express the cost behavior in formula form. What is the variable cost per patient? Compute and interpret the R^2 value for the regression.
3. Write a memo to the hospital administrator comparing the cost estimates using (*a*) least-squares regression, (*b*) the high-low method, and (*c*) the scatter diagram and visually fit semivariable-cost line from the preceding case (requirement (4)). Make a recommendation as to which estimate should be used, and support your recommendation. Make any other suggestions you feel are appropriate.
4. After receiving the memo comparing the three cost estimates, Mahoney called McDonough to discuss the matter. The following exchange occurred.

Mahoney: "As you know, Megan, I was never in favor of this clinic. It's going to be a drag on our administrative staff, and we'd have been far better off keeping the pediatrics operation here in the hospital."

McDonough: "I was aware that you felt the clinic was a mistake. Of course, the board of trustees had other issues to consider. I believe the board felt the clinic should be built to make pediatric care more accessible to the economically depressed area on the other side of the city."

Mahoney: "That's true, but the board doesn't realize how difficult it's going to make life for us here in the hospital. In any case, I called to tell you that when you and I report to the board next week, I'm going to recommend that the clinic be shut down. I want you to support my recommendation with one of your cost estimates showing that administrative costs will soar at high activity levels."

McDonough: "But that estimate was based on the high-low method. It's not an appropriate method for this situation."

Mahoney: "It *is* an estimate, Megan, and it's based on a well-known estimation method. This is just the ammunition I need to make the board see things my way."

McDonough: "I don't know, Jeff. I just don't think I can go along with that."

Mahoney: "Be a team player, Megan. I've got a meeting now. Got to run."

That night McDonough called to discuss the matter with her best friend, you. What would you advise her?

FOCUS COMPANY >>>

THIS CHAPTER'S FOCUS is on the Seattle Contemporary Theater. This nonprofit enterprise was formed to bring contemporary drama to the Seattle area. The theater operates in a historic theater building owned by the city, for which Seattle Contemporary Theater pays the city a fixed monthly rental charge and a portion of the price of each ticket sold. The theater must cover its operating expenses with ticket revenue in order to break even. Using the Seattle Contemporary Theater as an illustration, we will explore a technique called cost-volume-profit (or CVP) analysis, which the theater's managing director and business manager use to better understand the relationships between the theater's costs, ticket sales volume, and revenue.

7 Cost-Volume-Profit Analysis

IN CONTRAST >>>

In contrast to the nonprofit, entertainment-service setting of the Seattle Contemporary Theater, we explore the use of cost-volume-profit analysis by AccuTime Company. The management of this manufacturer of digital clocks uses CVP analysis to better understand the relationships between the company's costs, sales volume, and profit. The company's management also analyzes the firm's cost structure, which refers to the relative proportion of fixed and variable costs.

AFTER COMPLETING THIS CHAPTER, YOU SHOULD BE ABLE TO:

1 Compute a break-even point using the contribution-margin approach and the equation approach.

2 Compute the contribution-margin ratio and use it to find the break-even point in sales dollars.

3 Prepare a cost-volume-profit (CVP) graph and explain how it is used.

4 Apply CVP analysis to determine the effect on profit of changes in fixed expenses, variable expenses, sales prices, and sales volume.

5 Compute the break-even point and prepare a profit-volume graph for a multiproduct enterprise.

6 List and discuss the key assumptions of CVP analysis.

7 Prepare and interpret a contribution income statement.

8 Explain the role of cost structure and operating leverage in CVP relationships.

9 Understand the implications of activity-based costing for CVP analysis.

10 Be aware of the effects of advanced manufacturing technology on CVP relationships.

11 Understand the effect of income taxes on CVP analysis (appendix).

What effect on profit can United Airlines expect if it adds a flight on the Chicago to New York route? How will NBC's profit change if the ratings increase for its evening news program? How many patient days of care must Massachusetts General Hospital provide to break even for the year? What happens to this break-even patient load if the hospital leases a new computerized system for patient records?

Each of these questions concerns the effects on costs and revenues when the organization's activity changes. The analytical technique used by managerial accountants to address these questions is called **cost-volume-profit analysis.** Often called **CVP analysis** for short, this technique summarizes the effects of changes in an organization's *volume* of activity on its *costs,* revenue, and *profit.* Cost-volume-profit analysis can be extended to cover the effects on profit of changes in selling prices, service fees, costs, income-tax rates, and the organization's mix of products or services. What will happen to profit, for example, if the New York Yankees raise ticket prices for stadium seats? In short, CVP analysis provides management with a comprehensive overview of the effects on revenue and costs of all kinds of short-run financial changes.

Although the word *profit* appears in the term, cost-volume-profit analysis is not confined to profit-seeking enterprises. Managers in nonprofit organizations also routinely use CVP analysis to examine the effects of activity and other short-run changes on revenue and costs. For example, as the State of Florida gains approximately 1,000 people a day in population, the state's political leaders must analyze the effects of this change on sales-tax revenues and the cost of providing services, such as education, transportation, and police protection. Managers at such diverse nonprofit institutions as Massachusetts General Hospital, Stanford University, and the United Way all use CVP analysis as a routine operational tool.

Illustration of Cost-Volume-Profit Analysis

To illustrate the various analytical techniques used in cost-volume-profit analysis, we will focus on a performing arts organization. The Seattle Contemporary Theater was recently formed as a nonprofit enterprise to bring contemporary drama to the Seattle area. The organization has a part-time, unpaid board of trustees comprising local professional people who are avid theater fans. The board has hired the following full-time employees.

Managing director: Responsibilities include overall management of the organization; direction of six plays per year.

Artistic director: Responsibilities include hiring of actors and production crews for each play; direction of six plays per year.

Business manager and producer: Responsibilities include managing the organization's business functions and ticket sales; direction of the production crews, who handle staging, lighting, costuming, and makeup.

"Accounting is changing. You're no longer sitting behind a desk just working on a computer, just crunching the numbers. You're actually getting to be a part of the day-to-day functions of the business." (7a)
Abbott Laboratories

The board of trustees has negotiated an agreement with the city of Seattle to hold performances in a historic theater owned by the city. The theater has not been used for 30 years, but the city has agreed to refurbish it and to provide lighting and sound equipment. In return, the city will receive a rental charge of $10,000 per month plus $8 for each theater ticket sold.

Projected Expenses and Revenue

The theater's business manager and producer, Andrew Lloyd, has made the following projections for the first few years of operation.

Fixed expenses per month:	
Theater rental	$10,000
Employees' salaries and fringe benefits	8,000
Actors' wages	15,000
(to be supplemented with local volunteer talent)	
Production crew's wages	5,600
(to be supplemented with local volunteers)	
Playwrights' royalties for use of plays	5,000
Insurance	1,000
Utilities—fixed portion	1,400
Advertising and promotion	800
Administrative expenses	1,200
Total fixed expenses per month	$48,000
Variable expenses per ticket sold:	
City's charge per ticket for use of theater	$ 8
Other miscellaneous expenses (for example, printing of playbills and tickets, variable portion of utilities)	2
Total variable cost per ticket sold	$10
Revenue:	
Price per ticket	$16

Importance of Cost Behavior Notice that the theater's expenses have been categorized according to their cost behavior: fixed or variable. Analyzing an organization's cost behavior, the topic of Chapter 6, is a necessary first step in any cost-volume-profit analysis. As we proceed through this chapter, the data pertaining to Seattle Contemporary Theater will be an important part of our cost-volume-profit analysis.

The Break-Even Point

Learning Objective 1

Compute a break-even point using the contribution-margin approach and the equation approach.

As the first step in the CVP analysis for Seattle Contemporary Theater, we will find the **break-even point.** The break-even point is the volume of activity where the organization's revenues and expenses are equal. At this amount of sales, the organization has no profit or loss; it *breaks even.*

Suppose Seattle Contemporary Theater sells 8,000 tickets during a play's one-month run. The following income statement shows that the profit for the month will be zero; thus, the theater will break even.

Sales revenue (8,000 × $16)	$128,000
Less variable expenses (8,000 × $10)	80,000
Total contribution margin	$ 48,000
Less fixed expenses	48,000
Profit	$ 0

"Break-even analyses figure prominently in any discussion of new programs. Although we have programs that operate at a loss because of their importance educationally, overall our cash inflows have to be sufficient to support our total program." (7b)
Cornell University

Notice that this income statement highlights the distinction between variable and fixed expenses. The statement also shows the **total contribution margin,** which is defined as total sales revenue minus total variable expenses. This is the amount of revenue that is available to *contribute* to covering fixed expenses after all variable expenses have been covered. The contribution income statement will be covered in more depth later in the chapter. At this juncture, it provides a useful way to think about the meaning of breaking even.

How could we compute Seattle Contemporary Theater's break-even point if we did not already know it is 8,000 tickets per month? This is the question to which we turn our attention next.

Whether running a small business or a worldwide enterprise, understanding cost-volume-profit relationships is crucial in managing any organization.

Contribution-Margin Approach

Seattle Contemporary Theater will break even when the organization's revenue from ticket sales is equal to its expenses. How many tickets must be sold during one month (one play's run) for the organization to break even?

Each ticket sells for $16, but $10 of this is used to cover the variable expense per ticket. This leaves $6 per ticket to *contribute* to covering the fixed expenses of $48,000. When enough tickets have been sold in one month so that these $6 contributions per ticket add up to $48,000, the organization will break even for the month. Thus, we may compute the break-even volume of tickets as follows:

$$\frac{\text{Fixed expenses}}{\text{Contribution of each ticket toward covering fixed expenses}} = \frac{\$48{,}000}{\$6} = 8{,}000$$

Seattle Contemporary Theater must sell 8,000 tickets during a play's one-month run to break even for the month.

The $6 amount that remains of each ticket's price, after the variable expenses are covered, is called the **unit contribution margin.** The general formula for computing the break-even sales volume in units is given below.

$$\frac{\text{Fixed expenses}}{\text{Unit contribution margin}} = \text{Break-even point (in units)} \qquad (1)$$

Contribution-Margin Ratio Sometimes management prefers that the break-even point be expressed in sales *dollars* rather than *units.* Seattle Contemporary Theater's break-even point in sales dollars is computed as follows.

Learning Objective 2

Compute the contribution-margin ratio and use it to find the break-even point in sales dollars.

Break-even point in units (tickets)	8,000
Sales price per unit	× $16
Break-even point in sales dollars	$128,000

The following computation provides an alternative way to determine the break-even point in sales dollars.

$$\frac{\text{Fixed expenses}}{\left(\dfrac{\text{Unit contribution margin}}{\text{Unit sales price}}\right)} = \frac{\$48{,}000}{\left(\dfrac{\$6}{\$16}\right)} = \frac{\$48{,}000}{.375} = \$128{,}000$$

The unit contribution margin divided by the unit sales price is called the **contribution-margin ratio.** This ratio also can be expressed as a percentage, in which case it is called the *contribution-margin percentage.* Seattle Contemporary Theater's contribution-margin ratio is .375 (in percentage form, 37.5%). Thus, the organization's break-even point in sales dollars may be found by dividing its fixed expenses by its contribution-margin ratio. The logic behind this approach is that 37.5 percent of each sales dollar is available to make a contribution toward covering fixed expenses. The general formula is given below.

"Delta Air Lines computes a break-even load factor, which is the average percentage of available passenger seats that need to be occupied on our flights in order for the company to break even." (7c)
Delta Air Lines

$$\frac{\text{Fixed expenses}}{\text{Contribution-margin ratio}} = \text{Break-even point in sales dollars} \qquad (2)$$

Equation Approach

An alternative approach to finding the break-even point is based on the profit equation. Income (or profit) is equal to sales revenue minus expenses. If expenses are separated into variable and fixed expenses, the essence of the income (profit) statement is captured by the following equation.

Learning Objective 1

Compute a break-even point using the contribution-margin approach and the equation approach.

$$\text{Sales revenue} - \text{Variable expenses} - \text{Fixed expenses} = \text{Profit}$$

This equation can be restated as follows:

$$\left[\begin{pmatrix}\text{Unit}\\\text{sales}\\\text{price}\end{pmatrix}\times\begin{pmatrix}\text{Sales}\\\text{volume}\\\text{in units}\end{pmatrix}\right]-\left[\begin{pmatrix}\text{Unit}\\\text{variable}\\\text{expense}\end{pmatrix}\times\begin{pmatrix}\text{Sales}\\\text{volume}\\\text{in units}\end{pmatrix}\right]-\begin{pmatrix}\text{Fixed}\\\text{expenses}\end{pmatrix} = \text{Profit} \qquad (3)$$

To find Seattle Contemporary Theater's break-even volume of ticket sales per month, we define profit in equation (3) to be zero.

$$(\$16 \quad \times \quad X) \quad - \quad (\$10 \quad \times \quad X) \quad - \$48{,}000 \quad = 0$$

$$\left[\begin{pmatrix}\text{Unit}\\\text{sales}\\\text{price}\end{pmatrix}\times\begin{pmatrix}\text{Sales}\\\text{volume}\\\text{in units}\end{pmatrix}\right]-\left[\begin{pmatrix}\text{Unit}\\\text{variable}\\\text{expense}\end{pmatrix}\times\begin{pmatrix}\text{Sales}\\\text{volume}\\\text{in units}\end{pmatrix}\right]-\begin{pmatrix}\text{Fixed}\\\text{expenses}\end{pmatrix} = \begin{matrix}\text{Break-even}\\\text{profit (zero)}\end{matrix} \qquad (4)$$

where

X denotes the number of sales units (tickets) required to break even.

Equation (4) can be solved for X as shown below.

$$\$16X - \$10X - \$48{,}000 = 0$$

$$\$6X = \$48{,}000$$

$$X = \frac{\$48{,}000}{\$6} = 8{,}000$$

Using the equation approach, we have arrived at the same general formula for computing the break-even sales volume (formula (1)).

The contribution-margin and equation approaches are two equivalent techniques for finding the break-even point. Both methods reach the same conclusion, and so personal preference dictates which approach should be used.

Graphing Cost-Volume-Profit Relationships

Learning Objective 3

Prepare a cost-volume-profit (CVP) graph and explain how it is used.

While the break-even point conveys useful information to management, it does not show how profit changes as activity changes. To capture the relationship between profit and volume of activity, a **cost-volume-profit (CVP) graph** is commonly used. The following steps are used to prepare a CVP graph for Seattle Contemporary Theater. The graph is displayed in Exhibit 7–1. Notice that the graph shows the *relevant range,* which is the range of activity within which management expects the theater to operate.

Step 1: Draw the axes of the graph. Label the vertical axis in dollars and the horizontal axis in units of sales (tickets).

Step 2: Draw the fixed-expense line. It is parallel to the horizontal axis, since fixed expenses do not change with activity.

Step 3: Compute *total* expense at any convenient volume. For example, select a volume of 6,000 tickets.

Variable expenses (6,000 × $10 per ticket)	$ 60,000
Fixed expenses	48,000
Total expenses (at 6,000 tickets)	$108,000

Plot this point ($108,000 at 6,000 tickets) on the graph. See point *A* on the graph in Exhibit 7–1.

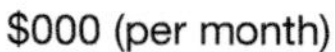

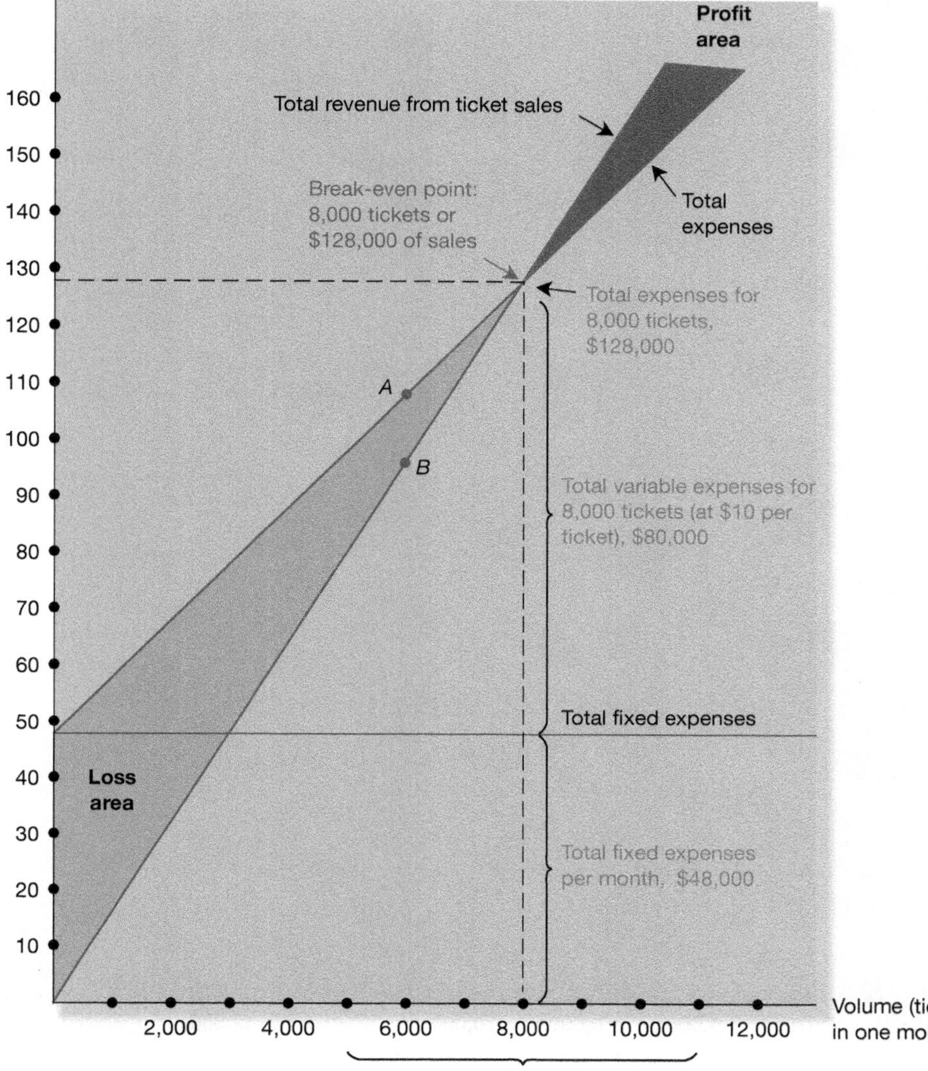

Exhibit 7–1
Cost-Volume-Profit Graph: Seattle Contemporary Theater

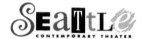

Step 4: Draw the total-expense line. This line passes through the point plotted in step 3 (point *A*) and the intercept of the fixed-expense line on the vertical axis ($48,000).

Step 5: Compute total sales revenue at any convenient volume. We will choose 6,000 tickets again. Total revenue is $96,000 (6,000 × $16 per ticket). Plot this point ($96,000 at 6,000 tickets) on the graph. See point *B* on the graph in Exhibit 7–1.

Step 6: Draw the total revenue line. This line passes through the point plotted in step 5 (point *B*) and the origin.

Step 7: Label the graph as shown in Exhibit 7–1.

Interpreting the CVP Graph

Several conclusions can be drawn from the CVP graph in Exhibit 7–1.

Learning Objective 3
Prepare a cost-volume-profit (CVP) graph and explain how it is used.

Break-Even Point The break-even point is determined by the intersection of the total-revenue line and the total-expense line. Seattle Contemporary Theater breaks even

Exhibit 7–2
Alternative Format for CVP Graph: Seattle Contemporary Theater

$000 (per month)

Profit area

Total revenue from ticket sales

Total expenses

Break-even point: 8,000 tickets or $128,000 of sales

Total expenses for 8,000 tickets, $128,000

Total fixed expenses per month, $48,000

Total variable expenses

Total variable expenses for 8,000 tickets (at $10 per ticket), $80,000

Loss area

A

B

160 150 140 130 120 110 100 90 80 70 60 50 40 30 20 10

2,000 4,000 6,000 8,000 10,000 12,000

Volume (tickets sold in one month)

Relevant range

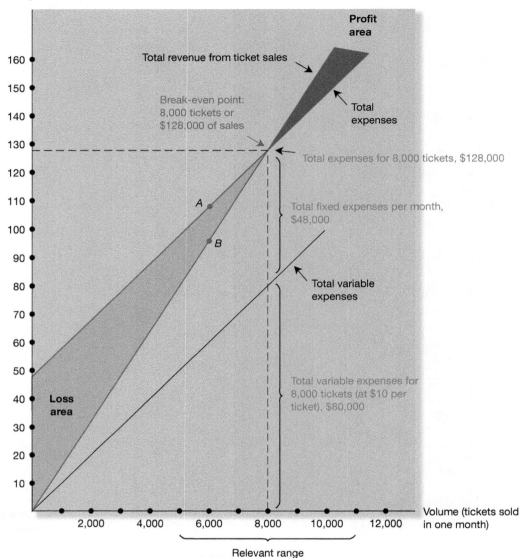

for the month at 8,000 tickets, or $128,000 of ticket sales. This agrees with our calculations in the preceding section.

Profit and Loss Areas The CVP graph discloses more information than the break-even calculation. From the graph, a manager can see the effects on profit of changes in volume. The vertical distance between the lines on the graph represents the profit or loss at a particular sales volume. If Seattle Contemporary Theater sells fewer than 8,000 tickets in a month, the organization will suffer a loss. The magnitude of the loss increases as ticket sales decline. The theater organization will have a profit if sales exceed 8,000 tickets in a month.

Implications of the Break-Even Point The position of the break-even point within an organization's relevant range of activity provides important information to management. The Seattle Contemporary Theater building seats 450 people. The agreement with the city of Seattle calls for 20 performances during each play's

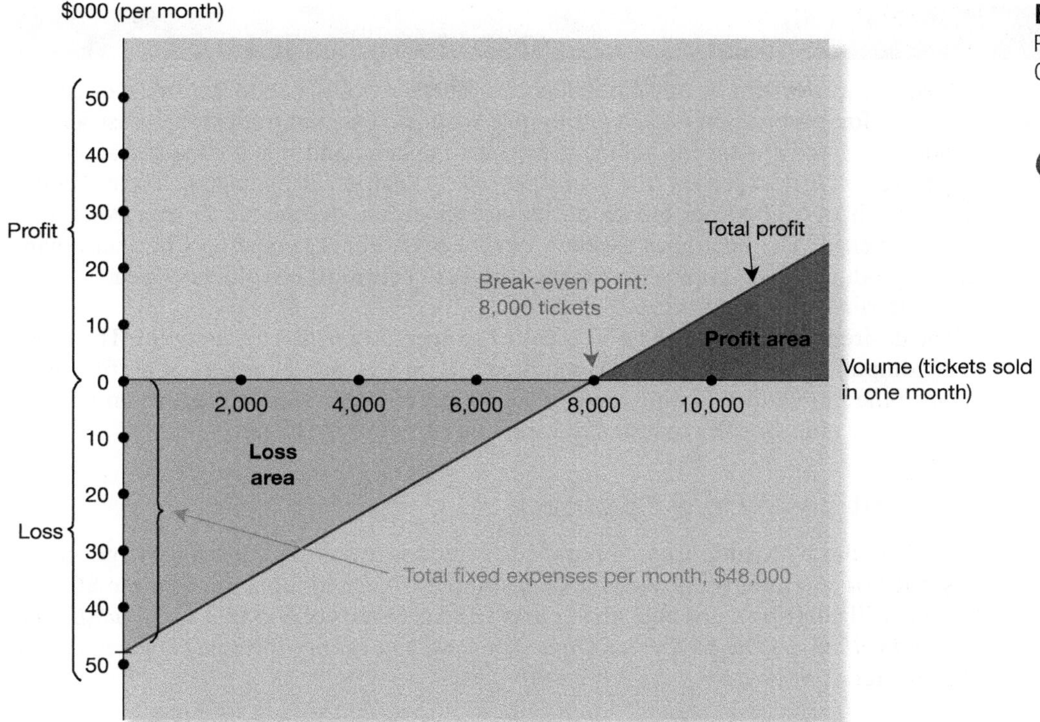

Exhibit 7–3
Profit-Volume Graph: Seattle Contemporary Theater

one-month run. Thus, the maximum number of tickets that can be sold each month is 9,000 (450 seats × 20 performances). The organization's break-even point is quite close to the maximum possible sales volume. This could be cause for concern in a nonprofit organization operating on limited resources.

What could management do to improve this situation? One possibility is to renegotiate with the city to schedule additional performances. However, this might not be feasible, because the actors need some rest each week. Also, additional performances would likely entail additional costs, such as increased theater-rental expenses and increased compensation for the actors and production crew. Other possible solutions are to raise ticket prices or reduce costs. These kinds of issues will be explored later in the chapter.

The CVP graph will not resolve this potential problem for the management of Seattle Contemporary Theater. However, the graph will *direct management's attention* to the situation.

Alternative Format for the CVP Graph

An alternative format for the CVP graph, preferred by some managers, is displayed in Exhibit 7–2. The key difference is that fixed expenses are graphed above variable expenses, instead of the reverse as they were in Exhibit 7–1.

Profit-Volume Graph

Yet another approach to graphing cost-volume-profit relationships is displayed in Exhibit 7–3. This format is called a **profit-volume graph,** since it highlights the amount of profit or loss. Notice that the graph intercepts the vertical axis at the amount equal to fixed expenses at the zero activity level. The graph crosses the horizontal axis at the break-even point. The vertical distance between the horizontal axis and the profit line, at a particular level of sales volume, is the profit or loss at that volume.

Target Net Profit

Learning Objective 4

Apply CVP analysis to determine the effect on profit of changes in fixed expenses, variable expenses, sales prices, and sales volume.

The board of trustees for Seattle Contemporary Theater would like to run free workshops and classes for young actors and aspiring playwrights. This program would cost \$3,600 per month in fixed expenses, including teachers' salaries and rental of space at a local college. No variable expenses would be incurred. If Seattle Contemporary Theater could make a profit of \$3,600 per month on its performances, the Seattle Drama Workshop could be opened. The board has asked Andrew Lloyd, the organization's business manager and producer, to determine how many theater tickets must be sold during each play's one-month run to make a profit of \$3,600.

The desired profit level of \$3,600 is called a **target net profit** (or **income).** The problem of computing the volume of sales required to earn a particular target net profit is very similar to the problem of finding the break-even point. After all, the break-even point is the number of units of sales required to earn a target net profit of zero.

Contribution-Margin Approach

Each ticket sold by Seattle Contemporary Theater has a unit contribution margin of \$6 (sales price of \$16 minus unit variable expense of \$10). Eight thousand of these \$6 contributions will contribute just enough to cover fixed expenses of \$48,000. *Each additional ticket sold will contribute \$6 toward profit.* Thus, we can modify formula (1) given earlier in the chapter as follows:

$$\frac{\text{Fixed expenses} + \text{Target net profit}}{\text{Unit contribution margin}} = \begin{array}{c}\text{Number of sales units required}\\ \text{to earn target net profit}\end{array} \qquad (5)$$

$$\frac{\$48{,}000 + \$3{,}600}{\$6} = 8{,}600 \text{ tickets}$$

If Seattle Contemporary Theater sells 8,600 tickets during each play's one-month run, the organization will make a monthly profit of \$3,600 on its performances. This profit can be used to fund the Seattle Drama Workshop. The total dollar sales required to earn a target net profit is found by modifying formula (2) given previously.

$$\frac{\text{Fixed expenses} + \text{Target net profit}}{\text{Contribution-margin ratio}} = \begin{array}{c}\text{Dollar sales required to earn}\\ \text{target net profit}\end{array} \qquad (6)$$

$$\frac{\$48{,}000 + \$3{,}600}{.375} = \$137{,}600$$

$$\text{where the contribution margin ratio} = \frac{\$6}{\$16} = .375$$

This dollar sales figure also can be found by multiplying the required sales of 8,600 tickets by the ticket price of \$16 (8,600 × \$16 = \$137,600).

Equation Approach

The equation approach also can be used to find the units of sales required to earn a target net profit. We can modify the profit equation given previously as follows:

$$\left[\begin{pmatrix}\text{Unit}\\ \text{sales}\\ \text{price}\end{pmatrix} \times \begin{pmatrix}\text{Sales volume}\\ \text{required to}\\ \text{earn target}\\ \text{net profit}\end{pmatrix}\right] - \left[\begin{pmatrix}\text{Unit}\\ \text{variable}\\ \text{expense}\end{pmatrix} \times \begin{pmatrix}\text{Sales volume}\\ \text{required to}\\ \text{earn target}\\ \text{net profit}\end{pmatrix}\right] - \begin{pmatrix}\text{Fixed}\\ \text{expenses}\end{pmatrix} = \text{Target net profit}$$

Filling in the values for Seattle Contemporary Theater, we have the following equation.

$$(\$16 \times X) - (\$10 \times X) - \$48{,}000 = \$3{,}600 \qquad (7)$$

where X denotes the sales volume required to earn the target net profit.

Equation (7) can be solved for X as follows:

$$\$16X - \$10X - \$48{,}000 = \$3{,}600$$
$$\$6X = \$51{,}600$$
$$X = \frac{\$51{,}600}{\$6} = 8{,}600$$

Graphical Approach

The profit-volume graph in Exhibit 7–3 also can be used to find the sales volume required to earn a target net profit. First, locate Seattle Contemporary Theater's target net profit of $3,600 on the vertical axis. Then move horizontally until the profit line is reached. Finally, move down from the profit line to the horizontal axis to determine the required sales volume.

Applying CVP Analysis

The cost-volume-profit relationships that underlie break-even calculations and CVP graphs have wide-ranging applications in management. We will look at several common applications illustrated by Seattle Contemporary Theater.

Learning Objective 4

Apply CVP analysis to determine the effect on profit of changes in fixed expenses, variable expenses, sales prices, and sales volume.

Safety Margin

The **safety margin** of an enterprise is the difference between the budgeted sales revenue and the break-even sales revenue. Suppose Seattle Contemporary Theater's business manager expects every performance of each play to be sold out. Then budgeted monthly sales revenue is $144,000 (450 seats × 20 performances of each play × $16 per ticket). Since break-even sales revenue is $128,000, the organization's safety margin is $16,000 ($144,000 − $128,000). The safety margin gives management a feel for how close projected operations are to the organization's break-even point. We will further discuss the safety margin concept later in the chapter.

"Basically the role of the [accountant] on the team [is] analyzing the financial impact of the business decision and providing advice. Does this make sense financially or not?" (7d)

Abbott Laboratories

Changes in Fixed Expenses

What would happen to Seattle Contemporary Theater's break-even point if fixed expenses change? Suppose the business manager is concerned that the estimate for fixed utilities expenses, $1,400 per month, is too low. What would happen to the break-even point if fixed utilities expenses prove to be $2,600 instead? The break-even calculations for both the original and the new estimate of fixed utilities expenses are as follows:

	Original Estimate	New Estimate
Fixed utilities expenses	$ 1,400	$ 2,600
Total fixed expenses	$48,000	$49,200
Break-even calculation	$48,000	$49,200
(Fixed expenses ÷ Unit contribution margin)	$6	$6
Break-even point (units)	8,000 tickets	8,200 tickets
Break-even point (dollars)	$128,000	$131,200

The estimate of fixed expenses has increased by 2.5 percent, since $1,200 is 2.5 percent of $48,000. Notice that the break-even point also increased by 2.5 percent (200 tickets is 2.5 percent of 8,000 tickets). This relationship will always exist.

$$\frac{\text{Fixed expenses}}{\text{Unit contribution margin}} = \text{Break-even point (in units)}$$

$$\frac{\text{Fixed expenses} \times 1.025}{\text{Unit contribution margin}} = \text{(Break-even point in units)} \times 1.025$$

Donations to Offset Fixed Expenses Nonprofit organizations often receive cash donations from people or organizations desiring to support a worthy cause. A donation is equivalent to a reduction in fixed expenses, and it reduces the organization's break-even point. In our original set of data, Seattle Contemporary Theater's monthly fixed expenses total $48,000. Suppose that various people pledge donations amounting to $6,000 per month. The new break-even point is computed as follows:

$$\frac{\text{Fixed expenses} - \text{Donations}}{\text{Unit contribution margin}} = \text{Break-even point (in units)}$$

$$\frac{\$48{,}000 - \$6{,}000}{\$6} = 7{,}000 \text{ tickets}$$

Changes in the Unit Contribution Margin

What would happen to Seattle Contemporary Theater's break-even point if miscellaneous variable expenses were $3 per ticket instead of $2? Alternatively, what would be the effect of raising the ticket price to $18?

Change in Unit Variable Expenses If the theater organization's miscellaneous variable expenses increase from $2 to $3 per ticket, the unit contribution margin will fall from $6 to $5. The original and new break-even points are computed as follows:

	Original Estimate	New Estimate
Miscellaneous variable expenses	$2 per ticket	$3 per ticket
Unit contribution margin	$6	$5
Break-even calculation	$48,000	$48,000
(Fixed expenses ÷ unit contribution margin)	$6	$5
Break-even point (units)	8,000 tickets	9,600 tickets
Break-even point (dollars)	$128,000	$153,600

If this change in unit variable expenses actually occurs, it will no longer be possible for the organization to break even. Only 9,000 tickets are available for each play's one-month run (450 seats × 20 performances), but 9,600 tickets would have to be sold to break even. Once again, CVP analysis will not solve this problem for management, but it will direct management's attention to potentially serious difficulties.

Change in Sales Price Changing the unit sales price will also alter the unit contribution margin. Suppose the ticket price is raised from $16 to $18. This change will raise the unit contribution margin from $6 to $8. The new break-even point will be 6,000 tickets ($48,000 ÷ $8).

A $2 increase in the ticket price will lower the break-even point from 8,000 tickets to 6,000 tickets. Is this change desirable? A lower break-even point decreases the risk of operating with a loss if sales are sluggish. However, the organization may be more likely to at least break even with a $16 ticket price than with an $18 ticket price. The reason is that the lower ticket price encourages more people to attend the theater's performances.

It could be that break-even sales of 8,000 tickets at $16 are more likely than break-even sales of 6,000 tickets at $18. Ultimately, the desirability of the ticket-price increase depends on management's assessment of the likely reaction by theater patrons.

Management's decision about the ticket price increase also will reflect the fundamental goals of Seattle Contemporary Theater. This nonprofit drama organization was formed to bring contemporary drama to the people of Seattle. The lower the ticket price, the more accessible the theater's productions will be to people of all income levels.

The point of this discussion is that CVP analysis provides valuable information, but it is only one of several elements that influence management's decisions.

Predicting Profit Given Expected Volume

So far, we have focused on finding the required sales volume to break even or achieve a particular target net profit. Thus, we have asked the following question.

$$\text{Given: } \begin{Bmatrix} \text{Fixed expenses} \\ \text{Unit contribution margin} \\ \text{Target net profit} \end{Bmatrix}, \text{ Find: } \{\text{required sales volume}\}$$

We also can use CVP analysis to turn this question around and make the following query.

$$\text{Given: } \begin{Bmatrix} \text{Fixed expenses} \\ \text{Unit contribution margin} \\ \text{Expected sales volume} \end{Bmatrix}, \text{ Find: } \{\text{expected profit}\}$$

Suppose the management of Seattle Contemporary Theater expects fixed monthly expenses of $48,000 and unit variable expenses of $10 per ticket. The organization's board of trustees is considering two different ticket prices, and the business manager has forecast monthly demand at each price.

Ticket Price	Forecast Monthly Demand
$16	9,000
$20	6,000

Expected profit may be calculated at each price as shown in the following table. In these profit calculations, the **total contribution margin** is the difference between *total* sales revenue and *total* variable expenses. This use of the term *contribution margin* is a "total" concept rather than the "per unit" concept used earlier in the chapter. The *total contribution margin* is the *total* amount left to contribute to covering fixed expenses after *total* variable expenses have been covered.

	Ticket Price	
	$16	**$20**
Sales revenue:		
9,000 × $16	$144,000	
6,000 × $20		$120,000
Less variable expenses:		
9,000 × $10	90,000	
6,000 × $10		60,000
Total contribution margin	$ 54,000	$ 60,000
Less fixed expenses	48,000	48,000
Profit	$ 6,000	$ 12,000

The difference in expected profit at the two ticket prices is due to two factors:

1. A different *unit* contribution margin, defined previously as *unit* sales price minus *unit* variable expenses
2. A different sales volume

Incremental Approach Rather than presenting the entire income statement under each ticket price alternative, we can use a simpler incremental approach. This analysis focuses only on the difference in the total contribution margin under the two prices. Thus, the combined effect of the change in unit contribution margin and the change in sales volume is as follows:

Expected *total* contribution margin at $20 ticket price:	
6,000 × ($20 − $10)	$60,000
Expected *total* contribution margin at $16 ticket price:	
9,000 × ($16 − $10)	54,000
Difference in *total* contribution margin	$ 6,000

The $6,000 difference in expected profit, at the two ticket prices, is due to a $6,000 difference in the total contribution margin. The board of trustees will consider these projected profits as it decides which ticket price is best. Even though Seattle Contemporary Theater is a nonprofit organization, it may still have legitimate reasons for attempting to make a profit on its theater performances. For example, the board might use these profits to fund a free drama workshop, provide scholarships for local young people to study drama in college, or produce a free outdoor play for Seattle's residents.

Interdependent Changes in Key Variables

Sometimes a change in one key variable will cause a change in another key variable. Suppose the board of trustees is choosing between ticket prices of $16 and $20, and the business manager has projected demand as shown in the preceding section. A famous retired actress who lives in Seattle has offered to donate $10,000 per month to Seattle Contemporary Theater if the board will set the ticket price at $16. The actress is interested in making the theater's performances affordable for as many people as possible. The facts are now as follows:

Ticket Price	Unit Contribution Margin	Forecast Monthly Demand	Net Fixed Expenses (after subtracting donation)
$16	$ 6	9,000	$38,000 ($48,000 − $10,000)
20	10	6,000	48,000

The organization's expected profit at each price is computed as follows:

	Ticket Price	
	$16	**$20**
Sales revenue:		
9,000 × $16	$144,000	
6,000 × $20		$120,000
Less variable expenses:		
9,000 × $10	90,000	
6,000 × $10		60,000
Total contribution margin	$ 54,000	$ 60,000
Less net fixed expenses (net of donation)	38,000	48,000
Profit	$ 16,000	$ 12,000

Now the difference in expected profit at the two ticket prices is due to three factors:

1. A different *unit* contribution margin.
2. A different sales volume.
3. A difference in the *net* fixed expenses, after deducting the donation.

Incremental Approach The combined effect of these factors is shown in the following analysis, which focuses on the effects of the price alternatives on the total contribution margin and the net fixed expenses.

Expected *total* contribution margin at $20 ticket price:	
6,000 × ($20 − $10)	$60,000
Expected *total* contribution margin at $16 ticket price:	
9,000 × ($16 − $10)	54,000
Difference in *total* contribution margin	$ 6,000
(higher with $20 ticket price)	
Net fixed expenses at $20 ticket price	$48,000
Net fixed expenses at $16 ticket price	38,000
Difference in net fixed expenses (higher with $20 ticket price)	$10,000

The expected total contribution margin is $6,000 higher with the $20 ticket price, but net fixed expenses are $10,000 higher. Thus, Seattle Contemporary Theater will make $4,000 more in profit at the $16 price ($10,000 − $6,000).

CVP Information in Published Annual Reports

Cost-volume-profit relationships are so important to understanding an organization's operations that some companies disclose CVP information in their published annual reports. The following illustration is from the airline industry.

Air France, Sabena, British Airways, and JetBlue

AIRLINES KEEP A CLOSE EYE ON BREAK-EVEN LOAD FACTORS

Airlines generally disclose their systemwide break-even load factors in their annual reports. British Airways, for example, listed its break-even load factor as 63.6 percent in a recent annual report. The large airlines, like British Airways, usually fill a smaller percentage of their seats than do the upstart, discount airlines. JetBlue is a good example. "The low-fare, low-cost carrier . . . now operates more than 100 flights a day to 18 cities in nine states."[1] Its load factor, or percentage of seats filled, is 76.1 percent.

"Air France has been able to make up for cutting Dallas and Miami flights with more flights and larger planes to African cities. The airline has also expanded its service to many French-speaking former destinations in the Caribbean and the Indian Ocean. Together with Africa, the former colonies should account for almost the same amount of Air France's revenue this year as North America, analysts say. Still, the operating costs of flying to Africa are 50 percent higher for Air France than flying to the U.S., and the logistical problems are much more challenging."

In recent years, "Sabena lost at least 8 percent on its flights to the U.S., but had margins above 10 percent on routes to its former colonies Congo, Rwanda, and Burundi, according to an internal Sabena study. That kind of difference in profit margins is common. Across the busy North Atlantic, where competition and seasonal variation force heavy discounting, all airlines are lucky to break even with a plane 75 percent full. For Kinshasa and other parts of Africa, where traffic is steadier, European carriers can break even with their planes barely 60 percent full, and planes often fly 85 percent full."[2]

[1]Susan Carey, "JetBlue, One of the Few U.S. Airlines to Buck the Downturn, Files for $125 Million IPO," *The Wall Street Journal,* February 13, 2002, p. B4. Also see "British Air's Net Soars Amid Strong Demand," *The Wall Street Journal,* February 4, 2008, P. A6.

[2]Daniel Michaels, "Kinshasa Is Poor, Scary, and a Boon for Air France," *The Wall Street Journal,* April 30, 2002, pp. A1, A8.

CVP Analysis with Multiple Products

Major airlines keep a close watch on the break-even passenger load factor.

Learning Objective 5

Compute the break-even point and prepare a profit-volume graph for a multiproduct enterprise.

Our CVP illustration for Seattle Contemporary Theater has assumed that the organization has only one product, a theater seat at a dramatic performance. Most firms have a *sales mix* consisting of more than one product, and this adds some complexity to their CVP analyses.

As we have seen, Seattle Contemporary Theater's monthly fixed expenses total $48,000, and the unit variable expense per ticket is $10. Now suppose that the city of Seattle has agreed to refurbish 10 theater boxes in the historic theater building. Each box has five seats, which are more comfortable and afford a better view of the stage than the theater's general seating. The board of trustees has decided to charge $16 per ticket for general seating and $20 per ticket for box seats. These facts are summarized as follows:

Seat Type	Ticket Price	Unit Variable Expense	Unit Contribution Margin	Seats in Theater	Seats Available per Month (20 performances)
Regular	$16	$10	$ 6	450	9,000
Box	20	10	10	50	1,000

Notice that 90 percent of the available seats are regular seats, and 10 percent are box seats. The business manager estimates that tickets for each type of seat will be sold in the same proportion as the number of seats available. If, for example, 5,000 tickets are sold during a month, sales will be as follows:

Regular seats:	90% × 5,000	4,500
Box seats:	10% × 5,000	500
Total		5,000

For any organization selling multiple products, the relative proportion of each type of product *sold* is called the **sales mix.** The business manager's estimate of Seattle Contemporary Theater's *sales mix* is 90 percent regular seats and 10 percent box seats.

The sales mix is an important assumption in multiproduct CVP analysis. The sales mix is used to compute a **weighted-average unit contribution margin.** This is the *average* of the several products' *unit contribution margins, weighted* by the relative sales proportion of each product. Seattle Contemporary Theater's weighted-average unit contribution margin is computed below.

$$\text{Weighted-average unit contribution margin} = (\$6 \times 90\%) + (\$10 \times 10\%) = \$6.40$$

The organization's break-even point in units is computed using the following formula.

$$\text{Break-even point} = \frac{\text{Fixed expenses}}{\text{Weighted-average unit contribution margin}} \qquad (8)$$

$$= \frac{\$48{,}000}{\$6.40} = 7{,}500 \text{ tickets}$$

The break-even point of 7,500 tickets must be interpreted in light of the sales mix. Seattle Contemporary Theater will break even for the month if it sells 7,500 tickets as follows:

Break-even sales in units	Regular seats: 7,500 × 90%	6,750 tickets
	Box seats: 7,500 × 10%	750 tickets
	Total	7,500 tickets

The following income calculation verifies the break-even point.

Sales revenue:	
Regular seats: 6,750 × $16	$108,000
Box seats: 750 × $20	15,000
Total revenue: 7,500 seats in total	$123,000
Less variable expenses: 7,500 × $10	75,000
Total contribution margin	$ 48,000
Less fixed expenses	48,000
Profit	$ 0

The break-even point of 7,500 tickets per month is *valid only for the sales mix assumed* in computing the weighted-average unit contribution margin. If 7,500 tickets are sold in any other mix of regular and box seats, the organization will not break even.

Notice that break-even formula (8) is a modification of formula (1) given earlier in the chapter. The only difference is that formula (8) uses the *weighted-average* unit contribution margin.

Seattle Contemporary Theater's business manager has constructed the profit-volume graph in Exhibit 7–4. The PV graph shows the organization's profit at any level of total monthly sales, assuming the sales mix of 90 percent regular seats and 10 percent box seats. For example, if 9,000 tickets are sold in total, at the assumed sales mix, the PV graph indicates that profit will be $9,600.

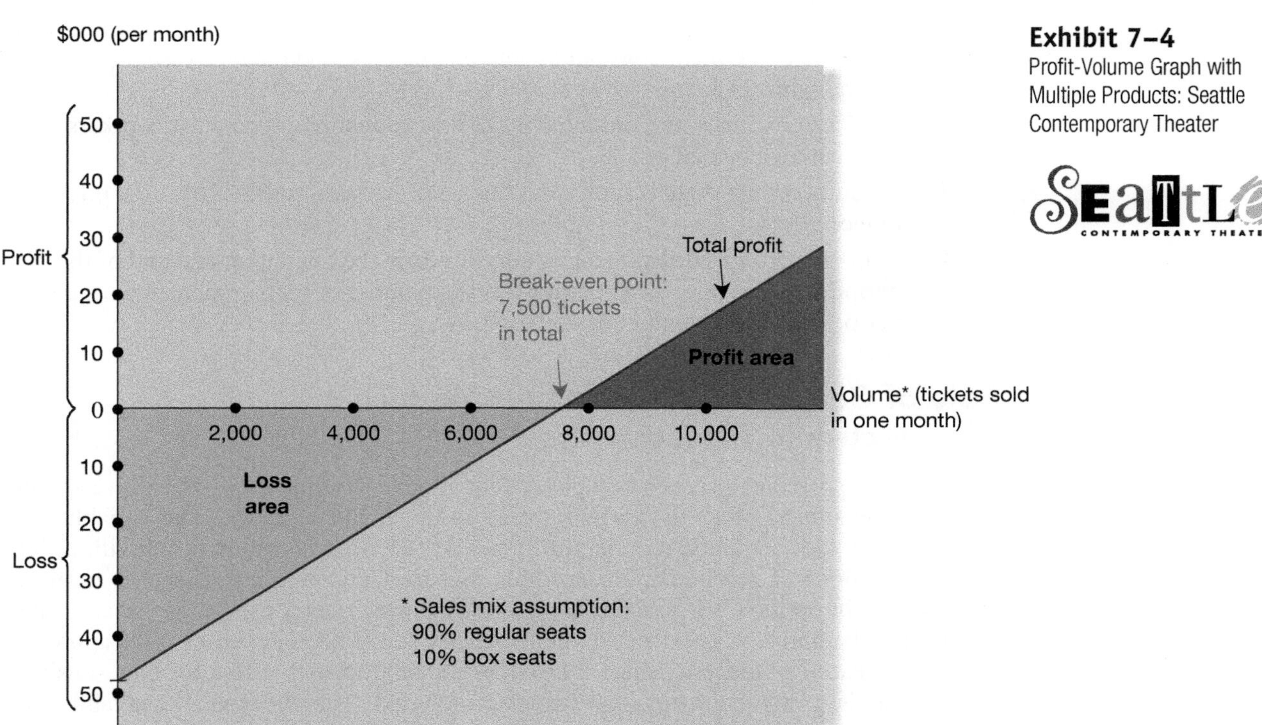

Exhibit 7–4
Profit-Volume Graph with Multiple Products: Seattle Contemporary Theater

SEaTtLe CONTEMPORARY THEATER

With multiproduct CVP analysis, a managerial accountant can investigate the impact on profit of changes in sales volume, prices, variable costs, fixed costs, or the sales mix itself. For example, what would be the effect on Seattle Contemporary Theater's break-even point if the sales mix were 95 percent regular seats and 5 percent box seats? With this sales mix, the weighted-average unit contribution margin is computed as follows:

$$\text{Weighted-average unit contribution margin} = (\$6 \times 95\%) + (\$10 \times 5\%) = \$6.20$$

The break-even point increases from 7,500 tickets to approximately 7,742 tickets as a result of the lower proportion of expensive seats in the sales mix.

$$\text{Break-even point} = \frac{\text{Fixed expenses}}{\text{Weighted-average unit contribution margin}} = \frac{\$48{,}000}{\$6.20} = 7{,}742 \text{ tickets*}$$

*Rounded

Assumptions Underlying CVP Analysis

Learning Objective 6

List and discuss the key assumptions of CVP analysis.

For any cost-volume-profit analysis to be valid, the following important assumptions must be reasonably satisfied *within the relevant range.*

1. The behavior of total revenue is linear (straight-line). This implies that the price of the product or service will not change as sales volume varies within the relevant range.
2. The behavior of total expenses is linear (straight-line) over the relevant range. This implies the following more specific assumptions.
   a. Expenses can be categorized as fixed, variable, or semivariable. *Total* fixed expenses remain constant as activity changes, and the *unit* variable expense remains unchanged as activity varies.
   b. The efficiency and productivity of the production process and workers remain constant.
3. In multiproduct organizations, the sales mix remains constant over the relevant range.
4. In manufacturing firms, the inventory levels at the beginning and end of the period are the same. This implies that the number of units produced during the period equals the number of units sold.

Role of Computerized Planning Models and Electronic Spreadsheets

Cost-volume-profit analysis is based on the four general assumptions listed above as well as specific estimates of all the variables used in the analysis. Since these variables are rarely known with certainty, it is helpful to run a CVP analysis many times with different combinations of estimates. For example, Seattle Contemporary Theater's business manager might do the CVP analysis using different estimates for the ticket prices, sales mix for regular and box seats, unit variable expenses, and fixed expenses. This approach is called **sensitivity analysis,** since it provides the analyst with a feel for how sensitive the analysis is to the estimates upon which it is based. The widespread availability of personal computers and electronic spreadsheet software has made sensitivity analysis relatively easy to do.

Exhibit 7–5
Income Statement: Traditional and Contribution Formats

A. Traditional Format

ACCUTIME COMPANY
Income Statement
For the Year Ended December 31, 20x1

Sales		$500,000
Less: Cost of goods sold		380,000
Gross margin		$120,000
Less: Operating expenses:		
Selling expenses	$ 35,000	
Administrative expenses	35,000	70,000
Net income		$ 50,000

B. Contribution Format

ACCUTIME COMPANY
Income Statement
For the Year Ended December 31, 20x1

Sales		$500,000
Less: Variable expenses:		
Variable manufacturing	$280,000	
Variable selling	15,000	
Variable administrative	5,000	300,000
Contribution margin		$200,000
Less: Fixed expenses:		
Fixed manufacturing	$100,000	
Fixed selling	20,000	
Fixed administrative	30,000	150,000
Net income		$ 50,000

CVP Relationships and the Income Statement

The management functions of planning, control, and decision making all are facilitated by an understanding of cost-volume-profit relationships. These relationships are important enough to operating managers that some businesses prepare income statements in a way that highlights CVP issues. Before we examine this new income-statement format, we will review the more traditional income statement used in the preceding chapters.

Traditional Income Statement

An income statement for AccuTime Company, a manufacturer of digital clocks, is shown in Exhibit 7–5 (panel A). During 20x1 the firm manufactured and sold 20,000 clocks at a price of $25 each. This income statement is prepared in the traditional manner. *Cost of goods sold* includes both variable and fixed manufacturing costs, as measured by the firm's product-costing system. The *gross margin* is computed by subtracting cost of goods sold from sales. Selling and administrative expenses are then subtracted; each expense includes both variable and fixed costs. *The traditional income statement does not disclose the breakdown of each expense into its variable and fixed components.*

Contribution Income Statement

Learning Objective 7

Prepare and interpret a contribution income statement.

Many operating managers find the traditional income-statement format difficult to use, because it does not separate variable and fixed expenses. Instead they prefer the **contribution income statement.** A contribution income statement for AccuTime is shown in Exhibit 7–5 (panel B). *The contribution format highlights the distinction between variable and fixed expenses.* The variable manufacturing cost of each clock is $14, and the total fixed manufacturing cost is $100,000. On the contribution income statement, all variable expenses are subtracted from sales to obtain the *contribution margin.* For AccuTime, $200,000 remains from total sales revenue, after all variable costs have been covered, to contribute to covering fixed costs and making a profit. All fixed costs are then subtracted from the contribution margin to obtain net income.

Comparison of Traditional and Contribution Income Statements

Operating managers frequently prefer the contribution income statement, because its separation of fixed and variable expenses highlights cost-volume-profit relationships. It is readily apparent from the contribution format statement how income will be affected when sales volume changes by a given percentage. Suppose management projects that sales volume in 20x2 will be 20 percent greater than in 20x1. No changes are anticipated in the sales price, variable cost per unit, or fixed costs. Examination of the contribution income statement shows that if sales volume increases by 20 percent, the following changes will occur. (Our discussion ignores income taxes, which are covered in the appendix at the end of this chapter.)

Income Statement Item	20x1 Amount	Change	20x2 Amount
Sales	$500,000	$100,000 (20% × $500,000)	$600,000
Total variable expenses	$300,000	$60,000 (20% × $300,000)	$360,000
Contribution margin	$200,000	$40,000 (20% × $200,000)	$240,000
Total fixed expenses	$150,000	–0– (no change in fixed expenses when volume changes)	$150,000
Net income	$ 50,000	$40,000 (income changes by the amount of the contribution-margin change)	$ 90,000

Notice that net income increases by the same amount as the increase in the contribution margin. Moreover, the contribution margin changes in direct proportion to the change in sales volume. These two facts enable us to calculate the increase in net income using the following shortcut. Recall that the *contribution-margin ratio* is the percentage of contribution margin to sales.

$$\begin{pmatrix}\text{Increase in}\\ \text{sales revenue}\end{pmatrix} \times \begin{pmatrix}\text{Contribution-margin}\\ \text{ratio}\end{pmatrix} = \begin{pmatrix}\text{Increase in}\\ \text{net income}\end{pmatrix}$$

$$\$100,000 \quad \times \quad .40 \quad = \quad \$40,000$$

$$\text{where} \quad \begin{pmatrix}\text{Contribution-margin}\\ \text{ratio}\end{pmatrix} = \frac{\text{Contribution margin}}{\text{Sales revenue}}$$

$$.40 = \frac{\$200,000}{\$500,000}$$

Exhibit 7–6
Comparison of Cost Structures

Microsoft Excel - Comparison of Cost Structures

B10 =B8-B9

	A	B	C	D	E	F	G
1		Company A		Company B		Company C	
2		(AccuTime Company)		(Manual System)		(Automated System)	
3							
4		Amount	%	Amount	%	Amount	%
5							
6	Sales	$ 500,000	100	$ 500,000	100	$ 500,000	100
7	Variable expenses	300,000	60	400,000	80	50,000	10
8	Contribution margin	$ 200,000	40	$ 100,000	20	$ 450,000	90
9	Fixed expenses	150,000	30	50,000	10	400,000	80
10	Net income	$ 50,000	10	$ 50,000	10	$ 50,000	10

Sheet1 / Sheet2 / Sheet3

Ready

The preceding analysis makes use of cost-volume-profit relationships that are disclosed in the contribution income statement. Such an analysis cannot be made with the information presented in the traditional income statement.

Cost Structure and Operating Leverage

Learning Objective 8

Explain the role of cost structure and operating leverage in CVP relationships.

The **cost structure** of an organization is the relative proportion of its fixed and variable costs. Cost structures differ widely among industries and among firms within an industry. A company using a computer-integrated manufacturing system has a large investment in plant and equipment, which results in a cost structure dominated by fixed costs. In contrast, a home building contractor's cost structure has a much higher proportion of variable costs. The highly automated manufacturing firm is capital-intensive, whereas the home building contractor is labor-intensive.

An organization's cost structure has a significant effect on the sensitivity of its profit to changes in volume. A convenient way to portray a firm's cost structure is shown in the Excel spreadsheet in Exhibit 7–6.[3] The data for AccuTime Company (company A) comes from the firm's 20x1 contribution income statement in Exhibit 7–5. For comparison purposes, two other firms' cost structures also are shown. Although these three firms have the same sales revenue ($500,000) and net income ($50,000), they have very different cost structures. Company B's production process is largely manual, and its cost structure is dominated by variable costs. It has a low contribution-margin ratio of only 20 percent. In contrast, company C employs a highly automated production process, and its cost structure is dominated by fixed costs. The firm's contribution-margin ratio is 90 percent. Company A falls between these two extremes with a contribution-margin ratio of 40 percent.

Suppose sales revenue increases by 10 percent, or $50,000, in each company. The resulting increase in each company's profit is calculated in Exhibit 7–7.

Notice that company B, with its high variable expenses and low contribution-margin ratio, shows a relatively low *percentage* increase in profit. In contrast, the high fixed expenses and large contribution-margin ratio of company C result in a relatively high *percentage* increase in profit. Company A falls in between these two extremes.

To summarize, the greater the proportion of fixed costs in a firm's cost structure, the greater the impact on profit will be from a given percentage change in sales revenue.

[3]This form of income statement, in which each item on the statement is expressed as a percentage of sales revenue, is often called a *common-size income statement.*

Exhibit 7–7
Effect on Profit of Increase in Sales Revenue

	(Increase In Sales Revenue)	×	(Contribution Margin Ratio)	=	(Increase In Net Income)	Percentage Increase in Net Income
Company A (AccuTime)	$50,000	×	40%	=	$20,000	40% ($20,000 ÷ $50,000)
Company B (high variable expenses)	$50,000	×	20%	=	$10,000	20% ($10,000 ÷ $50,000)
Company C (high fixed expenses)	$50,000	×	90%	=	$45,000	90% ($45,000 ÷ $50,000)

Operating Leverage

The extent to which an organization uses fixed costs in its cost structure is called **operating leverage.** The operating leverage is greatest in firms with a large proportion of fixed costs, low proportion of variable costs, and the resulting high contribution-margin ratio. Exhibit 7–6 shows that company B has low operating leverage, company C has high operating leverage, and company A falls in between. To a physical scientist, *leverage* refers to the ability of a small force to move a heavy weight. To the managerial accountant, *operating leverage* refers to the ability of the firm to generate an increase in net income when sales revenue increases.

Measuring Operating Leverage

The managerial accountant can measure a firm's operating leverage, *at a particular sales volume,* using the **operating leverage factor:**

$$\text{Operating leverage factor} = \frac{\text{Contribution margin}}{\text{Net income}}$$

Using the data in Exhibit 7–6, the operating leverage factors of companies A, B, and C are computed as follows:

	(Contribution Margin)	÷	(Net Income)	=	(Operating Leverage Factor)
Company A (AccuTime)	$200,000	÷	$50,000	=	4
Company B (high variable expenses)	$100,000	÷	$50,000	=	2
Company C (high fixed expenses)	$450,000	÷	$50,000	=	9

The operating leverage factor is a measure, at a particular level of sales, of the *percentage* impact on net income of a given *percentage* change in sales revenue. Multiplying the *percentage* change in sales revenue by the operating leverage factor yields the *percentage* change in net income.

	(Percentage Increase in Sales Revenue)	×	(Operating Leverage Factor)	=	(Percentage Change in Net Income)
Company A (AccuTime)	10%	×	4	=	40%
Company B (high variable expenses)	10%	×	2	=	20%
Company C (high fixed expenses)	10%	×	9	=	90%

The percentage change in net income shown above for each company may be verified by re-examining Exhibit 7–7.

Break-Even Point and Safety Margin A firm's operating leverage also affects its break-even point. Since a firm with relatively high operating leverage has proportionally high fixed expenses, the firm's break-even point will be relatively high. This fact is illustrated using the data from Exhibit 7–6.

	(Fixed Expenses)	÷	(Contribution Margin Ratio)	=	(Break-Even Sales Revenue)
Company A (AccuTime)	$150,000	÷	40%	=	$375,000
Company B (high variable expenses)	$ 50,000	÷	20%	=	$250,000
Company C (high fixed expenses)	$400,000	÷	90%	=	$444,444*

*Rounded

The safety margin also is affected by a firm's operating leverage. Suppose the budgeted sales revenue for each of the three companies is $500,000. Then the safety margin, defined as budgeted sales revenue minus break-even sales revenue, is calculated as shown on the next page:

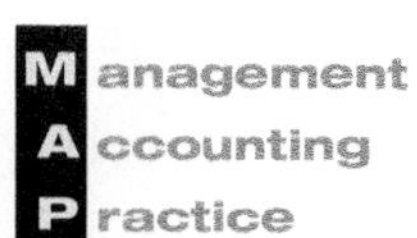

Expedia, Hotels.com, eBay, and Overture Services

OPERATING LEVERAGE HELPS WEB COMPANIES BECOME PROFITABLE

Four Web companies have made it into the Info Tech One Hundred: search engine Overture Services, auctioneer eBay, discount-hotel broker Hotels.com, and travel site Expedia. That's up from only one, and all of them are profitable. "The leaders of the Web pack are showing that once they turn profitable, they can quickly become big moneymakers. The reason is operating leverage. That's accounting-speak for a simple concept: Once you invest enough to build a Web site and your basic operations, you don't need to spend much money as sales rise. After you cover your fixed costs, the expense of processing each sale is so little that profits grow faster than revenues. That philosophy made for big Internet losses early on." The payoff, however, is at hand.

"Online travel agency Expedia Inc. is a textbook example of leverage in action." In one quarter alone, "Expedia doubled its sales, to $116 million. Yet its overhead, including administrative and marketing costs, rose only 8 percent, to $63 million. One big reason is that the company already had paid for the computing gear it needed to handle the higher volume of ticket sales."

Just a few years after the boom in e-commerce IPOs, "a clear pecking order of profitability has emerged. The biggest moneymakers: online travel, software, and financial-services firms." Why did these online companies turn profitable first? "Because software, financial services, and travel reservations are pure information products, without a physical widget to store or ship. Once overhead costs are covered, the expense in providing the service to one more customer is close to zero. Online retailers are making slower, yet tangible, progress toward profitability. What's holding Amazon.com Inc. and other e-tailers back is simple: Every time someone buys a book on Amazon, the company has to buy a new copy from the publisher. The upshot is that Amazon's gross margins are around 26 percent, compared with 70 percent at Expedia."

Every year, Web business writes a different story, "but now it's past the point where predictions of profitability are written in sand. Some Web businesses do work. The proof is in the black ink."[4]

[4]Timothy J. Mullaney and Robert D. Hof, "Finally, the Pot of Gold," *BusinessWeek,* June 24, 2002, p. 106.

Exhibit 7–8
Labor-Intensive Production Processes versus Advanced Manufacturing Systems

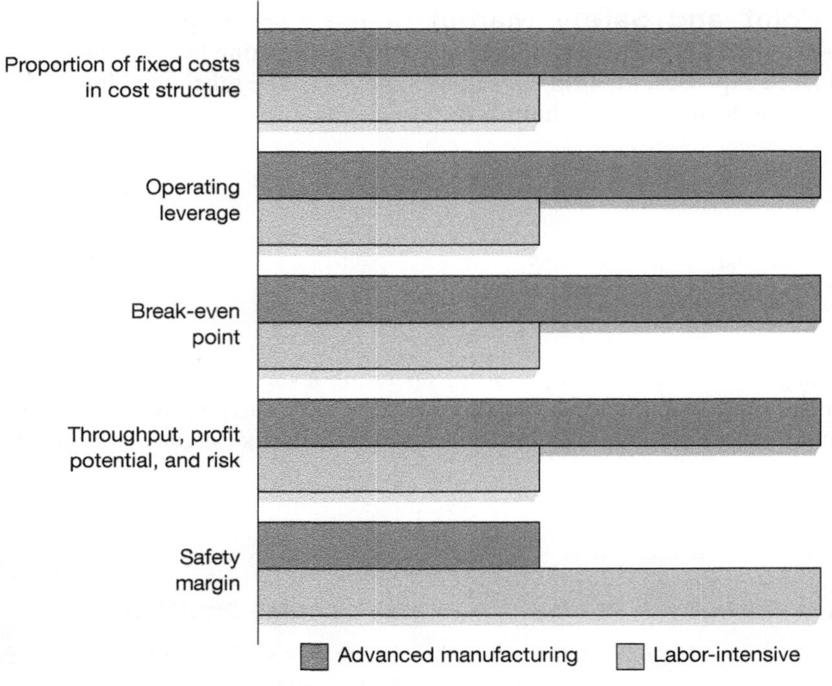

	Budgeted Sales Revenue	Break-Even Sales Revenue	Safety Margin
Company A (AccuTime)	$500,000	$375,000	$125,000
Company B (high variable expenses)	500,000	250,000	250,000
Company C (high fixed expenses)	500,000	444,444	55,556

To summarize, company C's high fixed expenses result in a high break-even point and low safety margin. Company B displays the opposite characteristics, and company A falls in between the two extremes.

Labor-Intensive Production Processes versus Advanced Manufacturing Systems The effects of labor-intensive (manual) production processes and highly automated, advanced manufacturing systems illustrated by companies A, B, and C are typical. As Exhibit 7–8 shows, a movement toward an advanced manufacturing environment often results in a higher break-even point, lower safety margin, and higher operating leverage. However, high-technology manufacturing systems generally have greater throughput, thus allowing greater potential for profitability. Along with the increased potential for profitability comes increased risk. In an economic recession, for example, a highly automated company with high fixed costs will be less able to adapt to lower consumer demand than will a firm with a more labor-intensive production process.

Cost Structure and Operating Leverage: A Cost-Benefit Issue

A firm's cost structure plays an important role in determining its cost-volume-profit relationships. A company with proportionately high fixed costs has relatively high operating leverage. The result of high operating leverage is that the firm can generate a large percentage increase in net income from a relatively small percentage increase in sales revenue. On the other hand, a firm with high operating leverage has a relatively high break-even point. This entails some risk to the firm.

The optimal cost structure for an organization involves a trade-off. Management must weigh the benefits of high operating leverage against the risks of large committed fixed costs and the associated high break-even point.

Management
Accounting
Practice

Kaiser Permanente

COST STRUCTURE AND OPERATING LEVERAGE

Kaiser Permanente was founded in 1945 to provide health care for workers at Henry F. Kaiser's West Coast shipyards and steel mills. It led the U.S. HMOs by building its own hospitals, marketing its own health insurance, and working with doctors in the Permanente Medical Group, who practice exclusively for Kaiser. Such a vertical integration allows Kaiser to control costs better than HMOs that contract with independent doctors and hospitals. This strategy results in Kaiser's cost structure being dominated by fixed costs. Kaiser has to focus on maintaining membership growth because of its high operating leverage.[5]

CVP Analysis, Activity-Based Costing, and Advanced Manufacturing Systems

Learning Objective 9

Understand the implications of activity-based costing for CVP analysis.

Traditional cost-volume-profit analysis focuses on the number of units sold as the only cost and revenue driver. Sales revenue is assumed to be linear in units sold. Moreover, costs are categorized as fixed or variable, with respect to the number of units sold, within the relevant range. This approach is consistent with traditional product-costing systems, in which cost assignment is based on a single, volume-related cost driver. In CVP analysis, as in product costing, the traditional approach can be misleading or provide less than adequate information for various management purposes. An activity-based costing system can provide a much more complete picture of cost-volume-profit relationships and thus provide better information to managers.

To illustrate the potential impact of activity-based costing on CVP analysis, we will continue our discussion of AccuTime Company. The basic data underlying the contribution income statement shown in Exhibit 7–5 are as follows:

AccuTime

Sales volume	20,000 units
Sales price	$25
Unit variable costs:	
Variable manufacturing	$14
Variable selling and administrative	1
Total unit variable cost	$15
Unit contribution margin	$10
Fixed costs:	
Fixed manufacturing	$100,000
Fixed selling and administrative	50,000
Total fixed costs	$150,000

These data are adequate for a traditional CVP analysis of various questions management may ask. For example, the break-even point is easily calculated as 15,000 units, as the following analysis shows:

$$\text{Break-even point} = \frac{\text{Fixed costs}}{\text{Unit contribution margin}} = \frac{\$150{,}000}{\$10} = 15{,}000 \text{ units}$$

"ABC was critical to the organization in helping us gain a better understanding of our costs. . . . It provided us with a foundation for managing expenses better." (7e)

BlueCross BlueShield of North Carolina

[5]Based on the author's research.

Alternatively, management may determine how many clocks must be sold to earn a target net profit of $200,000, as the following calculation demonstrates:

$$\text{Sales volume required to earn target net profit of \$200,000} = \frac{\text{Fixed costs} + \text{Target net profit}}{\text{Unit contribution margin}}$$

$$= \frac{\$150{,}000 + \$200{,}000}{\$10} = 35{,}000 \text{ units}$$

What do these questions have in common? They both focus on *sales volume* as the sole revenue and cost driver. The CVP analysis depends on a distinction between costs that are fixed and costs that are variable *with respect to sales volume.*

A Move Toward JIT and Flexible Manufacturing

Learning Objective 10

Be aware of the effects of advanced manufacturing technology on CVP relationships.

Now let's examine another question AccuTime's management could face. Suppose management is considering the installation of a *flexible manufacturing system* and a move toward just-in-time (JIT) production. A flexible manufacturing system uses highly automated material-handling and production equipment to manufacture a variety of similar products. In the new production process, setups would be quicker and more frequent and production runs would be smaller. Fewer inspections would be required, due to the total quality control (TQC) philosophy that often accompanies JIT. Variable manufacturing costs would be lower, due to savings in direct labor. Finally, general factory overhead costs would increase, due to the greater depreciation charges on the new production equipment.

Suppose management wants to answer the same two questions addressed previously, under the assumption that the production process changes are adopted. To properly address this issue, we need a much more detailed understanding of the impact of other, *non-volume-based cost drivers* on AccuTime's costs. This type of detail is the hallmark of an activity-based costing system. Suppose AccuTime's controller completes an ABC analysis of the company's 20x1 activity before the new equipment is installed. The results are shown in Exhibit 7–9.

There is a subtle but important point to realize about the cost behavior depicted in Exhibit 7–9. Setup, inspection, and material handling are listed as fixed costs. *They are*

Pictured here is a production cell in a flexible manufacturing system engaged in the production of disks for computer hard disk drives. In such a high-tech manufacturing environment, setups are quicker and more frequent, and production runs are smaller. An activity-based costing CVP analysis will give management a better understanding of cost-volume-profit relationships.

Exhibit 7–9
Activity-Based Costing Data under Current Production Process (20x1)

Sales price	$25
Unit variable costs:	
Variable manufacturing	$14
Variable selling and administrative	1
Total unit variable costs	$15
Unit contribution margin	$10
Fixed costs (fixed with respect to sales volume):	
General factory overhead (including depreciation on plant and equipment)	$ 60,000
Setup (52 setups at $100 per setup)*	5,200
Inspection [(52)(21) inspections at $20 per inspection]†	21,840
Material handling (1,080 hours at $12 per hour)	12,960
Total fixed manufacturing costs	$100,000
Fixed selling and administrative costs	50,000
Total fixed costs	$150,000

*One setup per week.
†Three inspections per day, seven days a week (52 weeks per year).

largely fixed with respect to sales volume. However, they are *not* fixed with respect to *other cost drivers,* such as the number of setups, inspections, and hours of material handling. This is the fundamental distinction between a traditional CVP analysis and an activity-based costing CVP analysis. The traditional CVP analysis recognizes a single, volume-based cost driver, namely, sales volume. The activity-based costing CVP analysis recognizes multiple cost drivers. As a result, some costs viewed as fixed under the traditional analysis are considered variable (with respect to the appropriate cost drivers) under the ABC approach.

Now let's return to management's decision regarding the installation of a flexible manufacturing system and the adoption of the JIT and TQC philosophies. The activity-based costing analysis of the proposed production technology is displayed in Exhibit 7–10. Due to the decreased use of direct labor, the unit variable manufacturing cost has declined from $14 to $9, thus bringing the total unit variable cost down to $10. This results in an increase in the unit contribution margin to $15. The installation of sophisticated new manufacturing equipment has more than tripled general factory overhead, from $60,000 to $184,000. Under the proposed JIT approach, setups will be daily instead of weekly; each setup will be quicker and less expensive. As a result of the emphasis on total quality control, only one inspection per day will be necessary, instead of three as before. Moreover, each inspection will be less expensive. Finally, the amount of material-handling activity will decline dramatically, although there will be a slight increase in the cost per hour. This is due to the higher skill grade of labor required to operate the new automated material-handling system.

Using the ABC data in Exhibit 7–10, we can answer the two CVP questions posed by management. If the new production technology is adopted, the following CVP computations will be appropriate.

$$\text{Break-even point} = \frac{\text{Fixed costs}}{\text{Unit contribution margin}} = \frac{\$250{,}000}{\$15} = \begin{array}{c}\text{16,667 units}\\ \text{(rounded)}\end{array}$$

$$\begin{array}{c}\text{Sales volume required to earn}\\ \text{target net profit of \$200,000}\end{array} = \frac{\text{Fixed costs} + \text{Target net profit}}{\text{Unit contribution margin}}$$

$$= \frac{\$250{,}000 + \$200{,}000}{\$15} = 30{,}000 \text{ units}$$

Exhibit 7–10
Activity-Based Costing Data under Proposed Production Technology

Sales price	$25
Unit variable costs:	
Variable manufacturing	$ 9
Variable selling and administrative	1
Total unit variable costs	$10
Unit contribution margin	$15
Fixed costs (fixed with respect to sales volume):	
General factory overhead (including depreciation on plant and equipment)	$184,000
Setup (365 setups at $30 per setup)	10,950
Inspection (365 inspections at $10 per inspection)	3,650
Material handling (100 hours at $14 per hour)	1,400
Total fixed manufacturing costs	$200,000
Fixed selling and administrative costs	50,000
Total fixed costs	$250,000

Notice that AccuTime's break-even point increased with the introduction of the advanced manufacturing system (from 15,000 to 16,667 units). However, the number of sales units required to earn a target net profit of $200,000 declined (from 35,000 to 30,000 units). These kinds of CVP changes are typical when firms install an advanced manufacturing system. Typically, the cost structure of an advanced manufacturing environment is characterized by a lower proportion of variable costs and a larger proportion of costs that are fixed (with respect to sales volume).

ABC Provides a Richer Understanding of Cost Behavior and CVP Relationships The point of this section is that activity-based costing provides a richer description of a company's cost behavior. AccuTime's traditional costing system treated setup, inspection, and material handling as fixed costs. However, the ABC analysis showed that while these costs are largely fixed with respect to sales volume, they are not fixed with respect to other appropriate cost drivers. In analyzing the cost-volume-profit implications of the proposed changes in manufacturing technology, it was crucial to have an understanding of how these costs would change with respect to such cost drivers as the number of setups, number of quality-assurance inspections, and amount of material-handling activity.

Just as ABC can improve an organization's product-costing system, it also can facilitate a deeper understanding of cost behavior and CVP relationships.

Chapter Summary

LO1 Compute a break-even point using the contribution-margin approach and the equation approach. These two approaches result in the same general formula for computing the break-even point (in units). Under the equation approach, the profit equation is specified as follows: Sales revenue − Variable expenses − Fixed expenses = Profit. When this equation is manipulated, the contribution-margin approach to the break-even point results, as follows: Break-even point (in units) = Fixed expenses ÷ Unit contribution margin.

LO2 Compute the contribution-margin ratio and use it to find the break-even point in sales dollars. The contribution-margin ratio is defined as follows: Unit contribution margin ÷ Unit sales price. The break-even point (in sales dollars) can be computed as follows: Fixed expenses ÷ Contribution-margin ratio.

LO3 Prepare a cost-volume-profit (CVP) graph and explain how it is used. A cost-volume-profit graph shows the break-even point (in sales dollars) as the intersection of the total revenue line and the total expense line. The graph can be used to help management understand how changes in the volume of activity affect cost and profit.

LO4 Apply CVP analysis to determine the effect on profit of changes in fixed expenses, variable expenses, sales prices, and sales volume. Management can use the break-even equation to predict the effects on the break-even point of changes in any component of the equation, e.g., sales price, unit variable cost, fixed cost, and so forth. Such prediction can help management in making a variety of operational decisions.

LO5 Compute the break-even point and prepare a profit-volume graph for a multiproduct enterprise. Break-even analysis in a multiproduct firm is accomplished by computing a weighted-average contribution margin, which is based on the expected sales mix. The same break-even formulas are used as in a single-product analysis, except that the unit contribution margin is replaced by the weighted-average contribution margin. This analysis is limited by the assumption of a constant sales mix across the range of total sales volume.

LO6 List and discuss the key assumptions of CVP analysis. CVP analysis involves several key assumptions, which follow: (1) Total revenue is linear (i.e., a straight line) with respect to changes in the volume of activity. (2) Total expense is linear (i.e., a straight line) with respect to changes in the volume of activity. An implication of this assumption is that the efficiency and productivity of the production process remains constant. (3) The sales mix remains constant over the relevant range. (4) The beginning and ending inventory levels are the same in a manufacturing firm.

LO7 Prepare and interpret a contribution income statement. Cost-volume-profit relationships are important enough to operating managers that some firms prepare a contribution income statement. This income-statement format separates fixed and variable expenses and computes the aggregate contribution margin. This statement format helps managers discern the effects on profit from changes in volume. The contribution income statement also discloses an organization's cost structure, which is the relative proportion of its fixed and variable costs.

LO8 Explain the role of cost structure and operating leverage in CVP relationships. An organization's cost structure is the relative proportions of its fixed and variable costs. The extent to which an organization uses fixed costs in its cost structure is called operating leverage. Firms with high operating leverage tend to have higher break-even points, other things being equal.

LO9 Understand the implications of activity-based costing for CVP analysis. Activity-based costing (ABC) provides a richer description of an organization's cost behavior and CVP relationships than is provided by a traditional costing system. An ABC cost-volume-profit analysis recognizes that some costs that are fixed with respect to sales volume may not be fixed with respect to other important cost drivers. In many cases, management can benefit substantially from such an improved understanding of cost behavior and CVP relationships.

LO10 Be aware of the effects of advanced manufacturing technology on CVP relationships. Companies with advanced manufacturing technology tend to have higher fixed costs, lower variable costs, and higher break-even points.

LO11 Understand the effect of income taxes on CVP analysis (Appendix). When a firm is required to pay taxes on income, it is important to distinguish between after-tax (AT) income and before-tax (BT) income. AT income is equal to BT income minus income tax expense. Therefore, BT income is equal to AT income ÷ (1 − tax rate). The number of units of sales required to earn a specified AT income is equal to (BT income + fixed expenses) ÷ unit contribution margin.

Review Problem on Cost-Volume-Profit Analysis

Overlook Inn is a small bed-and-breakfast inn located in the Great Smoky Mountains of Tennessee. The charge is $50 per person for one night's lodging and a full breakfast in the morning. The retired couple who own and manage the inn estimate that the variable expense per person is $20. This includes such expenses as food, maid service, and utilities. The inn's fixed expenses total $42,000 per year. The inn can accommodate 10 guests each night.

Required: Compute the following:

1. Contribution margin per unit of service. (A unit of service is one night's lodging for one guest.)
2. Contribution-margin ratio.

3. Annual break-even point in units of service and in dollars of service revenue.
4. The number of units of service required to earn a target net profit of $60,000 for the year. (Ignore income taxes.)

Solution to Review Problem

1. Contribution margin per unit of service = Nightly room charge − Variable expense per person

$$\$30 = \$50 - \$20$$

2. $$\text{Contribution-margin ratio} = \frac{\text{Contribution margin per unit}}{\text{Nightly room charge}}$$

$$.60 = \frac{\$30}{\$50}$$

3. $$\frac{\text{Break-even point}}{\text{in units of service}} = \frac{\text{Fixed expenses}}{\text{Contribution margin per unit}}$$

$$1{,}400 = \frac{\$42{,}000}{\$30}$$

$$\text{Break-even point in dollars of revenue} = \frac{\text{Fixed expenses}}{\text{Contribution-margin ratio}}$$

$$\$70{,}000 = \frac{\$42{,}000}{.60}$$

4. $$\text{Number of units of service required to earn target net profit} = \frac{\text{Fixed expenses} + \text{Target net profit}}{\text{Contribution margin per unit of service}}$$

$$3{,}400 = \frac{\$42{,}000 + \$60{,}000}{\$30}$$

Key Terms

For each term's definition refer to the indicated page, or turn to the glossary at the end of the text.

after-tax net income,* 304
before-tax income,* 304
break-even point, 278
contribution income statement, 293
contribution-margin ratio, 279
cost structure, 295
cost-volume-profit (CVP) analysis, 276
cost-volume-profit (CVP) graph, 280
operating leverage, 296
operating leverage factor, 296
profit-volume graph, 283
safety margin, 285
sales mix, 290
sensitivity analysis, 292
target net profit (or **income**), **284**
total contribution margin, 287
unit contribution margin, 279
weighted-average unit contribution margin, 290

*Term appears in the appendix.

APPENDIX TO CHAPTER 7

Effect of Income Taxes

Learning Objective 11

Understand the effect of income taxes on CVP analysis (Appendix).

Profit-seeking enterprises must pay income taxes on their profits. A firm's **after-tax net income,** the amount of income remaining after subtracting the firm's income-tax expense, is less than its **before-tax income.** This fact is expressed in the following formula.

$$(\text{After-tax net income}) = (\text{Before-tax income}) - t(\text{Before-tax income})$$

where t denotes the income-tax rate.

Rearranging this equation yields the following formula.

$$(\text{After-tax net income}) = (\text{Before-tax income})(1 - t) \qquad (9)$$

To illustrate this formula, suppose AccuTime Company must pay income taxes of 40 percent of its before-tax income. The company's contribution income statement for 20x1 appears below.

Sales, 20,000 units at $25 each	$500,000
Variable expenses, 20,000 units at $15 each*	300,000
Contribution margin	$200,000
Fixed expenses	150,000
Income before taxes	$ 50,000
Income-tax expense, .40 × $50,000	20,000
Net income, $50,000 × (1 − .40)	$ 30,000

*Variable cost per unit is $15: variable manufacturing cost of $14 plus variable selling and administrative costs of $1.

The requirement that companies pay income taxes affects their cost-volume-profit relationships. To earn a particular after-tax net income will require greater before-tax income than if there were no tax. For example, if AccuTime's target after-tax net income were $30,000, the company would have to earn before-tax income of $50,000. AccuTime's income statement shows this relationship.

How much before-tax income must be earned in order to achieve a particular target after-tax net income? Rearranging equation (9) above yields the following formula.

$$\text{Target after-tax net income} = \begin{pmatrix}\text{Target} \\ \text{before-tax} \\ \text{income}\end{pmatrix}(1 - t)$$

Divide both sides by $(1 - t)$

$$\frac{\text{Target after-tax net income}}{1 - t} = \begin{pmatrix}\text{Target} \\ \text{before-tax} \\ \text{income}\end{pmatrix}\frac{1 - t}{1 - t}$$

$$\frac{\text{Target after-tax net income}}{1 - t} = \text{Target before-tax income}$$

If AccuTime Company's target after-tax net income is $30,000, its target before-tax income is calculated as follows:

$$\frac{\text{Target after-tax net income}}{1 - t} = \frac{\$30{,}000}{1 - .40} = \$50{,}000 = \text{Target before-tax income}$$

Now we are in a position to compute the number of digital clocks that AccuTime must sell in order to achieve a particular after-tax net income. We begin with the following before-tax income equation.

$$\text{Sales} - \text{Variable expenses} - \text{Fixed expenses} = \text{Before-tax income}$$

Now we use our formula for before-tax income.

$$\text{Sales} - \text{Variable expenses} - \text{Fixed expenses} = \frac{\text{After-tax net income}}{1 - t}$$

$$\left[\begin{pmatrix}\text{Unit} \\ \text{sales} \\ \text{price}\end{pmatrix} \times \begin{pmatrix}\text{Sales} \\ \text{volume} \\ \text{in units}\end{pmatrix}\right] - \left[\begin{pmatrix}\text{Unit} \\ \text{variable} \\ \text{expense}\end{pmatrix} \times \begin{pmatrix}\text{Sales} \\ \text{volume} \\ \text{in units}\end{pmatrix}\right] - \begin{pmatrix}\text{Fixed} \\ \text{expenses}\end{pmatrix} = \frac{\text{After-tax net income}}{1 - t}$$

Using the data for AccuTime Company, and assuming target after-tax net income of $30,000:

$$(\$25 \times X) - (\$15 \times X) - \$150{,}000 = \frac{\$30{,}000}{1 - .40}$$

where X denotes the number of units that must be sold to achieve the target after-tax net income.

Now we solve for X as follows:

$$\underbrace{(\$25 - \$15)}\times X = \$150{,}000 + \frac{\$30{,}000}{1 - .40}$$

$$\$10 \times X = \$150{,}000 + \frac{\$30{,}000}{1 - .40}$$

$$X = \frac{\$150{,}000 + \dfrac{\$30{,}000}{1 - .40}}{\$10}$$

$$= 20{,}000 \text{ units}$$

In terms of sales revenue, AccuTime must achieve a sales volume of \$500,000 (20,000 units × \$25 sales price). We can verify these calculations by examining AccuTime's income statement given previously.

Notice in the calculations above that \$10 is the unit contribution margin (\$25 sales price minus \$15 variable expense). Thus, the general formula illustrated above is the following:

$$\begin{array}{c}\text{Number of units of sales}\\ \text{required to earn target}\\ \text{after-tax net income}\end{array} = \frac{\text{Fixed expenses} + \dfrac{\text{Target after-tax net income}}{1 - t}}{\text{Unit contribution margin}}$$

where t denotes the income tax rate.

Exhibit 7–11
Cost-Volume-Profit Graph (with income taxes)

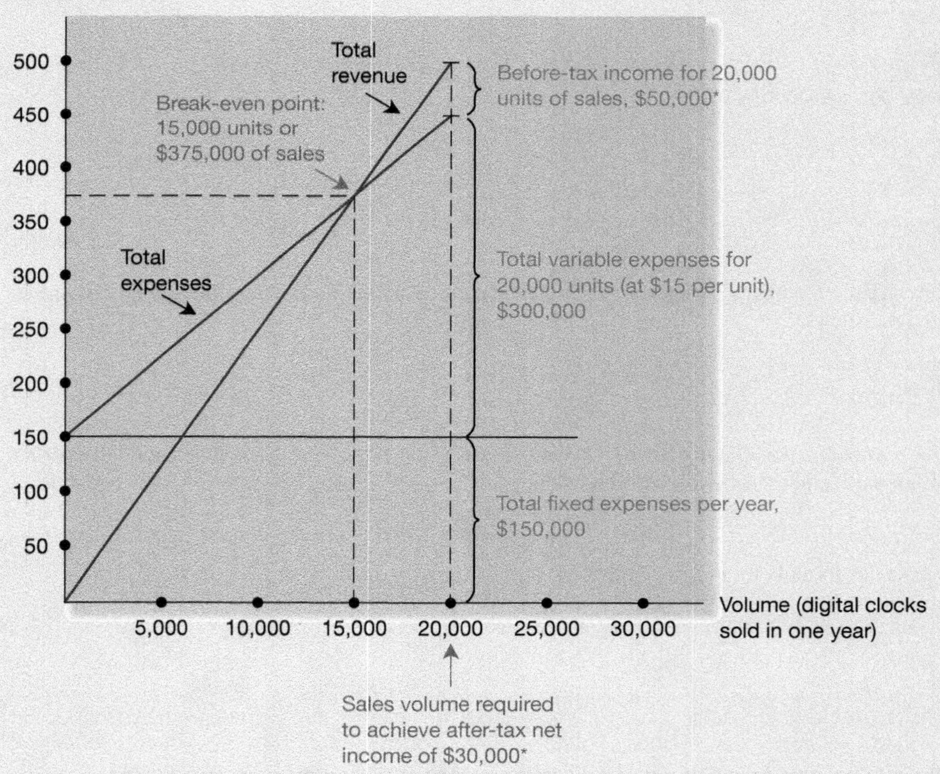

A cost-volume-profit graph for AccuTime Company is displayed in Exhibit 7–11. As the graph shows, 20,000 units must be sold to achieve $30,000 in after-tax net income. The company's break-even point is 15,000 units. The break-even point is not affected by income taxes, because at the break-even point, there is no income.

Notice that AccuTime Company must sell 5,000 units *beyond the break-even point* in order to achieve after-tax net income of $30,000. Each unit sold beyond the break-even point contributes $10 toward *before-tax* income. However, of that $10 contribution margin, $4 will have to be paid in income taxes. This leaves an *after-tax contribution* of $6 toward after-tax net income. Thus, selling 5,000 units beyond the break-even point results in after-tax net income of $30,000 (5,000 units × $6 after-tax contribution per unit).

Review Questions

7–1. Briefly explain each of the following methods of computing a break-even point in units: (*a*) contribution-margin approach, (*b*) equation approach, and (*c*) graphical approach.

7–2. What is the meaning of the term *unit contribution margin?* Contribution to what?

7–3. What information is conveyed by a cost-volume-profit graph in addition to a company's break-even point?

7–4. What does the term *safety margin* mean?

7–5. Suppose the fixed expenses of a travel agency increase. What will happen to its break-even point, measured in number of clients served? Why?

7–6. Delmarva Oyster Company has been able to decrease its variable expenses per pound of oysters harvested. How will this affect the firm's break-even sales volume?

7–7. In a strategy meeting, a manufacturing company's president said, "If we raise the price of our product, the company's break-even point will be lower." The financial vice president responded by saying, "Then we should raise our price. The company will be less likely to incur a loss." Do you agree with the president? Why? Do you agree with the financial vice president? Why?

7–8. What will happen to a company's break-even point if the sales price and unit variable cost of its only product increase by the same dollar amount?

7–9. An art museum covers its operating expenses by charging a small admission fee. The objective of the nonprofit organization is to break even. A local arts enthusiast has just pledged an annual donation of $10,000 to the museum. How will the donation affect the museum's break-even attendance level?

7–10. How can a profit-volume graph be used to predict a company's profit for a particular sales volume?

7–11. List the most important assumptions of cost-volume-profit analysis.

7–12. Why do many operating managers prefer a contribution income statement instead of a traditional income statement?

7–13. What is the difference between a manufacturing company's *gross margin* and its total *contribution margin?*

7–14. East Company manufactures VCRs using a completely automated production process. West Company also manufactures VCRs, but its products are assembled manually. How will these two firms' cost structures differ? Which company will have a higher operating leverage factor?

7–15. When sales volume increases, which company will experience a larger percentage increase in profit: company X, which has mostly fixed expenses, or company Y, which has mostly variable expenses?

7–16. What does the term *sales mix* mean? How is a *weighted-average unit contribution margin* computed?

7–17. A car rental agency rents subcompact, compact, and full-size automobiles. What assumptions would be made about the agency's sales mix for the purpose of a cost-volume-profit analysis?

7–18. How can a hotel's management use cost-volume-profit analysis to help in deciding on room rates?

7–19. How could cost-volume-profit analysis be used in budgeting? In making a decision about advertising?

7–20. Two companies have identical fixed expenses, unit variable expenses, and profits. Yet one company has set a much lower price for its product. Explain how this can happen.

7–21. A company with an advanced manufacturing environment typically will have a higher break-even point, greater operating leverage, and larger safety margin than a labor-intensive firm. True or false? Explain.

7–22. Explain briefly how activity-based costing (ABC) affects cost-volume-profit analysis.

Exercises

Exercise 7–23
Fill in Blanks; Basic CVP Relationships
(LO 1, 2)

Fill in the missing data for each of the following independent cases. (Ignore income taxes.)

	Sales Revenue	Variable Expenses	Total Contribution Margin	Fixed Expenses	Net Income	Break-Even Sales Revenue
1.	?	$40,000	?	$30,000	?	$40,000
2.	$ 80,000	?	$15,000	?	?	80,000
3.	?	40,000	80,000	?	$50,000	?
4.	110,000	22,000	?	?	38,000	?

Exercise 7–24
Pizza Delivery Business; Basic CVP Analysis
(LO 1, 2, 4)

College Pizza delivers pizzas to the dormitories and apartments near a major state university. The company's annual fixed expenses are $40,000. The sales price of a pizza is $10, and it costs the company $5 to make and deliver each pizza. (In the following requirements, ignore income taxes.)

Required:

1. Using the contribution-margin approach, compute the company's break-even point in units (pizzas).
2. What is the contribution-margin ratio?
3. Compute the break-even sales revenue. Use the contribution-margin ratio in your calculation.
4. How many pizzas must the company sell to earn a target net profit of $65,000? Use the equation method.

Exercise 7–25
Manufacturing; Using CVP Analysis
(LO 1, 4)

Rosario Company, which is located in Buenos Aires, Argentina, manufactures a component used in farm machinery. The firm's fixed costs are 4,000,000 *p* per year. The variable cost of each component is 2,000 *p,* and the components are sold for 3,000 *p* each. The company sold 5,000 components during the prior year. (*p* denotes the peso, Argentina's national currency. Several countries use the peso as their monetary unit. On the day this exercise was written, Argentina's peso was worth .327 U.S. dollar. In the following requirements, ignore income taxes.)

Required: Answer requirements (1) through (4) independently.

1. Compute the break-even point in units.
2. What will the new break-even point be if fixed costs increase by 10 percent?
3. What was the company's net income for the prior year?
4. The sales manager believes that a reduction in the sales price to 2,500 *p* will result in orders for 1,200 more components each year. What will the break-even point be if the price is changed?
5. Should the price change discussed in requirement (4) be made?

Exercise 7–26
Sports Franchise; CVP Graph
(LO 3, 4)

The Houston Armadillos, a minor-league baseball team, play their weekly games in a small stadium just outside Houston. The stadium holds 10,000 people and tickets sell for $10 each. The franchise owner estimates that the team's annual fixed expenses are $180,000, and the variable expense per ticket sold is $1. (In the following requirements, ignore income taxes.)

Required:

1. Draw a cost-volume-profit graph for the sports franchise. Label the axes, break-even point, profit and loss areas, fixed expenses, variable expenses, total-expense line, and total-revenue line.
2. If the stadium is half full for each game, how many games must the team play to break even?

Exercise 7–27
Continuation of Preceding Exercise; Profit-Volume Graph; Safety Margin
(LO 3, 4)

Refer to the data given in the preceding exercise. (Ignore income taxes.)

Required:

1. Prepare a fully labeled profit-volume graph for the Houston Armadillos.
2. What is the safety margin for the baseball franchise if the team plays a 12-game season and the team owner expects the stadium to be 30 percent full for each game?
3. If the stadium is half full for each game, what ticket price would the team have to charge in order to break even?

Exercise 7–28
Publishing; Contribution Income Statement
(LO 7, 8)

Europa Publications, Inc. specializes in reference books that keep abreast of the rapidly changing political and economic issues in Europe. The results of the company's operations during the prior year are given in the following table. All units produced during the year were sold. (Ignore income taxes.)

Sales revenue	$2,000,000
Manufacturing costs:	
Fixed	500,000
Variable	1,000,000
Selling costs:	
Fixed	50,000
Variable	100,000
Administrative costs:	
Fixed	120,000
Variable	30,000

Required:

1. Prepare a traditional income statement and a contribution income statement for the company.
2. What is the firm's operating leverage for the sales volume generated during the prior year?
3. Suppose sales revenue increases by 10 percent. What will be the percentage increase in net income?
4. Which income statement would an operating manager use to answer requirement (3)? Why?

Exercise 7–29
Retail; CVP Analysis with Multiple Products
(LO 1, 2, 5)

Tim's Bicycle Shop sells 21-speed bicycles. For purposes of a cost-volume-profit analysis, the shop owner has divided sales into two categories, as follows:

Product Type	Sales Price	Invoice Cost	Sales Commission
High-quality	$500	$275	$25
Medium-quality	300	135	15

Three-quarters of the shop's sales are medium-quality bikes. The shop's annual fixed expenses are $65,000. (In the following requirements, ignore income taxes.)

Required:

1. Compute the unit contribution margin for each product type.
2. What is the shop's sales mix?
3. Compute the weighted-average unit contribution margin, assuming a constant sales mix.
4. What is the shop's break-even sales volume in dollars? Assume a constant sales mix.
5. How many bicycles of each type must be sold to earn a target net income of $48,750? Assume a constant sales mix.

Exercise 7–30
Cost-Volume-Profit Analysis in an Airline; Use of Internet
(LO 4)

Use the Internet to access the Website of one of these airlines, or a different airline of your choosing.

American Airlines	www.aa.com
British Airways	www.britishairways.com
Delta Air Lines	www.delta.com
Northwest Airlines	www.nwa.com
Southwest Airlines	www.southwest.com

Required: Find the company's most recent annual report. Does the management discussion in the report disclose the airline's break-even load factor? If so, what is it for the most recent year reported?

Exercise 7–31
Hotel and Restaurant; Cost Structure and Operating Leverage
(LO 4, 8)

A contribution income statement for the Nantucket Inn is shown below. (Ignore income taxes.)

Revenue	$500,000
Less: Variable expenses	300,000
Contribution margin	$200,000
Less: Fixed expenses	150,000
Net income	$ 50,000

Required:

1. Show the hotel's cost structure by indicating the percentage of the hotel's revenue represented by each item on the income statement.
2. Suppose the hotel's revenue declines by 15 percent. Use the contribution-margin percentage to calculate the resulting decrease in net income.
3. What is the hotel's operating leverage factor when revenue is $500,000?
4. Use the operating leverage factor to calculate the increase in net income resulting from a 20 percent increase in sales revenue.

Exercise 7–32
Continuation of Preceding Exercise
(LO 4, 7)

Refer to the income statement given in the preceding exercise. Prepare a new contribution income statement for the Nantucket Inn in each of the following independent situations. (Ignore income taxes.)

1. The hotel's volume of activity increases by 20 percent, and fixed expenses increase by 40 percent.
2. The ratio of variable expenses to revenue doubles. There is no change in the hotel's volume of activity. Fixed expenses decline by $25,000.

Exercise 7–33
Consulting Firm; CVP Analysis with Income Taxes (Appendix)
(LO 1, 4, 11)

Hydro Systems Engineering Associates, Inc. provides consulting services to city water authorities. The consulting firm's contribution-margin ratio is 20 percent, and its annual fixed expenses are $120,000. The firm's income-tax rate is 40 percent.

Required:

1. Calculate the firm's break-even volume of service revenue.
2. How much before-tax income must the firm earn to make an after-tax net income of $48,000?
3. What level of revenue for consulting services must the firm generate to earn an after-tax net income of $48,000?
4. Suppose the firm's income-tax rate rises to 45 percent. What will happen to the break-even level of consulting service revenue?

Problems

All applicable Problems are available with McGraw-Hill's *Connect Accounting*™. 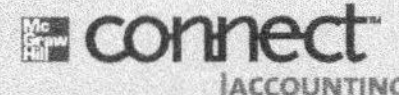

Problem 7–34
Basic CVP Relationships; Retailer
(LO 1, 2, 4)

2. Net income: $280,000

Disk City, Inc. is a retailer for digital video disks. The projected net income for the current year is $200,000 based on a sales volume of 200,000 video disks. Disk City has been selling the disks for $16 each. The variable costs consist of the $10 unit purchase price of the disks and a handling cost of $2 per disk. Disk City's annual fixed costs are $600,000.

Management is planning for the coming year, when it expects that the unit purchase price of the video disks will increase 30 percent. (Ignore income taxes.)

Required:

1. Calculate Disk city's break-even point for the current year in number of video disks.
2. What will be the company's net income for the current year if there is a 10 percent increase in projected unit sales volume?
3. What volume of sales (in dollars) must Disk City achieve in the coming year to maintain the same net income as projected for the current year if the unit selling price remains at $16?
4. In order to cover a 30 percent increase in the disk's purchase price for the coming year and still maintain the current contribution-margin ratio, what selling price per disk must Disk City establish for the coming year?
5. *Build a spreadsheet:* Construct an Excel spreadsheet to solve requirements (1), (2), and (3) above. Show how the solution will change if the following information changes: the selling price is $17 and the annual fixed costs are $640,000.

(CMA, adapted)

Problem 7–35
Basic CVP Computations
(LO 1, 2, 4)

2. Sales units required for $180,000 income: 54,000 units

CollegePak Company produced and sold 60,000 backpacks during the year just ended at an average price of $20 per unit. Variable manufacturing costs were $8 per unit, and variable marketing costs were $4 per unit sold. Fixed costs amounted to $180,000 for manufacturing and $72,000 for marketing. There was no year-end work-in-process inventory. (Ignore income taxes.)

Required:

1. Compute CollegePak's break-even point in sales dollars for the year.
2. Compute the number of sales units required to earn a net income of $180,000 during the year.
3. CollegePak's variable manufacturing costs are expected to increase by 10 percent in the coming year. Compute the firm's break-even point in sales dollars for the coming year.
4. If CollegePak's variable manufacturing costs do increase by 10 percent, compute the selling price that would yield the same contribution-margin ratio in the coming year.

(CMA, adapted)

Problem 7–36
CVP Relationships; Indifference Point
(LO 1, 4)

2. Net income, model no. 4399: $1,094,400

Corrigan Enterprises is studying the acquisition of two electrical component insertion systems for producing its sole product, the universal gismo. Data relevant to the systems follow.

Model no. 6754:

Variable costs, $16.00 per unit
Annual fixed costs, $985,600

Model no. 4399:

Variable costs, $12.80 per unit
Annual fixed costs, $1,113,600

Corrigan's selling price is $64 per unit for the universal gismo, which is subject to a 5 percent sales commission. (In the following requirements, ignore income taxes.)

Required:

1. How many units must the company sell to break even if Model 6754 is selected?
2. Which of the two systems would be more profitable if sales and production are expected to average 46,000 units per year?
3. Assume Model 4399 requires the purchase of additional equipment that is not reflected in the preceding figures. The equipment will cost $450,000 and will be depreciated over a five-year life by the straight-line method. How many units must Corrigan sell to earn $956,400 of income if Model 4399 is selected? As in requirement (2), sales and production are expected to average 46,000 units per year.
4. Ignoring the information presented in requirement (3), at what volume level will management be indifferent between the acquisition of Model no. 6754 and Model no. 4399? In other words, at what volume level will the annual total cost of each system be equal? (*Hint:* At any given sales volume, sales commissions will be the same amount regardless of which model is selected.)

Problem 7–37
CVP Analysis; Impact of Operating Changes
(LO 1, 4)

2. Break-even point: 32,000 units

Houston-based Advanced Electronics manufactures audio speakers for desktop computers. The following data relate to the period just ended when the company produced and sold 42,000 speaker sets:

Sales	$3,360,000
Variable costs	840,000
Fixed costs	2,280,000

Management is considering relocating its manufacturing facilities to northern Mexico to reduce costs. Variable costs are expected to average $18 per set; annual fixed costs are anticipated to be $1,984,000. (In the following requirements, ignore income taxes.)

Required:

1. Calculate the company's current income and determine the level of dollar sales needed to double that figure, assuming that manufacturing operations remain in the United States.
2. Determine the break-even point in speaker sets if operations are shifted to Mexico.
3. Assume that management desires to achieve the Mexican break-even point; however, operations will remain in the United States.
   a. If variable costs remain constant, what must management do to fixed costs? By how much must fixed costs change?
   b. If fixed costs remain constant, what must management do to the variable cost per unit? By how much must unit variable cost change?
4. Determine the impact (increase, decrease, or no effect) of the following operating changes.
   a. Effect of an increase in direct material costs on the break-even point.
   b. Effect of an increase in fixed administrative costs on the unit contribution margin.
   c. Effect of an increase in the unit contribution margin on net income.
   d. Effect of a decrease in the number of units sold on the break-even point.

Problem 7–38
Sales Mix and Employee Compensation; Operating Changes
(LO 4, 5)

2(c). Commissions, total: $535,600

Lawrence Corporation sells two ceiling fans, Deluxe and Basic. Current sales total 60,000 units, consisting of 39,000 Deluxe units and 21,000 Basic units. Selling price and variable cost information follow.

	Deluxe	Basic
Selling price	$86	$74
Variable cost	65	41

Salespeople currently receive flat salaries that total $400,000. Management is contemplating a change to a compensation plan that is based on commissions in an effort to boost the company's presence in the marketplace. Two plans are under consideration:

Plan A: 10% commission computed on gross dollar sales. Deluxe sales are expected to total 45,500 units; Basic sales are anticipated to be 19,500 units.

Plan B: 30% commission computed on the basis of production contribution margins. Deluxe sales are anticipated to be 26,000 units; Basic sales are expected to total 39,000 units.

Required:

1. Define the term *sales mix.*
2. Comparing Plan A to the current compensation arrangement:
   a. Will Plan A achieve management's objective of an increased presence in the marketplace? Briefly explain.
   b. From a sales-mix perspective, will the salespeople be promoting the product that one would logically expect? Briefly discuss.
   c. Will the sales force likely be satisfied with the results of Plan A? Why?
   d. Will Lawrence likely be satisfied with the resulting impact of Plan A on company profitability? Why?
3. Assume that Plan B is under consideration.
   a. Compare Plan A and Plan B with respect to total units sold and the sales mix. Comment on the results.
   b. In comparison with flat salaries, is Plan B more attractive to the sales force? To the company? Show calculations to support your answers.

Problem 7–39
Leverage; Analysis of Operating Change
(LO 1, 4, 8)

1. Plan B break-even point: 2,200 units
3. Operating leverage factor, plan A: 1.2

Consolidated Industries is studying the addition of a new valve to its product line. The valve would be used by manufacturers of irrigation equipment. The company anticipates starting with a relatively low sales volume and then boosting demand over the next several years. A new salesperson must be hired because Consolidated's current sales force is working at capacity. Two compensation plans are under consideration:

Plan A: An annual salary of $22,000 plus a 10% commission based on gross dollar sales.

Plan B: An annual salary of $66,000 and no commission.

Consolidated Industries will purchase the valve for $50 and sell it for $80. Anticipated demand during the first year is 6,000 units. (In the following requirements, ignore income taxes.)

Required:

1. Compute the break-even point for Plan A and Plan B.
2. What is meant by the term *operating leverage*?
3. Analyze the cost structures of both plans at the anticipated demand of 6,000 units. Which of the two plans has a higher operating leverage factor?
4. Assume that a general economic downturn occurred during year 2, with product demand falling from 6,000 to 5,000 units. Determine the percentage decrease in company net income if Consolidated had adopted Plan A.
5. Repeat requirement (4) for Plan B. Compare Plan A and Plan B, and explain a major factor that underlies any resulting differences.
6. Briefly discuss the likely profitability impact of an economic recession for highly automated manufacturers. What can you say about the risk associated with these firms?

Problem 7–40
Basic CVP Relationships
(LO 1, 2, 4)

3. Sales units required for target net profit: 140,000 units
6. Old contribution-margin ratio: .208

Serendipity Sound, Inc. manufactures and sells compact discs. Price and cost data are as follows:

Selling price per unit (package of two CDs)	$25.00
Variable costs per unit:	
Direct material	$10.50
Direct labor	5.00
Manufacturing overhead	3.00
Selling expenses	1.30
Total variable costs per unit	$19.80
Annual fixed costs:	
Manufacturing overhead	$ 192,000
Selling and administrative	276,000
Total fixed costs	$ 468,000
Forecasted annual sales volume (120,000 units)	$ 3,000,000

In the following requirements, ignore income taxes.

Required:

1. What is Serendipity Sound's break-even point in units?
2. What is the company's break-even point in sales dollars?
3. How many units would Serendipity Sound have to sell in order to earn $260,000?
4. What is the firm's margin of safety?
5. Management estimates that direct-labor costs will increase by 8 percent next year. How many units will the company have to sell next year to reach its break-even point?
6. If the company's direct-labor costs do increase by 8 percent, what selling price per unit of product must it charge to maintain the same contribution-margin ratio?

(CMA, adapted)

Problem 7–41
CVP Graph; Cost Structure; Operating Leverage
(LO 2, 3, 4, 8)

3. Margin of safety: $4,000,000

Athletico, Inc. manufactures warm-up suits. The company's projected income for the coming year, based on sales of 160,000 units, is as follows:

Sales		$8,000,000
Operating expenses:		
Variable expenses	$2,000,000	
Fixed expenses	3,000,000	
Total expenses		5,000,000
Net income		$3,000,000

Required: In completing the following requirements, ignore income taxes.

1. Prepare a CVP graph for Athletico, Inc. for the coming year.
2. Calculate the firm's break-even point for the year in sales dollars.
3. What is the company's margin of safety for the year?
4. Compute Athletico's operating leverage factor, based on the budgeted sales volume for the year.
5. Compute Athletico's required sales in dollars in order to earn income of $4,500,000 in the coming year.
6. Describe the firm's cost structure. Calculate the percentage relationships between variable and fixed expenses and sales revenue.

(CMA, adapted)

Problem 7–42
Break-Even Point; After-Tax Net Income; Profit-Volume Graph; International Issues (Appendix)
(LO 1, 2, 3, 4, 11)

3. Break-even point (units): 80,500 units

The European Division of Worldwide Reference Corporation produces a pocket dictionary containing popular phrases in six European languages. Annual budget data for the coming year follow. Projected sales are 100,000 books.

Sales			$1,000,000
Costs:	**Fixed**	**Variable**	
Direct material	$ –0–	$300,000	
Direct labor	–0–	200,000	
Manufacturing overhead	100,000	150,000	
Selling and administrative	110,000	50,000	
Total costs	$210,000	$700,000	910,000
Budgeted operating income			$ 90,000

Required:

1. Calculate the break-even point in units and in sales dollars.
2. If the European Division is subject to an income-tax rate of 40 percent, compute the number of units the company would have to sell to earn an after-tax profit of $90,000.
3. If fixed costs increased $31,500 with no other cost or revenue factor changing, compute the firm's break-even sales in units.
4. Prepare a profit-volume graph for the European Division.
5. Due to an unstable political situation in the country in which the European Division is located, management believes the country may split into two independent nations. If this happens, the tax rate could rise to 50 percent. Assuming all other data as in the original problem, how many pocket dictionaries must be sold to earn $90,000 after taxes?
6. *Build a spreadsheet:* Construct an Excel spreadsheet to solve requirements (1), (2), (3), and (5) above. Show how the solution will change if the following information changes: sales amounted to $1,100,000 and fixed manufacturing overhead was $110,000.

(CMA, adapted)

Problem 7–43
Break-Even Point; Safety Margin; Law Firm
(LO 1, 4)

1. Total fixed expenses: $1,491,980
2. Safety margin: $1,167,000

Terry Smith and two of his colleagues are considering opening a law office in a large metropolitan area that would make inexpensive legal services available to those who could not otherwise afford services. The intent is to provide easy access for their clients by having the office open 360 days per year, 16 hours each day from 7:00 a.m. to 11:00 p.m. The office would be staffed by a lawyer, paralegal, legal secretary, and clerk-receptionist for each of the two eight-hour shifts.

In order to determine the feasibility of the project, Smith hired a marketing consultant to assist with market projections. The results of this study show that if the firm spends $490,000 on advertising the first year, the number of new clients expected each day will be 50. Smith and his associates believe this number is reasonable and are prepared to spend the $490,000 on advertising. Other pertinent information about the operation of the office follows:

- The only charge to each new client would be $30 for the initial consultation. All cases that warrant further legal work will be accepted on a contingency basis with the firm earning 30 percent of any favorable settlements or judgments. Smith estimates that 20 percent of new client consultations will result in favorable settlements or judgments averaging $2,000 each. It is not expected that there will be repeat clients during the first year of operations.
- The hourly wages of the staff are projected to be $25 for the lawyer, $20 for the paralegal, $15 for the legal secretary, and $10 for the clerk-receptionist. Fringe benefit expense will be 40 percent of the wages paid. A total of 400 hours of overtime is expected for the year; this will be divided equally between the legal secretary and the clerk-receptionist positions. Overtime will be paid at one and one-half times the regular wage, and the fringe benefit expense will apply to the full wage.
- Smith has located 6,000 square feet of suitable office space that rents for $28 per square foot annually. Asssociated expenses will be $27,000 for property insurance and $37,000 for utilities.
- It will be necessary for the group to purchase malpractice insurance, which is expected to cost $180,000 annually.
- The initial investment in the office equipment will be $60,000. This equipment has an estimated useful life of four years.
- The cost of office supplies has been estimated to be $4 per expected new client consultation.

Required:

1. Determine how many new clients must visit the law office being considered by Terry Smith and his colleagues in order for the venture to break even during its first year of operations.
2. Compute the law firm's safety margin.

(CMA, adapted)

Problem 7–44
Break-Even Analysis; Operating Leverage; New Manufacturing Environment
(LO 1, 8, 10)

1(a). Computer-assisted manufacturing system, break-even point: 210,000 units

Celestial Products, Inc. has decided to introduce a new product, which can be manufactured by either a computer-assisted manufacturing system or a labor-intensive production system. The manufacturing method will not affect the quality of the product. The estimated manufacturing costs by the two methods are as follows:

	Computer-Assisted Manufacturing System		Labor-Intensive Production System	
Direct material		$5.00		$5.60
Direct labor (DLH denotes direct-labor hours)	.5DLH @ $12	6.00	.8DLH @ $9	7.20
Variable overhead	.5DLH @ $6	3.00	.8DLH @ $6	4.80
Fixed overhead*		$2,440,000		$1,320,000

*These costs are directly traceable to the new product line. They would not be incurred if the new product were not produced.

The company's marketing research department has recommended an introductory unit sales price of $30. Selling expenses are estimated to be $500,000 annually plus $2 for each unit sold. (Ignore income taxes.)

Required:

1. Calculate the estimated break-even point in annual unit sales of the new product if the company uses the (*a*) computer-assisted manufacturing system; (*b*) labor-intensive production system.
2. Determine the annual unit sales volume at which the firm would be indifferent between the two manufacturing methods.
3. Management must decide which manufacturing method to employ. One factor it should consider is operating leverage. Explain the concept of operating leverage. How is this concept related to Celestial Products' decision?
4. Describe the circumstances under which the firm should employ each of the two manufacturing methods.
5. Identify some business factors other than operating leverage that management should consider before selecting the manufacturing method.

(CMA, adapted)

Problem 7–45
Break-Even Analysis; Profit-Volume Graph; Movie Theaters
(LO 1, 3, 4)

1. Break-even sales volume, regular model: 27,500 tubs
3. Volume at which both machines produce same profit: 37,500 tubs

Silver Screen, Inc. owns and operates a nationwide chain of movie theaters. The 500 properties in the Silver Screen chain vary from low-volume, small-town, single-screen theaters to high-volume, urban, multiscreen theaters. The firm's management is considering installing popcorn machines, which would allow the theaters to sell freshly popped corn rather than prepopped corn. This new feature would be advertised to increase patronage at the company's theaters. The fresh popcorn will be sold for $1.75 per tub. The annual rental costs and the operating costs vary with the size of the popcorn machines. The machine capacities and costs are shown below. (Ignore income taxes.)

	Popper Model		
	Economy	**Regular**	**Super**
Annual capacity	45,000 tubs	90,000 tubs	140,000 tubs
Costs:			
Annual machine rental	$8,000	$11,000	$20,000
Popcorn cost per tub	.13	.13	.13
Other costs per tub	1.22	1.14	1.05
Cost of each tub	.08	.08	.08

Required:

1. Calculate each theater's break-even sales volume (measured in tubs of popcorn) for each model of popcorn popper.
2. Prepare a profit-volume graph for one theater, assuming that the Super Popper is purchased.
3. Calculate the volume (in tubs) at which the Economy Popper and the Regular Popper earn the same profit or loss in each movie theater.

(CMA, adapted)

Problem 7–46
CVP Analysis of Changes in Sales Prices and Costs
(LO 1, 4)

3. New break-even point: 19,125 units
5. New contribution-margin ratio: .40 (rounded)

Jupiter Game Company manufactures pocket electronic games. Last year Jupiter sold 25,000 games at $25 each. Total costs amounted to $525,000, of which $150,000 were considered fixed.

In an attempt to improve its product, the company is considering replacing a component part that has a cost of $2.50 with a new and better part costing $4.50 per unit in the coming year. A new machine also would be needed to increase plant capacity. The machine would cost $18,000 with a useful life of six years and no salvage value. The company uses straight-line depreciation on all plant assets. (Ignore income taxes.)

Required:

1. What was Jupiter's break-even point in number of units last year?
2. How many units of product would the company have had to sell in the last year to earn $140,000?
3. If management holds the sales price constant and makes the suggested changes, how many units of product must be sold in the coming year to break even?
4. If the firm holds the sales price constant and makes the suggested changes, how many units of product will the company have to sell to make the same net income as last year?
5. If Jupiter wishes to maintain the same contribution-margin ratio, what selling price per unit of product must it charge next year to cover the increased direct-material cost?

(CMA, adapted)

Problem 7–47
Continuation of Preceding Problem; Activity-Based Costing; Advanced Manufacturing Systems; Ethical Issues
(LO 4, 9, 10)

2. Break-even point: 17,000 units

Refer to the original data given for Jupiter Game Company in the preceding problem. An activity-based costing study has revealed that Jupiter's $150,000 of fixed costs include the following components:

Setup (40 setups at $400 per setup)	$ 16,000
Engineering (500 hours at $25 per hour)	12,500
Inspection (1,000 inspections at $30 per inspection)	30,000
General factory overhead	61,500
Total	$120,000
Fixed selling and administrative costs	30,000
Total fixed costs	$150,000

Management is considering the installation of new, highly automated manufacturing equipment that would significantly alter the production process. In addition, management plans a move toward just-in-time inventory and production management. If the new equipment is installed, setups will be quicker and less expensive. Under the proposed JIT approach, there would be 300 setups per year at $50 per setup. Since a total quality control program would accompany the move toward JIT, only 100 inspections would be anticipated annually, at a cost of $45 each. After the installation of the new production system, 800 hours of engineering would be required at a cost of $28 per hour. General factory overhead would increase to $166,100. However, the automated equipment would allow Jupiter to cut its unit variable cost by 20 percent. Moreover, the more consistent product quality anticipated would allow management to raise the price of electronic games to $26 per unit. (Ignore income taxes.)

Required:

1. Upon seeing the ABC analysis given in the problem, Jupiter's vice president for manufacturing exclaimed to the controller, "I thought you told me this $150,000 cost was fixed. These don't look like fixed costs at all. What you're telling me now is that setup costs us $400 every time we set up a production run. What gives?"

   As Jupiter's controller, write a short memo explaining to the vice president what is going on.
2. Compute Jupiter's new break-even point if the proposed automated equipment is installed.
3. Determine how many units Jupiter will have to sell to show a profit of $140,000, assuming the new technology is adopted.
4. If Jupiter adopts the new manufacturing technology, will its break-even point be higher or lower? Will the number of sales units required to earn a profit of $140,000 be higher or lower? (Refer to your answers for the first two requirements of the preceding problem.) Are the results in this case consistent with what you would typically expect to find? Explain.
5. The decision as to whether to purchase the automated manufacturing equipment will be made by Jupiter's board of directors. In order to support the proposed acquisition, the vice president for manufacturing asked the controller to prepare a report on the financial implications of the decision. As part of the report, the vice president asked the controller to compute the new break-even point, assuming the installation of the equipment. The controller complied, as in requirement (2) of this problem.

   When the vice president for manufacturing saw that the break-even point would increase, he asked the controller to delete the break-even analysis from the report. What should the controller do? Which ethical standards for managerial accountants are involved here?

Problem 7–48
CVP Relationships; Retail
(LO 1, 4)

2. Decrease in operating income: $(1,400)

Condensed monthly income data for Thurber Book Stores are presented in the following table for November 20x1. (Ignore income taxes.)

	Mall Store	Downtown Store	Total
Sales	$80,000	$120,000	$200,000
Less: Variable expenses	32,000	84,000	116,000
Contribution margin	$48,000	$ 36,000	$ 84,000
Less: Fixed expenses	20,000	40,000	60,000
Operating income	$28,000	$ (4,000)	$ 24,000

Additional Information:

- Management estimates that closing the downtown store would result in a 10 percent decrease in mall store sales, while closing the mall store would not affect downtown store sales.
- One-fourth of each store's fixed expenses would continue through December 31, 20x2, if either store were closed.
- The operating results for November 20x1 are representative of all months.

Required:

1. Calculate the increase or decrease in Thurber's monthly operating income during 20x2 if the downtown store is closed.
2. The management of Thurber Book Stores is considering a promotional campaign at the downtown store that would not affect the mall store. Annual promotional expenses at the downtown store would be increased by $60,000 in order to increase downtown store sales by 10 percent. What

would be the effect of this promotional campaign on the company's monthly operating income during 20x2?

3. One-half of the downtown store's dollar sales are from items sold at their variable cost to attract customers to the store. Thurber's management is considering the deletion of these items, a move that would reduce the downtown store's direct fixed expenses by 15 percent and result in the loss of 20 percent of the remaining downtown store's sales volume. This change would not affect the mall store. What would be the effect on Thurber's monthly operating income if the items sold at their variable cost are eliminated?
4. *Build a spreadsheet:* Construct an Excel spreadsheet to solve all of the preceding requirements. Show how the solution will change if the following information changes: the downtown store's sales amounted to $126,000 and its variable expenses were $86,000.

(CMA, adapted)

Problem 7–49
CVP; Multiple Products; Changes in Costs and Sales Mix
(LO 4, 5)

2. Total sales to break even: 162,500 units
3. Weighted-average unit contribution margin: $13.00

Cincinnati Tool Company (CTC) manufactures a line of electric garden tools that are sold in general hardware stores. The company's controller, Will Fulton, has just received the sales forecast for the coming year for CTC's three products: hedge clippers, weeders, and leaf blowers. CTC has experienced considerable variations in sales volumes and variable costs over the past two years, and Fulton believes the forecast should be carefully evaluated from a cost-volume-profit viewpoint. The preliminary budget information for 20x2 follows:

	Weeders	Hedge Clippers	Leaf Blowers
Unit sales	50,000	50,000	100,000
Unit selling price	$28	$36	$48
Variable manufacturing cost per unit	13	12	25
Variable selling cost per unit	5	4	6

For 20x2, CTC's fixed manufacturing overhead is budgeted at $2,000,000, and the company's fixed selling and administrative expenses are forecasted to be $600,000. CTC has a tax rate of 40 percent.

Required:

1. Determine CTC's budgeted net income for 20x2.
2. Assuming the sales mix remains as budgeted, determine how many units of each product CTC must sell in order to break even in 20x2.
3. After preparing the original estimates, management determined that its variable manufacturing cost of leaf blowers would increase by 20 percent, and the variable selling cost of hedge clippers could be expected to increase by $1.00 per unit. However, management has decided not to change the selling price of either product. In addition, management has learned that its leaf blower has been perceived as the best value on the market, and it can expect to sell three times as many leaf blowers as each of its other products. Under these circumstances, determine how many units of each product CTC would have to sell in order to break even in 20x2.

(CMA, adapted)

Problem 7–50
CVP Relationships; International Business; Automation
(LO 1, 4, 10)

3. Variable cost per ton: $275 per ton
6. Dollar sales required for target net profit: $1,140,000

Ohio Limestone Company produces thin limestone sheets used for cosmetic facing on buildings. The following income statement represents the operating results for the year just ended. The company had sales of 1,800 tons during the year. The manufacturing capacity of the firm's facilities is 3,000 tons per year. (Ignore income taxes.)

OHIO LIMESTONE COMPANY
Income Statement
For the Year Ended December 31, 20x1

Sales	$900,000
Variable costs:	
Manufacturing	$315,000
Selling costs	180,000
Total variable costs	$495,000
Contribution margin	$405,000
Fixed costs:	
Manufacturing	$100,000
Selling	107,500
Administrative	40,000
Total fixed costs	$247,500
Net income	$157,500

Required:

1. Calculate the company's break-even volume in tons for 20x1.
2. If the sales volume is estimated to be 2,100 tons in the next year, and if the prices and costs stay at the same levels and amounts, what is the net income that management can expect for 20x2?
3. Ohio Limestone has been trying for years to get a foothold in the European market. The company has a potential German customer that has offered to buy 1,500 tons at $450 per ton. Assume that all of the firm's costs would be at the same levels and rates as in 20x1. What net income would the firm earn if it took this order and rejected some business from regular customers so as not to exceed capacity?
4. Ohio Limestone plans to market its product in a new territory. Management estimates that an advertising and promotion program costing $61,500 annually would be needed for the next two or three years. In addition, a $25 per ton sales commission to the sales force in the new territory, over and above the current commission, would be required. How many tons would have to be sold in the new territory to maintain the firm's current net income? Assume that sales and costs will continue as in 20x1 in the firm's established territories.
5. Management is considering replacing its labor-intensive process with an automated production system. This would result in an increase of $58,500 annually in fixed manufacturing costs. The variable manufacturing costs would decrease by $25 per ton. Compute the new break-even volume in tons and in sales dollars.
6. Ignore the facts presented in requirement (5). Assume that management estimates that the selling price per ton would decline by 10 percent next year. Variable costs would increase by $40 per ton, and fixed costs would not change. What sales volume in dollars would be required to earn a net income of $94,500 next year?

(CMA, adapted)

Problem 7–51
Cost-Volume-Profit Analysis with Income Taxes and Multiple Products (Appendix)
(LO 1, 2, 4, 5, 11)

3. Break-even point, mountaineering model: 10,500 units

Alpine Thrills Ski Company recently expanded its manufacturing capacity. The firm will now be able to produce up to 15,000 pairs of cross-country skis of either the mountaineering model or the touring model. The sales department assures management that it can sell between 9,000 and 13,000 units of either product this year. Because the models are very similar, the company will produce only one of the two models.

The following information was compiled by the accounting department.

	Model	
	Mountaineering	**Touring**
Selling price per unit	$88.00	$80.00
Variable costs per unit	52.80	52.80

Fixed costs will total $369,600 if the mountaineering model is produced but will be only $316,800 if the touring model is produced. Alpine Thrills Ski Company is subject to a 40 percent income tax rate. (Round each answer to the nearest whole number.)

Required:

1. Compute the contribution-margin ratio for the touring model.
2. If Alpine Thrills Ski Company desires an after-tax net income of $22,080, how many pairs of touring skis will the company have to sell?
3. How much would the variable cost per unit of the touring model have to change before it had the same break-even point in units as the mountaineering model?
4. Suppose the variable cost per unit of touring skis decreases by 10 percent, and the total fixed cost of touring skis increases by 10 percent. Compute the new break-even point.
5. Suppose management decided to produce both products. If the two models are sold in equal proportions, and total fixed costs amount to $343,200, what is the firm's break-even point in units?

(CMA, adapted)

Problem 7–52
CVP Analysis; Marketing Decisions; Income Taxes (Appendix)
(LO 1, 4, 11)

2. Required sales dollars to break even: $19,692,308

Syracuse Telecom, Inc. manufactures telecommunications equipment. The company has always been production oriented and sells its products through agents. Agents are paid a commission of 15 percent of the selling price. Syracuse Telecom's budgeted income statement for 20x2 follows:

SYRACUSE TELECOM, INC.
Budgeted Income Statement
For the Year Ended December 31, 20x2
(in thousands)

Sales		$16,000
Manufacturing costs:		
Variable	$7,200	
Fixed overhead	2,340	9,540
Gross margin		$ 6,460
Selling and administrative expenses:		
Commissions	$2,400	
Fixed marketing expenses	140	
Fixed administrative expenses	1,780	4,320
Net operating income		$ 2,140
Less fixed interest expense		540
Income before income taxes		$ 1,600
Less income taxes (30%)		480
Net income		$ 1,120

After the profit plan was completed for the coming year, Syracuse Telecom's sales agents demanded that the commissions be increased to 22½ percent of the selling price. This demand was the latest in a series of actions that Vinnie McGraw, the company's president, believed had gone too far. He asked Maureen Elliott, the most sales-oriented officer in his production-oriented company, to estimate the cost to Syracuse Telecom of employing its own sales force. Elliott's estimate of the additional annual cost of employing its own sales force, exclusive of commissions, follows. Sales personnel would receive a commission of 10 percent of the selling price in addition to their salary.

Estimated Annual Cost of
Employing a Company Sales Force
(in thousands)

Salaries:	
Sales manager	$ 100
Sales personnel	1,000
Travel and entertainment	400
Fixed marketing costs	900
Total	$2,400

Required:

1. Calculate Syracuse Telecom's estimated break-even point in sales dollars for 20x2.
   a. If the events that are represented in the budgeted income statement take place.
   b. If the company employs its own sales force.
2. If Syracuse Telecom continues to sell through agents and pays the increased commission of 22½ percent of the selling price, determine the estimated volume in sales dollars for 20x2 that would be required to generate the same net income as projected in the budgeted income statement.
3. Determine the estimated volume in sales dollars that would result in equal net income for 20x2 regardless of whether the company continues to sell through agents and pays a commission of 22½ percent of the selling price or employs its own sales force.

(CMA, adapted)

Cases

Case 7–53
Break-Even Analysis; Hospital CVP Relationships
(LO 1, 4)

1. Contribution margin per patient day: $200
2. Increase in revenue: $540,000

Delaware Medical Center operates a general hospital. The medical center also rents space and beds to separately owned entities rendering specialized services, such as Pediatrics and Psychiatric Care. Delaware charges each separate entity for common services, such as patients' meals and laundry, and for administrative services, such as billings and collections. Space and bed rentals are fixed charges for the year, based on bed capacity rented to each entity. Delaware Medical Center charged the following costs to Pediatrics for the year ended June 30, 20x1:

	Patient Days (variable)	Bed Capacity (fixed)
Dietary	$ 600,000	—
Janitorial	—	$ 70,000
Laundry	300,000	—
Laboratory	450,000	—
Pharmacy	350,000	—
Repairs and maintenance	—	30,000
General and administrative	—	1,300,000
Rent	—	1,500,000
Billings and collections	300,000	—
Total	$2,000,000	$2,900,000

During the year ended June 30, 20x1, Pediatrics charged each patient an average of $300 per day, had a capacity of 60 beds, and had revenue of $6 million for 365 days. In addition, Pediatrics directly employed personnel with the following annual salary costs per employee: supervising nurses, $25,000; nurses, $20,000; and aides, $9,000.

Delaware Medical Center has the following minimum departmental personnel requirements, based on total annual patient days:

Annual Patient Days	Aides	Nurses	Supervising Nurses
Up to 22,000	20	10	4
22,001 to 26,000	25	14	5
26,001 to 29,200	31	16	5

Pediatrics always employs only the minimum number of required personnel. Salaries of supervising nurses, nurses, and aides are therefore fixed within ranges of annual patient days.

Pediatrics operated at 100 percent capacity on 90 days during the year ended June 30, 20x1. Administrators estimate that on these 90 days, Pediatrics could have filled another 20 beds above capacity. Delaware Medical Center has an additional 20 beds available for rent for the year ending June 30, 20x2. Such additional rental would increase Pediatrics' fixed charges based on bed capacity. (In the following requirements, ignore income taxes.)

Required:

1. Calculate the minimum number of patient days required for Pediatrics to break even for the year ending June 30, 20x2, if the additional 20 beds are not rented. Patient demand is unknown, but assume that revenue per patient day, cost per patient day, cost per bed, and salary rates will remain the same as for the year ended June 30, 20x1.
2. Assume that patient demand, revenue per patient day, cost per patient day, cost per bed, and salary rates for the year ending June 30, 20x2, remain the same as for the year ended June 30, 20x1. Prepare a schedule of Pediatrics' increase in revenue and increase in costs for the year ending June 30, 20x2. Determine the net increase or decrease in Pediatrics' earnings from the additional 20 beds if Pediatrics rents this extra capacity from Delaware Medical Center.

(CPA, adapted)

Case 7–54
CVP Analysis with Production and Marketing Decisions; Taxes (Appendix)
(LO 1, 4, 11)

1(b). To achieve after-tax profit objective, Oakley must sell 2,500 units
2. Alternative (3), after-tax profit: $204,000

Oakley Company manufactures and sells adjustable canopies that attach to motor homes and trailers. The market covers both new units as well as replacement canopies. Oakley developed its 20x2 business plan based on the assumption that canopies would sell at a price of $400 each. The variable cost of each canopy is projected at $200, and the annual fixed costs are budgeted at $100,000. Oakley's after-tax profit objective is $240,000; the company's tax rate is 40 percent.

While Oakley's sales usually rise during the second quarter, the May financial statements reported that sales were not meeting expectations. For the first five months of the year, only 350 units had been sold at the established price, with variable costs as planned. It was clear the 20x2 after-tax profit projection would not be reached unless some actions were taken. Oakley's president, Melanie Grand, assigned a management committee to analyze the situation and develop several alternative courses of action. The following mutually exclusive alternatives were presented to the president.

- Reduce the sales price by $40. The sales organization forecasts that with the significantly reduced sales price, 2,700 units can be sold during the remainder of the year. Total fixed and variable unit costs will stay as budgeted.
- Lower variable costs per unit by $25 through the use of less expensive raw materials and slightly modified manufacturing techniques. The sales price also would be reduced by $30, and sales of 2,200 units for the remainder of the year are forecast.
- Cut fixed costs by $10,000 and lower the sales price by 5 percent. Variable costs per unit will be unchanged. Sales of 2,000 units are expected for the remainder of the year.

Required:

1. If no changes are made to the selling price or cost structure, determine the number of units that Oakley Company must sell
   a. In order to break even.
   b. To achieve its after-tax profit objective.
2. Determine which one of the alternatives Oakley Company should select to achieve its annual after-tax profit objective.

(CMA, adapted)

Case 7–55
Sales Commissions in a Wholesale Firm; Income Taxes (Appendix)
(LO 1, 2, 4, 11)

1. Break-even point: $500,000
3. New contribution-margin ratio: .15

Niagra Falls Sporting Goods Company, a wholesale supply company, engages independent sales agents to market the company's products throughout New York and Ontario. These agents currently receive a commission of 20 percent of sales, but they are demanding an increase to 25 percent of sales made during the year ending December 31, 20x2. The controller already prepared the 20x2 budget before learning of the agents' demand for an increase in commissions. The budgeted 20x2 income statement is shown below. Assume that cost of goods sold is 100 percent variable cost.

NIAGRA FALLS SPORTING GOODS COMPANY
Budgeted Income Statement
For the Year Ended December 31, 20x2

Sales		$10,000,000
Cost of goods sold		6,000,000
Gross margin		$ 4,000,000
Selling and administrative expenses:		
Commissions	$2,000,000	
All other expenses (fixed)	100,000	2,100,000
Income before taxes		$ 1,900,000
Income tax (30%)		570,000
Net income		$ 1,330,000

The company's management is considering the possibility of employing full-time sales personnel. Three individuals would be required, at an estimated annual salary of $30,000 each, plus commissions of 5 percent of sales. In addition, a sales manager would be employed at a fixed annual salary of $160,000. All other fixed costs, as well as the variable cost percentages, would remain the same as the estimates in the 20x2 budgeted income statement.

Required:

1. Compute Niagra Falls Sporting Goods' estimated break-even point in sales dollars for the year ending December 31, 20x2, based on the budgeted income statement prepared by the controller.
2. Compute the estimated break-even point in sales dollars for the year ending December 31, 20x2, if the company employs its own sales personnel.
3. Compute the estimated volume in sales dollars that would be required for the year ending December 31, 20x2, to yield the same net income as projected in the budgeted income statement, if management continues to use the independent sales agents and agrees to their demand for a 25 percent sales commission.
4. Compute the estimated volume in sales dollars that would generate an identical net income for the year ending December 31, 20x2, regardless of whether Niagra Falls Sporting Goods Company employs its own sales personnel or continues to use the independent sales agents and pays them a 25 percent commission.

(CPA, adapted)

FOCUS COMPANY >>>

THIS CHAPTER'S FOCUS COMPANY is Quikmath.com, a manufacturer of Quikmath.com handheld calculators, pagers, and other electronic gadgetry. Quikmath specializes in the school-age and college markets, and virtually all of its sales are Web-based. In this chapter, we explore two product-costing systems called absorption and variable costing. Under absorption costing, all manufacturing costs, including fixed manufacturing overhead, are assigned as product costs and stored in inventory until the products are sold. Under variable costing, fixed manufacturing overhead is not included in inventory as a product cost. Instead, fixed manufacturing overhead is treated as a period cost, and it is expensed during the period in which it is incurred. The choice between absorption and variable costing arises only in manufacturing firms.

8 Absorption and Variable Costing

IN CONTRAST >>>

In contrast to the absorption and variable costing systems discussed in the first part of the chapter, we explore yet another product-costing method called throughput costing. We continue our illustration with Quikmath.com to explain how this product-costing method works. Throughput costing assigns only the unit-level spending for direct costs as the cost of a product. A unit-level cost is one that is incurred every time a unit is manufactured.

Quikmath.com

AFTER COMPLETING THIS CHAPTER, YOU SHOULD BE ABLE TO:

1 Explain the accounting treatment of fixed manufacturing overhead under absorption and variable costing.

2 Prepare an income statement under absorption costing.

3 Prepare an income statement under variable costing.

4 Reconcile reported income under absorption and variable costing.

5 Explain the implications of absorption and variable costing for cost-volume-profit analysis.

6 Evaluate absorption and variable costing.

7 Explain the rationale behind throughput costing.

8 Prepare an income statement under throughput costing.

Income is one of many important measures used to evaluate the performance of companies and segments of companies. There are two commonly used methods for determining product costs and reporting income in a manufacturing firm, depending on the accounting treatment of fixed manufacturing overhead. In this chapter, we will examine these two income-reporting alternatives, called *absorption costing* and *variable costing*. In addition, we will study a third alternative for product costing and income reporting, which is called *throughput costing*.

Product Costs

In the product-costing systems we have studied so far, manufacturing overhead is applied to Work-in-Process Inventory as a product cost along with direct material and direct labor. When the manufactured goods are finished, these product costs flow from Work-in-Process Inventory into Finished-Goods Inventory. Finally, during the accounting period when the goods are sold, the product costs flow from Finished-Goods Inventory into Cost of Goods Sold, an expense account. The following diagram summarizes this flow of costs.

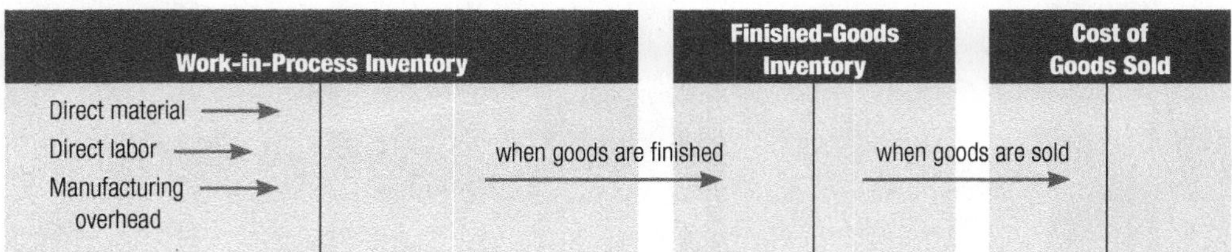

Since the costs of production are stored in inventory accounts until the goods are sold, these costs are said to be *inventoried costs*.

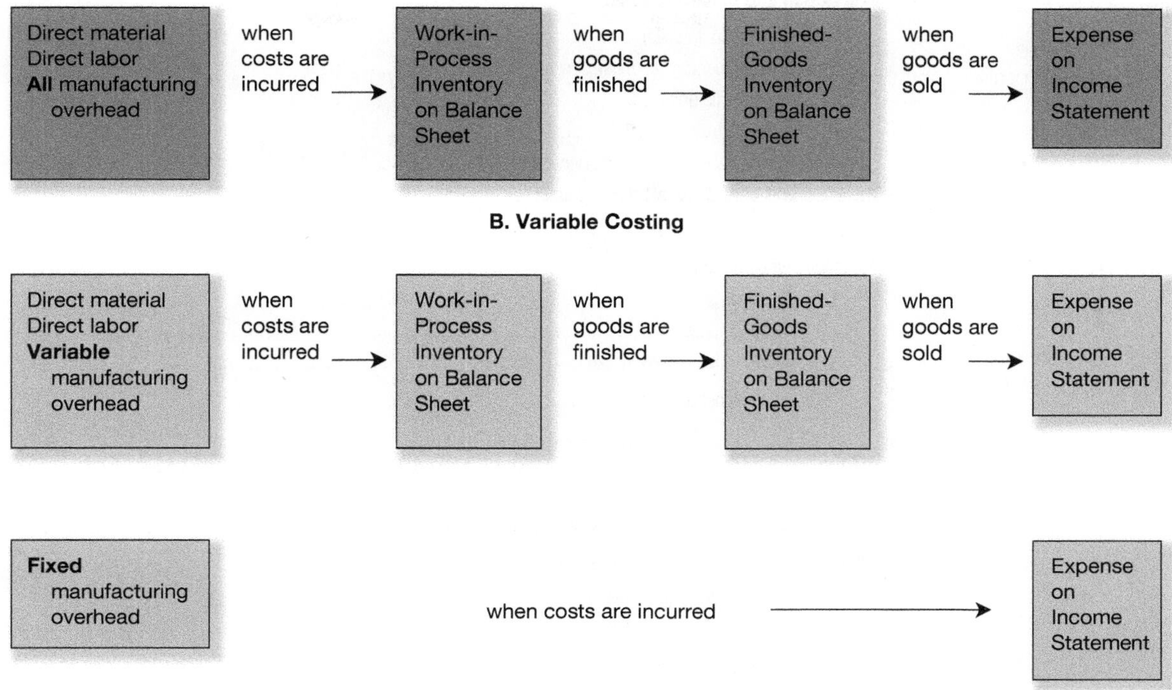

Exhibit 8–1
Absorption versus Variable Costing

Learning Objective 1

Explain the accounting treatment of fixed manufacturing overhead under absorption and variable costing.

Fixed Manufacturing Overhead: The Key In our study of product-costing systems, we have included both variable and fixed manufacturing overhead in the product costs that flow through the manufacturing accounts. This approach to product costing is called **absorption costing** (or **full costing**), because *all* manufacturing-overhead costs are applied to (or absorbed by) manufactured goods. An alternative approach to product costing is called **variable costing (or direct costing)**, in which *only variable* manufacturing overhead is applied to Work-in-Process Inventory as a product cost.

The distinction between absorption and variable costing is summarized in Exhibit 8–1. Notice that the distinction involves the *timing* with which fixed manufacturing overhead becomes an expense. Eventually, fixed overhead is expensed under both product-costing systems. Under variable costing, however, fixed overhead is expensed *immediately,* as it is incurred. Under absorption costing, fixed overhead is *inventoried* until the accounting period during which the manufactured goods are sold.

Illustration of Absorption and Variable Costing

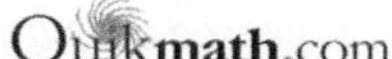

Quikmath.com began operations on January 1, 20x0, to manufacture handheld electronic calculators. The company uses a standard-costing system. Cost, production, and sales data for the first three years of Quikmath's operations are given in Exhibit 8–2. Comparative income statements for 20x0, 20x1, and 20x2 are presented in Exhibit 8–3, using both absorption and variable costing.

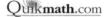

Exhibit 8–2
Data for Illustration: Quikmath.com

Quikmath.com

	20x0	20x1	20x2
Production and inventory data:			
Planned production (in units)	50,000	50,000	50,000
Finished-goods inventory (in units), January 1	–0–	–0–	15,000
Actual production (in units)	50,000	50,000	50,000
Sales (in units)	50,000	35,000	65,000
Finished-goods inventory (in units), December 31	–0–	15,000	–0–
Revenue and cost data, all three years:			
Sales price per unit			$12
Manufacturing costs per unit:			
Direct material			$ 3
Direct labor			2
Variable manufacturing overhead			1
Total variable cost per unit			$ 6
Used only under absorption costing: Fixed manufacturing overhead:			
Budgeted annual fixed overhead / Planned annual production*	$150,000 / 50,000		3
Total absorption cost per unit			$ 9
Variable selling and administrative cost per unit			$ 1
Fixed selling and administrative cost per year			$25,000

*Planned annual production of 50,000 units is management's estimate of the company's practical capacity for production.

Learning Objective 2

Prepare an income statement under absorption costing.

Absorption-Costing Income Statements

Examine the absorption-costing income statements in the upper half of Exhibit 8–3. Two features of these income statements are highlighted in the left-hand margin. First, notice that the Cost of Goods Sold expense for each year is determined by multiplying the year's sales by the absorption manufacturing cost per unit, $9. Included in the $9 cost per unit is the predetermined fixed manufacturing-overhead cost of $3 per unit. Second, notice that on Quikmath's absorption-costing income statements, the only period expenses are the selling and administrative expenses. There is no deduction of fixed-overhead costs as a lump-sum period expense at the bottom of each income statement. As mentioned above, fixed manufacturing-overhead costs are included in Cost of Goods Sold on these absorption-costing income statements.

The fixed costs of operating this manufacturing plant include such costs as the depreciation on plant and equipment, property taxes, insurance, and the salary of the plant manager. Fixed manufacturing costs are incurred in order to generate production capacity. Under absorption costing, these costs are treated as product costs and included in the cost of inventory. Under variable costing, they are expensed during the period incurred. Pictured here is a Kawasaki machine that presses steel at a heavy-duty truck factory in Maahshan, China.

Variable-Costing Income Statements

Now examine the income statements based on variable costing in the lower half of Exhibit 8–3. Notice that the format of the statements is different from the format used in the absorption-costing statements. In the variable-costing statements, the contribution format is used to highlight the separation of variable and fixed costs. Let's focus

Exhibit 8–3
Income Statements under Absorption and Variable Costing

Quikmath.com

QUIKMATH.COM
Absorption-Costing Income Statement

		20x0	20x1	20x2
	Sales revenue (at $12 per unit)	$600,000	$420,000	$780,000
1	Less: Cost of goods sold (at absorption cost of $9 per unit)	450,000	315,000	585,000
	Gross margin	$150,000	$105,000	$195,000
	Less: Selling and administrative expenses:			
2 No fixed overhead	Variable (at $1 per unit)	50,000	35,000	65,000
	Fixed	25,000	25,000	25,000
	Net income	$ 75,000	$ 45,000	$105,000

QUIKMATH.COM
Variable-Costing Income Statement

		20x0	20x1	20x2
	Sales revenue (at $12 per unit)	$600,000	$420,000	$780,000
	Less: Variable expenses:			
1	Variable manufacturing costs (at variable cost of $6 per unit)	300,000	210,000	390,000
	Variable selling and administrative costs (at $1 per unit)	50,000	35,000	65,000
	Contribution margin	$250,000	$175,000	$325,000
	Less: Fixed expenses:			
2	Fixed manufacturing overhead	150,000	150,000	150,000
	Fixed selling and administrative expenses	25,000	25,000	25,000
	Net income	$ 75,000	$ 0	$150,000

Learning Objective 3
Prepare an income statement under variable costing.

on the same two aspects of the variable-costing statements that we discussed for the absorption-costing statements. First, the manufacturing expenses subtracted from sales revenue each year include only the variable costs, which amount to $6 per unit. Second, fixed manufacturing overhead is subtracted as a lump-sum period expense at the bottom of each year's income statement.

Reconciling Income under Absorption and Variable Costing

Learning Objective 4
Reconcile reported income under absorption and variable costing.

Examination of Exhibit 8–3 reveals that the income reported under absorption and variable costing is sometimes different. Although income is the same for the two product-costing methods in 20x0, it is different in 20x1 and 20x2. Let's figure out why these results occur.

No Change in Inventory In 20x0 there is no change in inventory over the course of the year. Beginning and ending inventory are the same, because actual production and sales are the same. Think about the implications of the stable inventory level for the treatment of fixed manufacturing overhead. On the variable-costing statement, the $150,000 of fixed manufacturing overhead incurred during 20x0 is an expense in 20x0. Under absorption costing, however, fixed manufacturing overhead was applied to production at the predetermined rate of $3 per unit. Since all of the units produced in 20x0 also were sold in 20x0, all of the fixed manufacturing-overhead cost flowed through into Cost of Goods Sold. Thus, $150,000 of fixed manufacturing overhead was expensed in 20x0 under absorption costing also.

Exhibit 8–4
Reconciliation of Income under Absorption and Variable Costing: Quikmath.com

Quikmath.com

		20x0	20x1	20x2
1	Cost of goods sold under absorption costing	$450,000	$ 315,000	$585,000
	Variable manufacturing costs under variable costing	300,000	210,000	390,000
	Subtotal	$150,000	$ 105,000	$195,000
2	Fixed manufacturing overhead as period expense under variable costing	150,000	150,000	150,000
	Total	$ 0	$ (45,000)	$ 45,000
	Net income under variable costing	$ 75,000	$ 0	$150,000
	Net income under absorption costing	75,000	45,000	105,000
	Difference in net income	$ 0	$ (45,000)	$ 45,000

The 20x0 column of Exhibit 8–4 reconciles the 20x0 net income reported under absorption and variable costing. The reconciliation focuses on the two places in the income statements where differences occur between absorption and variable costing. The numbers in the left-hand margin of Exhibit 8–4 correspond to the numbers in the left-hand margin of the income statements in Exhibit 8–3.

Increase in Inventory In 20x1 inventory increased from zero on January 1 to 15,000 units on December 31. The increase in inventory was the result of production exceeding sales. Under variable costing, the $150,000 of fixed overhead cost incurred in 20x1 is expensed, just as it was in 20x0. Under absorption costing, however, only a portion of the 20x1 fixed manufacturing overhead is expensed in 20x1. Since the fixed overhead is inventoried under absorption costing, some of this cost *remains in inventory* at the end of 20x1.

The 20x1 column of Exhibit 8–4 reconciles the 20x1 net income reported under absorption and variable costing. As before, the reconciliation focuses on the two places in the income statements where differences occur between absorption and variable costing.

"The operational managers' bonuses are based on profitability, so they are keenly interested in the financial management reports' results." (8a)
John Deere Health Care, Inc.

Decrease in Inventory In 20x2 inventory decreased from 15,000 units to zero. Sales during the year exceeded production. As in 20x0 and 20x1, under variable costing, the $150,000 of fixed manufacturing overhead incurred in 20x2 is expensed in 20x2. Under absorption costing, however, *more than* $150,000 of fixed overhead is expensed in 20x2. Why? Because some of the fixed overhead incurred during the prior year, which was inventoried then, is now expensed in 20x2 as the goods are sold.

The 20x2 column of Exhibit 8–4 reconciles the 20x2 income under absorption and variable costing. Once again, the numbers on the left-hand side of Exhibit 8–4 correspond to those on the left-hand side of the income statements in Exhibit 8–3.

A Shortcut to Reconciling Income When inventory increases or decreases during the year, reported income differs under absorption and variable costing. This results from the fixed overhead that is inventoried under absorption costing but expensed immediately under variable costing. The following formula may be used to compute the difference in the amount of fixed overhead expensed in a given time period under the two product-costing methods.[1]

$$\text{Difference in fixed overhead expensed under absorption and variable costing} = \left(\text{Change in inventory, in units}\right) \times \left(\text{Predetermined fixed-overhead rate per unit}\right)$$

[1]This approach assumes that the predetermined fixed-overhead rate per unit does not change across time periods.

As the following table shows, this difference in the amount of fixed overhead expensed explains the difference in reported income under absorption and variable costing.

Year	Change in Inventory (in units)		Predetermined Fixed-Overhead Rate		Difference in Fixed Overhead Expensed		Absorption-Costing Income Minus Variable-Costing Income
20x0	–0–	×	$3	=	–0–	=	–0–
20x1	15,000 increase	×	$3	=	$ 45,000	=	$ 45,000
20x2	15,000 decrease	×	$3	=	$(45,000)	=	$(45,000)

Length of Time Period The discrepancies between absorption-costing and variable-costing income in Exhibit 8–3 occur because of the changes in inventory levels during 20x1 and 20x2. It is common for production and sales to differ over the course of a week, month, or year. Therefore, the income measured for those time periods often will differ between absorption and variable costing. This discrepancy is likely to be smaller over longer time periods. Over the course of a decade, for example, Quikmath.com cannot sell much more or less than it produces. Thus, the income amounts under the two product-costing methods, when added together over a lengthy time period, will be approximately equal under absorption and variable costing.

Notice in Exhibit 8–3 that Quikmath.com's total income over the three-year period is $225,000 under *both* absorption and variable costing. This results from the fact that the company produced and sold the same total amount over the three-year period.

Cost-Volume-Profit Analysis

Learning Objective 5

Explain the implications of absorption and variable costing for cost-volume-profit analysis.

One of the tools used by managers to plan and control business operations is cost-volume-profit analysis, which we studied in Chapter 7. Quikmath.com's break-even point in units can be computed as follows:

$$\text{Break-even point} = \frac{\text{Fixed costs}}{\text{Unit contribution margin}} = \frac{\$150{,}000 + \$25{,}000}{\$12 - \$6 - \$1}$$

$$= \frac{\$175{,}000}{\$5} = 35{,}000 \text{ units}$$

If Quikmath.com sells 35,000 calculators, net income should be zero, as Exhibit 8–5 confirms.

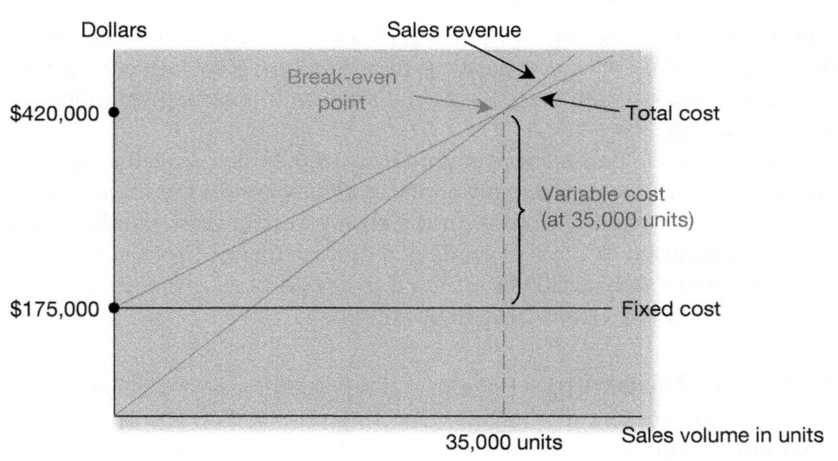

Exhibit 8–5
Break-Even Graph: Quikmath.com

Quikmath.com

Now return to Exhibit 8–3 and examine the 20x1 income statements under absorption and variable costing. In 20x1 Quikmath.com sold 35,000 units, the break-even volume. This fact is confirmed on the variable-costing income statement, since net income is zero. On the absorption-costing income statement, however, the 20x1 net income is $45,000. What has happened here?

The answer to this inconsistency lies in the different treatment of fixed manufacturing overhead under absorption and variable costing. Variable costing highlights the separation between fixed and variable costs, as do cost-volume-profit analysis and break-even calculations. Both of these techniques account for fixed manufacturing overhead as a lump sum. In contrast, *absorption costing is inconsistent with CVP analysis,* because fixed overhead is applied to goods as a product cost on a per-unit basis.

Evaluation of Absorption and Variable Costing

Learning Objective 6

Evaluate absorption and variable costing.

Some managers find the inconsistency between absorption costing and CVP analysis troubling enough to warrant using variable costing for internal income reporting. Variable costing dovetails much more closely than absorption costing with any operational analyses that require a separation between fixed and variable costs.

Pricing Decisions Many managers prefer to use absorption-costing data in cost-based pricing decisions. They argue that fixed manufacturing overhead is a necessary cost incurred in the production process. To exclude this fixed cost from the inventoried cost of a product, as is done under variable costing, is to understate the cost of the product. For this reason, most companies that use cost-based pricing base their prices on absorption-costing data.

Proponents of variable costing argue that a product's variable cost provides a better basis for the pricing decision. They point out that any price above a product's variable cost makes a positive contribution to covering fixed cost and profit.

Definition of an Asset Another controversy about absorption and variable costing hinges on the definition of an asset. An *asset* is a thing of value owned by the organization with future service potential. By accounting convention, assets are valued at their cost. Since fixed costs comprise part of the cost of production, advocates of absorption costing argue that inventory (an asset) should be valued at its full (absorption) cost of production. Moreover, they argue that these costs have future service potential since the inventory can be sold in the future to generate sales revenue.

Proponents of variable costing argue that the fixed-cost component of a product's absorption-costing value has no future service potential. Their reasoning is that the fixed manufacturing-overhead costs during the current period will not prevent these costs from having to be incurred again next period. Fixed-overhead costs will be incurred every period, regardless of production levels. In contrast, the incurrence of variable costs in manufacturing a product does allow the firm to avoid incurring these costs again.

To illustrate, Quikmath.com produced 15,000 more calculators in 20x1 than it sold. These units will be carried in inventory until they are sold in some future year. Quikmath.com will never again have to incur the costs of direct material, direct labor, and variable overhead incurred in 20x1 to produce those calculators. Yet Quikmath.com will have to incur approximately $150,000 of fixed-overhead costs every year, even though the firm has the 15,000 units from 20x1 in inventory.

External Reporting For external reporting purposes, generally accepted accounting principles require that income reporting be based on absorption costing. Federal tax laws also require the use of absorption costing in reporting income for tax purposes.

Management
Accounting
Practice

IRS

IRS: UNIQUE PRODUCT PACKAGING IS AN INVENTORIABLE COST

The Internal Revenue Service (IRS) requires absorption costing for tax purposes. Thus, absorption costing must be used in valuing inventory and in determining cost-of-goods-sold expense, which in turn affects taxable income. The IRS defines inventoriable costs (i.e., product costs) that must be included in valuing inventory and cost-of-goods-sold expense to include the following: (1) direct material consumed in the production of the product and (2) direct labor, and (3) all indirect costs deemed to be necessary for the production of the company's product. These necessary indirect costs include fixed-overhead costs. Thus, absorption costing is mandated by the IRS.

One interesting nuance in the IRS interpretation of what constitutes inventoriable costs concerns a company's expenditures on the design of the packaging for the company's products. Packaging design costs can run into hundreds of thousands of dollars for large consumer products companies. The IRS has specified that packaging design costs must be inventoried as product costs if the resulting design is successful—that is, it remains in use for several years. If, however, a package design fails in the marketplace, the company can deduct the package design costs early as an expense. Examples of products with unique packaging designs that would be affected by this IRS ruling include Pringles potato chips (sold in a can), Realemon and Realime (sold in plastic citrus-fruit-shaped containers), and L'eggs pantyhose (sold in the familiar plastic egg-shaped containers).

Why Not Both? Using computerized accounting systems, it is straightforward for a company to prepare income statements under both absorption and variable costing. Since absorption-costing statements are required for external reporting, managers will want to keep an eye on the effects of their decisions on financial reports to outsiders. Yet the superiority of variable-costing income reporting as a method for dovetailing with operational analyses cannot be denied. Preparation of both absorption-costing and variable-costing data is perhaps the best solution to the controversy.

JIT Manufacturing Environment In a just-in-time inventory and production management system, all inventories are kept very low. Since finished-goods inventories are minimal, there is little change in inventory from period to period. Thus, in a JIT environment, the income differences under absorption and variable costing generally will be insignificant.

Throughput Costing

Learning Objective 7

Explain the rationale behind throughput costing.

Some managers advocate *throughput costing* as an alternative to either absorption or variable costing for product costing and income reporting. **Throughput costing** assigns *only* the unit-level *spending* for direct costs as the cost of products or services. A unit-level cost is one that is incurred every time a unit of product is manufactured and will *not* be incurred if another unit is not manufactured.[2] Advocates of throughput costing argue that classifying any other past or committed cost as a product cost creates an

[2]See Chapter 5 for a thorough discussion of the concept of unit-level costs and cost hierarchies in the context of an activity-based costing system.

incentive to drive down the average cost per unit simply by manufacturing more units on nonbottleneck processes.

Throughput-Costing Income Statements

Learning Objective 8

Prepare an income statement under throughput costing.

Suppose Quikmath.com's management team decided that only direct material qualified as a throughput cost. This implies that Quikmath.com's management has *committed,* at least for the time being, to provide *all* other resources (i.e., direct labor and all manufacturing support costs included in manufacturing overhead) regardless of how many calculators and other devices Quikmath.com produces. Under throughput costing, then, Quikmath.com's income statements for the three years in our illustration would appear as in the Excel spreadsheet shown in Exhibit 8–6. Notice that all costs other than the throughput cost (only direct material in this hypothetical illustration) are considered to be operating cost of the period.

A comparison of the reported income under throughput costing (Exhibit 8–6) with the reported income under either variable or absorption costing (Exhibit 8–3) reveals substantial differences in the "bottom line" under the three methods for each year. Proponents of throughput costing argue that this method alone eliminates the incentive to produce excess inventory simply to reduce unit costs by spreading *committed* resource costs (i.e., direct labor and variable and fixed manufacturing overhead) across more units. The incentive for such overproduction disappears under throughput costing, because all nonthroughput costs (direct labor and manufacturing overhead in our illustration) will be expensed as period costs regardless of how many units are produced.

Exhibit 8–6
Income Statements under Throughput Costing

Quikmath.com

Microsoft Excel - Income Statements Under Throughput Costing

E17 =E9-E16

	A	B	C	D	E
1	QUIKMATH.COM				
2	Throughput-Costing Income Statement				
3					
4			20x0	20x1	20x2
5					
6	Sales revenue (at $12 per unit)		$ 600,000	$ 420,000	$ 780,000
7	Less: Cost of goods sold (at throughput cost:				
8	standard direct-material cost)[a]		150,000	105,000	195,000
9	Gross margin		$ 450,000	$ 315,000	$ 585,000
10	Less: Operating costs:				
11	Direct labor[b]		$ 100,000	$ 100,000	$ 100,000
12	Variable manufacturing overhead[c]		50,000	50,000	50,000
13	Fixed manufacturing overhead[c]		150,000	150,000	150,000
14	Variable selling and administrative costs[d]		50,000	35,000	65,000
15	Fixed selling and administrative costs[d]		25,000	25,000	25,000
16	Total operating costs		$ 375,000	$ 360,000	$ 390,000
17	Net income		$ 75,000	$ (45,000)	$ 195,000
18					
19	[a]Standard direct-material cost per unit of $3 multiplied by sales volume in units.				
20					
21	[b]Assumes management has committed to direct labor sufficient to produce the planned annual production				
22	volume of 50,000; direct-labor cost is used at a rate of $2 per unit produced.				
23					
24	[c]Assumes management has committed to support resources sufficient to produce the planned annual				
25	production volume of 50,000 units; variable-overhead cost is used at a rate of $1 per unit produced. Fixed				
26	overhead is $150,000 per year.				
27					
28	[d]Variable selling and administrative costs used amount to $1 per unit sold. Fixed selling and				
29	administrative costs are $25,000 per year.				

Sheet1 / Sheet2 / Sheet3

Ready

Focus on Ethics

INCENTIVE TO OVERPRODUCE INVENTORY

This classic case is based on an actual company's experience.* Brandolino Company uses an actual-cost system to apply all production costs to units produced. The plant has a maximum production capacity of 40 million units but produced and sold only 10 million units during year 1. There were no beginning or ending inventories. The company's absorption-costing income statement for year 1 follows:

BRANDOLINO COMPANY
Income Statement
For Year 1

Sales (10,000,000 units at $6)		$60,000,000
Cost of goods sold:		
Direct costs (material and labor) (10,000,000 at $2)	$20,000,000	
Manufacturing overhead	48,000,000	68,000,000
Gross margin		$ (8,000,000)
Less: Selling and administrative expenses		10,000,000
Operating profit (loss)		$(18,000,000)

The board of directors is upset about the $18 million loss. A consultant approached the board with the following offer: "I agree to become president for no fixed salary. But I insist on a year-end bonus of 10 percent of operating profit (before considering the bonus)." The board of directors agreed to these terms and hired the consultant as Brandolino's new president. The new president promptly stepped up production to an annual rate of 30 million units. Sales for year 2 remained at 10 million units. The resulting absorption-costing income statement for year 2 is displayed in the right-hand column.

The day after the year 2 statement was verified, the president took his check for $1,400,000 and resigned to take a job with another corporation. He remarked, "I enjoy challenges. Now that Brandolino Company is in the black, I'd prefer tackling another challenging situation." (His contract with his new employer is similar to the one he had with Brandolino Company.)

BRANDOLINO COMPANY
Income Statement
For Year 2

Sales (10,000,000 units at $6)		$60,000,000
Cost of goods sold:		
Costs of goods manufactured:		
Direct costs (material and labor) (30,000,000 at $2)	$ 60,000,000	
Manufacturing overhead	48,000,000	
Total cost of goods manufactured	$108,000,000	
Less: Ending inventory:		
Direct costs (material and labor) (20,000,000 at $2)	$ 40,000,000	
Manufacturing overhead (20/30 × $48,000,000)	32,000,000	
Total ending inventory costs	$ 72,000,000	
Cost of goods sold		36,000,000
Gross margin		$24,000,000
Less: Selling and administrative expenses		10,000,000
Operating profit before bonus		$14,000,000
Bonus		1,400,000
Operating profit after bonus		$12,600,000

What do you think is going on here? How would you evaluate the company's year 2 performance? Using variable costing, what would operating profit be for year 1? For year 2? (Assume that all selling and administrative costs are committed and unchanged.) Compare those results with the absorption-costing statements. Comment on the ethical issues in this scenario.

*This scenario is based on the case "I Enjoy Challenges," originally written by Michael W. Maher. It is used here with permission.

Chapter Summary

LO1 Explain the accounting treatment of fixed manufacturing overhead under absorption and variable costing. Under absorption (or full) costing, fixed overhead is applied to manufactured goods as a product cost. The fixed-overhead cost remains in inventory until the goods are sold. Under variable (or direct) costing, fixed overhead is a period cost expensed during the period when it is incurred.

LO2 Prepare an income statement under absorption costing. On an absorption-costing income statement, the cost of goods sold is measured at absorption cost (i.e., includes direct material, direct labor, and both variable and fixed manufacturing overhead) and, therefore, fixed overhead is not a period cost.

LO3 Prepare an income statement under variable costing. On a variable-costing income statement, the cost of goods sold is measured at variable cost (i.e., includes direct material, direct labor, and only variable manufacturing overhead), and fixed overhead is treated as a period cost.

LO4 Reconcile reported income under absorption and variable costing. Income reported under absorption and variable costing can be reconciled by focusing on the effects of the two places where the two statements differ: (1) calculation of cost of goods sold and (2) period costs.

LO5 Explain the implications of absorption and variable costing for cost-volume-profit analysis. Variable costing highlights the separation between fixed and variable costs, as do cost-volume-profit analysis and break-even calculations. Both of these techniques account for fixed manufacturing overhead as a lump-sum period cost. In contrast, absorption costing is inconsistent with CVP analysis, because fixed overhead is applied to goods as a product cost on a per-unit basis.

LO6 Evaluate absorption and variable costing. There are pros and cons to both costing methods. Variable costing dovetails much more closely than absorption costing with any operational analysis that requires a separation between fixed and variable costs (e.g., CVP analysis). On the other hand, variable costing understates a product's cost, because it excludes fixed manufacturing overhead from the unit cost calculation. In contrast, absorption costing alleviates that objection by including fixed overhead on a per-unit basis in a product's cost. However, this distorts the cost behavior of fixed costs, which do not in fact vary with production activity.

LO7 Explain the rationale behind throughput costing. Some accountants and managers advocate throughput costing, in which only throughput costs are inventoried as product costs. They argue that throughput costing reduces the incentive for management to produce excess inventory simply for the purpose of spreading committed (non-throughput) costs across a larger number of units produced.

LO8 Prepare an income statement under throughput costing. A throughput-costing income statement assigns only unit-level spending for direct costs as the cost of products or services. A unit-level cost is incurred every time a unit is manufactured and will not be incurred if another unit is not manufactured. All other costs are treated as period costs.

Review Problem on Absorption and Variable Costing

ScholasticPak Company manufactures backpacks used by students. A typical backpack has the following price and variable costs.

Sales price	$45
Direct material	15
Direct labor	6
Variable overhead	9

Budgeted fixed overhead in the company's first year of operations, was $900,000. Actual and planned production was 150,000 units, of which 125,000 were sold. ScholasticPak incurred the following selling and administrative expenses.

Fixed	$150,000 for the year
Variable	$3 per unit sold

Required:

1. Compute the product cost per backpack under (*a*) variable costing and (*b*) absorption costing.
2. Prepare income statements for the year using (*a*) variable costing and (*b*) absorption costing.
3. Reconcile the income reported under the two methods by analyzing the two key places where the income statements differ.

Solution to Review Problem

1. Predetermined fixed overhead rate $= \dfrac{\text{Budgeted fixed overhead}}{\text{Budgeted production}}$

$$= \frac{\$900{,}000}{150{,}000} = \$6 \text{ per unit}$$

Product Cost per Unit

Direct material	$15
Direct labor	6
Variable overhead	9
a. Cost per unit under variable costing	$30
Fixed overhead per unit under absorption costing	6
b. Cost per unit under absorption costing	$36

2. *a.* **Variable-Costing Income Statement**

Sales revenue (125,000 units sold at $45 per unit)	$5,625,000
Less: Variable expenses:	
Variable manufacturing costs (at variable cost of $30 per unit)	3,750,000
Variable selling and administrative costs (at $3 per unit × 125,000 units sold)	375,000
Contribution margin	$1,500,000
Less: Fixed expenses:	
Fixed manufacturing overhead	900,000
Fixed selling and administrative expenses	150,000
Net income	$ 450,000

b. **Absorption-Costing Income Statement**

Sales revenue (125,000 units sold at $45 per unit)	$5,625,000
Less: Cost of goods sold (at absorption cost of $36 per unit)	4,500,000
Gross margin	$1,125,000
Less: Selling and administrative expenses:	
Variable (at $3 per unit × 125,000 units sold)	375,000
Fixed	150,000
Net income	$ 600,000

3.

Cost of goods sold under absorption costing	$4,500,000
Less: Variable manufacturing costs under variable costing	3,750,000
Subtotal	$ 750,000
Less: Fixed manufacturing overhead as period expense under variable costing	900,000
Total	$ (150,000)
Net income under variable costing	$ 450,000
Less: Net income under absorption costing	600,000
Difference in net income	$ (150,000)

Key Terms

For each term's definition refer to the indicated page, or turn to the glossary at the end of the text.

absorption (or **full**) **costing, 327**

throughput costing, 333

variable (or **direct**) **costing, 327**

Review Questions

8–1. Briefly explain the difference between absorption costing and variable costing.

8–2. Timing is the key in distinguishing between absorption and variable costing. Explain this statement.

8–3. The term *direct costing* is a misnomer. *Variable costing* is a better term for the product-costing method. Do you agree or disagree? Why?

8–4. When inventory increases, will absorption-costing or variable-costing income be greater? Why?

8–5. Why do many managers prefer variable costing over absorption costing?

8–6. Explain how throughput costing differs from absorption and variable costing.

8–7. Explain why some management accountants believe that absorption costing may provide an incentive for managers to overproduce inventory. How does throughput costing avoid this problem?

8–8. Will variable and absorption costing result in significantly different income measures in a JIT setting? Why?

8–9. Why do proponents of absorption costing argue that absorption costing is preferable as the basis for pricing decisions?

8–10. Why do proponents of variable costing prefer variable costing when making pricing decisions?

8–11. Which is more consistent with cost-volume-profit analysis, variable costing or absorption costing? Why?

8–12. Explain how the accounting definition of an asset is related to the choice between absorption and variable costing.

Exercises

All applicable Exercises are available with McGraw-Hill's *Connect Accounting*™. 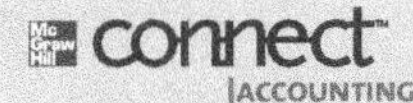

Exercise 8–13
Difference in Income under Absorption and Variable Costing
(LO 1, 4)

Manta Ray Company manufactures diving masks with a variable cost of $25. The masks sell for $34. Budgeted fixed manufacturing overhead for the most recent year was $792,000. Actual production was equal to planned production.

Required: Under each of the following conditions, state (*a*) whether income is higher under variable or absorption costing and (*b*) the amount of the difference in reported income under the two methods. Treat each condition as an independent case.

1.	Production	110,000 units
	Sales	108,000 units
2.	Production	90,000 units
	Sales	95,000 units
3.	Production	79,200 units
	Sales	79,200 units

Exercise 8–14
Absorption, Variable, and Throughput Costing
(LO 1, 7)

Information taken from Tuscarora Paper Company's records for the most recent year is as follows:

Direct material used	$290,000
Direct labor	100,000
Variable manufacturing overhead	50,000
Fixed manufacturing overhead	80,000
Variable selling and administrative costs	40,000
Fixed selling and administrative costs	20,000

Required:

1. Assuming Tuscarora Paper Company uses variable costing, compute the inventoriable costs for the year.
2. Compute the year's inventoriable costs using absorption costing.
3. Now assume that Tuscarora Paper Company uses throughput costing, and the company has *committed* to spending for direct labor, variable overhead, and fixed overhead in the amounts given in the problem. Under this scenario, compute the company's inventoriable costs for the year.

(CMA, adapted)

Exercise 8–15
Absorption and Variable Costing
(LO 1, 4)

Easton Pump Company's planned production for the year just ended was 20,000 units. This production level was achieved, and 21,000 units were sold. Other data follow:

Direct material used	$600,000
Direct labor incurred	300,000
Fixed manufacturing overhead	420,000
Variable manufacturing overhead	200,000
Fixed selling and administrative expenses	350,000
Variable selling and administrative expenses	105,000
Finished-goods inventory, January 1	2,000 units

There were no work-in-process inventories at the beginning or end of the year.

Required:

1. What would be Easton Pump Company's finished-goods inventory cost on December 31 under the variable-costing method?
2. Which costing method, absorption or variable costing, would show a higher operating income for the year? By what amount?

(CMA, adapted)

Exercise 8–16
Absorption, Variable, and Throughput Costing
(LO 1, 4, 7)

Pandora Pillow Company's planned production for the year just ended was 10,000 units. This production level was achieved, but only 9,000 units were sold. Other data follow:

Direct material used	$40,000
Direct labor incurred	20,000
Fixed manufacturing overhead	25,000
Variable manufacturing overhead	12,000
Fixed selling and administrative expenses	30,000
Variable selling and administrative expenses	4,500
Finished-goods inventory, January 1	None

There were no work-in-process inventories at the beginning or end of the year.

Required:

1. What would be Pandora Pillow Company's finished-goods inventory cost on December 31 under the variable-costing method?
2. Which costing method, absorption or variable costing, would show a higher operating income for the year? By what amount?
3. Suppose Pandora Pillow Company uses throughput costing, and direct material is its only unit-level cost. What would be Pandora's finished-goods inventory on December 31?

Exercise 8–17
Difference in Income under Absorption and Variable Costing
(LO 1, 4)

Bianca Bicycle Company manufactures mountain bikes with a variable cost of $200. The bicycles sell for $350 each. Budgeted fixed manufacturing overhead for the most recent year was $2,200,000. Planned and actual production for the year were the same.

Required: Under each of the following conditions, state (*a*) whether income is higher under variable or absorption costing and (*b*) the amount of the difference in reported income under the two methods. Treat each condition as an independent case.

1.	Production	20,000 units
	Sales	23,000 units
2.	Production	10,000 units
	Sales	10,000 units
3.	Production	11,000 units
	Sales	9,000 units

Exercise 8–18
Variable Costing and Cost-Volume-Profit Analysis
(LO 5)

Refer to the data given in the preceding exercise for Bianca Bicycle Company.

Required:

1. Prepare a cost-volume-profit graph for the company. (Scale the vertical axis in millions of dollars, and draw the CVP graph up through 15,000 units on the horizontal axis.)
2. Calculate Bianca Bicycle Company's break-even point in units, and show the break-even point on the CVP graph.
3. Explain why variable costing is more compatible with your CVP graph than absorption costing would be.

Exercise 8–19
Absorption versus Variable Costing
(LO 1)

Information taken from Allied Pipe Company's records for the most recent year is as follows:

Direct material used	$340,000
Direct labor	160,000
Variable manufacturing overhead	75,000
Fixed manufacturing overhead	125,000
Variable selling and administrative costs	70,000
Fixed selling and administrative costs	37,000

Required:

1. Assuming Allied Pipe Company uses absorption costing, compute the inventoriable costs for the year.
2. Compute the year's inventoriable costs using variable costing.

(CMA, adapted)

Exercise 8–20
Absorption, Variable, and Throughput Costing; Use of Internet
(LO 1, 6)

Visit the Web site for one of the following companies, or a different company of your choosing.

Coca-Cola	www.cocacola.com
Firestone	www.firestone.com
Motorola	www.motorola.com
Texas Instruments	www.ti.com
Toyota	www.toyota.com
Xerox Corporation	www.xerox.com

Required: Read about the company's products and operations. Discuss the pros and cons of absorption, variable, and throughput costing as the basis for product costing if the firm uses cost-based pricing.

Problems

All applicable Problems are available with McGraw-Hill's *Connect Accounting*™. 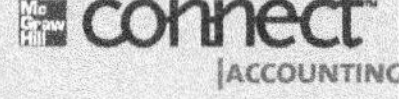

Problem 8–21
Straightforward Problem on Absorption versus Variable Costing
(LO 2, 3, 4)

2(a). Net income: $200,000
3. Cost of goods sold under absorption costing: $1,500,000

Skinny Dippers, Inc. produces nonfat frozen yogurt. The product is sold in five-gallon containers, which have the following price and variable costs.

Sales price	$15
Direct material	5
Direct labor	2
Variable overhead	3

Budgeted fixed overhead in 20x1, the company's first year of operations, was $300,000. Planned and actual production was 150,000 five-gallon containers, of which 125,000 were sold. Skinny Dippers, Inc. incurred the following selling and administrative expenses.

Fixed	$50,000 for the year
Variable	$1 per container sold

Required:

1. Compute the product cost per container of frozen yogurt under (*a*) variable costing and (*b*) absorption costing.
2. Prepare income statements for 20x1 using (*a*) absorption costing and (*b*) variable costing.
3. Reconcile the income reported under the two methods by listing the two key places where the income statements differ.
4. Reconcile the income reported under the two methods using the shortcut method.
5. *Build a spreadsheet:* Construct an Excel spreadsheet to solve all of the preceding requirements. Show how the solution will change if the following information changes: the selling price and direct-material cost per unit are $16.00 and $4.50, respectively.

Problem 8–22
Straightforward Problem on Throughput Costing
(LO 7, 8)

2. Net income: $25,000

Refer to the information given in the preceding problem for Skinny Dippers, Inc. Assume that the company has *committed* spending for direct labor and manufacturing overhead; direct material is the only unit-level production cost.

Required:

1. Compute the cost of Skinny Dippers' year-end finished-goods inventory using throughput costing.
2. Prepare an income statement for 20x1 using throughput costing.
3. Briefly explain the difference between gross margin computed under absorption costing and gross margin computed under throughput costing.
4. *Build a spreadsheet:* Construct an Excel spreadsheet to solve requirement (2) above. Show how the solution will change if the following information changes: the selling price and direct-material cost per unit are $16.00 and $4.50, respectively.

Problem 8–23
Absorption and Variable Costing; CVP Analysis
(LO 2, 3, 4, 5)

1. Total contribution margin: $320,000
2. Break-even point: 25,000 units

Yellowstone Company began operations on January 1 to produce a single product. It used an absorption costing system with a planned production volume of 100,000 units. During its first year of operations, the planned production volume was achieved, and there were no fixed selling or administrative expenses. Inventory on December 31 was 20,000 units, and net income for the year was $240,000.

Required:

1. If Yellowstone Company had used variable costing, its net income would have been $220,000. Compute the break-even point in units under variable costing.
2. Draw a profit-volume graph for Yellowstone Company. (Use variable costing.)

Problem 8–24
Variable versus Absorption Costing; JIT
(LO 1, 4)

2. Budgeted variable manufacturing costs: $3,500,000
3. Increase in inventory (in units): 5,000 units

Outback Corporation manufactures rechargeable flashlights in Brisbane, Australia. The firm uses an absorption costing system for internal reporting purposes; however, the company is considering using variable costing. Data regarding Outback's planned and actual operations for 20x1 follow:

	Budgeted Costs		
	Per Unit	**Total**	**Actual Costs**
Direct material	$12.00	$1,680,000	$1,560,000
Direct labor	9.00	1,260,000	1,170,000
Variable manufacturing overhead	4.00	560,000	520,000
Fixed manufacturing overhead	5.00	700,000	715,000
Variable selling expenses	8.00	1,120,000	1,000,000
Fixed selling expenses	7.00	980,000	980,000
Variable administrative expenses	2.00	280,000	250,000
Fixed administrative expenses	3.00	420,000	425,000
Total	$50.00	$7,000,000	$6,620,000

	Planned Activity	Actual Activity
Beginning finished-goods inventory in units	35,000	35,000
Sales in units	140,000	125,000
Production in units	140,000	130,000

The budgeted per-unit cost figures were based on Outback producing and selling 140,000 units in 20x1. Outback uses a predetermined overhead rate for applying manufacturing overhead to its product. A total manufacturing overhead rate of $9.00 per unit was employed for absorption costing purposes in 20x1. Any overapplied or underapplied manufacturing overhead is closed to the Cost of Goods Sold account at the end of the year. The 20x1 beginning finished-goods inventory for absorption costing purposes was valued at the 20x0 budgeted unit manufacturing cost, which was the same as the 20x1 budgeted unit manufacturing cost. There are no work-in-process inventories at either the beginning or the end of the year. The planned and actual unit selling price for 20x1 was $70 per unit.

Required: Was Outback's 20x1 income higher under absorption costing or variable costing? Why? Compute the following amounts.

1. The value of Outback Corporation's 20x1 ending finished-goods inventory under absorption costing.
2. The value of Outback Corporation's 20x1 ending finished-goods inventory under variable costing.
3. The difference between Outback Corporation's 20x1 reported income calculated under absorption costing and calculated under variable costing.
4. Suppose Outback Corporation had introduced a JIT production and inventory management system at the beginning of 20x1.
   a. What would likely be different about the scenario as described in the problem?
   b. Would reported income under variable and absorption costing differ by the magnitude you found in requirement (3)? Explain.

(CMA, adapted)

Problem 8–25
Variable-Costing and Absorption-Costing Income Statements; FMS; JIT
(LO 2, 3, 4, 6)

1. Total variable cost: $39
2(b). Net income: $320,000

Great Outdoze Company manufactures sleeping bags, which sell for $65 each. The variable costs of production are as follows:

Direct material	$20
Direct labor	11
Variable manufacturing overhead	8

Budgeted fixed overhead in 20x1 was $200,000 and budgeted production was 25,000 sleeping bags. The year's actual production was 25,000 units, of which 22,000 were sold. Variable selling and administrative costs were $1 per unit sold; fixed selling and administrative costs were $30,000. The firm does not prorate variances.

Required:

1. Calculate the product cost per sleeping bag under (*a*) absorption costing and (*b*) variable costing.
2. Prepare income statements for the year using (*a*) absorption costing and (*b*) variable costing.
3. Reconcile reported income under the two methods using the shortcut method.
4. Suppose that Great Outdoze Company implemented a JIT inventory and production management system at the beginning of 20x1. In addition, the firm installed a flexible manufacturing system. Would you expect reported income under variable and absorption costing to be different by as great a magnitude as you found in requirement (3)? Explain.

Problem 8–26
Throughput Costing
(LO 7, 8)

2. Net income: $263,000

Refer to the information given in the preceding problem for Great Outdoze Company. Assume that direct material is the *only unit-level* manufacturing cost. The company has *committed* its spending for direct labor and overhead (variable and fixed).

Required:

1. Calculate the product cost per sleeping bag under throughput costing.
2. Prepare a 20x1 income statement using throughput costing.
3. Give an argument for and against throughput costing.

Problem 8–27
Variable and Absorption Costing
(LO 1, 4)

2(a). Contribution margin per unit: $22
2(b). Projected net income for the year under absorption costing: $178,000

Dayton Lighting Company had net income for the first 10 months of the current year of $200,000. One hundred thousand units were manufactured during this period (the same as the planned production), and 100,000 units were sold. Fixed manufacturing overhead was $2,000,000 over the 10-month period (i.e., $200,000 per month). There are no selling and administrative expenses for Dayton Lighting Company. Both variable and fixed costs are expected to continue at the same rates for the balance of the year (i.e., fixed costs at $200,000 per month and variable costs at the same variable cost per unit). Twenty thousand units are to be produced and 19,000 units are to be sold in total over the last two months of the current year. Assume the unit variable cost is the same in the current year as in the previous year. (*Hint:* You cannot calculate revenue or cost of goods sold; you must work directly with contribution margin or gross margin.)

Required:

1. If operations proceed as described, will net income be higher under variable or absorption costing for the current year in total? Why?
2. If operations proceed as described, what will net income for the year *in total* be under (*a*) variable costing and (*b*) absorption costing? (Ignore income taxes.)
3. Discuss the advantages and disadvantages of absorption and variable costing.

Problem 8–28
Throughput Costing, Absorption Costing, and Variable Costing
(LO 1, 2, 3, 7, 8)

1. Total cost: $644,800
2. Year-end inventory, throughput costing: $4,800
4. Net income: $51,200

Emerson Corporation, which uses throughput costing, just completed its first year of operations. Planned and actual production equaled 10,000 units, and sales totaled 9,600 units at $72 per unit. Cost data for the year are as follows:

Direct material (per unit)	$12
Conversion cost:	
Direct labor	45,000
Variable manufacturing overhead	65,000
Fixed manufacturing overhead	220,000
Selling and administrative costs:	
Variable (per unit)	8
Fixed	118,000

The company classifies only direct material as a throughput cost.

Required:

1. Compute the company's total cost for the year assuming that variable manufacturing costs are driven by the number of units produced, and variable selling and administrative costs are driven by the number of units sold.
2. How much of this cost would be held in year-end inventory under (*a*) absorption costing, (*b*) variable costing, and (*c*) throughput costing?
3. How much of the company's total cost for the year would be included as an expense on the period's income statement under (*a*) absorption costing, (*b*) variable costing, and (*c*) throughput costing?
4. Prepare Emerson's throughput-costing income statement.
5. ***Build a spreadsheet:*** Construct an Excel spreadsheet to solve requirements (1) and (2) above. Show how the solution will change if the following information changes: the direct-material cost is $11 per unit, and the total direct-labor cost is $46,000.

Problem 8–29
Variable-Costing and Absorption Costing Income Statements; Reconciling Reported Income
(LO 2, 3, 4)

1(a). Absorption cost per case is $42
1(b). Variable costing, operating income, year 2: $145,000

Chataqua Can Company manufactures metal cans used in the food-processing industry. A case of cans sells for $50. The variable costs of production for one case of cans are as follows:

Direct material	$15
Direct labor	5
Variable manufacturing overhead	12
Total variable manufacturing cost per case	$32

Variable selling and administrative costs amount to $1 per case. Budgeted fixed manufacturing overhead is $800,000 per year, and fixed selling and administrative cost is $75,000 per year. The following data pertain to the company's first three years of operation.

	Year 1	Year 2	Year 3
Planned production (in units)	80,000	80,000	80,000
Finished-goods inventory (in units), January 1	0	0	20,000
Actual production (in units)	80,000	80,000	80,000
Sales (in units)	80,000	60,000	90,000
Finished-goods inventory (in units), December 31	0	20,000	10,000

Actual costs were the same as the budgeted costs.

Required:

1. Prepare operating income statements for Chataqua Can Company for its first three years of operations using:
   a. Absorption costing.
   b. Variable costing.
2. Reconcile Chataqua Can Company's operating income reported under absorption and variable costing for each of its first three years of operation. Use the shortcut method.
3. Suppose that during Chataqua's fourth year of operation actual production equals planned production, actual costs are equal to budgeted or standard costs, and the company ends the year with no inventory on hand.
   a. What will be the difference between absorption-costing income and variable-costing income in year 4?
   b. What will be the relationship between total operating income for the four-year period as reported under absorption and variable costing? Explain.

Problem 8–30
Throughput Costing
(LO 7, 8)

Net income, year 1: $485,000

Refer to the information in the preceding problem for Chataqua Can Company. Assume that direct material is the *only unit-level* manufacturing cost.

Required: Prepare income statements for all three years using throughput costing.

Cases

Case 8–31
Comparison of Absorption and Variable Costing; Actual Costing
(LO 2, 3, 4)

1. Operating income, year 1: $27,500
2. Operating income, year 2: $20,500

Lehighton Chalk Company manufactures blackboard chalk for educational uses. The company's product is sold by the box at $50 per unit. Lehighton uses an actual costing system, which means that the actual costs of direct material, direct labor, and manufacturing overhead are entered into work-in-process inventory. The actual application rate for manufacturing overhead is computed each year; actual manufacturing overhead is divided by actual production (in units) to compute the application rate. Information for Lehighton's first two years of operation is as follows:

	Year 1	Year 2
Sales (in units)	2,500	2,500
Production (in units)	3,000	2,000
Production costs:		
Variable manufacturing costs	$21,000	$14,000
Fixed manufacturing overhead	42,000	42,000
Selling and administrative costs:		
Variable	25,000	25,000
Fixed	20,000	20,000

Required: Lehighton Chalk Company had no beginning or ending work-in-process inventories for either year.

1. Prepare operating income statements for both years based on absorption costing.
2. Prepare operating income statements for both years based on variable costing.
3. Prepare a numerical reconciliation of the difference in income reported under the two costing methods used in requirements (1) and (2).

Case 8–32
Analysis of Differences in Absorption-Costing and Variable-Costing Income Statements; Continuation of Preceding Case
(LO 1, 6)

1. Cost of goods sold, year 1, absorption costing income statement: $52,500
Cost of goods sold, year 2, variable costing income statement: $17,500
5(a). Total sales revenue minus total costs expensed across both years, absorption costing: $41,000

Refer to the information given in the preceding case for Lehighton Chalk Company.

Required:

1. Reconcile Lehighton's income reported under absorption and variable costing, during each year, by comparing the following two amounts on each income statement:
   - Cost of goods sold
   - Fixed cost (expensed as a period expense)
2. What was Lehighton's total income across both years under absorption costing and under variable costing?
3. What was the total sales revenue across both years under absorption costing and under variable costing?
4. What was the total of all costs expensed on the income statements across both years under absorption costing and under variable costing?
5. Subtract the total costs expensed across both years [requirement (4)] from the total sales revenue across both years [requirement (3)]: (*a*) under absorption costing and (*b*) under variable costing.
6. Comment on the results obtained in requirements (1), (2), (3), and (4) in light of the following assertion: *Timing is the key in distinguishing between absorption and variable costing.*

Case 8–33
Absorption and Variable Costing; Effect on the Balance Sheet; Continuation of Preceding Case
(LO 1, 4)

4. Absorption costing, finished-goods inventory, end of year 1: $10,500
5. Variable costing, reported income for year 2, $20,500

Refer to the information given in Case 8–31 for Lehighton Chalk Company. Selected information from Lehighton's year-end balance sheets for its first two years of operation is as follows:

LEHIGHTON CHALK COMPANY
Selected Balance Sheet Information

Based on absorption costing	**End of Year 1**	**End of Year 2**
Finished-goods inventory	$10,500	$ 0
Retained earnings	16,500	24,600
Based on variable costing	**End of Year 1**	**End of Year 2**
Finished-goods inventory	$3,500	$ 0
Retained earnings	9,500	24,600

Required:

1. Why is the year 1 ending balance in finished-goods inventory higher if absorption costing is used than if variable costing is used?
2. Why is the year 2 ending balance in finished-goods inventory the same under absorption and variable costing?
3. Notice that the ending balance of finished-goods inventory under absorption costing is greater than or equal to the ending finished-goods inventory balance under variable costing *for both years 1 and 2.* Will this relationship always hold true at any balance sheet date? Explain.
4. Compute the amount by which the year-end balance in finished-goods inventory declined during year 2 (i.e., between December 31 of year 1 and December 31 of year 2):
   - Using the data from the balance sheet prepared under absorption costing.
   - Using the data from the balance sheet prepared under variable costing.
5. Refer to your calculations from requirement (4). Compute the difference in the amount by which the year-end balances in finished-goods inventory declined under absorption versus variable costing. Then compare the amount of this difference with the difference in the company's reported income for year 2 under absorption versus variable costing. (Refer to the income statements prepared in Case 8–31.)
6. Notice that the retained earnings balance at the end of both years 1 and 2 on the balance sheet prepared under absorption costing is greater than or equal to the corresponding retained earnings balance on the statement prepared under variable costing. Will this relationship hold true at any balance sheet date? Explain.

FOCUS COMPANY >>>

THIS CHAPTER'S FOCUS COMPANY is Suncoast Food Centers, a chain of retail grocery stores in Florida. The company has three divisions. The Gulf and Atlantic divisions operate individual grocery stores in six coastal Floridian cities. The Food Processing Division operates dairy plants, bakeries, and meat-processing facilities in Miami, Orlando, and Jacksonville in order to supply the Suncoast grocery stores with fresh food products. In this chapter, we will explore how companies evaluate the performance of investment centers, such as Suncoast's three divisions. Investment centers are organizational subunits whose managers have the authority to make significant investment decisions, such as building a new store or expanding an existing one.

13 Investment Centers and Transfer Pricing

IN CONTRAST >>>

In contrast to the evaluation of investment center performance explored in the first part of the chapter, we will turn our attention to transfer pricing. The amount charged when one division of a company sells products or services to another division is called a transfer price. We can continue to use Suncoast Food Centers for our illustration, because the Suncoast food processing facilities sell their dairy, bakery, and meat products to the Suncoast grocery stores at a transfer price. We will explore different ways to set such transfer prices.

Suncoast FOOD CENTERS

AFTER COMPLETING THIS CHAPTER, YOU SHOULD BE ABLE TO:

1 Explain the role of managerial accounting in achieving goal congruence.

2 Compute an investment center's return on investment (ROI), residual income (RI), and economic value added (EVA).

3 Explain how a manager can improve ROI by increasing either the sales margin or capital turnover.

4 Describe some advantages and disadvantages of both ROI and residual income as divisional performance measures.

5 Explain how to measure a division's income and invested capital.

6 Use the general economic rule to set an optimal transfer price.

7 Explain how to base a transfer price on market prices, costs, or negotiations.

8 Understand the behavioral issues of incentives, goal congruence, and internal controls.

How do the top managers of large companies such as Allstate Insurance Company and General Electric Company evaluate their divisions and other major subunits? The largest subunits within these and similar organizations usually are designated as **investment centers.** The manager of this type of *responsibility center* is held accountable not only for the investment center's *profit* but also for the *capital invested* to earn that profit. Invested capital refers to assets, such as buildings and equipment, used in a subunit's operations. In this chapter, we will study the methods that managerial accountants use to evaluate investment centers and the performance of their managers.[1]

In many organizations, one subunit manufactures a product or produces a service that is then transferred to another subunit in the same organization. For example, automobile parts manufactured in one division of General Motors are then transferred to another GM division that assembles vehicles.

The price at which products or services are transferred between two subunits in an organization is called a **transfer price.** Since a transfer price affects the profit of both the buying and selling divisions, the transfer price affects the performance evaluation of these responsibility centers. Later in this chapter, we will study the methods that managerial accountants use to determine transfer prices.

Delegation of Decision Making

Learning Objective 1

Explain the role of managerial accounting in achieving goal congruence.

Most large organizations are decentralized. Managers throughout these organizations are given autonomy to make decisions for their subunits. Decentralization takes advantage of the specialized knowledge and skills of managers, permits an organization to respond

[1]Recall from Chapter 12 that in practice the term *profit center* sometimes is used interchangeably with the term *investment center.* To be precise, however, the term *profit center* should be reserved for a subunit whose manager is held accountable for profit but not for invested capital.

quickly to events, and relieves top management of the need to direct the organization's day-to-day activities. The biggest challenge in making a decentralized organization function effectively is to obtain *goal congruence* among the organization's autonomous managers.

Obtaining Goal Congruence: A Behavioral Challenge

Goal congruence is obtained when the managers of subunits throughout an organization strive to achieve the goals set by top management. This desirable state of affairs is difficult to achieve for a variety of reasons. Managers often are unaware of the effects of their decisions on the organization's other subunits. Also, it is only human for people to be more concerned with the performance of their own subunit than with the effectiveness of the entire organization. The behavioral challenge in designing any management control system is to come as close as possible to obtaining goal congruence.

To obtain goal congruence, the behavior of managers throughout an organization must be directed toward top management's goals. Successful managers not only have their sights set on these organizational goals, but also have been given positive incentives to achieve them. *The managerial accountant's objective* in designing a responsibility-accounting system is to provide these incentives to the organization's subunit managers. *The key factor in deciding how well the responsibility-accounting system works is the extent to which it directs managers' efforts toward organizational goals.* Thus, the accounting measures used to evaluate investment-center managers should provide them with incentives to act in the interests of the overall organization.

Management by Objectives (MBO)

An emphasis on obtaining goal congruence is consistent with a broad managerial approach called **management by objectives,** or **MBO.** Under the MBO philosophy, managers participate in setting goals that they then strive to achieve. The goals usually are expressed in financial or other quantitative terms, and the responsibility-accounting system is used to evaluate performance in achieving them.

Adaptation of Management Control Systems

When an organization begins its operations, it is usually small and decision making generally is centralized. The chief executive can control operations without a formal responsibility-accounting system. It is relatively easy in a small organization for managers to keep in touch with routine operations through face-to-face contact with employees.

As an organization grows, however, its managers need more formal information systems, including managerial accounting information, in order to maintain control. Accounting systems are established to record events and provide the framework for internal and external financial reports. Budgets become necessary to plan the organization's activity. As the organization gains experience in producing its goods or services, cost standards and flexible budgets often are established to help control operations. As the organization continues to grow, some delegation of decision making becomes necessary. Decentralization is often the result of this tendency toward delegation. Ultimately, a fully developed responsibility-accounting system emerges. Managerial accountants designate cost centers, revenue centers, profit centers, and investment centers, and develop appropriate performance measures for each subunit.

Thus, an organization's accounting and managerial control systems usually adapt and become more complex as the organization grows and changes.

Measuring Performance in Investment Centers

In our study of investment-center performance evaluation, we will focus on Suncoast Food Centers. This Florida chain of retail grocery stores has three divisions, as depicted by the organization chart in Exhibit 13–1.

The Gulf and Atlantic divisions consist of individual grocery stores located in six coastal cities. The company's Food Processing Division operates dairy plants, bakeries, and meat-processing plants in Miami, Orlando, and Jacksonville. These facilities provide all Suncoast Food Centers with milk, ice cream, yogurt, cheese, breads and desserts, and packaged meat. These Suncoast-brand food products are transferred to the company's Gulf and Atlantic divisions at transfer prices established by the corporate controller's office.

"Accounting is changing. You're no longer sitting behind a desk just working on a computer, just crunching the numbers. You're actually getting to be a part of the day to day functions of the business." (13a)
Abbott Laboratories

Suncoast Food Centers' three divisions are investment centers. This responsibility-center designation is appropriate, because each division manager has the authority to make decisions that affect both profit and invested capital. For example, the Gulf Division manager approves the overall pricing policies in the Gulf Division's stores, and also has the autonomy to sign contracts to buy food and other products for resale. These actions influence the division's profit. In addition, the Gulf Division manager has the authority to build new Suncoast Food Centers, rent space in shopping centers, or close existing stores. These decisions affect the amount of capital invested in the division.

The primary goals of any profit-making enterprise include maximizing its profitability and using its invested capital as effectively as possible. Managerial accountants use three different measures to evaluate the performance of investment centers: return on investment (ROI), residual income (RI), and economic value added (EVA®). (EVA® is a registered trademark of Stern Stewart & Co.) We will illustrate each of these measures for Suncoast Food Centers.

Return on Investment

Learning Objective 2

Compute an investment center's return on investment (ROI), residual income (RI), and economic value added (EVA).

The most common investment-center performance measure is **return on investment,** or **ROI,** which is defined as follows:

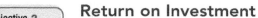

$$\text{Return on investment (ROI)} = \frac{\text{Income}}{\text{Invested capital}}$$

Exhibit 13–1
Organization Chart: Suncoast Food Centers

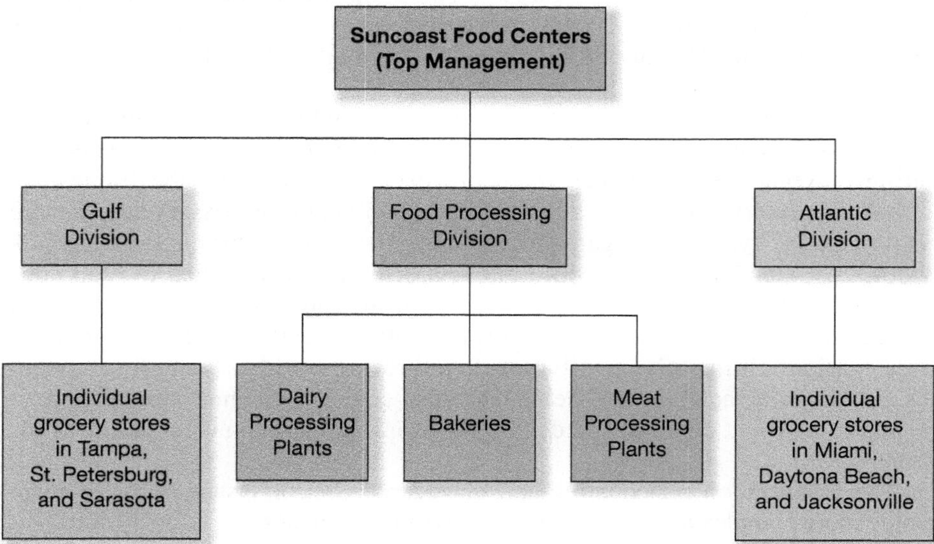

The most recent year's ROI calculations for Suncoast Food Centers' three divisions are:

	Income / Invested capital	=	Return on investment (ROI)
Gulf Division	$3,000,000 / $20,000,000	=	15%
Food Processing Division	$3,600,000 / $18,000,000	=	20%
Atlantic Division	$6,750,000 / $45,000,000	=	15%

Notice how the ROI calculation for each division takes into account *both divisional income and the capital invested* in the division. Why is this important? Suppose each division were evaluated only on the basis of its divisional profit. The Atlantic Division reported a higher divisional profit than the Gulf Division. Does this mean the Atlantic Division performed better than the Gulf Division? The answer is no. Although the Atlantic Division's profit exceeded the Gulf Division's profit, the Atlantic Division used a much larger amount of invested capital to earn its profit. The Atlantic Division's assets are more than two times the assets of the Gulf Division.

Considering the relative size of the two divisions, we should expect the Atlantic Division to earn a larger profit than the Gulf Division. The important question is not how much profit each division earned, but rather how effectively each division used its invested capital to earn a profit.

Factors Underlying ROI

We can rewrite the ROI formula as follows:

$$\text{Return on investment} = \frac{\text{Income}}{\text{Invested capital}} = \frac{\text{Income}}{\text{Sales revenue}} \times \frac{\text{Sales revenue}}{\text{Invested capital}}$$

Notice that the *sales revenue* term cancels out in the denominator and numerator when the two right-hand fractions are multiplied.

Writing the ROI formula in this way highlights the factors that determine a division's return on investment. Income divided by sales revenue is called the **sales margin.** This term measures the percentage of each sales dollar that remains as profit after all expenses are covered. Sales revenue divided by invested capital is called the **capital turnover.** This term focuses on the number of sales dollars generated by every dollar of invested capital. The sales margin and capital turnover for Suncoast Food Centers' three divisions are calculated below for the most recent year.

"The ROI of pollution prevention rises radically when 'hidden' environmental management costs are revealed." (13b)
Kestrel Management Services
(an environmental consulting firm)

	Sales margin	×	Capital turnover	=	ROI
	Income / Sales revenue	×	Sales revenue / Invested capital	=	ROI
Gulf Division	$3,000,000 / $60,000,000	×	$60,000,000 / $20,000,000	=	15%
Food Processing Division	$3,600,000 / $9,000,000	×	$9,000,000 / $18,000,000	=	20%
Atlantic Division	$6,750,000 / $135,000,000	×	$135,000,000 / $45,000,000	=	15%

The Gulf Division's sales margin is 5 percent ($3,000,000 of profit ÷ $60,000,000 of sales revenue). Thus, each dollar of divisional sales resulted in a five-cent profit. The division's capital turnover was 3 ($60,000,000 of sales revenue ÷ $20,000,000 of invested capital). Thus, three dollars of sales revenue were generated by each dollar of capital invested in the division's assets, such as store buildings, display shelves, checkout equipment, and inventory.

Learning Objective 3

Explain how a manager can improve ROI by increasing either the sales margin or capital turnover.

Improving ROI How could the Gulf Division manager improve the division's return on investment? Since ROI is the product of the sales margin and the capital turnover, ROI can be improved by increasing either or both of its components. For example, if the Gulf Division manager increased the division's sales margin to 6 percent while holding the capital turnover constant at 3, the division's ROI would climb from 15 percent to 18 percent, as follows:

$$\begin{aligned}\text{Gulf Division's improved ROI} &= \text{Improved sales margin} \times \text{Same capital turnover} \\ &= 6\% \times 3 = 18\%\end{aligned}$$

To bring about the improved sales margin, the Gulf Division manager would need to increase divisional profit to \$3,600,000 on sales of \$60,000,000 (\$3,600,000 ÷ \$60,000,000 = 6%). How could profit be increased without changing total sales revenue? There are two possibilities: increase sales prices while selling less quantity, or decrease expenses. Neither of these is necessarily easy to do. In increasing sales prices, the division manager must be careful not to lose sales to the extent that total sales revenue declines. Similarly, reducing the expenses must not diminish product quality, customer service, or overall store atmosphere. Any of these changes could also result in lost sales revenue.

An alternative way of increasing the Gulf Division's ROI would be to increase its capital turnover. Suppose the Gulf Division manager increased the division's capital turnover to 4 while holding the sales margin constant at 5 percent. The division's ROI would climb from 15 percent to 20 percent:

$$\begin{aligned}\text{Gulf Division's improved ROI} &= \text{Same Sales margin} \times \text{Improved capital turnover} \\ &= 5\% \times 4 = 20\%\end{aligned}$$

To obtain the improved capital turnover, the Gulf Division manager would need to either increase sales revenue or reduce the division's invested capital. For example, the improved ROI could be achieved by reducing invested capital to \$15,000,000 while maintaining sales revenue of \$60,000,000. This would be a very tall order. The division manager can lower invested capital somewhat by reducing inventories and can increase sales revenue by using store space more effectively. But reducing inventories may lead to stockouts and lost sales, and crowded aisles may drive customers away.

Improving ROI is a balancing act that requires all the skills of an effective manager. The ROI analysis above merely shows the arena in which the balancing act is performed.

Residual Income

Learning Objective 2

Compute an investment center's return on investment (ROI), residual income (RI), and economic value added (EVA).

Although ROI is the most popular investment-center performance measure, it has one major drawback. To illustrate, suppose Suncoast's Food Processing Division manager can buy a new food processing machine for \$500,000, which will save \$80,000 in operating expenses and thereby raise divisional profit by \$80,000. The return on this investment in new equipment is 16 percent:

$$\text{Return on investment in new equipment} = \frac{\text{Increase in divisional profit}}{\text{Increase in invested capital}} = \frac{\$80,000}{\$500,000} = 16\%$$

Now suppose it costs Suncoast Food Centers 12 cents for each dollar of capital to invest in operational assets. What is the optimal decision for the Food Processing Division manager to make, *viewed from the perspective of the company as a whole?* Since it costs Suncoast Food Centers 12 percent for every dollar of capital, and the return on investment in new equipment is 16 percent, the equipment should be purchased. For goal congruence, the autonomous division manager should decide to buy the new equipment.

Now consider what is likely to happen. The Food Processing Division manager's performance is evaluated on the basis of his division's ROI. Without the new equipment, the divisional ROI is 20 percent ($3,600,000 of divisional profit ÷ $18,000,000 of invested capital). If he purchases the new equipment, his divisional ROI will decline:

Food Processing Division's Return on Investment

Without Investment in New Equipment	With Investment in New Equipment
$\frac{\$3{,}600{,}000}{\$18{,}000{,}000} = 20\%$	$\frac{\$3{,}600{,}000 + \$80{,}000}{\$18{,}000{,}000 + \$500{,}000} < 20\%$

Why did this happen? Even though the investment in new equipment earns a return of 16 percent, which is greater than the company's cost of raising capital (12 percent), the return is less than the division's ROI without the equipment (20 percent). Averaging the new investment with those already in place in the Food Processing Division merely reduces the division's ROI. Since the division manager is evaluated using ROI, he will be reluctant to decide in favor of acquiring the new equipment.

The problem is that the ROI measure leaves out an important piece of information: it ignores the firm's cost of raising investment capital. For this reason, many managers prefer to use a different investment-center performance measure instead of ROI.

Computing Residual Income

An investment center's **residual income** is defined as follows:

$$\text{Residual income} = \text{Investment center's profit} - \left(\text{investment center's invested capital} \times \text{Imputed interest rate}\right)$$

where the imputed interest rate is the firm's cost of acquiring investment capital.

Residual income is a dollar amount, not a ratio like ROI. It is the amount of an investment center's profit that remains (as a residual) after subtracting an imputed interest charge. The term *imputed* means that the interest charge is estimated by the managerial accountant. This charge reflects the firm's minimum required rate of return on invested capital. In some firms, the imputed interest rate depends on the riskiness of the investment for which the funds will be used. Thus, divisions that have different levels of risk sometimes are assigned different imputed interest rates.

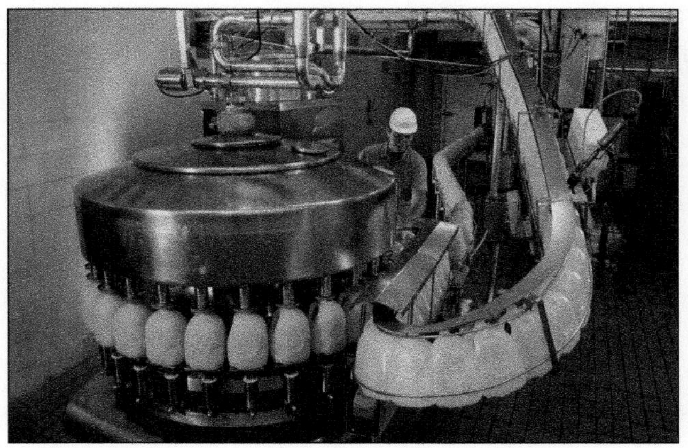

ROI and residual income are common performance measures for investment centers. Both measures relate the profit earned from selling the final product to the capital required to carry out production operations. Here the product is orange juice, and this bottling equipment represents the capital investment.

The residual income of Suncoast's Food Processing Division is computed below, both with and without the investment in the new equipment. The imputed interest rate is 12 percent.

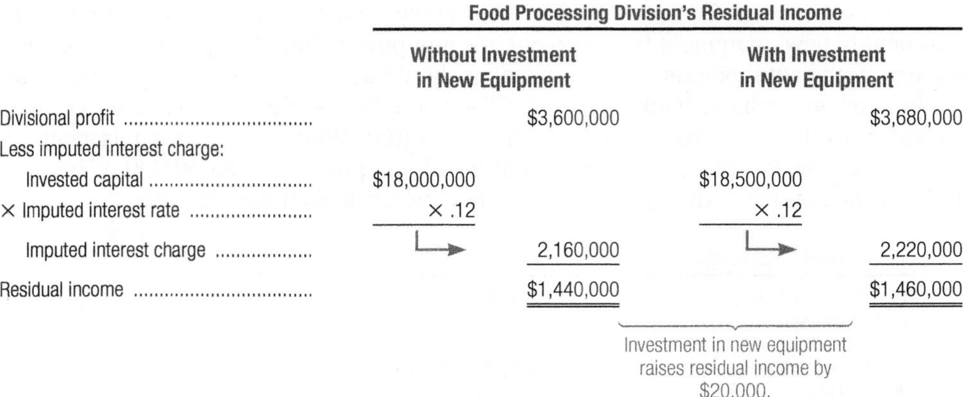

	Food Processing Division's Residual Income			
	Without Investment in New Equipment		With Investment in New Equipment	
Divisional profit		$3,600,000		$3,680,000
Less imputed interest charge:				
Invested capital	$18,000,000		$18,500,000	
× Imputed interest rate	× .12		× .12	
Imputed interest charge	→	2,160,000	→	2,220,000
Residual income		$1,440,000		$1,460,000

Investment in new equipment raises residual income by $20,000.

Notice that the Food Processing Division's residual income will *increase* if the new equipment is purchased. What will be the division manager's incentive if he is evaluated on the basis of residual income instead of ROI? He will want to make the investment because that decision will increase his division's residual income. Thus, goal congruence is achieved when the managerial accountant uses residual income to measure divisional performance.

Learning Objective 4

Describe some advantages and disadvantages of both ROI and residual income as divisional performance measures.

Why does residual income facilitate goal congruence while ROI does not? Because the residual-income formula incorporates an important piece of data that is excluded from the ROI formula: the firm's minimum required rate of return on invested capital. To summarize, ROI and residual income are compared as follows:

$$\text{ROI} = \frac{\text{Investment center's profit}}{\text{Investment center's invested capital}}$$

← Two pieces of data

$$\text{Residual income} = \text{Investment center's profit} - \left(\text{Investment center's invested capital} \times \text{Imputed interest rate}\right)$$

↑ Three pieces of data

Unfortunately, residual income also has a serious drawback: It should not be used to compare the performance of different-sized investment centers because it incorporates a bias in favor of the larger investment center. To illustrate, the following table compares the residual income of Suncoast Food Centers' Gulf and Atlantic divisions. Notice that the Atlantic Division's residual income is considerably higher than the Gulf Division's. This is entirely due to the much greater size of the Atlantic Division, as evidenced by its far greater invested capital.

	Comparison of Residual Income: Two Divisions			
	Gulf Division		Atlantic Division	
Divisional profit		$3,000,000		$6,750,000
Less imputed interest charge:				
Invested capital	$20,000,000		$45,000,000	
× Imputed interest rate	× .12		× .12	
Imputed interest charge	→	2,400,000	→	5,400,000
Residual income		$ 600,000		$1,350,000

The Atlantic Division's residual income is much higher simply because it is larger than the Gulf Division.

In short, neither ROI nor residual income provides a perfect measure of investment-center performance. ROI can undermine goal congruence. Residual income distorts comparisons between investment centers of different sizes. As a result, some companies routinely use both measures for divisional performance evaluation.

Shareholder Value Analysis Some companies apply the residual income concept to individual product lines. **Shareholder value analysis** calculates the residual income for a major product line, with the objective of determining how the product line affects the firm's value to the shareholders. Suppose, for example, that Suncoast Food Centers offers in-store, one-hour film development in selected stores. Let's say that the company's investment in this service is $200,000 and the annual profit is $40,000. Then the residual income on one-hour film development is $16,000 [$40,000 − ($200,000 × 12%)].

Economic Value Added

Learning Objective 2

Compute an investment center's return on investment (ROI), residual income (RI), and economic value added (EVA).

The most contemporary measure of investment center performance is **economic value added (EVA),** which is defined as follows:

$$\text{Economic value added} = \text{Investment center's after-tax operating income} - \left[\left(\text{Investment center's total assets} - \text{Investment center's current liabilities}\right) \times \text{Weighted-average cost of capital}\right]$$

Like residual income, the economic value added is a dollar amount. However, it differs from residual income in two important ways. First, an investment center's current liabilities are subtracted from its total assets. Second, the weighted-average cost of capital is used in the calculation.

Weighted-Average Cost of Capital Suncoast Food Centers has two sources of long-term capital: debt and equity. The cost to Suncoast of issuing debt is the after-tax cost of the interest payments on the debt, taking account of the fact that the interest payments are tax deductible. The cost of Suncoast's equity capital is the investment opportunity rate of Suncoast Food Centers' investors, that is, the rate they could earn on investments of similar risk to that of investing in Suncoast Food Centers. The **weighted-average cost of capital (WACC)** is defined as follows:

$$\text{Weighted-average cost of capital} = \frac{\left(\text{After-tax cost of debt capital}\right)\left(\text{Market value of debt}\right) + \left(\text{Cost of equity capital}\right)\left(\text{Market value of equity}\right)}{\text{Market value of debt} + \text{Market value of equity}}$$

The interest rate on Suncoast Food Centers' $40 million of debt is 9 percent, and the company's tax rate is 30 percent. Therefore, Suncoast's after-tax cost of debt is 6.3 percent [9% × (1 − 30%)]. Let's assume that the cost of Suncoast's equity capital is 12 percent. Moreover, the market value of the company's equity is $60 million.[2] The following calculation shows that Suncoast Food Centers' WACC is 9.72 percent.

[2]The *book value* of Suncoast Food Centers' equity is $41 million, but that amount does not reflect the current value of the company's assets or the value of intangible assets such as the Suncoast Food Centers name.

$$\text{Weighted-average cost of capital} = \frac{(.063)(\$40{,}000{,}000) + (.12)(\$60{,}000{,}000)}{\$40{,}000{,}000 + \$60{,}000{,}000} = .0972$$

Finally, Suncoast Food Centers had an average balance of $2 million in current liabilities, distributed as follows:

Division	Current Liabilities
Gulf Division	$ 400,000
Food Processing Division	1,000,000
Atlantic Division	600,000

Now we can compute the economic value added (or EVA) for each of Suncoast's three divisions.

Division	After-tax operating income (in millions)	− [(Total assets (in millions)	−	Current liabilities (in millions))	× WACC]	=	Economic value added
Gulf	$3.00 × (1 − .30) −	[($20	−	$ .4)	× .0972]	=	$194,880
Food Processing	$3.60 × (1 − .30) −	[($18	−	$1.0)	× .0972]	=	867,600
Atlantic	$6.75 × (1 − .30) −	[($45	−	$ .6)	× .0972]	=	409,320

The EVA analysis reveals that all three of Suncoast Food Centers' divisions are contributing substantially to the company's economic value.

What does an EVA analysis tell us? EVA indicates how much shareholder wealth is being created, as Roberto Goizueta, Coca-Cola's former CEO, explained: "We raise capital to make concentrate and sell it at an operating profit. Then we pay the cost of that capital. Shareholders pocket the difference (EVA amount)."

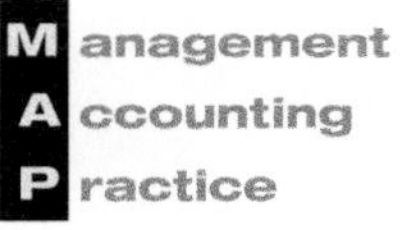

Siemens and Royal Bank of Canada

PAY FOR PERFORMANCE BASED ON EVA

In the wake of the excesses in top management compensation over the past few years, at many companies pay for performance is back in vogue. Top executives earn hefty bonuses when times are good, but are expected to share in the pain during a decline in business.

Siemens, a global electronics firm, links the compensation of its top 500 managers to their business units' economic value added (EVA) measure. Similarly, the Royal Bank of Canada, upon observing that its lower-level managers were not acting in accordance with the bank's overall strategy, began linking their compensation to the bank's EVA and revenue growth.[3]

[3]Kara Seannell and Joann Lublin, "SEC Unhappy with Answers on Executive Pay," *The Wall Street Journal,* January 29, 2008, p. 31; Louis Lavelle, "The Gravy Train Just Got Derailed—'Pay for Performance' Is Back in Vogue," *BusinessWeek,* November 19, 2001; and Tad Leahy, "All the Right Moves," *Business Finance* 6, no. 1 (April 2000), p. 32.

Measuring Income and Invested Capital

The ROI, residual-income, and economic value added (EVA) measures of investment-center performance all use profit and invested capital in their formulas. This raises the question of how to measure divisional profit and invested capital. This section will illustrate various approaches to resolving these measurement issues.

Invested Capital

Learning Objective 5

Explain how to measure a division's income and invested capital.

We will focus on Suncoast Food Centers' Food Processing Division to illustrate several alternative approaches to measuring an investment center's capital. Exhibit 13–2 lists the assets and liabilities associated with the Food Processing Division. Notice that Exhibit 13–2 does not constitute a complete balance sheet. First, there are no long-term liabilities, such as bonds payable, associated with the Food Processing Division. Although Suncoast Food Centers may have such long-term debt, it would not be meaningful to assign portions of that debt to the company's individual divisions. Second, there is no stockholders' equity associated with the Food Processing Division. The owners of the company own stock in Suncoast Food Centers, not in its individual divisions.

Average Balances ROI, residual income, and EVA are computed for a period of time, such as a year or a month. Asset balances, on the other hand, are measured at a point in time, such as December 31. Since divisional asset balances generally will change over time, we use average balances in calculating ROI, residual income, and EVA. For example, if the Food Processing Division's balance in invested capital was \$19,000,000 on January 1 and \$17,000,000 on December 31, we would use the year's average invested capital of \$18,000,000 in the ROI, residual income, and EVA calculations.

Should Total Assets Be Used? Exhibit 13–2 shows that the Food Processing Division had average balances during the year of \$2,000,000 in current assets, \$15,000,000 in long-lived assets, and \$1,000,000 tied up in a plant under construction. (Suncoast Food Centers is building a new high-tech dairy plant in Orlando to produce its innovative zero-calorie ice cream.) In addition, Exhibit 13–2 discloses that the Food Processing Division's average balance of current liabilities was \$1,000,000.

Exhibit 13–2
Assets and Liabilities Associated with Food Processing Division

Assets*		
Current assets (cash, accounts receivable, inventories, etc.)		\$ 2,000,000
Long-lived assets (land, buildings, equipment, vehicles, etc.):		
Gross book value (acquisition cost)	\$19,000,000	
Less: Accumulated depreciation	4,000,000	
Net book value		15,000,000
Plant under construction		1,000,000
Total assets		\$18,000,000
Liabilities		
Current liabilities (accounts payable, salaries payable, etc.)		\$ 1,000,000

*This is not a balance sheet, but rather a listing of certain assets and liabilities associated with the Food Processing Division.

What is the division's invested capital? Several possibilities exist.

1. ***Total assets.*** The management of Suncoast Food Centers has decided to use *average total assets* for the year in measuring each division's invested capital. Thus, $18,000,000 is the amount used in the ROI, residual-income, and EVA calculations discussed earlier in this chapter. This measure of invested capital is appropriate if the division manager has considerable authority in making decisions about *all* of the division's assets, *including nonproductive assets.* In this case, the Food Processing Division's partially completed dairy plant is a nonproductive asset. Since the division manager had considerable influence in deciding to build the new plant and he is responsible for overseeing the project, average total assets provides an appropriate measure.
2. ***Total productive assets.*** In other companies, division managers are directed by top management to keep nonproductive assets, such as vacant land or construction in progress. In such cases, it is appropriate to exclude nonproductive assets from the measure of invested capital. Then *average total productive assets* is used to measure invested capital. If Suncoast Food Centers had chosen this alternative, $17,000,000 would have been used in the ROI, residual-income, and EVA calculations (total assets of $18,000,000 less $1,000,000 for the plant under construction).
3. ***Total assets less current liabilities.*** Some companies allow division managers to secure short-term bank loans and other short-term credit. In such cases, invested capital often is measured by *average total assets less average current liabilities.* This approach encourages investment-center managers to minimize resources tied up in assets and maximize the use of short-term credit to finance operations. If this approach had been used by Suncoast Food Centers, the Food Processing Division's invested capital would have been $17,000,000, total assets of $18,000,000 less current liabilities of $1,000,000. (Note that current liabilities are always subtracted from total assets for the measure of invested capital used in the EVA measure.)

Gross or Net Book Value Another decision to make in choosing a measure of invested capital is whether to use the *gross book value (acquisition cost)* or the *net book value* of long-lived assets. (Net book value is the acquisition cost less accumulated depreciation.) Suncoast Food Centers' management has decided to use the average net book value of $15,000,000 to value the Food Processing Division's long-lived assets. If gross book value had been used instead, the division's measure of invested capital would have been $22,000,000, as the following calculation shows.

Current assets	$ 2,000,000
Long-lived assets (at gross book value)	19,000,000
Plant under construction	1,000,000
Total assets (at gross book value)	$22,000,000

There are advantages and disadvantages associated with both gross and net book value as a measure of invested capital. The advantages of net book value are:

1. Using net book value maintains consistency with the balance sheet prepared for external reporting purposes. This allows for more meaningful comparisons of return-on-investment measures across different companies.
2. Using net book value to measure invested capital is also more consistent with the definition of income, which is the numerator in ROI calculations. In computing income, the current period's depreciation on long-lived assets is deducted as an expense.

Exhibit 13–3
Increase in ROI over Time (when net book value is used)

Acquisition cost of equipment	$500,000
Useful life	5 years
Salvage value at end of useful life	0
Annual straight-line depreciation	$100,000
Annual income generated by asset (before deducting depreciation)	$150,000

Year	Income before Depreciation	Annual Depreciation	Income Net of Depreciation	Average Net Book Value*	ROI Based on Net Book Value†	Average Gross Book Value	ROI Based on Gross Book Value
1	$150,000	$100,000	$50,000	$450,000	11.1%	$500,000	10%
2	150,000	100,000	50,000	350,000	14.3	500,000	10
3	150,000	100,000	50,000	250,000	20.0	500,000	10
4	150,000	100,000	50,000	150,000	33.3	500,000	10
5	150,000	100,000	50,000	50,000	100.0	500,000	10

*Average net book value is the average of the beginning and ending balances for the year in net book value. In year 1, for example, the average net book value is

$$\frac{\$500{,}000 + \$400{,}000}{2}$$

†ROI rounded to nearest tenth of 1 percent.

The following two advantages are often associated with using gross book value:

1. The usual methods of computing depreciation, such as the straight-line and the declining-balance methods, are arbitrary. Hence, they should not be allowed to affect ROI, residual-income, or EVA calculations.
2. When long-lived assets are depreciated, their net book value declines over time. This results in a misleading increase in ROI, residual income, and EVA across time. Exhibit 13–3 provides an illustration of this phenomenon for the ROI calculated on an equipment purchase under consideration by the Food Processing Division manager. Notice that the ROI rises steadily across the five-year horizon if invested capital is measured by net book value. However, using gross book value eliminates this problem. If an accelerated depreciation method were used instead of the straight-line method, the increasing trend in ROI would be even more pronounced.

A Behavioral Problem The tendency for net book value to produce a misleading increase in ROI over time can have a serious effect on the incentives of investment-center managers. Investment centers with old assets will show much higher ROIs than investment centers with relatively new assets. This can discourage investment-center managers from investing in new equipment. If this behavioral tendency persists, a division's assets can become obsolete, making the division uncompetitive.

Allocating Assets to Investment Centers Some companies control certain assets centrally, although these assets are needed to carry on operations in the divisions. Common examples are cash and accounts receivable. Divisions need cash in order to operate, but many companies control cash balances centrally in order to minimize their total cash holdings. Some large retail firms manage accounts receivable centrally. A credit customer of some national department store chains can make a payment either at the local store or by mailing the payment to corporate headquarters.

When certain assets are controlled centrally, some allocation basis generally is chosen to allocate these asset balances to investment centers, for the purpose of measuring invested capital. For example, cash may be allocated based on the budgeted cash needs in each division or on the basis of divisional sales. Accounts receivable usually are allocated on the basis of divisional sales. Divisions with less stringent credit terms are allocated proportionately larger balances of accounts receivable.

Measuring Investment-Center Income

Learning Objective 5

Explain how to measure a division's income and invested capital.

In addition to choosing a measure of investment-center capital, an accountant must also decide how to measure a center's income. The key issue is controllability; the choice involves the extent to which uncontrollable items are allowed to influence the income measure. The Excel spreadsheet in Exhibit 13–4 illustrates several different possibilities for measuring the income of Suncoast Food Centers' Food Processing Division.

Suncoast Food Centers' top management uses the *profit margin controllable by division manager,* $3,600,000, to evaluate the Food Processing Division manager. This profit measure is used in calculating ROI, residual income, or EVA. Some fixed costs traceable to the division have not been deducted from this $3,600,000 amount, but the division manager cannot control or significantly influence these costs. Hence they are excluded from the ROI calculation in evaluating the division manager. In calculating EVA, the $3,600,000 profit-margin amount is converted to an after-tax basis by multiplying it by 1 minus the tax rate of 30 percent.

Pay for Performance Some companies reward investment-center managers with **cash bonuses** if they meet a predetermined target on a specified performance criterion, such as residual income, ROI, or EVA. Such payments often are referred to as **pay for performance, merit pay,** or **incentive compensation.** These cash bonuses generally are single payments, independent of a manager's base salary.

As the result of public outrage over the recent nearly catastrophic financial meltdown, as well as other perceived corporate excesses, many companies are beginning to rein in top management compensation packages. The U.S. government also reacted to the negative public mood by appointing a "pay czar" whose job it was to oversee top management compensation for the various companies that received "bailout" funds from government coffers during the recent financial crisis.[4]

Exhibit 13–4

Divisional Income Statement: Food Processing Division

Microsoft Excel - Divisional Income Statement - Food Processing Division

File Edit View Insert Format Tools Data Window Help

H16 fx =H14-H15

	A	B	H
1		FOOD PROCESSING DIVISION	
2		Divisional Income Statement	
3			
4		Sales revenue	$9,000,000
5		Variable expenses	3,800,000
6	(1)	Divisional contribution margin	$5,200,000
7		Fixed expenses controllable by division manager	1,600,000
8	(2)	Profit margin controllable by division manager	$3,600,000
9		Fixed expenses, traceable to division, but controlled by others	1,200,000
10	(3)	Profit margin traceable to division	$2,400,000
11		Common fixed expenses, allocated from corporate headquarters	400,000
12	(4)	Divisional income before interest and taxes	$2,000,000
13		Interest expense allocated from corporate headquarters	250,000
14	(5)	Divisional income before taxes	$1,750,000
15		Income taxes allocated from corporate headquarters	700,000
16	(6)	Divisional net income	$1,050,000

Sheet1 / Sheet2 / Sheet3 /

Ready

[4]See, for example, G. Chazan, "Shell Plans to Reduce Executive Salaries," *The Wall Street Journal,* February 17, 2010, p. B1; and D. Brady, "The Pay Czar on the End of His Empire," *Bloomberg Businessweek,* January 4, 2010, p. 15.

Managers versus Investment Centers It is important to make a distinction between an investment center and its manager. In evaluating the *manager's* performance, only revenues and costs that the manager can control or significantly influence should be included in the profit measure. Remember that the overall objective of the performance measure is to provide incentives for goal-congruent behavior. No performance measure can motivate a manager to make decisions about costs he or she cannot control. This explains why Suncoast Food Centers' top management relies on the profit margin controllable by division manager to compute the manager's ROI performance measure.

Evaluating the Food Processing Division as a viable economic investment is a different matter altogether. In this evaluation, traceability of costs, rather than controllability, is the issue. For this purpose, Suncoast Food Centers' top management uses the profit margin traceable to division to compute the divisional ROI, residual income, or EVA. As Exhibit 13–4 shows, this amount is $2,400,000.

Other Profit Measures The other measures of divisional profit shown in Exhibit 13–4 (lines 4, 5, and 6) also are used by some companies. The rationale behind these divisional income measures is that all corporate costs have to be covered by the operations of the divisions. Allocating corporate costs, interest, and income taxes to the divisions makes division managers aware of these costs.

Inflation: Historical-Cost versus Current-Value Accounting

Whether measuring investment-center income or invested capital, the impact of price-level changes should not be forgotten. During periods of inflation, historical-cost asset values soon cease to reflect the cost of replacing those assets. Therefore, some accountants argue that investment-center performance measures based on historical-cost accounting are misleading. Yet surveys of corporate managers indicate that an accounting system based on current values would not alter their decisions. Most managers believe that measures based on historical-cost accounting are adequate when used in conjunction with budgets and performance targets. As managers prepare those budgets, they build their expectations about inflation into the budgets and performance targets.

Another reason for using historical-cost accounting for internal purposes is that it is required for external reporting. Thus, historical-cost data already are available, while installing current-value accounting would add substantial incremental costs to the organization's information system.

Other Issues in Segment Performance Evaluation

Alternatives to ROI, Residual Income, and Economic Value Added (EVA)

ROI, residual income, and EVA are short-run performance measures. They focus on only one period of time. Yet an investment center is really a collection of assets (investments), each of which has a multiperiod life. Exhibit 13–5 portrays this perspective of an investment center.

To evaluate any one of these individual investments correctly requires a multiperiod viewpoint, which takes into account the timing of the cash flows from the investment. For example, investment E in Exhibit 13–5 may start out slowly in years 4 and 5, but it may be economically justified by its expected high performance in years 8, 9, and 10. Any evaluation of the investment center in year 5 that ignores the long-term performance of its various investments can result in a misleading conclusion. Thus, single-period

Exhibit 13–5
Investment Center Viewed as a Collection of Investments

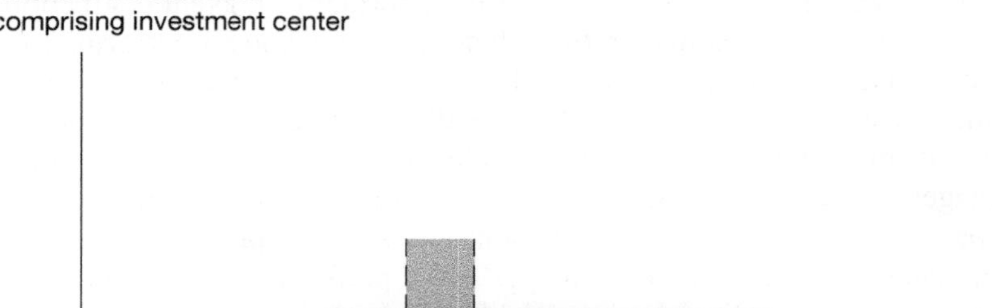

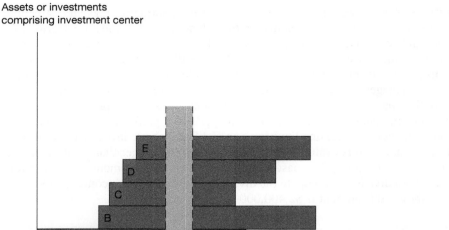

performance measures suffer from myopia. They focus on only a short time segment that slices across the division's investments as portrayed in Exhibit 13–5.

To avoid this short-term focus, some organizations downplay ROI, residual income, and EVA in favor of an alternative approach. Instead of relating profit to invested capital in a single measure, these characteristics of investment-center performance are evaluated separately. Actual divisional profit for a time period is compared to a flexible budget, and variances are used to analyze performance. The division's major investments are evaluated through a *postaudit* of the investment decisions. For example, investment E may have been undertaken because of expected high performance in years 8, 9, and 10. When that time comes, a review will determine whether the project lived up to expectations.

Evaluating periodic profit through flexible budgeting and variance analysis, coupled with postaudits of major investment decisions, is a more complicated approach to evaluating investment centers. However, it does help management avoid the myopia of single-period measures such as ROI, residual income, and EVA.

Importance of Nonfinancial Information

Although financial measures such as segment profit, ROI, residual income, and EVA are widely used in performance evaluation, nonfinancial measures are important also. Manufacturers collect data on rates of defective products, airlines record information on lost bags and aircraft delays, and hotels keep track of occupancy rates. The proper evaluation of an organization and its segments requires that multiple performance measures be defined and used. The *balanced scorecard,* with its *lead* and *lag measures* of performance, is one tool that is more and more widely used as a means of introducing nonfinancial measures into performance evaluation. See Chapter 10 for a discussion of the balanced scorecard.

Measuring Performance in Nonprofit Organizations

Management control in a nonprofit organization presents a special challenge. Such organizations often are managed by professionals, such as physicians in a hospital. Moreover, many people participate in a nonprofit organization at some personal sacrifice, motivated by humanitarian or public service ideals. Often, such people are less receptive to formal control procedures than their counterparts in business.

The goals of nonprofit organizations often are less clear-cut than those of businesses. Public service objectives may be difficult to specify with precision and even more difficult to measure in terms of achievement. For example, one community health center was established in an economically depressed area with three stated goals:

1. To reduce costs in a nearby hospital by providing a clinic for people to use instead of the hospital emergency room.
2. To provide preventive as well as therapeutic care, and establish outreach programs in the community.
3. To become financially self-sufficient.

There is some conflict between these objectives, since goal 2 does not provide revenue to the center, while goals 1 and 3 focus on financial efficiency. Moreover, the health center was staffed with physicians who could have achieved much greater incomes in private practice. The management control tools described in this and the preceding three chapters can be used in nonprofit organizations. However, the challenges in doing so effectively often are greater.

Transfer Pricing

Measuring performance in profit centers or investment centers is made more complicated by transfers of goods or services between responsibility centers. The amount charged when one division sells goods or services to another division is called a *transfer price.* This price affects the profit measurement for both the selling division and the buying division. A high transfer price results in high profit for the selling division and low profit for the buying division. A low transfer price has the opposite effect. Consequently, the transfer-pricing policy *can* affect the *incentives* of autonomous division managers as they decide whether to make the transfer. Exhibit 13–6 depicts this scenario.

Goal Congruence

What should be management's goal in setting transfer prices for internally transferred goods or services? In a decentralized organization, the managers of profit centers and investment centers often have considerable autonomy in deciding whether to accept or reject orders and whether to buy inputs from inside the organization or from outside. For example, a large manufacturer of farm equipment allows its Assembly Division managers to buy parts either from another division of the company or from independent manufacturers. The goal in setting transfer prices is to establish incentives for autonomous division managers to make decisions that support the overall goals of the organization.

Suppose it is in the best interests of Suncoast Food Centers for the baked goods produced by the Food Processing Division's Orlando Bakery to be transferred to the Gulf Division's stores in the Tampa Bay area. Thus, if the firm were centralized, bakery products would be transferred from the Food Processing Division to the Gulf Division. However, Suncoast Food Centers is a decentralized company, and the Gulf Division manager is free to buy baked goods either from the Food Processing Division or from an outside bakery company. Similarly, the Food Processing Division manager is free to accept or reject an order for baked goods, at any given price, from the Gulf Division. The goal of the company's controller in setting the transfer price is to provide incentives for each of these division managers to act in the company's best interests.

The transfer price should be chosen so that each division manager, when striving to maximize his or her own division's profit, makes the decision that maximizes the company's profit.

Transfer pricing is widely used in all kinds of businesses. When the chassis for this GM automobile was transferred from the manufacturing division to the assembly division, a transfer price was specified.

Exhibit 13–6
The Transfer-Pricing Scenario

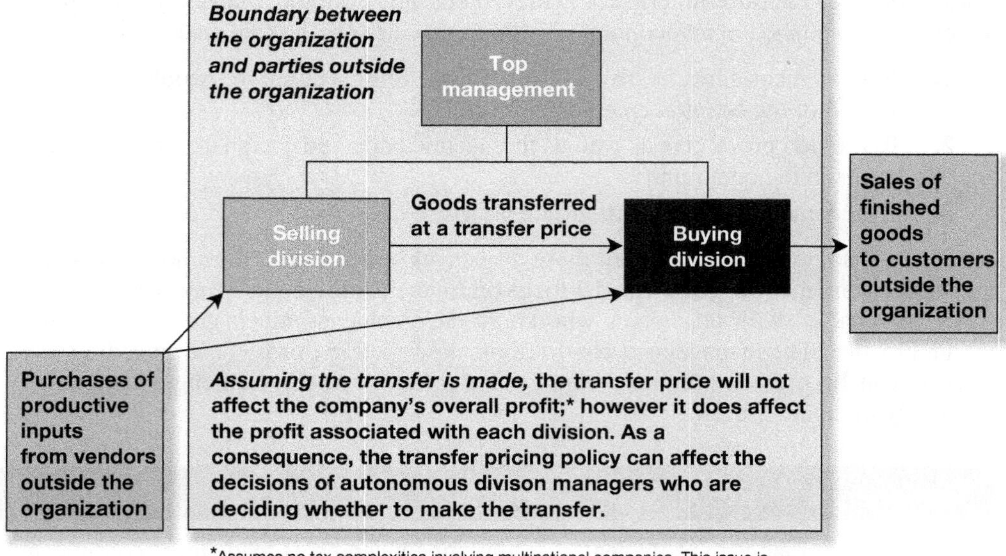

*Assumes no tax complexities involving multinational companies. This issue is addressed later in the chapter.

General Transfer-Pricing Rule

Learning Objective 6

Use the general economic rule to set an optimal transfer price.

Management's objective in setting a transfer price is to encourage goal congruence among the division managers involved in the transfer. A general rule that will ensure goal congruence is given below.

Transfer price = Additional *outlay cost* per unit incurred because good are transferred + *Opportunity cost* per unit to the organization because of the transfer

The general rule specifies the transfer price as the sum of two cost components. The first component is the outlay cost incurred by the division that produces the goods or services to be transferred. Outlay costs will include the direct variable costs of the product or service and any other outlay costs that are incurred only as a result of the transfer. The second component in the general transfer-pricing rule is the opportunity cost incurred by the organization as a whole because of the transfer. Recall from Chapter 2 that an *opportunity cost* is a benefit that is forgone as a result of taking a particular action.

"Transfer pricing is a business issue as well as a tax issue that should be considered in the board room." (13c)
Ernst & Young

We will illustrate the general transfer-pricing rule for Suncoast Food Centers. The company's Food Processing Division produces bread in its Orlando Bakery. The division transfers some of its products to the company's Gulf and Atlantic divisions, and sells some of its products to other companies in the *external market* under different labels.

Bread is transported to stores in racks containing one dozen loaves of packaged bread. In the Orlando bakery, the following variable costs are incurred to produce bread and transport it to a buyer.

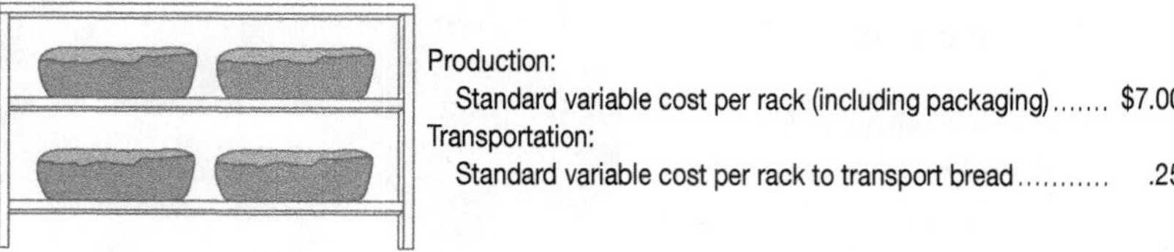

Production:	
Standard variable cost per rack (including packaging)	$7.00
Transportation:	
Standard variable cost per rack to transport bread	.25

In applying the general transfer-pricing rule, we will distinguish between two different scenarios.

Scenario I: No Excess Capacity Suppose the Food Processing Division can sell all the bread it can produce to outside buyers at a market price of $11 per rack. Since the division can sell all of its production, it has *no excess capacity. Excess capacity* exists only when more goods can be produced than the producer is able to sell, due to low demand for the product.

What transfer price does the general rule yield under this scenario of no excess capacity? The transfer price is determined as follows:

Outlay cost:	
Standard variable cost of production	$ 7.00 per rack
Standard variable cost of transportation	.25 per rack
Total outlay cost	$ 7.25 per rack
Opportunity cost:	
Selling price per unit in external market	$11.00 per rack
Less: Variable cost of production and transportation	7.25 per rack
Opportunity cost (forgone contribution margin)	$ 3.75 per rack

General transfer-pricing rule:

Transfer price	=	Outlay cost	+	Opportunity cost
$11.00	=	$7.25	+	$3.75

The *outlay cost* incurred by the Food Processing Division in order to transfer a rack of bread includes the standard variable production cost of $7.00 and the standard variable transportation cost of $.25. The *opportunity cost* incurred by Suncoast Food Centers when its Food Processing Division transfers a rack of bread to the Gulf Division *instead* of selling it in the external market is the forgone contribution margin from the lost sale, equal to $3.75. Why does the company lose a sale in the external market for every rack of bread transferred to the Gulf Division? The sale is lost because there is *no excess capacity* in the Food Processing Division. Every rack of bread transferred to another company division results in one less rack of bread sold in the external market.

Goal Congruence How does the general transfer-pricing rule promote goal congruence? Suppose the Gulf Division's grocery stores can sell a loaf of bread for $1.50, or $18 for a rack of 12 loaves ($18 = 12 × $1.50). What is the best way for Suncoast Food Centers to use the limited production capacity in the Food Processing Division's Orlando bakery? The answer is determined as follows:

Contribution to Suncoast Food Centers from Sale in External Market		Contribution to Suncoast Food Centers from Transfer to Gulf Division	
Wholesale selling price per rack	$11.00	Retail selling price per rack	$18.00
Less: Variable costs	7.25	Less: Variable costs	7.25
Contribution margin	$ 3.75	Contribution margin	$10.75

The best use of the bakery's limited production capacity is to produce bread for transfer to the Gulf Division. If the transfer price is set at $11.00, as the general rule specifies, goal congruence is maintained. The Food Processing Division manager is willing to transfer bread to the Gulf Division, because the transfer price of $11.00 is equal to the external market price. The Gulf Division manager is willing to buy the bread, because her division will have a contribution margin of $7.00 on each rack of bread transferred ($18.00 sales price minus the $11.00 transfer price).

Now consider a different situation. Suppose a local organization makes a special offer to the Gulf Division manager to buy several hundred loaves of bread to sell in a promotional campaign. The organization offers to pay $.80 per loaf, which is $9.60 per rack of a dozen loaves. What will the Gulf Division manager do? She must pay a transfer price of $11.00 per rack, so the Gulf Division would lose $1.40 per rack if the special offer were accepted ($1.40 = $11.00 − $9.60). The Gulf Division manager will decline the special offer. Is this decision in the best interests of Suncoast Food Centers as a whole? If the offer were accepted, the company as a whole would make a positive contribution of $2.35 per rack, as shown below.

Contribution to Suncoast Food Centers If Special Offer Is Accepted

Special price per rack	$9.60 per rack
Less: Variable cost to company	7.25 per rack
Contribution to company, per rack	$2.35 per rack

However, the company can make even more if its Food Processing Division sells bread directly in its external market. Then the contribution to the company is $3.75, as we have just seen. (The external market price of $11.00 per rack minus a variable cost of $7.25 per rack equals $3.75 per rack.) Thus, Suncoast Food Centers is better off, as a whole, if the Gulf Division's special offer is rejected. Once again, the general transfer-pricing rule results in goal-congruent decision making.

Scenario II: Excess Capacity Now let's change our basic assumption, and suppose the Food Processing Division's Orlando bakery has excess production capacity. This means that the total demand for its bread from all sources, including the Gulf and Atlantic divisions and the external market, is less than the bakery's production capacity. Under this scenario of excess capacity, what does the general rule specify for a transfer price?

$$\text{Transfer price} = \text{Outlay cost} + \text{Opportunity cost}$$
$$\$7.25 = \$7.25 + 0$$

The *outlay cost* in the Food Processing Division's Orlando bakery is still $7.25, since it does not depend on whether there is idle capacity or not. The *opportunity cost,* however, is now zero. There is no opportunity cost to the company when a rack of bread is transferred to the Gulf Division, because the Food Processing Division can still satisfy all of its external demand for bread. Thus, the general rule specifies a transfer price of $7.25, the total standard variable cost of production and transportation.

"It is difficult for people 'doing the business' to stop and consult about the transfer pricing implications of their moves, but they have to." (13d)

Respondent, Ernst & Young Survey

Goal Congruence Let's reconsider what will happen when the Gulf Division manager receives the local organization's special offer to buy bread at $9.60 per rack. The Gulf Division will now show a positive contribution of $2.35 per rack on the special order.

Special price per rack	$9.60 per rack
Less: Transfer price paid by Gulf Division	7.25 per rack
Contribution to Gulf Division	$2.35 per rack

The Gulf Division manager will accept the special offer. This decision is also in the best interests of Suncoast Food Centers. The company, as a whole, also will make a contribution of $2.35 per rack on every rack transferred to the Gulf Division to satisfy the special order. Once again, the general transfer-pricing rule maintains goal-congruent decision-making behavior.

Notice that the general rule yields a transfer price that leaves the Food Processing Division manager indifferent as to whether the transfer will be made. At a transfer price of \$7.25, the contribution to the Food Processing Division will be zero (transfer price of \$7.25 less variable cost of \$7.25). To avoid this problem, we can view the general rule as providing a lower bound on the transfer price. Some companies allow the producing division to add a markup to this lower bound in order to provide a positive contribution margin. This in turn provides a positive incentive to make the transfer.

Difficulty in Implementing the General Rule The general transfer-pricing rule will always promote goal-congruent decision making *if the rule can be implemented.* However, the rule is often difficult or impossible to implement due to the difficulty of measuring opportunity costs. Such a cost-measurement problem can arise for a number of reasons. One reason is that the external market may not be perfectly competitive. Under **perfect competition,** the market price does not depend on the quantity sold by any one producer. Under **imperfect competition,** a single producer or group of producers can affect the market price by varying the amount of product available in the market. In such cases, the external market price depends on the production decisions of the producer. This in turn means that the opportunity cost incurred by the company as a result of internal transfers depends on the quantity sold externally. These interactions may make it impossible to measure accurately the opportunity cost caused by a product transfer.

Other reasons for difficulty in measuring the opportunity cost associated with a product transfer include uniqueness of the transferred goods or services, a need for the producing division to invest in special equipment in order to produce the transferred goods, and interdependencies among several transferred products or services. For example, the producing division may provide design services as well as production of the goods for a buying division. What is the opportunity cost associated with each of these related outputs of the producing division? In many such cases, it is difficult to sort out the opportunity costs.

The general transfer-pricing rule provides a good conceptual model for the managerial accountant to use in setting transfer prices. Moreover, in many cases, it can be implemented. When the general rule cannot be implemented, organizations turn to other transfer-pricing methods, as we shall see next.

Transfers Based on the External Market Price

Learning Objective 7

Explain how to base a transfer price on market prices, costs, or negotiations.

A common approach is to set the transfer price equal to the price in the external market. In the Suncoast Food Centers illustration, the Food Processing Division would set the transfer price for bread at \$11.00 per rack, since that is the price the division can obtain in its external market. When the producing division has no excess capacity and perfect competition prevails, where no single producer can affect the market price, the general transfer-pricing rule and the external market price yield the same transfer price. This fact is illustrated for Suncoast Food Centers as follows:

Transfer price	=	Outlay cost	+	Opportunity cost	
	=	Variable cost of production and transportation	+	Forgone contribution margin of an external sale	
	=	\$7.25	+	(\$11.00 − \$7.25)	= \$11.00

Transfer price = External market price = \$11.00

If the producing division has excess capacity or the external market is imperfectly competitive, the general rule and the external market price will not yield the same transfer price.

If the transfer price is set at the market price, the producing division should have the option of either producing goods for internal transfer or selling in the external market. The buying division should be required to purchase goods from inside its organization if the producing division's goods meet the product specifications. Otherwise, the buying division should have the autonomy to buy from a supplier outside its own organization. To handle pricing disputes that may arise, an arbitration process should be established.

Transfer prices based on market prices are consistent with the responsibility-accounting concepts of profit centers and investment centers. In addition to encouraging division managers to focus on divisional profitability, market-based transfer prices help to show the contribution of each division to overall company profit. Suppose the Food Processing Division of Suncoast Food Centers transfers bread to the Gulf Division at a market-based transfer price of $11.00 per rack. The following contribution margins will be earned by the two divisions and the company as a whole.

Food Processing Division		Gulf Division	
Transfer price	$11.00 per rack	Retail sales price	$18.00 per rack
Less: Variable costs	7.25 per rack	Less: Transfer price	11.00 per rack
Contribution margin	$ 3.75 per rack	Contribution margin	$ 7.00 per rack

Suncoast Food Centers	
Retail sales price	$18.00 per rack
Less: Variable costs	7.25 per rack
Contribution margin	$10.75 per rack

When aggregate divisional profits are determined for the year, and ROI and residual income are computed, the use of a market-based transfer price helps to assess the contributions of each division to overall corporate profits.

Distress Market Prices Occasionally an industry will experience a period of significant excess capacity and extremely low prices. For example, when gasoline prices soared due to a foreign oil embargo, the market prices for recreational vehicles and power boats fell temporarily to very low levels.

Under such extreme conditions, basing transfer prices on market prices can lead to decisions that are not in the best interests of the overall company. Basing transfer prices on artificially *low distress market prices* could lead the producing division to sell or close the productive resources devoted to producing the product for transfer. Under distress market prices, the producing division manager might prefer to move the division into a more profitable product line. While such a decision might improve the division's profit in the short run, it could be contrary to the best interests of the company overall. It might be better for the company as a whole to avoid divesting itself of any productive resources and to ride out the period of market distress. To encourage an autonomous division manager to act in this fashion, some companies set the transfer price equal to the long-run average external market price, rather than the current (possibly depressed) market price.

Negotiated Transfer Prices

Many companies use negotiated transfer prices. Division managers or their representatives actually negotiate the price at which transfers will be made. Sometimes they start with the external market price and then make adjustments for various reasons. For example, the producing division may enjoy some cost savings on internal transfers that are not obtained on external sales. Commissions may not have to be paid to sales personnel on internally transferred products. In such cases, a negotiated transfer price may split the cost savings between the producing and buying divisions.

In other instances, a negotiated transfer price may be used because no external market exists for the transferred product.

Two drawbacks sometimes characterize negotiated transfer prices. First, negotiations can lead to divisiveness and competition between participating division managers. This can undermine the spirit of cooperation and unity that is desirable throughout an organization. Second, although negotiating skill is a valuable managerial talent, it should not be the sole or dominant factor in evaluating a division manager. If, for example, the producing division's manager is a better negotiator than the buying division's manager, then the producing division's profit may look better than it should, simply because of its manager's superior negotiating ability.

Cost-Based Transfer Prices

Organizations that do not base prices on market prices or negotiations often turn to a cost-based transfer-pricing approach.

Variable Cost One approach is to set the transfer price equal to the standard variable cost. The problem with this approach is that even when the producing division has excess capacity, it is not allowed to show any contribution margin on the transferred products or services. To illustrate, suppose the Food Processing Division has excess capacity and the transfer price is set at the standard variable cost of $7.25 per rack of bread. There is no positive incentive for the division to produce and transfer bread to the Gulf Division. The Food Processing Division's contribution margin from a transfer will be zero (transfer price of $7.25 minus variable costs of $7.25 equals zero). Some companies avoid this problem by setting the transfer price at standard variable cost plus a markup to allow the producing division a positive contribution margin.

Full Cost An alternative is to set the transfer price equal to the *full cost* of the transferred product or service. **Full** (or **absorption**) **cost** is equal to the product's variable cost plus an allocated portion of fixed overhead.

Suppose the Food Processing Division's Orlando bakery has budgeted annual fixed overhead of $500,000 and budgeted annual production of 200,000 racks of bread. The full cost of the bakery's product is computed as follows:

$$\begin{aligned}\text{Full cost} &= \text{Variable cost} + \text{Allocated fixed overhead}\\ &= \$7.25 \text{ per rack} + \frac{\$500{,}000 \text{ budgeted fixed overhead}}{200{,}000 \text{ budgeted racks of bread}}\\ &= \$7.25 + \$2.50\\ &= \$9.75 \text{ per rack}\end{aligned}$$

Under this approach, the transfer price is set at $9.75 per rack of bread.

Dysfunctional Decision-Making Behavior Basing transfer prices on full cost entails a serious risk of causing dysfunctional decision-making behavior. Full-cost-based transfer prices lead the buying division to view costs that are fixed for the company as a whole as variable costs to the buying division. This can cause faulty decision making.

To illustrate, suppose the Food Processing Division has excess capacity, and the transfer price of bread is equal to the full cost of $9.75 per rack. What will happen if the Gulf Division receives the special offer discussed previously, where it can sell bread to a local organization at a special price of $9.60 per rack? The Gulf Division manager will reject the special order, since otherwise her division would incur a loss of $.15 per rack.

Special price per rack	$9.60 per rack
Less: Transfer price based on full cost	9.75 per rack
Loss	$ .15 per rack

What is in the best interests of the company as a whole? Suncoast Food Centers would make a positive contribution of $2.35 per rack on the bread sold in the special order.

Special price per rack	$9.60 per rack
Less: Variable cost in Food Processing Division	7.25 per rack
Contribution to company as a whole	$2.35 per rack

What has happened here? Setting the transfer price equal to the full cost of $9.75 has turned a cost that is fixed in the Food Processing Division, and hence is fixed for the company as a whole, into a variable cost from the viewpoint of the Gulf Division manager. The manager would tend to reject the special offer, even though accepting it would benefit the company as a whole.

Although the practice is common, transfer prices should not be based on full cost. The risk is too great that the cost behavior in the producing division will be obscured. This can all too easily result in poor decisions in the buying division.

Standard versus Actual Costs

Throughout our discussion of transfer prices, we have used standard costs rather than actual costs. This was true in our discussion of the general transfer-pricing rule as well as for cost-based transfer prices. Transfer prices should not be based on actual costs, because such a practice would allow an inefficient producing division to pass its excess production costs on to the buying division in the transfer price. When standard costs are used in transfer-pricing formulas, the buying division is not forced to pick up the tab for the producer's inefficiency. Moreover, the producing division is given an incentive to control its costs, since any costs of inefficiency cannot be passed on.

Undermining Divisional Autonomy

Suppose the manager of Suncoast Food Centers' Food Processing Division has excess capacity but insists on a transfer price of $9.75, based on full cost. The Gulf Division manager is faced with the special offer for bread at $9.60 per rack. She regrets that she will have to decline the offer because it would cause her division's profit to decline, even though the company's interests would be best served by accepting the special order. The Gulf Division manager calls the company president and explains the situation. She asks the president to intervene and force the Food Processing Division manager to lower his transfer price.

"[Transfer pricing] affects nearly every aspect of multinational operations—R&D, manufacturing, marketing and distribution, after-sale services." (13e)
Ernst & Young

As the company president, what would you do? If you stay out of the controversy, your company will lose the contribution on the special order. If you intervene, you will run the risk of undermining the autonomy of your division managers. You established a decentralized organization structure for Suncoast Centers and hired competent managers because you believed in the benefits of decentralized decision making.

There is no obvious answer to this dilemma. In practice, central managers are reluctant to intervene in such disputes unless the negative financial consequences to the organization are quite large. Most managers believe the benefits of decentralized decision making are important to protect, even if it means an occasional dysfunctional decision.

An International Perspective

Two international issues arise in the case of multinational firms setting transfer prices between divisions in different countries.

Income-Tax Rates Multinational companies often consider domestic and foreign income-tax rates when setting transfer prices. For example, suppose a company based in

TRANSFER PRICING AND TAX ISSUES

The most difficult transfer-pricing issues arise in multinational corporations because of the complexity of the tax issues involved. According to a survey by Ernst & Young LLP, "transfer pricing is the top tax issue facing multinational corporations. Of the international tax directors at 582 multinational organizations polled in the survey, 75 percent expect their company to face a transfer-pricing audit within the next two years. Respondents cited related-party transactions (including the intercompany transfer of goods, services, properties, loans, and leases) involving administrative and management services as the most likely to be audited. Moreover, there has been an increase in transfer pricing audit activity in recent years.[5]

"The Internal Revenue Service (IRS) is concerned that companies could use transfer prices to shift profits between related entities through cost of goods sold. Thus, transfer pricing manipulation could be used by taxpayers to shift income from high tax jurisdictions like the U.S. to low tax jurisdictions. The right price from the IRS's perspective is the market value price. Because it's difficult to prove that the transfer price was equal to the market price, companies often find themselves in disputes with the IRS. But now there's help. The IRS's Advanced Pricing Agreement Program provides companies an opportunity to avoid costly audits and litigation by allowing them to negotiate a prospective agreement with the IRS regarding the facts, the transfer pricing methodology, and an acceptable range of results. The program is aimed at multinational corporations interested in avoiding penalties, managing risk, and determining their tax liability with certainty."[6]

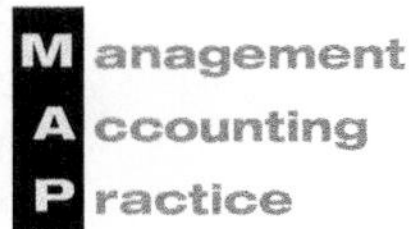

Ernst & Young, IRS

Europe also has a division in Asia. A European division produces a subassembly, which is transferred to the Asian division for assembly and sale of the final product. Suppose also that the income-tax rate for the company's European division is higher than the rate in the Asian division's country. How would these different tax rates affect the transfer price for the subassembly?

The company's management has an incentive to set a low transfer price for the subassembly. This will result in relatively low profits for the company's European division and a relatively high income for the Asian division. Since the tax rate is lower in the Asian country, the overall company will save on income tax. By setting a low transfer price, the company will shift a portion of its income to a country with a lower tax rate. Tax laws vary among countries with regard to flexibility in setting transfer prices. Some countries' tax laws prohibit the behavior described in our example, while other countries' laws permit it.

"Transfer pricing has become the most difficult area of international taxation." (13f)
Ernst & Young

Import Duties Another international issue that can affect a firm's transfer pricing policy is the imposition of import duties, or tariffs. These are fees charged to an importer, generally on the basis of the reported value of the goods being imported. Consider again the example of a firm with divisions in Europe and Asia. If the Asian country imposes an import duty on goods transferred in from the European division, the company has an incentive to set a relatively low transfer price on the transferred goods. This will minimize

[5]Maheudra Gujarathi, "GlaxoSmithkline Plc.: International Transfer Pricing and Taxation," *Issues in Accounting Education* 22, no. 4 (November 2007), pp. 749–759; and Eric Krell, "Scrutiny of Transfer Pricing Grows," *Business Finance* 6, no. 4 (August 2000), p. 12.

[6]Steven C. Wrappe, Ken Milani, and Julie Joy, "The Transfer Price Is Right," *Strategic Finance* 81, no. 1 (July 1999), p. 40.

the duty to be paid and maximize the overall profit for the company as a whole. As in the case of taxation, countries sometimes pass laws to limit a multinational firm's flexibility in setting transfer prices for the purpose of minimizing import duties.

Transfer prices are used in the service industry as well as in manufacturing. Cornell University, for example, charges an accessory instruction fee to a campus unit when one of its students enrolls in a course offered in a different unit.

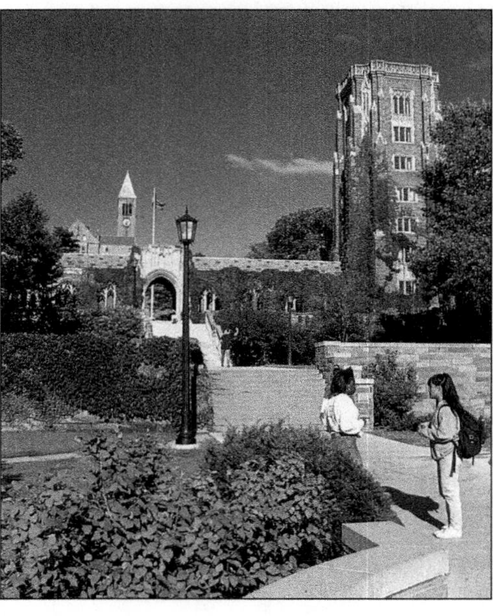

Transfer Pricing in the Service Industry

Service industry firms and nonprofit organizations also use transfer pricing when services are transferred between responsibility centers. In banks, for example, the interest rate at which depositors' funds are transferred to the loan department is a form of transfer price. At Cornell University, if a student in the law school takes a course in the business school, a transfer price is charged to the law school for the credit hours of instruction provided to the law student. Since the transfer price is based on tuition charges, it is a market-price-based transfer price.

Behavioral Issues: Risk Aversion and Incentives

Learning Objective 8

Understand the behavioral issues of incentives, goal congruence, and internal controls.

The designer of a performance-evaluation system for responsibility-center managers must consider many factors. Trade-offs often must be made between competing objectives. The overall objective is to achieve goal congruence by providing *incentives* for managers to act in the best interests of the organization as a whole. Financial performance measures such as divisional income, ROI, and residual income go a long way toward achieving this objective. However, these measures do have the disadvantage of imposing *risk* on a manager, because the measures also are affected by factors beyond the manager's control. For example, the income of an orange-growing division of an agricultural company will be affected not only by the manager's diligence and ability, but also by the weather and insect infestations.

Since most people exhibit *risk aversion,* managers must be compensated for the risk they must bear. This compensation comes in the form of higher salaries or bonuses. Thus, the design of a managerial performance evaluation and reward system involves a trade-off between the following two factors:

Evaluation of a manager on the basis of financial performance measures, which provide incentives for the manager to act in the organization's interests.	Imposition of risk on a manager who exhibits risk aversion, because financial performance measures are controllable only partially by the manager.

Trade-offs in designing managerial performance evaluation and reward system.

Achieving the optimal trade-off between risk and incentives is a delicate balancing act that requires the skill and experience of top management.

Goal Congruence and Internal Control Systems

Although most business professionals have high ethical standards, there are unfortunately those who will cut corners. An **internal control system** is designed to provide reasonable assurance of the achievement of objectives in: (1) the effectiveness and efficiency of operations; (2) reliability of financial reporting; and (3) compliance with laws and regulations. Internal control procedures are designed to prevent the major lapses in responsible behavior described below.

Fraud Theft or misuse of an organization's resources constitutes *fraud.* To prevent and detect fraud, organizations establish well-defined procedures that prescribe how valuable resources will be handled. For example, many organizations require all checks above a particular amount to be authorized by two people.

Financial Misrepresentation Internal control systems also are designed to prevent managers from intentionally (or accidentally) misstating an organization's financial records. Most companies have an *internal audit* staff, which reviews financial records throughout the organization to ensure their accuracy. (Appendix I on pages 766–771 explores the Sarbanes-Oxley Act and internal controls over financial reporting.)[7]

Corruption Activities such as bribery, deceit, illegal political campaign contributions, and kickbacks constitute *corruption.* Most organizations have internal control procedures and codes of conduct to prevent and detect corrupt practices. For example, many organizations forbid their purchasing personnel from accepting gifts or gratuities from the sales personnel with whom they conduct business. The Foreign Corrupt Practices Act, passed by the U.S. Congress in 1977, prohibits a variety of corrupt practices in foreign business operations. For example, the law prohibits a company's management from bribing officials of a foreign government in return for favorable treatment of their company.

Unauthorized Action Sometimes a well-meaning employee is tempted to take an action that is not illegal or even unethical, but it is contrary to the organization's policies. Internal control procedures also are designed to detect and prevent unauthorized actions by an organization's employees, when those actions could reflect unfavorably on the organization. For example, a company may prohibit its employees from using company facilities for a rally in support of a controversial social cause.

An internal control system constitutes an integral part of an organization's efforts to achieve its goals. To be effective, internal control procedures require top management's full support and intolerance of intentional violations.

[7]The Sarbanes-Oxley Act, passed by the U.S. Congress in 2002, is designed to ensure that a company's financial statements accurately portray its financial condition.

Chapter Summary

LO1 Explain the role of managerial accounting in achieving goal congruence. An important objective of any organization's managerial accounting system is to promote goal congruence among its employees. Thus, the primary criterion for judging the effectiveness of performance measures for responsibility-center managers is the extent to which the measures promote goal congruence.

LO2 Compute an investment center's return on investment (ROI), residual income (RI), and economic value added (EVA). An investment center's ROI is equal to its income divided by its invested capital. The investment center's RI is equal to its profit minus the product of its invested capital and an imputed interest rate. The investment center's EVA is computed as follows: After-tax operating income − [(Total assets − Current liabilities) × Weighted-average cost of capital].

LO3 Explain how a manager can improve ROI by increasing either the sales margin or capital turnover. An investment center's ROI equals sales margin multiplied by capital turnover. Therefore, an investment center's ROI may be improved by increasing either the sales margin or capital turnover.

LO4 Describe some advantages and disadvantages of both ROI and residual income as divisional performance measures. Each of these performance measures relates an investment center's income to the capital invested to earn it. However, residual income and EVA have the additional advantage of incorporating the organization's cost of acquiring capital in the performance measure.

LO5 Explain how to measure a division's income and invested capital. There are several ways that investment centers' invested capital is measured in practice. Among the commonly observed measures are: total assets, total productive assets, and total assets less current liabilities. Similarly, several measures of investment center income are observed in practice. As explained in the chapter, these income measures differ on the degree to which certain expenses are controllable at the investment center level.

LO6 Use the general economic rule to set an optimal transfer price. The general rule states that the transfer price should be equal to the outlay cost incurred to make the transfer plus the organization's opportunity cost associated with the transfer.

LO7 Explain how to base a transfer price on market prices, costs, or negotiations. Due to difficulties in implementing the general transfer pricing rule, most companies base transfer prices on external market prices, costs, or negotiations. Market prices may be the best practical measure, as long as an external market for the transferred product exists. Alternatively, transfer prices may be based on full, absorption product costs or variable product costs. Negotiation, although widely used in setting transfer prices, can be time-consuming and divisive.

LO8 Understand the behavioral issues of incentives, goal congruence, and internal controls. In general, companies use investment center performance measures and transfer pricing methods to provide incentives to managers to make goal-congruent decisions. In some cases, both investment center performance measures and transfer prices may result in dysfunctional decisions by mid-level managers. Top management then must weigh the benefits of intervening to prevent suboptimal decisions and the costs of undermining divisional autonomy. Internal controls also are used in organizations to promote the effectiveness and efficiency of operations, the reliability of financial reporting, and compliance with laws and regulations.

Review Problems on Investment Centers and Transfer Pricing

Problem 1

Stellar Systems Company manufactures guidance systems for rockets used to launch commercial satellites. The company's Software Division reported the following results for 20x7.

Income	$ 300,000
Sales revenue	2,000,000
Invested capital (total assets)	3,000,000
Average balance in current liabilities	20,000

Stellar Systems' weighted-average cost of capital (WACC) is 9 percent, and the company's tax rate is 40 percent. Moreover, the company's required rate of return on invested capital is 9 percent.

Required:

1. Compute the Software Division's sales margin, capital turnover, return on investment (ROI), residual income, and economic value added (EVA) for 20x7.
2. If income and sales remain the same in 20x8, but the division's capital turnover improves to 80 percent, compute the following for 20x8: (*a*) invested capital and (*b*) ROI.

Problem 2

Stellar Systems Company's Microprocessor Division sells a computer module to the company's Guidance Assembly Division, which assembles completed guidance systems. The Microprocessor Division has no excess capacity. The computer module costs $10,000 to manufacture, and it can be sold in the external market to companies in the computer industry for $13,500.

Required: Compute the transfer price for the computer module using the general transfer-pricing rule.

Solutions to Review Problems

Problem 1

1.
$$\text{Sales margin} = \frac{\text{Income}}{\text{Sales revenue}} = \frac{\$300{,}000}{\$2{,}000{,}000} = 15\%$$

$$\text{Capital turnover} = \frac{\text{Sales revenue}}{\text{Invested capital}} = \frac{\$2{,}000{,}000}{\$3{,}000{,}000} = 67\%$$

$$\text{Return on investment} = \frac{\text{Income}}{\text{Invested capital}} = \frac{\$300{,}000}{\$3{,}000{,}000} = 10\%$$

Residual income:

Divisional income		$300,000
Less: Imputed interest charge:		
Invested capital	$3,000,000	
× Imputed interest rate	× .09	
Imputed interest charge		270,000
Residual income		$ 30,000

Economic value added (EVA):

$$\text{EVA} = \begin{matrix}\text{Investment center's}\\ \text{after-tax}\\ \text{operating income}\end{matrix} - \left[\left(\begin{matrix}\text{Investment center's}\\ \text{total assets}\end{matrix} - \begin{matrix}\text{Investment center's}\\ \text{current liabilities}\end{matrix}\right) \times \begin{matrix}\text{Weighted-average}\\ \text{cost of capital}\end{matrix}\right]$$

$$= \$300{,}000\,(1 - .40) - [(\$3{,}000{,}000 - \$20{,}000) \times .09]$$

$$= \$(88{,}200)$$

2. *a.*
$$\text{Capital turnover} = \frac{\text{Sales revenue}}{\text{Invested capital}} = \frac{\$2{,}000{,}000}{?} = 80\%$$

$$\text{Therefore:} \quad \text{Invested capital} = \frac{\$2{,}000{,}000}{.80} = \$2{,}500{,}000$$

b. New ROI = 15% × 80% = 12%

Problem 2

$$\text{Transfer price} = \text{Outlay cost} + \text{Opportunity cost}$$
$$= \$10{,}000 + (\$13{,}500 - \$10{,}000)$$
$$= \$13{,}500$$

The $3,500 opportunity cost of a transfer is the contribution margin that will be forgone if a computer module is transferred instead of sold in the external market.

Key Terms

For each term's definition refer to the indicated page, or turn to the glossary at the end of the text.

capital turnover, 551
cash bonus, 560
economic value added (EVA), 555
full (or absorption) cost, 569
goal congruence, 549
imperfect competition, 567
incentive compensation, 560
internal control system, 573
investment center, 548
management by objectives (MBO), 549
merit pay, 560
pay for performance, 560
perfect competition, 567
residual income, 553
return on investment (ROI), 550
sales margin, 551
shareholder value analysis, 555
transfer price, 548
weighted-average cost of capital (WACC), 555

Review Questions

13–1. What is the managerial accountant's primary objective in designing a responsibility-accounting system?

13–2. Define *goal congruence,* and explain why it is important to an organization's success.

13–3. Describe the managerial approach known as *management by objectives* or *MBO*.

13–4. Define and give three examples of an *investment center.*

13–5. Write the formula for ROI, showing sales margin and capital turnover as its components.

13–6. Explain how the manager of the Automobile Division of an insurance company could improve her division's ROI.

13–7. Make up an example showing how residual income is calculated. What information is used in computing residual income that is not used in computing ROI?

13–8. What is the chief disadvantage of ROI as an investment-center performance measure? How does the residual-income measure eliminate this disadvantage?

13–9. Why is there typically a rise in ROI or residual income across time in a division? What undesirable behavioral implications could this phenomenon have?

13–10. Define the term *economic value added.* How does it differ from residual income?

13–11. Distinguish between the following measures of invested capital, and briefly explain when each should be used: (*a*) total assets, (*b*) total productive assets, and (*c*) total assets less current liabilities.

13–12. Why do some companies use gross book value instead of net book value to measure a division's invested capital?

13–13. Explain why it is important in performance evaluation to distinguish between investment centers and their managers.

13–14. How do organizations use pay for performance to motivate managers?

13–15. Describe an alternative to using ROI or residual income to measure investment-center performance.

13–16. How does inflation affect investment-center performance measures?

13–17. List three nonfinancial measures that could be used to evaluate a division of an insurance company.

13–18. Discuss the importance of nonfinancial information in measuring investment-center performance.

13–19. Identify and explain the managerial accountant's primary objective in choosing a transfer-pricing policy.

13–20. Describe four methods by which transfer prices may be set.

13–21. Explain the significance of excess capacity in the transferring division when transfer prices are set using the general transfer-pricing rule.

13–22. Why might income-tax laws affect the transfer-pricing policies of multinational companies?

13–23. Explain the role of import duties, or tariffs, in affecting the transfer-pricing policies of multinational companies.

Exercises

Exercise 13–24
Components of ROI
(LO 2)

The following data pertain to Dakota Division's most recent year of operations.

Income	$ 4,000,000
Sales revenue	50,000,000
Average invested capital	20,000,000

Required: Compute Dakota Division's sales margin, capital turnover, and return on investment for the year.

Exercise 13–25
Improving ROI
(LO 3)

Refer to the preceding exercise.

Required: Demonstrate two ways Dakota Division's manager could improve the division's ROI to 25 percent.

Exercise 13–26
Residual Income
(LO 2)

Refer to the data for Exercise 13–24. Assume that the company's minimum desired rate of return on invested capital is 11 percent.

Required: Compute Dakota Division's residual income for the year.

Exercise 13–27
Calculate Weighted-Average Cost of Capital for EVA
(LO 2)

Golden Gate Construction Associates, a real estate developer and building contractor in San Francisco, has two sources of long-term capital: debt and equity. The cost to Golden Gate of issuing debt is the after-tax cost of the interest payments on the debt, taking into account the fact that the interest payments are tax deductible. The cost of Golden Gate's equity capital is the investment opportunity rate of Golden Gate's investors, that is, the rate they could earn on investments of similar risk to that of investing in Golden Gate Construction Associates. The interest rate on Golden Gate's $60 million of long-term debt is 10 percent, and the company's tax rate is 40 percent. The cost of Golden Gate's equity capital is 15 percent. Moreover, the market value (and book value) of Golden Gate's equity is $90 million.

Required: Calculate Golden Gate Construction Associates' weighted-average cost of capital.

Exercise 13–28
Economic Value Added (EVA); Continuation of Preceding Exercise
(LO 2)

Refer to the data in the preceding exercise for Golden Gate Construction Associates. The company has two divisions: the real estate division and the construction division. The divisions' total assets, current liabilities, and before-tax operating income for the most recent year are as follows:

Division	Total Assets	Current Liabilities	Before-Tax Operating Income
Real estate	$100,000,000	$6,000,000	$20,000,000
Construction	60,000,000	4,000,000	18,000,000

Required: Calculate the economic value added (EVA) for each of Golden Gate Construction Associates' divisions. (You will need to use the weighted-average cost of capital, which was computed in the preceding exercise.)

Exercise 13–29
ROI; Residual Income
(LO 1, 2)

Wyalusing Industries has manufactured prefabricated houses for over 20 years. The houses are constructed in sections to be assembled on customers' lots. Wyalusing expanded into the precut housing market when it acquired Fairmont Company, one of its suppliers. In this market, various types of lumber are precut into the appropriate lengths, banded into packages, and shipped to customers' lots for assembly. Wyalusing designated the Fairmont Division as an investment center. Wyalusing uses return on investment (ROI) as a performance measure with investment defined as average productive assets. Management bonuses are based in part on ROI. All investments are expected to earn a minimum return of 15 percent before income taxes. Fairmont's ROI has ranged from 19.3 to 22.1 percent since it was acquired. Fairmont had an investment opportunity in 20x1 that had an estimated ROI of 18 percent. Fairmont's management decided against the investment because it believed the investment would decrease the division's overall ROI. The 20x1 income statement for Fairmont Division follows. The division's productive assets were $12,600,000 at the end of 20x1, a 5 percent increase over the balance at the beginning of the year.

FAIRMONT DIVISION
Income Statement
For the Year Ended December 31, 20x1
(in thousands)

Sales revenue		$24,000
Cost of goods sold		15,800
Gross margin		$ 8,200
Operating expenses:		
Administrative	$2,140	
Selling	3,600	5,740
Income from operations before income taxes		$ 2,460

Required:

1. Calculate the following performance measures for 20x1 for the Fairmont Division.
   a. Return on investment (ROI).
   b. Residual income.
2. Would the management of Fairmont Division have been more likely to accept the investment opportunity it had in 20x1 if residual income were used as a performance measure instead of ROI? Explain your answer.
3. ***Build a spreadsheet:*** Construct an Excel spreadsheet to solve requirement (1) above. Show how the solution will change if income from operations was $2,700,000.

(CMA, adapted)

Exercise 13–30
ROI and Residual Income; Annual Reports; Use of Internet
(LO 2)

Select one of the following companies (or any company of your choosing) and use the Internet to explore the company's most recent annual report.

American Airlines	www.americanair.com
Deere and Company	www.deere.com
Firestone	www.firestone.com
IBM	www.ibm.com
Pizza Hut	www.pizzahut.com
Wyndham Hotels	www.wyndham.com
Walmart	www.wal-mart.com

Required:

1. Calculate the company's overall return on investment (ROI). Also, calculate the company's overall residual income. (Assume an imputed interest rate of 10 percent.) List and explain any assumptions you make.
2. Does the company include a calculation of ROI in its online annual report? If it does, do your calculations agree with those of the company? If not, what would be some possible explanations?

Exercise 13–31
Increasing ROI over Time
(LO 2, 4, 5)

Refer to Exhibit 13–3. Assume that you are a consultant who has been hired by Suncoast Food Centers.

Required: Write a memorandum to the company president explaining why the ROI based on net book value (in Exhibit 13–3) behaves as it does over the five-year time horizon.

Exercise 13–32
Internal Control
(LO 8)

Dryden Company is an auto parts supplier. At the end of each month, the employee who maintains all of the inventory records takes a physical inventory of the firm's stock. When discrepancies occur between the recorded inventory and the physical count, the employee changes the physical count to agree with the records.

Required:

1. What problems could arise as a result of Dryden Company's inventory procedures?
2. How could the internal control system be strengthened to eliminate the potential problems?

Exercise 13–33
Improving ROI
(LO 2, 3)

The following data pertain to British Isles Aggregates Company, a producer of sand, gravel, and cement, for the year just ended.

Sales revenue	£2,000,000
Cost of goods sold	1,100,000
Operating expenses	800,000
Average invested capital	1,000,000

£ denotes the British pound sterling, the national monetary unit of Great Britain.

Required:

1. Compute the company's sales margin, capital turnover, and ROI.
2. If the sales and average invested capital remain the same during the next year, to what level would total expenses have to be reduced in order to improve the firm's ROI to 15 percent?
3. Assume expenses are reduced, as calculated in requirement (2). Compute the firm's new sales margin. Show how the new sales margin and the old capital turnover together result in a new ROI of 15 percent.

Exercise 13–34
General Transfer-Pricing Rule
(LO 6)

Illinois Metallurgy Corporation has two divisions. The Fabrication Division transfers partially completed components to the Assembly Division at a predetermined transfer price. The Fabrication Division's standard variable production cost per unit is $300. The division has no excess capacity, and it could sell all of its components to outside buyers at $380 per unit in a perfectly competitive market.

Required:

1. Determine a transfer price using the general rule.
2. How would the transfer price change if the Fabrication Division had excess capacity?

Exercise 13–35
Cost-Based Transfer Pricing
(LO 7)

Refer to the preceding exercise. The Fabrication Division's full (absorption) cost of a component is $340, which includes $40 of applied fixed-overhead costs. The transfer price has been set at $374, which is the Fabrication Division's full cost plus a 10 percent markup.

The Assembly Division has a special offer for its product of $465. The Assembly Division incurs variable costs of $100 in addition to the transfer price for the Fabrication Division's components. Both divisions currently have excess production capacity.

Required:

1. What is the Assembly Division's manager likely to do regarding acceptance or rejection of the special offer? Why?
2. Is this decision in the best interests of the company as a whole? Why?
3. How could the situation be remedied using the transfer price?

Problems

All applicable Problems are available with McGraw-Hill's *Connect Accounting*™. 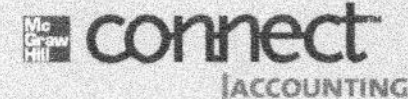

Problem 13–36
Comparing the Performance of Two Divisions
(LO 2, 4)

Long Beach Pharmaceutical Company has two divisions, which reported the following results for the most recent year.

	Division I	Division II
Income	$ 900,000	$ 200,000
Average invested capital	$6,000,000	$1,000,000
ROI	15%	20%

Required: Which was the more successful division during the year? Think carefully about this, and explain your answer.

Problem 13–37
ROI and Residual Income; Missing Data
(LO 2)

Residual income, division A: $240,000

The following data pertain to three divisions of Nevada Aggregates, Inc. The company's required rate of return on invested capital is 8 percent.

	Division A	Division B	Division C
Sales revenue	?	$10,000,000	?
Income	$400,000	$2,000,000	?
Average investment	?	$2,500,000	?
Sales margin	20%	?	25%
Capital turnover	1	?	?
ROI	?	?	20%
Residual income	?	?	$120,000

Required: Fill in the blanks above.

Problem 13–38
Improving ROI
(LO 3)

2. ROI: 25%

Refer to the preceding problem about Nevada Aggregates, Inc.

Required:

1. Explain three ways the Division B manager could improve her division's ROI. Use numbers to illustrate these possibilities.
2. Suppose Division A's sales margin increased to 25 percent, while its capital turnover remained constant. Compute the division's new ROI.

Problem 13–39
Residual Income
(LO 2, 4)

Refer to the data for problem 13–36 regarding Long Beach Pharmaceutical Company.

Required: Compute each division's residual income for the year under each of the following assumptions about the firm's cost of acquiring capital.

1. 12 percent.
2. 15 percent.
3. 18 percent.

Which division was more successful? Explain your answer.

Problem 13–40
Increasing ROI over Time; Accelerated Depreciation
(LO 2, 4, 5)

Year 2, ROI based on net book value: 12.5%

Refer to Exhibit 13–3. Prepare a similar table of the changing ROI assuming the following accelerated depreciation schedule. Assume the same income before depreciation as shown in Exhibit 13–3. (If there is a loss, leave the ROI column blank.)

Year	Depreciation
1	$200,000
2	120,000
3	72,000
4	54,000
5	54,000
Total	$500,000

Required:

1. How does your table differ from the one in Exhibit 13–3? Why?
2. What are the implications of the ROI pattern in your table?

Problem 13–41
Increasing Residual Income over Time
(LO 2, 4, 5)

Year 1, residual income (based on net book value): $5,000

Prepare a table similar to Exhibit 13–3, which focuses on residual income. Use a 10 percent rate to compute the imputed interest charge. The table should show the residual income on the investment during each year in its five-year life. Assume the same income before depreciation and the same depreciation schedule as shown in Exhibit 13–3.

Problem 13–42
ROI and Residual Income; Investment Evaluation
(LO 2, 3, 4, 8)

3. Income: $150,000
5. Current residual income of the Northeast Division: $148,000

Megatronics Corporation, a massive retailer of electronic products, is organized in four separate divisions. The four divisional managers are evaluated at year-end, and bonuses are awarded based on ROI. Last year, the company as a whole produced a 13 percent return on its investment.

During the past week, management of the company's Northeast Division was approached about the possibility of buying a competitor that had decided to redirect its retail activities. (If the competitor is acquired, it will be acquired at its book value.) The data that follow relate to recent performance of the Northeast Division and the competitor:

	Northeast Division	Competitor
Sales	$8,400,000	$5,200,000
Variable costs	70% of sales	65% of sales
Fixed costs	$2,150,000	$1,670,000
Invested capital	$1,850,000	$625,000

Management has determined that in order to upgrade the competitor to Megatronics' standards, an additional $375,000 of invested capital would be needed.

Required: As a group, complete the following requirements.

1. Compute the current ROI of the Northeast Division and the division's ROI if the competitor is acquired.
2. What is the likely reaction of divisional management toward the acquisition? Why?
3. What is the likely reaction of Megatronics' corporate management toward the acquisition? Why?
4. Would the division be better off if it didn't upgrade the competitor to Megatronics' standards? Show computations to support your answer.
5. Assume that Megatronics uses residual income to evaluate performance and desires a 12 percent minimum return on invested capital. Compute the current residual income of the Northeast Division and the division's residual income if the competitor is acquired. Will divisional management be likely to change its attitude toward the acquisition? Why?

Problem 13–43
ROI and Performance Evaluations
(LO 2, 4, 8)

1. Capital turnover: 80%

Kenneth Washburn, head of the Sporting Goods Division of Reliable Products, has just completed a miserable nine months. "If it could have gone wrong, it did. Sales are down, income is down, inventories are bloated, and quite frankly, I'm beginning to worry about my job," he moaned. Washburn is evaluated on the basis of ROI. Selected figures for the past nine months follow.

Sales	$4,800,000
Operating income	360,000
Invested capital	6,000,000

In an effort to make something out of nothing and to salvage the current year's performance, Washburn was contemplating implementation of some or all of the following four strategies:

a. Write off and discard $60,000 of obsolete inventory. The company will take a loss on the disposal.
b. Accelerate the collection of $80,000 of overdue customer accounts receivable.
c. Stop advertising through year-end and drastically reduce outlays for repairs and maintenance. These actions are expected to save the division $150,000 of expenses and will conserve cash resources.
d. Acquire two competitors that are expected to have the following financial characteristics:

	Projected Sales	Projected Operating Expenses	Projected Invested Capital
Anderson Manufacturing	$3,000,000	$2,400,000	$5,000,000
Palm Beach Enterprises	4,500,000	4,120,000	4,750,000

Required:

1. Briefly define sales margin, capital turnover, and return on investment and then compute these amounts for Reliable's Sporting Goods Division over the past nine months.
2. Evaluate each of the first two strategies listed, with respect to its effect on the Reliable's last nine months' performance, and make a recommendation to Washburn regarding which, if any, to adopt.
3. Are there possible long-term problems associated with strategy (c)? Briefly explain.
4. Determine the ROI of the investment in Anderson Manufacturing and do the same for the investment in Palm Beach Enterprises. Should Washburn reject both acquisitions, acquire one company, or acquire both companies? Assume that sufficient capital is available to fund investments in both organizations.

Problem 13–44
Weighted-Average Cost of Capital; Economic Value Added (EVA)
(LO 2)

1. Weighted-average cost of capital: .1056

Cape Cod Lobster Shacks, Inc. (CCLS) is a seafood restaurant chain operating throughout the northeast. The company has two sources of long-term capital: debt and equity. The cost to CCLS of issuing debt is the after-tax cost of the interest payments on the debt, taking into account the fact that the interest payments are tax deductible. The cost of CCLS's equity capital is the investment opportunity rate of CCLS's investors, that is, the rate they could earn on investments of similar risk to that of investing in Cape Cod Lobster Shacks, Inc. The interest rate on CCLS's $80 million of long-term debt is 9 percent, and the company's tax rate is 40 percent. The cost of CCLS's equity capital is 14 percent. Moreover, the market value (and book value) of CCLS's equity is $120 million.

Cape Cod Lobster Shacks, Inc. consists of two divisions, the properties division and the food service division. The divisions' total assets, current liabilities, and before-tax operating income for the most recent year are as follows:

Division	Total Assets	Current Liabilities	Before-Tax Operating Income
Properties	$145,000,000	$3,000,000	$29,000,000
Food Service	64,000,000	6,000,000	15,000,000

Required:

1. Calculate the weighted-average cost of capital for Cape Cod Lobster Shacks, Inc.
2. Calculate the economic value added (EVA) for each of CCLS's divisions.
3. *Build a spreadsheet:* Construct an Excel spreadsheet to solve both of the preceding requirements. Show how the solution will change if the following information changes: before-tax operating income was $30,000,000 and $14,000,000 for Properties and Food Service, respectively.

Problem 13–45
Weighted-Average Cost of Capital; Economic Value Added (EVA)
(LO 2)

1. The weighted-average cost of capital: .0972
2. Atlantic Division, economic value added: $(12,181,200)

All-Canadian, Ltd. is a multiproduct company with three divisions: Pacific Division, Plains Division, and Atlantic Division. The company has two sources of long-term capital: debt and equity. The interest rate on All-Canadian's $400 million debt is 9 percent, and the company's tax rate is 30 percent. The cost of All-Canadian's equity capital is 12 percent. Moreover, the market value of the company's equity is $600 million. (The book value of All-Canadian's equity is $430 million, but that amount does not reflect the current value of the company's assets or the value of intangible assets.)

The following data (in millions) pertain to All-Canadian's three divisions.

Division	Operating Income	Current Liabilities	Total Assets
Pacific	$14	$6	$ 70
Plains	45	5	300
Atlantic	48	9	480

Required:

1. Compute All-Canadian's weighted-average cost of capital (WACC).
2. Compute the economic value added (or EVA) for each of the company's three divisions.
3. What conclusions can you draw from the EVA analysis?

Problem 13–46
Comprehensive Transfer-Pricing Problem; Ethics
(LO 6, 7, 8)

2(a). Transfer price: $65

Clearview Window Company manufactures windows for the home-building industry. The window frames are produced in the Frame Division. The frames are then transferred to the Glass Division, where the glass and hardware are installed. The company's best-selling product is a three-by-four-foot, doublepaned operable window.

The Frame Division also can sell frames directly to custom home builders, who install the glass and hardware. The sales price for a frame is $80. The Glass Division sells its finished windows for $190. The markets for both frames and finished windows exhibit perfect competition.

The standard variable cost of the window is detailed as follows:

	Frame Division	Glass Division
Direct material	$15	$30*
Direct labor	20	15
Variable overhead	30	30
Total	$65	$75

*Not including the transfer price for the frame.

Required:

1. Assume that there is no excess capacity in the Frame Division.
   a. Use the general rule to compute the transfer price for window frames.
   b. Calculate the transfer price if it is based on standard variable cost with a 10 percent markup.
2. Assume that there is excess capacity in the Frame Division.
   a. Use the general rule to compute the transfer price for window frames.
   b. Explain why your answers to requirements (1*a*) and (2*a*) differ.

c. Suppose the predetermined fixed-overhead rate in the Frame Division is 125 percent of direct-labor cost. Calculate the transfer price if it is based on standard full cost plus a 10 percent markup.

d. Assume the transfer price established in requirement (2c) is used. The Glass Division has been approached by the U.S. Army with a special order for 1,000 windows at $155. From the perspective of Clearview Window Company as a whole, should the special order be accepted or rejected? Why?

e. Assume the same facts as in requirement (2d). Will an autonomous Glass Division manager accept or reject the special order? Why?

f. Comment on any ethical issues you see in the questions raised in requirements (2*d*) and (2*e*).

3. Comment on the use of full cost as the basis for setting transfer prices.

Problem 13–47
Transfer Pricing; Negotiation
(LO 7, 8)

4. Produce diode and sell externally, contribution margin: $275

Cortez Enterprises has two divisions: Birmingham and Tampa. Birmingham currently sells a diode reducer to manufacturers of aircraft navigation systems for $775 per unit. Variable costs amount to $500, and demand for this product currently exceeds the division's ability to supply the marketplace.

Despite this situation, Cortez is considering another use for the diode reducer, namely, integration into a satellite positioning system that would be made by Tampa. The positioning system has an anticipated selling price of $1,400 and requires an additional $670 of variable manufacturing costs. A transfer price of $750 has been established for the diode reducer.

Top management is anxious to introduce the positioning system; however, unless the transfer is made, an introduction will not be possible because of the difficulty of obtaining needed diode reducers. Birmingham and Tampa are in the process of recovering from previous financial problems, and neither division can afford any future losses. The company uses responsibility accounting and ROI in measuring divisional performance, and awards bonuses to divisional management.

Required:

1. How would Birmingham's divisional manager likely react to the decision to transfer diode reducers to Tampa? Show computations to support your answer.

2. How would Tampa's divisional management likely react to the $750 transfer price? Show computations to support your answer.

3. Assume that a lower transfer price is desired. Should top management lower the price or should the price be lowered by another means? Explain.

4. From a contribution margin perspective, does Cortez benefit more if it sells the diode reducers externally or transfers the reducers to Tampa? By how much?

Problem 13–48
Setting a Transfer Price; International Setting; Differential Tax Rates
(LO 6, 7)

2. U.S. operation, income after tax: $24.00
3. German operation, income after tax: $36.00

Alpha Communications, Inc., which produces telecommunications equipment in the United States, has a very strong local market for its circuit board. The variable production cost is $130, and the company can sell its entire supply domestically for $170. The U.S. tax rate is 40 percent.

Alternatively, Alpha can ship the circuit board to its division in Germany, to be used in a product that the German division will distribute throughout Europe. Information about the German product and the division's operating environment follows.

Selling price of final product: $360
Shipping fees to import circuit board: $20
Labor, overhead, and additional material costs of final product: $115
Import duties levied on circuit board (to be paid by the German division): 10% of transfer price
German tax rate: 60%

Assume that U.S. and German tax authorities allow a transfer price for the circuit board set at either U.S. variable manufacturing cost or the U.S. market price. Alpha's management is in the process of exploring which transfer price is better for the firm as a whole.

Required:

1. Compute overall company profitability per unit if all units are transferred and U.S. variable manufacturing cost is used as the transfer price. Show separate calculations for the U.S. operation and the German division.

2. Repeat requirement (1), assuming the use of the U.S. market price as the transfer price. Which of the two transfer prices is better for the firm?

3. Assume that the German division can obtain the circuit board in Germany for $155.
   a. If you were the head of the German division, would you rather do business with your U.S. division or buy the circuit board locally? Why?
   b. Rather than proceed with the transfer, is it in the best interest of Alpha to sell its goods domestically and allow the German division to acquire the circuit board in Germany? Why? Show computations to support your answer.
4. Generally speaking, when tax rates differ between countries, what strategy should a company use in setting its transfer prices?
5. *Build a spreadsheet:* Construct an Excel spreadsheet to solve requirements (1) and (2) above. Show how the solution will change if the following information changes: the U.S. tax rate is 35 percent, the German tax rate is 55 percent, and the import duties are 8 percent of the transfer price.

Problem 13–49
Transfer Pricing; Management Behavior
(LO 6, 7, 8)

2. Total contribution margin, Mining Division: $15,200,000

Provo Consolidated Resources Company (PCRC) has several divisions. However, only two divisions transfer products to other divisions. The Mining Division refines toldine, which is then transferred to the Metals Division. The toldine is processed into an alloy by the Metals Division, and the alloy is sold to customers at a price of $150 per unit. The Mining division is currently required by PCRC to transfer its total yearly output of 400,000 units of toldine to the Metals Division at total actual manufacturing cost plus 10 percent. Unlimited quantities of toldine can be purchased and sold on the open market at $90 per unit. While the Mining Division could sell all the toldine it produces at $90 per unit on the open market, it would incur a variable selling cost of $5 per unit.

Brian Jones, manager of the Mining Division, is unhappy with having to transfer the entire output of toldine to the Metals Division at 110 percent of cost. In a meeting with the management of Provo, he said, "Why should my division be required to sell toldine to the Metals Division at less than market price? For the year just ended in May, Metals' contribution margin was over $19 million on sales of 400,000 units, while Mining's contribution was just over $5 million on the transfer of the same number of units. My division is subsidizing the profitability of the Metals Division. We should be allowed to charge the market price for toldine when transferring to the Metals Division."

The following table shows the detailed unit cost structure for both the Mining and Metals divisions during the most recent year.

	Mining Division	Metals Division
Transfer price from Mining Division	—	$ 66
Direct material	$12	6
Direct labor	16	20
Manufacturing overhead	32*	25†
Total cost per unit	$60	$117

*Manufacturing-overhead cost in the Mining Division is 25 percent fixed and 75 percent variable.
†Manufacturing-overhead cost in the Metals Division is 60 percent fixed and 40 percent variable.

Required:

1. Explain why transfer prices based on total actual costs are not appropriate as the basis for divisional performance measurement.
2. Using the market price as the transfer price, determine the contribution margin for both the Mining Division and the Metals Division.
3. If Provo Consolidated Resources Company were to institute the use of negotiated transfer prices and allow divisions to buy and sell on the open market, determine the price range for toldine that would be acceptable to both the Mining Division and the Metals Division. Explain your answer.
4. Use the general transfer-pricing rule to compute the lowest transfer price that would be acceptable to the Mining Division. Is your answer consistent with your conclusion in requirement (3)? Explain.
5. Identify which one of the three types of transfer prices (cost-based, market-based, or negotiated) is most likely to elicit desirable management behavior at PCRC. Explain your answer.

(CMA, adapted)

Cases

Case 13–50
ROI versus Residual Income; Incentive Effects
(LO 1, 2, 4, 8)

2. Residual income, RLI: $120,000

Holiday Entertainment Corporation (HEC), a subsidiary of New Age Industries, manufactures go-carts and other recreational vehicles. Family recreational centers that feature not only go-cart tracks but miniature golf, batting cages, and arcade games as well have increased in popularity. As a result, HEC has been receiving some pressure from New Age's management to diversify into some of these other recreational areas. Recreational Leasing, Inc. (RLI), one of the largest firms that leases arcade games to family recreational centers, is looking for a friendly buyer. New Age's top management believes that RLI's assets could be acquired for an investment of $3.2 million and has strongly urged Bill Grieco, division manager of HEC, to consider acquiring RLI.

Grieco has reviewed RLI's financial statements with his controller, Marie Donnelly, and they believe the acquisition may not be in the best interest of HEC. "If we decide not to do this, the New Age people are not going to be happy," said Grieco. "If we could convince them to base our bonuses on something other than return on investment, maybe this acquisition would look more attractive. How would we do if the bonuses were based on residual income, using the company's 15 percent cost of capital?"

New Age Industries traditionally has evaluated all of its divisions on the basis of return on investment. The desired rate of return for each division is 20 percent. The management team of any division reporting an annual increase in the ROI is automatically eligible for a bonus. The management of divisions reporting a decline in the ROI must provide convincing explanations for the decline in order to be eligible for a bonus. Moreover, this bonus is limited to 50 percent of the bonus paid to divisions reporting an increase in ROI.

In the following table are condensed financial statements for both HEC and RLI for the most recent year.

	RLI	HEC
Sales revenue	—	$9,500,000
Leasing revenue	$3,100,000	—
Variable expenses	(1,300,000)	(6,000,000)
Fixed expenses	(1,200,000)	(1,500,000)
Operating income	$ 600,000	$2,000,000
Current assets	$1,900,000	$2,300,000
Long-lived assets	1,100,000	5,700,000
Total assets	$3,000,000	$8,000,000
Current liabilities	$ 850,000	$1,400,000
Long-term liabilities	1,200,000	3,800,000
Stockholders' equity	950,000	2,800,000
Total liabilities and stockholders' equity	$3,000,000	$8,000,000

Required:

1. If New Age Industries continues to use ROI as the sole measure of divisional performance, explain why Holiday Entertainment Corporation would be reluctant to acquire Recreational Leasing, Inc.
2. If New Age Industries could be persuaded to use residual income to measure the performance of HEC, explain why HEC would be more willing to acquire RLI.
3. Discuss how the behavior of division managers is likely to be affected by the use of the following performance measures: (*a*) return on investment and (*b*) residual income.

(CMA, adapted)

Case 13–51
Interdivisional Transfers; IPricing the Final Product
(LO 6, 7, 8)

1. Increase in net income before taxes: $132,000
3. Increase in net income before taxes for InterGlobal Industries: $312,500

InterGlobal Industries is a diversified corporation with separate operating divisions. Each division's performance is evaluated on the basis of profit and return on investment.

The Air Comfort Division manufactures and sells air-conditioner units. The coming year's budgeted income statement, which follows, is based upon a sales volume of 15,000 units.

AIR COMFORT DIVISION
Budgeted Income Statement
(In thousands)

	Per Unit	Total
Sales revenue	$400	$6,000
Manufacturing costs:		
Compressor	$ 70	$1,050
Other direct material	37	555
Direct labor	30	450
Variable overhead	45	675
Fixed overhead	32	480
Total manufacturing costs	$214	$3,210
Gross margin	$186	$2,790
Operating expenses:		
Variable selling	$ 18	$270
Fixed selling	19	285
Fixed administrative	38	570
Total operating expenses	$ 75	$1,125
Net income before taxes	$111	$1,665

Air Comfort's division manager believes sales can be increased if the price of the air-conditioners is reduced. A market research study by an independent firm indicates that a 5 percent reduction in the selling price would increase sales volume 16 percent, or 2,400 units. The division has sufficient production capacity to manage this increased volume with no increase in fixed costs.

The Air Comfort Division uses a compressor in its units, which it purchases from an outside supplier at a cost of $70 per compressor. The Air Comfort Division manager has asked the manager of the Compressor Division about selling compressor units to Air Comfort. The Compressor Division currently manufactures and sells a unit to outside firms that is similar to the unit used by the Air Comfort Division. The specifications of the Air Comfort Division compressor are slightly different, which would reduce the Compressor Division's direct material cost by $1.50 per unit. In addition, the Compressor Division would not incur any variable selling costs in the units sold to the Air Comfort Division. The manager of the Air Comfort Division wants all of the compressors it uses to come from one supplier and has offered to pay $50 for each compressor unit.

The Compressor Division has the capacity to produce 75,000 units. Its budgeted income statement for the coming year, which follows, is based on a sales volume of 64,000 units without considering Air Comfort's proposal.

COMPRESSOR DIVISION
Budgeted Income Statement
(In thousands)

	Per Unit	Total
Sales revenue	$100	$6,400
Manufacturing costs:		
Direct material	$ 12	$ 768
Direct labor	8	512
Variable overhead	10	640
Fixed overhead	11	704
Total manufacturing costs	$ 41	$2,624
Gross margin	$ 59	$3,776
Operating expenses:		
Variable selling	$ 6	$ 384
Fixed selling	4	256
Fixed administrative	7	448
Total operating expenses	$ 17	$1,088
Net income before taxes	$ 42	$2,688

Required:

1. Should the Air Comfort Division institute the 5 percent price reduction on its air-conditioner units even if it cannot acquire the compressors internally for $50 each? Support your conclusion with appropriate calculations.
2. Independently of your answer to requirement (1), assume the Air Comfort Division needs 17,400 units. Should the Compressor Division be willing to supply the compressor units for $50 each? Support your conclusions with appropriate calculations.
3. Independently of your answer to requirement (1), assume Air Comfort needs 17,400 units. Suppose InterGlobal's top management has specified a transfer price of $50. Would it be in the best interest of *InterGlobal Industries* for the Compressor Division to supply the compressor units at $50 each to the Air Comfort Division? Support your conclusions with appropriate calculations.
4. Is $50 a goal-congruent transfer price? [Refer to your answers for requirements (2) and (3).]

(CMA, adapted)

Case 13–52
Minimum and Maximum Acceptable Transfer Prices; Multinational
(LO 6, 7, 8)

2. Unit contribution margin, LDP: $6
5. Net savings if TCH-320 is produced using an HDP: $112.00

General Instrumentation Company manufactures dashboard instruments for heavy construction equipment. The firm is based in Baltimore, but operates several divisions in the United States, Canada, and Europe. The Hudson Bay Division manufactures complex electrical panels that are used in a variety of the firm's instruments. There are two basic types of panels. The high-density panel (HDP) is capable of many functions and is used in the most sophisticated instruments, such as tachometers and pressure gauges. The low-density panel (LDP) is much simpler and is used in less-complicated instruments. Although there are minor differences among the different high-density panels, the basic manufacturing process and production costs are the same. The high-density panels require considerably more skilled labor than the low-density panels, but the unskilled labor needs are about the same. Moreover, the direct materials in the high-density panel run substantially more than the cost of materials in the low-density panels. Production costs are summarized as follows:

	LDP	HDP
Unskilled labor (.5 hour @ $10)	$ 5	$ 5
Skilled labor:		
LDP (.25 hour @ $20)	5	
HDP (1.5 hours @ $20)		30
Raw material	3	8
Purchased components	4	12
Variable overhead	5	15
Total variable cost	$22	$70

The annual fixed overhead in the Hudson Bay Division is $1,000,000. There is a limited supply of skilled labor available in the area, and the division must constrain its production to 40,000 hours of skilled labor each year. This has been a troublesome problem for Jacqueline Ducharme, the division manager. Ducharme has successfully increased demand for the LDP line to the point where it is essentially unlimited. Each LDP sells for $28. Business also has increased in recent years for the HDP, and Ducharme estimates the division could now sell anywhere up to 6,000 units per year at a price of $115.

On the other side of the Atlantic, General Instrumentation operates its Volkmar Tachometer Division in Berlin. A recent acquisition of General Instrumentation, the division was formerly a German company known as Volkmar Construction Instruments. The division's main product is a sophisticated tachometer used in heavy-duty cranes, bulldozers, and backhoes. The instrument, designated as a TCH–320, has the following production costs.

	TCH–320
Unskilled labor (.5 hour @ $9)	$ 4.50
Skilled labor (3 hours @ $17)	51.00
Raw material	11.50
Purchased components	150.00
Variable overhead	11.00
Total variable cost	$228.00

The cost of purchased components includes a $145 control pack currently imported from Japan. Fixed overhead in the Volkmar Tachometer Division runs about $800,000 per year. Both skilled and unskilled labor are in abundant supply. The TCH–320 sells for $270.

Bertram Mueller, the division manager of the Volkmar Tachometer Division, recently attended a high-level corporate meeting in Baltimore. In a conversation with Jacqueline Ducharme, it was apparent that Hudson Bay's high-density panel might be a viable substitute for the control pack currently imported from Japan and used in Volkmar's TCH–320. Upon returning to Berlin, Mueller asked his chief engineer to look into the matter. Hans Schmidt obtained several HDP units from Hudson Bay, and a minor R&D project was mounted to determine if the HDP could replace the Japanese control pack. Several weeks later, the following conversation occurred in Mueller's office:

Schmidt: There's no question that Hudson Bay's HDP unit will work in our TCH–320. In fact, it could save us some money.

Mueller: That's good news. If we can buy our components within the company, we'll help Baltimore's bottom line without hurting ours. Also, it will look good to the brass at corporate if they see us working hard to integrate our division into General Instrumentation's overall production program.

Schmidt: I've also been worried about the reliability of supply of the control pack. I don't like being dependent on such a critical supplier that way.

Mueller: I agree. Let's look at your figures on the HDP replacement.

Schmidt: I got together with the controller's people, and we worked up some numbers. If we replace the control pack with the HDP from Canada, we'll avoid the $145 control pack cost we're now incurring. In addition, I figure we'll save $5.50 on the basic raw materials. There is one catch, though. The HDP will require some adjustments in order to use it in the TCH–320. We can make the adjustments here in Berlin. I'm guessing it will require an additional two hours of skilled labor to make the necessary modifications. I don't think variable overhead would be any different. Then there is the cost of transporting the HDPs to Berlin. Let's figure on $4.50 per unit.

Mueller: Sounds good. I'll give Jacqueline Ducharme a call and talk this over. We can use up to 10,000 of the HDP units per year given the demand for the TCH–320. I wonder what kind of a transfer price Hudson Bay will want.

Required:

1. Draw a simple diagram depicting the two divisions and their products. Also show the two alternatives that the Volkmar Tachometer Division has in the production of its TCH–320.
2. From the perspective of General Instrumentation's top management, should any of the TCH–320 units be produced using the high-density panel? If so, how many?
3. Suppose Hudson Bay transfers 10,000 HDP units per year to Volkmar. From the perspective of General Instrumentation's top management, what effect will the transfer price have on the company's income?
4. What is the minimum transfer price that the Hudson Bay Division would find acceptable for the HDP?
5. What is the maximum transfer price that the Volkmar Tachometer Division would find acceptable for the HDP?
6. As the corporate controller for General Instrumentation, recommend a transfer price.

FOCUS COMPANY >>>

THIS CHAPTER'S FOCUS COMPANY is Worldwide Airways, an international airline based in Atlanta, Georgia. Using this service-industry company for our illustration, we will explore a variety of decisions that managers make routinely. Examples of such decisions are accepting or rejecting a special offer for the company's services, outsourcing a service, and adding or dropping a service or department. We will find in this chapter that different kinds of cost information are relevant, depending on the type of decision to be made.

14 Decision Making: Relevant Costs and Benefits

IN CONTRAST >>>

In contrast to the transportation-services setting of Worldwide Airways, we will explore certain types of decisions that most often arise in a manufacturing setting. Our illustration will be based on International Chocolate Company, which produces a variety of chocolate products. In addition to producing chocolate candy, the company processes cocoa beans into cocoa powder and cocoa butter. The cocoa powder can then be processed further into instant cocoa mix. We will explore a variety of decisions faced by International Chocolate Company's management.

AFTER COMPLETING THIS CHAPTER, YOU SHOULD BE ABLE TO:

1. Describe seven steps in the decision-making process and the managerial accountant's role in that process.
2. Explain the relationship between quantitative and qualitative analyses in decision making.
3. List and explain two criteria that must be satisfied by relevant information.
4. Identify relevant costs and benefits, giving proper treatment to sunk costs, opportunity costs, and unit costs.
5. Prepare analyses of various special decisions, properly identifying the relevant costs and benefits.
6. Analyze manufacturing decisions involving joint products and limited resources.
7. Explain the impact of an advanced manufacturing environment and activity-based costing on a relevant-cost analysis.
8. Formulate a linear program to solve a product-mix problem with multiple constraints (appendix).

Decision making is a fundamental part of management. Decisions about the acquisition of equipment, mix of products, methods of production, and pricing of products and services confront managers in all types of organizations. This chapter covers the role of managerial accounting information in a variety of common decisions. The next chapter examines pricing decisions.

The Managerial Accountant's Role in Decision Making

Managerial accountants are increasingly playing important roles as full-fledged members of cross-functional management teams. These management teams face a broad array of decisions, including production, marketing, financial, and other decisions. All managers and management teams need information pertinent to their decisions. In support of the decision-making process, managerial accountants play a specific role in providing relevant information. Thus, the managerial accountant must have a good understanding of the decisions faced by managers throughout the organization.

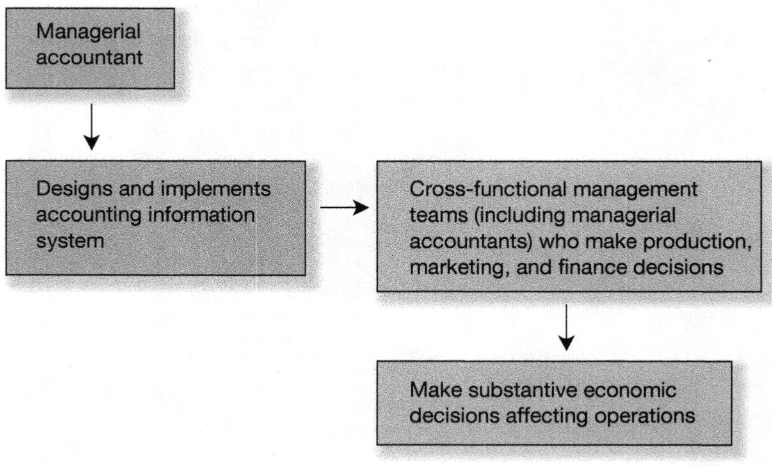

Steps in the Decision-Making Process

Seven steps characterize the decision-making process:

Learning Objective 1

Describe seven steps in the decision-making process and the managerial accountant's role in that process.

1. ***Clarify the decision problem.*** Sometimes the decision to be made is clear. For example, if a company receives a special order for its product at a price below the usual price, the decision problem is to accept or reject the order. But the decision problem is seldom so clear and unambiguous. Perhaps demand for a company's most popular product is declining. What exactly is causing this problem? Increasing competition? Declining quality control? A new alternative product on the market? Before a decision can be made, the problem needs to be clarified and defined in more specific terms. Considerable managerial skill is required to define a decision problem in terms that can be addressed effectively.
2. ***Specify the criterion.*** Once a decision problem has been clarified, the manager should specify the criterion upon which a decision will be made. Is the objective to maximize profit, increase market share, minimize cost, or improve public service? Sometimes the objectives are in conflict, as in a decision problem where production cost is to be minimized but product quality must be maintained. In such cases, one objective is specified as the decision criterion—for example, cost minimization. The other objective is established as a constraint—for example, product quality must not be worse than one defective part in 1,000 manufactured units.

"We are looked upon as more business advisors than just accountants, and that has a lot to do with the additional analysis and the forward looking goals we are setting." (14a)

Caterpillar

3. ***Identify the alternatives.*** A decision involves selecting between two or more alternatives. If a machine breaks down, what are the alternative courses of action? The machine can be repaired or replaced, or a replacement can be leased. But perhaps repair will turn out to be more costly than replacement. Determining the possible alternatives is a critical step in the decision process.
4. ***Develop a decision model.*** A *decision model* is a simplified representation of the choice problem. Unnecessary details are stripped away, and the most important elements of the problem are highlighted. Thus, the decision model brings together the elements listed above: the criterion, the constraints, and the alternatives.
5. ***Collect the data.*** Although the managerial accountant often is involved in steps 1 through 4, he or she is chiefly responsible for step 5. Selecting data pertinent to decisions is one of the managerial accountant's most important roles in an organization.
6. ***Select an alternative.*** Once the decision model is formulated and the pertinent data are collected, the appropriate manager makes a decision.
7. ***Evaluate decision effectiveness.*** After a decision has been implemented, the results of the decision are evaluated with the objective of improving future decisions.

Quantitative versus Qualitative Analysis

Learning Objective 2

Explain the relationship between quantitative and qualitative analyses in decision making.

Decision problems involving accounting data typically are specified in quantitative terms. The criteria in such problems usually include objectives such as profit maximization or cost minimization. When a manager makes a final decision, however, the qualitative characteristics of the alternatives can be just as important as the quantitative measures. **Qualitative characteristics** are the factors in a decision problem that cannot be expressed effectively in numerical terms. To illustrate, suppose Worldwide Airways' top management is considering the elimination of its hub operation in London. Airlines establish hubs at airports where many of their routes intersect. Hub operations include facilities for in-flight food preparation, aircraft maintenance and storage, and administrative offices. A careful quantitative analysis indicates that Worldwide Airways' profit-maximizing alternative is to eliminate the London hub. In making its decision, however, the company's managers will consider such qualitative issues as the effect of the closing on its London employees and on the morale of its remaining employees in the airline's Paris, Atlanta, and Tokyo hubs.

To clarify what is at stake in such qualitative analyses, quantitative analysis can allow the decision maker to put a "price" on the sum total of the qualitative characteristics. For example, suppose Worldwide Airways' controller gives top management a quantitative analysis showing that elimination of the London hub will increase annual profits by $2,000,000. However, the qualitative considerations favor the option of continuing the London operation. How important are these qualitative considerations to the top managers? If they decide to continue the London operation, the qualitative considerations must be worth at least $2,000,000 to them. Weighing the quantitative and qualitative considerations in making decisions is the essence of management. The skill, experience, judgment, and ethical standards of managers all come to bear on such difficult choices.

Exhibit 14–1 depicts the seven steps in the decision process, and the relationship between quantitative and qualitative analysis.

Obtaining Information: Relevance, Accuracy, and Timeliness

What criteria should the managerial accountant use in designing the accounting information system that supplies data for decision making? Three characteristics of information determine its usefulness.

Relevance Information is **relevant** if it is *pertinent* to a decision problem. Different decisions typically will require different data. The primary theme of this chapter is how to decide what information is relevant to various common decision problems.

Accuracy Information that is pertinent to a decision problem also must be **accurate,** or it will be of little use. This means the information must be precise. For example, the cost incurred by Worldwide Airways to rent facilities at London's Heathrow Airport is

Exhibit 14–1
The Decision-Making Process

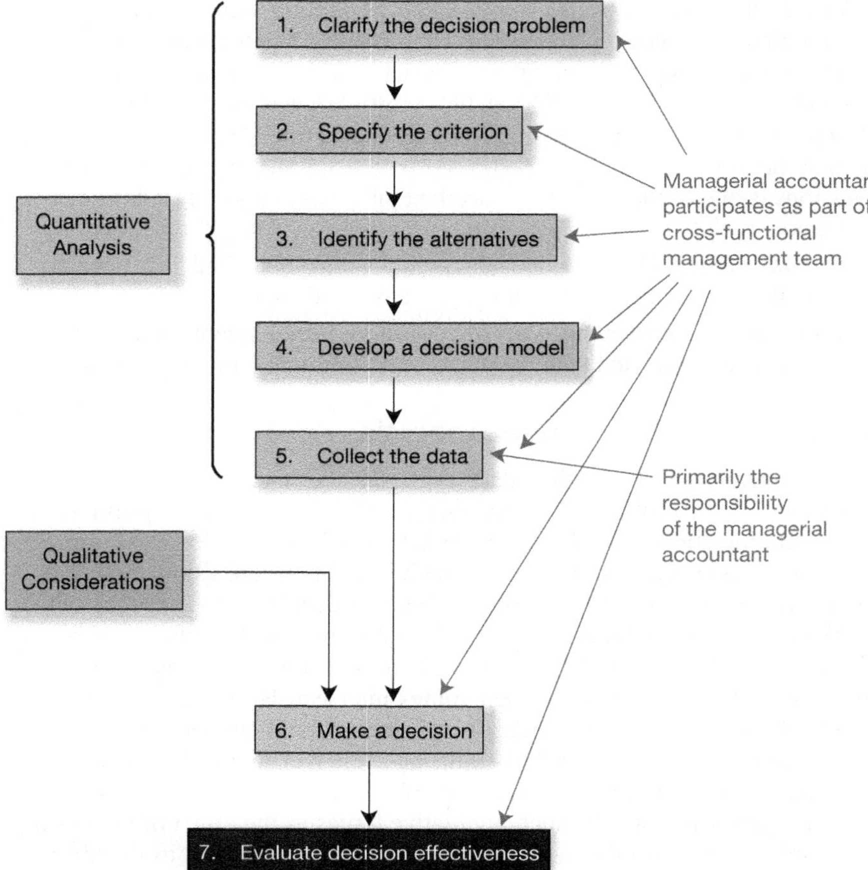

relevant to a decision about eliminating the airline's London hub. However, if the rental cost data are imprecise, due to incomplete or misplaced records, the usefulness of the information will be diminished.

Conversely, highly accurate but irrelevant data are of no value to a decision maker. Suppose Worldwide Airways will continue its daily round-trip flight between New York and London regardless of its decision about eliminating the London hub. Precise data about fuel consumption on the New York–London route are irrelevant to the decision about closing down the London hub.

Timeliness Relevant and accurate data are of value only if they are **timely,** that is, available in time for a decision. Thus, timeliness is the third important criterion for determining the usefulness of information. Some situations involve a trade-off between the accuracy and the timeliness of information. More accurate information may take longer to produce. Therefore, as accuracy improves, timeliness suffers, and vice versa. For example, a company may test-market a potential new product in a particular city. The longer the test-marketing program runs, the more accurate will be the marketing data generated. However, a long wait for the accurate marketing report may unduly delay management's decision to launch the new product nationally.

To summarize, the managerial accountant's primary role in the decision-making process is twofold:

1. Decide what information is *relevant* to each decision problem.
2. Provide *accurate* and *timely* data, keeping in mind the proper balance between these often-conflicting criteria.

Relevant Information

What makes information relevant to a decision problem? Two criteria are important.

Learning Objective 3

List and explain two criteria that must be satisfied by relevant information.

Bearing on the Future The consequences of decisions are borne in the future, not the past. To be relevant to a decision, cost or benefit information must involve a future event. The cost information relevant to Worldwide Airways' decision concerning its London operations involves the costs that *will be incurred in the future* under the airline's two alternatives. Costs incurred in the past in the airline's London operations will not change regardless of management's decision, and they are irrelevant to the decision at hand.

Since relevant information involves future events, the managerial accountant must predict the amounts of the relevant costs and benefits. In making these predictions, the accountant often will use estimates of cost behavior based on historical data. There is an important and subtle issue here. *Relevant* information must involve costs and benefits to be realized in the *future.* However, the accountant's *predictions* of those costs and benefits often are based on data from the *past.*

Different under Competing Alternatives Relevant information must involve costs or benefits that *differ among the alternatives.* Costs or benefits that are the same across all the available alternatives have no bearing on the decision. For example, suppose Worldwide Airways' management decides to keep its reservations and ticketing office in London regardless of whether its London hub is eliminated. Then the costs of the reservations and ticketing office will not differ between the two alternatives regarding elimination of the London hub. Hence, those costs are irrelevant to that decision.

"You have to try to summarize numbers. You can't just give numbers. People in marketing are going to make decisions based on your numbers. They have to understand what those numbers mean." (14b)
Abbott Laboratories

Unique versus Repetitive Decisions

Unique decisions arise infrequently or only once. Worldwide Airways' decision regarding its London hub is an example. Compiling data for unique decisions usually requires a special analysis by the managerial accountant. The relevant information often will be found in many diverse places in the organization's overall information system.

In contrast, *repetitive decisions* are made over and over again, at either regular or irregular intervals. For example, Worldwide Airways makes route-scheduling decisions every six months. Such a routine decision makes it worthwhile for the managerial accountant to keep a special file of the information relevant to the scheduling decision.

Cost predictions relevant to repetitive decisions typically can draw on a large amount of historical data. Since the decisions have been made repeatedly in the past, the data from those decisions should be readily available. Information relevant to unique decisions is harder to generate. The managerial accountant typically will have to give more thought to deciding which data are relevant, and will have less historical data available upon which to base predictions.

Importance of Identifying Relevant Costs and Benefits

Why is it important for the managerial accountant to isolate the relevant costs and benefits in a decision analysis? The reasons are twofold. First, generating information is a costly process. The relevant data must be sought, and this requires time and effort. By focusing on only the relevant information, the managerial accountant can simplify and shorten the data-gathering process.

Second, people can effectively use only a limited amount of information. Beyond this, they experience **information overload,** and their decision-making effectiveness declines. By routinely providing only information about relevant costs and benefits, the managerial accountant can reduce the likelihood of information overload.

Identifying Relevant Costs and Benefits

Learning Objective 4

Identify relevant costs and benefits, giving proper treatment to sunk costs, opportunity costs, and unit costs.

To illustrate how managerial accountants determine relevant costs and benefits, we will consider several decisions faced by the management of Worldwide Airways. Based in Atlanta, the airline flies routes between the United States and Europe, between various cities in Europe, and between the United States and several Asian cities.

Sunk Costs

Sunk costs are costs that have already been incurred. They do not affect any future cost and cannot be changed by any current or future action. Sunk costs are irrelevant to decisions, as the following two examples show.

Book Value of Equipment At Charles de Gaulle Airport in Paris, Worldwide Airways has a three-year-old loader truck used to load in-flight meals onto airplanes. The box on the truck can be lifted hydraulically to the level of a jumbo jet's side doors. The *book value* of this loader, defined as the asset's acquisition cost less the accumulated depreciation to date, is computed as follows:

Acquisition cost of old loader	$100,000
Less: Accumulated depreciation	75,000
Book value	$ 25,000

The loader has one year of useful life remaining, after which its salvage value will be zero. However, it could be sold now for $5,000. In addition to the annual depreciation of $25,000, Worldwide Airways annually incurs $80,000 in variable costs to operate the loader. These include the costs of operator labor, gasoline, and maintenance.

John Orville, Worldwide Airways' ramp manager at Charles de Gaulle Airport, faces a decision about replacement of the loader. A new kind of loader uses a conveyor belt to move meals into an airplane. The new loader is much cheaper than the old hydraulic loader and costs less to operate. However, the new loader would be operable for only one year before it would need to be replaced. Pertinent data about the new loader are as follows:

Acquisition cost of new loader	$15,000
Useful life	1 year
Salvage value after one year	0
Annual depreciation	$15,000
Annual operating costs	$45,000

Orville's initial inclination is to continue using the old loader for another year. He exclaims, "We can't dump that equipment now. We paid $100,000 for it, and we've only used it three years. If we get rid of that loader now, we'll lose $20,000 on the disposal." Orville reasons that the old loader's book value of $25,000, less its current salvage value of $5,000, amounts to a loss of $20,000.

Fortunately, Orville's comment is overheard by Joan Wilbur, the managerial accountant in the company's Charles de Gaulle Airport administrative offices. Wilbur points out to Orville that the book value of the old loader is a *sunk cost.* It cannot affect any future cost the company might incur. To convince Orville that she is right, Wilbur prepares the analysis shown in Exhibit 14–2.

Regardless of which alternative is selected, the $25,000 book value of the old loader will be an expense or loss in the next year. If the old loader is kept in service, the $25,000 will be recognized as depreciation expense; otherwise, the $25,000 cost will be incurred by the company as a write-off of the asset's book value. Thus, the current book value of the old loader is a *sunk cost* and irrelevant to the replacement decision.

Notice that the *relevant* data in the equipment replacement decision are items (3), (4), and (5). Each of these items meets the two tests of relevant information:

1. The costs or benefits relate to the future.
2. The costs or benefits differ between the alternatives.

"[We are continually moving] from being the scorekeeper to being an active, involved participant in crafting business solutions." (14c)
Boeing

The proceeds from selling the old loader, item (3), will be received in the future only under the "replace" alternative. Similarly, the acquisition cost (depreciation) of the new loader,

Exhibit 14–2
Equipment Replacement Decision: Worldwide Airways

		Costs of Two Alternatives		
		(a) Do Not Replace Old Loader*	(b) Replace Old Loader*	(c) Differential Cost: (a) − (b)
Sunk cost	(1) Depreciation of old loader	$ 25,000		
	OR			–0–
	(2) Write-off of old loader's book value		$25,000	
Relevant data	(3) Proceeds from disposal of old loader	–0–	(5,000)†	$ 5,000
	(4) Depreciation (cost) of new loader	–0–	15,000	(15,000)
	(5) Operating costs	80,000	45,000	35,000
	Total cost	$105,000	$80,000	$25,000

*Since costs are the focus of the analysis in this exhibit, costs are shown in columns (a) and (b) without parentheses.
†Parentheses denote a cash inflow in this case.

item (4), is a future cost incurred only under the "replace" alternative. The operating cost, item (5), is also a future cost that differs between the two alternatives.

Differential Costs Exhibit 14–2 includes a column entitled *Differential Cost.* A **differential cost** is the difference in a cost item under two decision alternatives. The computation of differential costs is a convenient way of summarizing the relative advantage of one alternative over the other. John Orville can make a correct equipment-replacement decision in either of two ways: (1) by comparing the total cost of the two alternatives, shown in columns (a) and (b); or (2) by focusing on the total differential cost, shown in column (c), which favors the "replacement" option.

Cost of Inventory on Hand Never having taken a managerial accounting course in college, John Orville is slow to learn how to identify sunk costs. The next week he goofs again.

The inventory of spare aircraft parts held by Worldwide Airways at Charles de Gaulle includes some obsolete parts originally costing $20,000. The company no longer uses the planes for which the parts were purchased. The obsolete parts include spare passenger seats, luggage racks, and galley equipment. The spare parts could be sold to another airline for $17,000. However, with some modifications, the obsolete parts could still be used in the company's current fleet of aircraft. Using the modified parts would save Worldwide Airways the cost of purchasing new parts for its airplanes.

John Orville decides not to dispose of the obsolete parts, because doing so would entail a loss of $3,000. Orville reasons that the $20,000 book value of the parts, less the $17,000 proceeds from disposal, would result in a $3,000 loss on disposal. Joan Wilbur, the managerial accountant, comes to the rescue again, demonstrating that the right decision is to dispose of the parts. Wilbur's analysis is shown in Exhibit 14–3.

Notice that the book value of the obsolete inventory is a sunk cost. If the parts are modified, the $20,000 book value will be an expense during the period when the parts are used. Otherwise, the $20,000 book value of the asset will be written off when the parts are sold. As a sunk cost, the book value of the obsolete inventory will not affect any future cash flow of the company.

As the managerial accountant's analysis reveals, the relevant data include the $17,000 proceeds from disposal, the $12,000 cost to modify the parts, and the $26,000 cost to buy new parts. All of these data meet the two tests of relevance: they affect future cash flows and they differ between the two alternatives. As Joan Wilbur's analysis shows, Worldwide Airways' cost will be $3,000 less if the obsolete parts are sold and new parts are purchased.

Exhibit 14–3
Obsolete Inventory Decision: Worldwide Airways

		Costs of Two Alternatives		
		(a) Modify and Use Parts*	(b) Dispose of Parts*	(c) Differential Cost: (a) − (b)
Sunk cost	Book value of parts inventory: asset value written off whether parts are used or not	$20,000	$20,000	$ -0-
Relevant data	Proceeds from disposal of parts	-0-	(17,000)†	17,000
	Cost to modify parts	12,000	-0-	12,000
	Cost incurred to buy new parts for current aircraft fleet	-0-	26,000	(26,000)
	Total cost	$32,000	$29,000	$ 3,000

*Since costs are the focus of the analysis in this exhibit, costs are shown in columns (a) and (b) without parentheses.
†Parentheses denote a cash inflow in this case.

Exhibit 14–4
Flight-Route Decision: Worldwide Airways

Relevant or Irrelevant			(a) Nonstop Route*	(b) With Stop in San Francisco*	(c) Differential Amount†: (a) – (b)
			Revenues and Costs under Two Alternatives		
Relevant		(1) Passenger revenue	$240,000	$258,000	$(18,000)
	Irrelevant	(2) Cargo revenue	80,000	80,000	–0–
Relevant		(3) Landing fee in San Francisco	–0–	(5,000)	5,000
Relevant		(4) Use of airport gate facilities	–0–	(3,000)	3,000
Relevant		(5) Flight crew cost	(2,000)	(2,500)	500
Relevant		(6) Fuel	(21,000)	(24,000)	3,000
Relevant		(7) Meals and services	(4,000)	(4,600)	600
	Irrelevant	(8) Aircraft maintenance	(1,000)	(1,000)	–0–
		Total revenue less costs	$292,000	$297,900	$ (5,900)

*In columns (a) and (b), parentheses denote costs and numbers without parentheses are revenues.
†In column (c), parentheses denote differential items favoring option (b).

Irrelevant Future Costs and Benefits

At Worldwide Airways' headquarters in Atlanta, Amy Earhart, manager of flight scheduling, is in the midst of making a decision about the Atlanta to Honolulu route. The flight is currently nonstop, but she is considering a stop in San Francisco. She feels that the route would attract additional passengers if the stop is made, but there also would be additional variable costs. Her analysis appears in Exhibit 14–4.

The analysis indicates that the preferable alternative is the route that includes a stop in San Francisco. Notice that the cargo revenue [item (2)] and the aircraft maintenance cost [item (8)] are irrelevant to the flight-route decision. Although these data do affect future cash flows, they *do not differ between the two alternatives.* All of the other data in Exhibit 14–4 are relevant to the decision, because they do differ between the two alternatives. The analysis in Exhibit 14–4 could have ignored the irrelevant data; the same decision would have been reached. (Exercise 14–30, at the end of the chapter, will ask you to prove this assertion by redoing the analysis without the irrelevant data.)

Opportunity Costs

Another decision confronting Amy Earhart is whether to add two daily round-trip flights between Atlanta and Montreal. Her initial analysis of the relevant costs and benefits indicates that the additional revenue from the flights will exceed their costs by $30,000 per month. Hence, she is ready to add the flights to the schedule. However, Chuck Lindbergh, Worldwide Airways' hangar manager in Atlanta, points out that Earhart has overlooked an important consideration.

Worldwide Airways currently has excess space in its hangar. A commuter airline has offered to rent the hangar space for $40,000 per month. However, if the Atlanta-to-Montreal flights are added to the schedule, the additional aircraft needed in Atlanta will require the excess hangar space.

If Worldwide Airways adds the Atlanta-to-Montreal flights, it will forgo the opportunity to rent the excess hangar space for $40,000 per month. Thus, the $40,000 in rent forgone is an *opportunity cost* of the alternative to add the new flights. An **opportunity cost** is the potential benefit given up when the choice of one action precludes a different action. Although people tend to overlook or underestimate the importance of opportunity costs, they are just as relevant as out-of-pocket costs in evaluating decision alternatives. In Worldwide Airways' case, the best action is to rent the excess warehouse space to the commuter airline, rather than adding the new flights. The analysis in Exhibit 14–5 supports this conclusion.

Exhibit 14–5
Decision to Add Flights: Worldwide Airways

	(a) Add Flights	(b) Do Not Add Flights	(c) Differential Amount: (a) − (b)
Additional revenue from new flights less additional costs	$30,000	–0–	$ 30,000
Rental of excess hangar space	–0–	$40,000	(40,000)*
Total	$30,000	$40,000	$(10,000)

*Parentheses denote that differential benefit favors option (b).

It is a common mistake for people to overlook or underweigh opportunity costs. The $40,000 hangar rental, which will be forgone if the new flights are added, is an *opportunity cost* of the option to add the flights. It is a *relevant cost* of the decision, and it is just as important as any out-of-pocket expenditure.

Summary

Relevant costs and benefits satisfy the following two criteria:

1. They affect the future.
2. They differ between alternatives.

"I would say that they [line managers] view us as business partners." (14d)
Boeing

Sunk costs are *not* relevant costs, because they do not affect the future. An example of a sunk cost is the book value of an asset, either equipment or inventory. *Future costs or benefits that are identical across all decision alternatives are not relevant.* They can be ignored when making a decision. *Opportunity costs are relevant costs.* Such costs deserve particular attention because many people tend to overlook them when making decisions.

Analysis of Special Decisions

Learning Objective 5

Prepare analyses of various special decisions, properly identifying the relevant costs and benefits.

What are the relevant costs and benefits when a manager must decide whether to add or drop a product or service? What data are relevant when deciding whether to produce or buy a service or component? These decisions and certain other nonroutine decisions merit special attention in our discussion of relevant costs and benefits.

Accept or Reject a Special Offer

Jim Wright, Worldwide Airways' vice president for operations, has been approached by a Japanese tourist agency about flying chartered tourist flights from Japan to Hawaii. The tourist agency has offered Worldwide Airways $150,000 per round-trip flight on a jumbo jet. Given the airline's usual occupancy rate and air fares, a round-trip jumbo-jet flight between Japan and Hawaii typically brings in revenue of $250,000. Thus, the tourist agency's specially priced offer requires a special analysis by Jim Wright.

Wright knows that Worldwide Airways has two jumbo jets that are not currently in use. The airline has just eliminated several unprofitable routes, freeing these aircraft for other uses. The airline was not currently planning to add any new routes, and therefore the two jets were idle. To help make his decision, Wright asks for cost data from the controller's office. The controller provides the information in Exhibit 14–6, which pertains to a typical round-trip jumbo-jet flight between Japan and Hawaii.

The variable costs cover aircraft fuel and maintenance, flight-crew costs, in-flight meals and services, and landing fees. The fixed costs allocated to each flight cover Worldwide Airways' fixed costs, such as aircraft depreciation, maintenance and depreciation of facilities, and fixed administrative costs.

Revenue:		
Passenger	$250,000	
Cargo	30,000	
Total revenue		$280,000
Expenses:		
Variable expenses of flight	$ 90,000	
Fixed expenses allocated to each flight	100,000	
Total expenses		190,000
Profit		$ 90,000

Exhibit 14–6
Data for Typical Flight Between Japan and Hawaii: Worldwide Airways

If Jim Wright had not understood managerial accounting, he might have done the following *incorrect analysis.*

Special price for charter	$150,000
Total cost per flight	190,000
Loss on charter flight	$ (40,000)

This calculation suggests that the special charter offer should be rejected. What is the error in this analysis? The mistake is the inclusion of allocated fixed costs in the cost per flight. This is an error, because the *fixed costs will not increase in total* if the charter flight is added. Since the fixed costs will not change under either of the alternate choices, they are irrelevant.

Fortunately, Jim Wright does not make this mistake. He knows that only the variable costs of the proposed charter are relevant. Moreover, Wright determines that the variable cost of the charter would be less than that of a typical flight, because Worldwide Airways would not incur the variable costs of reservations and ticketing. These variable expenses amount to $5,000 for a scheduled flight. Thus, Wright's analysis of the charter offer is as shown below.

Assumes excess capacity (idle aircraft)

Special price for charter		$150,000
Variable cost per routine flight	$90,000	
Less: Savings on reservations and ticketing	5,000	
Variable cost of charter		85,000
Contribution from charter		$ 65,000

Wright's analysis shows that the special charter flight will contribute $65,000 toward covering the airline's fixed costs and profit. Since the airline has excess flight capacity, due to the existence of idle aircraft, the optimal decision is to accept the special charter offer.

"I've seen it (managerial accounting) evolve to become more of a team player and being involved in major projects and being looked to as a business advisor or consultant to help leverage our expertise on profitability of certain products or sourcing decisions." (14e)

Caterpillar

No Excess Capacity Now let's consider how Wright's analysis would appear if Worldwide Airways had no idle aircraft. Suppose that in order to fly the charter between Japan and Hawaii, the airline would have to cancel its least profitable route, which is between Japan and Hong Kong. This route contributes $80,000 toward covering the airline's fixed costs and profit. Thus, if the charter offer is accepted, the airline will incur an opportunity cost of $80,000 from the forgone contribution of the Japan–Hong Kong route. Now Wright's analysis should appear as shown below.

Assumes no excess capacity (no idle aircraft)

Special price for charter		$150,000
Variable cost per routine flight	$90,000	
Less: Savings on reservations and ticketing	5,000	
Variable cost of charter	$85,000	
Add: Opportunity cost, forgone contribution on canceled Japan–Hong Kong route	80,000	165,000
Loss from charter		$ (15,000)

Thus, if Worldwide Airways has no excess flight capacity, Jim Wright should reject the special charter offer.

Summary The decision to accept or reject a specially priced order is common in both service-industry and manufacturing firms. Manufacturers often are faced with decisions about selling products in a special order at less than full price. The correct analysis of such decisions focuses on the relevant costs and benefits. Fixed costs, which often are allocated to individual units of product or service, are usually irrelevant. Fixed costs typically will not change in total, whether the order is accepted or rejected.

When excess capacity exists, the only relevant costs usually will be the variable costs associated with the special order. When there is no excess capacity, the opportunity cost of using the firm's facilities for the special order is also relevant to the decision.

Outsource a Product or Service

Ellie Rickenbacker is Worldwide Airways' manager of in-flight services. She supervises the airline's flight attendants and all of the firm's food and beverage operations. Rickenbacker currently faces a decision regarding the preparation of in-flight dinners at the airline's Atlanta hub. In the Atlanta flight kitchen, full-course dinners are prepared and packaged for long flights that pass through Atlanta. In the past, all of the desserts were baked and packaged in the flight kitchen. However, Rickenbacker has received an offer from an Atlanta bakery to bake the airline's desserts. Thus, her decision is whether to *outsource* the dessert portion of the in-flight dinners. An **outsourcing decision,** also called a **make-or-buy decision,** entails a choice between producing a product or service in-house and purchasing it from an outside supplier. To help guide her decision, Rickenbacker has assembled the cost information in Exhibit 14–7, which shows a total cost per dessert of 25 cents.

The Atlanta bakery has offered to supply the desserts for 21 cents each. Rickenbacker's initial inclination is to accept the bakery's offer, since it appears that the airline would save 4 cents per dessert. However, the controller reminds Rickenbacker that not all of the costs listed in Exhibit 14–7 are relevant to the outsourcing decision. The controller modifies Rickenbacker's analysis as shown in Exhibit 14–8.

If Worldwide Airways stops making desserts, it will save all of the variable costs but only 1 cent of fixed costs. The 1-cent saving in supervisory salaries would result because the airline could get along with two fewer kitchen supervisors. The remainder of the fixed costs would be incurred even if the desserts were purchased. These remaining fixed costs of supervision and depreciation would have to be reallocated to the flight kitchen's other products. In light of the controller's revised analysis, Rickenbacker realizes that the airline should continue to make its own desserts. To outsource the desserts would require an expenditure of 21 cents per dessert, but only 15 cents per dessert would be saved.

Exhibit 14–7
Cost of In-Flight Desserts: Worldwide Airways

	Cost per Dessert
Variable costs:	
Direct material (food and packaging)	$.06
Direct labor	.04
Variable overhead	.04
Fixed costs (allocated to products):	
Supervisory salaries	.04
Depreciation of flight-kitchen equipment	.07
Total cost per dessert	$.25

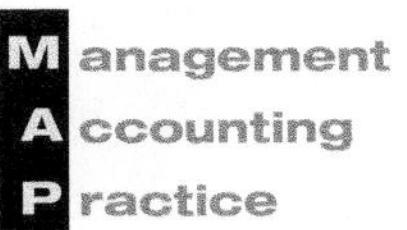

Northwest, JetBlue, America West, Apple, Dell, Hewlett-Packard, Motorola, Nokia, Canon, Kodak, and Nikon

OUTSOURCING

Outsourcing is widely used in a variety of businesses. The management at Northwest Airlines, for example, has decided to outsource some of its flight attendants in order to reduce the cost of filling the most expensive of these positions. According to *The Wall Street Journal,* it's a sign "that Northwest, which has filed for bankruptcy protection, wants to become a 'virtual airline,' with all sorts of jobs previously claimed by organized labor outsourced to cheaper workers, some overseas."

Other airlines are outsourcing key maintenance operations. JetBlue Airways "will fly at least 17 of its 68 Airbus A320 jets to" El Salvador. "There, over six days, local mechanics working for an aircraft-overhaul shop under contract to JetBlue will inspect each plane nose to tail." After any required maintenance is performed, the jets will fly back to the U.S. America West Airlines also is flying its planes to El Salvador for inspections required by the FAA. "Northwest Airlines flies its wide-body jets to Singapore and Hong Kong for service by outside contractors."

BusinessWeek reports that many technology manufacturers are outsourcing research and development and product design to outside contractors in Taiwan and other countries. Among the companies outsourcing some of these key design functions are computer manufacturers Apple, Dell, and Hewlett-Packard, and wireless phone manufacturers Motorola and Nokia. Camera manufacturers Canon, Kodak, and Nikon also outsource designs of some low-end models.[1]

To clarify her decision further, Rickenbacker asks the controller to prepare an analysis of the *total costs* per month of making or buying desserts. The controller's report, displayed in Exhibit 14–9, shows the total cost of producing 1,000,000 desserts, the flight kitchen's average monthly volume.

The total-cost analysis confirmed Rickenbacker's decision to continue making desserts in the airline's flight kitchen.

Exhibit 14–8
Cost Savings from Buying In-Flight Desserts: Worldwide Airways

	Cost per Dessert	Costs Saved by Purchasing Desserts
Variable costs:		
Direct material	$ .06	$ .06
Direct labor	.04	.04
Variable overhead	.04	.04
Fixed costs (allocated to products):		
Supervisory salaries	.04	.01
Depreciation of flight-kitchen equipment	.07	–0–
Total cost per dessert	$ .25	$ .15
Cost of purchasing desserts (per dessert)		$ .21
Loss per dessert if desserts are purchased (savings per dessert minus purchase cost per dessert, or $.15 – $.21)		$(.06)

[1]The sources for these anecdotes are S. Carey, "Northwest Targets Flight Attendants for Outsourcing," *The Wall Street Journal,* October, 26, 2005, pp. A1, A8; S. Carey and A. Frangos, "Airlines, Facing Cost Pressure, Outsource Crucial Safety Tasks," *The Wall Street Journal,* January 21, 2005, pp. A1, A5; and P. Engardio and B. Einhorn, "Outsourcing Innovation," *BusinessWeek,* March 21, 2005, pp. 82–94.

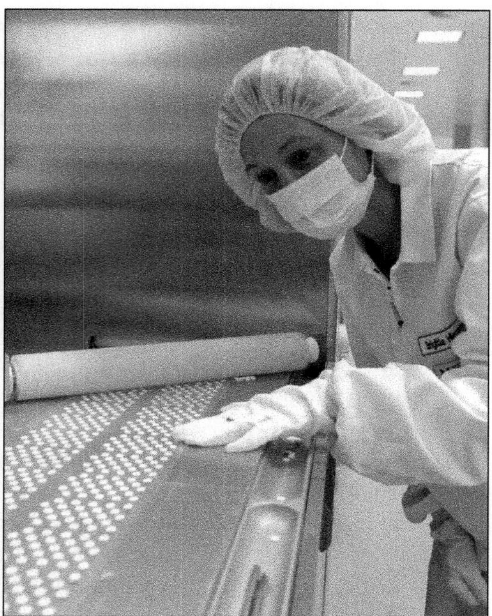

In today's global economy, more and more companies are outsourcing significant products and services. Gallo Winery, for example, buys a significant portion of its grapes from other vintners. Kodak outsources its entire data processing operation. Cummins Engine outsources many of its pistons, and Intel Corporation buys microchips. Chase Bank outsources its cafeteria and legal services. Many pharmaceutical companies, such as Japan's Yamanouchi Pharmaceutical, have outsourced much of their production to cut costs.[2] Pictured here are grape harvesting and pharmaceutical production.

Beware of Unit-Cost Data Fixed costs often are allocated to individual units of product or service for product-costing purposes. For decision-making purposes, however, unitized fixed costs can be misleading. As the total-cost analysis in Exhibit 14–9 shows, only $10,000 in fixed monthly cost will be saved if the desserts are purchased. The remaining $100,000 in monthly fixed cost will continue whether the desserts are made or

Exhibit 14–9
Total-Cost Analysis of Outsourcing Decision: Worldwide Airways

	Cost per Month	Costs Saved by Purchasing Desserts
Variable costs:		
Direct material	$ 60,000	$ 60,000
Direct labor	40,000	40,000
Variable overhead	40,000	40,000
Fixed costs (allocated to products):		
Supervisory salaries	40,000	10,000*
Depreciation of flight-kitchen equipment	70,000	–0–
Total cost per month	$250,000	$150,000
Cost of purchasing desserts (per month)		$210,000
Total loss if desserts are purchased (total savings minus total cost of purchasing, or $150,000 − $210,000)		$ (60,000)

*Cost of monthly compensation for two kitchen supervisors, who will not be needed if desserts are purchased.

[2]Peter Landers, "Japan's Local Drug Makers to Outsource to Suppliers," *The Wall Street Journal,* March 26, 2002, p. A20.

purchased. Rickenbacker's initial cost analysis in Exhibit 14–7 implies that each dessert costs the airline 25 cents, but that 25-cent cost includes 11 cents of unitized fixed costs. Most of these costs will remain unchanged regardless of the outsourcing decision. By allocating fixed costs to individual products or services, they are made to appear variable even though they are not.

Add or Drop a Service, Product, or Department

Worldwide Airways offers its passengers the opportunity to join its World Express Club. Club membership entitles a traveler to use the club facilities at the airport in Atlanta. Club privileges include a private lounge and restaurant, discounts on meals and beverages, and use of a small health spa.

Jayne Wing, the president of Worldwide Airways, is worried that the World Express Club might not be profitable. Her concern is caused by the statement of monthly operating income shown in the Excel spreadsheet in Exhibit 14–10.

In her weekly staff meeting, Wing states her concern about the World Express Club's profitability. The controller responds by pointing out that not all of the costs on the club's income statement would be eliminated if the club were discontinued. The vice president for sales adds that the club helps Worldwide Airways attract passengers who it might otherwise lose to a competitor. As the meeting adjourns, Wing asks the controller to prepare an analysis of the relevant costs and benefits associated with the World Express Club. The controller's analysis is displayed in Exhibit 14–11.

The controller's analysis in Exhibit 14–11 contains two parts. Part I focuses on the relevant costs and benefits of the World Express Club only, while ignoring any impact of the club on other airline operations. In column (a), the controller has listed the club's revenues and expenses from the income statement presented in Exhibit 14–10. Column (b) in Exhibit 14–11 lists the expenses that will continue if the club is eliminated. These expenses are called **unavoidable expenses.** In contrast, the expenses appearing in column (a) but not column (b) are **avoidable expenses.** The airline will no longer incur these expenses if the club is eliminated.

Exhibit 14–10
World Express Club Monthly Operating Income Statement: Worldwide Airways

Microsoft Excel - World Express Club - Monthly Operating Income Statement

File Edit View Insert Format Tools Data Window Help

F16 =F9-F15

	A–D	E	F
1	WORLDWIDE AIRWAYS: WORLD EXPRESS CLUB		
2	Monthly Operating Income Statement		
3			
4	Sales revenue		$ 200,000
5	Less: Variable expenses:		
6	Food and beverages	$ 70,000	
7	Personnel	40,000	
8	Variable overhead	25,000	135,000
9	Contribution margin		$ 65,000
10	Less: Fixed expenses:		
11	Depreciation	$ 30,000	
12	Supervisory salaries	20,000	
13	Insurance	10,000	
14	Airport fees	5,000	
15	General overhead (allocated)	10,000	75,000
16	Loss		$ (10,000)

Sheet1 / Sheet2 / Sheet3 /

Ready

Exhibit 14–11
Relevant Costs and Benefits of World Express Club: Worldwide Airways

	(a) Keep Club	(b) Eliminate Club	(c) Differential Amount: (a) − (b)
Part I:			
Sales revenue	$200,000	–0–	$200,000
Less: Variable expenses:			
Food and beverages	(70,000)	–0–	(70,000)
Personnel	(40,000)	–0–	(40,000)
Variable overhead	(25,000)	–0–	(25,000)
Contribution margin	$ 65,000	–0–	$ 65,000
Less: Fixed expenses:			
Depreciation	$ (30,000)	$(30,000)	$ –0–
Supervisory salaries	(20,000)	–0–	(20,000)
Insurance	(10,000)	(10,000)	–0–
Airport fees	(5,000)	–0–	(5,000)
General overhead (allocated)	(10,000)	(10,000)	–0–
Total fixed expenses	$ (75,000)	$(50,000)	$ (25,000)
Profit (loss)	$ (10,000)	$(50,000)	$ 40,000*
		Expenses in the column above are **unavoidable** expenses	Expenses in the column above are **avoidable** expenses
Part II:			
Contribution margin from general airline operations that will be forgone if club is eliminated	$ 60,000	–0–	$ 60,000

*The *positive* $40,000 differential amount reflects the fact that the company is $40,000 *better off* by keeping the club.

Notice that all of the club's variable expenses are avoidable. The depreciation expense, $30,000, is an allocated portion of the depreciation on a Worldwide Airways building, part of which is used by the World Express Club. If the Club is discontinued, the airline will continue to own and use the building, and the depreciation expense will continue. Thus, it is an unavoidable expense. The fixed supervisory salaries are avoidable, since these employees will no longer be needed if the club is eliminated. The fixed insurance expense of $10,000 is not avoidable; the $5,000 fee paid to the airport for the privilege of operating the club is avoidable. Finally, the club's allocated portion of general overhead expenses, $10,000, is not avoidable. Worldwide Airways will incur these expenses regardless of its decision about the World Express Club.

The conclusion shown by Part I of the controller's report is that the club should not be eliminated. If the club is closed, the airline will lose more in contribution margin, $65,000, than it saves in avoidable fixed expenses, $25,000. Thus, the club's $65,000 contribution margin is enough to cover the avoidable fixed expenses of $25,000 and still contribute $40,000 toward covering the overall airline's fixed expenses.

World Express Club's contribution margin	$65,000
Avoidable fixed expenses	25,000
Contribution of club toward covering overall airline's fixed expenses	$40,000

Now consider Part II of the controller's analysis in Exhibit 14–11. As the vice president for sales pointed out, the World Express Club is an attractive feature to many travelers. The controller estimates that if the club were discontinued, the airline would lose $60,000 each month in forgone contribution margin from general airline operations.

Management
Accounting
Practice

FedEx and Caterpillar

ADDING A SERVICE

Changing business conditions can cause a company to rethink its business model and add new services. Federal Express, for example, found that a sizable portion of its overnight letter delivery business was eliminated by e-mail. Customers no longer needed to ship a hard-copy document overnight, when the same document could be sent instantaneously via e-mail. FedEx also found a decline in the need for overnight repair parts shipments. Many customers' improved supply chain systems resulted in better spare parts preparedness and less need for last-minute overnight shipments. FedEx responded by adding slower ground shipment services to compete more directly with UPS and the U.S. Postal Service. While FedEx still excels when an overnight shipment is needed, its ground transport business is becoming an increasing part of its operations. FedEx also is adding new technology-based services that give customers greater ability to track shipments in transit.

Caterpillar has added heavy equipment overhaul services to its already successful manufacturing operations. The company uses available capacity in its manufacturing plants to disassemble and rebuild heavy diesel engines, after cleaning, inspecting, and repairing them. This new service component of Caterpillar's operations has become the company's fastest-growing business unit, with annual revenue topping $1 billion.[3]

This loss in contribution margin would result from losing to a competing airline current passengers who are attracted to Worldwide Airways by its World Express Club. This $60,000 in forgone contribution margin is an *opportunity cost* of the option to close down the club.

Considering both Parts I and II of the controller's analysis, Worldwide Airways' monthly profit will be greater by $100,000 if the club is kept open. Recognition of two issues is key to this conclusion:

1. Only the avoidable expenses of the club will be saved if it is discontinued.
2. Closing the club will adversely affect the airline's other operations.

Special Decisions in Manufacturing Firms

Learning Objective 6

Analyze manufacturing decisions involving joint products and limited resources.

Some types of decisions are more likely to arise in manufacturing companies than in service-industry firms. We will examine two of these decisions.

Joint Products: Sell or Process Further

A **joint production process** results in two or more products, called *joint products.* An example is the processing of cocoa beans into cocoa powder and cocoa butter. Cocoa beans constitute the input to the joint production process, and the two joint products are cocoa powder and cocoa butter. The point in the production process where the joint

[3]"Delivering the Goods at FedEx," *BusinessWeek,* June 13, 2005, pp. 60–62; D. Foust, "The Ground War at FedEx," *BusinessWeek,* November 28, 2005, pp. 42, 43; "Overnight, Everything Changed for FedEx; Can It Reinvent Itself?" *The Wall Street Journal,* November 4, 1999, p. A1; and M. Arndt, "Cat Sinks Its Claws into Services," *BusinessWeek,* December 5, 2005, pp. 56–59.

products are identifiable as separate products is called the **split-off point.** Other examples of joint production processes include the slaughtering of animals for various cuts of meat and the processing of petroleum into various products, such as kerosene and gasoline.

Manufacturers with joint production processes sometimes must decide whether a joint product should be sold at the split-off point or processed further before being sold. Such a decision recently confronted Bill Candee, the president of International Chocolate Company. Candee's firm imports cocoa beans and processes them into cocoa powder and cocoa butter. Only a portion of the cocoa powder is used by International Chocolate Company in the production of chocolate candy. The remainder of the cocoa powder is sold to an ice cream producer. Candee is considering the possibility of processing his remaining cocoa powder into an instant cocoa mix to be marketed under the brand name ChocoTime. Data pertaining to Candee's decision are displayed in Exhibit 14–12.

Notice from the diagram that cocoa beans are processed in 1-ton batches. The total cost of the cocoa beans and the joint processing is $1,100. This is called the **joint cost.** The output of the joint process is 1,500 pounds of cocoa butter and 500 pounds of cocoa powder.

How should Bill Candee approach the decision about processing the cocoa powder into instant cocoa mix? What are the relevant costs and benefits? First, let's consider the joint cost of $1,100. Is this a relevant cost in the decision at hand? *The joint cost is not a relevant cost,* because it will not change regardless of the decision Candee makes.

Suppose the $1,100 joint cost had been allocated to the two joint products for product-costing purposes. A common method of allocating a joint cost is the **relative-sales-value method,** in which the joint cost is allocated between the joint products in proportion to their sales value at the split-off point.[4] International Chocolate Company would make the following joint cost allocation.

Joint Cost	Joint Products	Sales Value at Split-Off Point	Relative Proportion	Allocation of Joint Cost
	Cocoa butter	$750	.60	$ 660
$1,100	Cocoa powder	500	.40	440
	Total joint cost allocated			$1,100

Exhibit 14–12
Joint Processing of Cocoa Beans: International Chocolate Company

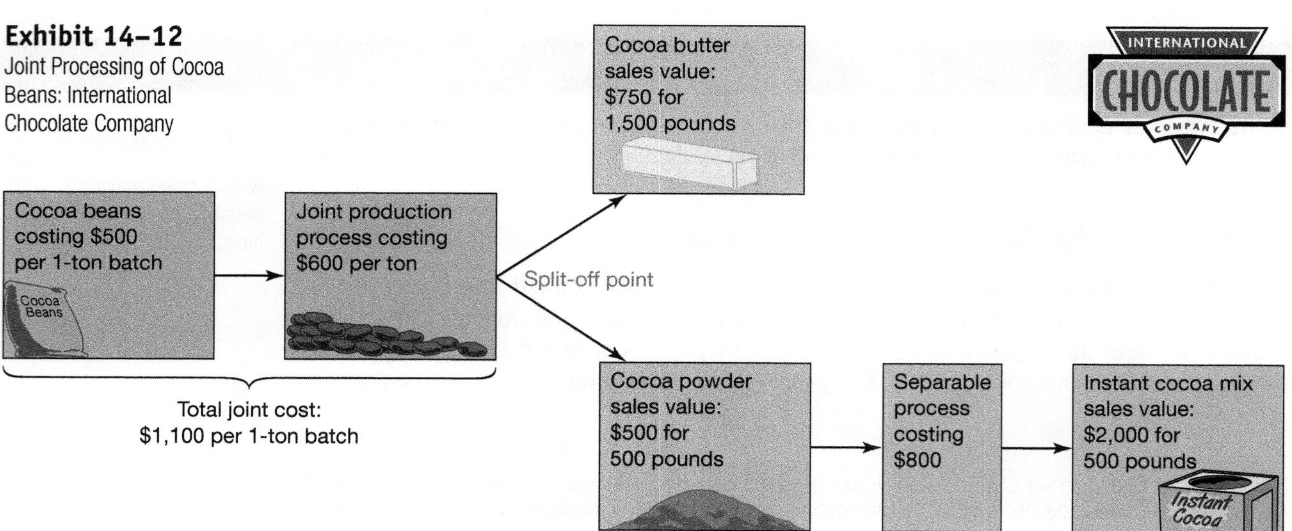

[4]Other methods of allocating joint costs are covered in Chapter 17.

Exhibit 14–13
Decision to Sell or Process Further: International Chocolate Company

Relevant or Irrelevant			(a) Process Cocoa Powder into Instant Cocoa Mix	(b) Sell Cocoa Powder at Split-Off Point	(c) Differential Amount: (a) − (b)
		Sales revenue:			
	Irrelevant	Cocoa butter	$ 750	$ 750	–0–
Relevant		Instant cocoa mix	2,000		$1,500
Relevant		Cocoa powder		500	
		Less: Costs:			
	Irrelevant	Joint cost	(1,100)	(1,100)	–0–
Relevant		Separable cost of processing cocoa powder into instant cocoa mix	(800)	–0–	(800)
		Total	$ 850	$ 150	$ 700

Does this allocation of the $1,100 joint cost make it relevant to the decision about processing cocoa powder into instant cocoa mix? The answer is no. *The $1,100 joint cost still does not change in total,* whether the cocoa powder is processed further or not. The joint cost is irrelevant to the decision at hand.

The only costs and benefits relevant to Candee's decision are those that differ between the two alternatives. The proper analysis is shown in Exhibit 14–13.

There is a shortcut method that arrives at the same conclusion as Exhibit 14–13. In this approach, the incremental revenue from the further processing of cocoa powder is compared with the **separable processing cost,** which is the cost incurred after the split-off point, as follows:

Sales value of instant cocoa mix	$2,000
Sales value of cocoa powder	500
Incremental revenue from further processing	$1,500
Less: Separable processing cost	(800)
Net benefit from further processing	$ 700

Both analyses indicate that Bill Candee should process his excess cocoa powder into instant cocoa mix. The same conclusion is reached if the analysis is done on a per-unit basis rather than a total basis:

Sales value of instant cocoa mix ($2,000 ÷ 500 pounds)	$4.00 per pound
Sales value of cocoa powder ($500 ÷ 500 pounds)	1.00 per pound
Incremental revenue from further processing	$3.00 per pound
Less: Separable processing cost ($800 ÷ 500 pounds)	(1.60) per pound
Net benefit from further processing	$1.40 per pound

Once again, the analysis shows that Bill Candee should decide to process the cocoa powder into instant cocoa mix.

Decisions Involving Limited Resources

Organizations typically have limited resources. Limitations on floor space, machine time, labor hours, or raw materials are common. Operating with limited resources, a firm often must choose between sales orders, deciding which orders to fill and which ones to decline. In making such decisions, managers must decide which product or service is the most profitable.

Exhibit 14–14
Contribution Margin per Case: International Chocolate Company

	Chewies	Chompo Bars
Sales price	$10.00	$14.00
Less: Variable costs:		
Direct material	$ 3.00	$ 3.75
Direct labor	2.00	2.50
Variable overhead	3.00	3.75
Variable selling and administrative costs	1.00	2.00
Total variable costs	$ 9.00	$12.00
Contribution margin per case	$ 1.00	$ 2.00

Exhibit 14–15
Contribution Margin per Machine Hour: International Chocolate Company

		Chewies	Chompo Bars
(a)	Contribution margin per case	$1.00	$2.00
(b)	Machine hours required per case	.02	.05
(a) ÷ (b)	Contribution margin per machine hour	$50	$40

To illustrate, suppose International Chocolate Company's Phoenix plant makes two candy-bar products, Chewies and Chompo Bars. The contribution margin for a case of each of these products is computed in Exhibit 14–14.

A glance at the contribution-margin data suggests that Chompo Bars are more profitable than Chewies. It is true that a case of Chompo Bars contributes more toward covering the company's fixed cost and profit. However, an important consideration has been ignored in the analysis so far. The Phoenix plant's capacity is limited by its available machine time. Only 700 machine hours are available in the plant each month. International Chocolate Company can sell as many cases of either candy bar as it can produce, so production is limited only by the constraint on machine time.

To maximize the plant's total contribution toward covering fixed cost and profit, management should strive to use each machine hour as effectively as possible. This realization alters the analysis of product profitability. The relevant question is *not,* Which candy bar has the highest contribution margin *per case?* The pertinent question is, Which product has the highest contribution margin *per machine hour?* This question is answered with the calculation in Exhibit 14–15.

A machine hour spent in the production of Chewies will contribute $50 toward covering fixed cost and profit, while a machine hour devoted to Chompo Bars contributes only $40. Hence, the Phoenix plant's most profitable product is Chewies, when the plant's scarce resource is taken into account.

Suppose International Chocolate Company's Phoenix plant manager, Candace Barr, is faced with a choice between two sales orders, only one of which can be accepted. Only 100 hours of unscheduled machine time remains in the month, and it can be used to produce either Chewies or Chompos. The analysis in Exhibit 14–16 shows that Barr should devote the 100-hour block of machine time to filling the order for Chewies.

As Exhibit 14–16 demonstrates, a decision about the best use of a limited resource should be made on the basis of the *contribution margin per unit of the scarce resource.*

Multiple Scarce Resources Suppose the Phoenix plant had a limited amount of *both* machine hours *and* labor hours. Now the analysis of product profitability is more complicated. The choice as to which product is most profitable typically will involve a trade-off between the two scarce resources. Solving such a problem requires a powerful mathematical tool called *linear programming,* which is covered in the appendix to this chapter.

Exhibit 14–16
Total Contribution from 100 Machine Hours: International Chocolate Company

	Chewies	Chompo Bars
Contribution margin per case	$1.00	$2.00
Number of cases produced in 100 hours of machine time	× 5,000*	× 2,000†
Total contribution toward covering fixed cost and profit	$5,000	$4,000

*Chewies: 100 hours ÷ .02 hour per case = 5,000 cases
†Chompo Bars: 100 hours ÷ .05 hour per case = 2,000 cases

Theory of Constraints As the previous analysis suggests, a binding constraint can limit a company's profitability. For example, a manufacturing company may have a *bottleneck operation,* through which every unit of a product must pass before moving on to other operations. The *theory of constraints (TOC)* calls for identifying such limiting constraints and seeking ways to relax them. Also referred to as *managing constraints,* this management approach can significantly improve an organization's level of goal attainment. Among the ways that management can relax a constraint by expanding the capacity of a bottleneck operation are the following:

- *Outsourcing* (subcontracting) all or part of the bottleneck operation.
- Investing in additional production equipment and employing *parallel processing,* in which multiple product units undergo the same production operation simultaneously.
- Working *overtime* at the bottleneck operation.
- *Retraining* employees and shifting them to the bottleneck.
- Eliminating any *non-value-added activities* at the bottleneck operation.

Uncertainty

Our analyses of the decisions in this chapter assumed that all relevant data were known with certainty. In practice, of course, decision makers are rarely so fortunate. One common technique for addressing the impact of uncertainty is *sensitivity analysis.* **Sensitivity analysis** is a technique for determining what would happen in a decision analysis if a key prediction or assumption proved to be wrong.

To illustrate, let's return to Candace Barr's decision about how to use the remaining 100 hours of machine time in International Chocolate Company's Phoenix plant. The calculation in Exhibit 14–15 showed that Chewies have the higher contribution margin per machine hour. Suppose Barr is uncertain about the contribution margin per case of Chewies. A sensitivity analysis shows how sensitive her decision is to the value of this uncertain parameter. As Exhibit 14–17 shows, the Chewies contribution margin could decline to $.80 per case before Barr's decision would change. As long as the contribution

Exhibit 14–17
Sensitivity Analysis: International Chocolate Company

		Chewies	Chompo Bars
Original Analysis			
(a)	Contribution margin per case predicted	$1.00	$2.00
(b)	Machine hours required per case	.02	.05
(a) ÷ (b)	Contribution per machine hour	$50.00	$40.00
Sensitivity Analysis			
(c)	Contribution margin per case hypothesized in sensitivity analysis	$.80	
(d)	Machine hours required per case	.02	same
(c) ÷ (d)	Contribution per machine hour	$40.00	

Exhibit 14–18
Use of Expected Values: International Chocolate Company

	Chewies		Chompo Bars	
	Possible Values of Contribution Margin	Probability	Possible Values of Contribution Margin	Probability
	$ .75	.5	$1.50	.3
	1.25	.5	2.00	.4
			2.50	.3
Expected value	(.5)($.75) + (.5)($1.25) = $1.00		(.3)($1.50) + (.4)($2.00) + (.3)($2.50) = $2.00	
Machine hours required per case	.02		.05	
Expected value of contribution per machine hour	$50	>	$40	

margin per case of Chewies exceeds $.80 per case, the 100 hours of available machine time should be devoted to Chewies.

Sensitivity analysis can help the managerial accountant decide which parameters in an analysis are most critical to estimate accurately. In this case, the managerial accountant knows that the contribution margin per case of Chewies could be as much as 20 percent lower than the original $1.00 prediction without changing the outcome of the analysis.

Expected Values Another approach to dealing explicitly with uncertainty is to base the decision on expected values. The **expected value** of a random variable is equal to the sum of the possible values for the variable, each weighted by its probability. To illustrate, suppose the contribution margins per case for Chewies and Chompos are uncertain, as shown in Exhibit 14–18. As the exhibit shows, the choice as to which product to produce with excess machine time may be based on the *expected value* of the contribution per machine hour. Statisticians have developed many other methods for dealing with uncertainty in decision making. These techniques are covered in statistics and decision analysis courses.

Activity-Based Costing and Today's Advanced Manufacturing Environment

Learning Objective 7

Explain the impact of an advanced manufacturing environment and activity-based costing on a relevant-cost analysis.

In this chapter we have explored how to identify the relevant costs and benefits in various types of decisions. How will the relevant-costing approach change in the new manufacturing environment, characterized by just-in-time (JIT) production methods and flexible manufacturing systems (FMS)? How would a relevant-costing analysis change if a company uses an activity-based costing (ABC) system?[5]

The *concepts* underlying a relevant-costing analysis continue to be completely valid in an advanced manufacturing setting and in a situation where activity-based costing is used. The objective of the decision analysis is to determine the costs and benefits that are relevant to the decision. As we found earlier in this chapter, relevant costs and benefits *have a bearing on the future and differ among the decision alternatives.*

What *will* be different in a setting where activity-based costing is used is the decision maker's ability to determine what costs are relevant to a decision. Under ABC, the decision maker typically can associate costs with the activities that drive them much more accurately than under a conventional product-costing system. Let's explore these issues with an illustration.

[5]Activity-based costing (ABC), which was introduced conceptually in Chapter 3, is thoroughly explored in Chapter 5. This section can be studied most effectively after completing Chapter 5.

Conventional Outsourcing (Make-or-Buy) Analysis

International Chocolate Company makes fine chocolates in its Savannah plant. The chocolates are packaged in two-pound and five-pound gift boxes. The company also manufactures the gift boxes in the Savannah plant. The plant manager, Marsha Mello, was approached recently by a packaging company with an offer to supply the gift boxes at a price of $.45 each. Mello concluded that the offer should be rejected on the basis of the relevant-costing analysis in Exhibit 14–19. International Chocolate Company's traditional, volume-based product-costing system showed a unit product cost of $.80 per box. However, Mello realized that not all of the costs would be avoided. She reasoned that all of the direct material, direct labor, and variable overhead would be avoided, but only a small part of the assigned fixed overhead would be saved. She concluded that $60,000 of supervisory salaries and $20,000 of machinery depreciation could be traced directly to gift package production. These costs would be avoided, she felt, but the remaining

Exhibit 14–19
Conventional Product-Costing Data and Outsourcing Analysis: International Chocolate Company

A. Manufacturing Overhead Budget for Savannah Plant	
Variable overhead:	
Electricity	$ 700,000
Oil and lubricants	120,000
Equipment maintenance	180,000
Total variable overhead	$1,000,000
Variable overhead rate: $1,000,000 ÷ 100,000 direct-labor hours = $10 per hour	
Fixed overhead:	
Plant depreciation	$1,650,000
Product development	300,000
Supervisory salaries	600,000
Material handling	800,000
Purchasing	250,000
Inspection	300,000
Setup	400,000
Machinery depreciation	200,000
Total fixed overhead	$4,500,000
Fixed overhead rate: $4,500,000 ÷ 100,000 direct-labor hours = $45 per hour	
B. Conventional Product-Costing Data: Gift Boxes	
Direct material	$ 100,000
Direct labor (10,000 hr. at $15 per hr.)	150,000
Variable overhead ($10 per direct-labor hr.)	100,000
Fixed overhead ($45 per direct-labor hr.)	450,000
Total cost	$ 800,000
Unit cost: $800,000 ÷ 1,000,000 boxes = $.80 per box	
C. Conventional Outsourcing Analysis: Gift Boxes	
Relevant costs (costs that will be avoided if the gift boxes are purchased):	
Direct material	$ 100,000
Direct labor	150,000
Variable overhead	100,000
Fixed overhead:	
Supervision	60,000
Machinery depreciation	20,000
Total costs to be avoided by purchasing	$ 430,000
Total cost of purchasing (1,000,000 boxes × $.45 per box)	$ 450,000

fixed costs would not. Mello concluded that only $430,000 of costs would be avoided by purchasing, while $450,000 would be spent to buy the boxes. The decision was clear; the supplier's offer should be rejected.

Activity-Based Costing Analysis of the Outsourcing Decision

At a staff meeting, Mello mentioned her tentative decision to Dave Mint, the plant controller. Mint then explained to Mello that he was completing a pilot project using activity-based costing. Mint offered to analyze the outsourcing decision using the new ABC database. Mello agreed, and Mint proceeded to do the ABC analysis shown in Exhibit 14–20.

In stage one of the ABC analysis, Mint designated 11 activity cost pools corresponding to the major items in the Savannah plant's overhead budget. These activity cost pools were categorized as facility-level, product-sustaining level, batch-level, or unit-level activities. In stage two of the ABC project, cost drivers were identified and pool rates were computed. The ABC analysis showed that $243,000 of overhead should be assigned to the gift boxes, rather than $550,000 as the conventional product-costing system had indicated.

Using the ABC database, Mint completed a new relevant-costing analysis of the outsourcing decision. Mint felt that all of the overhead costs assigned to the gift box operation

Exhibit 14–20
Activity-Based Costing Analysis of Outsourcing Decision: International Chocolate Company

A. Activity Cost Pools and Pool Rates

Activity Cost Pools	Budgeted Cost	Pool Rate and Cost Driver	Cost Assigned to Gift Boxes	
Facility level:				
Plant depreciation	$1,650,000	—		
Product-sustaining level:				
Product development	300,000	$600 per product spec	$600 × 5* =	$ 3,000
Supervisory salaries	600,000	$40 per supervisory hour	$40 × 1,500 =	60,000
Batch level:				
Material handling	800,000	$8 per material-handling hour	$8 × 5,000 =	40,000
Purchasing	250,000	$250 per purchase order	$250 × 40 =	10,000
Inspection	300,000	$300 per inspection	$300 × 20 =	6,000
Setup	400,000	$400 per setup	$400 × 10 =	4,000
Unit level:				
Electricity	700,000	$1.40 per machine hour	$1.40 × 50,000 =	70,000
Oil and lubrication	120,000	$.24 per machine hour	$.24 × 50,000 =	12,000
Equipment maintenance	180,000	$.36 per machine hour	$.36 × 50,000 =	18,000
Machinery depreciation	200,000	$.40 per machine hour	$.40 × 50,000 =	20,000
Total overhead for Savannah plant	$5,500,000			
Total overhead assigned to gift box production				$243,000

*The numbers in this column are the quantities of each cost driver required for gift box production.

B. ABC Outsourcing Analysis: Gift Boxes

Relevant costs (costs that will be avoided if the gift boxes are purchased):	
Direct material	$100,000
Direct labor	150,000
Overhead (from ABC analysis in panel A, above)	243,000
Total costs to be avoided by purchasing	$493,000
Total cost of purchasing (1,000,000 boxes × $.45 per box)	$450,000

could be avoided if the boxes were purchased. Notice that none of the facility-level costs are relevant to the analysis. They will not be avoided by purchasing the gift boxes. Mint's ABC analysis showed that a total of $493,000 of costs could be avoided by purchasing the boxes at a cost of $450,000. This would result in a net saving of $43,000.

Mint showed the ABC relevant-costing analysis to Mello. After some discussion, they agreed that various qualitative issues needed to be explored before a final decision was made. For example, would the new supplier be reliable, and would the gift boxes be of good quality? Nevertheless, Mello and Mint agreed that the ABC data cast an entirely different light on the decision.

The Key Point What has happened here? Why did the conventional and ABC analyses of this decision reach different conclusions? Is the relevant-costing concept faulty?

The answer is no; the relevant-costing idea is alive and well. Both analyses sought to identify the relevant costs as those that would be avoided by purchasing the gift boxes. That approach is valid. The difference in the analyses lies in the superior ability of the ABC data to properly identify what the avoidable costs are. This is the key point. The conventional analysis relied on a traditional, volume-based product-costing system. That system lumps all of the fixed overhead costs together and assigns them using a single, unit-based cost driver (i.e., direct-labor hours). That analysis simply failed to note that many of the so-called fixed costs are *not* really fixed with respect to the appropriate cost driver. The more accurate ABC system correctly showed this fact, and identified additional costs that could be avoided by purchasing.

To summarize, under activity-based costing, the concepts underlying relevant-costing analysis remain valid. However, the ABC system does enable the decision maker to apply the relevant-costing decision model more accurately.

Other Issues in Decision Making

Incentives for Decision Makers

In this chapter, we studied how managers should make decisions by focusing on the relevant costs and benefits. In previous chapters, we covered accounting procedures for evaluating managerial performance. There is an important link between *decision making* and *managerial performance evaluation.* Managers typically will make decisions that maximize their perceived performance evaluations and rewards. This is human nature. If we want managers to make optimal decisions by properly evaluating the relevant costs and benefits, then the performance evaluation system and reward structure had better be consistent with that perspective.

The proper treatment of sunk costs in decision making illustrates this issue. Earlier in this chapter, we saw that sunk costs should be ignored as irrelevant. For example, the book value of an outdated machine is irrelevant in making an equipment-replacement decision. Suppose, however, that a manager correctly ignores an old machine's book value and decides on early replacement of the machine he purchased a few years ago. Now suppose the hapless manager is criticized by his superior for "taking a loss" on the old machine, or for "buying a piece of junk" in the first place. What is our manager likely to do the next time he faces a similar decision? If he is like many people, he will tend to keep the old machine in order to justify his prior decision to purchase it. In so doing, he will be compounding his error. However, he also may be avoiding criticism from a superior who does not understand the importance of goal congruence.

The point is simply that if we want managers to make optimal decisions, we must give them incentives to do so. This requires that managerial performance be judged on the same factors that should be considered in making correct decisions.

Short-Run versus Long-Run Decisions

The decisions we have examined in this chapter were treated as short-run decisions. *Short-run decisions* affect only a short time period, typically a year or less. In reality, many of these decisions would have longer-term implications. For example, managers usually make a decision involving the addition or deletion of a product or service with a relatively long time frame in mind. The process of identifying relevant costs and benefits is largely the same whether the decision is viewed from a short-run or long-run perspective. One important factor that does change in a long-run analysis, however, is the *time value of money.* When several time periods are involved in a decision, the analyst should account for the fact that a $1.00 cash flow today is different from a $1.00 cash flow in five years. A dollar received today can be invested to earn interest, while the dollar received in five years cannot be invested over the intervening time period. The analysis of long-run decisions requires a tool called *capital budgeting,* which is covered in Chapter 16.

Pitfalls to Avoid

Identification of the relevant costs and benefits is an important step in making any economic decision. Nonetheless, analysts often overlook relevant costs or incorrectly include irrelevant data. In this section, we review four common mistakes to avoid in decision making.

1. ***Sunk costs.*** The book value of an asset, defined as its acquisition cost less the accumulated depreciation, is a sunk cost. Sunk costs cannot be changed by any current or future course of action, so they are irrelevant in decision making. Nevertheless, a common behavioral tendency is to give undue importance to book values in decisions that involve replacing an asset or disposing of obsolete inventory. People often seek to justify their past decisions by refusing to dispose of an asset, even if a better alternative has been identified. *The moral: Ignore sunk costs.*
2. ***Unitized fixed costs.*** For product-costing purposes, fixed costs often are divided by some activity measure and assigned to individual units of product. The result is to make a fixed cost appear variable. While there are legitimate reasons for this practice from a *product-costing* perspective, it can create havoc in *decision making.* Therefore, in a decision analysis, it is usually wise to include a fixed cost in its total amount, rather than as a per-unit cost. *The moral: Beware of unitized fixed costs in decision making.*
3. ***Allocated fixed costs.*** It is also common to allocate fixed costs across divisions, departments, or product lines. A possible result is that a product or department may appear unprofitable when in reality it does make a contribution toward covering fixed costs and profit. Before deciding to eliminate a department, be sure to ask which costs will be *avoided* if a particular alternative is selected. A fixed cost that has been allocated to a department may continue, in total or in part, even after the department has been eliminated. *The moral: Beware of allocated fixed costs; identify the avoidable costs.*
4. ***Opportunity costs.*** People tend to overlook opportunity costs, or to treat such costs as less important than out-of-pocket costs. Yet opportunity costs are just as real and important to making a correct decision as are out-of-pocket costs. *The moral: Pay special attention to identifying and including opportunity costs in a decision analysis.*

Focus on Ethics

EFFECTS OF DECISION TO CLOSE A DEPARTMENT AND OUTSOURCE

Outsourcing has become a common way of reducing costs in many organizations. Such decisions, though, often have repercussions that may not be captured "by the numbers." Employee morale, product quality, and vendor reliability are some of the issues that should be considered. Let's revisit the scenario described earlier at the International Chocolate Company. Recall that the Savannah plant manager, Marsha Mello (M), was considering outsourcing the production of gift boxes for the company's fine chocolates. A conventional analysis of the decision pointed toward keeping the production operation in-house. Now let's change the scenario a bit, and consider the following conversation between Dave Mint, plant controller (C), and Jack Edgeworth, supervisor of the gift box production department (SG). The conversation takes place after the two friends' weekly tennis game.

Mint (C): "Well, you took me again, Jack. I'm starting to feel old."

Edgeworth (SG): "It was a close match, Dave. Always is. Fortunately, it looks like we'll be able to keep our matches up, too."

Mint (C): "What do you mean?"

Edgeworth (SG): "I'm talking about the outsourcing decision Marsha was considering. Fortunately, the analysis showed her that we should keep making our own gift boxes. So my department stays in business. And I won't have to consider a transfer. My wife's very happy about that, with the twins in middle school and all."

Mint (C): "Uh, Jack, I think there's something you need to know about."

Edgeworth (SG): "What's that?"

Mint (C): "I've been doing some preliminary studies using a technique called activity-based costing. I think it could improve our decision making in a lot of areas."

Edgeworth (SG): "So?"

Mint (C): "That outsourcing decision is one of the areas where I tried out the new ABC approach. I just finished the analysis yesterday. I was going to schedule an appointment with Marsha and you next week to discuss it."

Edgeworth (SG): "I'm getting queasy about where this is going, Jack. What did your analysis show?"

Mint (C): "It changes the conclusion—pretty dramatically, in fact. The ABC study shows that we'd save over $40,000 each year by outsourcing."

Edgeworth (SG): "Is that really all that much, Dave? Among friends, I mean?"

Mint (C): "It's not a trivial amount, Jack."

Edgeworth (SG): "Look, Dave, I don't think I've ever asked anything of you before. But can't you bury this one for me? Our family really doesn't need another move. And I've got people working for me who will probably lose their jobs. We've done a good job for the company. Our product is top notch. Nobody's ever complained about a thing."

Mint (C): "I don't see how I can withhold the analysis from Marsha, Jack. She has a right to all the information I have."

Edgeworth (SG): "But you said you were just doing preliminary studies, Dave. Marsha doesn't know anything about this one, does she?"

Mint (C): "Not yet, Jack, but I've got a professional obligation to show it to her."

Edgeworth (SG): "You're opening a Pandora's box, Dave. What about employee morale if you close my department? And what about product quality, and reliability of the supply?"

Mint (C): "Those are valid issues, Jack. But they need to be addressed on their own merits, in a full and open discussion."

Edgeworth (SG): "Could you at least share this so-called ABC study with me before you show it to Marsha? Maybe I'll see something you've missed."

Mint (C): "I don't see why not, Jack. Come by my office tomorrow morning—say about 10:00."

Identify any ethical issues you see in this scenario. How would you resolve them? What should the controller do?

Chapter Summary

LO1 Describe seven steps in the decision-making process and the managerial accountant's role in that process. The decision-making steps are: (1) clarify the decision problem; (2) specify the criterion; (3) identify the alternatives; (4) develop a decision model; (5) collect the data; (6) select an alternative; and (7) evaluate decision effectiveness.

LO2 Explain the relationship between quantitative and qualitative analyses in decision making. The managerial accountant's key role in the decision-making process is to provide data relevant to the decision. Managers can then use these data in preparing a quantitative analysis of the decision. Qualitative factors also are considered in making the final decision.

LO3 List and explain two criteria that must be satisfied by relevant information. In order to be relevant to a decision, a cost or benefit must (1) bear on the future and (2) differ under the various decision alternatives.

LO4 Identify relevant costs and benefits, giving proper treatment to sunk costs, opportunity costs, and unit costs. Sunk costs, such as the book value of equipment or inventory, are not relevant to decisions. Such costs do not have any bearing on the future. Opportunity costs frequently are relevant to decisions, but they often are overlooked by decision makers. Unit costs bear particular scrutiny in decision-making situations. Fixed costs often are unitized and assigned to products or services for product-costing purposes. For decision-making purposes, however, unit costs can be misleading, since the total fixed cost will not increase as the total number of units produced increases.

LO5 Prepare analyses of various special decisions, properly identifying the relevant costs and benefits. To analyze any special decision, the proper approach is to determine all of the costs and benefits that will differ among the alternatives. Common decisions include the following: (1) accept or reject a special offer; (2) outsource a product or service; and (3) add or drop a service, product, or department.

LO6 Analyze manufacturing decisions involving joint products and limited resources. A common decision that arises in a joint-product environment is whether to sell a joint product at the split-off point or process it further. This decision should be based on the incremental costs and benefits occurring after the split-off point. A common decision involving limited resources is which of several products to produce. The correct decision is to produce the product with the highest contribution margin per unit of the scarce resource.

LO7 Explain the impact of an advanced manufacturing environment and activity-based costing on a relevant-cost analysis. The concepts underlying a relevant-cost analysis remain valid in an advanced manufacturing environment and in situations where activity-based costing is used. However, an ABC system typically enables a decision maker to estimate the relevant costs in a decision problem more accurately.

LO8 Formulate a linear program to solve a product-mix problem with multiple constraints (appendix). A linear program can be used to solve a firm's product-mix problem when the production process is constrained by scarce resources. A linear program consists of a linear objective function and a set of linear constraints. The solution to the optimization problem consists of finding the optimal solution point within the feasible region, as determined by the constraints.

Review Problem on Relevant Costs

Lansing Camera Company has received a special order for photographic equipment it does not normally produce. The company has excess capacity, and the order could be manufactured without reducing production of the firm's regular products. Discuss the relevance of each of the following items in computing the cost of the special order.

1. Equipment to be used in producing the order has a book value of $2,000. The equipment has no other use for Lansing Camera Company. If the order is not accepted, the equipment will be sold for $1,500. If the equipment is used in producing the order, it can be sold in three months for $800.

2. If the special order is accepted, the operation will require some of the storage space in the company's plant. If the space is used for this purpose, the company will rent storage space temporarily in a nearby warehouse at a cost of $18,000. The building depreciation allocated to the storage space to be used in producing the special order is $12,000.
3. If the special order is accepted, it will require a subassembly. Lansing Camera can purchase the subassembly for $24 per unit from an outside supplier or make it for $30 per unit. The $30 cost per unit was determined as follows:

Direct material	$10.00
Direct labor	6.00
Variable overhead	6.00
Allocated fixed overhead	8.00
Total unit cost of subassembly	$30.00

Solution to Review Problem

1. The book value of the equipment is a sunk cost, irrelevant to the decision. The relevant cost of the equipment is $700, determined as follows:

Sales value of equipment now	$1,500
Sales value after producing special order	800
Differential cost	$ 700

2. The $12,000 portion of building depreciation allocated to the storage space to be used for the special order is irrelevant. First, it is a sunk cost. Second, any costs relating to the company's factory building will continue whether the special order is accepted or not. The relevant cost is the $18,000 rent that will be incurred only if the special order is accepted.
3. Lansing Camera should make the subassembly. The subassembly's relevant cost is $22 per unit.

Relevant Cost of Making Subassembly (per unit)		Relevant Cost of Purchasing Subassembly (per unit)	
Direct material	$10.00	Purchase price	$24.00
Direct labor	6.00		
Variable overhead	6.00		
Total	$22.00		

Notice that the unitized fixed overhead, $8, is not a relevant cost of the subassembly. Lansing Camera Company's *total* fixed cost will not change, whether the special order is accepted or not.

Key Terms

For each term's definition refer to the indicated page, or turn to the glossary at the end of the text.

accurate information, 594
avoidable expenses, 605
constraints,* 620
decision variables,* 620
differential cost, 598
expected value, 612
feasible region,* 620
information overload, 596
joint cost, 608
joint production process, 607
make-or-buy decision, 602
objective function,* 620
opportunity cost, 599
outsourcing decision, 602
qualitative characteristics, 593
relative-sales-value method, 608
relevant information, 594
sensitivity analysis, 611
separable processing cost, 609
split-off point, 608
sunk costs, 596
timely information, 595
unavoidable expenses, 605

*Term appears in the appendix.

APPENDIX TO CHAPTER 14

Linear Programming

Learning Objective 8

Formulate a linear program to solve a product-mix problem with multiple constraints (appendix).

When a firm produces multiple products, management must decide how much of each output to produce. In most cases, the firm is limited in the total amount it can produce, due to constraints on resources such as machine time, direct labor, or raw materials. This situation is known as a *product-mix problem.*

To illustrate, we will use International Chocolate Company's Phoenix plant, which produces Chewies and Chompo Bars. Exhibit 14–21 provides data pertinent to the problem.

Linear programming is a powerful mathematical tool, well suited to solving International Chocolate Company's product-mix problem. The steps in constructing the linear program are as follows:

1. Identify the **decision variables,** which are the variables about which a decision must be made. International Chocolate's decision variables are as follows:

   Decision variables X = Number of cases of Chewies to produce each month
   Y = Number of cases of Chompo Bars to produce each month

2. Write the **objective function,** which is an algebraic expression of the firm's goal. International Chocolate's goal is to *maximize its total contribution margin.* Since Chewies bring a contribution margin of $1 per case, and Chompos result in a contribution margin of $2 per case, the firm's objective function is the following:

   Objective function Maximize $Z = X + 2Y$

3. Write the **constraints,** which are algebraic expressions of the limitations faced by the firm, such as those limiting its productive resources. International Chocolate has a constraint for machine time and a constraint for direct labor.

   Machine-time constraint $.02X + .05Y \leq 700$
   Labor-time constraint $.20X + .25Y \leq 5{,}000$

Suppose, for example, that management decided to produce 20,000 cases of Chewies and 6,000 cases of Chompos. The machine-time constraint would appear as follows:

$$(.02)(20{,}000) + (.05)(6{,}000) = 700$$

Thus, at these production levels, the machine-time constraint would just be satisfied, with no machine hours to spare.

Graphical Solution

To understand how the linear program described above will help International Chocolate's management solve its product-mix problem, examine the graphs in Exhibit 14–22. The two colored lines in panel A represent the constraints. The colored arrows indicate that the production quantities, X and Y, must lie on or below these lines. Since the production quantities must be nonnegative, colored arrows also appear on the graphs' axes. Together, the axes and constraints form an area called the **feasible region,** in which the solution to the linear program must lie.

The black slanted line in panel A represents the objective function. Rearrange the objective function equation as follows:

$$Z = X + 2Y \longrightarrow Y = \frac{Z}{2} - \frac{1}{2}X$$

Exhibit 14–21
Data for Product-Mix Problem: International Chocolate Company

	Chewies	Chompo Bars
Contribution margin per case	$1.00	$2.00
Machine hours per case	.02	.05
Direct-labor hours per case	.20	.25
	Machine Hours	**Direct-Labor Hours**
Limited resources: hours available per month	700	5,000

Exhibit 14–22
Product-Mix Problem Expressed as Linear Program: International Chocolate Company

Y (cases of Chompos)

Labor-time constraint
.20X + .25Y ≤ 5,000

Machine-time constraint
.02X + .05Y ≤ 700

Feasible region

20,000
15,000
10,000
5,000

5,000 10,000 15,000 20,000 25,000 30,000 35,000

X (cases of Chewies)

Objective function:
Z = X + 2Y

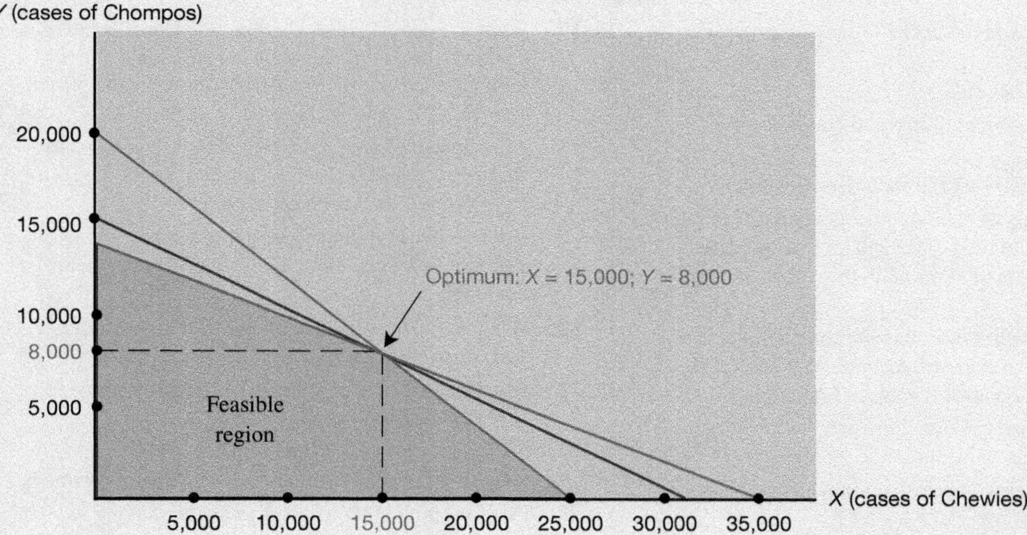

This form of the objective function shows that the slope of the equation is −½, which is the slope of the objective-function line in the exhibit. Management's goal is to maximize total contribution margin, denoted by Z. To achieve the maximum, the objective-function line must be moved as far outward and upward in the feasible region as possible, while maintaining the same slope. This goal is represented in panel A by the arrow that points outward from the objective-function line.

Solution The result of moving the objective-function line as far as possible in the indicated direction is shown in panel B of the exhibit. The objective-function line intersects the feasible region at exactly one point, where *X* equals 15,000 and *Y* equals 8,000. Thus, International Chocolate's optimal product mix is 15,000 cases of Chewies and 8,000 cases of Chompos per month. The total contribution margin is calculated as shown below.

Total contribution margin = (15,000)($1) + (8,000)($2) = $31,000

Simplex Method and Sensitivity Analysis Although the graphical method is instructive, it is a cumbersome technique for solving a linear program. Fortunately, mathematicians have developed a more efficient solution method called the *simplex algorithm.* A computer can apply the algorithm to a complex linear program and determine the solution in seconds. In addition, most linear programming computer packages provide a sensitivity analysis of the problem. This analysis shows the decision maker the extent to which the estimates used in the objective function and constraints can change without changing the solution.

Managerial Accountant's Role

What is the managerial accountant's role in International Chocolate's product-mix decision? The production manager in the company's Phoenix plant makes this decision, with the help of a linear program. However, the linear program uses *information supplied by the managerial accountant.* The coefficients of X and Y in the objective function are unit contribution margins. Exhibit 14–14 shows that calculating these contribution margins requires estimates of direct-material, direct-labor, variable-overhead, and variable selling and administrative costs. These estimates were provided by a managerial accountant, along with estimates of the machine time and direct-labor time required to produce a case of Chewies or Chompos. All of these estimates were obtained from the standard-costing system, upon which the Phoenix plant's product costs are based. Thus, the managerial accountant makes the product-mix decision possible by providing the relevant cost data.

Linear programming is widely used in business decision making. Among the applications are blending in the petroleum and chemical industries; scheduling of personnel, railroad cars, and aircraft; and the mixing of ingredients in the food industry. In all of these applications, managerial accountants provide information crucial to the analysis.

Review Questions

14–1. List the seven steps in the decision-making process.

14–2. Describe the managerial accountant's role in the decision-making process.

14–3. Distinguish between qualitative and quantitative decision analyses.

14–4. Explain what is meant by the term *decision model.*

14–5. A quantitative analysis enables a decision maker to put a "price" on the sum total of the qualitative characteristics in a decision situation. Explain this statement, and give an example.

14–6. What is meant by each of the following potential characteristics of information: relevant, accurate, and timely? Is objective information always relevant? Accurate?

14–7. List and explain two important criteria that must be satisfied in order for information to be relevant.

14–8. Explain why the book value of equipment is not a relevant cost.

14–9. Is the book value of inventory on hand a relevant cost? Why?

14–10. Why might a manager exhibit a behavioral tendency to inappropriately consider sunk costs in making a decision?

14–11. Give an example of an irrelevant future cost. Why is it irrelevant?

14–12. Define the term *opportunity cost,* and give an example of one.

14–13. What behavioral tendency do people often exhibit with regard to opportunity costs?

14–14. How does the existence of excess production capacity affect the decision to accept or reject a special order?

14–15. What is meant by the term *differential cost analysis?*

14–16. Briefly describe the proper approach for making a decision about adding or dropping a product line.

14–17. What is a *joint production process?* Describe a special decision that commonly arises in the context of a joint production process. Briefly describe the proper approach for making this type of decision.

14–18. Are allocated joint processing costs relevant when making a decision to sell a joint product at the split-off point or process it further? Why?

14–19. Briefly describe the proper approach to making a production decision when limited resources are involved.

14–20. What is meant by the term *contribution margin per unit of scarce resource?*

14–21. How is sensitivity analysis used to cope with uncertainty in decision making?

14–22. There is an important link between *decision making* and *managerial performance evaluation.* Explain.

14–23. List four potential pitfalls in decision making, which represent common errors.

14–24. Why can unitized fixed costs cause errors in decision making?

14–25. Give two examples of sunk costs, and explain why they are irrelevant in decision making.

14–26. "Accounting systems should produce only relevant data and forget about the irrelevant data. Then I'd know what was relevant and what wasn't!" Comment on this remark by a company president.

14–27. Are the concepts underlying a relevant-cost analysis still valid in an advanced manufacturing environment? Are these concepts valid when activity-based costing is used? Explain.

14–28. List five ways that management can seek to relax a constraint by expanding the capacity of a bottleneck operation.

Exercises

All applicable Exercises are available with McGraw-Hill's *Connect Accounting*™. 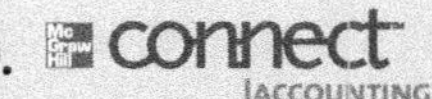

Exercise 14–29
Steps in Decision-Making Process
(LO 1)

Choose an organization and a particular decision situation. Then give examples, using that decision context, of each step illustrated in Exhibit 14–1. For example, you could choose a decision that would be made by a retailer, such as Best Buy or Borders. Or you could focus on a service provider, such as Hertz rent-a-car or Marriott Hotels. Alternatively, select a manufacturer, such as Nike or Nokia. Or consider a decision to be made by your college or home city.

Exercise 14–30
Irrelevant Future Costs and Benefits
(LO 3, 4)

Redo Exhibit 14–4 without the irrelevant data.

Exercise 14–31
Machine Replacement
(LO 4, 5)

Valley Pizza's owner bought his current pizza oven two years ago for $9,000, and it has one more year of life remaining. He is using straight-line depreciation for the oven. He could purchase a new oven for $1,900, but it would last only one year. The owner figures the new oven would save him $2,600 in annual operating expenses compared to operating the old one. Consequently, he has decided against buying the new oven, since doing so would result in a "loss" of $400 over the next year.

Required:

1. How do you suppose the owner came up with $400 as the loss for the next year if the new pizza oven were purchased? Explain.
2. Criticize the owner's analysis and decision.
3. Prepare a correct analysis of the owner's decision.

Exercise 14–32
Joint Products
(LO 4, 5, 6)

Lamont Industries produces chemicals for the swimming pool industry. In one joint process, 10,000 gallons of GSX are processed into 7,000 gallons of xenolite and 3,000 gallons of banolide. The cost of the joint process, including the GSX, is $19,000. The firm allocates $13,300 of the joint cost to the xenolite and $5,700 of the cost to the banolide. The 3,000 gallons of banolide can be sold at the split-off point for $2,500, or be processed further into a product called kitrocide. The sales value of 3,000 gallons of kitrocide is $10,000, and the additional processing cost is $8,100.

Required: Lamont's president has asked your consulting firm to make a recommendation as to whether the banolide should be sold at the split-off point or processed further. Write a letter providing an analysis and a recommendation.

Exercise 14–33
Drop Product Line
(LO 4, 5)

Day Street Deli's owner is disturbed by the poor profit performance of his ice cream counter. He has prepared the following profit analysis for the year just ended.

Sales		$45,000
Less: Cost of food		20,000
Gross profit		$25,000
Less: Operating expenses:		
Wages of counter personnel	$12,000	
Paper products (e.g., napkins)	4,000	
Utilities (allocated)	2,900	
Depreciation of counter equipment and furnishings	2,500	
Depreciation of building (allocated)	4,000	
Deli manager's salary (allocated)	3,000	
Total		28,400
Loss on ice cream counter		$ (3,400)

Required: Criticize and correct the owner's analysis.

Exercise 14–34
Outsourcing Decision; Use of Internet
(LO 1, 2, 5)

Visit the Web site of one of the following companies, or a different company of your choosing.

Burger King	www.burgerking.com
Compaq	www.compaq.com
Corning	www.corning.com
Kmart	www.kmart.com
Kodak	www.kodak.com
NBC	www.nbc.com

Required: Read about the company's activities and operations. Choose an activity that is necessary for the company's operations, and then discuss the pros and cons of outsourcing that activity.

Exercise 14–35
Obsolete Inventory
(LO 4, 5)

Armstrong Corporation manufactures bicycle parts. The company currently has a $21,000 inventory of parts that have become obsolete due to changes in design specifications. The parts could be sold for $9,000, or modified for $12,000 and sold for $22,300.

Required:

1. Which of the data above are relevant to the decision about the obsolete parts?
2. Prepare an analysis of the decision.

Exercise 14–36
Special Order
(LO 4, 5)

Intercontinental Chemical Company, located in Buenos Aires, Argentina, recently received an order for a product it does not normally produce. Since the company has excess production capacity, management is considering accepting the order. In analyzing the decision, the assistant controller is compiling the relevant costs of producing the order. Production of the special order would require 8,000 kilograms of theolite. Intercontinental does not use theolite for its regular product, but the firm has 8,000 kilograms of the chemical on hand from the days when it used theolite regularly. The theolite could be sold to a chemical wholesaler for 14,500 *p*. The book value of the theolite is 2.00 *p* per kilogram. Intercontinental could buy theolite for 2.40 *p* per kilogram. (*p* denotes the peso, Argentina's national monetary unit. Many countries use the peso as their unit of currency. On the day this exercise was written, Argentina's peso was worth .3274 U.S. dollar.)

Required:

1. What is the relevant cost of theolite for the purpose of analyzing the special-order decision? (Remember to express your answer in terms of Argentina's peso.)
2. Discuss each of the numbers given in the exercise with regard to its relevance in making the decision.

Exercise 14–37
Continuation of Preceding Exercise
(LO 4, 5)

Intercontinental's special order also requires 1,000 kilograms of genatope, a solid chemical regularly used in the company's products. The current stock of genatope is 8,000 kilograms at a book value of 8.10 *p* per kilogram. If the special order is accepted, the firm will be forced to restock genatope earlier than expected, at a predicted cost of 8.70 *p* per kilogram. Without the special order, the purchasing manager predicts that the price will be 8.30 *p* when normal restocking takes place. Any order of genatope must be in the amount of 5,000 kilograms.

Required:

1. What is the relevant cost of genatope?
2. Discuss each of the figures in the exercise in terms of its relevance to the decision.

Exercise 14–38
Closing a Department
(LO 4, 5)

Fusion Metals Company is considering the elimination of its Packaging Department. Management has received an offer from an outside firm to supply all Fusion's packaging needs. To help her in making the decision, Fusion's president has asked the controller for an analysis of the cost of running Fusion's Packaging Department. Included in that analysis is $9,100 of rent, which represents the Packaging Department's allocation of the rent on Fusion's factory building. If the Packaging Department is eliminated, the space it used will be converted to storage space. Currently Fusion rents storage space in a nearby warehouse for $11,000 per year. The warehouse rental would no longer be necessary if the Packaging Department were eliminated.

Required:

1. Discuss each of the figures given in the exercise with regard to its relevance in the department-closing decision.
2. What type of cost is the $11,000 warehouse rental, from the viewpoint of the costs of the Packaging Department?

Exercise 14–39
Continuation of Preceding Exercise
(LO 4, 5)

If Fusion Metals Company closes its Packaging Department, the department manager will be appointed manager of the Cutting Department. The Packaging Department manager makes $45,000 per year. To hire a new Cutting Department manager will cost Fusion $60,000 per year.

Required: Discuss the relevance of each of these salary figures to the department-closing decision.

Exercise 14–40
Joint Products; Relevant Costs; Cost-Volume-Profit Analysis
(LO 4, 6)

Zytel Corporation produces cleaning compounds and solutions for industrial and household use. While most of its products are processed independently, a few are related. Grit 337, a coarse cleaning powder with many industrial uses, costs $1.60 a pound to make and sells for $2.00 a pound. A small portion of the annual production of this product is retained for further processing in the Mixing Department, where it is combined with several other ingredients to form a paste, which is marketed as a silver polish selling for $4.00 per jar. This further processing requires ¼ pound of Grit 337 per jar. Costs of other ingredients, labor, and variable overhead associated with this further processing amount to $2.50 per jar. Variable selling costs are $.30 per jar. If the decision were made to cease production of the silver polish, $5,600 of Mixing Department fixed costs could be avoided. Zytel has limited production capacity for Grit 337, but unlimited demand for the cleaning powder.

Required: Calculate the minimum number of jars of silver polish that would have to be sold to justify further processing of Grit 337.

(CMA, adapted)

Exercise 14–41
Limited Resource
(LO 6)

Duo Company manufactures two products, Uno and Dos. Contribution margin data follow.

	Uno	Dos
Unit sales price	$13.00	$31.00
Less variable cost:		
Direct material	$ 7.00	$ 5.00
Direct labor	1.00	6.00
Variable overhead	1.25	7.50
Variable selling and administrative cost	.75	.50
Total variable cost	$10.00	$19.00
Unit contribution margin	$ 3.00	$12.00

Duo company's production process uses highly skilled labor, which is in short supply. The same employees work on both products and earn the same wage rate.

Required: Which of Duo Company's products is more profitable? Explain.

Exercise 14–42
Linear Programming (Appendix)
(LO 6, 8)

Refer to the data given in the preceding exercise for Duo Company. Assume that the direct-labor rate is $24 per hour, and 10,000 labor hours are available per year. In addition, the company has a short supply of machine time. Only 8,000 hours are available each year. Uno requires 1 machine hour per unit, and Dos requires 2 machine hours per unit.

Required: Formulate the production planning problem as a linear program. Specifically identify (1) the decision variables, (2) the objective function, and (3) the constraints.

Exercise 14–43
Linear Programming; Formulate and Solve wvwwGraphically (Appendix)
(LO 8)

Southern California Chemical Company manufactures two industrial chemical products, called kreolite-red and kreolite-blue. Two machines are used in the process, and each machine has 24 hours of capacity per day. The following data are available:

	Kreolite-Red	Kreolite-Blue
Selling price per drum	$36	$42
Variable cost per drum	$28	$28
Hours required per drum on machine I	2 hr	2 hr
Hours required per drum on machine II	1 hr	3 hr

The company can produce and sell partially full drums of each chemical. For example, a half drum of kreolite-red sells for $18.

Required:

1. Formulate the product-mix problem as a linear program.
2. Solve the problem graphically.

Problems

All applicable Problems are available with McGraw-Hill's *Connect Accounting*™.

Problem 14–44
Production Decisions; Limited Capacity
(LO 5, 6)

Kitchen Magician, Inc. has assembled the following data pertaining to its two most popular products.

	Blender	Electric Mixer
Direct material	$ 6	$11
Direct labor	4	9
Manufacturing overhead @ $16 per machine hour	16	32
Cost if purchased from an outside supplier	20	38
Annual demand (units)	20,000	28,000

Past experience has shown that the fixed manufacturing overhead component included in the cost per machine hour averages $10. Kitchen Magician's management has a policy of filling all sales orders, even if it means purchasing units from outside suppliers.

Required:

1. If 50,000 machine hours are available, and management desires to follow an optimal strategy, how many units of each product should the firm manufacture? How many units of each product should be purchased?
2. With all other things constant, if management is able to reduce the direct material for an electric mixer to $6 per unit, how many units of each product should be manufactured? Purchased?
3. *Build a spreadsheet:* Construct an Excel spreadsheet to solve requirement (1) above. Show how the solution will change if the following information changes: the unit cost if purchased from an outside supplier is $22 for the blender and $40 for the electric mixer.

(CMA, adapted)

Problem 14–45
Special Order; Financial and Production Considerations
(LO 4, 5)

1. Net contribution to profit: $34,050

Jupiter Corporation manufactures skateboards. Several weeks ago, the firm received a special-order inquiry from Venus, Inc. Venus desires to market a skateboard similar to one of Jupiter's and has offered to purchase 11,000 units if the order can be completed in three months. The cost data for Jupiter's model no. 43 skateboard follow.

Direct material	$ 8.20
Direct labor: .25 hour at $9.00	2.25
Total manufacturing overhead:	
.5 hour at $20	10.00
Total	$20.45

Additional data:

- The normal selling price of model no. 43 is $26.50; however, Venus has offered Jupiter only $15.75 because of the large quantity it is willing to purchase.
- Venus requires a modification of the design that will allow a $2.10 reduction in direct-material cost.
- Jupiter's production supervisor notes that the company will incur $3,700 in additional setup costs and will have to purchase a $2,400 special device to manufacture these units. The device will be discarded once the special order is completed.
- Total manufacturing overhead costs are applied to production at the rate of $20 per machine hour. This figure is based, in part, on budgeted yearly fixed overhead of $750,000 and planned production activity of 60,000 machine hours (5,000 per month).
- Jupiter will allocate $1,800 of existing fixed administrative costs to the order as ". . . part of the cost of doing business."

Required:

1. Assume that present sales will not be affected. Should the order be accepted from a financial point of view (i.e., is it profitable)? Why? Show calculations.
2. Assume that Jupiter's current production activity consumes 70 percent of planned machine-hour activity. Can the company accept the order and meet Venus' deadline?
3. What options might Jupiter consider if management truly wanted to do business with Venus in hopes of building a long-term relationship with the firm?

Problem 14–46
Introducing a New Product
(LO 4, 5)

1. Unit contribution margin, Enhanced Model, $200

Johnson and Gomez, Inc. is a small firm involved in the production and sale of electronic business products. The company is well known for its attention to quality and innovation.

During the past 15 months, a new product has been under development that allows users handheld access to e-mail and video images. Johnson and Gomez code named the product the Wireless Wizard and has been quietly designing two models: Basic and Enhanced. Development costs have amounted to $121,000 and $175,000, respectively. The total market demand for each model is expected to be 40,000 units, and management anticipates being able to obtain the following market shares: Basic, 25 percent; Enhanced, 20 percent. Forecasted data follow.

	Basic	Enhanced
Projected selling price	$ 250	$ 330
Per-unit production costs:		
Direct material	28	45
Direct labor	15	20
Variable overhead	24	32
Marketing and advertising	130,000	200,000
Sales salaries	57,000	57,000
Sales commissions*	10%	10%

*Computed on the basis of sales dollars.

Since the start of development work on the Wireless Wizard, advances in technology have altered the market somewhat, and management now believes that the company can introduce only one of the two models. Consultants confirmed this fact not too long ago, with Johnson and Gomez paying $23,000 for an in-depth market study. The total fixed overhead is expected to be the same, regardless of which product is manufactured.

Required:

1. Compute the per-unit contribution margin for both models.
2. Which of the data in the table above should be ignored in making the product-introduction decision? For what reason?
3. Prepare a financial analysis and determine which of the two models should be introduced.
4. What other factors should Johnson and Gomez, Inc. consider before a final decision is made?

Problem 14–47
Closing an Unprofitable Department
(LO 4, 5)

1. Income (loss) from closure: $(12,800)

Tipton One-Stop Decorating sells paint and paint supplies, carpet, and wallpaper at a single-store location in suburban Des Moines. Although the company has been very profitable over the years, management has seen a significant decline in wallpaper sales and earnings. Much of this decline is attributable to the Internet and to companies that advertise deeply discounted prices in magazines and offer customers free shipping and toll-free telephone numbers. Recent figures follow.

	Paint and Supplies	Carpeting	Wallpaper
Sales	$380,000	$460,000	$140,000
Variable costs	$228,000	$322,000	$112,000
Fixed costs	56,000	75,000	45,000
Total costs	$284,000	$397,000	$157,000
Operating income (loss)	$ 96,000	$ 63,000	$ (17,000)

Tipton is studying whether to drop wallpaper because of the changing market and accompanying loss. If the line is dropped, the following changes are expected to occur:

- The vacated space will be remodeled at a cost of $12,400 and will be devoted to an expanded line of high-end carpet. Sales of carpet are expected to increase by $120,000, and the line's overall contribution margin ratio will rise by five percentage points.
- Tipton can cut wallpaper's fixed costs by 40 percent. Remaining fixed costs will continue to be incurred.
- Customers who purchased wallpaper often bought paint and paint supplies. Sales of paint and paint supplies are expected to fall by 20 percent.
- The firm will increase advertising expenditures by $25,000 to promote the expanded carpet line.

Required:

1. Should Tipton close its wallpaper operation? Show computations to support your answer.
2. Assume that Tipton's wallpaper inventory at the time of the closure decision amounted to $23,700. How would you have treated this additional information in making the decision?
3. What advantages might Internet- and magazine-based firms have over Tipton that would allow these organizations to offer deeply discounted prices—prices far below what Tipton can offer?
4. *Build a spreadsheet:* Construct an Excel spreadsheet to solve requirement (1) above. Show how the solution will change if the following information changes: sales were $400,000, $450,000, and $130,000, for paint and supplies, carpeting, and wallpaper, respectively.

Problem 14–48
Excess Production Capacity
(LO 5, 6)

2. Contribution margin per direct-labor hour, Deluxe Model: $12

Carpenter's Mate, Inc. manufactures electric carpentry tools. The Production Department has met all production requirements for the current month and has an opportunity to produce additional units of product with its excess capacity. Unit selling prices and unit costs for three different drill models are as follows:

	Home Model	Deluxe Model	Pro Model
Selling price	$58	$65	$80
Direct material	16	20	19
Direct labor ($10 per hour)	10	15	20
Variable overhead	8	12	16
Fixed overhead	16	5	15

Variable overhead is applied on the basis of direct-labor dollars, while fixed overhead is applied on the basis of machine hours. There is sufficient demand for the additional production of any model in the product line.

Required:

1. If Carpenter's Mate, Inc. has excess machine capacity and can add more labor as needed (i.e., neither machine capacity nor labor is a constraint), the excess production capacity should be

devoted to producing which product? (Assume that the excess capacity will be used for a single product line.)

2. If Carpenter's Mate has excess machine capacity but a limited amount of labor time, the excess production capacity should be devoted to producing which product or products?

(CMA, adapted)

Problem 14–49
Make or Buy
(LO 4, 5)

Casting Technology Resources (CTR) has purchased 10,000 pumps annually from Kobec, Inc. Because the price keeps increasing and reached $68.00 per unit last year, CTR's management has asked for an estimate of the cost of manufacturing the pump in CTR's facilities. CTR makes stampings and castings and has little experience with products requiring assembly.

The engineering, manufacturing, and accounting departments have prepared a report for management that includes the following estimate for an assembly run of 10,000 pumps. Additional production employees would be hired to manufacture the pumps but no additional equipment, space, or supervision would be needed.

The report states that total costs for 10,000 units are estimated at $957,000, or $95.70 per unit. The current purchase price is $68.00 per unit, so the report recommends continued purchase of the product.

Components (outside purchases)	$120,000
Assembly labor*	300,000
Manufacturing overhead†	450,000
General and administrative overhead‡	87,000
Total costs	$957,000

*Assembly labor consists of hourly production workers.

†Manufacturing overhead is applied to products on a direct-labor-dollar basis. Variable-overhead costs vary closely with direct-labor dollars.

Fixed overhead	50% of direct-labor dollars
Variable overhead	100% of direct-labor dollars
Manufacturing-overhead rate	150% of direct-labor dollars

‡General and administrative overhead is applied at 10 percent of the total cost of material (or components), assembly labor, and manufacturing overhead.

Required: Was the analysis prepared by Casting Technology Resources' engineering, manufacturing, and accounting departments and their recommendation to continue purchasing the pumps correct? Explain your answer and include any supporting calculations you consider necessary.

(CMA, adapted)

Problem 14–50
Outsourcing Decision; Relevant Costs; Ethics
(LO 3, 4, 5)

1(a). Savings if purchased from Marley: $(15,440)

The Midwest Division of the Paibec Corporation manufactures subassemblies that are used in the corporation's final products. Lynn Hardt of Midwest's Profit Planning Department has been assigned the task of determining whether a component, MTR–2000, should continue to be manufactured by Midwest or purchased from Marley Company, an outside supplier. MTR–2000 is part of a subassembly manufactured by Midwest.

Marley has submitted a bid to manufacture and supply the 32,000 units of MTR–2000 that Paibec will need for 20x1 at a unit price of $17.30. Marley has assured Paibec that the units will be delivered according to Paibec's production specifications and needs. While the contract price of $17.30 is only applicable in 20x1, Marley is interested in entering into a long-term arrangement beyond 20x1.

Hardt has gathered the following information regarding Midwest's cost to manufacture MTR–2000 in 20x0. These annual costs will be incurred to manufacture 30,000 units.

Direct material	$195,000
Direct labor	120,000
Factory space rental	84,000
Equipment leasing costs	36,000
Other manufacturing overhead	225,000
Total manufacturing costs	$660,000

Hardt has collected the following additional information related to manufacturing MTR–2000.

- Direct materials used in the production of MTR–2000 are expected to increase 8 percent in 20x1.
- Midwest's direct-labor contract calls for a 5 percent increase in 20x1.
- The facilities used to manufacture MTR–2000 are rented under a month-to-month rental agreement. Thus, Midwest can withdraw from the rental agreement without any penalty. Midwest will have no need for this space if MTR–2000 is not manufactured.
- Equipment leasing costs represent special equipment that is used in the manufacture of MTR–2000. This lease can be terminated by paying the equivalent of one month's lease payment for each year left on the lease agreement. Midwest has two years left on the lease agreement, through the end of the year 20x2.
- Forty percent of the other manufacturing overhead is considered variable. Variable overhead changes with the number of units produced, and this rate per unit is not expected to change in 20x1. The fixed manufacturing overhead costs are not expected to change regardless of whether MTR–2000 is manufactured. Equipment other than the leased equipment can be used in Midwest's other manufacturing operations.

John Porter, divisional manager of Midwest, stopped by Hardt's office to voice his concern regarding the outsourcing of MTR–2000. Porter commented, "I am really concerned about outsourcing MTR–2000. I have a son-in-law and a nephew, not to mention a member of our bowling team, who work on MTR–2000. They could lose their jobs if we buy that component from Marley. I really would appreciate anything you can do to make sure the cost analysis comes out right to show we should continue making MTR–2000. Corporate is not aware of the material increases and maybe you can leave out some of those fixed costs. I just think we should continue making MTR–2000!"

Required:

1. *a.* Prepare an analysis of relevant costs that shows whether or not the Midwest Division of Paibec Corporation should make MTR–2000 or purchase it from Marley Company for 20x1.
   b. Based solely on the financial results, recommend whether the 32,000 units of MTR–2000 for 20x1 should be made by Midwest or purchased from Marley.
2. Identify and briefly discuss three qualitative factors that the Midwest Division and Paibec Corporation should consider before agreeing to purchase MTR–2000 from Marley Company.
3. By referring to the standards of ethical conduct for managerial accountants given in Chapter 1, explain why Lynn Hardt would consider the request of John Porter to be unethical.

(CMA, adapted)

Problem 14–51
Joint Products; Sell or Process Further
(LO 6)

Total revenue from further processing $460,000

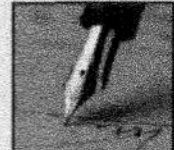

Connecticut Chemical Company is a diversified chemical processing company. The firm manufactures swimming pool chemicals, chemicals for metal processing, specialized chemical compounds, and pesticides.

Currently, the Noorwood plant is producing two derivatives, RNA–1 and RNA–2, from the chemical compound VDB developed by the company's research labs. Each week, 1,200,000 pounds of VDB are processed at a cost of $246,000 into 800,000 pounds of RNA–1 and 400,000 pounds of RNA–2. The proportion of these two outputs cannot be altered, because this is a joint process. RNA–1 has no market value until it is converted into a pesticide with the trade name Fastkil. Processing RNA–1 into Fastkil costs $240,000. Fastkil wholesales at $50 per 100 pounds.

RNA–2 is sold as is for $80 per hundred pounds. However, management has discovered that RNA–2 can be converted into two new products by adding 400,000 pounds of compound LST to the 400,000 pounds of RNA–2. This joint process would yield 400,000 pounds each of DMZ–3 and Pestrol, the two new products. The additional direct-material and related processing costs of this joint process would be $120,000. DMZ–3 and Pestrol would each be sold for $57.50 per 100 pounds. The company's management has decided not to process RNA–2 further based on the analysis presented in the following schedule.

	Process Further			
	RNA–2	**DMZ–3**	**Pestrol**	**Total**
Production in pounds	400,000	400,000	400,000	
Revenue	$320,000	$230,000	$230,000	$ 460,000
Costs:				
VDB costs	$ 82,000*	$ 61,500	$ 61,500	$ 123,000†
Additional direct materials (LST) and processing of RNA–2	—	60,000	60,000	120,000
Total costs	$ 82,000	$121,500	$121,500	$ 243,000
Weekly gross profit	$238,000	$108,500	$108,500	$ 217,000

*$82,000 is one-third of the $246,000 cost of processing VDB. When RNA–2 is not processed further, one-third of the final output is RNA–2 (400,000 out of a total of 1,200,000 pounds).

†$123,000 is one-half of the $246,000 cost of processing VDB. When RNA–2 is processed further, one-half of the final output consists of DMZ–3 and Pestrol. The final products then are: 800,000 pounds of RNA–1; 400,000 pounds of DMZ–3; and 400,000 pounds of Pestrol.

Required: Evaluate Connecticut Chemical Company's analysis, and make any revisions that are necessary. Your critique and analysis should indicate:

a. Whether management made the correct decision.

b. The gross savings or loss per week resulting from the decision not to process RNA–2 further, if different from management's analysis.

(CMA, adapted)

Problem 14–52
Add a Product Line
(LO 4, 5)

1. Incremental contribution margin: $42,945

Manhattan Fashions, Inc., a high-fashion dress manufacturer, is planning to market a new cocktail dress for the coming season. Manhattan Fashions supplies retailers in the east and mid-Atlantic states.

Four yards of material are required to lay out the dress pattern. Some material remains after cutting, which can be sold as remnants. The leftover material also could be used to manufacture a matching cape and handbag. However, if the leftover material is to be used for the cape and handbag, more care will be required in the cutting operation, which will increase the cutting costs.

The company expects to sell 1,250 dresses. Market research reveals that dress sales will be 20 percent higher if a matching cape and handbag are available. The market research indicates that the cape and handbag will be salable only as accessories with the dress. The combination of dresses, capes, and handbags expected to be sold by retailers are as follows:

	Percent of Total
Complete sets of dress, cape, and handbag	70%
Dress and cape	6
Dress and handbag	15
Dress only	9
Total	100%

The material used in the dress costs $12.50 a yard, or $50.00 for each dress. The cost of cutting the dress if the cape and handbag are not manufactured is estimated at $20.00 a dress, and the resulting remnants can be sold for $5.00 per dress. If the cape and handbag are manufactured, the cutting costs will be increased by $9.00 per dress and there will be no salable remnants. The selling prices and the costs to complete the three items once they are cut are as follows:

	Selling Price per Unit	Unit Cost to Complete (excludes costs of material and cutting operation)
Dress	$200.00	$80.00
Cape	27.50	19.50
Handbag	9.50	6.50

Required:

1. Calculate Manhattan Fashions' incremental profit or loss from manufacturing the capes and handbags in conjunction with the dresses.
2. Identify any qualitative factors that could influence the company's management in its decision to manufacture capes and handbags to match the dresses.

(CMA, adapted)

Problem 14–53
Outsourcing Decision
(LO 4, 5)

1. Total variable cost per unit: $10.50
2. Quantity of component B81 to be purchased: 4,000 units

Upstate Mechanical, Inc. has been producing two bearings, components T79 and B81, for use in production. Data regarding these two components follow.

	T79	B81
Machine hours required per unit	2.5	3.0
Standard cost per unit:		
Direct material	$ 2.25	$ 3.75
Direct labor	4.00	4.50
Manufacturing overhead		
Variable*	2.00	2.25
Fixed†	3.75	4.50
Total	$12.00	$15.00

*Variable manufacturing overhead is applied on the basis of direct-labor hours.
†Fixed manufacturing overhead is applied on the basis of machine hours.

Upstate Mechanical's annual requirement for these components is 8,000 units of T79 and 11,000 units of B81. Recently, management decided to devote additional machine time to other product lines, leaving only 41,000 machine hours per year for producing the bearings. An outside company has offered to sell Upstate Mechanical its annual supply of bearings at prices of $11.25 for T79 and $13.50 for B81. Management wants to schedule the otherwise idle 41,000 machine hours to produce bearings so that the firm can minimize costs (maximize net benefits).

Required:

1. Compute the net benefit (loss) per machine hour that would result if Upstate Mechanical accepts the supplier's offer of $13.50 per unit for component B81.
2. Choose the correct answer. Upstate Mechanical will maximize its net benefits by:
   a. purchasing 4,800 units of T79 and manufacturing the remaining bearings.
   b. purchasing 8,000 units of T79 and manufacturing 11,000 units of B81.
   c. purchasing 11,000 units of B81 and manufacturing 8,000 units of T79.
   d. purchasing 4,000 units of B81 and manufacturing the remaining bearings.
   e. purchasing and manufacturing some amounts other than those given above.
3. Suppose management has decided to drop product T79. Independently of requirements (1) and (2), assume that the company's idle capacity of 41,000 machine hours has a traceable, avoidable annual fixed cost of $44,000, which will be incurred only if the capacity is used. Calculate the maximum price Upstate Mechanical should pay a supplier for component B81.

(CMA, adapted)

Problem 14–54
Outsource a Component; Relevant Costs, Opportunity Costs, and Quality Control
(LO 3, 4, 5)

2. Increase in monthly cost: $23,000

Chenango Industries uses 10 units of part JR63 each month in the production of radar equipment. The cost of manufacturing one unit of JR63 is the following:

Direct material	$ 1,000
Material handling (20% of direct-material cost)	200
Direct labor	8,000
Manufacturing overhead (150% of direct labor)	12,000
Total manufacturing cost	$21,200

Material handling represents the direct variable costs of the Receiving Department that are applied to direct materials and purchased components on the basis of their cost. This is a separate charge in addition to manufacturing overhead. Chenango Industries' annual manufacturing overhead budget is one-third variable and two-thirds fixed. Scott Supply, one of Chenango Industries' reliable vendors, has offered to supply part number JR63 at a unit price of $15,000.

Required:

1. If Chenango Industries purchases the JR63 units from Scott, the capacity Chenango Industries used to manufacture these parts would be idle. Should Chenango Industries decide to purchase the parts from Scott, the unit cost of JR63 would increase (or decrease) by what amount?
2. Assume Chenango Industries is able to rent out all its idle capacity for $25,000 per month. If Chenango Industries decides to purchase the 10 units from Scott Supply, Chenango's monthly cost for JR63 would increase (or decrease) by what amount?
3. Assume that Chenango Industries does not wish to commit to a rental agreement but could use its idle capacity to manufacture another product that would contribute $52,000 per month. If Chenango's management elects to manufacture JR63 in order to maintain quality control, what is the net amount of Chenango's cost from using the space to manufacture part JR63?

(CMA, adapted)

Problem 14–55
Analysis of Special Order
(LO 4, 5)

2. Contribution from sale to Kaytell: $53,848

Miami Industries received an order for a piece of special machinery from Jay Company. Just as Miami completed the machine, Jay Company declared bankruptcy, defaulted on the order, and forfeited the 10 percent deposit paid on the selling price of $72,500.

Miami's manufacturing manager identified the costs already incurred in the production of the special machinery for Jay Company as follows:

Direct material		$16,600
Direct labor		21,400
Manufacturing overhead applied:		
Variable	$10,700	
Fixed	5,350	16,050
Fixed selling and administrative costs		5,405
Total		$59,455

Another company, Kaytell Corporation, will buy the special machinery if it is reworked to Kaytell's specifications. Miami Industries offered to sell the reworked machinery to Kaytell as a special order for $68,400. Kaytell agreed to pay the price when it takes delivery in two months. The additional identifiable costs to rework the machinery to Kaytell's specifications are as follows:

Direct material	$ 6,200
Direct labor	4,200
Total	$10,400

A second alternative available to Miami's management is to convert the special machinery to the standard model, which sells for $62,500. The additional identifiable costs for this conversion are as follows:

Direct material	$2,850
Direct labor	3,300
Total	$6,150

A third alternative for Miami Industries is to sell the machine as is for a price of $52,000. However, the potential buyer of the unmodified machine does not want it for 60 days. This buyer has offered a $7,000 down payment, with the remainder due upon delivery.

The following additional information is available regarding Miami's operations.

- The sales commission rate on sales of standard models is 2 percent, while the rate on special orders is 3 percent.
- Normal credit terms for sales of standard models are 2/10, net/30. This means that a customer receives a 2 percent discount if payment is made within 10 days, and payment is due no later than 30 days after billing. Most customers take the 2 percent discount. Credit terms for a special order are negotiated with the customer.

- The allocation rates for manufacturing overhead and fixed selling and administrative costs are as follows:

Manufacturing costs:	
Variable	50% of direct-labor cost
Fixed	25% of direct-labor cost
Fixed selling and administrative costs	10% of the total of direct-material, direct-labor, and manufacturing-overhead costs

- Normal time required for rework is one month.

Required:

1. Determine the dollar contribution each of the three alternatives will add to Miami Industries' before-tax profit.
2. If Kaytell makes Miami Industries a counteroffer, what is the lowest price Miami should accept for the reworked machinery from Kaytell? Explain your answer.
3. Discuss the influence fixed manufacturing-overhead cost should have on the sales price quoted by Miami Industries for special orders.

(CMA, adapted)

Problem 14–56
Special Order; Ethics
(LO 3, 4, 5)

2. Accepting the special order will result in a total additional contribution margin of $37,500

Winner's Circle, Inc. manufactures medals for winners of athletic events and other contests. Its manufacturing plant has the capacity to produce 10,000 medals each month. Current monthly production is 7,500 medals. The company normally charges $175 per medal. Variable costs and fixed costs for the current activity level of 75 percent of capacity are as follows:

Production Costs

Variable costs:	
Manufacturing:	
Direct labor	$ 375,000
Direct material	262,500
Marketing	187,500
Total variable costs	$ 825,000
Fixed costs:	
Manufacturing	$ 275,000
Marketing	175,000
Total fixed costs	$ 450,000
Total costs	$1,275,000
Variable cost per unit	$110
Fixed cost per unit	60
Average unit cost	$170

Winner's Circle has just received a special one-time order for 2,500 medals at $100 per medal. For this particular order, no variable marketing costs will be incurred. Cathy Donato, a management accountant with Winner's Circle, has been assigned the task of analyzing this order and recommending whether the company should accept or reject it. After examining the costs, Donato suggested to her supervisor, Gerard LePenn, who is the controller, that they request competitive bids from vendors for the raw material as the current quote seems high. LePenn insisted that the prices are in line with other vendors and told her that she was not to discuss her observations with anyone else. Donato later discovered that LePenn is a brother-in-law of the owner of the current raw-material supply vendor.

Required:

1. Identify and explain the costs that will be relevant to Cathy Donato's analysis of the special order being considered by Winner's Circle, Inc.
2. Determine if Winner's Circle should accept the special order. In explaining your answer, compute both the new average unit cost and the incremental unit cost for the special order.
3. Discuss any other considerations that Donato should include in her analysis of the special order.

4. What steps could Donato take to resolve the ethical conflict arising out of the controller's insistence that the company avoid competitive bidding?

5. *Build a spreadsheet:* Construct an Excel spreadsheet to solve requirement (2). Show how the solution will change if the sales price is $170 per medal.

(CMA, adapted)

Problem 14–57
Production Planning
(LO 5, 6)

2. Contribution margin, product M07: $93
2. Total contribution margin: $113,250

Ozark Industries manufactures and sells three products, which are manufactured in a factory with four departments. Both labor and machine time are applied to the products as they pass through each department. The machines and labor skills required in each department are so specialized that neither machines nor labor can be switched from one department to another.

Ozark Industries' management is planning its production schedule for the next few months. The planning is complicated, because there are labor shortages in the community and some machines will be down several months for repairs.

Management has assembled the following information regarding available machine and labor time by department and the machine hours and direct-labor hours required per unit of product. These data should be valid for the next six months.

		Department			
Monthly Capacity Availability		**1**	**2**	**3**	**4**
Normal machine capacity in machine hours		3,500	3,500	3,000	3,500
Capacity of machines being repaired in machine hours		(500)	(400)	(300)	(200)
Available machine capacity in machine hours		3,000	3,100	2,700	3,300
Available labor in direct-labor hours		3,700	4,500	2,750	2,600
Labor and Machine Specifications per Unit of Product					
Product	**Labor and Machine Time**				
M07	Direct-labor hours	2	3	3	1
	Machine hours	1	1	2	2
T28	Direct-labor hours	1	2	—	2
	Machine hours	1	1	—	2
B19	Direct-labor hours	2	2	2	1
	Machine hours	2	2	1	1

The sales department believes that the monthly demand for the next six months will be as follows:

Product	Monthly Unit Sales
M07	500
T28	400
B19	1,000

Inventory levels are satisfactory and need not be increased or decreased during the next six months. Unit price and cost data that will be valid for the next six months are as follows:

	Product		
	M07	**T28**	**B19**
Unit costs:			
Direct material	$ 7	$ 13	$ 17
Direct labor:			
Department 1	12	6	12
Department 2	21	14	14
Department 3	24	—	16
Department 4	9	18	9
Variable overhead	27	20	25
Fixed overhead	15	10	32
Variable selling expenses	3	2	4
Unit selling price	196	123	167

Required:

1. Calculate the monthly requirement for machine hours and direct-labor hours for the production of products M07, T28, and B19 to determine whether the monthly sales demand for the three products can be met by the factory.
2. What monthly production schedule should Ozark Industries select in order to maximize its dollar profits? Explain how you selected this production schedule, and present a schedule of the contribution to profit that would be generated by your production schedule.
3. Identify the alternatives Ozark Industries might consider so it can supply its customers with all the product they demand.

(CMA, adapted)

Problem 14–58
Conventional versus Activity-Based-Costing Analyses; Relevant Costs
(LO 5, 7)

2. Costs to be avoided by purchasing (ABC analysis), total: $810,750

In addition to fine chocolate, International Chocolate Company also produces chocolate-covered pretzels in its Savannah plant. This product is sold in five-pound metal canisters, which also are manufactured at the Savannah facility. The plant manager, Marsha Mello, was recently approached by Catawba Canister Company with an offer to supply the canisters at a price of $1.00 each. International Chocolate's traditional product-costing system assigns the following costs to canister production.

Direct material	$ 300,000
Direct labor (12,000 hrs. at $15 per hr.)	180,000
Variable overhead ($10 per direct-labor hr.)	120,000
Fixed overhead ($45 per direct-labor hr.)	540,000
Total cost	$1,140,000

Unit costs: $1,140,000 ÷ 760,000 canisters = $1.50 per canister

Mello's conventional make-or-buy analysis indicated that Catawba's offer should be rejected, since only $708,000 of costs would be avoided (including $80,000 of supervisory salaries and $28,000 of machinery depreciation). In contrast, the firm would spend $760,000 buying the canisters. The controller, Dave Mint, came to the rescue with an activity-based costing analysis of the decision. Mint concluded that the cost driver levels associated with canister production are as follows:

10 product specs	30 inspections
2,000 supervisory hours	15 setups
6,000 material-handling hours	70,000 machine hours
55 purchase orders	

Additional conventional and ABC data from the Savannah plant are given in Exhibits 14–19 and 14–20.

Required:

1. Show how Mello arrived at the $708,000 of cost savings in her conventional make-or-buy analysis.
2. Determine the costs that will be saved by purchasing canisters, using Mint's ABC data.
3. Complete the ABC relevant-costing analysis of the make-or-buy decision. Should the firm buy from Catawba?
4. If the conventional and ABC analyses yield different conclusions, briefly explain why.

Problem 14–59
Linear Programming; Formulate and Solve Graphically (Appendix)
(LO 8)

3. Total contribution margin: $55,000

Deru Chocolate Company manufactures two popular candy bars, the Venus bar and the Comet bar. Both candy bars go through a mixing operation where the various ingredients are combined, and the Coating Department where the bars from the Mixing Department are coated with chocolate. The Venus bar is coated with both white and dark chocolate to produce a swirled effect. A material shortage of an ingredient in the Comet bar limits production to 300 batches per day. Production and sales data are presented in the following table. Both candy bars are produced in batches of 200 bars.

		Use of Capacity in Hours per Batch of Product	
Department	**Available Daily Capacity in Hours**	**Venus**	**Comet**
Mixing	525	1.5	1.5
Coating	500	2.0	1.0

Management believes that Deru Chocolate can sell all of its daily production of both the Venus and Comet bars. Other data follow.

	Venus	Comet
Selling price per batch	$ 300	$ 350
Variable cost per batch	100	225
Monthly fixed costs (allocated evenly between both products)	375,000	375,000

Required:

1. Formulate the objective function and all of the constraints in order to maximize contribution margin. Be sure to define the variables.
2. How many batches of each type of candy bar (Venus and Comet) should be produced to maximize the total contribution margin?
3. Calculate the contribution margin at the optimal solution.

(CMA, adapted)

Problem 14–60
Linear Programming (Appendix)
(LO 8)

4. Contribution margin at the optimal solution: $4,500

Meals for Professionals, Inc. offers monthly service plans providing prepared meals that are delivered to the customers' homes. The target market for these meal plans includes double-income families with no children and retired couples in upper income brackets. The firm offers two monthly plans: Premier Cuisine and Haute Cuisine. The Premier Cuisine plan provides frozen meals that are delivered twice each month; this plan generates a contribution margin of $120 for each monthly plan sold. The Haute Cuisine plan provides freshly prepared meals delivered on a daily basis and generates a contribution margin of $90 for each monthly plan sold. The company's reputation provides a market that will purchase all the meals that can be prepared. All meals go through food preparation and cooking steps in the company's kitchens. After these steps, the Premier Cuisine meals are flash frozen. The time requirements per monthly meal plan and hours available per month are as follows:

	Preparation	Cooking	Freezing
Hours required:			
Premier Cuisine	2	2	1
Haute Cuisine	1	3	0
Hours available	60	120	45

For planning purposes, Meals for Professionals, Inc. uses linear programming to determine the most profitable number of Premier Cuisine and Haute Cuisine monthly meal plans to produce.

Required:

1. Using the notation P for Premier Cuisine and H for Haute Cuisine, state the objective function and the constraints that management should use to maximize the total contribution margin generated by the monthly meal plans.
2. Graph the constraints on the meal preparation process. Be sure to clearly label the graph.
3. Using the graph prepared in requirement (2), determine the optimal solution to the company's production planning problem in terms of the number of each type of meal plan to produce.
4. Calculate the value of the objective function at the optimal solution.
5. If the constraint on preparation time could be eliminated, determine the revised optimal solution.

(CMA, adapted)

Problem 14–61
Linear Programming; Formulate and Discuss (Appendix)
(LO 8)

2(a). Contribution margin, R_L: $10.30

Colonial Corporation manufactures two types of electric coffeemakers, Regular and Deluxe. The major difference between the two appliances is capacity. Both are considered top-quality units and sell for premium prices. Both coffeemakers pass through two manufacturing departments: Plating and Assembly. Colonial has two assembly operations, one automated and one manual. The Automated Assembly Department has been in operation for one year and was intended to replace the Labor Assembly Department. However, Colonial's business has expanded rapidly in recent months,

and both assembly operations are still being used. Workers have been trained for both operations and can be used in either department. The only difference between the two departments is the proportion of machine time versus direct labor used. Data regarding the two coffeemakers are presented in the following schedule.

Sales Data

	Regular Model	Deluxe Model
Selling price per unit	$ 45.00	$ 60.00
Variable selling cost per unit	3.00	3.00
Annual allocated fixed overhead	900,000	900,000

Unit Variable Manufacturing Costs

	Plating Department		Labor	Automated
	Regular	Deluxe	Assembly	Assembly
Raw material:				
Casing	$7.75	$14.50	—	—
Heating element	6.00	6.00	—	—
Other	8.25	8.25	—	—
Direct labor:				
At $10 per hour	2.00	2.00	—	—
At $12 per hour	—	—	$3.00	$ .60
Manufacturing overhead:				
Supplies	1.25	1.25	1.50	1.50
Power	1.20	1.20	.75	1.80

Machine Hour Data

	Plating	Labor Assembly	Automated Assembly
Machine hours required per unit	.15	.02	.05
Machine hours available per month	25,000	1,500	5,000
Annual machine hours available	300,000	18,000	60,000

Colonial produced and sold 600,000 Deluxe coffeemakers and 900,000 Regular coffemakers last year. Management estimates that total unit sales could increase by 20 percent or more if the units can be produced. Colonial already has contracts to produce and sell 35,000 units of each model each month. Colonial has a monthly maximum labor capacity of 30,000 direct-labor hours in the Plating Department and 40,000 direct-labor hours for the assembly operation (Automated Assembly and Labor Assembly, combined). Sales, production, and costs occur uniformly throughout the year.

Required:

1. Colonial Corporation's management believes that linear programming could be used to determine the optimum mix of Regular and Deluxe coffeemakers to produce and sell. Explain why linear programming is appropriate to use in this situation.
2. Management has decided to use linear programming to determine the optimal product mix. Formulate and label the following:
   a. Objective function
   b. Constraints

   Be sure to define your variables.

(CMA, adapted)

Cases

Case 14–62
Adding a Product Line
(LO 4, 5)

1. Contribution per hour, tackle boxes: $26.40
2. Improvement in contribution margin: $236,250

Bo Vonderweidt, the production manager for Sportway Corporation, had requested to have lunch with the company president. Vonderweidt wanted to put forward his suggestion to add a new product line. As they finished lunch, Meg Thomas, the company president, said, "I'll give your proposal some serious thought, Bo. I think you're right about the increasing demand for skateboards. What I'm not sure about is whether the skateboard line will be better for us than our tackle boxes. Those have been our bread and butter the past few years."

Vonderweidt responded with, "Let me get together with one of the controller's people. We'll run a few numbers on this skateboard idea that I think will demonstrate the line's potential."

Sportway is a wholesale distributor supplying a wide range of moderately priced sports equipment to large chain stores. About 60 percent of Sportway's products are purchased from other companies while the remainder of the products are manufactured by Sportway. The company has a Plastics Department that is currently manufacturing molded fishing tackle boxes. Sportway is able to manufacture and sell 8,000 tackle boxes annually, making full use of its direct-labor capacity at available work stations. The selling price and costs associated with Sportway's tackle boxes are as follows:

Selling price per box		$86.00
Costs per box:		
Molded plastic	$ 8.00	
Hinges, latches, handle	9.00	
Direct labor ($15.00 per hour)	18.75	
Manufacturing overhead	12.50	
Selling and administrative cost	17.00	65.25
Profit per box		$20.75

Because Sportway's sales manager believes the firm could sell 12,000 tackle boxes if it had sufficient manufacturing capacity, the company has looked into the possibility of purchasing the tackle boxes for distribution. Maple Products, a steady supplier of quality products, would be able to provide up to 9,000 tackle boxes per year at a price of $68.00 per box delivered to Sportway's facility.

Bo Vonderweidt, Sportway's production manager, has come to the conclusion that the company could make better use of its Plastics Department by manufacturing skateboards. Vonderweidt has a market study that indicates an expanding market for skateboards and a need for additional suppliers. Vonderweidt believes that Sportway could expect to sell 17,500 skateboards annually at a price of $45.00 per skateboard.

After his lunch with the company president, Vonderweidt worked out the following estimates with the assistant controller.

Selling price per skateboard		$45.00
Costs per skateboard:		
Molded plastic	$5.50	
Wheels, hardware	7.00	
Direct labor ($15.00 per hour)	7.50	
Manufacturing overhead	5.00	
Selling and administrative cost	9.00	34.00
Profit per skateboard		$11.00

In the Plastics Department, Sportway uses direct-labor hours as the application base for manufacturing overhead. Included in the manufacturing overhead for the current year is $50,000 of factorywide, fixed manufacturing overhead that has been allocated to the Plastics Department. For each unit of product that Sportway sells, regardless of whether the product has been purchased or is manufactured by Sportway, there is an allocated $6.00 fixed overhead cost per unit for distribution that is included in the selling and administrative cost for all products. Total selling and administrative costs for the purchased tackle boxes would be $10.00 per unit.

Required: In order to maximize the company's profitability, prepare an analysis that will show which product or products Sportway Corporation should manufacture or purchase.

1. First determine which of Sportway's options makes the best use of its scarce resources. How many skateboards and tackle boxes should be manufactured? How many tackle boxes should be purchased?
2. Calculate the improvement in Sportway's total contribution margin if it adopts the optimal strategy rather than continuing with the status quo.

(CMA, adapted)

Case 14–63
Drop a Product Line
(LO 4, 5)

Unit contribution, E-gauge: $19.00

Alberta Gauge Company, Ltd., a small manufacturing company in Calgary, Alberta, manufactures three types of electrical gauges used in a variety of machinery. For many years the company has been profitable and has operated at capacity. However, in the last two years, prices on all gauges were reduced and selling expenses increased to meet competition and keep the plant operating at capacity. Second-quarter results for the current year, which follow, typify recent experience.

ALBERTA GAUGE COMPANY, LTD.
Income Statement
Second Quarter
(in thousands)

	Q-Gauge	E-Gauge	R-Gauge	Total
Sales	$1,600	$900	$ 900	$3,400
Cost of goods sold	1,048	770	950	2,768
Gross margin	$ 552	$130	$ (50)	$ 632
Selling and administrative expenses	370	185	135	690
Income before taxes	$ 182	$ (55)	$(185)	$ (58)

Alice Carlo, the company's president, is concerned about the results of the pricing, selling, and production prices. After reviewing the second-quarter results, she asked her management staff to consider the following three suggestions:

- Discontinue the R-gauge line immediately. R-gauges would not be returned to the product line unless the problems with the gauge can be identified and resolved.
- Increase quarterly sales promotion by $100,000 on the Q-gauge product line in order to increase sales volume by 15 percent.
- Cut production on the E-gauge line by 50 percent, and cut the traceable advertising and promotion for this line to $20,000 each quarter.

Jason Sperry, the controller, suggested a more careful study of the financial relationships to determine the possible effects on the company's operating results of the president's proposed course of action. The president agreed and assigned JoAnn Brower, the assistant controller, to prepare an analysis. Brower has gathered the following information.

- All three gauges are manufactured with common equipment and facilities.
- The selling and administrative expense is allocated to the three gauge lines based on average sales volume over the past three years.
- Special selling expenses (primarily advertising, promotion, and shipping) are incurred for each gauge as follows:

	Quarterly Advertising and Promotion	Shipping Expenses
Q-gauge	$210,000	$10 per unit
E-gauge	100,000	4 per unit
R-gauge	40,000	10 per unit

- The unit manufacturing costs for the three products are as follows:

	Q-Gauge	E-Gauge	R-Gauge
Direct material	$ 31	$17	$ 50
Direct labor	40	20	60
Variable manufacturing overhead	45	30	60
Fixed manufacturing overhead	15	10	20
Total	$131	$77	$190

- The unit sales prices for the three products are as follows:

Q-gauge	$200
E-gauge	90
R-gauge	180

- The company is manufacturing at capacity and is selling all the gauges it produces.

Required:

1. JoAnn Brower says that Alberta Gauge Company's product-line income statement for the second quarter is not suitable for analyzing proposals and making decisions such as the ones suggested by Alice Carlo. Write a memo to Alberta Gauge's president that addresses the following points.
   a. Explain why the product-line income statement as presented is not suitable for analysis and decision making.
   b. Describe an alternative income-statement format that would be more suitable for analysis and decision making, and explain why it is better.
2. Use the operating data presented for Alberta Gauge Company and assume that the president's proposed course of action had been implemented at the beginning of the second quarter. Then evaluate the president's proposal by specifically responding to the following points.
   a. Are each of the three suggestions cost-effective? Support your discussion with an analysis that shows the net impact on income before taxes for each of the three suggestions.
   b. Was the president correct in proposing that the R-gauge line be eliminated? Explain your answer.
   c. Was the president correct in promoting the Q-gauge line rather than the E-gauge line? Explain your answer.
   d. Does the proposed course of action make effective use of the company's capacity? Explain your answer.
3. Are there any qualitative factors that Alberta Gauge Company's management should consider before it drops the R-gauge line? Explain your answer.

(CMA, adapted)

CONTENTS

Garrison: *Managerial Accounting,* 14/e
ISBN: 0-07-811100-5

Standard Costs and Variances 454

Chapter 12

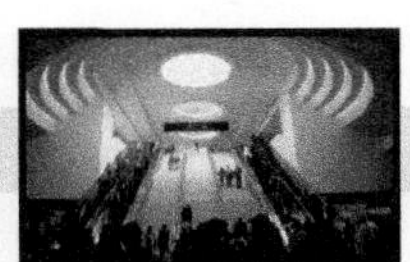

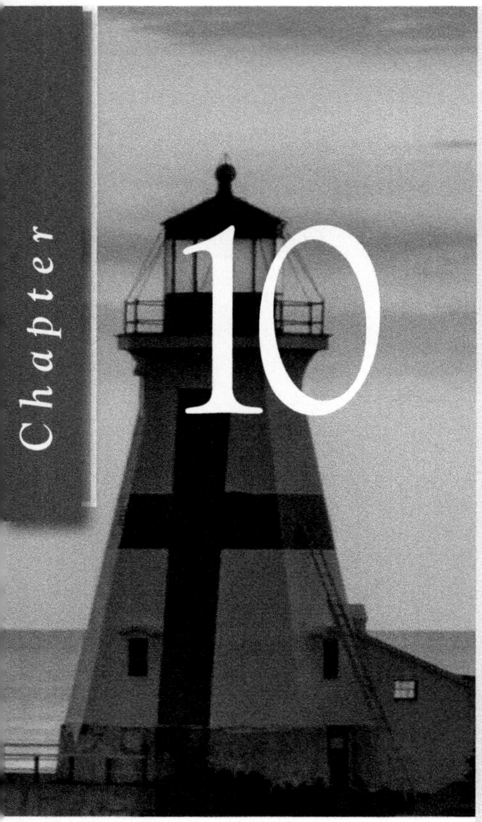

Chapter 10

Standard Costs and Variances

Managing Materials and Labor

BUSINESS FOCUS

Schneider Electric's Oxford, Ohio, plant manufactures *busways* that transport electricity from its point of entry into a building to remote locations throughout the building. The plant's managers pay close attention to direct material costs because they are more than half of the plant's total manufacturing costs. To help control scrap rates for direct materials such as copper, steel, and aluminum, the accounting department prepares direct materials quantity variances. These variances compare the standard quantity of direct materials that should have been used to make a product (according to computations by the plant's engineers) to the amount of direct materials that were actually used. Keeping a close eye on these differences helps to identify and deal with the causes of excessive scrap, such as an inadequately trained machine operator, poor quality raw material inputs, or a malfunctioning machine.

Because direct labor is also a significant component of the plant's total manufacturing costs, the management team daily monitors the direct labor efficiency variance. This variance compares the standard amount of labor time allowed to make a product to the actual amount of labor time used. When idle workers cause an unfavorable labor efficiency variance, managers temporarily move workers from departments with slack to departments with a backlog of work to be done. ■

Source: Author's conversation with Doug Taylor, plant controller, Schneider Electric's Oxford, Ohio, plant.

LEARNING OBJECTIVES

After studying Chapter 10, you should be able to:

LO1 Compute the direct materials quantity and price variances and explain their significance.

LO2 Compute the direct labor efficiency and rate variances and explain their significance.

LO3 Compute the variable manufacturing overhead efficiency and rate variances and explain their significance.

LO4 (Appendix 10A) Compute and interpret the fixed overhead volume and budget variances.

LO5 (Appendix 10B) Prepare journal entries to record standard costs and variances.

In the last chapter, we investigated flexible budget variances. These variances provide feedback concerning how well an organization performed in relation to its budget. The impact on profit of a change in the level of activity is captured in the overall net operating income activity variance. The revenue and spending variances indicate how well revenues and costs were controlled—given the actual level of activity. In the case of many of the spending variances, we can get even more detail about how well costs were controlled. For example, at Rick's Hairstyling, an unfavorable spending variance for hairstyling supplies could be due to using too many supplies or to paying too much for the supplies, or some combination of the two. It would be useful to separate those two different effects, particularly if different people are responsible for using the supplies and for purchasing them. In this chapter, we will learn how that can be done for some costs; basically, we will decompose spending variances into two parts—a part that measures how well resources were used and a part that measures how well the acquisition prices of those resources were controlled.

Companies in highly competitive industries like Federal Express, Southwest Airlines, Dell, and Toyota must be able to provide high-quality goods and services at low cost. If they do not, their customers will buy from more efficient competitors. Stated in the starkest terms, managers must obtain inputs such as raw materials and electricity at the lowest possible prices and must use them as effectively as possible—while maintaining or increasing the quality of what they sell. If inputs are purchased at prices that are too high or more input is used than is really necessary, higher costs will result.

How do managers control the prices that are paid for inputs and the quantities that are used? They could examine every transaction in detail, but this obviously would be an inefficient use of management time. For many companies, the answer to this control problem lies at least partially in standard costs.

Standard Costs—Setting the Stage

A *standard* is a benchmark or "norm" for measuring performance. Standards are found everywhere. Your doctor evaluates your weight using standards for individuals of your age, height, and gender. The food we eat in restaurants is prepared using standardized recipes. The buildings we live in conform to standards set in building codes. Standards are also widely used in managerial accounting where they relate to the *quantity* and *cost* (or acquisition price) of inputs used in manufacturing goods or providing services.

Quantity and price standards are set for each major input such as raw materials and labor time. *Quantity standards* specify how much of an input should be used to make a product or provide a service. *Price standards* specify how much should be paid for each unit of the input. Actual quantities and actual costs of inputs are compared to these standards. If either the quantity or the cost of inputs departs significantly from the standards, managers investigate the discrepancy to find the cause of the problem and eliminate it. This process is called **management by exception.**

In our daily lives, we often operate in a management by exception mode. Consider what happens when you sit down in the driver's seat of your car. You put the key in the ignition, you turn the key, and your car starts. Your expectation (standard) that the car will start is met; you do not have to open the car hood and check the battery, the connecting cables, the fuel lines, and so on. If you turn the key and the car does not start, then you have a discrepancy (variance). Your expectations are not met, and you need to investigate why. Note that even if the car starts after a second try, it still would be wise to investigate. The fact that the expectation was not met should be viewed as an opportunity to uncover the cause of the problem rather than as simply an annoyance. If the underlying cause is not discovered and corrected, the problem may recur and become much worse.

This basic approach to identifying and solving problems is the essence of the *variance analysis cycle,* which is illustrated in Exhibit 10–1. The cycle begins with the preparation of standard cost performance reports in the accounting department. These reports

EXHIBIT 10–1
The Variance Analysis Cycle

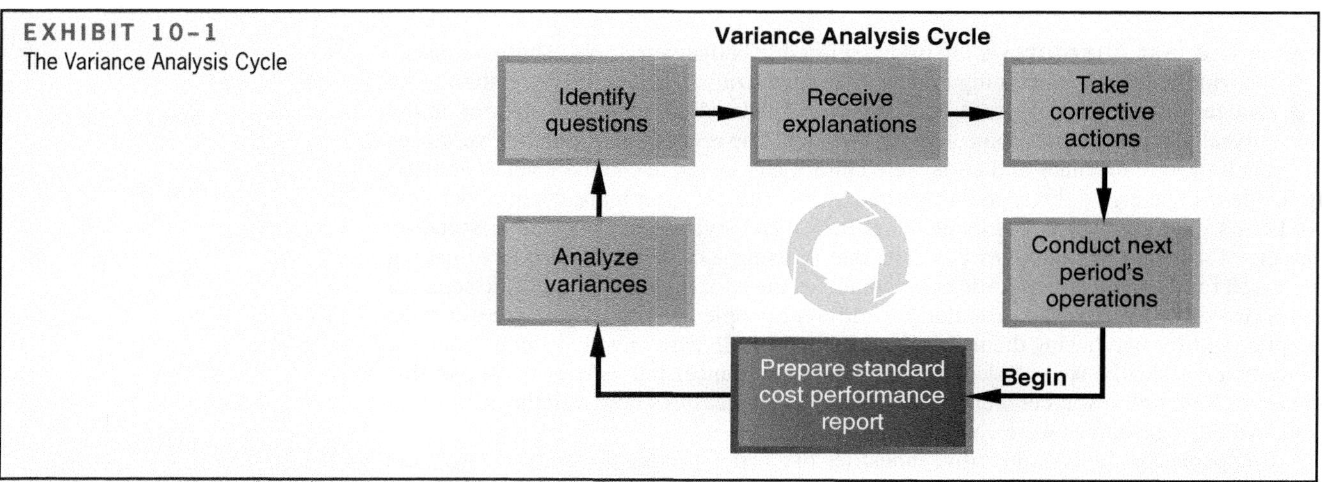

highlight the *variances,* which are the differences between actual results and what should have occurred according to the standards. The variances raise questions. Why did this variance occur? Why is this variance larger than it was last period? The significant variances are investigated to discover their root causes. Corrective actions are taken. And then next period's operations are carried out. The cycle begins again with the preparation of a new standard cost performance report for the latest period. The emphasis should be on highlighting problems, finding their root causes, and then taking corrective action. The goal is to improve operations—not to assign blame.

Who Uses Standard Costs?

Manufacturing, service, food, and not-for-profit organizations all make use of standards to some extent. Auto service centers like Firestone and Sears, for example, often set specific labor time standards for the completion of certain tasks, such as installing a carburetor or doing a valve job, and then measure actual performance against these standards. Fast-food outlets such as McDonald's have exacting standards for the quantity of meat going into a sandwich, as well as standards for the cost of the meat. Hospitals have standard costs for food, laundry, and other items, as well as standard time allowances for certain routine activities, such as laboratory tests. In short, you are likely to run into standard costs in virtually any line of business.

Manufacturing companies often have highly developed standard costing systems in which standards for direct materials, direct labor, and overhead are created for each product. A **standard cost card** shows the standard quantities and costs of the inputs required to produce a unit of a specific product. In the following section, we provide an example of a standard cost card.

Setting Standard Costs

Standards should be designed to encourage efficient *future* operations, not just a repetition of *past* operations that may or may not have been efficient. Standards tend to fall into one of two categories—either ideal or practical.

Ideal standards can be attained only under the best circumstances. They allow for no machine breakdowns or other work interruptions, and they call for a level of effort that can be attained only by the most skilled and efficient employees working at peak effort 100% of the time. Some managers feel that such standards spur continual improvement. These managers argue that even though employees know they will rarely meet the standard, it is a constant reminder of the need for ever-increasing efficiency and effort. Few organizations use ideal standards. Most managers feel that ideal standards tend to discourage even the most diligent workers. Moreover, variances from ideal standards are difficult to interpret. Large variances from the ideal are normal and it is therefore difficult to "manage by exception."

Practical standards are standards that are "tight but attainable." They allow for normal machine downtime and employee rest periods, and they can be attained through reasonable, though highly efficient, efforts by the average worker. Variances from practical standards typically signal a need for management attention because they represent deviations that fall outside of normal operating conditions. Furthermore, practical standards can serve multiple purposes. In addition to signaling abnormal conditions, they can also be used in forecasting cash flows and in planning inventory. By contrast, ideal standards cannot be used for these purposes because they do not allow for normal inefficiencies and result in unrealistic forecasts.

Throughout the remainder of this chapter, we will assume that practical rather than ideal standards are in use.

MANAGERIAL ACCOUNTING IN ACTION
The Issue

Colonial Pewter Company

The Colonial Pewter Company was organized a year ago. The company's only product is an elaborate reproduction of an eighteenth century pewter bookend. The bookend is made largely by hand, using traditional metalworking tools. Consequently, the manufacturing process is labor intensive and requires a high level of skill.

Colonial Pewter has recently expanded its workforce to take advantage of unexpected demand for the bookends as gifts. The company started with a small cadre of experienced pewter workers but has had to hire less experienced workers as a result of the expansion. The president of the company, J. D. Wriston, has called a meeting to discuss production problems. Attending the meeting are Tom Kuchel, the production manager; Janet Warner, the purchasing manager; and Terry Sherman, the corporate controller.

J. D.: I've got a feeling that we aren't getting the production we should out of our new people.

Tom: Give us a chance. Some of the new people have been with the company for less than a month.

Janet: Let me add that production seems to be wasting an awful lot of material—particularly pewter. That stuff is very expensive.

Tom: What about the shipment of defective pewter that you bought—the one with the iron contamination? That caused us major problems.

Janet: How was I to know it was off-grade? Besides, it was a great deal.

J. D.: Calm down everybody. Let's get the facts before we start attacking each other.

Tom: I agree. The more facts the better.

J. D.: Okay, Terry, it's your turn. Facts are the controller's department.

Terry: I'm afraid I can't provide the answers off the top of my head, but if you give me about a week I can set up a system that can routinely answer questions relating to worker productivity, material waste, and input prices.

J. D.: Let's mark it on our calendars.

Setting Direct Materials Standards

Terry Sherman's first task was to prepare price and quantity standards for the company's only significant raw material, pewter ingots. The **standard price per unit** for direct materials should reflect the final, delivered cost of the materials. After consulting with purchasing manager Janet Warner, Terry set the standard price of pewter at $4.00 per pound.

The **standard quantity per unit** for direct materials should reflect the amount of material required for each unit of finished product as well as an allowance for unavoidable waste.[1] After consulting with the production manager, Tom Kuchel, Terry set the quantity standard for pewter at 3.0 pounds per pair of bookends.

---

[1] Although allowances for waste, spoilage, and rejects are often built into standards, this practice is often criticized because it contradicts the zero defects goal that underlies many process improvement programs. If allowances for waste, spoilage, and rejects are built into the standard cost, those allowances should be periodically reviewed and reduced over time to reflect improved processes, better training, and better equipment.

IN BUSINESS

SKYROCKETING TRANSPORTATION COSTS AFFECT DIRECT MATERIALS STANDARDS

Direct materials price standards should reflect the final delivered cost of the materials. Given increases in the costs of shipping raw materials across oceans, many companies have increased their price standards. For example, the average cost to rent a ship to transport raw materials from Brazil to China has increased from $65,000 to $180,000. In some instances, shipping costs now exceed the cost of the cargo itself. It costs about $88 to ship a ton of iron ore from Brazil to Asia; however, the iron ore itself only costs $60 per ton.

Source: Robert Guy Matthews, "Ship Shortage Pushes Up Prices of Raw Materials," *The Wall Street Journal*, October 22, 2007, pp. A1 and A12.

Once Terry established the price and quantity standards he computed the standard cost of material per unit of the finished product as follows:

3.0 pounds per unit × $4.00 per pound = $12.00 per unit

This $12.00 cost will appear on the product's standard cost card.

Setting Direct Labor Standards

Direct labor price and quantity standards are usually expressed in terms of a labor rate and labor-hours. The **standard rate per hour** for direct labor should include hourly wages, employment taxes, and fringe benefits. Using wage records and in consultation with the production manager, Terry Sherman determined the standard rate per direct labor-hour to be $22.00.

Many companies prepare a single standard rate per hour for all employees in a department. This standard rate reflects the expected "mix" of workers, even though the actual wage rates may vary somewhat from individual to individual due to differing skills or seniority.

The standard direct labor time required to complete a unit of product (called the **standard hours per unit**) is perhaps the single most difficult standard to determine. One approach is to break down each task into elemental body movements (such as reaching, pushing, and turning over). Published tables of standard times for such movements can be used to estimate the total time required to complete the task. Another approach is for an industrial engineer to do a time and motion study, actually clocking the time required for each task. As stated earlier, the standard time should include allowances for breaks, personal needs of employees, cleanup, and machine downtime.

After consulting with the production manager, Terry set the standard for direct labor time at 0.50 direct labor-hours per pair of bookends.

Once Terry established the rate and time standards, he computed the standard direct labor cost per unit of product as follows:

0.50 direct labor-hours per unit × $22.00 per direct labor-hour = $11.00 per unit

This $11.00 per unit standard direct labor cost appears along with direct materials on the standard cost card for a pair of pewter bookends.

Setting Variable Manufacturing Overhead Standards

As with direct labor, the price and quantity standards for variable manufacturing overhead are usually expressed in terms of rate and hours. The rate represents *the variable portion of the predetermined overhead rate* discussed in the job-order costing

EXHIBIT 10–2
Standard Cost Card—Variable Manufacturing Costs

Inputs	(1) Standard Quantity or Hours	(2) Standard Price or Rate	Standard Cost (1) × (2)
Direct materials	3.0 pounds	$4.00 per pound	$12.00
Direct labor	0.50 hours	$22.00 per hour	11.00
Variable manufacturing overhead	0.50 hours	$6.00 per hour	3.00
Total standard cost per unit			$26.00

chapter; the hours relate to the activity base that is used to apply overhead to units of product (usually machine-hours or direct labor-hours). At Colonial Pewter, the variable portion of the predetermined overhead rate is $6.00 per direct labor-hour. Therefore, Terry computed the standard variable manufacturing overhead cost per unit as follows:

0.50 direct labor-hours per unit × $6.00 per direct labor-hour = $3.00 per unit

This $3.00 per unit cost for variable manufacturing overhead appears along with direct materials and direct labor on the standard cost card in Exhibit 10–2. Observe that the **standard cost per unit** for variable manufacturing overhead is computed the same way as for direct materials or direct labor—the standard quantity allowed per unit of the output is multiplied by the standard price. In this case, the standard quantity is expressed as 0.5 direct labor-hours per unit and the standard price (or rate) is expressed as $6.00 per direct labor-hour.

Using Standards in Flexible Budgets

The standard costs of $12.00 per unit for materials, $11.00 per unit for direct labor, and $3.00 per unit for variable manufacturing overhead can be used to compute activity and spending variances as described in the previous chapter. To illustrate, Colonial Pewter's flexible budget performance report for June is shown in Exhibit 10–3. Notice, the report includes an activity variance and a spending variance for direct materials, direct labor, and variable overhead. This performance report is based on the following data:

Originally budgeted output in June	2,100 units
Actual output in June	2,000 units
Actual direct materials cost in June*	$24,700
Actual direct labor cost in June	$22,680
Actual variable manufacturing overhead cost in June	$7,140

*There were no beginning or ending inventories of raw materials in June; all materials purchased were used.

For example, the direct labor cost for the planning budget in Exhibit 10–3 is $23,100 (= $11.00 per unit × 2,100 units).

While the performance report in Exhibit 10–3 is useful, it would be even more useful if the spending variances could be broken down into their price-related and quantity-related components. For example, the direct materials spending variance in the report is $700 unfavorable. This means that, given the actual level of production for the period, direct materials costs were too high by $700—at least according to the standard costs. Was this due to higher than expected prices for materials? Or was it due to too much material being used? The standard cost variances we will be discussing in the rest of the chapter are designed to answer these questions.

EXHIBIT 10–3
Flexible Budget Performance Report for Manufacturing Costs

Colonial Pewter
Flexible Budget Performance Report—Manufacturing Costs Only
For the Month Ended June 30

	Planning Budget	Activity Variances	Flexible Budget	Spending Variances	Actual Results
Bookends produced (q)	2,100		2,000		2,000
Direct materials (12.00q$)	$25,200	$1,200 F	$24,000	$700 U	$24,700
Direct labor (11.00q$)	$23,100	$1,100 F	$22,000	$680 U	$22,680
Variable manufacturing overhead (3.00q$)	$6,300	$300 F	$6,000	$1,140 U	$7,140

A General Model for Standard Cost Variance Analysis

The basic idea in standard cost variance analysis is to decompose spending variances from the flexible budget into two elements—one due to the amount of the input that is used and the other due to the price paid for the input. Using too much of the input results in an unfavorable quantity variance. Paying too much for the input results in an unfavorable price variance. A **quantity variance** is the difference between how much of an input was actually used and how much should have been used and is stated in dollar terms using the standard price of the input. A **price variance** is the difference between the actual price of an input and its standard price, multiplied by the actual amount of the input purchased.

Why are standards separated into two categories—quantity and price? Quantity variances and price variances usually have different causes. In addition, different managers are usually responsible for buying and for using inputs. For example, in the case of a raw material, a purchasing manager is responsible for its price. However, the production manager is responsible for the amount of the raw material actually used to make products. As we shall see, setting up separate quantity and price standards allows us to better separate the responsibilities of these two managers. It also allows us to prepare more timely reports. The purchasing manager's tasks are completed when the material is delivered for use in the factory. A performance report for the purchasing manager can be prepared at that point. However, the production manager's responsibilities have just begun at that point. A performance report for the production manager must be delayed until production is completed and it is known how much raw material was used in the final product. Therefore, it is important to clearly distinguish between deviations from price standards (the responsibility of the purchasing manager) and deviations from quantity standards (the responsibility of the production manager).

Exhibit 10–4 presents a general model that can be used to decompose the spending variance for a variable cost into a *quantity variance* and a *price variance.* Column (1) in this exhibit corresponds with the Flexible Budget column in Exhibit 10–3. Column (3) corresponds with the Actual Results column in Exhibit 10–3. Column (2) has been inserted into Exhibit 10–4 to enable separating the spending variance into a quantity variance and a price variance.

Three things should be noted from Exhibit 10–4. First, a quantity variance and a price variance can be computed for each of the three variable cost elements—direct materials, direct labor, and variable manufacturing overhead—even though the variances have different names. For example, a price variance is called a *materials price variance* in the case of direct materials but a *labor rate variance* in the case of direct labor and a *variable overhead rate variance* in the case of variable manufacturing overhead.

EXHIBIT 10–4
A General Model for Standard Cost Variance Analysis—Variable Manufacturing Costs

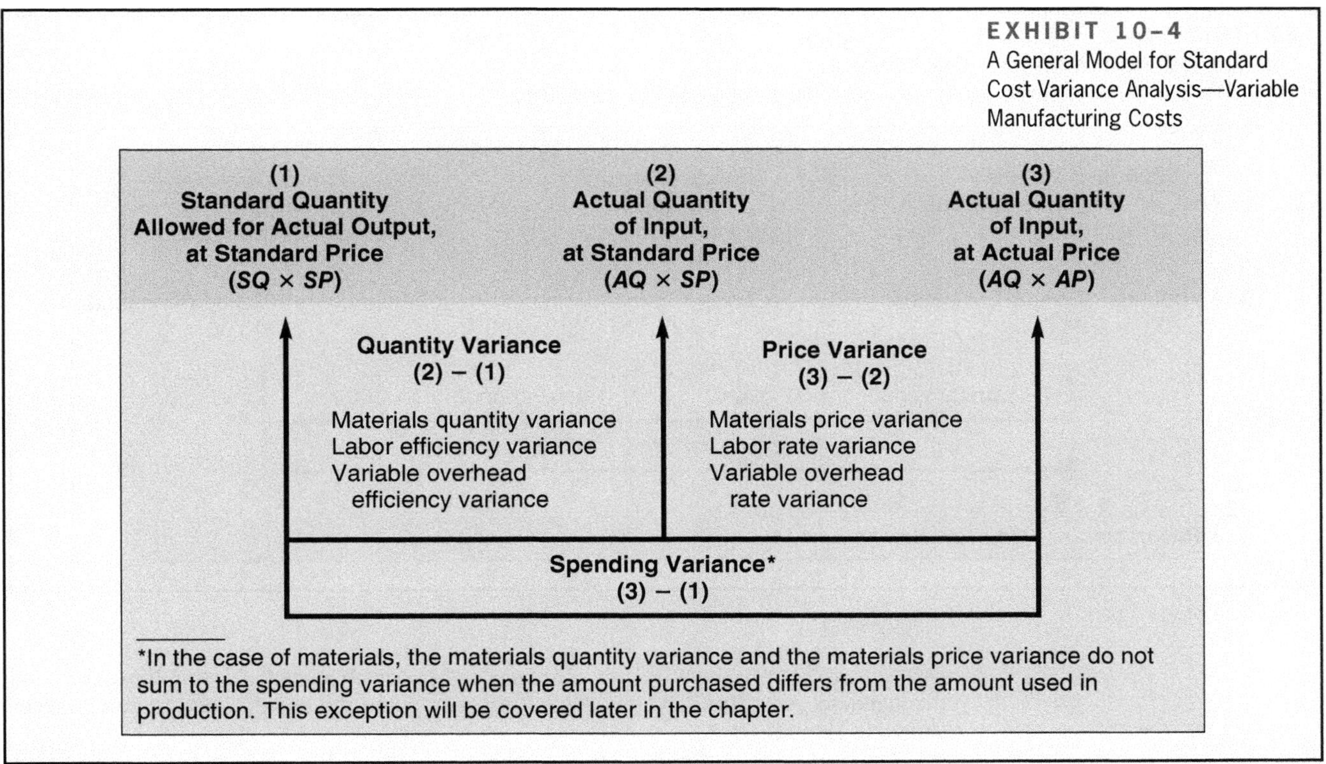

Second, the quantity variance—regardless of what it is called—is computed in exactly the same way regardless of whether one is dealing with direct materials, direct labor, or variable manufacturing overhead. The same is true of the price variance.

Third, the input is the actual quantity of direct materials or direct labor purchased; the output is the good production of the period, expressed in terms of the *standard quantity* (or the *standard hours) allowed for the actual output* (see column 1 in Exhibit 10–4). The **standard quantity allowed** or **standard hours allowed** means the amount of an input *that should have been used* to produce the actual output of the period. This could be more or less than the actual amount of the input, depending on the efficiency or inefficiency of operations. The standard quantity allowed is computed by multiplying the actual output in units by the standard input allowed per unit of output.

With this general model as the foundation, we will now calculate Colonial Pewter's quantity and price variances.

Using Standard Costs—Direct Materials Variances

LEARNING OBJECTIVE 1
Compute the direct materials quantity and price variances and explain their significance.

After determining Colonial Pewter Company's standard costs for direct materials, direct labor, and variable manufacturing overhead, Terry Sherman's next step was to compute the company's variances for June. As discussed in the preceding section, variances are computed by comparing standard costs to actual costs. Terry referred to the standard cost card in Exhibit 10–2 that shows the standard cost of direct materials was computed as follows:

$$3.0 \text{ pounds per unit} \times \$4.00 \text{ per pound} = \$12.00 \text{ per unit}$$

Colonial Pewter's records for June showed that 6,500 pounds of pewter were purchased at a cost of $3.80 per pound, for a total cost of $24,700. All of the material purchased was

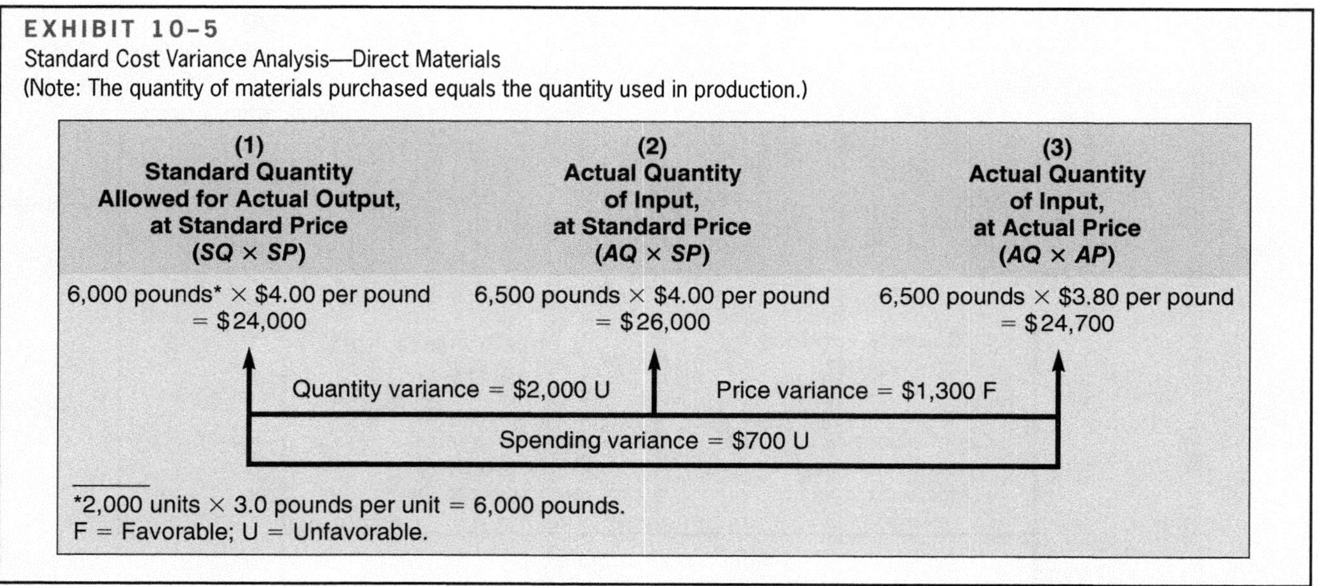

EXHIBIT 10–5
Standard Cost Variance Analysis—Direct Materials
(Note: The quantity of materials purchased equals the quantity used in production.)

used during June to manufacture 2,000 pairs of pewter bookends.[2] Using these data and the standard costs from Exhibit 10–2, Terry computed the quantity and price variances shown in Exhibit 10–5.

The variances in Exhibit 10–5 are based on three different total costs—$24,000, $26,000, and $24,700. The first, $24,000, refers to how much should have been spent on pewter to produce the actual output of 2,000 units. The standards call for 3 pounds of pewter per unit. Because 2,000 units were produced, 6,000 pounds of pewter should have been used. This is referred to as the *standard quantity allowed for the actual output.* If this 6,000 pounds of pewter had been purchased at the standard price of $4.00 per pound, the company would have spent $24,000. This is the amount that appears in the company's flexible budget for the month.

The third total cost figure, $24,700, is the actual amount paid for the actual amount of pewter purchased. The difference between the $24,700 actually spent and the amount that should have been spent, $24,000, is the spending variance for the month of $700. This variance is unfavorable (denoted by U) because the amount that was actually spent exceeded the amount that should have been spent.

The second total cost figure, $26,000, is the key that allows us to decompose the spending variance into two distinct elements—one due to quantity and one due to price. It represents how much the company should have spent if it had purchased the actual amount of input, 6,500 pounds, at the standard price of $4.00 a pound rather than the actual price of $3.80 a pound.

The Materials Quantity Variance

Using the $26,000 total cost figure in column (2), we can make two comparisons—one with the total cost of $24,000 in column (1) and one with the total cost of $24,700 in column (3). The difference between the $24,000 in column (1) and the $26,000 in column (2) is the quantity variance of $2,000, which is labeled as unfavorable (denoted by U).

[2] Throughout this section, we assume zero beginning and ending inventories of materials and that all materials purchased during a period are used during that period. The more general case in which there are beginning and ending inventories of materials and materials are not necessarily used during the period in which they are purchased is considered later in the chapter.

To understand this quantity variance, note that the actual amount of pewter used in production was 6,500 pounds. However, the standard amount of pewter allowed for the actual output is 6,000 pounds. Therefore, too much pewter was used to produce the actual output—by a total of 500 pounds. To express this in dollar terms, the 500 pounds is multiplied by the standard price of $4.00 per pound to yield the quantity variance of $2,000. Why is the standard price of the pewter, rather than the actual price, used in this calculation? The production manager is ordinarily responsible for the quantity variance. If the actual price were used in the calculation of the quantity variance, the production manager would be held responsible for the efficiency or inefficiency of the purchasing manager. Apart from being unfair, fruitless arguments between the production manager and purchasing manager would occur every time the actual price of an input was above its standard price. To avoid these arguments, the standard price is used when computing the quantity variance. The quantity variance in Exhibit 10–5 is labeled unfavorable (U) because more pewter was used to produce the actual output than the standard allows. A quantity variance is labeled favorable (F) if the actual quantity is less than the standard quantity.

The Materials Price Variance

The difference between the $26,000 in column (2) and the $24,700 in column (3) is the price variance of $1,300, which is labeled as favorable (denoted by F).

To understand the price variance, note that the $3.80 per pound price paid for the pewter is $0.20 less than the $4.00 per pound standard price allowed for the pewter. Because 6,500 pounds were purchased, the total amount of the variance is $1,300 (= $0.20 per pound × 6,500 pounds). This variance is labeled favorable (F) because the actual purchase price was less than the standard purchase price. A price variance is labeled unfavorable (U) if the actual purchase price exceeds the standard purchase price.

The computations in Exhibit 10–5 reflect the fact that all of the material purchased during June was also used during June. If the amount of material purchased differs from the amount that is used, the computation of the price variance is a bit different. This slight complication is covered at the end of this chapter.

IN BUSINESS

DIRECT MATERIAL PURCHASES: A RISK MANAGEMENT PERSPECTIVE

Shenzhen Hepalink manufactures heparin, a blood-thinning medication that is injected directly into the bloodstream of some surgical patients. The company relies on suppliers to extract its raw material, called crude heparin, from the intestines of slaughtered pigs. The harvesting of crude heparin is susceptible to contamination if the process is improperly managed and monitored. For example, Baxter International recently recalled tainted heparin that some people believe caused illnesses, allergic reactions, and deaths in some patients in the United States and Germany.

Shenzhen Hepalink strives to reduce contamination risks by buying crude heparin only from Chinese government-regulated slaughterhouses instead of rural unregulated slaughterhouses. The company also maintains quality assurance laboratories on each supplier's premises to ensure compliance with applicable rules. These safeguards increase Shenzhen Hepalink's raw materials cost, but they also reduce the risk of contaminated heparin eventually being injected into a patient's bloodstream.

Source: Gordon Fairclough, "How a Heparin Maker in China Tackles Risks," *The Wall Street Journal*, March 10, 2009, pp. B1 and B5.

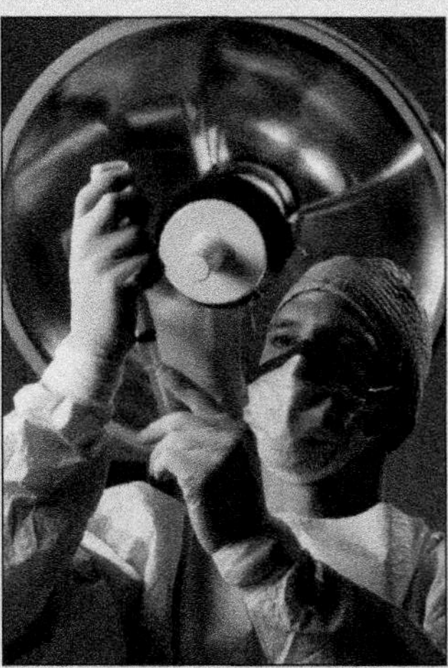

Materials Quantity Variance—A Closer Look

The **materials quantity variance** measures the difference between the quantity of materials used in production and the quantity that should have been used according to the standard. Although the variance is concerned with the physical usage of materials, as shown in Exhibit 10–5, it is generally stated in dollar terms to help gauge its importance. The formula for the materials quantity variance is as follows:

$$\text{Materials quantity variance} = (AQ \times SP) - (SQ \times SP)$$

Actual quantity used — Standard price — Standard quantity allowed for actual output

The formula can be factored as follows:

$$\text{Materials quantity variance} = (AQ - SQ)SP$$

Using the data from Exhibit 10–5 in the formula, we have the following:

$$SQ = 2{,}000 \text{ units} \times 3.0 \text{ pounds per unit} = 6{,}000 \text{ pounds.}$$

$$\text{Materials quantity variance} = (6{,}500 \text{ pounds} - 6{,}000 \text{ pounds}) \times \$4.00 \text{ per pound}$$
$$= \$2{,}000\ \text{U}$$

The answer, of course, is the same as that shown in Exhibit 10–5.

Variance reports are often presented in the form of a table. An excerpt from Colonial Pewter's variance report is shown below along with the production manager's explanation for the materials quantity variance.

Colonial Pewter Company
Variance Report—Production Department

Type of Material	(1) Standard Price	(2) Actual Quantity	(3) Standard Quantity Allowed	(4) Difference in Quantity (2) − (3)	Total Quantity Variance (1) × (4)	Explanation
Pewter	$4.00	6,500 pounds	6,000 pounds	500 pounds	$2,000 U	Low-quality materials unsuitable for production.

F = Favorable; U = Unfavorable.

It is best to isolate the materials quantity variance when materials are used in production. Materials are drawn for the number of units to be produced, according to the standard bill of materials for each unit. Any additional materials are usually drawn with an excess materials requisition slip, which differs from the normal requisition slips. This procedure calls attention to the excessive usage of materials *while production is still in process* and provides an opportunity to correct any developing problem.

Excessive materials usage can result from many factors, including faulty machines, inferior materials quality, untrained workers, and poor supervision. Generally speaking, it is the responsibility of the production department to see that material usage is kept in line with standards. There may be times, however, when the *purchasing* department is responsible for an unfavorable materials quantity variance. For example, if the purchasing department buys inferior materials at a lower price, the materials may be unsuitable for use and may result in excessive waste. Thus, purchasing rather than production would be responsible for the quantity variance. At Colonial Pewter, the production manager, Tom Kuchel, claimed on the Production Department's Performance Report that low-quality materials were the cause of the unfavorable materials quantity variance for June.

Materials Price Variance—A Closer Look

A **materials price variance** measures the difference between what is paid for a given quantity of materials and what should have been paid according to the standard. From Exhibit 10–5, this difference can be expressed by the following formula:

$$\text{Materials price variance} = (AQ \times AP) - (AQ \times SP)$$

Actual quantity purchased · Actual price · Standard price

The formula can be factored as follows:

$$\text{Materials price variance} = AQ(AP - SP)$$

Using the data from Exhibit 10–5 in this formula, we have the following:

Materials price variance = 6,500 pounds ($3.80 per pound − $4.00 per pound) = $1,300 F

Notice that the answer is the same as that shown in Exhibit 10–5. Also note that when using this formula approach, a negative variance is always labeled as favorable (F) and a positive variance is always labeled as unfavorable (U). This will be true of all variance formulas in this chapter.

An excerpt from Colonial Pewter's variance report is shown below along with the purchasing manager's explanation for the materials price variance.

Colonial Pewter Company
Variance Report—Purchasing Department

Item Purchased	(1) Quantity Purchased	(2) Actual Price	(3) Standard Price	(4) Difference in Price (2) − (3)	Total Price Variance (1) × (4)	Explanation
Pewter	6,500 pounds	$3.80	$4.00	$0.20	$1,300 F	Bargained for an especially good price.

F = Favorable; U = Unfavorable.

Isolation of Variances

Variances should be isolated and brought to the attention of management as quickly as possible so that problems can be promptly identified and corrected. The most significant variances should be viewed as "red flags"; an exception has occurred that requires explanation by the responsible manager and perhaps follow-up effort. The performance report itself may contain explanations for the variances, as illustrated above. In the case of Colonial Pewter Company, the purchasing manager said that the favorable price variance resulted from bargaining for an especially good price.

Responsibility for the Variance

Who is responsible for the materials price variance? Generally speaking, the purchasing manager has control over the price paid for goods and is therefore responsible for the materials price variance. Many factors influence the prices paid for goods including how many units are ordered, how the order is delivered, whether the order is a rush order, and the quality of materials purchased. If any of these factors deviates from what was assumed when the standards were set, a price variance can result. For example, purchasing second-grade materials rather than top-grade materials may result in a favorable price variance because the lower-grade materials may be less costly. However, we should keep in mind that the lower-grade materials may create production problems.

IN BUSINESS

MANAGING MATERIALS PRICE VARIANCES

When Tata Motors lost $110 million in 2000, the company's executives mandated a 10% reduction in costs. Tata's purchasing managers responded by using reverse auctions to buy raw materials. Reverse auctions require suppliers to bid against one another for the right to sell raw material inputs to Tata Motors. The supplier who places the lowest bid wins the contract. Tata's purchasing managers have used 750 reverse auctions a year to lower the company's average purchase prices by 7%. While this practice produces favorable purchase price variances and higher profits in the short run, these benefits may eventually be offset by greater scrap, rework, warranty repairs, customer complaints, and lost sales.

Source: Robyn Meredith, "The Next People's Car," *Forbes*, April 16, 2007, pp. 70–74.

However, someone other than the purchasing manager could be responsible for a materials price variance. For example, due to production problems beyond the purchasing manager's control, the purchasing manager may have to use express delivery. In these cases, the production manager should be held responsible for the resulting price variances.

A word of caution is in order. Variance analysis should not be used to assign blame. The emphasis should be on *supporting* the line managers and *assisting* them in meeting the goals that they have participated in setting for the company. In short, the emphasis should be positive rather than negative. Excessive dwelling on what has already happened, particularly in terms of trying to find someone to blame, can destroy morale and kill any cooperative spirit.

Using Standard Costs—Direct Labor Variances

LEARNING OBJECTIVE 2
Compute the direct labor efficiency and rate variances and explain their significance.

Terry Sherman's next step in determining Colonial Pewter's variances for June was to compute the direct labor variances for the month. Recall from Exhibit 10–2 that the standard direct labor cost per unit of product is $11, computed as follows:

$$0.50 \text{ hours per unit} \times \$22.00 \text{ per hour} = \$11.00 \text{ per unit}$$

During June, the company paid its direct labor workers $22,680, including payroll taxes and fringe benefits, for 1,050 hours of work. This was an average of $21.60 per hour. Using these data and the standard costs from Exhibit 10–2, Terry computed the direct labor efficiency and rate variances that appear in Exhibit 10–6.

Notice that the column headings in Exhibit 10–6 are the same as those used in the prior two exhibits, except that in Exhibit 10–6 the terms *hours* and *rate* are used in place of the terms *quantity* and *price.*

Labor Efficiency Variance—A Closer Look

The **labor efficiency variance** attempts to measure the productivity of direct labor. No variance is more closely watched by management because it is widely believed that increasing direct labor productivity is vital to reducing costs. The formula for the labor efficiency variance is expressed as follows:

$$\text{Labor efficiency variance} = (AH \times SR) - (SH \times SR)$$

AH = Actual hours; SR = Standard rate; SH = Standard hours allowed for actual output

EXHIBIT 10–6
Standard Cost Variance Analysis—Direct Labor

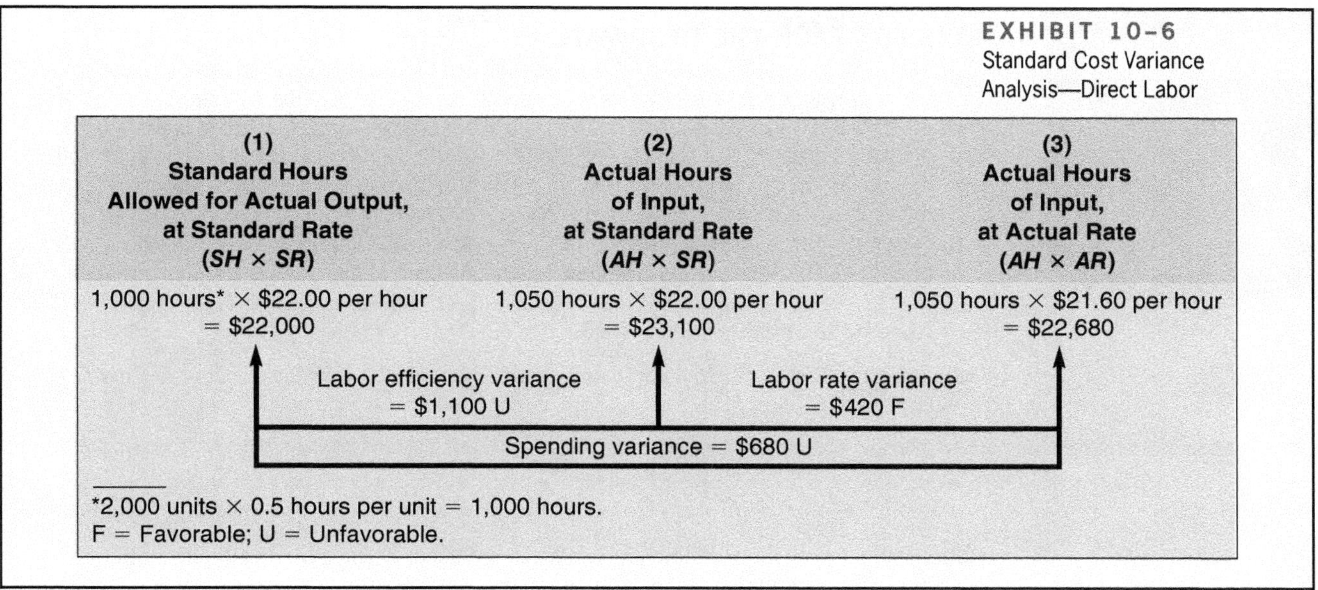

The formula can be factored as follows:

$$\text{Labor efficiency variance} = (AH - SH)SR$$

Using the data from Exhibit 10–6 in the formula, we have the following:

$$SH = 2{,}000 \text{ units} \times 0.5 \text{ hours per unit} = 1{,}000 \text{ hours.}$$

$$\text{Labor efficiency variance} = (1{,}050 \text{ hours} - 1{,}000 \text{ hours}) \$22.00 \text{ per hour} = \$1{,}100 \text{ U}$$

Possible causes of an unfavorable labor efficiency variance include poorly trained or motivated workers; poor quality materials, requiring more labor time; faulty equipment, causing breakdowns and work interruptions; poor supervision of workers; and inaccurate standards. The managers in charge of production would usually be responsible for control of the labor efficiency variance. However, the purchasing manager could be held responsible if the purchase of poor-quality materials resulted in excessive labor processing time.

Another important cause of an unfavorable labor efficiency variance may be insufficient demand for the company's products. Managers in some companies argue that it is difficult, and perhaps unwise, to constantly adjust the workforce in response to changes in the amount of work that needs to be done. In such companies, the direct labor workforce is essentially fixed in the short run. If demand is insufficient to keep everyone busy, workers are not laid off and an unfavorable labor efficiency variance will often be recorded.

If customer orders are insufficient to keep the workers busy, the work center manager has two options—either accept an unfavorable labor efficiency variance or build inventory.[3] A central lesson of Lean Production is that building inventory with no immediate prospect of sale is a bad idea. Excessive inventory—particularly work in process inventory—leads to high defect rates, obsolete goods, and inefficient operations. As a consequence, when the workforce is basically fixed in the short term, managers must be

[3] For further discussion, see Eliyahu M. Goldratt and Jeff Cox, *The Goal*, 2nd rev. ed. (Croton-on-Hudson, NY: North River Press, 1992).

IN BUSINESS

CASHIERS FACE THE STOPWATCH

Operations Workforce Optimization (OWO) writes software that uses engineered labor standards to determine how long it should take a cashier to check out a customer. The software measures an employee's productivity by continuously comparing actual customer checkout times to pre-established labor efficiency standards. For example, the cashiers at Meijer, a regional retailer located in the Midwest, may be demoted or terminated if they do not meet or exceed labor efficiency standards for at least 95% of customers served. In addition to Meijer, OWO has attracted other clients such as Gap, Limited Brands, Office Depot, Nike, and Toys "R" Us, based on claims that its software can reduce labor costs by 5–15%. The software has also attracted the attention of the United Food and Commercial Workers Union, which represents 27,000 Meijer employees. The union has filed a grievance against Meijer related to its cashier monitoring system.

Source: Vanessa O'Connell, "Stores Count Seconds to Cut Labor Costs," *The Wall Street Journal*, November 17, 2008, pp. A1–A15.

cautious about how labor efficiency variances are used. Some experts advocate eliminating labor efficiency variances in such situations—at least for the purposes of motivating and controlling workers on the shop floor.

Labor Rate Variance—A Closer Look

As explained earlier, the price variance for direct labor is commonly called the **labor rate variance.** This variance measures any deviation from standard in the average hourly rate paid to direct labor workers. The formula for the labor rate variance is expressed as follows:

$$\text{Labor rate variance} = (AH \times AR) - (AH \times SR)$$

Actual hours; Actual rate; Standard rate

The formula can be factored as follows:

$$\text{Labor rate variance} = AH(AR - SR)$$

Using the data from Exhibit 10–6 in the formula, the labor rate variance can be computed as follows:

Labor rate variance = 1,050 hours (\$21.60 per hour − \$22.00 per hour) = \$420 F

In most companies, the wage rates paid to workers are quite predictable. Nevertheless, rate variances can arise because of the way labor is used. Skilled workers with high hourly rates of pay may be given duties that require little skill and call for lower hourly rates of pay. This will result in an unfavorable labor rate variance because the actual hourly rate of pay will exceed the standard rate specified for the particular task. In contrast, a favorable rate variance would result when workers who are paid at a rate lower than specified in the standard are assigned to the task. However, the lower-paid workers may not be as efficient. Finally, overtime work at premium rates will result in an unfavorable rate variance if the overtime premium is charged to the direct labor account.

Who is responsible for controlling the labor rate variance? Because labor rate variances generally arise as a result of how labor is used, production supervisors are usually responsible for seeing that labor rate variances are kept under control.

Using Standard Costs—Variable Manufacturing Overhead Variances

LEARNING OBJECTIVE 3
Compute the variable manufacturing overhead efficiency and rate variances and explain their significance.

The final step in Terry Sherman's analysis of Colonial Pewter's variances for June was to compute the variable manufacturing overhead variances. The variable portion of manufacturing overhead can be analyzed using the same basic formulas that we used to analyze direct materials and direct labor. Recall from Exhibit 10–2 that the standard variable manufacturing overhead is $3.00 per unit of product, computed as follows:

0.5 hours per unit × $6.00 per hour = $3.00 per unit

Colonial Pewter's cost records showed that the total actual variable manufacturing overhead cost for June was $7,140. Recall from the earlier discussion of the direct labor variances that 1,050 hours of direct labor time were recorded during the month and that the company produced 2,000 pairs of bookends. Terry's analysis of this overhead data appears in Exhibit 10–7.

Notice the similarities between Exhibits 10–6 and 10–7. These similarities arise from the fact that direct labor-hours are being used as the base for allocating overhead cost to units of product; thus, the same hourly figures appear in Exhibit 10–7 for variable manufacturing overhead as in Exhibit 10–6 for direct labor. The main difference between the two exhibits is in the standard hourly rate being used, which in this company is much lower for variable manufacturing overhead than for direct labor.

Manufacturing Overhead Variances—A Closer Look

The formula for the **variable overhead efficiency variance** is expressed as follows:

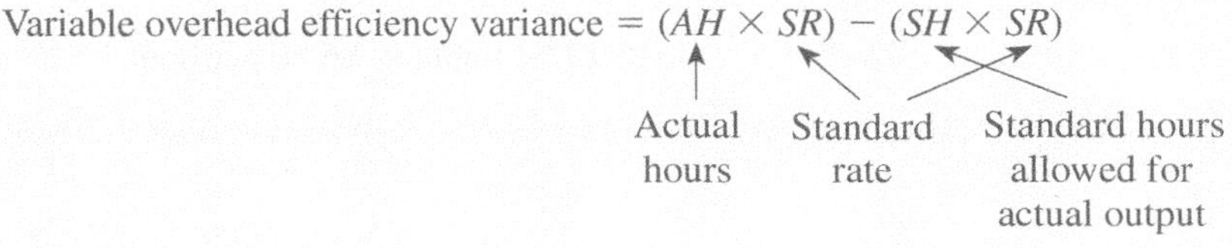

EXHIBIT 10–7
Standard Cost Variance Analysis—Variable Manufacturing Overhead

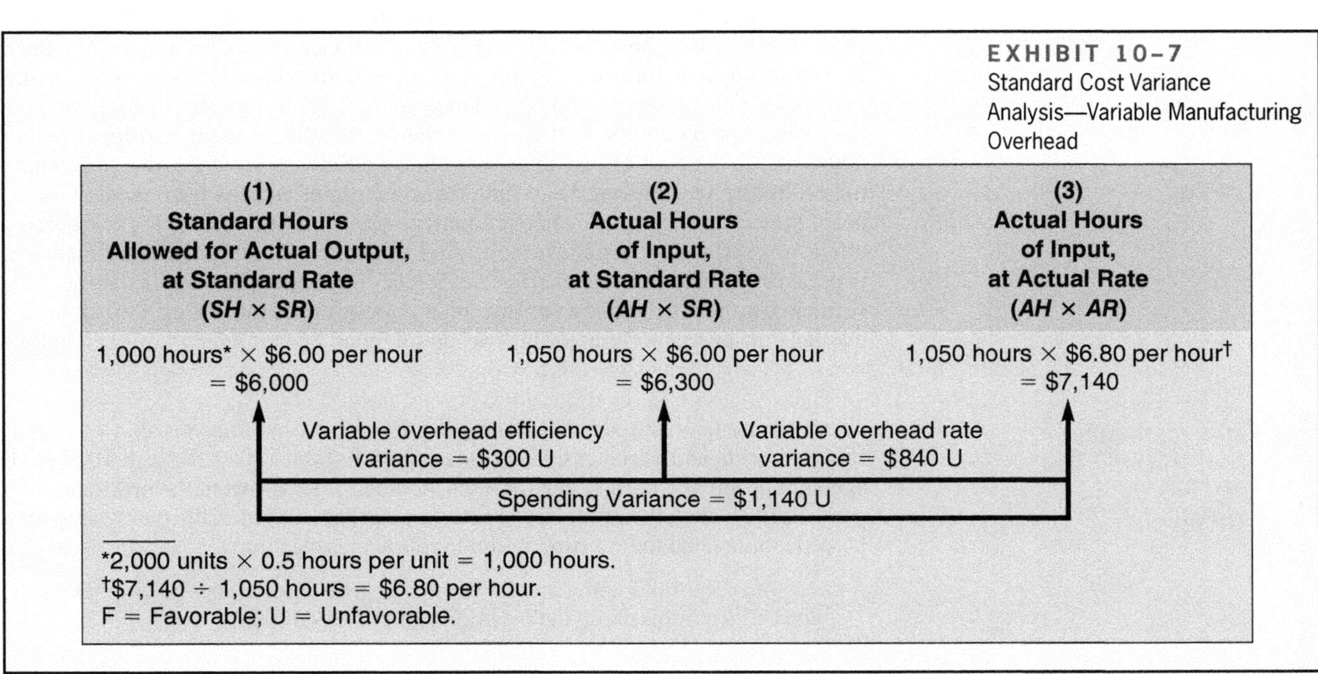

This formula can be factored as follows:

$$\text{Variable overhead efficiency variance} = (AH - SH)SR$$

Again using the data from Exhibit 10–7, the variance can be computed as follows:

$$SH = 2{,}000 \text{ units} \times 0.5 \text{ hours per unit} = 1{,}000 \text{ hours}$$

$$\text{Variable overhead efficiency variance} = (1{,}050 \text{ hours} - 1{,}000 \text{ hours})\ \$6.00 \text{ per hour}$$
$$= \$300\ \text{U}$$

The formula for the **variable overhead rate variance** is expressed as follows:

$$\text{Variable overhead rate variance} = (\underset{\text{Actual hours}}{AH} \times \underset{\text{Actual rate}}{AR}) - (AH \times \underset{\text{Standard rate}}{SR})$$

This formula can be factored as follows:

$$\text{Variable overhead rate variance} = AH(AR - SR)$$

Using the data from Exhibit 10–7 in the formula, the variable overhead rate variance can be computed as follows:

$$AR = \$7{,}140 \div 1{,}050 \text{ hours} = \$6.80 \text{ per hour}$$

$$\text{Variable overhead rate variance} = 1{,}050 \text{ hours } (\$6.80 \text{ per hour} - \$6.00 \text{ per hour})$$
$$= \$840\ \text{U}$$

The interpretation of the variable overhead variances is not as clear as the direct materials and direct labor variances. In particular, the variable overhead efficiency variance is exactly the same as the direct labor efficiency variance except for one detail—the rate that is used to translate the variance into dollars. In both cases, the variance is the difference between the actual hours worked and the standard hours allowed for the actual output. In the case of the direct labor efficiency variance, this difference is multiplied by the direct labor rate. In the case of the variable overhead efficiency variance, this difference is multiplied by the variable overhead rate. So when direct labor is used as the base for overhead, whenever the direct labor efficiency variance is favorable, the variable overhead efficiency variance will be favorable. And whenever the direct labor efficiency variance is unfavorable, the variable overhead efficiency variance will be unfavorable. Indeed, the variable overhead efficiency variance really doesn't tell us anything about how efficiently overhead resources were used. It depends solely on how efficiently direct labor was used.

MANAGERIAL ACCOUNTING IN ACTION
The Wrap-up

In preparation for the scheduled meeting to discuss his analysis of Colonial Pewter's standard costs and variances, Terry distributed Exhibits 10–2 through 10–7 to the management group of Colonial Pewter. This included J. D. Wriston, the president of the company; Tom Kuchel, the production manager; and Janet Warner, the purchasing manager. J. D. Wriston opened the meeting with the following question:

J. D.: Terry, I think I understand the report you distributed, but just to make sure, would you mind summarizing the highlights of what you found?

Colonial Pewter Company

Terry: As you can see, the biggest problems are the unfavorable materials quantity variance of $2,000 and the unfavorable labor efficiency variance of $1,100.

J. D.: Tom, you're the production boss. What do you think is causing the unfavorable labor efficiency variance?

Tom: It has to be the new production workers. Our experienced workers shouldn't have much problem meeting the standard of half an hour per unit. We all knew that there would be some inefficiency for a while as we brought new people on board. My plan for overcoming the problem is to pair up each of the new guys with one of our old-timers and have them work together for a while. It would slow down our older guys a bit, but I'll bet the unfavorable variance disappears and our new workers would learn a lot.

J. D.: Sounds good. Now, what about that $2,000 unfavorable materials quantity variance?

Terry: Tom, are the new workers generating a lot of scrap?

Tom: Yeah, I guess so.

J. D.: I think that could be part of the problem. Can you do anything about it?

Tom: I can watch the scrap closely for a few days to see where it's being generated. If it is the new workers, I can have the old-timers work with them on the problem when I team them up.

J. D.: Janet, the favorable materials price variance of $1,300 isn't helping us if it is contributing to the unfavorable materials quantity and labor efficiency variances. Let's make sure that our raw material purchases conform to our quality standards.

Janet: Fair enough.

J. D.: Good. Let's reconvene in a few weeks to see what has happened. Hopefully, we can get those unfavorable variances under control.

An Important Subtlety in the Materials Variances

Most companies compute the materials price variance when materials are purchased rather than when they are used in production. There are two reasons for this practice. First, delaying the computation of the price variance until the materials are used would result in less timely variance reports. Second, computing the price variance when the materials are purchased allows materials to be carried in the inventory accounts at their standard cost. This greatly simplifies bookkeeping. (See Appendix 10B at the end of the chapter for an explanation of how the bookkeeping works in a standard costing system.)

The equations presented earlier that define the direct materials quantity and price variances are correct and are reproduced below:

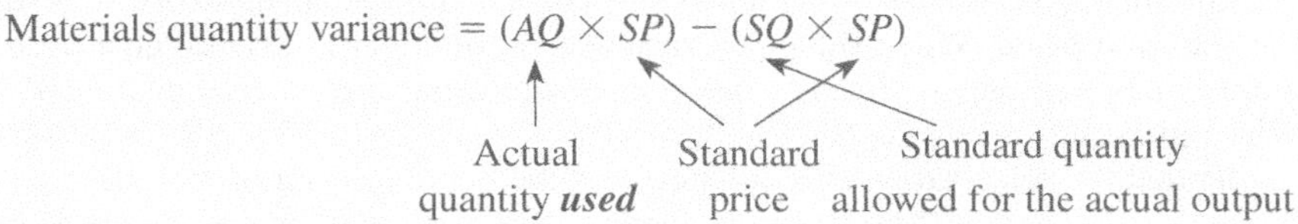

Materials price variance = $(AQ \times AP) - (AQ \times SP)$

Actual quantity ***purchased*** — Actual price — Standard price

Carefully note that the materials quantity variance is based on the actual quantity *used,* whereas the materials price variance is based on the actual quantity *purchased.* This is a subtle, but important, distinction. It didn't matter in the earlier example because the amount purchased (6,500 pounds of pewter) was the same as the amount used (again, 6,500 pounds of pewter). It *does* matter when the quantity purchased differs from the quantity used.

To illustrate, assume that during June Colonial Pewter purchased 7,000 pounds of materials at \$3.80 per pound instead of 6,500 pounds as assumed earlier in the chapter. In this case, the quantity and price variances for direct materials would be computed as shown below:

Materials quantity variance = (*AQ used* × *SP*) − (*SQ* × *SP*)

= (6,500 pounds × \$4.00 per pound) − (6,000 pounds × \$4.00 per pound)

= (6,500 pounds − 6,000 pounds) × \$4.00 per pound

= \$2,000 U

Materials price variance = (*AQ purchased* × *AP*) − (*AQ purchased* × *SP*)

= (7,000 pounds × \$3.80 per pound) − (7,000 pounds × \$4.00 per pound)

= 7,000 pounds × (\$3.80 per pound − \$4.00 per pound)

= \$1,400 F

This distinction between the actual quantity purchased and actual quantity used is perhaps clearer in Exhibit 10–8.

Note that the format of Exhibit 10–8 differs from the format of Exhibit 10–5—both of which are used to compute the direct materials variances. *Exhibit 10–8 can always be used to compute the direct materials variances. Exhibit 10–5 can only be used to compute the direct materials variances when the amount purchased equals the amount used.*

In Exhibit 10–8, the computation of the quantity variance is based on the actual input used whereas the computation of the price variance is based on the amount of the input purchased. Column (2) of Exhibit 10–8 contains two different total costs for this reason. When the quantity variance is computed, the total cost used from column (2) is \$26,000—which is the cost of the actual input *used,* evaluated at the standard price. When the price variance is computed, the total cost used from column (2) is \$28,000—which is the cost of the input *purchased,* evaluated at the standard price.

Note that the price variance is computed on the entire amount of material purchased (7,000 pounds), whereas the quantity variance is computed only on the amount of materials used in production during the month (6,500 pounds). What about the other 500 pounds of material that were purchased during the period, but that have not yet been used? When those materials are used in future periods, a quantity variance will be computed. However, a price variance will not be computed when the materials are finally used because the price variance was computed when the materials were purchased.

Finally, because the quantity variance is based on the amount used whereas the price variance is based on the amount purchased, the two variances do not generally

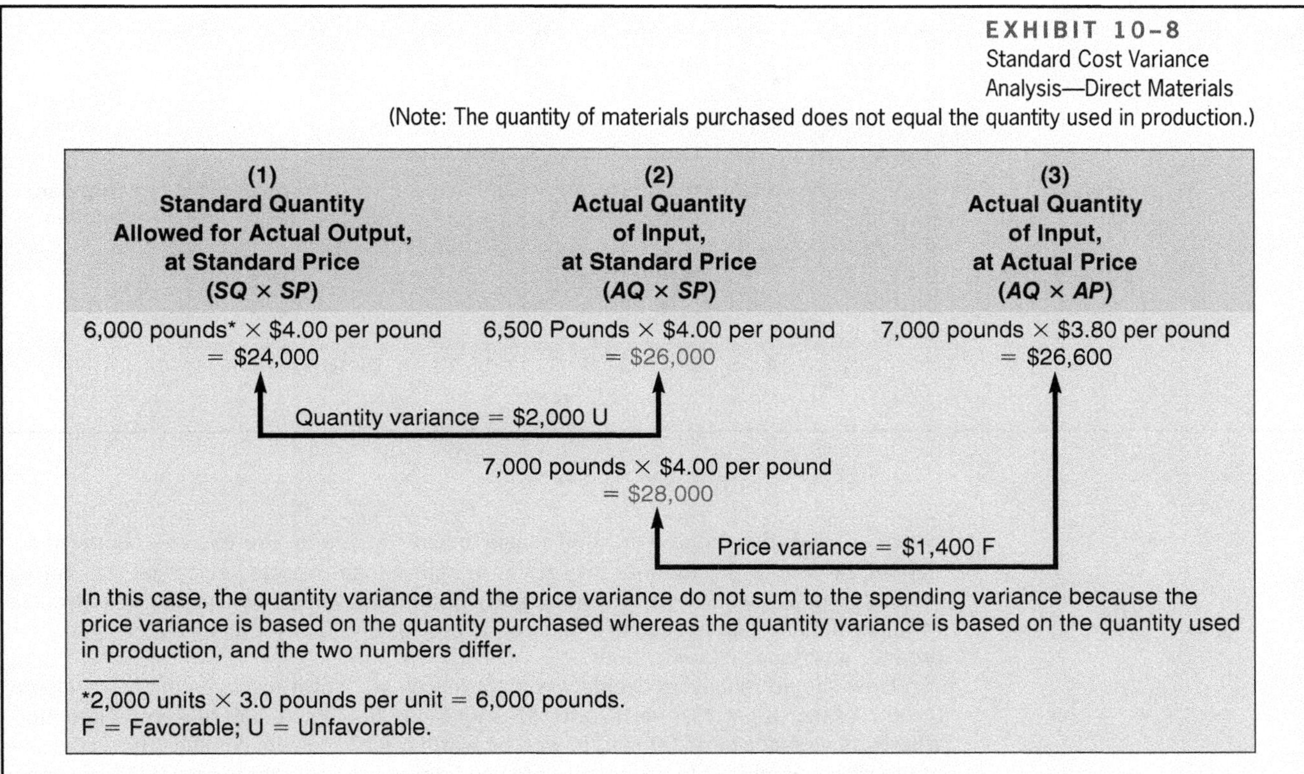

EXHIBIT 10–8
Standard Cost Variance Analysis—Direct Materials
(Note: The quantity of materials purchased does not equal the quantity used in production.)

(1) Standard Quantity Allowed for Actual Output, at Standard Price (SQ × SP)	(2) Actual Quantity of Input, at Standard Price (AQ × SP)	(3) Actual Quantity of Input, at Actual Price (AQ × AP)
6,000 pounds* × \$4.00 per pound = \$24,000	6,500 Pounds × \$4.00 per pound = \$26,000	7,000 pounds × \$3.80 per pound = \$26,600
	7,000 pounds × \$4.00 per pound = \$28,000	

Quantity variance = \$2,000 U

Price variance = \$1,400 F

In this case, the quantity variance and the price variance do not sum to the spending variance because the price variance is based on the quantity purchased whereas the quantity variance is based on the quantity used in production, and the two numbers differ.

*2,000 units × 3.0 pounds per unit = 6,000 pounds.
F = Favorable; U = Unfavorable.

sum to the spending variance from the flexible budget, which is wholly based on the amount used.

We would like to repeat that the variance formulas and Exhibit 10–8 can always be used. *However, Exhibit 10–5 can only be used in the special case when the quantity of materials purchased equals the quantity of materials used!*

Variance Analysis and Management by Exception

Variance analysis and performance reports are important elements of *management by exception,* which is an approach that emphasizes focusing on those areas of responsibility where goals and expectations are not being met.

The budgets and standards discussed in this chapter and in the preceding chapter reflect management's plans. If all goes according to plan, there will be little difference between actual results and the results that would be expected according to the budgets and standards. If this happens, managers can concentrate on other issues. However, if actual results do not conform to the budget and to standards, the performance reporting system sends a signal to managers that an "exception" has occurred. This signal is in the form of a variance from the budget or standards.

However, are all variances worth investigating? The answer is no. Differences between actual results and what was expected will almost always occur. If every variance were investigated, management would waste a great deal of time tracking down nickel-and-dime differences. Variances may occur for a variety of reasons—only some of

EXHIBIT 10–9
A Statistical Control Chart

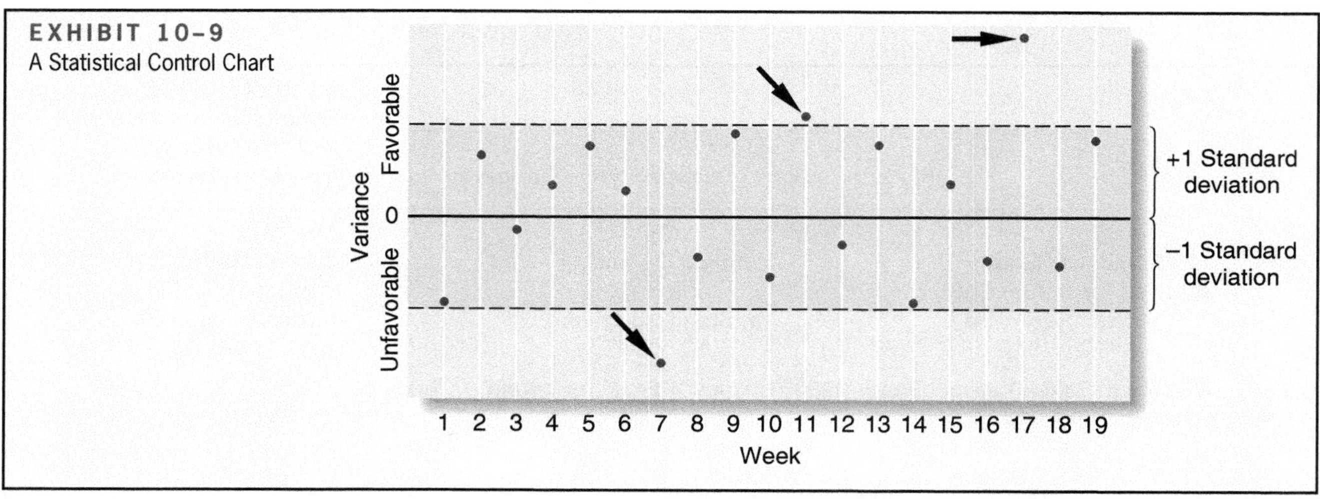

which are significant and worthy of management's attention. For example, hotter-than-normal weather in the summer may result in higher-than-expected electrical bills for air conditioning. Or, workers may work slightly faster or slower on a particular day. Because of unpredictable random factors, one can expect that virtually every cost category will produce a variance of some kind.

How should managers decide which variances are worth investigating? One clue is the size of the variance. A variance of $5 is probably not big enough to warrant attention, whereas a variance of $5,000 might well be worth tracking down. Another clue is the size of the variance relative to the amount of spending. A variance that is only 0.1% of spending on an item is likely to be well within the bounds one would normally expect due to random factors. On the other hand, a variance of 10% of spending is much more likely to be a signal that something is wrong.

A more dependable approach is to plot variance data on a statistical control chart, such as illustrated in Exhibit 10–9. The basic idea underlying a statistical control chart is that some random fluctuations in variances from period to period are normal. A variance should only be investigated when it is unusual relative to that normal level of random fluctuation. Typically, the standard deviation of the variances is used as the measure of the normal level of fluctuations. A rule of thumb is adopted such as "investigate all variances that are more than X standard deviations from zero." In the control chart in Exhibit 10–9, X is 1.0. That is, the rule of thumb in this company is to investigate all variances that are more than one standard deviation in either direction (favorable or unfavorable) from zero. This means that the variances in weeks 7, 11, and 17 would have been investigated, but none of the others.

What value of X should be chosen? The bigger the value of X, the wider the band of acceptable variances that would not be investigated. Thus, the bigger the value of X, the less time will be spent tracking down variances, but the more likely it is that a real out-of-control situation will be overlooked. Ordinarily, if X is selected to be 1.0, roughly 30% of all variances will trigger an investigation even though there is no real problem. If X is set at 1.5, the figure drops to about 13%. If X is set at 2.0, the figure drops all the way to about 5%. Don't forget, however, that selecting a big value of X will result not only in fewer false alarms but also in a higher probability that a real problem will be overlooked.

In addition to watching for unusually large variances, the pattern of the variances should be monitored. For example, a run of steadily mounting variances should trigger an investigation even though none of the variances is large enough by itself to warrant investigation.

International Uses of Standard Costs

Standard costs are used by companies throughout the world. One study found that three-fourths of the companies surveyed in the United Kingdom, two-thirds of the companies surveyed in Canada, and 40% of the companies surveyed in Japan used standard cost systems.[4]

Standard costs were first introduced in Japan after World War II, with Nippon Electronics Company (NEC) being one of the first Japanese companies to adopt standard costs for all of its products. Many other Japanese companies followed NEC's lead and developed standard cost systems. The ways in which these standard costs are used in Japan—and also in the other countries cited above—are shown in Exhibit 10–10.

Over time, the pattern of use shown in Exhibit 10–10 may change, but at present managers can expect to encounter standard costs in most industrialized nations. Moreover, the most important uses are for cost management and budgetary planning purposes.

EXHIBIT 10–10
Uses of Standard Costs in Four Countries

	United States	United Kingdom	Canada	Japan
Cost management	1*	2	2	1
Budgetary planning and control†	2	3	1	3
Pricing decisions	3	1	3	2
Financial statement preparation	4	4	4	4

*The numbers 1 through 4 denote importance of use of standard costing systems, from greatest to least.
†Includes management planning.
Source: Compiled from data in a study by Shin'ichi Inoue, "Comparative Studies of Recent Development of Cost Management Problems in U.S.A., U.K., Canada, and Japan," Research Paper No. 29, Kagawa University, p. 20.

Evaluation of Controls Based on Standard Costs

Advantages of Standard Costs

Standard cost systems have a number of advantages.

1. Standard costs are a key element in a management by exception approach. If costs conform to the standards, managers can focus on other issues. When costs are significantly outside the standards, managers are alerted that problems may exist that require attention. This approach helps managers focus on important issues.
2. Standards that are viewed as reasonable by employees can promote economy and efficiency. They provide benchmarks that individuals can use to judge their own performance.
3. Standard costs can greatly simplify bookkeeping. Instead of recording actual costs for each job, the standard costs for direct materials, direct labor, and overhead can be charged to jobs.
4. Standard costs fit naturally in an integrated system of "responsibility accounting." The standards establish what costs should be, who should be responsible for them, and whether actual costs are under control.

---

[4] Shin'ichi Inoue, "Comparative Studies of Recent Development of Cost Management Problems in U.S.A., U.K., Canada, and Japan," Research Paper No. 29, Kagawa University, p. 17. The study included 95 United States companies, 52 United Kingdom companies, 82 Canadian companies, and 646 Japanese companies.

Potential Problems with the Use of Standard Costs

The improper use of standard costs can present a number of potential problems.

1. Standard cost variance reports are usually prepared on a monthly basis and often are released days or even weeks after the end of the month. As a consequence, the information in the reports may be so outdated that it is almost useless. Timely, frequent reports that are approximately correct are better than infrequent reports that are very precise but out of date by the time they are released. Some companies are now reporting variances and other key operating data daily or even more frequently.

2. If managers are insensitive and use variance reports as a club, morale may suffer. Employees should receive positive reinforcement for work well done. Management by exception, by its nature, tends to focus on the negative. If variances are used as a club, subordinates may be tempted to cover up unfavorable variances or take actions that are not in the best interests of the company to make sure the variances are favorable. For example, workers may put on a crash effort to increase output at the end of the month to avoid an unfavorable labor efficiency variance. In the rush to produce more output, quality may suffer.
3. Labor quantity standards and efficiency variances make two important assumptions. First, they assume that the production process is labor-paced; if labor works faster, output will go up. However, output in many companies is not determined by how fast labor works; rather, it is determined by the processing speed of machines. Second, the computations assume that labor is a variable cost. However, direct labor may be essentially fixed. If labor is fixed, then an undue emphasis on labor efficiency variances creates pressure to build excess inventories.
4. In some cases, a "favorable" variance can be as bad or worse than an "unfavorable" variance. For example, McDonald's has a standard for the amount of hamburger meat that should be in a Big Mac. A "favorable" variance would mean that less meat was used than the standard specifies. The result is a substandard Big Mac and possibly a dissatisfied customer.
5. Too much emphasis on meeting the standards may overshadow other important objectives such as maintaining and improving quality, on-time delivery, and customer satisfaction. This tendency can be reduced by using supplemental performance measures that focus on these other objectives.
6. Just meeting standards may not be sufficient; continual improvement may be necessary to survive in a competitive environment. For this reason, some companies focus on the trends in the standard cost variances—aiming for continual improvement rather than just meeting the standards. In other companies, engineered standards are replaced either by a rolling average of actual costs, which is expected to decline, or by very challenging target costs.

In sum, managers should exercise considerable care when using a standard cost system. It is particularly important that managers go out of their way to focus on the positive, rather than just on the negative, and to be aware of possible unintended consequences.

Summary

A standard is a benchmark, or "norm," for measuring performance. Standards are set for both the quantity and the cost of inputs needed to manufacture goods or to provide services. Quantity standards indicate how much of an input, such as labor time or raw materials, should be used to make a product or provide a service. Cost standards indicate what the cost of the input should be.

Standards are normally set so that they can be attained by reasonable, though highly efficient, efforts. Such "practical" standards are believed to positively motivate employees.

When standards are compared to actual performance, the difference is referred to as a *variance*. Variances are computed and reported to management on a regular basis for both the quantity and the price elements of direct materials, direct labor, and variable overhead. Quantity variances are computed by taking the difference between the actual amount of the input used and the amount of input that is allowed for the actual output, and then multiplying the result by the standard price of the input. Price variances are computed by taking the difference between actual and standard prices and multiplying the result by the amount of input purchased.

Not all variances require management attention. Only unusual or particularly significant variances should be investigated—otherwise a great deal of time would be spent investigating unimportant matters. Additionally, it should be emphasized that the point of the investigation should not be to find someone to blame. The point of the investigation is to pinpoint the problem so that it can be fixed and operations improved.

Traditional standard cost variance reports are often supplemented with other performance measures. Overemphasis on standard cost variances may lead to problems in other critical areas such as product quality, inventory levels, and on-time delivery.

Review Problem: Standard Costs

Xavier Company produces a single product. Variable manufacturing overhead is applied to products on the basis of direct labor-hours. The standard costs for one unit of product are as follows:

Direct material: 6 ounces at $0.50 per ounce	$ 3.00
Direct labor: 0.6 hours at $30.00 per hour	18.00
Variable manufacturing overhead: 0.6 hours at $10.00 per hour	6.00
Total standard variable cost per unit	$27.00

During June, 2,000 units were produced. The costs associated with June's operations were as follows:

Material purchased: 18,000 ounces at $0.60 per ounce	$10,800
Material used in production: 14,000 ounces	—
Direct labor: 1,100 hours at $30.50 per hour	$33,550
Variable manufacturing overhead costs incurred	$12,980

Required:

Compute the direct materials, direct labor, and variable manufacturing overhead variances.

Solution to Review Problem

Direct Materials Variances

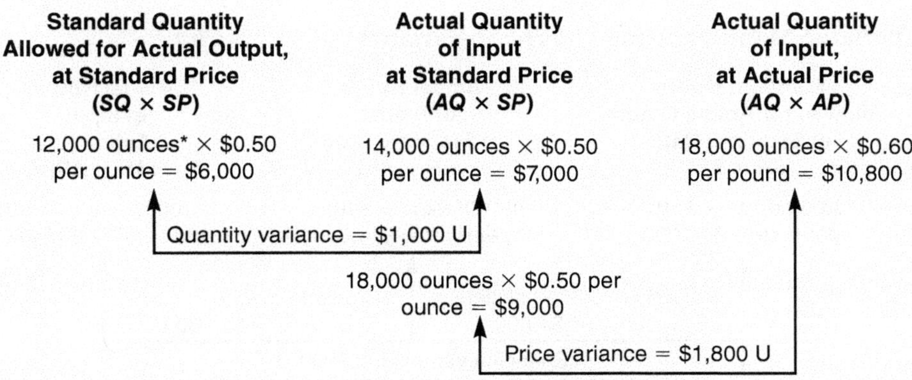

*2,000 units × 6 ounces per unit = 12,000 ounces.

Using the formulas in the chapter, the same variances would be computed as follows:

Materials quantity variance = $(AQ - SQ)SP$

(14,000 ounces − 12,000 ounces) $0.50 per ounce = $1,000 U

Materials price variance = $AQ(AP - SP)$

18,000 ounces ($0.60 per ounce − $0.50 per ounce) = $1,800 U

Direct Labor Variances

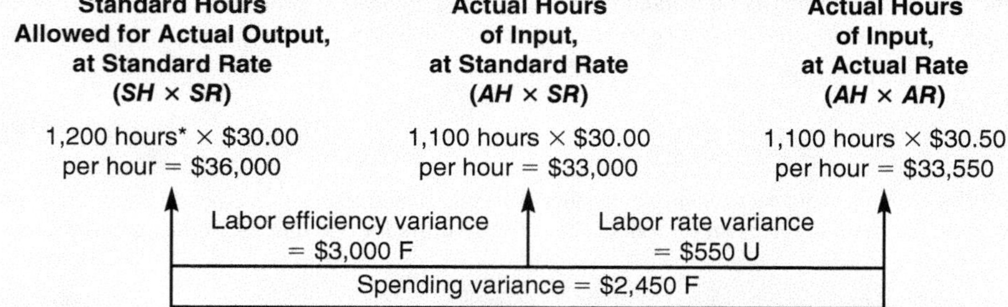

*2,000 units × 0.6 hours per unit =1,200 hours.
F = Favorable; U = Unfavorable.

Using the formulas in the chapter, the same variances can be computed as follows:

Labor efficiency variance = $(AH \times SR) - (SH \times SR)$

= (1,100 hours × $30.00 per hour) − (1,200 hours × $30.00 per hour)

= (1,100 hours − 1,200 hours) × $30.00 per hour

= $3,000 F

Labor rate variance = $(AH \times AR) - (AH \times SR)$

= (1,100 hours × $30.00 per hour) − (1,100 hours × $30.50 per hour)

= 1,100 hours × ($30.00 per hour − $30.50 per hour)

= $550 U

Variable Manufacturing Overhead Variances

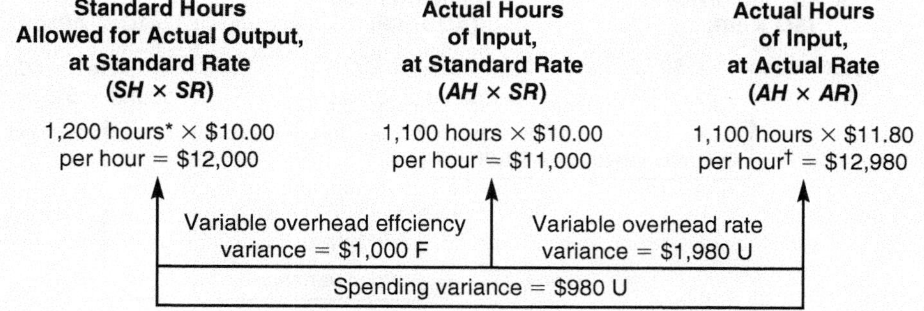

*2,000 units × 0.6 hours per unit = 1,200 hours.
†$12,980 ÷ 1,100 hours = $11.80 per hour.
F = Favorable; U = Unfavorable.

Using the formulas in the chapter, the same variances can be computed as follows:

Variable overhead efficiency variance $= (AH \times SR) - (SH \times SR)$

$= (1{,}100 \text{ hours} \times \$10.00 \text{ per hour}) - (1{,}200 \text{ hours} \times \$10.00 \text{ per hour})$

$= (1{,}100 \text{ hours} - 1{,}200 \text{ hours}) \times \$10.00 \text{ per hour}$

$= \$1{,}000$ F

Variable overhead rate variance $= (AH \times AR) - (AH \times SR)$

$= (1{,}100 \text{ hours} \times \$10.00 \text{ per hour}) - (1{,}100 \text{ hours} \times \$11.80 \text{ per hour})$

$= 1{,}100 \text{ hours} \times (\$10.00 \text{ per hour} - \$11.80 \text{ per hour})$

$= \$1{,}980$ U

Glossary

Ideal standards Standards that assume peak efficiency at all times. (p. 420)

Labor efficiency variance The difference between the actual hours taken to complete a task and the standard hours allowed for the actual output, multiplied by the standard hourly labor rate. (p. 430)

Labor rate variance The difference between the actual hourly labor rate and the standard rate, multiplied by the number of hours worked during the period. (p. 432)

Management by exception A management system in which standards are set for various activities, with actual results compared to these standards. Significant deviations from standards are flagged as exceptions. (p. 419)

Materials price variance The difference between the actual unit price paid for an item and the standard price, multiplied by the quantity purchased. (p. 429)

Materials quantity variance The difference between the actual quantity of materials used in production and the standard quantity allowed for the actual output, multiplied by the standard price per unit of materials. (p. 427)

Practical standards Standards that allow for normal machine downtime and other work interruptions and that can be attained through reasonable, though highly efficient, efforts by the average worker. (p. 421)

Price variance A variance that is computed by taking the difference between the actual price and the standard price and multiplying the result by the actual quantity of the input. (p. 424)

Quantity variance A variance that is computed by taking the difference between the actual quantity of the input used and the amount of the input that should have been used for the actual level of output and multiplying the result by the standard price of the input. (p. 424)

Standard cost card A detailed listing of the standard amounts of inputs and their costs that are required to produce one unit of a specific product. (p. 420)

Standard cost per unit The standard quantity allowed of an input per unit of a specific product, multiplied by the standard price of the input. (p. 423)

Standard hours allowed The time that should have been taken to complete the period's output. It is computed by multiplying the actual number of units produced by the standard hours per unit. (p. 425)

Standard hours per unit The amount of direct labor time that should be required to complete a single unit of product, including allowances for breaks, machine downtime, cleanup, rejects, and other normal inefficiencies. (p. 422)

Standard price per unit The price that should be paid for an input. (p. 421)

Standard quantity allowed The amount of an input that should have been used to complete the period's actual output. It is computed by multiplying the actual number of units produced by the standard quantity per unit. (p. 425)

Standard quantity per unit The amount of an input that should be required to complete a single unit of product, including allowances for normal waste, spoilage, rejects, and other normal inefficiencies. (p. 421)

Standard rate per hour The labor rate that should be incurred per hour of labor time, including employment taxes and fringe benefits. (p. 422)

Variable overhead efficiency variance The difference between the actual level of activity (direct labor-hours, machine-hours, or some other base) and the standard activity allowed, multiplied by the variable part of the predetermined overhead rate. (p. 433)

Variable overhead rate variance The difference between the actual variable overhead cost incurred during a period and the standard cost that should have been incurred based on the actual activity of the period. (p. 434)

Questions

10–1 What is a quantity standard? What is a price standard?

10–2 Distinguish between ideal and practical standards.

10–3 What is meant by the term *management by exception?*

10–4 Why are separate price and quantity variances computed?

10–5 Who is generally responsible for the materials price variance? The materials quantity variance? The labor efficiency variance?

10–6 The materials price variance can be computed at what two different points in time? Which point is better? Why?

10–7 If the materials price variance is favorable but the materials quantity variance is unfavorable, what might this indicate?

10–8 Should standards be used to identify who to blame for problems?

10–9 "Our workers are all under labor contracts; therefore, our labor rate variance is bound to be zero." Discuss.

10–10 What effect, if any, would you expect poor-quality materials to have on direct labor variances?

10–11 If variable manufacturing overhead is applied to production on the basis of direct labor-hours and the direct labor efficiency variance is unfavorable, will the variable overhead efficiency variance be favorable or unfavorable, or could it be either? Explain.

10–12 What is a statistical control chart, and how is it used?

10–13 Why can undue emphasis on labor efficiency variances lead to excess work in process inventories?

Multiple-choice questions are provided on the text website at www.mhhe.com/garrison14e.

Applying Excel connect ACCOUNTING

LEARNING OBJECTIVES 1, 2, 3

Available with McGraw-Hill's *Connect™ Accounting*.

The Excel worksheet form that appears on the next page is to be used to recreate the main example in the text on pages 423–433. Download the workbook containing this form from the Online Learning Center at www.mhhe.com/garrison14e. *On the website you will also receive instructions about how to use this worksheet form.*

You should proceed to the requirements below only after completing your worksheet.

Required:

1. Check your worksheet by changing the direct materials standard quantity in cell B6 to 2.9 pounds, the direct labor quantity standard quantity in cell B7 to 0.6 hours, and the variable

	A	B	C	D	E	F	G
1	**Chapter 10: Applying Excel**						
2							
3	**Data**						
4	***Exhibit 10-2: Standard Cost Card***						
5	*Inputs*	*Standard Quantity*		*Standard Price*			
6	Direct materials	3.0	pounds	$4.00	per pound		
7	Direct labor	0.50	hours	$22.00	per hour		
8	Variable manufacturing overhead	0.50	hours	$6.00	per hour		
9							
10	Actual results:						
11	Actual output	2,000	units				
12	Actual variable manufacturing overhead cost	$7,140					
13		*Actual Quantity*		*Actual price*			
14	Actual direct materials cost	6,500	pounds	$3.80	per pound		
15	Actual direct labor cost	1,050	hours	$21.60	per hour		
16							
17	*Enter a formula into each of the cells marked with a ? below*						
18	**Main Example: Chapter 10**						
19							
20	***Exhibit 10-5: Standard Cost Variance Analysis–Direct Materials***						
21	Standard Quantity Allowed for the Actual Output, at Standard Price	?	pounds ×	?	per pound =	?	
22	Actual Quantity of Input, at Standard Price	?	pounds ×	?	per pound =	?	
23	Actual Quantity of Input, at Actual Price	?	pounds ×	?	per pound =	?	
24	Direct materials variances:						
25	Materials quantity variance	?					
26	Materials price variance	?					
27	Materials spending variance	?					
28							
29	***Exhibit 10-6: Standard Cost Variance Analysis–Direct Labor***						
30	Standard Hours Allowed for the Actual Output, at Standard Rate	?	hours ×	?	per hour =	?	
31	Actual Hours of Input, at Standard Rate	?	hours ×	?	per hour =	?	
32	Actual Hours of Input, at Actual Rate	?	hours ×	?	per hour =	?	
33	Direct labor variances:						
34	Labor efficiency variance	?					
35	Labor rate variance	?					
36	Labor spending variance	?					
37							
38	***Exhibit 10-7: Standard Cost Variance Analysis–Variable Manufacturing Overhead***						
39	Standard Hours Allowed for the Actual Output, at Standard Rate	?	hours ×	?	per hour =	?	
40	Actual Hours of Input, at Standard Rate	?	hours ×	?	per hour =	?	
41	Actual Hours of Input, at Actual Rate	?	hours ×	?	per hour =	?	
42	Variable overhead variances:						
43	Variable overhead efficiency variance	?					
44	Variable overhead rate variance	?					
45	Variable overhead spending variance	?					
46							

Chapter 10 Form | Filled in Chapter 10 Form | Chapter 10 Formulas

manufacturing overhead in cell B8 to 0.6 hours. The materials spending variance should now be $1,500 U, the labor spending variance should now be $3,720 F, and the variable overhead spending variance should now be $60 F. If you do not get these answers, find the errors in your worksheet and correct them.

a. What is the materials quantity variance? Explain this variance.

b. What is the labor rate variance? Explain this variance.

2. Revise the data in your worksheet to reflect the results for the subsequent period:

Data Exhibit 10–2: Standard Cost Card		
Inputs	Standard Quantity	Standard Price
Direct materials	3.0 pounds	$4.00 per pound
Direct labor	0.50 hours	$22.00 per hour
Variable manufacturing overhead	0.50 hours	$6.00 per hour
Actual results:		
Actual output	2,100 units	
Actual variable manufacturing overhead cost	$5,100	
	Actual Quantity	Actual price
Actual direct materials cost	6,350 pounds	$4.10 per pound
Actual direct labor cost	1,020 hours	$22.10 per hour

a. What is the materials quantity variance? What is the materials price variance?
b. What is the labor efficiency variance? What is the labor rate variance?
c. What is the variable overhead efficiency variance? What is the variable overhead rate variance?

Exercises connect ACCOUNTING

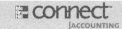

All applicable exercises are available with McGraw-Hill's *Connect™ Accounting*.

EXERCISE 10–1 Material Variances [LO1]

Harmon Household Products, Inc., manufactures a number of consumer items for general household use. One of these products, a chopping board, requires an expensive hardwood. During a recent month, the company manufactured 4,000 chopping boards using 11,000 board feet of hardwood. The hardwood cost the company $18,700.

The company's standards for one chopping board are 2.5 board feet of hardwood, at a cost of $1.80 per board foot.

Required:

1. According to the standards, what cost for wood should have been incurred to make 4,000 chopping blocks? How much greater or less is this than the cost that was incurred?
2. Break down the difference computed in (1) above into a materials price variance and a materials quantity variance.

EXERCISE 10–2 Direct Labor Variances [LO2]

AirMeals, Inc., prepares in-flight meals for a number of major airlines. One of the company's products is stuffed cannelloni with roasted pepper sauce, fresh baby corn, and spring salad. During the most recent week, the company prepared 6,000 of these meals using 1,150 direct labor-hours. The company paid these direct labor workers a total of $11,500 for this work, or $10 per hour.

According to the standard cost card for this meal, it should require 0.20 direct labor-hours at a cost of $9.50 per hour.

Required:

1. According to the standards, what direct labor cost should have been incurred to prepare 6,000 meals? How much does this differ from the actual direct labor cost?
2. Break down the difference computed in (1) above into a labor rate variance and a labor efficiency variance.

EXERCISE 10–3 Variable Overhead Variances [LO3]

Order Up, Inc., provides order fulfillment services for dot.com merchants. The company maintains warehouses that stock items carried by its dot.com clients. When a client receives an order from a customer, the order is forwarded to Order Up, which pulls the item from storage, packs it, and ships it to the customer. The company uses a predetermined variable overhead rate based on direct labor-hours.

In the most recent month, 140,000 items were shipped to customers using 5,800 direct labor-hours. The company incurred a total of $15,950 in variable overhead costs.

According to the company's standards, 0.04 direct labor-hours are required to fulfill an order for one item and the variable overhead rate is $2.80 per direct labor-hour.

Required:

1. According to the standards, what variable overhead cost should have been incurred to fill the orders for the 140,000 items? How much does this differ from the actual variable overhead cost?
2. Break down the difference computed in (1) above into a variable overhead rate variance and a variable overhead efficiency variance.

EXERCISE 10–4 Labor and Variable Manufacturing Overhead Variances [LO2, LO3]

Hollowell Audio, Inc., manufactures military-specification compact discs. The company uses standards to control its costs. The labor standards that have been set for one disc are as follows:

Standard Hours	Standard Rate per Hour	Standard Cost
6 minutes	$24.00	$2.40

During July, 2,125 hours of direct labor time were required to make 20,000 discs. The direct labor cost totaled $49,300 for the month.

Required:

1. According to the standards, what direct labor cost should have been incurred to make the 20,000 discs? By how much does this differ from the cost that was incurred?
2. Break down the difference in cost from (1) above into a labor rate variance and a labor efficiency variance.
3. The budgeted variable manufacturing overhead rate is $16.00 per direct labor-hour. During July, the company incurred $39,100 in variable manufacturing overhead cost. Compute the variable overhead rate and efficiency variances for the month.

EXERCISE 10–5 Working Backwards from Labor Variances [LO2]

The Worldwide Credit Card, Inc., uses standards to control the labor time involved in opening mail from card holders and recording the enclosed remittances. Incoming mail is gathered into batches, and a standard time is set for opening and recording each batch. The labor standards relating to one batch are as follows:

	Standard Hours	Standard Rate	Standard Cost
Per batch	1.25	$12.00	$15.00

The record showing the time spent last week in opening batches of mail has been misplaced. However, the batch supervisor recalls that 168 batches were received and opened during the week, and the controller recalls the following variance data relating to these batches:

Total labor spending variance	$330 U
Labor rate variance	$150 F

Required:

1. Determine the number of actual labor-hours spent opening batches during the week.
2. Determine the actual hourly rate paid to employees for opening batches last week.

(Hint: A useful way to proceed would be to work from known to unknown data either by using the variance formulas or by using the columnar format shown in Exhibit 10–6.)

EXERCISE 10–6 Material and Labor Variances [LO1, LO2]

Sonne Company produces a perfume called Whim. The direct materials and direct labor standards for one bottle of Whim are given below:

	Standard Quantity or Hours	Standard Price or Rate	Standard Cost
Direct materials	7.2 ounces	$2.50 per ounce	$18.00
Direct labor	0.4 hours	$10.00 per hour	$4.00

During the most recent month, the following activity was recorded:

a. Twenty thousand ounces of material were purchased at a cost of $2.40 per ounce.
b. All of the material was used to produce 2,500 bottles of Whim.
c. Nine hundred hours of direct labor time were recorded at a total labor cost of $10,800.

Required:

1. Compute the direct materials price and quantity variances for the month.
2. Compute the direct labor rate and efficiency variances for the month.

EXERCISE 10–7 Material Variances [LO1]

Refer to the data in Exercise 10–6. Assume that instead of producing 2,500 bottles of Whim during the month, the company produced only 2,000 bottles using 16,000 ounces of material. (The rest of the material purchased remained in raw materials inventory.)

Required:

Compute the direct materials price and quantity variances for the month.

EXERCISE 10–8 Material and Labor Variances [LO1, LO2]

Topper Toys has developed a new toy called the Brainbuster. The company has a standard cost system to help control costs and has established the following standards for the Brainbuster toy:

Direct materials: 8 diodes per toy at $0.30 per diode
Direct labor: 0.6 hours per toy at $14.00 per hour

During August, the company produced 5,000 Brainbuster toys. Production data on the toy for August follow:

Direct materials: 70,000 diodes were purchased at a cost of $0.28 per diode. 20,000 of these diodes were still in inventory at the end of the month.
Direct labor: 3,200 direct labor-hours were worked at a cost of $48,000.

Required:

1. Compute the following variances for August:
   a. Direct materials price and quantity variances.
   b. Direct labor rate and efficiency variances.
2. Prepare a brief explanation of the possible causes of each variance.

Problems

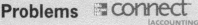

All applicable problems are available with McGraw-Hill's *Connect™ Accounting*.

PROBLEM 10–9 Comprehensive Variance Analysis [LO1, LO2, LO3]

Portland Company's Ironton Plant produces precast ingots for industrial use. Carlos Santiago, who was recently appointed general manager of the Ironton Plant, has just been handed the plant's contribution format income statement for October. The statement is shown below:

	Budgeted	Actual
Sales (5,000 ingots)	$250,000	$250,000
Variable expenses:		
Variable cost of goods sold*	80,000	96,390
Variable selling expenses	20,000	20,000
Total variable expenses	100,000	116,390
Contribution margin	150,000	133,610
Fixed expenses:		
Manufacturing overhead	60,000	60,000
Selling and administrative	75,000	75,000
Total fixed expenses	135,000	135,000
Net operating income (loss)	$ 15,000	$ (1,390)

*Contains direct materials, direct labor, and variable manufacturing overhead.

Mr. Santiago was shocked to see the loss for the month, particularly because sales were exactly as budgeted. He stated, "I sure hope the plant has a standard cost system in operation. If it doesn't, I won't have the slightest idea of where to start looking for the problem."

The plant does use a standard cost system, with the following standard variable cost per ingot:

	Standard Quantity or Hours	Standard Price or Rate	Standard Cost
Direct materials	4.0 pounds	$2.50 per pound	$10.00
Direct labor	0.6 hours	$9.00 per hour	5.40
Variable manufacturing overhead	0.3 hours*	$2.00 per hour	0.60
Total standard variable cost			$16.00

*Based on machine-hours.

During October the plant produced 5,000 ingots and incurred the following costs:

a. Purchased 25,000 pounds of materials at a cost of $2.95 per pound. There were no raw materials in inventory at the beginning of the month.
b. Used 19,800 pounds of materials in production. (Finished goods and work in process inventories are insignificant and can be ignored.)
c. Worked 3,600 direct labor-hours at a cost of $8.70 per hour.
d. Incurred a total variable manufacturing overhead cost of $4,320 for the month. A total of 1,800 machine-hours was recorded.

It is the company's policy to close all variances to cost of goods sold on a monthly basis.

Required:

1. Compute the following variances for October:
   a. Direct materials price and quantity variances.
   b. Direct labor rate and efficiency variances.
   c. Variable overhead rate and efficiency variances.
2. Summarize the variances that you computed in (1) above by showing the net overall favorable or unfavorable variance for October. What impact did this figure have on the company's income statement?
3. Pick out the two most significant variances that you computed in (1) above. Explain to Mr. Santiago possible causes of these variances.

PROBLEM 10–10 Variance Analysis in a Hospital [LO1, LO2, LO3]

"What's going on in that lab?" asked Derek Warren, chief administrator for Cottonwood Hospital, as he studied the prior month's reports. "Every month the lab teeters between a profit and a loss. Are we going to have to increase our lab fees again?"

"We can't," replied Lois Ankers, the controller. "We're getting *lots* of complaints about the last increase, particularly from the insurance companies and governmental health units. They're now paying only about 80% of what we bill. I'm beginning to think the problem is on the cost side."

To determine if lab costs are in line with other hospitals, Mr. Warren has asked you to evaluate the costs for the past month. Ms. Ankers has provided you with the following information:

a. Two basic types of tests are performed in the lab—smears and blood tests. During the past month, 2,700 smears and 900 blood tests were performed in the lab.
b. Small glass plates are used in both types of tests. During the past month, the hospital purchased 16,000 plates at a cost of $38,400. This cost is net of a 4% purchase discount. A total of 2,000 of these plates were unused at the end of the month; no plates were on hand at the beginning of the month.
c. During the past month, 1,800 hours of labor time were used in performing smears and blood tests. The cost of this labor time was $18,450.
d. The lab's variable overhead cost last month totaled $11,700.

Cottonwood Hospital has never used standard costs. By searching industry literature, however, you have determined the following nationwide averages for hospital labs:

Plates: Three plates are required per lab test. These plates cost $2.50 each and are disposed of after the test is completed.

Labor: Each smear should require 0.3 hours to complete, and each blood test should require 0.6 hours to complete. The average cost of this lab time is $12 per hour.

Overhead: Overhead cost is based on direct labor-hours. The average rate of variable overhead is $6 per hour.

Required:

1. Compute the materials price variance for the plates purchased last month, and compute a materials quantity variance for the plates used last month.
2. For labor cost in the lab:
   a. Compute a labor rate variance and a labor efficiency variance.
   b. In most hospitals, three-fourths of the workers in the lab are certified technicians and one-fourth are assistants. In an effort to reduce costs, Cottonwood Hospital employs only one-half certified technicians and one-half assistants. Would you recommend that this policy be continued? Explain.
3. Compute the variable overhead rate and efficiency variances. Is there any relation between the variable overhead efficiency variance and the labor efficiency variance? Explain.

PROBLEM 10-11 Basic Variance Analysis [LO1, LO2, LO3]
Barberry, Inc., manufactures a product called Fruta. The company uses a standard cost system and has established the following standards for one unit of Fruta:

	A	B	C	D	E	F
1		*Standard Quantity*		*Standard Price or Rate*		*Standard Cost*
2	Direct materials	1.5	pounds	$6.00	per pound	$ 9.00
3	Direct labor	0.6	hours	$12.00	per hour	7.20
4	Variable manufacturing overhead	0.6	hours	$2.50	per hour	1.50
5						$ 17.70
6						

Sheet1 Sheet2 Sheet3

During June, the company recorded this activity related to production of Fruta:

a. The company produced 3,000 units during June.
b. A total of 8,000 pounds of material were purchased at a cost of $46,000.
c. There was no beginning inventory of materials; however, at the end of the month, 2,000 pounds of material remained in ending inventory.
d. The company employs 10 persons to work on the production of Fruta. During June, they worked an average of 160 hours at an average rate of $12.50 per hour.
e. Variable manufacturing overhead is assigned to Fruta on the basis of direct labor-hours. Variable manufacturing overhead costs during June totaled $3,600.

The company's management is anxious to determine the efficiency of Fruta production activities.

Required:

1. For direct materials:
   a. Compute the price and quantity variances.
   b. The materials were purchased from a new supplier who is anxious to enter into a long-term purchase contract. Would you recommend that the company sign the contract? Explain.
2. For labor employed in the production of Fruta:
   a. Compute the rate and efficiency variances.
   b. In the past, the 10 persons employed in the production of Fruta consisted of 4 senior workers and 6 assistants. During June, the company experimented with 5 senior workers and 5 assistants. Would you recommend that the new labor mix be continued? Explain.
3. Compute the variable overhead rate and efficiency variances. What relation can you see between this efficiency variance and the labor efficiency variance?

PROBLEM 10–12 Basic Variance Analysis; the Impact of Variances on Unit Costs [LO1, LO2, LO3]
Landers Company manufactures a number of products. The standards relating to one of these products are shown below, along with actual cost data for May.

	Standard Cost per Unit		Actual Cost per Unit
Direct materials:			
Standard: 1.80 feet at $3.00 per foot	$ 5.40		
Actual: 1.75 feet at $3.20 per foot			$ 5.60
Direct labor:			
Standard: 0.90 hours at $18.00 per hour	16.20		
Actual: 0.95 hours at $17.40 per hour			16.53
Variable overhead:			
Standard: 0.90 hours at $5.00 per hour	4.50		
Actual: 0.95 hours at $4.60 per hour.			4.37
Total cost per unit	$26.10		$26.50
Excess of actual cost over standard cost per unit		$0.40	

The production superintendent was pleased when he saw this report and commented: "This $0.40 excess cost is well within the 2 percent limit management has set for acceptable variances. It's obvious that there's not much to worry about with this product."

Actual production for the month was 12,000 units. Variable overhead cost is assigned to products on the basis of direct labor-hours. There were no beginning or ending inventories of materials.

Required:

1. Compute the following variances for May:
   a. Materials price and quantity variances.
   b. Labor rate and efficiency variances.
   c. Variable overhead rate and efficiency variances.
2. How much of the $0.40 excess unit cost is traceable to each of the variances computed in (1) above.
3. How much of the $0.40 excess unit cost is traceable to apparent inefficient use of labor time?
4. Do you agree that the excess unit cost is not of concern?

PROBLEM 10–13 Materials and Labor Variances; Computations from Incomplete Data [LO1, LO2]
Topaz Company makes one product and has set the following standards for materials and labor:

	Direct Materials	Direct Labor
Standard quantity or hours per unit	? pounds	2.5 hours
Standard price or rate	? per pound	$9.00 per hour
Standard cost per unit	?	$22.50

During the past month, the company purchased 6,000 pounds of direct materials at a cost of $16,500. All of this material was used in the production of 1,400 units of product. Direct labor cost totaled $28,500 for the month. The following variances have been computed:

Materials quantity variance	$1,200 U
Total materials spending variance	$300 F
Labor efficiency variance.	$4,500 F

Required:

1. For direct materials:
   a. Compute the standard price per pound for materials.
   b. Compute the standard quantity allowed for materials for the month's production.
   c. Compute the standard quantity of materials allowed per unit of product.
2. For direct labor:
   a. Compute the actual direct labor cost per hour for the month.
   b. Compute the labor rate variance.

(Hint: In completing the problem, it may be helpful to move from known to unknown data either by using the variance formulas or by using the columnar format shown in Exhibits 10–5 and 10–6.)

PROBLEM 10–14 Comprehensive Variance Analysis [LO1, LO2, LO3]
Vitalite, Inc., produces a number of products, including a body-wrap kit. Standard variable costs relating to a single kit are given below:

	Standard Quantity or Hours	Standard Price or Rate	Standard Cost
Direct materials	?	$6 per yard	$?
Direct labor	?	?	?
Variable manufacturing overhead	?	$2 per direct labor-hour	?
Total standard cost per kit			$42

During August, 500 kits were manufactured and sold. Selected information relating to the month's production is given below:

	Materials Used	Direct Labor	Variable Manufacturing Overhead
Total standard cost*	?	$8,000	$1,600
Actual costs incurred	$10,000	?	$1,620
Materials price variance	?		
Materials quantity variance	$600 U		
Labor rate variance		?	
Labor efficiency variance		?	
Variable overhead rate variance			?
Variable overhead efficiency variance			?

*For the month's production.

The following additional information is available for August's production of kits:

Actual direct labor-hours	900
Difference between standard and actual cost per kit produced during August	$0.14 U

Required:

1. What was the total standard cost of the materials used during August?
2. How many yards of material are required at standard per kit?
3. What was the materials price variance for August if there were no beginning or ending inventories of materials?
4. What is the standard direct labor rate per hour?
5. What was the labor rate variance for August? The labor efficiency variance?
6. What was the variable overhead rate variance for August? The variable overhead efficiency variance?
7. Complete the standard cost card for one kit shown at the beginning of the problem.

PROBLEM 10–15 Comprehensive Variance Analysis [LO1, LO2, LO3]
Helix Company produces several products in its factory, including a karate robe. The company uses a standard cost system to assist in the control of costs. According to the standards that have

been set for the robes, the factory should work 780 direct labor-hours each month and produce 1,950 robes. The standard costs associated with this level of production are as follows:

	Total	Per Unit of Product
Direct materials	$35,490	$18.20
Direct labor	$7,020	3.60
Variable manufacturing overhead (based on direct labor-hours)	$2,340	1.20
		$23.00

During April, the factory worked only 760 direct labor-hours and produced 2,000 robes. The following actual costs were recorded during the month:

	Total	Per Unit of Product
Direct materials (6,000 yards)	$36,000	$18.00
Direct labor	$7,600	3.80
Variable manufacturing overhead	$3,800	1.90
		$23.70

At standard, each robe should require 2.8 yards of material. All of the materials purchased during the month were used in production.

Required:

Compute the following variances for April:

1. The materials price and quantity variances.
2. The labor rate and efficiency variances.
3. The variable manufacturing overhead rate and efficiency variances.

PROBLEM 10–16 Multiple Products, Materials, and Processes [LO1, LO2]

Monte Rosa Corporation produces two products, Alpha8s and Zeta9s, which pass through two operations, Sintering and Finishing. Each of the products uses two raw materials, X342 and Y561. The company uses a standard cost system, with the following standards for each product (on a per unit basis):

	Raw Material		Standard Labor Time	
Product	X342	Y561	Sintering	Finishing
Alpha8	1.8 kilos	2.0 liters	0.20 hours	0.80 hours
Zeta9	3.0 kilos	4.5 liters	0.35 hours	0.90 hours

Information relating to materials purchased and materials used in production during May follows:

Material	Purchases	Purchase Cost	Standard Price	Used in Production
X342	14,000 kilos	$51,800	$3.50 per kilo	8,500 kilos
Y561	15,000 liters	$19,500	$1.40 per liter	13,000 liters

The following additional information is available:

a. The company recognizes price variances when materials are purchased.
b. The standard labor rate is $20.00 per hour in Sintering and $19.00 per hour in Finishing.
c. During May, 1,200 direct labor-hours were worked in Sintering at a total labor cost of $27,000, and 2,850 direct labor-hours were worked in Finishing at a total labor cost of $59,850.
d. Production during May was 1,500 Alpha8s and 2,000 Zeta9s.

Required:

1. Prepare a standard cost card for each product, showing the standard cost of direct materials and direct labor.
2. Compute the materials quantity and price variances for each material.
3. Compute the direct labor efficiency and rate variances for each operation.

Case connect ACCOUNTING

All applicable cases are available with McGraw-Hill's *Connect™ Accounting.*

CASE 10–17 Working Backwards from Variance Data [LO1, LO2, LO3]

You have recently accepted a position with Lorthen Inc. As part of your duties, you review the variances that are reported for each period and make a presentation to the company's executive committee.

Earlier this morning you received the variances for one of the company's major products for the most recent period. After reviewing the variances and organizing the data for your presentation, you accidentally placed the material on top of some papers that were going to the shredder. In the middle of lunch you suddenly realized your mistake and dashed to the shredding room. There you found the operator busily feeding your pages through the machine. You managed to pull only part of one page from the feeding chute, which contains the following information:

Standard Cost Card	
Direct materials, 2.0 meters at $16.00 per meter	$32.00
Direct labor, 1.0 hours at $15.00 per hour	$15.00
Variable overhead, 1.0 hours at $9.00 per hour	$9.00

	Total Standard Cost	Quantity or Efficiency Variance	Price or Rate Variance
Direct materials	$608,000	$32,000 U	$11,600 F
Direct labor	$285,000	$15,000 U	$4,000 U
Variable overhead	$171,000	Ruined by shredder	$4,000 F

The standard for variable overhead is based on direct labor-hours. All of the materials purchased during the period were used in production.

At lunch your supervisor said how pleased she was with your work and that she was looking forward to your presentation that afternoon. You realize that to avoid looking like a bungling fool you must somehow generate the necessary "backup" data for the variances before the executive committee meeting starts in one hour.

Required:

1. How many units were produced during the period?
2. How many meters of direct materials were purchased and used in production?
3. What was the actual cost per meter of material?
4. How many actual direct labor-hours were worked during the period?
5. What was the actual rate per direct labor-hour?
6. How much actual variable manufacturing overhead cost was incurred during the period?

Appendix 10A: Predetermined Overhead Rates and Overhead Analysis in a Standard Costing System

LEARNING OBJECTIVE 4
Compute and interpret the fixed overhead volume and budget variances.

In this appendix, we will investigate how the predetermined overhead rates that we discussed in the job-order costing chapter earlier in the book can be used in a standard costing system. Throughout this appendix, we assume that an absorption costing system is used in which *all* manufacturing costs—both fixed and variable—are included in product costs.

EXHIBIT 10A–1
MicroDrive Corporation Data

Budgeted production	25,000 motors
Standard machine-hours per motor	2 machine-hours per motor
Budgeted machine-hours (2 machine-hours per motor × 25,000 motors)	50,000 machine-hours
Actual production	20,000 motors
Standard machine-hours allowed for the actual production (2 machine-hours per motor × 20,000 motors)	40,000 machine-hours
Actual machine-hours.	42,000 machine-hours
Budgeted variable manufacturing overhead . . .	$75,000
Budgeted fixed manufacturing overhead	$300,000
Total budgeted manufacturing overhead	$375,000
Actual variable manufacturing overhead	$71,000
Actual fixed manufacturing overhead	$308,000
Total actual manufacturing overhead	$379,000

Predetermined Overhead Rates

The data in Exhibit 10A–1 pertain to MicroDrive Corporation, a company that produces miniature electric motors. Note that the company budgeted for 50,000 machine-hours based on production of 25,000 motors. At this level of activity, the budgeted variable manufacturing overhead was $75,000 and the budgeted fixed manufacturing overhead was $300,000.

Recall from the job-order costing chapter that the following formula is used to set the predetermined overhead rate at the beginning of the period:

$$\frac{\text{Predetermined}}{\text{overhead rate}} = \frac{\text{Estimated total manufacturing overhead cost}}{\text{Estimated total amount of the allocation base}}$$

The estimated total amount of the allocation base in the formula for the predetermined overhead rate is called the **denominator activity.**

As discussed in the job-order costing chapter, once the predetermined overhead rate has been determined, it remains unchanged throughout the period, even if the actual level of activity differs from what was estimated. Consequently, the amount of overhead applied to each unit of product is the same regardless of when it is produced during the period.

MicroDrive Corporation uses budgeted machine-hours as its denominator activity in the predetermined overhead rate. Consequently, the company's predetermined overhead rate would be computed as follows:

$$\frac{\text{Predetermined}}{\text{overhead rate}} = \frac{\$375{,}000}{50{,}000\text{ MHs}} = \$7.50\text{ per MH}$$

This predetermined overhead rate can be broken down into its variable and fixed components as follows:

$$\frac{\text{Variable componenet of the}}{\text{predetermined overhead rate}} = \frac{\$75{,}000}{50{,}000\text{ MHs}} = \$1.50\text{ per MH}$$

$$\frac{\text{Fixed component of the}}{\text{predetermined overhead rate}} = \frac{\$300{,}000}{50{,}000\text{ MHs}} = \$6.00\text{ per MH}$$

For every standard machine-hour recorded, work in process is charged with $7.50 of manufacturing overhead, of which $1.50 represents variable manufacturing overhead and

$6.00 represents fixed manufacturing overhead. In total, MicroDrive Corporation would apply $300,000 of overhead to work in process as shown below:

$$\text{Overhead applied} = \frac{\text{Predetermined}}{\text{overhead rate}} \times \frac{\text{Standard hours allowed}}{\text{for the actual output}}$$

$$= \$7.50 \text{ per machine-hour} \times 40{,}000 \text{ machine-hours}$$

$$= \$300{,}000$$

Overhead Application in a Standard Cost System

To understand fixed overhead variances, we first have to understand how overhead is applied to work in process in a standard cost system. Recall that in the job-order costing chapter we applied overhead to work in process on the basis of the actual level of activity. This procedure was correct because at the time we were dealing with a normal cost system.[1] However, we are now dealing with a standard cost system. In such a system, overhead is applied to work in process on the basis of the *standard hours allowed for the actual output of the period* rather than on the basis of the actual number of hours worked. Exhibit 10A–2 illustrates this point. In a standard cost system, every unit of a particular product is charged with the same amount of overhead cost, regardless of how much time the unit actually requires for processing.

EXHIBIT 10A–2
Applied Overhead Costs: Normal Cost System versus Standard Cost System

Normal Cost System		Standard Cost System	
Manufacturing Overhead		Manufacturing Overhead	
Actual overhead costs incurred.	Applied overhead costs: Actual hours × Predetermined overhead rate.	Actual overhead costs incurred.	Applied overhead costs: Standard hours allowed for actual output × Predetermined overhead rate.
Underapplied or overapplied overhead		Underapplied or overapplied overhead	

Budget Variance

Two fixed manufacturing overhead variances are computed in a standard costing system—a *budget variance* and a *volume variance.* These variances are computed in Exhibit 10A–3. The **budget variance** is simply the difference between the actual fixed manufacturing overhead and the budgeted fixed manufacturing overhead for the period. The formula is:

$$\text{Budget variance} = \text{Actual fixed overhead} - \text{Budgeted fixed overhead}$$

If the actual fixed overhead cost exceeds the budgeted fixed overhead cost, the budget variance is labeled unfavorable. If the actual fixed overhead cost is less than the budgeted fixed overhead cost, the budget variance is labeled favorable.

Applying the formula to the MicroDrive Corporation data, the budget variance is computed as follows:

$$\text{Budget variance} = \$308{,}000 - \$300{,}000 = \$8{,}000 \text{ U}$$

[1] Normal cost systems are discussed on page 90 in the job-order costing chapter.

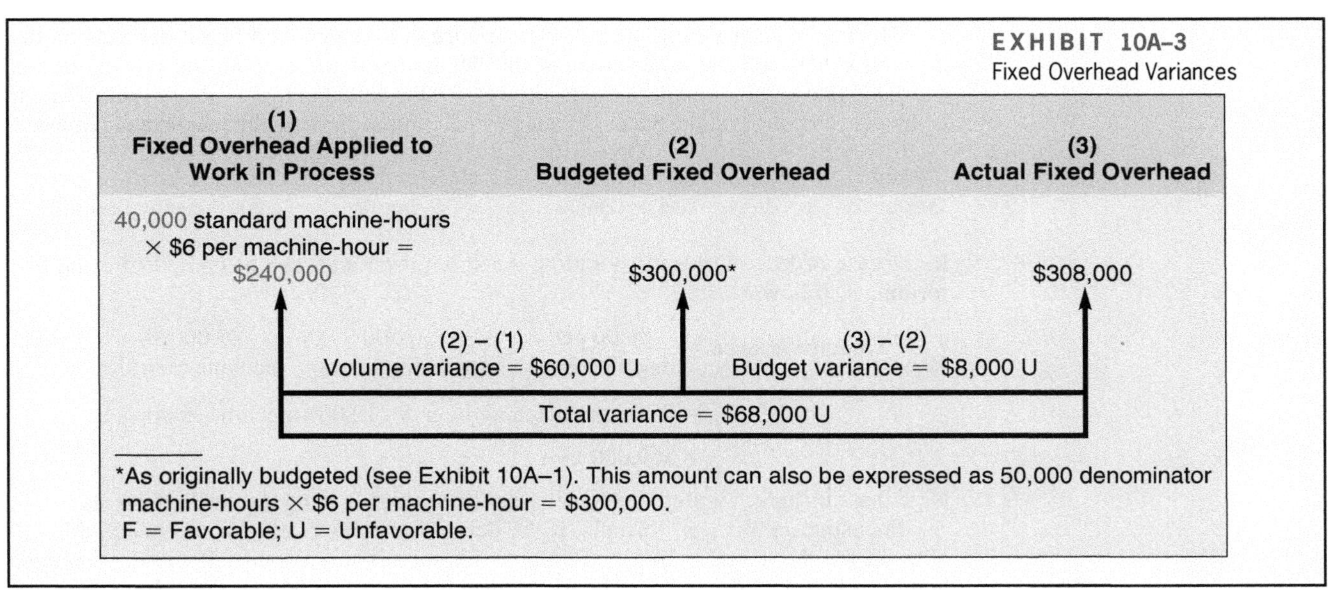

EXHIBIT 10A–3
Fixed Overhead Variances

According to the budget, the fixed manufacturing overhead should have been $300,000, but it was actually $308,000. Because the actual cost exceeds the budget by $8,000, the variance is labeled as unfavorable; however, this label does not automatically signal ineffective managerial performance. For example, this variance may be the result of waste and inefficiency, or it may be due to an unforeseen yet prudent investment in fixed overhead resources that improves product quality or manufacturing cycle efficiency.

Volume Variance

The **volume variance** is defined by the following formula:

$$\text{Volume variance} = \frac{\text{Budgeted fixed}}{\text{overhead}} - \frac{\text{Fixed overhead applied}}{\text{to work in process}}$$

When the budgeted fixed manufacturing overhead exceeds the fixed manufacturing overhead applied to work in process, the volume variance is labeled as unfavorable. When the budgeted fixed manufacturing overhead is less than the fixed manufacturing overhead applied to work in process, the volume variance is labeled as favorable. As we shall see, caution is advised when interpreting this variance.

To understand the volume variance, we need to understand how fixed manufacturing overhead is applied to work in process in a standard costing system. As discussed earlier, fixed manufacturing overhead is applied to work in process on the basis of the standard hours allowed for the actual output of the period. In the case of MicroDrive Corporation, the company produced 20,000 motors and the standard for each motor is 2 machine-hours. Therefore, the standard hours allowed for the actual output is 40,000 machine-hours (= 20,000 motors × 2 machine-hours). As shown in Exhibit 10A–3, the predetermined fixed manufacturing overhead rate of $6.00 per machine-hour is multiplied by the 40,000 standard machine-hours allowed for the actual output to arrive at $240,000 of fixed manufacturing overhead applied to work in process. Another way to think of this is that the standard for each motor is 2 machine-hours. Because the predetermined fixed manufacturing overhead rate is $6.00 per machine-hour, each motor is assigned $12.00 (= 2 machine-hours × $6.00 per machine-hour) of fixed manufacturing overhead. Consequently, a total of $240,000 of fixed manufacturing overhead is applied to the 20,000 motors that are actually produced. Under either explanation, the volume variance according to the formula is:

$$\text{Volume variance} = \$300{,}000 - \$240{,}000 = \$60{,}000\text{ U}$$

The key to interpreting the volume variance is to understand that it depends on the difference between the hours used in the denominator to compute the predetermined overhead rate and the standard hours allowed for the actual output of the period. While it is not obvious, the volume variance can also be computed using the following formula:

$$\text{Volume variance} = \text{Fixed component of the predetermined overhead rate} \times \left(\text{Denominator hours} - \text{Standard hours allowed for the actual output}\right)$$

In the case of MicroDrive Corporation, the volume variance can be computed using this formula as follows:

$$\begin{aligned}\text{Volume variance} &= \frac{\$6.00 \text{ per}}{\text{machine-hour}} \times \left(\frac{50{,}000}{\text{machine-hours}} - \frac{40{,}000}{\text{machine-hours}}\right)\\ &= \$6.00 \text{ per machine-hour} \times (10{,}000 \text{ machine-hours})\\ &= \$60{,}000 \text{ U}\end{aligned}$$

Note that this agrees with the volume variance computed using the earlier formula.

Focusing on this new formula, if the denominator hours exceed the standard hours allowed for the actual output, the volume variance is unfavorable. If the denominator hours are less than the standard hours allowed for the actual output, the volume variance is favorable. Stated differently, the volume variance is unfavorable if the actual level of activity is less than expected. The volume variance is favorable if the actual level of activity is greater than expected. It is important to note that the volume variance does not measure overspending or underspending. A company should incur the same dollar amount of fixed overhead cost regardless of whether the period's activity was above or below the planned (denominator) level.

The volume variance is often viewed as a measure of the utilization of facilities. If the standard hours allowed for the actual output are greater than (less than) the denominator hours, it signals efficient (inefficient) usage of facilities. However, other measures of utilization—such as the percentage of capacity utilized—are easier to compute and understand. Perhaps a better interpretation of the volume variance is that it is the error that occurs when the level of activity is incorrectly estimated and the costing system assumes fixed costs behave as if they are variable. This interpretation may be clearer in the next section that graphically analyses the fixed manufacturing overhead variances.

Graphic Analysis of Fixed Overhead Variances

Exhibit 10A–4 shows a graphic analysis that offers insights into the fixed overhead budget and volume variances. As shown in the graph, fixed overhead cost is applied to work in process at the predetermined rate of $6.00 for each standard hour of activity. (The applied-cost line is the upward-sloping line on the graph.) Because a denominator level of 50,000 machine-hours was used in computing the $6.00 rate, the applied-cost line crosses the budget-cost line at exactly 50,000 machine-hours. If the denominator hours and the standard hours allowed for the actual output are the same, there is no volume variance. It is only when the standard hours differ from the denominator hours that a volume variance arises.

In MicroDrive's case, the standard hours allowed for the actual output (40,000 hours) are less than the denominator hours (50,000 hours). The result is an unfavorable volume variance because less cost was applied to production than was originally budgeted. If the situation had been reversed and the standard hours allowed for the actual output had exceeded the denominator hours, then the volume variance on the graph would have been favorable.

Cautions in Fixed Overhead Analysis

A volume variance for fixed overhead arises because when applying the costs to work in process, we act *as if* the fixed costs are variable. The graph in Exhibit 10A–4 illustrates this point. Notice from the graph that fixed overhead costs are applied to work in process at a rate of $6 per hour *as if* they are variable. Treating these costs as if they are variable

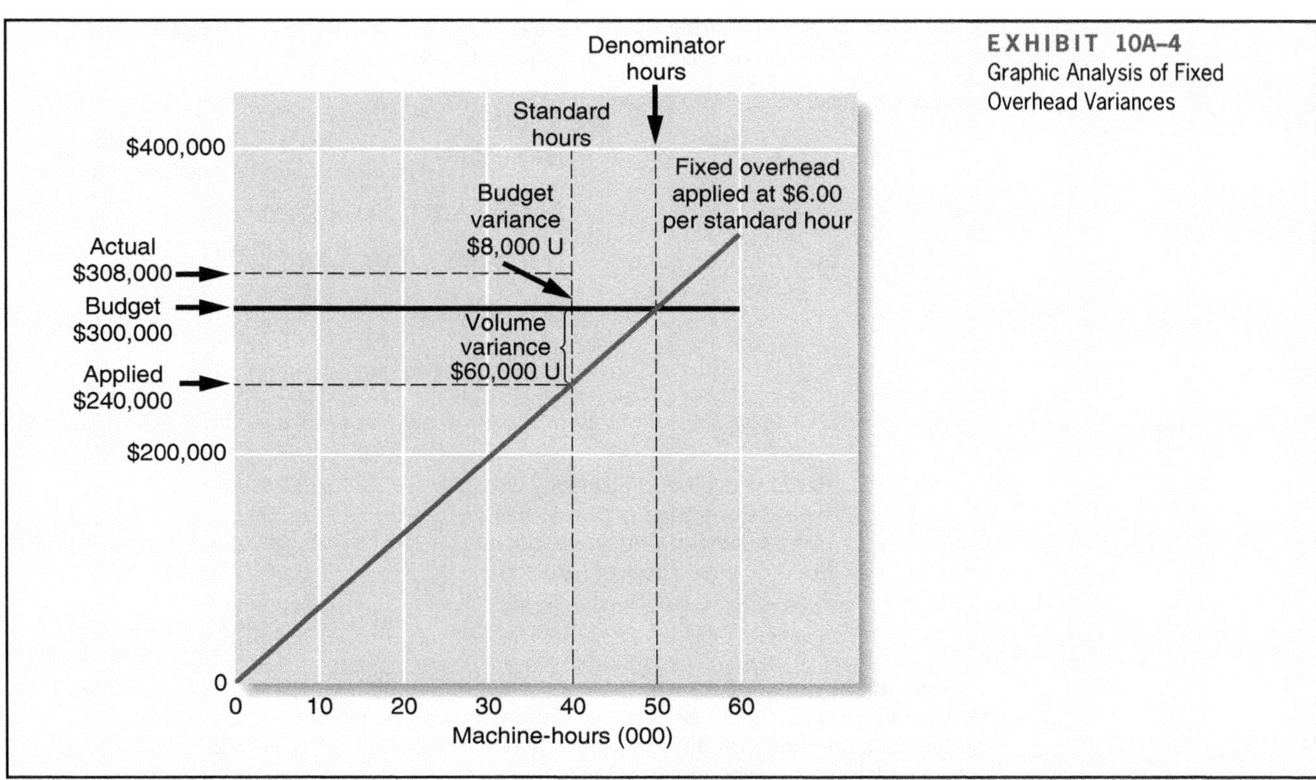

EXHIBIT 10A–4
Graphic Analysis of Fixed Overhead Variances

is necessary for product costing purposes, but some real dangers lurk here. Managers can easily be misled into thinking that fixed costs are *in fact* variable.

Keep clearly in mind that fixed overhead costs come in large chunks. Expressing fixed costs on a unit or per hour basis, though necessary for product costing for external reports, is artificial. Increases or decreases in activity in fact have no effect on total fixed costs within the relevant range of activity. Even though fixed costs are expressed on a unit or per hour basis, they are *not* proportional to activity. In a sense, the volume variance is the error that occurs as a result of treating fixed costs as variable costs in the costing system.

Reconciling Overhead Variances and Underapplied or Overapplied Overhead

In a standard cost system, the underapplied or overapplied overhead for a period equals the sum of the overhead variances. To see this, we will return to the MicroDrive Corporation example.

As discussed earlier, in a standard cost system, overhead is applied to work in process on the basis of the standard hours allowed for the actual output of the period. The following table shows how the underapplied or overapplied overhead for MicroDrive is computed.

Predetermined overhead rate (a)	$7.50 per machine-hour
Standard hours allowed for the actual output [Exhibit 10A–1] (b)	40,000 machine-hours
Manufacturing overhead applied (a) × (b)	$300,000
Actual manufacturing overhead [Exhibit 10A–1]	$379,000
Manufacturing overhead underapplied or overapplied	$79,000 underapplied

We have already computed the budget variance and the volume variance for this company. We will also need to compute the variable manufacturing overhead variances. The data for these computations are contained in Exhibit 10A–1. Recalling the formulas for the variable manufacturing overhead variances from earlier in this chapter, we can compute the variable overhead efficiency and rate variances as follows:

$$\text{Variable overhead efficiency variance} = (AH \times SR) - (SH \times SR)$$

$$= (\$63{,}000) - \left(\begin{matrix}40{,}000 \\ \text{machine-hours}\end{matrix} \times \begin{matrix}\$1.50\text{ per} \\ \text{machine-hour}\end{matrix}\right)$$

$$= \$63{,}000 - \$60{,}000 = \$3{,}000\text{ U}$$

$$\text{Variable overhead rate variance} = (AH \times AR) - (AH \times SR)$$

$$= (\$71{,}000) - \left(\begin{matrix}42{,}000 \\ \text{machine-hours}\end{matrix} \times \begin{matrix}\$1.50\text{ per} \\ \text{machine-hour}\end{matrix}\right)$$

$$= \$71{,}000 - \$63{,}000 = \$8{,}000\text{ U}$$

We can now compute the sum of all of the overhead variances as follows:

Variable overhead efficiency variance	$ 3,000 U
Variable overhead rate variance	8,000 U
Fixed overhead volume variance	60,000 U
Fixed overhead budget variance	8,000 U
Total of the overhead variances	$79,000 U

Note that the total of the overhead variances is $79,000, which equals the underapplied overhead of $79,000. In general, if the overhead is underapplied, the total of the standard cost overhead variances is unfavorable. If the overhead is overapplied, the total of the standard cost overhead variances is favorable.

Glossary

Budget variance The difference between the actual fixed overhead costs and the budgeted fixed overhead costs for the period. (p. 456)

Denominator activity The level of activity used to compute the predetermined overhead rate. (p. 455)

Volume variance The variance that arises whenever the standard hours allowed for the actual output of a period are different from the denominator activity level that was used to compute the predetermined overhead rate. It is computed by multiplying the fixed component of the predetermined overhead rate by the difference between the denominator hours and the standard hours allowed for the actual output. (p. 457)

Appendix 10A Exercises and Problems 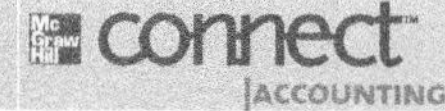

All applicable exercises and problems are available with McGraw-Hill's *Connect™ Accounting*.

EXERCISE 10A–1 Applying Overhead in a Standard Costing System [LO4]

Mosbach Corporation has a standard cost system in which it applies overhead to products based on the standard direct labor-hours allowed for the actual output of the period. Data concerning the most recent year are as follows:

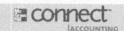

Variable overhead cost per direct labor-hour	$3.50
Total fixed overhead cost per year	$600,000
Budgeted standard direct labor-hours (denominator level of activity)	80,000
Actual direct labor-hours	84,000
Standard direct labor-hours allowed for the actual output	82,000

Required:

1. Compute the predetermined overhead rate for the year.
2. Determine the amount of overhead that would be applied to the output of the period.

EXERCISE 10A–2 Fixed Overhead Variances [LO4]

Lusive Corporation has a standard cost system in which it applies overhead to products based on the standard direct labor-hours allowed for the actual output of the period. Data concerning the most recent year appear below:

Total budgeted fixed overhead cost for the year	$400,000
Actual fixed overhead cost for the year	$394,000
Budgeted standard direct labor-hours (denominator level of activity)	50,000
Actual direct labor-hours	51,000
Standard direct labor-hours allowed for the actual output	48,000

Required:

1. Compute the fixed portion of the predetermined overhead rate for the year.
2. Compute the fixed overhead budget and volume variances.

EXERCISE 10A–3 Fixed Overhead Variances [LO4]

Selected operating information on three different companies for a recent period is given below:

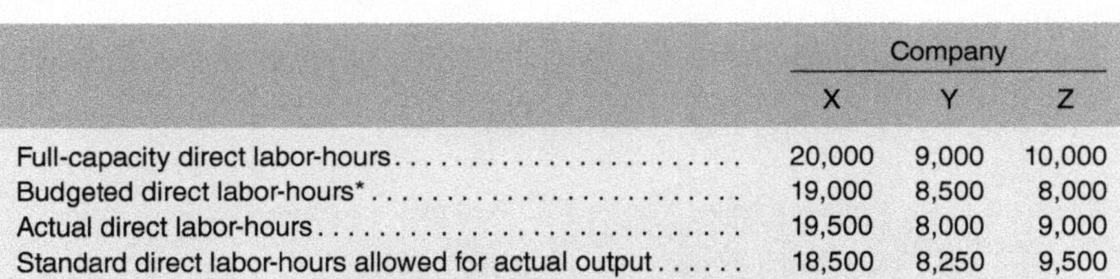

	Company		
	X	Y	Z
Full-capacity direct labor-hours	20,000	9,000	10,000
Budgeted direct labor-hours*	19,000	8,500	8,000
Actual direct labor-hours	19,500	8,000	9,000
Standard direct labor-hours allowed for actual output	18,500	8,250	9,500

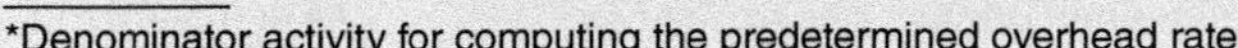

*Denominator activity for computing the predetermined overhead rate.

Required:

For each company, state whether the volume variance would be favorable or unfavorable and explain why.

EXERCISE 10A–4 Relations Among Fixed Overhead Variances [LO4]

Selected information relating to the fixed overhead costs of Westwood Company for the most recent year is given below:

Activity:	
Number of units produced	9,500
Standard machine-hours allowed per unit	2
Denominator activity (machine-hours)	20,000
Costs:	
Actual fixed overhead costs incurred	$79,000
Budget variance	$1,000 F

Overhead cost is applied to products on the basis of standard machine-hours.

Required:
1. What was the fixed portion of the predetermined overhead rate?
2. What were the standard machine-hours allowed for the period's production?
3. What was the volume variance?

EXERCISE 10A–5 Predetermined Overhead Rates [LO4]
Operating at a normal level of 24,000 direct labor-hours per year, Trone Company produces 8,000 units of product. The direct labor wage rate is $12.60 per hour. Two pounds of raw materials go into each unit of product at a cost of $4.20 per pound. Variable manufacturing overhead should be $1.60 per standard direct labor-hour. Fixed manufacturing overhead should be $84,000 per year.

Required:
1. Using 24,000 direct labor-hours as the denominator activity, compute the predetermined overhead rate and break it down into fixed and variable elements.
2. Complete the standard cost card below for one unit of product:

Direct materials, 2 pounds at $4.20 per pound	$8.40
Direct labor, ?	?
Variable manufacturing overhead, ?	?
Fixed manufacturing overhead, ?	?
Total standard cost per unit	$?

EXERCISE 10A–6 Predetermined Overhead Rate; Overhead Variances [LO3, LO4]
Weller Company's variable manufacturing overhead should be $1.05 per standard machine-hour and its fixed manufacturing overhead should be $24,800 per month. The following information is available for a recent month:

a. The denominator activity of 8,000 machine-hours was chosen to compute the predetermined overhead rate.
b. At the 8,000 standard machine-hours level of activity, the company should produce 3,200 units of product.
c. The company's actual operating results were as follows:

Number of units produced	3,500
Actual machine-hours	8,500
Actual variable manufacturing overhead cost	$9,860
Actual fixed manufacturing overhead cost	$25,100

Required:
1. Compute the predetermined overhead rate and break it down into variable and fixed cost elements.
2. What were the standard hours allowed for the year's actual output?
3. Compute the variable overhead rate and efficiency variances and the fixed overhead budget and volume variances.

EXERCISE 10A–7 Using Fixed Overhead Variances [LO4]
The standard cost card for the single product manufactured by Prince Company is given below:

Standard Cost Card—Per Unit	
Direct materials, 3.5 feet at $4.00 per foot	$14.00
Direct labor, 0.8 direct labor-hours at $18.00 per direct labor-hour	14.40
Variable overhead, 0.8 direct labor-hours at $2.50 per direct labor-hour	2.00
Fixed overhead, 0.8 direct labor-hours at $6.00 per direct labor-hour	4.80
Total standard cost per unit	$35.20

Last year, the company produced 10,000 units of product and worked 8,200 actual direct labor-hours. Manufacturing overhead cost is applied to production on the basis of direct labor-hours. Selected data relating to the company's fixed manufacturing overhead cost for the year are shown below:

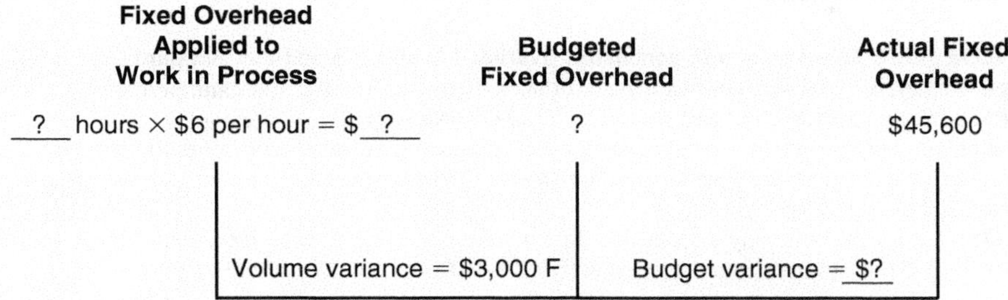

Required:

1. What were the standard hours allowed for the year's production?
2. What was the amount of budgeted fixed overhead cost for the year?
3. What was the budget variance for the year?
4. What denominator activity level did the company use in setting the predetermined overhead rate for the year?

PROBLEM 10A–8 Comprehensive Standard Cost Variances [LO1, LO2, LO3, LO4]

"It certainly is nice to see that small variance on the income statement after all the trouble we've had lately in controlling manufacturing costs," said Linda White, vice president of Molina Company. "The $12,250 overall manufacturing variance reported last period is well below the 3% limit we have set for variances. We need to congratulate everybody on a job well done."

The company produces and sells a single product. The standard cost card for the product follows:

Standard Cost Card—Per Unit	
Direct materials, 4 yards at $3.50 per yard	$14.00
Direct labor, 1.5 direct labor-hours at $12.00 per direct labor-hour	18.00
Variable overhead, 1.5 direct labor-hours at $2.00 per direct labor-hour	3.00
Fixed overhead, 1.5 direct-labor hours at $6.00 per direct labor-hour	9.00
Standard cost per unit	$44.00

The following additional information is available for the year just completed:

a. The company manufactured 20,000 units of product during the year.
b. A total of 78,000 yards of material was purchased during the year at a cost of $3.75 per yard. All of this material was used to manufacture the 20,000 units. There were no beginning or ending inventories for the year.
c. The company worked 32,500 direct labor-hours during the year at a cost of $11.80 per hour.
d. Overhead cost is applied to products on the basis of standard direct labor-hours. Data relating to manufacturing overhead costs follow:

Denominator activity level (direct labor-hours)	25,000
Budgeted fixed overhead costs	$150,000
Actual fixed overhead costs	$148,000
Actual variable overhead costs	$68,250

Required:

1. Compute the direct materials price and quantity variances for the year.
2. Compute the direct labor rate and efficiency variances for the year.

3. For manufacturing overhead, compute the following:
   a. The variable overhead rate and efficiency variances for the year.
   b. The fixed overhead budget and volume variances for the year.
4. Total the variances you have computed, and compare the net amount with the $12,250 mentioned by the vice president. Do you agree that everyone should be congratulated for a job well done? Explain.

PROBLEM 10A–9 Selection of a Denominator; Overhead Analysis; Standard Cost Card [LO3, LO4]
Scott Company's variable manufacturing overhead should be $2.50 per standard direct labor-hour and fixed manufacturing overhead should be $320,000 per year.

The company produces a single product that requires 2.5 direct labor-hours to complete. The direct labor wage rate is $20 per hour. Three yards of raw material are required for each unit of product, at a cost of $5 per yard.

Demand for the company's product differs widely from year to year. Expected activity for this year is 50,000 direct labor-hours; normal activity is 40,000 direct labor-hours per year.

Required:

1. Assume that the company chooses 40,000 direct labor-hours as the denominator level of activity. Compute the predetermined overhead rate, breaking it down into fixed and variable cost components.
2. Assume that the company chooses 50,000 direct labor-hours as the denominator level of activity. Repeat the computations in (1) above.
3. Complete two standard cost cards as outlined below.

Denominator Activity: 40,000 DLHs	
Direct materials, 3 yards at $5 per yard	$15.00
Direct labor, ?	?
Variable manufacturing overhead, ?.	?
Fixed manufacturing overhead, ?	?
Total standard cost per unit.	$?

Denominator Activity: 50,000 DLHs	
Direct materials, 3 yards at $5 per yard	$15.00
Direct labor, ?	?
Variable manufacturing overhead, ?.	?
Fixed manufacturing overhead, ?	?
Total standard cost per unit.	$?

4. Assume that 48,000 actual hours are worked during the year, and that 18,500 units are produced. Actual manufacturing overhead costs for the year are as follows:

Variable manufacturing overhead cost	$124,800
Fixed manufacturing overhead cost.	321,700
Total manufacturing overhead cost.	$446,500

   a. Compute the standard hours allowed for the year's actual output.
   b. Compute the missing items from the Manufacturing Overhead account below. Assume that the company uses 40,000 direct labor-hours (normal activity) as the denominator activity figure in computing overhead rates, as you have used in (1) above.

Manufacturing Overhead

Debit	Credit
Actual costs 446,500	?
?	?

c. Analyze your underapplied or overapplied overhead balance in terms of variable overhead rate and efficiency variances and fixed overhead budget and volume variances.

5. Looking at the variances that you have computed, what appears to be the major disadvantage of using normal activity rather than expected actual activity as a denominator in computing the predetermined overhead rate? What advantages can you see to offset this disadvantage?

PROBLEM 10A–10 Applying Overhead; Overhead Variances [LO3, LO4]

Highland Shortbread, Ltd., of Aberdeen, Scotland, produces a single product and uses a standard cost system to help control costs. Manufacturing overhead is applied to production on the basis of standard machine-hours. According to the company's flexible budget, the following overhead costs should be incurred at an activity level of 18,000 machine-hours (the denominator activity level chosen for the year):

Variable manufacturing overhead cost	£ 31,500
Fixed manufacturing overhead cost	72,000
Total manufacturing overhead cost	£103,500

During the year, the following operating results were recorded:

Actual machine-hours worked	15,000
Standard machine-hours allowed	16,000
Actual variable manufacturing overhead cost incurred	£26,500
Actual fixed manufacturing overhead cost incurred	£70,000

At the end of the year, the company's Manufacturing Overhead account contained the following data:

Manufacturing Overhead

Actual costs	96,500	Applied costs	92,000
	4,500		

Management would like to determine the cause of the £4,500 underapplied overhead.

Required:

1. Compute the predetermined overhead rate for the year. Break it down into variable and fixed cost elements.
2. Show how the £92,000 "Applied costs" figure in the Manufacturing Overhead account was computed.
3. Analyze the £4,500 underapplied overhead figure in terms of the variable overhead rate and efficiency variances and the fixed overhead budget and volume variances.
4. Explain the meaning of each variance that you computed in (3) above.

PROBLEM 10A–11 Applying Overhead; Overhead Variances [LO3, LO4]

Wymont Company produces a single product that requires a large amount of labor time. Overhead cost is applied on the basis of standard direct labor-hours. Variable manufacturing overhead should be $2.00 per standard direct labor-hour and fixed manufacturing overhead should be $180,000 per year.

The company's product requires 4 feet of direct material that has a standard cost of $3.00 per foot. The product requires 1.5 hours of direct labor time. The standard labor rate is $12.00 per hour.

During the year, the company had planned to operate at a denominator activity level of 30,000 direct labor-hours and to produce 20,000 units of product. Actual activity and costs for the year were as follows:

Number of units produced	22,000
Actual direct labor-hours worked	35,000
Actual variable manufacturing overhead cost incurred	$63,000
Actual fixed manufacturing overhead cost incurred	$181,000

Required:

1. Compute the predetermined overhead rate for the year. Break the rate down into variable and fixed components.
2. Prepare a standard cost card for the company's product; show the details for all manufacturing costs on your standard cost card.
3. *a.* Compute the standard direct labor-hours allowed for the year's production.
   b. Complete the following Manufacturing Overhead T-account for the year:

Manufacturing Overhead	
?	?
?	?

4. Determine the reason for the underapplied or overapplied overhead from (3) above by computing the variable overhead rate and efficiency variances and the fixed overhead budget and volume variances.
5. Suppose the company had chosen 36,000 direct labor-hours as the denominator activity rather than 30,000 hours. State which, if any, of the variances computed in (4) above would have changed, and explain how the variance(s) would have changed. No computations are necessary.

PROBLEM 10A–12 Comprehensive Standard Cost Variances [LO1, LO2, LO3, LO4]

Dresser Company uses a standard cost system and sets predetermined overhead rates on the basis of direct labor-hours. The following data are taken from the company's budget for the current year:

Denominator activity (direct labor-hours)	9,000
Variable manufacturing overhead cost at 9,000 direct labor-hours	$34,200
Fixed manufacturing overhead cost	$63,000

The standard cost card for the company's only product is given below:

Direct materials, 4 pounds at $2.60 per pound	$10.40
Direct labor, 2 direct labor-hours at $9.00 per hour	18.00
Overhead, 2 direct labor-hours at $10.80 per hour	21.60
Standard cost per unit	$50.00

During the year, the company produced 4,800 units of product and incurred the following costs:

Materials purchased, 30,000 pounds at $2.50 per pound	$75,000
Materials used in production (in pounds)	20,000
Direct labor cost incurred, 10,000 direct labor-hours at $8.60 per direct labor-hour	$86,000
Variable manufacturing overhead cost incurred	$35,900
Fixed manufacturing overhead cost incurred	$64,800

Required:

1. Redo the standard cost card in a clearer, more usable format by detailing the variable and fixed overhead cost elements.
2. Prepare an analysis of the variances for materials and labor for the year.
3. Prepare an analysis of the variances for variable and fixed overhead for the year.
4. What effect, if any, does the choice of a denominator activity level have on standard unit costs? Is the volume variance a controllable variance from a spending point of view? Explain.

Appendix 10B: Journal Entries to Record Variances

LEARNING OBJECTIVE 5
Prepare journal entries to record standard costs and variances.

Although standard costs and variances can be computed and used by management without being formally entered into the accounting records, many organizations prefer to make formal journal entries. Formal entry tends to give variances a greater emphasis than informal, off-the-record computations. This emphasis signals management's desire to keep costs within the limits that have been set. In addition, formal use of standard costs simplifies the bookkeeping process enormously. Inventories and cost of goods sold can be valued at their standard costs—eliminating the need to keep track of the actual cost of each unit.

Direct Materials Variances

To illustrate the journal entries needed to record standard cost variances, we will return to the data contained in the review problem at the end of the chapter. The entry to record the purchase of direct materials would be as follows:

Raw Materials (18,000 ounces at $0.50 per ounce)	9,000	
Materials Price Variance (18,000 ounces at $0.10 per ounce U)	1,800	
Accounts Payable (18,000 ounces at $0.60 per ounce)		10,800

Notice that the price variance is recognized when purchases are made, rather than when materials are actually used in production and that the materials are carried in the inventory account at standard cost. As direct materials are later drawn from inventory and used in production, the quantity variance is isolated as follows:

Work in Process (12,000 ounces at $0.50 per ounce)	6,000	
Materials Quantity Variance (2,000 ounces U at $0.50 per ounce)	1,000	
Raw Materials (14,000 ounces at $0.50 per ounce)		7,000

Thus, direct materials are added to the Work in Process account at the standard cost of the materials that should have been used to produce the actual output.

Notice that both the price variance and the quantity variance above are unfavorable and are debit entries. If either of these variances had been favorable, it would have appeared as a credit entry.

Direct Labor Variances

Referring again to the cost data in the review problem at the end of the chapter, the journal entry to record the incurrence of direct labor cost would be:

Work in Process (1,200 hours at $30.00 per hour)	36,000	
Labor Rate Variance (1,100 hours at $0.50 U)	550	
Labor Efficiency Variance (100 hours F at $30.00 per hour)		3,000
Wages Payable (1,100 hours at $30.50 per hour)		33,550

Thus, as with direct materials, direct labor costs enter into the Work in Process account at standard, both in terms of the rate and in terms of the hours allowed for the actual production of the period. Note that the unfavorable labor efficiency variance is a debit entry whereas the favorable labor rate variance is a credit entry.

Cost Flows in a Standard Cost System

The flow of costs through the company's accounts are illustrated in Exhibit 10B–1. Note that entries into the various inventory accounts are made at standard cost—not actual cost. The differences between actual and standard costs are entered into special accounts that

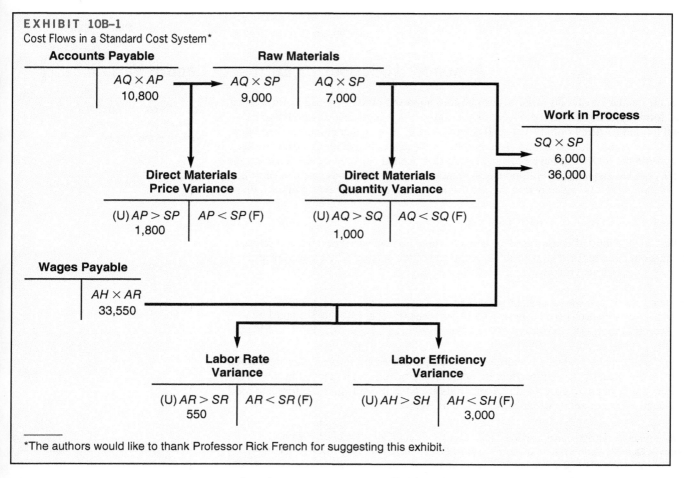

EXHIBIT 10B–1
Cost Flows in a Standard Cost System*

Accounts Payable

	$AQ \times AP$ 10,800

Raw Materials

$AQ \times SP$ 9,000	$AQ \times SP$ 7,000

Work in Process

$SQ \times SP$ 6,000 36,000	

Direct Materials Price Variance

(U) $AP > SP$ 1,800	$AP < SP$ (F)

Direct Materials Quantity Variance

(U) $AQ > SQ$ 1,000	$AQ < SQ$ (F)

Wages Payable

	$AH \times AR$ 33,550

Labor Rate Variance

(U) $AR > SR$ 550	$AR < SR$ (F)

Labor Efficiency Variance

(U) $AH > SH$	$AH < SH$ (F) 3,000

*The authors would like to thank Professor Rick French for suggesting this exhibit.

accumulate the various standard cost variances. Ordinarily, these standard cost variance accounts are closed out to Cost of Goods Sold at the end of the period. Unfavorable variances increase Cost of Goods Sold, and favorable variances decrease Cost of Goods Sold.

Appendix 10B Exercises and Problems

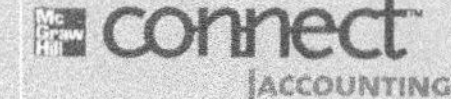

All applicable exercises and problems are available with McGraw-Hill's *Connect™ Accounting*.

EXERCISE 10B–1 Recording Variances in the General Ledger [LO5]

Kinkel Corporation makes a product with the following standard costs for direct material and direct labor:

Direct material: 1.50 meters at $5.40 per meter	$8.10
Direct labor: 0.25 hours at $14.00 per hour	$3.50

During the most recent month, 8,000 units were produced. The costs associated with the month's production of this product were as follows:

Material purchased: 15,000 meters at $5.60 per meter	$84,000
Material used in production: 11,900 meters	—
Direct labor: 1,950 hours at $14.20 per hour	$27,690

The standard cost variances for direct material and direct labor are:

Materials price variance: 15,000 meters at $0.20 per meter U.	$3,000 U
Materials quantity variance: 100 meters at $5.40 per meter F	$540 F
Labor rate variance: 1,950 hours at $0.20 per hour U	$390 U
Labor efficiency variance: 50 hours at $14.00 per hour F.	$700 F

Required:

1. Prepare the journal entry to record the purchase of materials on account for the month.
2. Prepare the journal entry to record the use of materials for the month.
3. Prepare the journal entry to record the incurrence of direct labor cost for the month.

EXERCISE 10B–2 Material and Labor Variances; Journal Entries [LO1, LO2, LO5]
Aspen Products, Inc., began production of a new product on April 1. The company uses a standard cost system and has established the following standards for one unit of the new product:

	Standard Quantity or Hours	Standard Price or Rate	Standard Cost
Direct materials.	3.5 feet	$6.00 per foot	$21.00
Direct labor	0.4 hours	$10.00 per hour	$4.00

During April, the following activity was recorded regarding the new product:

a. Purchased 7,000 feet of material at a cost of $5.75 per foot.
b. Used 6,000 feet of material to produce 1,500 units of the new product.
c. Worked 725 direct labor-hours on the new product at a cost of $8,120.

Required:

1. For direct materials:
   a. Compute the direct materials price and quantity variances.
   b. Prepare journal entries to record the purchase of materials and the use of materials in production.
2. For direct labor:
   a. Compute the direct labor rate and efficiency variances.
   b. Prepare journal entries to record the incurrence of direct labor cost for the month.
3. Post the entries you have prepared to the T-accounts below:

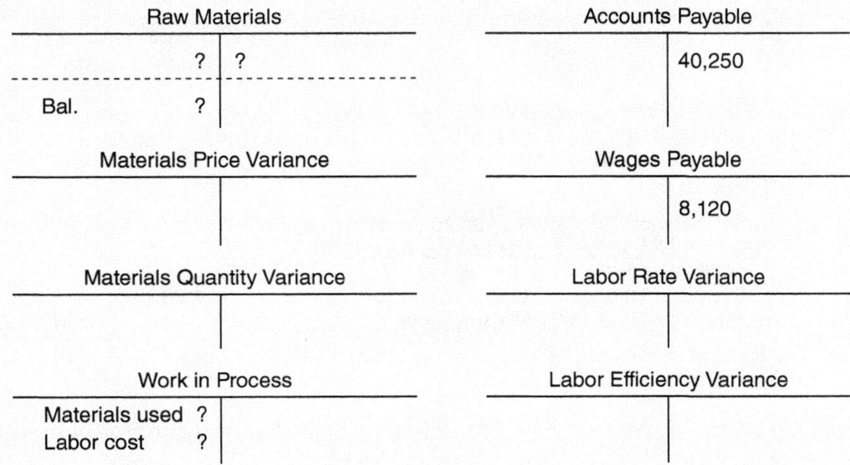

PROBLEM 10B–3 Comprehensive Variance Analysis with Incomplete Data; Journal Entries [LO1, LO2, LO3, LO5]

Topline Surf Boards manufactures a single product. The standard cost of one unit of this product is as follows:

Direct materials: 6 feet at $1.00 per foot	$ 6.00
Direct labor: 1 hour at $4.50 per hour.	4.50
Variable manufacturing overhead: 1 hour at $3.00 per hour.	3.00
Total standard variable cost per unit.	$13.50

During October, 6,000 units were produced. Selected data relating to the month's production follow:

Material purchased: 60,000 feet at $0.95 per foot.	$57,000
Material used in production: 38,000 feet	—
Direct labor: _?_ hours at $ _?_ per hour	$27,950
Variable manufacturing overhead cost incurred	$20,475
Variable manufacturing overhead efficiency variance	$1,500 U

There was no beginning inventory of raw materials. The variable manufacturing overhead rate is based on direct labor-hours.

Required:

1. For direct materials:
   a. Compute the price and quantity variances for October.
   b. Prepare journal entries to record activity for October.
2. For direct labor:
   a. Compute the rate and efficiency variances for October.
   b. Prepare a journal entry to record labor activity for October.
3. For variable manufacturing overhead:
   a. Compute the spending variance for October, and verify the efficiency variance given above.
   b. If manufacturing overhead is applied to production on the basis of direct labor-hours, is it possible to have a favorable direct labor efficiency variance and an unfavorable variable overhead efficiency variance? Explain.
4. State possible causes of each variance that you have computed.

PROBLEM 10B–4 Comprehensive Variance Analysis; Journal Entries [LO1, LO2, LO3, LO5]

Vermont Mills, Inc., is a large producer of men's and women's clothing. The company uses standard costs for all of its products. The standard costs and actual costs for a recent period are given below for one of the company's product lines (per unit of product):

	Standard Cost	Actual Cost
Direct materials:		
Standard: 4.0 yards at $3.60 per yard	$14.40	
Actual: 4.4 yards at $3.35 per yard		$14.74
Direct labor:		
Standard: 1.6 hours at $4.50 per hour.	7.20	
Actual: 1.4 hours at $4.85 per hour.		6.79
Variable manufacturing overhead:		
Standard: 1.6 hours at $1.80 per hour	2.88	
Actual: 1.4 hours at $2.15 per hour		3.01
Total cost per unit.	$24.48	$24.54

During this period, the company produced 4,800 units of product. A comparison of standard and actual costs for the period on a total cost basis is given below:

Actual costs: 4,800 units at $24.54.	$117,792
Standard costs: 4,800 units at $24.48.	117,504
Difference in cost—unfavorable.	$ 288

There was no inventory of materials on hand to start the period. During the period, 21,120 yards of materials were purchased and used in production.

Required:

1. For direct materials:
   a. Compute the price and quantity variances for the period.
   b. Prepare journal entries to record all activity relating to direct materials for the period.
2. For direct labor:
   a. Compute the rate and efficiency variances.
   b. Prepare a journal entry to record the incurrence of direct labor cost for the period.
3. Compute the variable manufacturing overhead rate and efficiency variances.
4. On seeing the $288 total cost variance, the company's president stated, "This variance of $288 is only 0.2% of the $117,504 standard cost for the period. It's obvious that our costs are well under control." Do you agree? Explain.
5. State possible causes of each variance that you have computed.

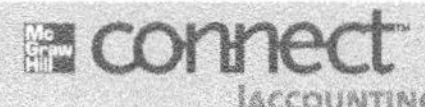

Case

All applicable cases are available with McGraw-Hill's *Connect™ Accounting*.

CASE 10B–5 Ethics and the Manager; Rigging Standards [LO5]

Stacy Cummins, the newly hired controller at Merced Home Products, Inc., was disturbed by what she had discovered about the standard costs at the Home Security Division. In looking over the past several years of quarterly earnings reports at the Home Security Division, she noticed that the first-quarter earnings were always poor, the second-quarter earnings were slightly better, the third-quarter earnings were again slightly better, and the fourth quarter always ended with a spectacular performance in which the Home Security Division managed to meet or exceed its target profit for the year. She also was concerned to find letters from the company's external auditors to top management warning about an unusual use of standard costs at the Home Security Division.

When Ms. Cummins ran across these letters, she asked the assistant controller, Gary Farber, if he knew what was going on at the Home Security Division. Gary said that it was common knowledge in the company that the vice president in charge of the Home Security Division, Preston Lansing, had rigged the standards at his division in order to produce the same quarterly earnings pattern every year. According to company policy, variances are taken directly to the income statement as an adjustment to cost of goods sold.

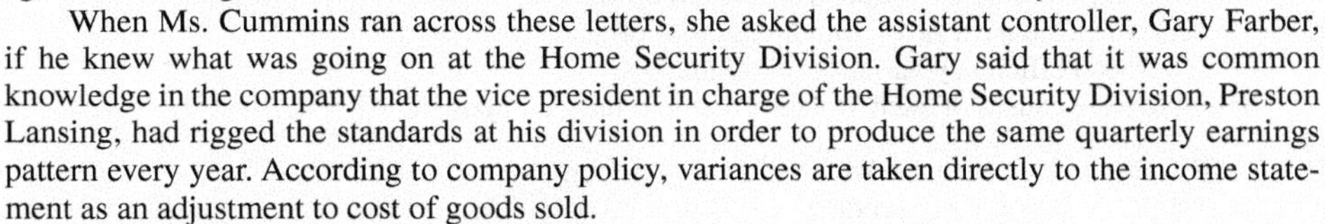

Favorable variances have the effect of increasing net operating income, and unfavorable variances have the effect of decreasing net operating income. Lansing had rigged the standards so that there were always large favorable variances. Company policy was a little vague about when these variances have to be reported on the divisional income statements. While the intent was clearly to recognize variances on the income statement in the period in which they arise, nothing in the company's accounting manuals actually explicitly required this. So for many years, Lansing had followed a practice of saving up the favorable variances and using them to create a nice smooth pattern of earnings growth in the first three quarters, followed by a big "Christmas present" of an extremely good fourth quarter. (Financial reporting regulations forbid carrying variances forward from one year to the next on the annual audited financial statements, so all of the variances must appear on the divisional income statement by the end of the year.)

Ms. Cummins was concerned about these findings and attempted to bring up the subject with the president of Merced Home Products but was told that "we all know what Lansing's doing, but as long as he continues to turn in such good reports, don't bother him." When Ms. Cummins asked if the board of directors was aware of the situation, the president somewhat testily replied, "Of course they are aware."

Required:

1. How did Preston Lansing probably "rig" the standard costs—are the standards set too high or too low? Explain.
2. Should Preston Lansing be permitted to continue his practice of managing reported earnings?
3. What should Stacy Cummins do in this situation?

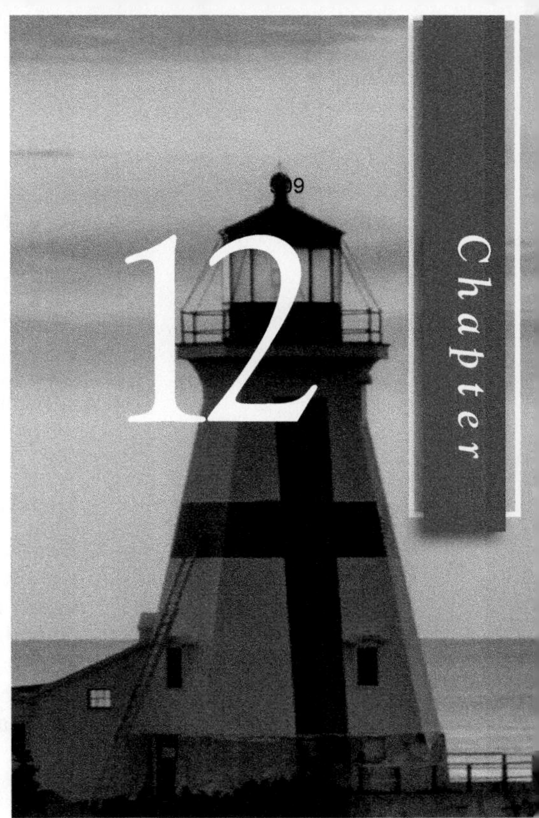

Differential Analysis: The Key to Decision Making

Utilization of a Constrained Resource

LEARNING OBJECTIVE 5
Determine the most profitable use of a constrained resource.

Managers routinely face the problem of deciding how constrained resources are going to be used. A department store, for example, has a limited amount of floor space and therefore cannot stock every product that may be available. A manufacturer has a limited number of machine-hours and a limited number of direct labor-hours at its disposal. When a limited resource of some type restricts the company's ability to satisfy demand, the company has a **constraint.** Because the company cannot fully satisfy demand, managers must decide which products or services should be cut back. In other words, managers must decide which products or services make the best use of the constrained resource. Fixed costs are usually unaffected by such choices, so the course of action that will maximize the company's total contribution margin should ordinarily be selected.

Contribution Margin per Unit of the Constrained Resource

If some products must be cut back because of a constraint, the key to maximizing the total contribution margin may seem obvious—favor the products with the highest unit contribution margins. Unfortunately, that is not quite correct. Rather, the correct solution is to favor the products that provide the highest *contribution margin per unit of the constrained resource.* To illustrate, in addition to its other products, Mountain Goat Cycles makes saddlebags for bicycles called *panniers.* These panniers come in two models—a touring model and a mountain model. Cost and revenue data for the two models of panniers follow:

	Mountain Pannier	Touring Pannier
Selling price per unit.	$25	$30
Variable cost per unit.	10	18
Contribution margin per unit.	$15	$12
Contribution margin (CM) ratio	60%	40%

The mountain pannier appears to be much more profitable than the touring pannier. It has a $15 per unit contribution margin as compared to only $12 per unit for the touring model, and it has a 60% CM ratio as compared to only 40% for the touring model.

But now let us add one more piece of information—the plant that makes the panniers is operating at capacity. This does not mean that every machine and every person in the plant is working at the maximum possible rate. Because machines have different capacities, some machines will be operating at less than 100% of capacity. However, if the plant as a whole cannot produce any more units, some machine or process must be operating at capacity. The machine or process that is limiting overall output is called the **bottleneck**—it is the constraint.

At Mountain Goat Cycles, the bottleneck (i.e., constraint) is a stitching machine. The mountain pannier requires two minutes of stitching time per unit, and the touring pannier requires one minute of stitching time per unit. The stitching machine is available for 12,000 minutes per month, and the company can sell up to 4,000 mountain panniers and 7,000 touring panniers per month. Producing up to this demand for both products would require 15,000 minutes, as shown below:

	Mountain Pannier	Touring Pannier	Total
Monthly demand (a).	4,000 units	7,000 units	
Stitching machine time required to produce one unit (b).	2 minutes	1 minute	
Total stitching time required (a) × (b)	8,000 minutes	7,000 minutes	15,000 minutes

Producing up to demand would require 15,000 minutes, but only 12,000 minutes are available. This simply confirms that the stitching machine is the bottleneck. By definition, because the stitching machine is a bottleneck, the stitching machine does not have enough capacity to satisfy the existing demand for mountain panniers and touring panniers Therefore, some orders for the products will have to be turned down. Naturally, managers will want to know which product is less profitable. To answer this question, they should focus on the contribution margin per unit of the constrained resource. This figure is computed by dividing a product's contribution margin per unit by the amount of the constrained resource required to make a unit of that product. These calculations are carried out below for the mountain and touring panniers:

	Mountain Pannier	Touring Pannier
Contribution margin per unit (a)	$15.00	$12.00
Stitching machine time required to produce one unit (b)	2 minutes	1 minute
Contribution margin per unit of the constrained resource, (a) ÷ (b)	$7.50 per minute	$12.00 per minute

It is now easy to decide which product is less profitable and should be deemphasized. Each minute on the stitching machine that is devoted to the touring pannier results in an increase of $12.00 in contribution margin and profits. The comparable figure for the mountain pannier is only $7.50 per minute. Therefore, the touring model should be emphasized. Even though the mountain model has the larger contribution margin per unit and the larger CM ratio, the touring model provides the larger contribution margin in relation to the constrained resource.

To verify that the touring model is indeed the more profitable product, suppose an hour of additional stitching time is available and that unfilled orders exist for both products. The additional hour on the stitching machine could be used to make either 30 mountain panniers (60 minutes ÷ 2 minutes per mountain pannier) or 60 touring panniers (60 minutes ÷ 1 minute per touring pannier), with the following profit implications:

	Mountain Pannier	Touring Pannier
Contribution margin per unit	$ 15	$ 12
Additional units that can be processed in one hour	× 30	× 60
Additional contribution margin	$450	$720

Because the additional contribution margin would be $720 for the touring panniers and only $450 for the mountain panniers, the touring panniers make the most profitable use of the company's constrained resource—the stitching machine.

The stitching machine is available for 12,000 minutes per month, and producing the touring panniers is the most profitable use of the stitching machine. Therefore, to maximize profits, the company should produce all of the touring panniers the market will demand (7,000 units) and use any remaining capacity to produce mountain panniers. The computations to determine how many mountain panniers can be produced are as follows:

Monthly demand for touring panniers (a)	7,000 units
Stitching machine time required to produce one touring pannier (b)	1 minute
Total stitching time required to produce touring panniers (a) × (b)	7,000 minutes
Remaining stitching time available (12,000 minutes − 7,000 minutes) (c)	5,000 minutes
Stitching machine time required to produce one mountain pannier (d)	2 minutes
Production of mountain panniers (c) ÷ (d)	2,500 units

Therefore, profit would be maximized by producing 7,000 touring panniers and then using the remaining capacity to produce 2,500 mountain panniers.

This example clearly shows that looking at unit contribution margins alone is not enough; the contribution margin must be viewed in relation to the amount of the constrained resource each product requires.

IN BUSINESS

BOEING IS CONSTRAINED BY A SUPPLIER

Boeing Co. had to delay delivery of its model 777 airplanes to Emirates airline because the German supplier Sell GmbH could not provide the equipment for cooking galleys to Boeing on time. The production bottleneck forced Emirates to repeatedly postpone its planned expansion into the U.S. west coast. It also forced Boeing to accept payment delays for airplanes that sell for more than $200 million apiece. In response, Sell GmbH hired 250 more employees and invested millions of euros in new machine tools and factory space to expand its production capacity.

Source: Daniel Michaels and J. Lynn Lunsford, "Lack of Seats, Galleys Stalls Boeing, Airbus," *The Wall Street Journal*, August 8, 2008, pp. B1 and B4.

LEARNING OBJECTIVE 6
Determine the value of obtaining more of the constrained resource.

Managing Constraints

Effectively managing an organization's constraints is a key to increased profits. As discussed above, when a constraint exists in the production process, managers can increase profits by producing the products with the highest contribution margin per unit of the constrained resource. However, they can also increase profits by increasing the capacity of the bottleneck operation.

When a manager increases the capacity of the bottleneck, it is called **relaxing (or elevating) the constraint.** In the case of Mountain Goat Cycles, the company is currently working one eight-hour shift. To relax the constraint, the stitching machine operator could be asked to work overtime. No one else would have to work overtime. Because all of the other operations involved in producing panniers have excess capacity, up to a point, the additional panniers processed through the stitching machine during overtime could be finished during normal working hours in the other operations.

The benefits from relaxing the constraint are often enormous and can be easily quantified—the key is the contribution margin per unit of the constrained resource that we have already computed. This number, which was originally stated in terms of minutes in the Mountain Goat Cycles example, is restated below in terms of hours for easier interpretation:

	Mountain Pannier	Touring Pannier
Contribution margin per unit of the constrained resource (in minutes) . . .	$7.50 per minute × 60 minutes per hour	$12.00 per minute × 60 minutes per hour
Contribution margin per unit of the constrained resource (in hours) . . .	= $450 per hour	= $720 per hour

So what is the value of relaxing the constraint—the time on the stitching machine? The manager should first ask, "What would I do with additional capacity at the bottleneck if it were available?" If the time were to be used to make additional mountain panniers, it would be worth $450 per hour. If the time were to be used to make additional touring panniers, it would be worth $720 per hour. In this latter case, the company should be willing to pay an overtime *premium* to the stitching machine operator of up to $720 per hour! Suppose, for example, that the stitching machine operator is paid $20 per hour during normal working hours and time-and-a-half, or $30 per hour, for overtime. In this case, the premium for overtime is only $10 per hour, whereas in principle, the company should be willing to pay a premium of up to $720 per hour. The difference between what the company should be willing to pay as a premium, $720 per hour, and what it would actually have to pay, $10 per hour, is pure profit of $710 per hour.

To reinforce this concept, suppose that there are only unfilled orders for the mountain pannier. How much would it be worth to the company to run the stitching machine overtime in this situation? Because the additional capacity would be used to make the mountain pannier, the value of that additional capacity would drop to $7.50 per minute or $450 per hour. Nevertheless, the value of relaxing the constraint would still be quite high and the company should be willing to pay an overtime premium of up to $450 per hour.

These calculations indicate that managers should pay great attention to the bottleneck operation. If a bottleneck machine breaks down or is ineffectively utilized, the losses to the company can be quite large. In our example, for every minute the stitching machine is down due to breakdowns or setups, the company loses between $7.50 and $12.00.[2] The losses on an hourly basis are between $450 and $720! In contrast, there is no such loss of contribution margin if time is lost on a machine that is not a bottleneck—such machines have excess capacity anyway.

The implications are clear. Managers should focus much of their attention on managing the bottleneck. As we have discussed, managers should emphasize products that most profitably utilize the constrained resource. They should also make sure that products are processed smoothly through the bottleneck, with minimal lost time due to breakdowns and setups. And they should try to find ways to increase the capacity at the bottleneck.

[2] Setups are required when production switches from one product to another. For example, consider a company that makes automobile side panels. The panels are painted before shipping them to an automobile manufacturer for final assembly. The customer might require 100 blue panels, 50 black panels, and 20 yellow panels. Each time the color is changed, the painting equipment must be purged of the old paint color, cleaned with solvents, and refilled with the new paint color. This takes time. In fact, some equipment may require such lengthy and frequent setups that it is unavailable for actual production more often than not.

The capacity of a bottleneck can be effectively increased in a number of ways, including:

- Working overtime on the bottleneck.
- Subcontracting some of the processing that would be done at the bottleneck.
- Investing in additional machines at the bottleneck.
- Shifting workers from processes that are not bottlenecks to the process that is the bottleneck.
- Focusing business process improvement efforts on the bottleneck.
- Reducing defective units. Each defective unit that is processed through the bottleneck and subsequently scrapped takes the place of a good unit that could have been sold.

The last three methods of increasing the capacity of the bottleneck are particularly attractive because they are essentially free and may even yield additional cost savings.

The methods and ideas discussed in this section are all part of the Theory of Constraints, which was introduced in Chapter 1. A number of organizations have successfully used the Theory of Constraints to improve their performance, including Avery Dennison, Bethlehem Steel, Binney & Smith, Boeing, Champion International, Ford Motor Company, General Motors, ITT, Monster Cable, National Semiconductor, Pratt and Whitney Canada, Pretoria Academic Hospital, Procter and Gamble, Texas Instruments, United Airlines, United Electrical Controls, the United States Air Force Logistics Command, and the United States Navy Transportation Corps.

IN BUSINESS

ELEVATING A CONSTRAINT

The Odessa Texas Police Department was having trouble hiring new employees. Its eight-step hiring process was taking 117 days to complete and the best-qualified job applicants were accepting other employment offers before the Odessa Police Department could finish evaluating their candidacy. The constraint in the eight-step hiring process was the background investigation that required an average of 104 days. The other seven steps—filling out an application and completing a written exam, an oral interview, a polygraph exam, a medical exam, a psychological exam, and a drug screen—took a combined total of only 13 days. The Odessa Police Department elevated its constraint by hiring additional background checkers. This resulted in slashing its application processing time from 117 days to 16 days.

Source: Lloyd J. Taylor III, Brian J. Moersch, and Geralyn McClure Franklin, "Applying the Theory of Constraints to a Public Safety Hiring Process," *Public Personnel Management*, Fall 2003, pp. 367–382.

The Problem of Multiple Constraints

What does a company do if it has more than one potential constraint? For example, a company may have limited raw materials, limited direct labor-hours available, limited floor space, and limited advertising dollars to spend on product promotion. How would it determine the right combination of products to produce? The proper combination or "mix" of products can be found by use of a quantitative method known as *linear programming,* which is covered in quantitative methods and operations management courses.

Contents

Credits

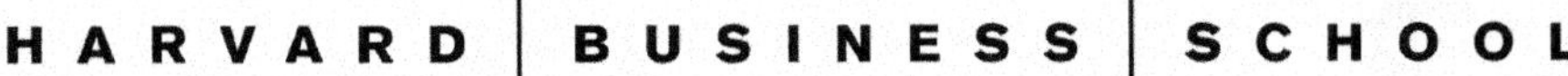

9-205-060
REV: MARCH 27, 2006

ROBIN GREENWOOD
LUCY WHITE

Decision Trees

Most business decisions involve uncertainties of some kind. A drug company may decide to invest in research and development (R&D), for example, not knowing whether it will be able to obtain Food and Drug Administration (FDA) approval for its product. An automobile maker may choose to build a large factory to exploit scale economies without knowing whether the market will be large enough to allow the factory to work at full capacity. Although uncertainty can be daunting, you will see that by laying out the set of events that can occur in a systematic way and anticipating your actions following the resolution of uncertainty, you can make better decisions.

This note outlines a set of techniques to analyze decisions under uncertainty. You will be able to apply the techniques to classes of decisions that have three properties:

1. The *alternatives* are well-defined,

2. The critical *uncertainties* can be quantified,

3. The *objectives* are clear.

Not all decisions have these characteristics. However, many, and perhaps all, decisions can be simplified in such a way that these three properties hold. Because decisions with these three properties are straightforward to solve, you will find that good decision makers are distinguished by their ability to cast complex problems in a way that highlights these properties.

You will learn how to construct a graphical device called a *decision tree*. Decision trees serve two primary purposes. First, they tell you which alternatives to choose. Second, they identify the value of having those alternatives in the first place.

A Simple Business Problem

Allison Tate runs a small company that manufactures low-cost ergonomic chairs, sold via the Internet. Her firm has several popular models, each with annual sales of $200,000 to $450,000.

Her research staff has produced a prototype that improves on the top-of-the-line model in several ways. However, because of the number of innovations in the new chair, Tate does not expect to be able to produce it using her existing manufacturing facility. Tate knows that a new facility will cost $300,000 and is unsure whether there will be sufficient demand for the chair to cover this large

---

Professors Robin Greenwood and Lucy White prepared this note as the basis for class discussion.

investment. If the market is good, she thinks she might sell 8,000 chairs at a profit of $100 each, generating a cash flow with present value of $800,000.[1] On the other hand, if the market is poor, she thinks she might sell only 1,000 chairs, generating a cash flow with present value of only $100,000. How should she make this decision?

Before we can determine how to make a decision where the outcome of the decision is uncertain, we need a way of determining the value of uncertain prospects. Uncertain gains and losses can be evaluated using a device known as a *probability tree*. In the next section we show how Tate can use a probability tree to evaluate the value of investment. Then, in the following section, we allow Tate to make a *sequence of decisions*. This is done using a device known as a *decision tree*.

Probability Trees

What Is the Value of Tate's Investment Opportunity?

If Tate invests in the factory to produce the new chairs, this will cost $300,000. If the market is large, cash flows from sales will total $800,000. If Tate is certain that the market will be large, then her decision will be easy: she should go ahead and invest, since the project is worth $500,000 ($800,000 minus the cost of investment of $300,000).

Her decision is more difficult, however, since she is not certain whether the market will be large or small. If the market for the chairs is small, cash flows from sales will be only $100,000. In this case, she will lose $200,000 ($100,000 minus the cost of investment of $300,000). How should she think about the opportunity to invest now? She begins by laying out the alternative outcomes if she invests, shown in **Figure A** below. (Costs and benefits in all the figures are expressed in thousands.)

Figure A

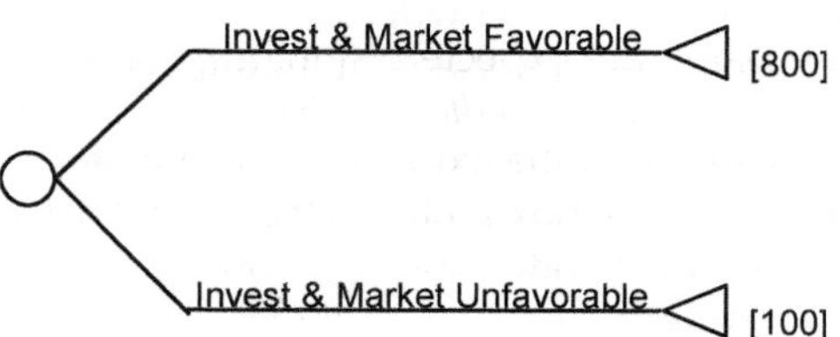

How should she trade off the possibility of gaining $800,000 versus gaining $100,000 in relation to her certain cost of investment of $300,000? Intuitively, Tate will be more inclined to make the investment the more likely it is that the market will be large. The likelihood of such an *event* occurring is expressed mathematically by its *probability*. If an event is impossible, we assign it probability of zero. At the other end of the spectrum, if an event is certain to occur, we assign it probability of one. Most real-world events are between these two extremes—and the probability that they occur is between zero and one, with more likely events being assigned higher probabilities.

In order to decide whether to invest in the factory, Tate needs to decide just how likely it is that the market will be large. Considering what she knows about the market, she reasons that the chairs

[1] To simplify matters, all cash flows in this note are discounted to the time of the investment decision.

are a new design and it is a little more likely that the market will be small than that it will be large; that is, the probability of a small market is more than half. On the other hand, there is still a decent chance that the market will be large. She decides that the probability of a large market is around 0.40. Since the sum of the probabilities of the two outcomes must equal one, the probability of a small market is therefore 0.60. Assessing a 40% probability of a large market means that she thinks that this is as likely to occur as a draw of a red ball from a jar containing 40 red and 60 black balls. Armed with this information, she can now construct a simple probability tree to represent the value of the investment opportunity:

Figure B

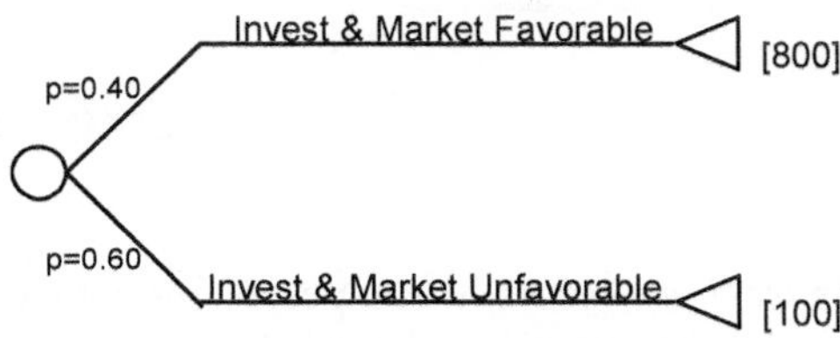

What is the expected value of her investment? Suppose we were to replay the scenario many times. Forty percent of the time Tate would expect to make $800,000, and 60% of the time, she would expect to get $100,000. However, she always incurs the cost of investment of $300,000. On average she expects cash flows of

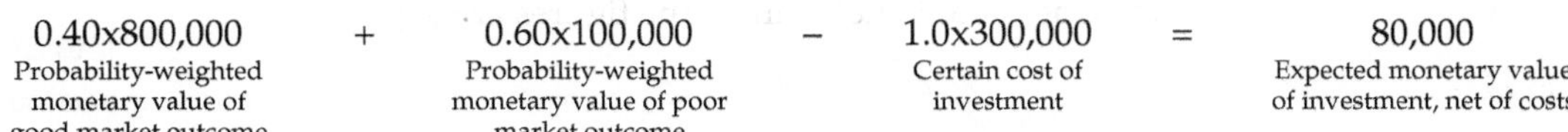

0.40x800,000
Probability-weighted monetary value of good market outcome
+
0.60x100,000
Probability-weighted monetary value of poor market outcome
–
1.0x300,000
Certain cost of investment
=
80,000
Expected monetary value of investment, net of costs

The equation above calculates the expected monetary value of the investment opportunity. *The expected monetary value of a probability tree is the probability-weighted average of the outcomes.* The expected monetary value of Tate's *investment* is the expected monetary value of the tree minus the cost of her investment. Tate's opportunity thus has an expected monetary value of $80,000. To maximize the expected returns to her shareholders, Tate should choose to invest, since this offers a higher expected monetary value than not investing.

Evaluating More Complicated Probability Trees

Other more complicated, risky prospects can be evaluated in the same way as the simple problem above. Suppose that there is a chance that the innovative and controversial chairs will be shown on national television. This will increase sales fourfold: that is, to $3.2 million if the market is large and to $400,000 if the market is small. Tate estimates that the chance of her product's being featured on TV is 10% if the market is large and only 1% if the market is small. We can extend the tree as follows:

Figure C

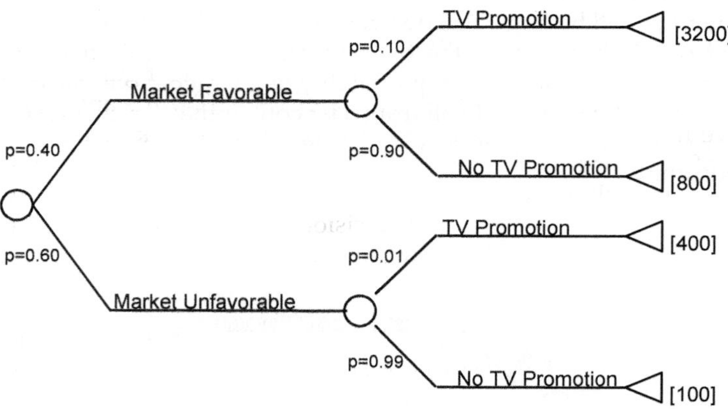

What is the value of this tree? As before, the expected monetary value of a probability tree is the probability-weighted average of the outcomes. To get the probability of an outcome, we multiply the probabilities along the branches of the tree. Thus, the probability that the market is favorable and there is a TV promotion is equal to 0.40 x 0.10 = 0.04. Similarly, the probability that the market is favorable and there is no TV promotion is equal to 0.40 x 0.90 = 0.36. We can do this calculation for each of the branches of the tree, as follows:

Figure D

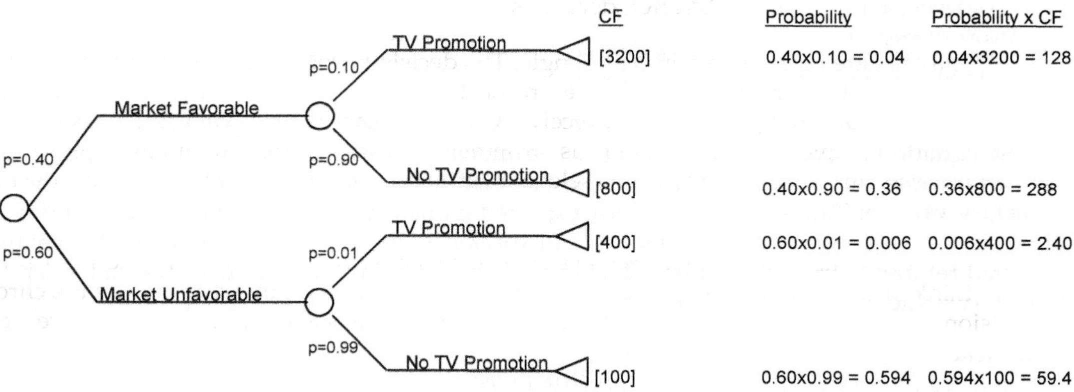

If done correctly, the sum of the probabilities of the outcomes should equal 1. We can check that indeed 0.04 + 0.36 + 0.006 + 0.594 = 1. To get the expected monetary value, we take the probability-weighted average of the four outcomes (summing the product of the outcomes with the probability of each outcome). This gives us 0.04x3,200,000 + 0.36x800,000 + 0.006x400,000 + 0.594x100,000 = 477,800. Thus the value of this investment opportunity, net of costs, is $477,800 – $300,000 = $177,800.

Decision Trees

In the probability tree we just analyzed, Tate did not have to make any decisions, as uncertainty was resolved. She just had to figure out the value of the investment opportunity by calculating the expected monetary value of the probability tree, and having figured out this value, she simply compared it to the cost of investment. How would we modify the analysis to take into account the fact that often we may be able to partially control events by making decisions as time goes on? To analyze a series of decisions where there is uncertainty, decision makers often use a device called a *decision tree.* Like a probability tree, a decision tree represents a chronological sequence of events presented in a simple graphical manner. A decision tree also allows for decisions along the way as uncertainty is resolved. We typically draw the decision tree from left to right, emphasizing the chronological nature of decisions.

Decision trees serve two primary goals. First, they help you decide which decision to make. At each decision node, you will be faced with several alternatives. Using a tree, you will be able to decide which of these alternatives is the right one to choose. Second, the decision tree identifies the value of any particular decision or set of options. For example, you may want to know not only whether you prefer one alternative to another, but by how much. At other times, you might also want to know how valuable the right to make a decision at a particular point is.

There are three important elements in the decision tree:

□ A decision is represented by a square, or *decision node*. This node could refer to the decision to invest or not invest, to purchase a piece of equipment or not to purchase, or how much to offer in an auction.

○ Uncertain events are represented with a circle, or *chance node*. Uncertain events may occur before or after, or both before and after, decisions.

◁ *Outcomes* are represented with a triangle. The decision process arrives at an outcome when all uncertainties have been resolved and there are no further decisions to be made; at this point the decision maker knows the payoff he will receive. Outcomes can occur at various stages of a complex decision. For example, if the decision is whether to continue or abandon, the selection of abandonment is an outcome, while the selection of continuance may lead to future decisions or uncertainties.

The three elements of a decision tree are connected with lines. Although we do not draw them, you can think of the lines as arrows that go from left to right, in the same direction as the chronology of decisions. The lines are often called "branches" because decisions may lead to future decisions, which lead to future decisions . . . and so on.

The order in which the shapes in the decision tree are connected is very important. A square that is followed by a circle, for example, means that the decision is made before the uncertainty is resolved. In contrast, a circle that is followed by a square denotes a decision that occurs after uncertainty is resolved.

A Simple Decision Problem: Tate's Ergonomic Chairs

Let us go back to our simple example to illustrate the principles involved in constructing and solving a decision tree. We saw earlier that Tate was faced with deciding whether to invest $300,000 in a new manufacturing facility when she was unsure whether there would be sufficient demand for the chair it would produce to cover the large investment. She knows that if the market is large, she will sell 8,000 chairs at a profit of $100 each, generating a cash flow with present value of $800,000. On the other hand, if the market is small, she will sell only 1,000 chairs, generating a cash flow with a present value of only $100,000.

A market research firm has submitted a proposal to evaluate the potential market for the chair. Tate is confident that this will resolve her uncertainty about whether the market for the chair will be large or small. But she does not know whether it is worth the $50,000 that the firm is asking to carry out the survey. How should she decide whether to pay for the market research?

Designing the Tree

Step 1: Lay out the alternatives Decision trees are designed forwards, one branch at a time, starting with the first decision. Tate must begin by deciding whether to invest in market research or not. (There would be no point in investing in market research after making her investment decision, since the value of the research is in helping to make the investment decision.) Because we start with a decision and there are two alternatives, we draw a square with two lines coming out of it:

Figure E

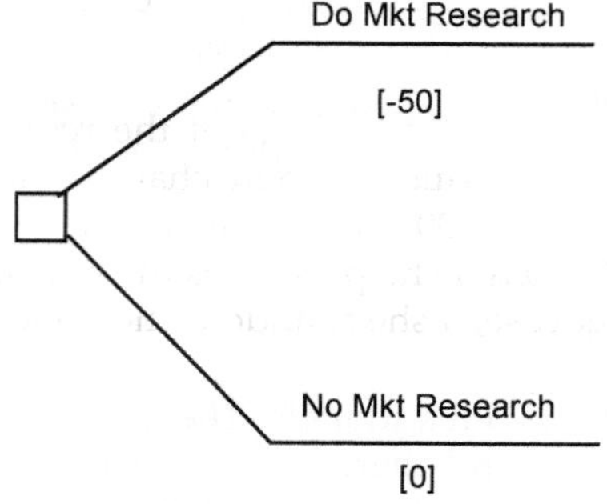

We keep track of costs (and benefits) as they occur. Below the top branch, we note the cost of $50,000. If Tate does no research, she incurs no costs. Thus we write a zero under the bottom branch.

Now what? We start with the top branch. The market research will identify the market opportunities to be either good or bad. Tate is unsure which of these events will occur.

Figure F

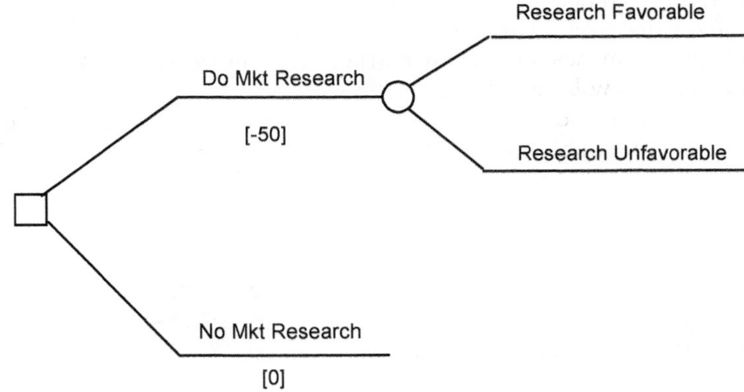

Because the results of the market research are out of her control, we mark the resolution of uncertainty with a circle. Why are there no cash flows associated with either of these two branches? Even though the research results may influence her course of action, there are no direct cash flows associated with the results from the research survey.

What happens next? Armed with the results of the research survey, Tate can purchase a new facility or abandon her efforts to produce the new chair. If the market is large, then if she purchases the new facility this will cost $300,000 and she will receive $800,000 in revenue subsequently. In contrast, if the market is small, then if she purchases the new facility this will cost $300,000 and yield cash flows of $100,000. In either case, if she abandons the project, her cash flows will be zero.

Figure G

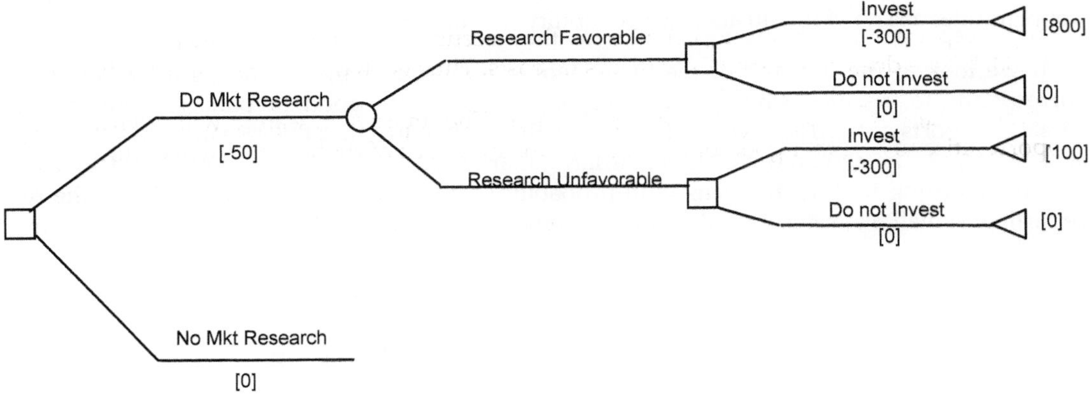

Finally, we repeat these steps for the case for which Tate does not purchase the market research. Notice that this part of the tree contains no further decisions and is just like the probability tree we analyzed earlier. The difference between the upper and lower sections of the tree is that in the lower half Tate must make a decision *before* the uncertainty about the size of the market is resolved, whereas in the upper half she already knows the market size before she makes her investment decision. Therefore, the final decision tree is:

Figure H

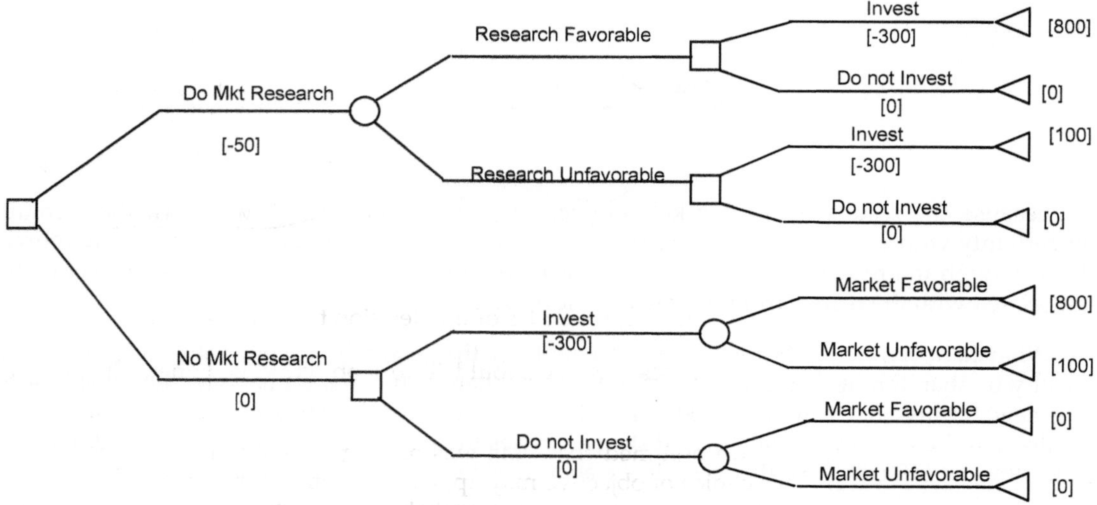

Step 2: Quantify the uncertainties As with probability trees, Tate must estimate the probability that each of the branches of uncertain outcomes occurs. We have already done this for the lower half of the tree in the previous section. Recall that Tate believes that the probability that opportunities are good is 0.40 and the probability that opportunities are bad is 0.60.

If we look at the top half of the tree, there is only one chance node, with two outcomes, that corresponds to research saying that sales opportunities are good or bad. Tate believes that the research reports are 100% accurate. So what is the probability that the research says that the market will be large? The research will report a large market precisely when the market actually is large, which, according to Tate, happens with probability 0.40. Similarly, the probability of the research's reporting a small market is 0.60. We now have enough information to fill out the rest of the tree.

Figure I Tate's Decision Tree

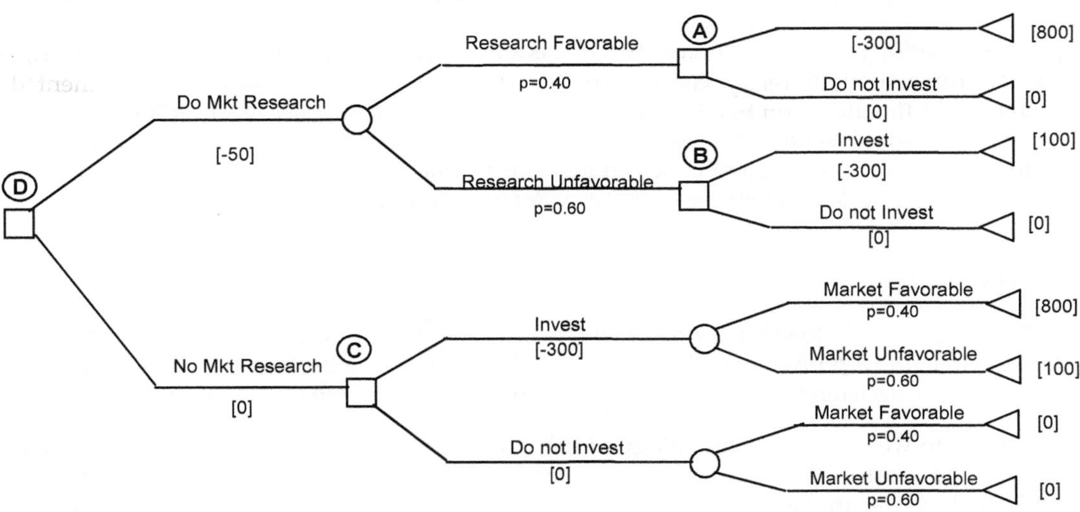

For easy reference, we label the important nodes of the decision tree **A**, **B**, **C**, and **D**.

Step 3: Specify the objectives What should Tate's objective be when choosing among alternatives?

In our previous analysis, we assumed that Tate was aiming to make the decision offering the highest monetary value. This choice of objective may appear problematic, because it seems to assume that Tate is *risk neutral*, which is to say, she values a probability tree at its expected monetary value. Tate treated a 40% chance at $800,000 and a 60% chance of $100,000, an expected monetary value of $380,000, as being equivalent to $380,000 for sure. Most people, however, are *risk averse*, meaning that they would prefer to receive the expected value of a gamble to the gamble itself. In Tate's case, it means that she may prefer to invest $300,000 and receive $380,000 for sure than to invest and take her chances. To take a simpler case, most people would prefer to receive $100 for sure than to take a 50% chance at receiving $200.

Nevertheless, the maximization of expected value is a reasonable starting point for most business decisions. Underlying this decision rule are two important assumptions. First, we assume that the decision maker is trying to make the best decision on behalf of diversified investors. If each investor holds only a very small part of his portfolio in Tate's company, the risks that Tate's company takes have very little impact on the investor's overall wealth. Second, we assume that the uncertainties in the tree are not related to the riskiness of the investor's portfolio. In the context of our example, this means that the probability that the market for ergonomic chairs is favorable is not related to the overall performance of the stock market.[2]

Of course, these assumptions may sometimes be violated. If Tate is the sole owner of her company and most of her wealth is tied up in the company, then she may act in a risk-averse way, avoiding investments with a positive expected monetary value if they are very risky. Risk aversion can be incorporated into our analysis by having the decision maker specify a *utility* for each final outcome (a

[2] These intuitions are formalized by the Capital-Asset Pricing Model, or CAPM.

measure of how happy or unhappy she would feel about her enhanced or diminished wealth level at that outcome) and then allowing her to maximize *expected utility* rather than expected value.

Maximization of expected monetary value is a much simpler decision rule, however, and is a good first approximation in most cases where the risks the decision maker faces are not too large. Therefore, in this note, we will continue to assume Tate values a set of uncertain alternatives at its expected monetary value. This means that, when faced with two or more alternatives, she always prefers the one with the highest expected monetary value, no matter what the risks. *At a decision node, we always choose the branch with the highest expected monetary value.*

Solving the Tree

Tate is now ready to solve the decision tree. To solve any complex decision problem, we break the decision tree into a series of smaller decision problems. Looking back on the decision tree in **Figure I**, we count four decision nodes: **A, B, C,** and **D**. Tate must decide what to do at each.

Where do we start? The chronology of the tree makes it easy. We start on the right-hand side of the tree and work backwards. Why do we start at the end? While it may seem counterintuitive to work backwards, in fact we often do this in making day-to-day decisions. Suppose you are considering whether it is worth the extra time and effort of going into town to eat, versus eating at your local restaurant. In making this decision, you might think first about what you would eat if you went to town, versus what you would eat if you ate locally. In other words, you would imagine that you had already gone into town and consider how you would act next. Then, having solved this problem, you would work backwards to make your first decision, comparing how much more you would enjoy your selected meal in town to your selected local meal considering the extra time and effort of going into town.

In a similar way, Tate starts by imagining that she has already invested in market research and discovered that the market is favorable. That is to say, she first supposes that she is in position **A** in the tree below. What would she do then?

Figure J

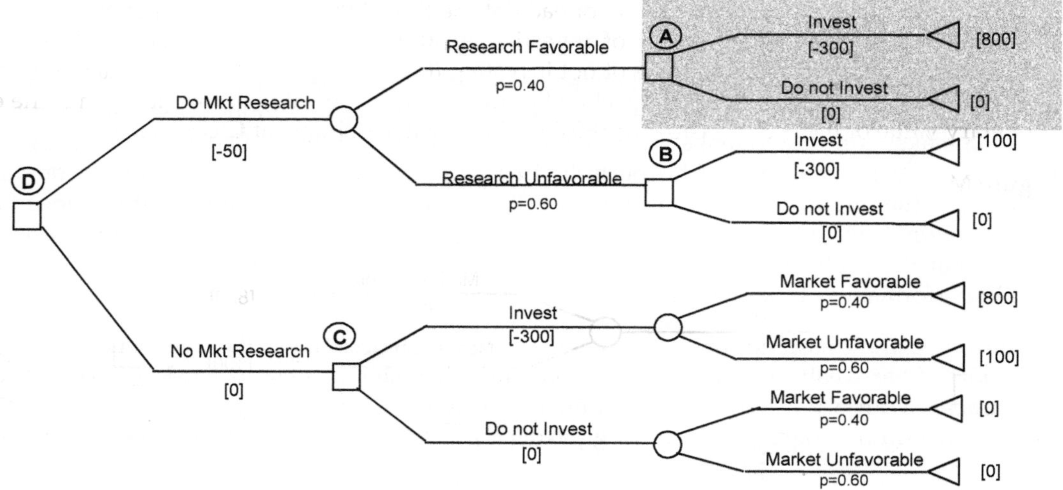

If Tate found herself at **A**, she would have to choose between investing and not investing. By virtue of being in this position, she knows that the market is good and that investing would yield a cash flow of $500,000 compared with not investing, which would yield zero. Therefore, she knows that if she were to reach point **A**, she would always choose to invest.

Figure K

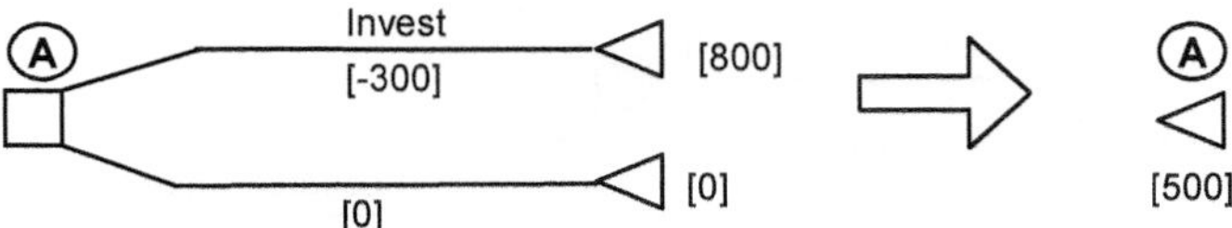

Because she knows what she would do if she were at **A**, she knows that the value of being at that point is equal to the value when she makes the best decision available there: $500,000.

Following the same technique, she thinks about what she would do if she invested in market research and found that it was unfavorable, at point **B**. Comparing the certain loss of 200 (-300 plus 100) if she invests with 0 if she does not invest, she chooses not to invest.

Figure L

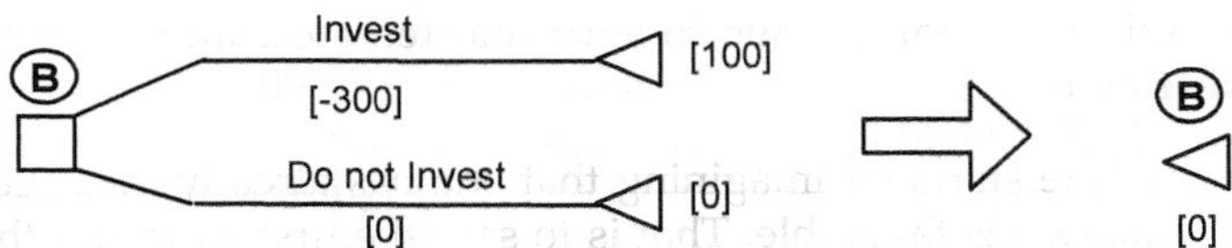

Finally, she thinks about what she would do if she were at point **C**. Here, her decision is more complicated because she does not know for sure what the consequences of her actions will be. She compares the expected monetary value of each of the branches of the tree and chooses the best one. Since the expected monetary value of investing (0.40x800,000 + 0.60x100,000 – 300,000 = 80,000) exceeds the expected monetary value of not investing (0.40 x 0 + 0.60 x 0 – 0 = 0), she would choose to invest. As we saw in our analysis of probability trees earlier, the value of this decision is the expected monetary value of the best decision, or $80,000. Tate's value of being at **C** is $80,000.

Figure M

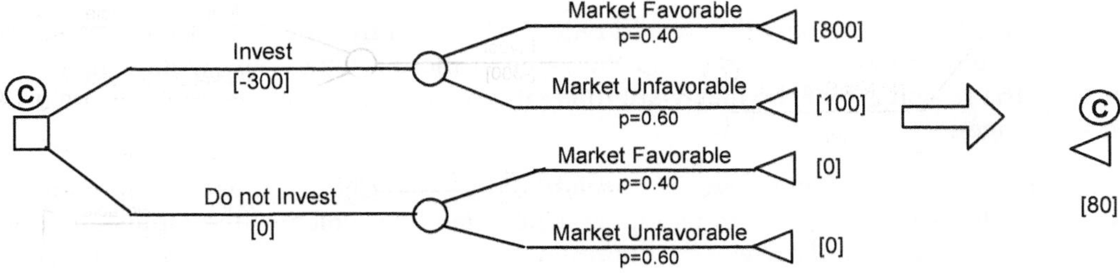

At this point, we know what Tate would do at points **A**, **B**, and **C**. We can condense the tree into a smaller set of decisions as follows:

Figure N

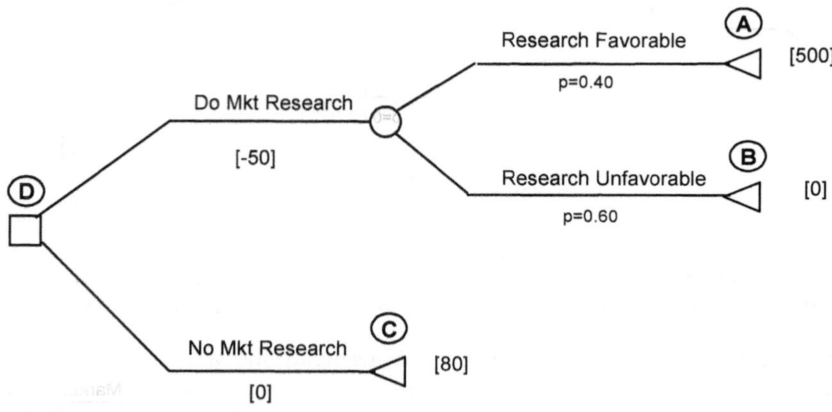

With our simplified tree, we can now ask what Tate should do at **D.** She compares the expected monetary value of the first path (doing market research) with the expected monetary value of the second path (not doing market research). In the top path, she gets 500,000 with a probability of 0.40 and 0 with a probability of 0.60 but incurs a certain cost of 50,000. The expected cash flow after choosing to commission the market research is therefore $500{,}000 \times 0.4 + 0 \times 0.6 = 200{,}000$, less the cost of the research itself, 50,000, yielding a net expected cash flow of $150,000. In the bottom path, she has an expected cash flow of $80,000. Therefore, she should pay for the market research, as it increases her expected cash flows by $70,000, from $80,000 to $150,000.

Figure O summarizes the steps involved in solving Tate's decision problem.

Sensitivity Analysis

Having written down and solved the decision tree for her business problem, Tate is ready to proceed. However, she may want to know how her decision would change if there were an intermediate stage of the market, in which cash flows from sales were $400,000 rather than limited to the $100,000 and $800,000 extremes. Alternatively, she may want to know whether she would still want to purchase the information if the price were raised by $30,000. Finally, she may want to analyze how her decision would change if the probabilities of the market's being high or low were different.

To answer these questions, Tate would redo the decision tree for each of these scenarios. In each case, she would analyze her actions and the value of those actions. Why would she go to so much trouble? The reason is that she may want to identify what the crucial assumptions are on which her decision hinges.

In many business decisions, *sensitivity analysis* of this kind can be extremely important. Remember that the model is only as good as its inputs. Understanding which of the inputs are crucial to the decision can help you clarify where the uncertainties are and ultimately make better decisions.

Figure O Solving the Tree Backwards

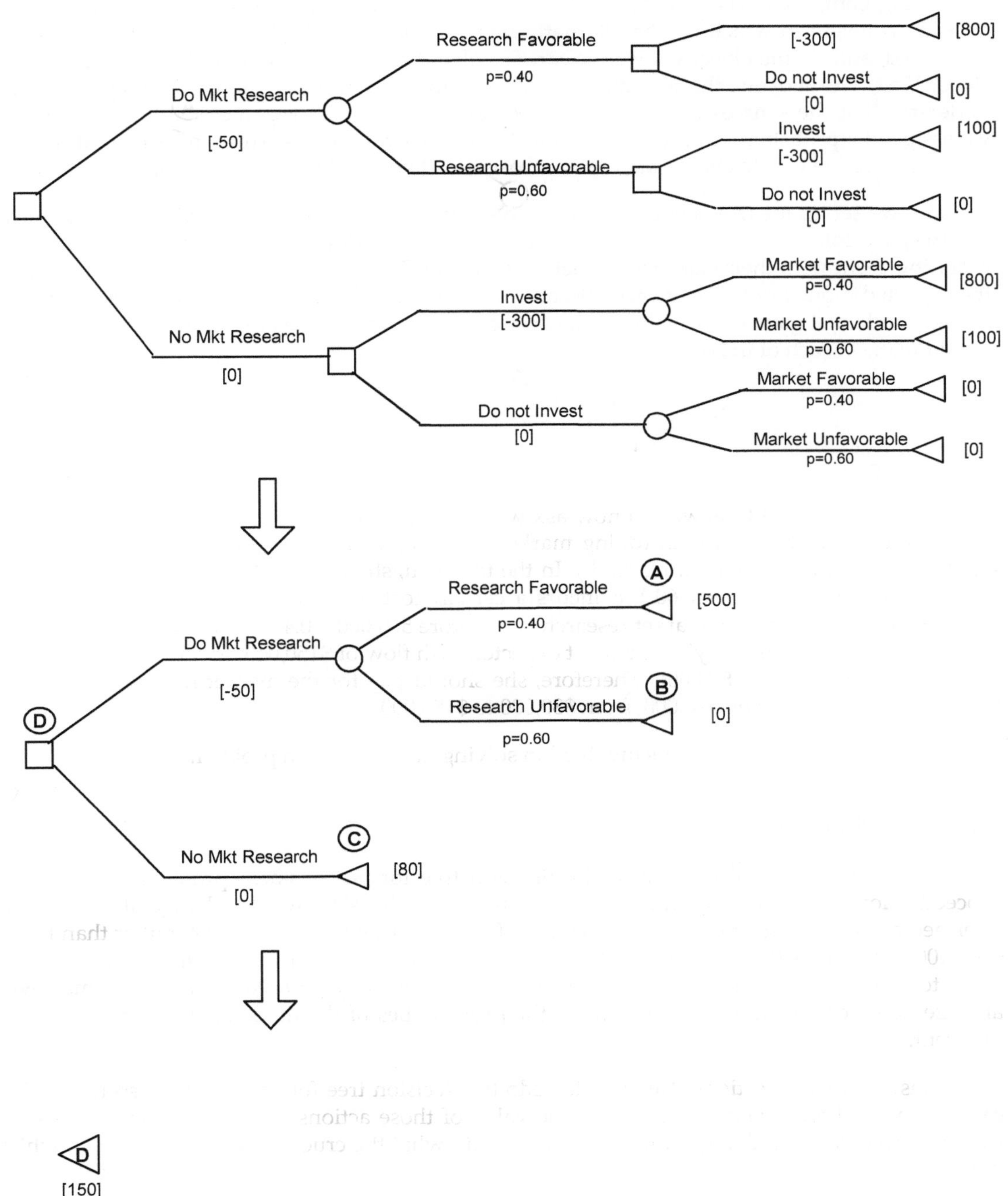

Summary

Solving complex decision problems is easy with a few simple tools. In this note, we solved a decision problem in which (1) the alternatives were well-defined, (2) the critical uncertainties were quantified, and (3) the objectives were clear. To solve the problem, we built the decision tree in three steps. First, we laid out the alternatives, paying close attention to the chronology of events and understanding the sources of uncertainty. Second, we quantified the uncertainties. This meant that we assigned a probability to each of the branches of the event nodes. Third, we said that the decision maker's objective was to choose alternatives based on their expected monetary value.

Once we set up the tree, solving it was simple (see **Figure O** for a summary). Starting at the end of the tree, we folded back the event nodes and decision nodes. Event nodes were folded back by replacing them with their expected monetary value. Decision nodes were folded back by calculating the expected monetary value of each alternative and selecting the best one. Finally, we were left with a single node that gave us the value of the project. In the process, we also learned which decisions we would make at each of the decision nodes.

Harvard Business School **9-191-138**

Rev. April 6, 1994

The Value of Information

Collecting information is a valuable tool for decision makers. Information is sometimes collected to aid general understanding, and often purely out of curiosity, but on occasion information is collected to aid in making a particular decision. For example, a consumer products company might survey customers about the design of a new product that is still not finalized for production. A purchasing manager might learn about the costs other industries face before putting pressure on her suppliers to lower their prices.

Information is usually obtained only at some cost. Marketing research costs money and time: test markets are expensive to conduct and (often more important) they can delay introduction even of successful products. The decision to collect information can be analyzed to see if the ***expected value*** of the information exceeds its cost of collection.

Information is seldom perfect. ***Sample*** information may be inaccurate for several reasons: pure sampling error; measurement bias (what respondents say is not necessarily what they will do); and selection bias (the sample is not representative of the population). The results of a test market, for example, may not be a perfect indicator of the outcome of a new-product introduction for any or all of the above reasons.

Michelle's Movers

Michelle's Movers (MM) rents out trucks with a crew of two on a daily basis, usually to homeowners who are moving house, or to companies with delivery problems. On one particular day Michelle is a truck short and intends hiring one from a local truck rental firm. The question she faces is, how big a truck should she hire? A large truck costs $200 per day (including insurance, fuel, etc.), a small truck $130/day. The advantage of hiring the small truck may be offset if the load is too big, necessitating that the crew make two trips. The additional cost of making two trips (overtime, truck mileage) she assesses at $150. She assesses the probability that two trips will be necessary as 0.40.

Question 1 Assuming there are no other ramifications to her decision, should she rent a large truck or a small truck?

Professor David E. Bell prepared this note as a basis for class discussion.

Question 2 What would it be worth to Michelle to know for sure whether a small truck would be adequate for the job? [For example, she might send someone a day in advance to examine the job at first hand.]

To answer question 1 we may draw the following tree:

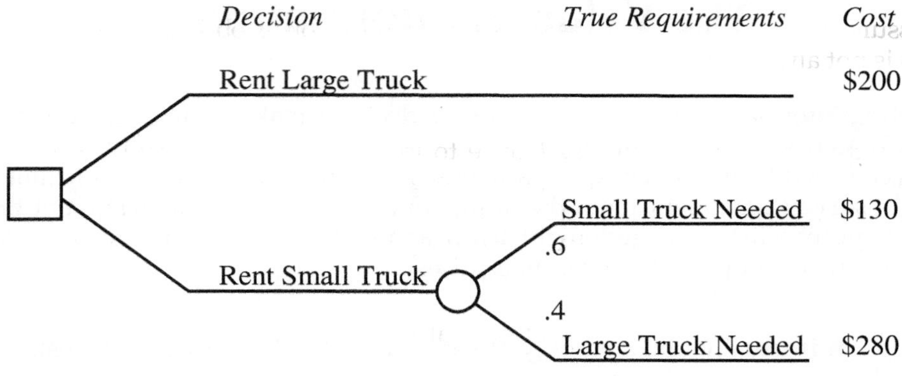

The expected cost of renting a small truck is 0.6 * 130 + 0.4 * 280 = $190. Thus she should rent a small truck.

To answer question 2, let's first assume that the information Michelle gets suffers from none of the possible inaccuracies discussed above: it is "perfect" information. To analyze Michelle's problem, we must draw a more complex tree:

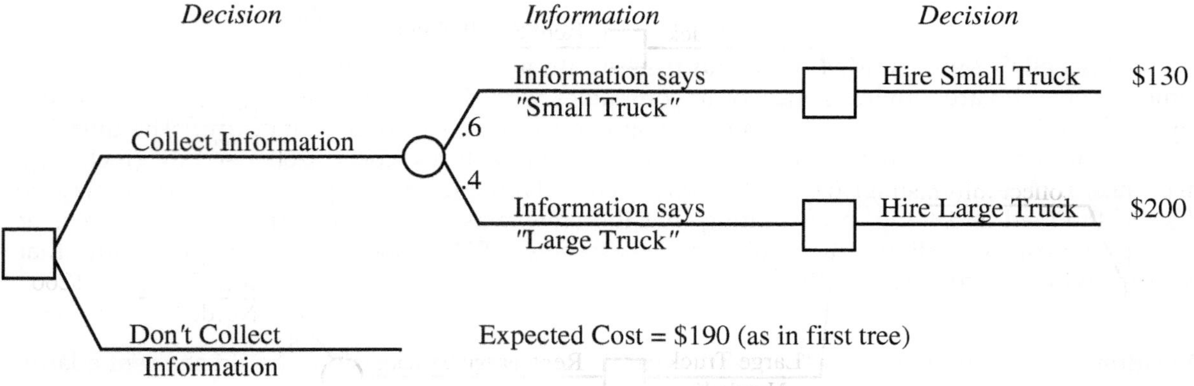

The expected value of the "Collect Information" decision is 0.6 * 130 + 0.4 * 200 = $158. This is $32 cheaper than the expected cost without the information. Thus the expected value of information is $32. Michelle would be better off first getting the information and then deciding what to do if the cost of getting it were less than $32; if it exceeded $32, however, she would be better off just going ahead and renting a small truck.

A way to see this directly is to recognize that we save $80 by collecting the information if a large truck is needed, and this occurs with probability 0.4 (and 0.4 x $80 = $32). In more complicated settings it may not be possible to deduce the answer so easily.

The Value of Imperfect Information

We assumed in our example that the information, once obtained, would be perfectly accurate. This is not always the case.

Suppose that the person sent in advance to inspect the job is known to make mistakes. Michelle believes that even if this person reports "Large Truck Needed" then the probability that a large truck is indeed needed is 0.80. Similarly if the person reports "Small Truck Needed" then there is only an 80% chance that a small truck is needed.

How much is advance information of this nature worth?

Before proceeding with the analysis, note that it will certainly be true that this information is worth less than $32. We may solve this problem with the following tree:

Exhibit 1

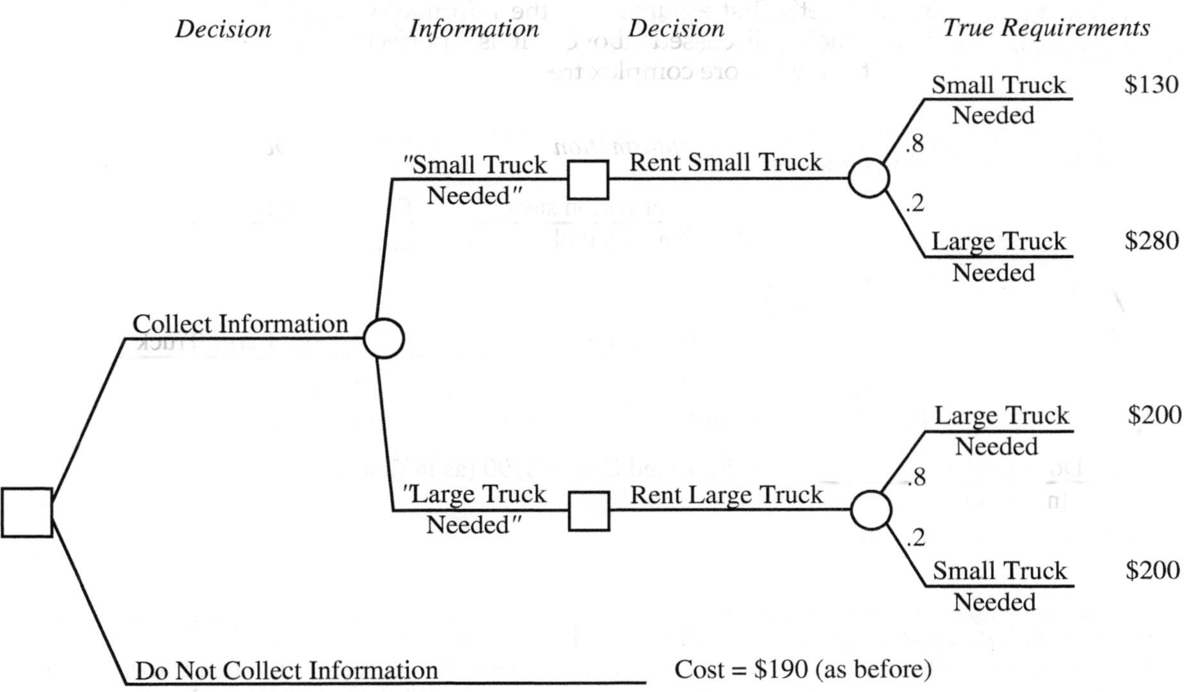

This tree is almost complete. It lacks, however, one piece of probabilistic information: how likely is our informant to say "Small Truck" versus "Large Truck"? You may think that the appropriate probabilities ought to be .6 and .4 respectively because these are the probabilities of a small and large truck being needed. But this is not entirely consistent. Consider the following tree:

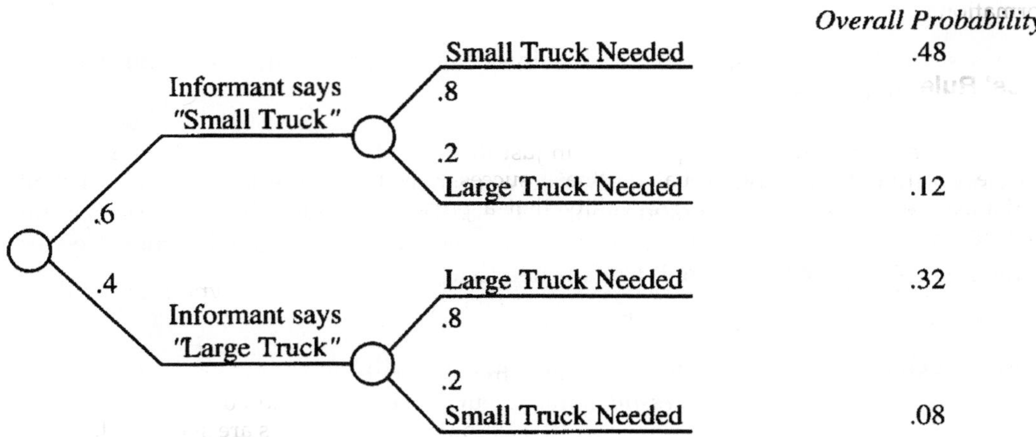

According to this tree there is a 0.56 probability that a small truck will in fact be needed (0.48 + 0.08) and a 0.44 probability that a large truck will be needed (.12 + .32). These aren't quite the same as 0.6 and 0.4 respectively. To see this problem more clearly, suppose our informant is right half the time and wrong half the time, then even if we almost certainly needed a large truck, our informant is just as likely to ***say*** "Large" or "Small".

To find the correct probability p that our informant will ***say*** "Large Truck Needed" we need to solve the following equation

$$p * 0.8 + (1-p) * 0.2 = 0.4$$

or in words:

*Probability Informant says "Large Truck" * Probability this is correct*
*+ Probability Informant says "Small Truck" * Probability this is wrong*
= Overall Probability of Large Truck.

The solution to this equation is $p = \frac{1}{3}$.

Placing this information in *Exhibit 1* we may fold back the tree to find the expected value of the "Collect Information" branch:

$$\frac{2}{3}[0.8 * 130 + 0.2 * 280] + 1/3 * 200 = \underline{\$173\frac{1}{3}}$$

This means we would be prepared to pay up to $16.67 (the $190 expected cost of acting without further information less the $173.33 cost of acting with imperfect information) for this "imperfect" information.

Bayes' Rule

Information is not always provided in just the format you need for a decision tree. For example, you might know the probability that a successful entrepreneur has an MBA, when what you'd really like to know is the probability that a person with an MBA will be a successful entrepreneur.

The thinking process by which one converts probabilities of one type into the other is known as Bayes' Rule (Bayes invented the rule!).

Let's suppose that 60% of all successful entrepreneurs have MBAs (and 40% don't). Let's suppose further that 20% of ***unsuccessful*** entrepreneurs have MBAs and 80% don't. To find the answer we want, we still need to know what proportion of entrepreneurs are successful. Let's say 5%. Now we draw the following tree:

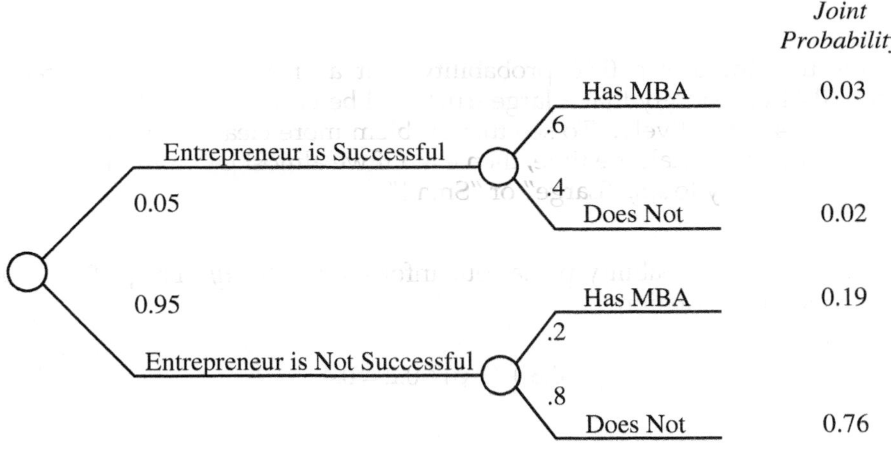

Instead of payoffs we write down the joint probabilities, for example the probability that an entrepreneur is successful ***and*** has an MBA is 0.03.

The question we want to answer is "what proportion of MBAs who are entrepreneurs are successful?" From the tree we see that a proportion 0.22 of entrepreneurs have MBAs (= .19 + .03). Of this 0.22, 0.03 are successful, so $\frac{0.03}{0.22}$ is the answer we seek, or 13.6%. [These numbers also suggest that entrepreneurs without an MBA have only a $\frac{0.02}{0.78}$ = 2.6% chance of success.]

There is a substantial discrepancy between the number 60% (proportion of successful entrepreneurs who have MBAs) and 13.6% (proportion of entrepreneurs with MBAs that are successful) yet the two statements are often viewed as interchangeable by a lay audience!